From Dāśarājña to Kurukṣetra

From Dāśarājña to Kurukṣetra

Making of a Historical Tradition

KANAD SINHA

OXFORD
UNIVERSITY PRESS

OXFORD
UNIVERSITY PRESS

Oxford University Press is a department of the University of Oxford. It furthers the University's objective of excellence in research, scholarship, and education by publishing worldwide. Oxford is a registered trademark of Oxford University Press in the UK and in certain other countries

Published in India by
Oxford University Press
22 Workspace, 2nd Floor, 1/22 Asaf Ali Road, New Delhi 110002, India

First Edition published in 2021

Second impression 2023

ISBN–13 (print edition): 978–0–19–013069–5

ISBN–10 (print edition): 0–19–013069–5

ISBN–13 (eBook): 978–0–19–099346–7

ISBN–10 (eBook): 0–19–099346–4

DOI: 10.1093/oso/9780190130695.001.0001

Typeset in Minion Pro 10.5/14
by Newgen Knowledge Works, Chennai
Printed in India by Replika Press Pvt. Ltd.

The poet who could turn the grief of a bird into poetry . . .
The seer who could make an encyclopedia of human experience
out of a family feud . . .
The nameless bards who kept millennium-old stories alive . . .
And those who still keep on telling the stories . . .

Contents

Foreword ix
Romila Thapar
Preface xvii
List of Diacritical Marks Used xxiii
List of Abbreviations xxv

1. The *Mahābhārata* and the End of an Era 1
1.1 Where the 'Past' Ends, Where the 'Future' Starts: The Journey from *Dāśarājña* to Kurukṣetra 1
1.2 Understanding an *Itihāsa*: A Historiographical Survey 11

2. Bharatas, Pūrus, Kurus, and the Vedas: A Politico-textual History 43
2.1 The Ṛgvedic Poets and Their World 43
2.2 Viśvāmitra's Poetry 49
2.3 Thus Spake Vasiṣṭha 52
2.4 Sudās and the Ten Tribes: Reflections on the *Dāśarājña* 57
2.5 The Kurus and the Later Vedas 63
2.6 From Saudāsas to Śunaḥśepa: Viśvāmitra and Vasiṣṭha in the Later Vedic World 66

3. The Great Saga of the Bharatas 81
3.1 Searching for a Lost History of 'Time': Layering the *Mahābhārata* 81
3.2 Heroes, Forest, and the Vedic Deities: Revisiting the *Khāṇḍavadāhana* 111
3.3 Dice, Duel, and *Dharma*: Contextualizing Yudhiṣṭhira's *Rājasūya* 129
3.4 When the *Bhūpati* Sought the *Gopati*'s Wealth: Locating the *Mahābhārata* Economy 152
3.5 Cousins, Clans, and Kingdoms: Studying the Kurukṣetra War 159
3.6 Constituting the 'Fifth Veda': The Voice of Vyāsa 179

4. New Text, New Era, New Hero: Vāsudeva Kṛṣṇa and His *Svadharma* 237
4.1 Kṛṣṇa or the Kṛṣṇas?: Questioning a Deified Hero 237
4.2 'There Is No Song without Kānu': Sourcing Vāsudeva Kṛṣṇa 244
4.3 'I Am Born as Thy Friend': Kṛṣṇa the Cowherd 256
4.4 Vāsudeva, *Prativāsudeva*, and the False *Vāsudeva*: Tracing the Rise of a Legend 276
4.5 From Butter Thief to Jewel Thief: Kṛṣṇa the Vṛṣṇi Diplomat 302
4.6 Leader, Teacher, and Envoy: Kṛṣṇa in the 'Udyogaparvan' 311
4.7 *Svadharma, Karman*, and Kṛṣṇa: (Re)reading the *Bhagavad Gītā* 333
4.8 '*Yatra yogeśvaraḥ kṛṣṇaḥ yatra pārthaḥ dhanurdharaḥ*': Kṛṣṇa at Kurukṣetra and Beyond 388

5. The *Bhārata* beyond the Bhārata War 423
5.1 Śaunaka and the *Sūta*: Bhārgavizing the *Bhārata* 423
5.2 Viśvāmitra versus Vasiṣṭha: Reshaping a Vedic Legend 437
5.3 The Axe-Wielding Hero of the Bhṛgus 450
5.4 From the Lost *Itihāsa* of the Bhāratas to the Great Epic of Bhārata: An Epilogue 461

Bibliography 475
Index 499

Foreword

Romila Thapar

I have read Kanad Sinha's book *From Dāśarājña to Kurukṣetra: Making of a Historical Tradition* with considerable interest as it presents an extension of our understanding of the texts he uses as sources. His proposed reconstruction of events is suggestive of fresh ways of envisaging this segment of the past. It is a significant departure from most studies reconstructing the history of the second and first millennia BCE as his focus is on the question of how the sources reflect what we today refer to as either history, historical consciousness, or historical tradition. His purpose is not in proving whether or not the various persons described and the events narrated were historical and did actually exist and happen. This is what is often spoken of when the question of the historicity of the *Mahābhārata*, for instance, is raised. His is a far more probing question, namely, how the *Mahābhārata* reflects society at given moments of historical time. The issue is not whether the epic encapsulates reliable history but rather what it tells us about how people in the past viewed what they regarded as their past. We need to take this view seriously; although not necessarily as reliable history but as how at a certain time a certain society perceived what it constructed as its past. An important distinction is therefore made between history as we understand it today and historical traditions as they have been understood in earlier times. The distinction applies to many early societies.

These views of the past, as found in the text, took many centuries to evolve. Then, at a certain point, they were taken as given. This is normal with the many reflections brought to bear on constructions of the past. In this the form and purpose of the composition had a role. The epic form is characterized as being open. A single poet or bard may originally have composed a long narrative poem, but often the related compositions of others are stitched into it—what we now call interpolations. It, therefore, may begin as the articulation of a single author and is often attributed to a single author, but in effect, with various additions, it becomes the extended statement of a society and generally of the elite of that society. In the process, the text is seen to be interpreting the past and, while doing so, keeping in view the perspective of the present. The text therefore becomes a complicated interplay of the past and the present. This contributes to the making of a tradition. The epic is seldom only a contemporary description. It is more often an attempt to capture what a society likes to recall about its past, and this may be done at more than one point in time.

The interpolations are at least of two recognizable kinds. One explains in further detail that part of the narrative or activities that have perhaps become unfamiliar to later generations. An example of this is the marriage of Draupadī conforming to polyandry. It had to be explained, and this is done in a variety of ways. Or sometimes the discussions of the time are reflected in the narrative. For example, the subject that is being much debated by scholars these days is that of the scene where, after the conclusion of the battle at Kurukṣetra, Bhīṣma, still lying on a bed of arrows, is trying to persuade Yudhiṣṭhira to accept the validity of *rāja-dharma* (Śāntiparvan Mbh., XII). Yudhiṣṭhira is averse to taking up the kingship after the termination of the battle, because he disapproves of violence and kingship in various ways involves the use of violence by the king.

This was not a question that was central to the *Vedas* nor to the dominant *kṣatriya* ethos that pervaded heroic society, but it was nevertheless central to the thinking of the new sects—the Śramaṇas of various kinds—that were questioning Vedic Brahmanism and whom the *brāhmaṇas* were to refer to as the *nāstikas*. The debate continued through the Mauryan period as is evident from the edicts of Aśoka and into the post-Mauryan period as, for example, indicated by the Hathigumpha inscription of Khāravela as well as in other sources. Since the Śāntiparvan was a later addition to the *Mahābhārata* and is generally dated to the post-Mauryan period, it is plausible that this debate is linked to what appears to have been current debates on the subject of violence and non-violence.

Apart from the debate on *ahiṃsā*, Kanad Sinha reminds us that the concepts of *ānṛśaṃsya* and *anukrośa*, compassion and empathy, were also discussed, both in the putting together of the text and currently in its analyses. These ideas are also not alien to Buddhist thought. Discussions on the need for compassion and empathy often subsequent to the debates on the legitimacy of violence seem to hover over the narrative even when not being spoken about. Could it be argued that the recital of the narratives of conflict replete with violence, where such conflicts do not provide solutions to problems, are intended to lead to a kind of purgation of violence and eventually to discarding the belief that violent conflicts can be solutions?

The *Mahābhārata* in some ways can be seen as reflecting the transition from the society of the *Ṛg Veda* to that of the later *Vedas* and occasionally also the post-Vedic as is reflected in the multiple narratives that are accretions to the story. The transition from one kind of society to another was not a simple linear movement. In all such changes one has to ask what was carried forward and in what form and what was discarded despite the belief that everything was present in the changed society. This is reflected in our own times when we insist that 'traditions' are age old, were created centuries ago, and have survived intact and unchanged to the present day, forgetting that traditions are more frequently invented precisely to meet contemporary problems posed by social and cultural change, and therefore inevitably have to change accordingly. But the change has to be legitimized by giving it an ancient ancestry.

A fundamental change in political forms is present in the conflict described in the epic, which is, as Kanad Sinha points out, the conflict between the legitimacy of lineage essential to clan society and the gradual change to a focus on primogeniture that becomes a requirement in monarchy. One could add to this the explicit hierarchy of status central to caste. I have elsewhere referred to it as the gradual mutation from clan-based or lineage-based societies to kingdoms representing the coming into existence of states. It represents foundational mutations in the structure of societies. A few recent studies suggest that this is now a subject of interest to historians.

Change of course is not limited to what evolves within a single culture. It is affected both by those that are dissenters within the culture as well as those who live in the vicinity but have distinctively different patterns of living. These latter are recognizably the 'Other'. Those recorded as the Other in the Vedic sources are the *dāsas*. Even where the *dāsa* was the subordinate, there was nevertheless an interface between the cultures, and some of the differences that creep into elite cultural items are taken from the culture of the Other. There is the example of the *dāsyaḥ-putraḥ-brāhmaṇa*, the *brāhmaṇa* who was the son of a *dāsī*, such as Kavaṣa Ailuṣa, and yet was inducted into the *brāhmaṇa varṇa*. Inevitably the question that comes to mind is that such instances would have resulted in, to some extent, the interface of cultures. What were the likely changes that this might have brought about in either of the two societies?

Epic literature of earlier times frequently focuses on conflict between the important clans in a region, and this encapsulates much of their pattern of living—that is, their culture. In the *Mahābhārata*, the Kurus and the Pāṇḍavas battle for land rights in the Doab. The actual area that each comes to control is not extensive but with the listing of allied and hostile clans on each side, whether actually present or not, the strife in the epic takes on a bigger dimension than what might have been involved in realistic terms. This is another characteristic of the epic form: a small conflict can easily be enlarged into a far bigger confrontation with participants from every part of the known geography. How this geography is expanded is of much historical interest. A dramatic illustration is provided in the *Odyssey* of Homer, where a large part of the Mediterranean is inducted into the narrative.

The other way of extending the geography is to send the protagonists into exile for a period. The location of the exile need not be too distant but preferably should have the potential of being culturally alien so as to introduce expanded geographies and multiple cultures. This gives scope to the imagination of the bard to invent diverse societies with a license to colour realism with fantasy where needed. The ostensible purpose of this is to entertain the audience, but it can also be used as expressing a comment on the society of the protagonists. Exile to the forest in both the Indian epics is to a place where the pattern of living, the culture, is different from that of the protagonists. The latter may be sympathetic to this pattern or may treat it as antithetical. If it is the former, the people of the forest become allies, but if it is the latter, they have to be subdued.

Arjuna's experiences as he travels and his marriages to various women were to some degree a commentary on the culture of the Pāṇḍavas, as was Bhīma's marriage to Hiḍimbā. The voyage home of Ulysses from Troy to Ithaca was a matter of a few weeks, but the poet extends it to a few years with the ship constantly being taken off course by wind and wave. The cultures they meet with in these travels are diverse and extraordinarily different from their own. Distant places have always been an excuse to let the imagination run. Exile extends the context and implies that the narrating of epic events is not to be restricted. It also allows the bard/poet to present vignettes of situations that may otherwise merely divert from the main narrative.

The entry of Kṛṣṇa of the Vṛṣṇi clan into the story was what might be called a significant accretion. It has been suggested that he may not originally have been one of the central figures when the story was first composed. By the time it became a much known and quoted epic, it appears to have been taken up by the Bhārgavas who found it possible to weave into the epic the Vaiṣṇava cult of Vāsudeva. Many questions arise if one even considers the possibility of this happening. Why at this point was it necessary to give authority and publicity to the cult of Kṛṣṇa? The historical context would have been that of the post-Mauryan period given Sukthankar's dating of the *Mahābhārata* as having been composed during the period from 400 BCE to 400 CE. This was a time when the Śramaṇic religions were riding high with the patronage of an emperor and subsequent royalty as well, and that of wealthy merchants. Aśoka's edicts suggest tension between the *brāhmaṇas* and the *śramaṇas*, and other sources indicate a conflict.

The epic genre, because it is open to interpolations, can support more than one narrative even in its current Critical Edition. There is the original epic of the clash of clans and the ultimate victory of the Pāṇḍavas. Built into this is the narrative of Vaiṣṇavism through divinizing Kṛṣṇa and giving him a more central role. This is in part reinforced by the somewhat different trajectory of what have been called the narrative sections and the didactic sections, where some of the latter seem to be add-ons. This has been discussed by many scholars of the epics, among them V.S. Sukthankar and R.N. Dandekar. However, the differentiation cannot be made in a literal manner where all the early sections are taken as narrative and all the later sections as didactic, or alternatively all the narratives are taken as early and the discussions as didactic and therefore late. Kanad Sinha's study takes care not to automatically assign them as early or late without considering other features. This involves a careful analysis of both the text and its context.

The core of the narrative revolves around what probably were to begin with handed-down narratives claiming to be memories of the clan societies. The use of the term 'tribe' can be somewhat confusing since it can include aspects of a society that were not present at that time. Some historians therefore prefer to use the term 'clan society' either prior to the beginnings of kingship and caste society or contemporary with the initial evolving of both.

One of the more interesting aspects of the Vedic and epic texts are the references to the processes of migration and settlement. These are sometimes major episodes and the descriptions can be quite dramatic. The description of the burning of the Khāṇḍava-vana in the *Mahābhārata* could not have been captured in a more dramatic fashion. It is virtually a battle against nature with the burning of the forest and the dying of the animals in the flames. So severe was the devastation that those animals that were normally the prey of the predators were now together, both predator and its prey, jointly seeking refuge from the fire. Burning the forest was the technique of clearing land and opening up a new area to settlement and cultivation. The settlers were groups of migrants looking for places to settle. So, the Khāṇḍava-vana had to be burnt to clear the location for constructing the town of Indraprastha. Apart from the town, the rest of the clearing would have been cultivated, leaving the edge of the forest as pasturage.

The *Śatapatha Brāhmaṇa* mentions a migration from the Doab to the middle Gaṅgā plain led by a chief called Videgha Maṭhava. He too, on arrival in the region of what came to be called Videha, began the process of settlement by first burning the forest and clearing the marshes. It is said that he carried Agni in his mouth, a highly symbolic statement as it could refer to the worship of Agni or else, as some have suggested, to the language of the migrating *āryas* coming from the Doab.

Kanad Sinha's study draws not only on his careful reading of the *Mahābhārata* and related texts but also on his extensive reading of much that has been written on the *Mahābhārata* as well as on epic as a genre in other early cultures and histories. His reading covers both early writings on the subject and also more recent works. Such extensive reading has now become essential as it opens up so many new avenues of research. There have been wide-ranging works on various aspects of the *Mahābhārata* and these have taken the study of the text way beyond what it was in the past century. That scholars should be familiar with these studies is essential to further the understanding of the epic.

Kanad Sinha's study is impressive both because of his reading of the texts and because of the kinds of questions he asks and the answers he provides that help to illumine the text. His questions are challenging and fresh, and his answers to these beckon us towards new perspectives of examining the texts. And that is what is required at the cutting edge of research.

New Delhi
September 2020

Preface

This book has developed out of my PhD thesis. Therefore, it cannot begin without the acknowledgement that it would not be anywhere without the care and guidance of my supervisor Prof. Kunal Chakrabarti, who had been a pillar of support and my go-to person over the past decade. He was the first person to listen to the initial draft of my PhD proposal, and, till the submission, his suggestions and guidance have been invaluable in shaping up this thesis as well as several aspects of my life. I am extremely grateful to Prof. Kumkum Roy for guiding me in preparing my historiography, and sections of this book grew out of two seminar papers I had done with her. At every stage of my research, I have benefitted from the feedback and comments of Prof. Ranabir Chakravarti regarding academics, literature, and beyond. I am thankful to Prof. Vijaya Ramaswamy for introducing me to the idea of reading devotion as dissent and for her thoughtful insights about shaping up my research proposal; I mourn her untimely demise before this book materialized. Dr. Supriya Varma had kindly guided me through the reports of the excavations at Hastinapur and Atranjikhera. Many of my teachers at the Centre for Historical Studies, including Profs R. Mahalakshmi, Aditya Mukherjee, Janaki Nair, Neeladri Bhattacharya, Rajat Datta, Najaf Haider, Indivar Kamtekar, and Heeraman Tiwari, have been ready to help always, and I have gained a lot from their valuable comments in the formal setting of seminars and conferences as well as in informal discussions. Prof. Romila Thapar, whose writings had oriented me towards the methodological approach adopted in this thesis, has always been kind enough to offer her comments and lead me towards new research questions; she most graciously agreed to write the foreword for this book. As she is introducing the book, any further attempt on my part to introduce it will be redundant.

The preface, therefore, could end here, but that would have been an unfair and incomplete story. After all, a PhD thesis turned into a book is not only about the work done over a few years but also about the culmination of a long journey. It has been an eventful journey where several helping hands have been invaluable in channelizing it to the course it has taken, and the acknowledgement cannot but be a humble opportunity to express my gratitude to all of them. The list is long and must start with my parents, Mr. Asanta Sinha and Mrs. Nupur Datta Sinha, who have not only allowed me complete freedom about every choice in my academics and life, and have remained extremely supportive in everything I choose to do, but also were the first people to introduce me to the contents of the Indian epics through stories, children's books, and my mother's daily recital of the *Gītā*. Thanks to listening to my mother teaching her students Bengali classics, for example, Michael Madhusudan Dutt's *Meghanādavadhakābya* or Rabindranath Tagore's *Karṇakuntīsaṃvāda* and *Gāndhārīr Ābedan*, I first came to realize how the epics were not about singular monolithic narratives but could be read and recreated in multiple ways. My grandmother, Mrs. Pratimarani Datta, had been the earliest recipient of my first childish engagement with my favourite texts and remained a keen listener until she passed away. I have been fortunate to enjoy all the privileges the youngest member of a generation enjoys in an Indian joint family, and my work has always been received with appreciation, encouragement, and enthusiasm by my family members, both paternal and maternal, including the ones with a background in history and the ones pursuing completely different professions. It is unfortunate that some of the most enthusiastic enquirers of my research, particularly my cousin Atanu Sinha, have left us before they could see its culmination. In the final days of finishing the thesis and in the long process of turning it into a book, my wife Debasree Sarkar's patient support and active efforts have been a great help.

It is difficult to decide when my serious engagement with the topic of my research started. Perhaps it was the day in my childhood when the rickshaw-puller named Samar Sinha, who would satisfy every asthma-induced whim of mine, took me to the local bookshop. The owner of the shop, Mohammad Mosharaf Hossain, had always been generous in handing over to me any book that caught my fancy, and from him I had received the volumes of Kṛttibāsa's Bengali *Rāmāyaṇa* and Kāśirām Dās's Bengali *Mahābhārata*, which introduced me to the world of epic grandeur, even though in the vernacular. The curiosity generated then blossomed into genuine interest in the conducive atmosphere of my school, Ramakrishna Mission Vivekananda Vidyamandir, Malda, where my teachers, especially my headmaster Swami Sumanasananda, provided all the support necessary for nurturing my love for humanities in general and Sanskrit texts in particular. I am particularly grateful to Mr. Maheshwar Bhattacharya for inculcating in us a spirit of rational and critical thinking and original writing and to Dr. Radhagobinda Ghosh for guiding my first endeavours to understand the Sanskrit language. Thus, my amateurish ideas about historical research were forming, and my friends—Supratim Nandy, Tapas Shil, Sagnik Saha, Tamoghna Majumdar, Priyabrata Halder, Priyam Ghosh, Sandipan Chakraborty, Shreya Sarkar, and many others—had to be patient listeners.

It was at the Presidency College, Calcutta, that Dr. Kaushik Roy bluntly pointed out to us, in the very first class, the difference between amateurish historical interest in certain texts and critical historical study of particular sources. A few days later, Prof. Rajat Kanta Ray had taken us around the college to remind us of a legacy, of commitment to truth and rational thinking, that the 'Derozian community' stood for. Teachers like them, as well as the ones like Profs Subhash Ranjan Chakraborty, Uttara Chakraborty, Jayashree Mukherjee, and Sugata Nandy, were the reasons why, alongside learning the business trick of predicting and memorizing the answers of the set of questions the Calcutta University was likely to ask, we developed a keen interest in trying to grasp and understand the 'historian's craft'. During my college days, it became my habit to talk to 'Subhashbabu' and 'Uttara ma'am' before taking any major academic decision and to share with them every piece of writing I could come up with. Therefore, it is heartbreaking for me that Uttara ma'am has been taken away from us before this book could come out.

But when was Presidency only about its teachers? Growing up around the tradition of the balance of the 'three Ps: *parashona* (study), *prem* (romance), and politics', received from our seniors, we hardly realized when the aspirations of historical research pervaded our minds at both the conscious and the unconscious levels to such a degree that even the chitchats and jokes shared with friends such as Sanmitra Ghosh, Dipanjan Mazumdar, and Apurba Chatterjee became full of allusions and references to our budding research interests and historical perceptions. Following one such casual conversation, Torsa Chakraborty introduced me to Prof. Nrisinha Prasad Bhaduri, who has not only contributed immensely in popularizing epic studies to the Bengali readership but has also helped me immensely in engaging with the epics. I had shared the first rudimentary ideas about what this book discusses with Elora Tribedy and Jayati Halder, both of whom helped me with their ideas, and the former has continuously supplemented my textual interest with relevant information from the field of archaeology, especially the findings from her first-hand field experience at Ahichchhatra.

As my journey moved to the Jawaharlal Nehru University (JNU), not just an educational institution but an identity one gradually adopts and can hardly get out of, I became part of a fraternity not limited to my very own Centre for Historical Studies. I fondly remember how Prof. S.K. Sopory, the former vice chancellor, would bring to my notice any new research on my field of interest he would come across. Prof. Santosh Kumar Shukla, of the Special Centre for Sanskrit Studies, was my pathfinder in the wilderness of Vedic Sanskrit. Profs Robert P. Goldman and Sally J. Sutherland Goldman, of the University of Berkeley, California, have been kind enough to provide thorough critical comments and suggestions about any piece of writing I had shared with them. I am thankful to Profs Simon Brodbeck, Brian Black, and John Brockington and Dr. Vishwa Adluri for liberally supplying me with their writings whenever I faced any difficulty in accessing them. I am grateful to Profs Suchandra Ghosh and Uma Chakravarti, my PhD examiners, for their detailed reviews and insightful comments which helped me reshape the book. As bits and pieces of my research started to be presented in various seminars and conferences, I gradually benefitted from exchange of ideas with many brilliant minds, including Profs Michael Witzel, B.D. Chattopadhyaya, Patrick Olivelle, Upinder Singh, and Daniel Bell.

I have benefitted no less from being with my students than from being with my teachers. I must thank all my students from Miranda House, St. Stephen's College, Presidency University, Udaynarayanpur Madhabilata Mahavidyalaya, and the Sanskrit College and University for being the best company of my life so far. My former colleagues Dr. Bharati Jagannathan (of Miranda House) and Dr. Naina Dayal (of St. Stephen's College) have been consistent in advising, guiding, and scolding me to keep both my teaching and research on track. Dr. Valson Thampu (former principal, St. Stephen's College), Dr. Arabinda Ghosh (principal, Udaynarayanpur Madhabilata Mahavidyalaya), and Prof. Paula Banerjee (former vice chancellor, the Sanskrit College and University) have been tremendously supportive in helping me balance my teaching and research.

Just like the *Mahābhārata* is not just about the Bhārata War but also about a panoramic view of everything that it considers significant about *dharma*, *artha*, *kāma*, or *mokṣa*, a thesis coming out of JNU cannot be about the routine exercises of academic research alone. It is equally a product of the night-long debates, discussions, and adventures, nocturnal walks around the Ring Road, heated discussions over cups of coffee at Ganga Dhaba or 24x7—with Archisman Chaudhuri and Biswadev Banerjee, Byapti Sur and Anwesha Saha, Titas De Sarkar and Shounak Ghosh, Siddhartha Mukherjee and Deepro Chakraborty, Pintu Parui and Amartya Pal, Virendra Singh Charan and Vipin Krishna, Mahashweta Chakraborty and Shatavisha Mustafi, friends from the discipline and beyond. Suvajit Halder and Dev Kumar Jhanjh provided tremendous logistical, intellectual, and emotional support in times of need. Friends like Ritadhi Chakravarti and Saronik Basu ensured that resources in the foreign libraries were never inaccessible. Last but not the least, I must thank Ashis Kumar Das for his constant supply of photocopies and printouts that made research at JNU seem so easy. This book comes out at a time when the teachers and students of JNU are facing one onslaught after another while standing strong as a bastion against fanaticism, unreason, and authoritarianism. It being the space that inevitably inculcates in one the spirits of tolerance and free thinking expressed in every academic production coming out of the campus, this book would have been incomplete without a full-throated thanksgiving to JNU.

This book is the culmination of a long eventful journey, a journey blessed with the help and cooperation of numerous brilliant minds and excellent souls, some of whom I have mentioned and many more I might have missed out. The final round of help came from the staff of the Oxford University Press—including Nandini Ganguli, Nadita Krishnamurthy, Emma Collison, and Rajakumari Ganessin—who did a marvellous job amidst a pandemic to keep this book project going. The overwhelming task of preparing an index was possible only because of the tireless help from Debasree, and prompt support from Suvajit, Anuja Saha, Shubhranil Ghosh, Debankita Das, and Sreetama Sau. The journey had its ups and downs, highs and lows, satisfactions and disappointments. Yet, the disappointments seem too meagre in front of the immense amount of help, goodwill, love, and affection I received in the journey and scarcely deserved. For what I did not get, I would like to repeat the words of Tagore:[1]

> What you have given me without asking:
> The sky, the light, the mind, body and life—
> Day by day you are turning me into worthy of that great gift,
> Saving me from the danger of wishing for too much.
> I ask wholeheartedly in extreme desire, you have saved me through deprivation.

Note

1. My translation of a passage from Rabindranath Tagore, *Gitanjali*, Patra Bharati, Kolkata, 2010 edition, Song No. 2, p. 16.

List of Diacritical Marks Used

Method of Transliteration from Sanskrit to English

अ	आ	इ	ई	उ	ऊ	ऋ	ॠ	ए	ऐ	ओ	औ	अं	अः
a	ā	i	ī	u	ū	ṛ	ṝ	e	ai	o	au	aṃ	aḥ

क	ख	ग	घ	ङ
ka	kha	ga	gha	ṅa
च	छ	ज	झ	ञ
ca	cha	ja	jha	ña
ट	ठ	ड	ढ	ण
ṭa	ṭha	ḍa	ḍha	ṇa
त	थ	द	ध	न
ta	tha	da	dha	na
प	फ	ब	भ	म
pa	pha	ba	bha	ma
य	र	ल	व	
ya	ra	la	va	
श	ष	स	ह	
śa	ṣa	sa	ha	

Abbreviations

AB	*Aitareya Brāhmaṇa*
ĀŚS	*Āśvalāyana Śrauta Sūtra*
AV	*Atharva Veda Saṃhitā*
ĀGS	*Āśvalāyana Gṛhya Sūtras*
BGS	*Baudhāyana Gṛhya Sūtra*
BŚS	*Baudhāyana Śrauta Sūtra*
BU	*Bṛhadāraṇyaka Upaniṣad*
CU	*Chāndogya Upaniṣad*
GB	*Gopatha Brāhmaṇa*
ĪU	*Īśa Upaniṣad*
JB	*Jaiminīya Brāhmaṇa*
JUB	*Jaiminīya Upaniṣad Brāhmaṇa*
KB	*Kauśitakī Brāhmaṇa*
KS	*Kaṭhaka Saṃhitā*
KU	*Kaṭha Upaniṣad*
MS	*Maitrāyaṇī Saṃhitā*
MŚS	*Mānava Śrauta Sūtra*
MU	*Muṇḍaka Upaniṣad*
PB	*Pañcaviṃśa Brāhmaṇa*
ṚV	*Ṛg Veda Saṃhitā*
ŚB	*Śatapatha Brāhmaṇa*
ŚŚS	*Śāṅkhāyana Śrauta Sūtra*
ŚU	*Śvetāśvatara Upaniṣad*
TĀ	*Taittirīya Āraṇyaka*
TB	*Taittirīya Brāhmaṇa*
TS	*Taittirīya Saṃhitā*
E	Kanad Sinha

1

The *Mahābhārata* and the End of an Era

1.1 Where the 'Past' Ends, Where the 'Future' Starts: The Journey from *Dāśarājña* to Kurukṣetra

The period from *c.* 1000 to 600 BCE is marked by a kind of vacuum in Indian history. Prior to that stands the age of the *Ṛg Veda*, characterized by a predominantly pastoral economy supported by rudimentary agriculture, tribal sociopolitical organization, a sacrificial religion, and very little social stratification. However, in *c.* sixth century BCE, when Vardhamāna Mahāvīra and Gautama Buddha were preaching their ideas, the North Indian landscape was witnessing a fully developed complex state society of the *mahājanapadas*, settled agrarian economy, luxurious urban centres, and rampant speculative and philosophical debates. The transition, definitely, did not happen overnight, and the four centuries that lay in between must have witnessed one of the most significant shifts in Indian history—the shift from lineage to state, as noted by Romila Thapar.[1]

Thus, this period—conveniently called the Later Vedic Age—has been seen as a time when the Aryan settlers moved eastwards from Brahmāvarta to Āryāvarta, when agriculture gained relatively more importance than pastoralism, when the cattle-raiding chieftain (*gopati*) became the tax-claiming monarch (*bhūpati*), and when the validity of the sacrificial Vedic religion began to be questioned. However, this highly significant history can hardly be recovered as all the safely dateable sources relating to the period are religious literature.

The information discussed here is mainly gleaned from Vedic texts, which are religious in nature and provide only occasional and incidental information about historical events. Though lacking in historical consciousness or orientation, they are favoured as source materials

From Dāśarājña to Kurukṣetra. Kanad Sinha, Oxford University Press. © Oxford University Press 2021.
DOI: 10.1093/oso/9780190130695.003.0001

by several scholars because of their better preserved state and relative freedom from 'textual corruption'. However, a parallel tradition, called *itihāsa-purāṇa*, consciously recording traditional history, existed at least from the Later Vedic Age. It was an oral tradition, primarily based on the compositions of the bards like the *sūtas*, *māgadhas*, and *kuśīlavas*, who might have received patronage from the *kṣatriyas* who held political authority. However, the texts containing remnants of this tradition—namely the *Rāmāyaṇa*, the *Mahābhārata*, the *Harivaṃśa*, and the eighteen/nineteen major Purāṇas—received their present shape much later, after several revisions, alterations, additions, and interpolations, mainly at the hands of the *brāhmaṇas* who provided a religious character to these texts. This is why scholars such as A.B. Keith, V. Gordon Childe, and H.C. Raychaudhuri doubt their usefulness as historical source material. Childe views them as 'hardly an unpolluted source of history'.[2] Moreover, they contain several serious errors, for instance, depicting collateral rulers as successors. F.E. Pargiter, on the other hand, strongly criticized this tendency of depending more on Vedic texts than on the Purāṇic tradition:

> Hitherto opinions about ancient India have been based on a study of the Veda and Vedic literature without much regard for historical tradition outside that ... To make the former the chief and more authoritative basis of historical reconstruction is much the same as to write European history mainly from theological works—an undertaking that would not receive a moment's acceptance.[3]

The way Pargiter and some other scholars uncritically accept the entire Purāṇic tradition—against many verifiable historical facts and without separating the different layers of the composition of the concerned texts—is not fully acceptable.[4] Pargiter's thesis depended on the conviction that Vedic tradition represented the Brahmanical tradition, which lacked historical consciousness, while the Purāṇic tradition (at least the genealogies and ballads about kings) contained more historically oriented *kṣatriya* traditions preserved by the *sūta* bards. However, despite acknowledging that the *kṣatriya* tradition was eventually Brahmanized, he did not consider that the presently available Purāṇic texts, produced not earlier than mid-first millennium CE, are as much Brahmanical production as the Vedic literature is and neglected the necessity to corroborate the information with the parallel Buddhist and Jaina traditions which he dismissed as religious. As a result, Pargiter ended up constructing a historical narrative based on one kind of religious tradition, ignoring all other which were actually older and better preserved, and his genealogies and narratives could be exposed by comparing them with the information gathered from other sources. This problem was faced by the Indian scholars who tried to follow Pargiter and to construct early Indian genealogical tables on the basis of the Purāṇas. S.N. Pradhan had to repeatedly rectify the errors in the Purāṇic tables on the basis of the information gathered from Vedic, Buddhist, and Jaina sources, leaving much room for doubt about the details of the information for which no such corroborative or corrective source is available.[5] A.D. Pusalkar, arguing against dismissing Purāṇic tradition altogether and preparing a chronological arrangement for traditional history up to the Bhārata War, divided in eight phases, and ranging from 3100 to 1400 BCE, himself acknowledges that while the Purāṇic accounts show a picture of massive conquests across the subcontinent and up to South India and Sri Lanka by kings like Māndhātṛ, Sagara, and Rāma, contemporary records up to the end of the Vedic period show that the Aryans had not advanced much beyond the central plains of North India till then. Therefore, the authenticity of the Purāṇic tradition was suspect even in the eyes of some of their ardent supporters.[6] Under such circumstances, works such as P.L. Bhargava's, attempting to synchronize Purāṇic chronology with the information known from Vedic sources and accounting for the mismatch as textual corruption in the hands of the priestly class who canonized the present texts, becomes a tacit acknowledgement of the unreliable nature of the presently available Purāṇic texts and the priority of the Vedic sources over them.[7]

However, Pargiter's objection about the handling of the sources still holds ground. Though none of the aforementioned works succeeded in presenting a reliable historical narrative, they rightly pointed out that ancient India might have contained historical traditions of secular origin, which may offer us valuable insight if their content can be ploughed out from their canonized Brahmanical forms. Thapar points out the character of this historical tradition as 'embedded history', more representative of a lineage-based society, as different from 'externalised history' produced by state societies.[8] Scholars sometimes undertook ambitious projects to fill up the vacuum. H.C. Raychaudhuri sought to reconstruct the history of the Kuru kings Parikṣit and Janamejaya and of the Janakas of Videha on the basis of stray references found in Later Vedic texts.[9] However, much of the vacuum still remains.[10]

The *Mahābhārata* is traditionally called an *itihāsa*, the closest Sanskrit equivalent to 'history'. However, treating the *Mahābhārata* as a historical text is a problematic task. The dating of the *Mahābhārata*, a text composed over more than a thousand years, which acknowledges to have undergone at least three retellings, is almost impossible. Therefore, the dominant perception that ancient Indians failed to produce a history remains almost intact.

Drawing from comments made by medieval travellers and historians like Al-biruni and Firishta, both the scholars and the administrators working in colonial India (the categories were often overlapping) firmly believed in India's lack in historical consciousness. A.A. Macdonell emphatically proclaimed, 'Early India wrote no history because it never made any'.[11] E.J. Rapson's opinion sounds a little bit tempered but shares similar sentiment:

> In all the large and varied literatures of the Brahmans, Jains and Buddhists, there is not to be found a single work which can be compared to the *Histories* in which Herodotus recounts the struggle between the Greeks and the Persians or to the *Annals* in which Livy traces the growth and progress of Roman power ... But this is not because the people of India had no history ... We know from other sources that the ages were filled with stirring events; but these events found no systematic record.[12]

The first generation of Nationalist historians accepted this framework without much objection, since their perception of history was also shaped by the model presented by colonial education. Therefore, R.C. Majumdar, usually very proud of the achievements of the early Indians, grimly accepts the absence of historical texts:

> It is a well-known fact that with the single exception of the *Rājataraṅgiṇī* ... there is no historical text in Sanskrit dealing with the

whole or even parts of India. But ideas of history and historical literature were not altogether lacking.[13]

The only notable exception to this tendency among the Nationalist historians was U.N. Ghoshal. He had painstakingly pointed out that there were historical narratives present in early Indian literature, even though not in a very organized form. Therefore, the Vedic literature contained genealogical tables of teachers and students, as well as praises of the chiefs and their achievements in *dāna-stuti* hymns of the *Ṛg Veda* and the *gāthā* and *nārāśaṃsī* hymns of Later Vedic literature. The narratives known as the *itihāsas* and *purāṇas* were self-consciously more historical in orientation. Thus, there are occasional references to historical incidents, such as the Battle of Ten Kings, in the ṚV itself and allusions to statements of ritualistic authorities, historical examples of efficacy of rituals, historical explanations of the emergence of certain rituals, and memories of theological disputes and intellectual debates. Thus, despite many defects, a mass of genuine tradition was collected and memorized. Similarly, early Buddhist literature in Pali does not contain any full-length historical biography of the Buddha but treats him as a man and preserves scattered historical memories and traditions about the most important incidents of his life. The Purāṇic genealogies contain too many defects to be relied on, but nevertheless they were attempts to preserve a traditional memory. All these traditions contributed to the eventual making of early Indian historiography as manifested in Bāṇa's biography of King Harṣa or, in a more systematic manner, Kalhaṇa's chronicle about the history of Kashmir.[14]

However, Ghoshal remained an exception. The dominant attitude hardly changed in the relatively recent attempts to account for this absence of history by various justifications, including a deliberate hiding of the low-caste origin of the rulers by the priestly elite,[15] bifurcation between the low-caste keepers of scribal records and the *brāhmaṇa* intelligentsia,[16] the Mimāṃsā school of philosophy underplaying the role of history,[17] the Western variety of knowledge called 'history' not being important in the Indian scenario,[18] wilful amnesia to forget subjugation by foreign rulers,[19] and the colonial power cutting off the newly educated from their traditional past.[20]

However, our conception of history has drastically changed from the period when Macdonnell or Rapson was writing. History is hardly seen any more as a Positivist enterprise whose task is collecting a huge amount of supposedly objective facts. Still, there has been little re-examination of the stereotype of ancient India not having any historical literature in the light of the new turns in our understanding of history.

If we take history as an intellectual form, as Jan Huizinga defines it, in which a civilization renders account to itself of its past, and consider historical memory as a creation of the interplay of the past with the present,[21] the early Indian tradition called *itihāsa-purāṇa* may very well qualify as history. Probably, there was no historical text composed in ancient India to qualify as 'history' in its sense as an Occidental academic discipline. However, Romila Thapar has shown in her book *The Past before Us* that even the entire corpus of Occidental historical tradition can hardly be accommodated within any single definition of history. The understanding, definition, and methodology of history practised by Herodotus and other Classical historians were starkly different from the discipline practised by the Medieval European church historians or the post-Renaissance and post-Enlightenment Positivistic history popularized in the nineteenth century.[22] Similarly, there were diverse methods of perceiving the past within the Mesopotamian, Chinese, or Islamic cultures. Al-biruni's comment about the Indians not having any history may therefore be a result of his unawareness of the historical traditions of the Indian society and his search for a parallel to his familiar model of history. His main informants being the ritual specialists did not help him either.[23] Therefore, Thapar thinks that historical consciousness does not need to conform to any particular model. It begins with a society showing consciousness of both past and future and starting to record the past.[24] She rightly says:

> To argue over whether a particular society had a sense of history or not on the basis of our recognition of the presence or absence of a particular kind of historical tradition—one which has been predetermined as being properly historical in perpetuity—seems somewhat beside the point. It is more purposeful to try and ascertain what each culture regards as its historical tradition and why it does so; and to analyse its constituents and functions as well as assess how it contends with competing or parallel traditions.[25]

Following this approach, we can agree with Thapar that many early Indian texts reflect a consciousness of history and subsequently there came into existence recognizable forms of historical writing. Both varieties of texts were used in early times to reconstruct the past and were drawn upon as cultural, political, religious, or other such resources at various times, in various situations, and for a variety of reasons.[26] Ancient India, thus, had a good range of historical traditions emanating from a sense of the past and including the three essential aspects of a historical tradition, namely consciousness of the past events as relevant or significant by a particular society (the reasons for such choice being implicit); the placing of these events in an approximately chronological framework, which would tend to reflect elements of the idea of causality; and the recording of these events in a form which meets the requirements of that society.[27] A historical tradition is therefore an authentic record, if not of actual events, then certainly of the believed assumptions about the past. It is created from the intellectual and social assumptions of a society. Consciously selected events are enveloped in a deliberately created tradition which may only be partially factual.[28]

Since the different interpretations of the past are shaped by the social and intellectual background of the compilers of the traditions, the choice of the materials and their interpretations differ. Early India seems to have at least three distinct historical traditions from a very early period: the Vedic-Brahmanic, the bardic tradition called *itihāsa-purāṇa* (Brahmanized later), and the Śramaṇic (within which the Buddhist and the Jaina traditions can be differentiated). Occurrence of an event/tradition across these traditions invariably would empower them with a greater claim of historicity, but each of these traditions represents a unique historical consciousness in its own right.

The beginning of Indian historical traditions can be traced in its earliest literary composition, the *Ṛg Veda*. Though the text's primary concern was not recording history, certain Vedic poets left valuable historical accounts about their families and patrons. Such information often helps us to reconstruct bits of early Indian history. For instance, the history of a significant political event, the *dāśarājña* or the Battle of Ten Kings, can be satisfactorily reconstructed from the accounts given by the poet-priests of both the contending parties, Viśvāmitra and Vasiṣṭha. The event was a landmark, demarcating the hegemony of the Bharata tribe over vast regions of the North Indian plains after the victory of their chief Sudās over a confederacy of ten tribes. Gradually, the Vedic composers felt a need to record certain historical accounts, and Thapar identifies the *dānastutis*, *gāthās*, *nārāśaṃśīs*, and *ākhyānas* of the Vedic texts as the earliest forms of 'embedded history'.[29] Whereas the *dānastutis* were celebrations of lavish gifts given by the generous patrons and the *gāthās* and *nārāśaṃśīs* repetitions of brilliant achievements (ritual or military) by certain individuals, the *ākhyānas* were properly formed narratives for narration during the sacrifices. Some of these narratives were identified as *itihāsas* (it happened like this), indicating that they had some truth-claim about their historicity unlike the other *ākhyānas*. The *ākhyānas* about Purūravas and Urvaśī (ṚV 10.95) or Śaṃtanu and Devāpi (ṚV 10.98) are examples of such *itihāsas*.[30]

However, *itihāsa* was also considered a separate discipline in its own right from a very early period. It was considered a tradition different from the Vedic one but of almost equal importance. The *Atharva Veda* considers it as emanating from the Supreme Being, just like the Vedas.[31] The *Bṛhadāraṇyaka Upaniṣad* treats it on par with the Vedas,[32] whereas the *Chāndogya Upaniṣad* calls it the 'fifth Veda'.[33] The *Āśvalāyana Śrauta Sūtra* (X.7), the *Gopatha Brāhmaṇa* (I.10), the *Śāṅkhāyana* (I.24.8), and *Āśvalāyana Gṛhya Sūtras* (IV.6.6) prescribe the hearing of *itihāsa* in certain ritual contexts.[34] The *Arthaśāstra* includes it in the curriculum of princely education.[35] The early composers and transmitters of the *itihāsa* were various bardic groups such as the *sūtas*, *māgadhas*, and *kuśīlavas*, who were the custodians of its sister tradition *purāṇa* (tales from old) as well. Both the traditions were orally transmitted initially. Later, they were formalized and written down under Brahmanical control. Therefore, gradually they lost their original character. The present Purāṇas, for instance, are characteristically devotional Brahmanical texts rather than accounts of the past.

What was the character of *itihāsa*? Is there any text retaining some elements of that tradition? The traditional definitions of *itihāsa* take it very close to what we now understand as historical tradition. The *Nāṭyaśāstra*, for instance, almost defines it as a dialogue between the past and the present by saying that *itihāsa* is the past being visualized as if it is happening in the present.[36] The traditional definition of *itihāsa*, quoted by Taranatha Tarkavachaspati in his *Vācaspatyam*, describes it as a comprehensive discipline which not only contains the accounts of the past but can provide guidelines for social duties, political economy, pleasure, and salvation:

dharmārthakāmamokṣāṇaṃ upadeśasamanvitam/
puravṛttakathāyuktam itihāsaṃ pracakṣate.[37]

The *Nirukta* of Yāska shows that the truth-claim in *itihāsa* had been a source of lively debate from a very early time. The school called the *aitihāsikas* focused on historicity, while the *nairuktakas* insisted that the *itihāsas* should be interpreted figuratively.[38] Though the discipline called *itihāsa* was not exactly a part of the Śramaṇic tradition, its truth-claim was so well known that the Jaina scholar Jinasena defined it as relating that which actually happened.[39] Thus, *itihāsa* had a claim of authenticity but not the kind of factual authenticity around which Positivist historiography was formed. As Sibesh Chandra Bhattacharya has pointed out, *itihāsa* is much more explicitly didactic in nature than history. It teaches, and it teaches by example. *Itihāsa* is not interested in the past for its own sake, it is not interested in the whole of the past, but in what is exemplary. The past that is devoid of didactic value is not given a place in *itihāsa*.[40] Therefore, the historical tradition named *itihāsa* narrated what it believed to be authentic account of the past, but the claim to authenticity lay not in factual or chronological accuracy but in the lesson to be learnt about *dharma*, *artha*, *kāma*, and *mokṣa* from an exemplary and comprehensive account of the past.

The only complete text described in Indian tradition as an *itihāsa* is the *Mahābhārata*.[41] In fact, the *Mahābhārata* has a central position within early Indian historical tradition. It revolves around an event which marks the culmination of the Vedic historical tradition and the starting point of the Purāṇic one. As mentioned earlier, the Early Vedic period witnessed the establishment of Bharata hegemony. The Bharatas and their allies the Pūrus gradually evolved in the Kuru tribe. The Kurus and their Pañcāla dominated the Later Vedic landscape. The *Mahābhārata* is the *itihāsa* of the Kurus in the period between the reigns of Śaṃtanu (the last Kuru chief known to the *Ṛg Veda*) and Parikṣit (the Kuru chief celebrated as a contemporary in the *Atharva Veda*). Two of the prominent Vedic *ākhyānas* known as *itihāsa*, those of Purūravas-Urvaśī and

Śaṃtanu-Devāpi, are also integrally connected with the *Mahābhārata* narrative. Can the *Mahābhārata* then serve as our major source to document the history of the transition which took place in the Later Vedic period?

The text itself took its role as *itihāsa* very seriously. Thus, it promises to have fulfilled its role most comprehensively, according to the traditional definition of *itihāsa*:

dharme cārthe ca kāme ca mokṣe ca bharatarṣabha/
yad ihāsti tad anyatra yan nehāsti na kutracit//

(Bull among Bharatas, whatever is here, on Law, on Profit, on Pleasure, and on Salvation, that is found elsewhere. But what is not here is nowhere else.)[42]

Not only that, the text also is consciously proud of generating an effective communication between the past and the present:

ācakhyuḥ kavayaḥ kecit saṃpratyācakṣate pare/
ākhyāsyanti tathaivānye itihāsam imaṃ bhūvi//

(Poets have told it before, poets are telling it now, other poets shall tell this *itihāsa* on earth in the future.)[43]

Moreover, the *Mahābhārata* knows itself as a text of transition, a witness to the shift from the Dvāpara Age to the Kali Age.[44] Traditionally also, the Bhārata War is regarded as a watershed. In Purāṇic literature, incidents prior to the Bhārata War are usually narrated in the past tense, while incidents after it are generally in the future tense. In early Indian historical consciousness, the battlefield of Kurukṣetra marks a highly significant boundary where the 'past' ends and the 'future' begins. However, can we use the present text of the *Mahābhārata* to understand which great shift it deals with, how it portrays that shift, and what is the text's commentary on it? We will seek the answer. However, as indicated already, the history that culminates at Kurukṣetra has a long prehistory. Therefore, our work will focus not only on the decisive moment of the Bhārata War but also on the long journey from the *dāśarājña* to Kurukṣetra.

1.2 Understanding an *Itihāsa*: A Historiographical Survey

While we have outlined our intention to look at the *Mahābhārata* as an *itihāsa*, we must also remember the enormous body of research that has developed around the text. In this section, we shall attempt to outline some of the major interpretations of the text. The biggest obstacle to using the *Mahābhārata* for historical purpose is dating. It is a text that internally acknowledges three retellings. It must have undergone many more before its final codification after a journey which is at least a millennium long. Its mammoth size and self-contradictory nature led Maurice Winternitz to describe it as 'literary nonsense'.[45] R.C. Dutt laments the loss of the 'epic nucleus', while some scholars try to find the nucleus by distinguishing old and new layers.[46]

Christian Lassen speaks of an older text named *Bhārata*, composed between 460 and 400 BCE and mentioned in the *Āśvalāyana Gṛhya Sūtra*, to which were added the 'Krishnite' elements.[47] Walter Ruben saw Kṛṣṇa—whose conflict with the Magadha king Jarāsaṃdha might have some historical basis—as a superimposed inessential absentee hero on the Pāṇḍava-Kaurava narrative.[48] R.N. Dandekar also thinks that the bardic tradition of the *sūtas* got crystallised around the historical battle of Kurukṣetra in an epic named *Jaya*, to which was redacted the new and popular practical religion of Kṛṣṇa.[49]

However, removing Kṛṣṇa from the epic without destroying its core is hardly possible, and the attempt sometimes takes absurd proportions. For instance, though Kṛṣṇa does not fight in the Bhārata War, generally taken as the central event of the text, he plays a major role in the downfall of the four great Kaurava warriors—Bhīṣma, Droṇa, Karṇa, and Duryodhana. Ruben, in order to construct a Kṛṣṇaless *Mahābhārata*, argues that Śalya's death at the hands of Yudhiṣṭhira—in a 'just combat' and without Kṛṣṇa's intervention—represents the oldest single battle of the original epic.[50] It is absurd to suggest that a Kuru-Pañcāla or Kuru-Pāṇḍava battle was decided by the death of the least important of all Kaurava commandants, who was not even a member of the Kuru clan. J. Kennedy's attempt to distinguish several Kṛṣṇas—one of solar myths, another non-Aryan hero of Indus Valley, yet another derived from the legends of Christ, and so on—is not at all convincing.[51]

Sören Sörensen tried to construct an ur-text of the *Mahābhārata*, with 8,800 *ślokas*.[52] But this number is found in a very late tradition about difficult *ślokas* of the *Mahābhārata*. E. Washburn Hopkins dates the composition of the epic between 400 BCE and 400 CE and assumes five phases of composition. His general assumption is that a *Mahābhārata* tale was constructed around the Pāṇḍavas, and it incorporated other legends between 400 and 200 BCE. Kṛṣṇa was not yet considered the Supreme Deity. Between 200 BCE and 200 CE, the text was reworked with Kṛṣṇa as the Supreme Divinity. Puranic material and didactic matters were added to the text between 200 and 400 CE. In this phase, the last books were composed, the first book was enlarged, and the 'Anuśāsanaparvan' was separated from the 'Śāntiparvan'. This dating is more or less accepted.[53] But, V.S. Sukthankar points out that Hopkins did not show any concrete evidence to defend his phases.[54]

Adolf Holtzmann and, following him, Leopold von Schröder note the misdeeds by the Pāṇḍavas and Kṛṣṇa in the epic and use them to argue for an 'Inversion Theory', suggesting that the Kauravas were the initial heroes of the epic which was later inverted by Vaiṣṇava priests.[55] However, the misdeeds of the Kauravas are no less than those of the Pāṇḍavas, and therefore Sukthankar considers this theory unacceptable.[56] Moreover, as Oldenberg has pointed out, the instances of trickery by the Devas in the Vedic myths cannot mean that Vedic poets originally sided with the Asuras.[57] Thus, he tries to trace the old version, corroborated by Vedic references, as a representation of some events of the Vedic Age.[58]

F.E. Pargiter considers the *Mahābhārata* as a historical account of Kuru-Pañcāla and *brāhmaṇa-kṣatriya* conflict,[59] a view supported by George Grierson[60] but opposed by A.B. Keith.[61] Criticizing this approach, D.D. Kosambi says that the *Mahābhārata* converted trifling incidents into world-shattering events. He views in the text a transition from food-gathering to food-producing society and representation of interactions with the autochthonous Nāgas. The epic began as a Kuru lament converted into a Pāṇḍu song of victory, absorbed Nāga myths during acculturation, acquired fresh myths from the Mathuran Kṛṣṇa saga, and was eventually Brahmanized by the Kāśyapas and the Bhṛgus.[62]

All these views are usually bracketed under the 'Analytical Theory' of understanding the *Mahābhārata*. They are quite valuable since they approached the text critically and addressed the need to stratify the text to contextualize its historical layers. However, none of these aforementioned studies could provide a satisfactory methodology to do so. Extreme views, like that of Pargiter, can easily be nullified because of the nature of the text. An overwhelming amount of mythical elements, a long period of composition of over a millennium with several additions, alterations, omissions, and interpolations, confused genealogical details, and mixing up of fact with fiction are some of the pertinent criticisms of accepting the text as history in its present form. On the other hand, the overambitious 'Inversion Theory' and Kosambi's analysis remain just interesting speculations due to a dearth of supporting evidence. Washburn Hopkins's stratification is still largely followed but lack of a clear-cut methodology for dating the layers leaves room for questioning the chronology.

Some other scholars speak against stratification of the text. Early medieval commentators such as Ānandavardhana and Abhinavagupta saw the entire text as a single whole.[63] Joseph Dahlmann initiated a 'Synthetic Theory' claiming unity of the text—with both the narrative and the didactic sections—which he views primarily as a didactic work invented not later than fifth century BCE to propagate the maxims of law.[64] However, the manuscript used by Dahlmann could by no means be a production of the fifth century BCE, and he overstretched the point of legal symbolism (like explaining Draupadī's polyandry as common ownership in a joint family).

Ludwig attempts to explain the *Mahābhārata* as a season-myth[65] without making it clear why a poem of about 200,000 lines should be composed to allegorically represent some nature myth. Sukthankar takes the text of the *Mahābhārata* as a whole which has three levels of meaning—mundane, ethical, and metaphysical. The mundane plain is about effective characterization, the ethical plain represents the struggle of *dharma* and *adharma*, and the metaphysical plane—mainly the *Bhagavad Gītā*—represents the Upaniṣadic idea of the unity of *jīvātman* and *paramātman*. The 'epic nucleus' with its historical content, he thinks, has been swallowed up by the Bhṛgus.[66]

Patricia M. Greer argues for an inherent integrity of the *Mahābhārata*, with a brilliantly constructed narrative pattern which is self-referential, plastic in time and space, wonderfully rich, and tightly fabricated.[67] For K. Kunjunni Raja, the text in its present form has a unity despite diversity, based on the ultimate *śānta rasa*.[68] A.K. Ramanujan analyses the structure of the text in its repetitive patterns about characters, events, actions, and consequences of actions.[69] Radhavallabh Tripathi also prefers to view the *Mahābhārata* as a synthetic whole.[70]

However, still the need to stratify the text could not be neglected by even Sukthankar. Rather, he became the General Editor of the Critical Edition of the text, the most ambitious attempt to reach the original text. Therefore, the need of an analytical approach is inevitable in a historical study, even if approaching the text as a synthetic whole can be useful from the literary point of view.

The creation of the Critical Edition itself has been viewed by some supporters of the 'Synthetic Theory' as the termination point of the analytical studies on the *Mahābhārata*. After all, a thorough laborious exercise by Sukthankar and his colleagues produced a text which is an approximation of the oldest possible model from which the varied available manuscripts of the *Mahābhārata* received their present shape. With a single text in hand, these scholars would like to focus on studying it hermeneutically and on 'lower criticism' based on the reading of the text itself rather than on 'higher criticism' guided by philology and various tools of historical analysis often used to stratify the text. Vishwa Adluri, one of the major recent advocates of the model, vehemently opposes higher criticism on the ground that 'higher criticism creates a "new text" according to the author's particular ideological preference, arguing duplicitously for a text that never existed while denying the text that actually exists'.[71] Adluri thinks that, in doing so, higher criticism employs 'fantastic and unscientific' figures of speech, such as layers, threads, cores, accretions, interpolations, rings, and nodes.[72] This kind of exercise, after the creation of the Critical Edition, is an 'intellectual embarrassment' to Adluri.[73] He thinks that higher criticism is 'unscientific' and often 'ideologically tainted', while 'lower criticism is an honourable endeavour to which great minds have dedicated considerable labor'.[74] In fact, Adluri takes a strong stance against any kind of historical analysis of the text, arguing that

> [n]o one denies that modern historical sciences in the sense of 'Geisteswissenschaften' have provided a wealth of information in diverse fields, but what is often overlooked is that these sciences are by no means as objective as they claim. Their origin is itself tied to specific historical conditions, to an intellectual climate and to specific needs and

> aims. What the historical method claims to be the only 'objective' approach, it forgets that it too has a history. By believing that it sets itself above all prejudices, it falls prey to the greatest prejudice of all: that of being free of prejudice.[75]

Therefore, Adluri decides that hermeneutics is the richest among all textual approaches, since it is the 'most scientific and the most gentle(wo) manly'.[76] Simon Brodbeck has also opined that the creation of the Critical Edition has exhausted the possibility of analytically studying the *Mahābhārata*.[77]

A major problem with Adluri's opinion is his misunderstanding of the discipline of history. His criticism is valid for some of the early analytic attempts in studying the text in an atmosphere where Positivistic search for 'objective' and 'scientific' 'facts' dominated historical exercises. However, the discipline of history has moved much beyond the way a Rankean Positivist would have approached it about a couple of centuries back. Clearly, Adluri's understanding of history somehow missed the developments in the two intervening centuries. History, after all, is no longer perceived as 'historical sciences' claiming to present an accumulated body of objective, scientific facts. A historian denying that every history is a product of its (and the historian's) context and that no history can be absolutely objective or unprejudiced will be taken with little seriousness nowadays.[78] Thus, by presenting arguments that would have hit the bull's eye in the nineteenth century, in a twenty-first-century work, Adluri has caused himself a great 'intellectual embarrassment'. While no student with sensitivity to literature would deny the importance of hermeneutics, Adluri's advocacy of the method being the most 'scientific' also points out how he failed to get out of the framework Positivism had created in the nineteenth century. While no historical work can be without the prejudices of the historian, Adluri's veiled claim of hermeneutical analyses being 'scientific' and unprejudiced deserves little serious engagement, less so when he himself has demonstrated the extent of prejudice working in his writing by giving the verdict that only lower criticism is an 'honorable endeavour' in which 'great minds' devoted considerable labour but higher criticism is not so.

However, the creation of the Critical Edition is no doubt a point of culmination in the analytical studies of the *Mahābhārata*. The creation of a single available text, possibly approximating the oldest archetype for the extant manuscripts, is also extremely useful for reading the text using hermeneutics and various other tools of literary criticism. However, the purpose of historically enquiring a text/tradition does not end in the construction of a text. The purpose of the historical enquiry, after all, is not just to see what the text might have looked like at a certain point in history but also to learn how it came into being from a bardic oral tradition. It is true that sometimes historical analysis goes overboard and tries to artificially create a text that never existed at the cost of the text that exists, for instance, the attempts to create an ur-*Mahābhārata* or Holtzmann's 'Inversion Theory' or Muneo Tokunaga's attempt to relocate Bhīṣma's discourse to Yudhiṣṭhira to a different context in an assumed earlier version of the *Mahābhārata*.[79] Such reconstructions are problematic, not because they claim any objective singular fact but because they present speculations regarding earlier versions of the text without any corroborative evidence from any existent manuscript or external sources. But there is ample scope, and necessity, to historically enquire into the coming into being of a massive tradition like the *Mahābhārata* and the process of its textualization, which is in no way in contradiction with literary criticism of the existent text as a whole. After all, the Critical Edition itself is a hypothetically constructed text that never existed before its coming into being in the twentieth century. That the Analytic and Synthetic methods are not mutually exclusive is best illustrated by the fact that Alf Hiltebeitel, a big supporter of the hermeneutical model, himself made different attempts to historically contextualize the time and process of the *Mahābhārata*'s creation.[80]

If we now shift our attention to the studies which viewed the *Mahābhārata* as a unified text, much attention has been paid to the mythical and religious aspects of the epic. Stig Wikander and Georges Dümezil view the epic as reminiscent of an old Indo-European mythology. Yudhiṣṭhira, Bhīma and Arjuna, and Nakula and Sahadeva, respectively, represent the three major aspects of Indo-European religion and society: the sacerdotal-legislative (Mitra/Dharma), the martial-kingly (Indra and Vāyu), and the fertile-popular (the Aśvins), which later assumed the shape of the duties of the *brāhmaṇas*, *kṣatriyas*, and *vaiśyas*. Draupadī is the primeval female deity associated with the male gods of these three functions, comparable with the Iranian goddess Anāhitā.[81]

However, many of these connections are questionable, like the identification of Dhṛtarāṣṭra, Pāṇḍu, and Vidura as Bhaga, Varuṇa, and Aryaman. Draupadī is clearly identified with Śrī in the epic, and the presence of the solar figure—Karṇa—on the evil side is not likely in an Indo-European myth. Jan Gonda criticized Dümezil's selective use of material,[82] and F.B.J. Kuiper points out that the three-tier structure within the Pāṇḍavas—as indicated by Wikander and Dümezil—is secondary to their contrast, as a group, to the Kauravas.[83] Similarly problematic is Gesta Johnson's identification of Dhṛtarāṣṭra as Varuṇa.[84]

N.J. Allen, who has extended Dümezil's model of three functions to a developed model of four functions in analysing Bhīṣma's role as a matchmaker, also notes striking similarities between the journeys of Arjuna and Odysseus, regarding particularly their dealings with women, to argue for common Indo-European inheritances.[85] However, there are much more to these voyages apart from those dealings, and—for the *Mahābhārata*—Arjuna's wandering is nothing but a tiny section. Julian Baldick goes even further in seeking a universal theme for several epics, but sometimes his comparisons are a bit overambitious, such as the one between Kumbhakarṇa and Hector.[86] Josette Lallement's suggestion of Virgil's borrowings from the '*Mahābhārata*' is also not very conclusive. More important comparative studies on epics include Pavel Grinster's,[87] which emphasizes the uniformity of motifs and plots in heroic epics, and Yaroslav Vassilkov's, which traces all three forms of historical development of an epic—archaic, classical, and late—in the '*Mahābhārata*'.[88]

Fernando Alonso Wulff, in his recent works, has resurrected the claims of the Eurocentric thinkers and Evangelists of the nineteenth century who claimed that most of the notable works of the early Indian authors were modelled on/borrowed from Occidental literature. This kind of attitude, expressed in Weber's claim of the *Rāmāyaṇa* being an imitation of the *Iliad* or Lorinser's attempts to show the *Bhagavad Gītā* as a paraphrase of the *New Testament*, is resurrected by Wulff's claim that

> [t]he Mahābhārata was written with a great quantity (and quality) of Greek materials near at hand, specially using the *Iliad* as a kind of guideline or reference point. Nevertheless, it is important to stress that the Mahābhārata's author/s use this Greek 'repertoire' brilliantly, creating

a new and unique world for a new political, religious and ideological purpose.[89]

Wulff stresses on the *Mahābhārata* story about how the Earth was overburdened by powerful *kṣatriyas*, necessitating the incarnation of the divine and demonic beings as the various *Mahābhārata* characters to cause a great war which would involve massive killing and would mark the coming of the decadent Kali Age. He notes its similarities with the *Cypria*'s representation of the secret behind the Trojan War: the Earth, being overburdened by the human race, requested Zeus for help, and Zeus plotted successive wars in Thebes and Troy. Zeus's plan involved the birth of the son of a goddess and a man (Achilles) and the supernatural birth of a beautiful and powerful woman (Helen). The ensuing battle ended the 'age of heroes' and brought a decadent age.[90]

There is no doubt that there is a similarity between these stories, but the two texts unfold in very different ways. For instance, while the plan of Zeus culminates in two wars, the *Mahābhārata* involves only one Great War. Wulff tries to present the destruction of the Yādavas in the 'Mauṣalaparvan' as the second war, but the text shows it as nothing more than a heated intra-family fighting during a picnic. To further the range of the similarities, Wulff thinks that Achilles and Helen have their counterparts in the son of a goddess and a man (Bhīṣma) and a beautiful woman with supernatural birth (Draupadī), respectively. His stretched comparison between Helen and Draupadī cannot move beyond the supernatural quality of their births and their beauty,[91] too common for epic heroines. Wulff attempts a full-scale comparison of Bhīṣma and Achilles, noting that both were born out of an unusual wedding brought about by a divine manoeuvre, both had a water-goddess as mother who abandoned the father's place at some point and killed all the brothers of the hero but spared him, both were raised in non-human environment, both were not crowned as king despite deserving the throne, both were not married, both died at an odd age (Achilles too young and Bhīṣma too old), both are described as a shining warrior full of light and a general of the forces, both had problems with the king in power, both had an enemy—accompanied by a deity—visiting his tent before his death, both were killed with arrows, both expected and welcomed death, and both had elaborate singular funerals and were lamented by their mothers.[92]

The similarities are well noted but most of them are too generic. A great warrior being a general or being described as a 'shining warrior' or having a singular funeral cannot be any concrete evidence of borrowing. Since almost all births are results of divine manoeuvres in both the epics, that cannot be a special point to mention either. A mother lamenting her child is nothing unusual, and we can see Kuntī lamenting Karṇa, Subhadrā lamenting Abhimanyu, and Gāndhārī lamenting Duryodhana as well. Some of the similarities are of course interesting. However, the field of comparative mythology has shown us that such similarities can be seen among various characters across cultures. For instance, whereas Wulff noted the similarities between Bhīṣma and Achilles, Dümezil and Allen noted Bhīṣma's similarities with Sarpedon in the *Iliad*, Zeus and Ouranos in Hesiod's *Theogony*, Romulus of Roman mythology, and Heimdall of the Eddic poem *Rigspula*.[93] The characters share some common motifs as well as some drastic points of difference. For instance, it needs blind conviction to take Achilles's extreme youth and Bhīṣma's extreme old age as a point of similarity or to think that Achilles, whose strife with Agamemnon over the control of a woman is at the heart of the *Iliad*, can be a model for the celibate Bhīṣma whose refusal to break his vow of celibacy was at the root of both his own death and of the *Mahābhārata* war. Similarly, it is impossible to imagine Achilles without his possibly homoerotic friendship with Patroclus, and it is impossible to conceive Bhīṣma in any role remotely similar. Would Bhīṣma, whose commitment to the code of warfare (which he himself had outlined) led to his death, ever degrade the dead body of his fallen opponent the way Achilles disgraced Hector's body is another question Wulff's hypothesis fails to answer.

To defend the untenable, Wulff thinks that where parallelism does not work, it is because of borrowing from some other Greek myth. Thus, acknowledging that Gaṅgā, Bhīṣma's mother, does not resemble Thetis (the mother of Achilles), he thinks that Gaṅgā's character is modelled on Aphrodite of the *Homeric Hymn to Aphrodite* and some features of Demeter. Following this line, he goes on making confused parallelisms in which Aśvatthāman becomes Diomedes at some point, Belerophontes in some other, and the Trojan Horse (because of the *aśva* with which his name begins!) in another context (that of the nocturnal attack).[94] Similarly, poor Diomedes is sometimes Aśvatthāman and sometimes Kṛtavarman, while Arjuna is sometimes Odysseus and sometimes Heracles.[95] Even the extremely generic coincidences, such as that Nārada praised Yudhiṣṭhira's palace in the *Mahābhārata* while Telemachus praised Menelaus's palace in the *Odyssey*, are referred to as examples of borrowing, with the courage that is needed to imagine the young Telemachus as equivalent to the eternal globe-trotting sage Nārada.[96] Even the facts that positive virtues are shared by the two antagonistic parties, victory is bittersweet, and the survivors are depressed by the trauma of the war—which would have been the case in any good literature anywhere in the world—are presented in support of Wulff's hypothesis.[97] Though Helen and Draupadī both had multiple husbands, imagining Menelaus and Paris as brothers like Yudhiṣṭhira and Arjuna would take a level of insensitivity towards both the texts which few will manage. The places where even such stretched comparisons could not be made are seen as examples of borrowings from Greek sources no longer available to us.[98]

If Wulff's model were true, it would have been astonishing to think what an authority on Greek mythology the author of the *Mahābhārata* would have been. However, any conclusion based on such vague similarities will be a joke, because any text can be reconstructed as borrowed from some motif or other in one or the other myth of the entire repertoire of a culture (especially with a concession that where the exercise fails, the borrowing is still assumed from a source now inaccessible). There is no doubt that there were some similar motifs of heroic culture and contingent myths of India and Greece. When the two cultures met, there were definite mutual influences as well. However, why should that be a case of direct borrowing, why necessarily one way (Greek to Indian), and why the source of borrowing must be a Greek myth (and not Indian or Semitic or Chinese or Egyptian or anything else) are questions which beg answers. As long as there are no satisfactory answers to such questions, the most polite assessment of such works would be to designate them as futile.

Madeleine Biardeau, on the other hand, focuses on the ideology of *bhakti*, and stresses on the concept of *avatāra*.[99] She believes in the integrity of the *Mahābhārata* as a tradition rather than as a text and questions the entire analytical project of creating a Critical Edition, arguing that there was never a single written text of the *Mahābhārata* as an archetype from which all the manuscripts have evolved, but the various manuscripts are simply written versions of the story.[100] Hiltebeitel shows the important presence of Kṛṣṇa in several crucial episodes of the epic and considers the complementarity of Viṣṇu and Śiva too essential for the epic to be interpolated. He, like Biardeau, goes on to understand the text with religious ideas like *pralaya* and *avatāra*, with high importance placed on Kṛṣṇa's divinity and Draupadī's identification with Śrī.[101] Heino Gehrts has viewed the epic as modelled on a sacrificial theme, mainly as an extended *rājasūya*.[102] Buddhadeb Basu has shown the structural unity of the *Mahābhārata* in the gradual development of the character of Yudhiṣṭhira as its principal hero.[103] Adluri and Joydeep Bagchee have shown how the text may provide hermeneutical and etymological tools for its holistic interpretation.[104]

James Fitzgerald combines the views of Dahlmann (Deva-Asura conflict), Dümezil (allegories of Indo-European deities), Biardeau (importance of *avatāra*), and Hiltebeitel (the significant role of three Kṛṣṇas: Vāsudeva, Dvaipāyana, and Draupadī) in a grand interpretation that the *Mahābhārata* is primarily a religious epic, a response of the 'Brahmanical Renaissance' to the empires of Pāṭaliputra, which patronized the heterodox religions. The principal agenda is to espouse an ideal polity under a king who subjects himself under the *brāhmaṇas* whom he supports materially and preserves from all harm. The ideal society is conceived as one where all the *varṇas* perform their specified duties. The Brahmanical rage against the contemporary ruling class is presented within an overall narrative of demonic, unlawful *kṣatriyas* being purged by the divine *kṣatriyas* allied with the *brāhmaṇas*. The narration unfolds in genocidal hatred of a sacrifice to kill all the world's snakes, with Rāma Jāmadagnya's genocidal rampage against all *kṣatriyas* as the backdrop, gradually moving towards the violent purge of the *kṣatriyas* in the Bhārata War. The demons born as the unlawful Dhārtarāṣṭras are eradicated in a mortal conflict with the divine incarnations—the lawful Pāṇḍavas—who appear in the epic both as children begotten by deities and as a combined incarnation of Indra. Favourite of the *brāhmaṇas*, they are aided by three 'dark', 'obscure', 'secret' holy agents—the Viṣṇu-incarnate Kṛṣṇa Vāsudeva, the Śrī-incarnate Kṛṣṇā Draupadī, and the Vedic *brāhmaṇa* Kṛṣṇa Dvaipāyana Vyāsa.[105] However, Fitzgerald's overemphasis on Divine and Demonic birth—a secondary element to the main narrative—made him overlook the main narrative where the major characters rarely adhere to their prescribed *varṇa* duties.

Thus, various major researches on the *Mahābhārata* bypassed or negated a possibility of historicizing the text. However, B.B. Lal shows that the major sites of the epic event—including Hastināpura, Indraprastha, Vārāṇāvata, Pāṇiprastha, Tilaprastha, Kurukṣetra, Mathurā, and Vairāṭa—had a common habitational level in the Painted Grey Ware (PGW) using culture which belonged to *c.* 1200–600 BCE. Moreover, archaeology attests the epic account of a flood in Hastināpura which led to the shift of capital to Kauśāmbī, and the latter site also shows evidence of a late PGW culture.[106] Moreover, the great city of Pāṭaliputra—the prime city of Magadha, as well as of entire North India, from the fourth century BCE—is not mentioned as the metropolis of the Magadha of the *Mahābhārata*. The Magadha king Jarāsaṃdha ruled not even from Rājagṛha, the capital of Magadha in the sixth century BCE, but from Girivraja, the earliest power centre of Magadha, which indicates a date prior to sixth century BCE.

B.D. Chattopadhyaya questions Lal's procedure and quotes V. Gordon Childe to claim a priority of the Vedic sources over the 'polluted' epic-Purāṇic tradition. The Vedic and the Buddhist texts show an unmistakable shift from tribe to territory, and what the archaeology of the epic sites establishes is—to him—nothing but the archaeology of the emergence of *janapadas* in the Gaṅgā basin. He quotes Amalananda Ghosh's note of caution in his editorial notes on the Hastinapur excavation report. Ghosh, in his note, warns against taking the report as an official archaeological attestation of the epic narrative and points out that the only facts the report can attest are that Hastināpura—the reputed Kaurava capital—was occupied by PGW users in a period roughly synchronizing with the original narrative of the epic; the site was indeed deserted because of a great flood; and the same ceramic is found in many early sites connected with the epic. This information, to Chattopadhyaya, is not as important as they seem, except in their usefulness as a corrective to the exaggerated accounts of the epics. In fact, he thinks that a one-to-one correlation between archaeology and textual tradition is not possible. As Schliemann's Troy is not the same as Homer's, the Hastināpura and Indraprastha of archaeology hardly correspond with their epic description. Thus, methodologically, archaeology should be based on its own academic consideration rather than in a pursuit to search for the epic heroes. A digging at Kaveripattinam, for instance, should be the excavation of a site in the littoral region of the Saṅgam sources and not a search for the heroes and heroines of the *Cilappaṭikāram*.[107]

However, despite full agreement with Chattopadhyaya's archaeological standpoint, one cannot help wondering how the scholar, after emphasizing again and again the impossibility of correlation between literary tradition and archaeology, himself follows the same model. His identification of Hastināpura, Indraprastha, Kośala, and Videha as emergent *janapadas* of Later Vedic time or his marking of Kaveripattinam as a Saṅgam site is no less based on textual tradition than the identification of these sites as centres of epic activity. Therefore, in the end, it seems to be the case of privileging one set of literary sources (in this case the Vedic literature, the Buddhist texts, and the Saṅgam literature) over another (the *Rāmāyaṇa*, the *Mahābhārata*, the Purāṇas, and the *Cilappaṭikāram*), a tendency against which Chattopadhyaya himself speaks so vehemently. No doubt, archaeological excavations in search of Rāma or Kṛṣṇa, Hector or Achilles, Kovālan or Kannagī are amateurish and futile exercises. But the sites of Troy, Hastināpura, and Kaveripaṭṭinam must not necessarily be seen as corresponding to certain specific kinds of sources only, and not as a part of the geographical landscape of the *Iliad*, the *Mahābhārata*, and the *Cilappaṭikāram*, however different the sites' material culture may be from the poetic exaggerations and imaginations. Schliemann's Troy may not be the same as Homer's Troy, Lal's Hastinapur not the same as Vyāsa's. But whether that means that they cannot be the same Troy or Hastināpura at all is questionable.

As the flood occurred in around 800 BCE, Lal dates the war in the ninth century BCE.[108] Interestingly, Pargiter's dating, based on the Puranic tradition,[109] and Raychaudhuri's dating, based on Upaniṣadic genealogy,[110] point to a similar date. The *Atharva Veda* mentions Parikṣit, the descendent of the *Mahābhārata* heroes, as an active ruler.[111] The *Śatapatha Brāhmaṇa* refers to the horse sacrifice of Janamejaya—Parikṣit's son and successor—and his brothers Ugrasena, Bhīmasena, and Śrutasena.[112] Janamejaya, a great conqueror, is said to have been consecrated by the priest Tura Kāvaṣeya with *Aindra Mahābhiṣeka* in the AB.[113] The BU says that the descendants of Parikṣit are gone.[114] All these references together also place the events in the ninth to eighth centuries BCE. Remembering that the first recitation of the *Mahābhārata* was probably in a sacrifice organized by Janamejaya, J.A.B. van Buitenen thus remarks:

> It seems more likely than not that the origins of the *Mahābhārata* fall somewhere in the eighth or ninth century.[115]

Bhattacharya also dates the origin of the *Mahābhārata* tradition during the transition taking place around 1000 BCE.[116]

The legend of the recitation of the *Mahābhārata* in Janamejaya's sacrifice is corroborated by the *Āśvalāyana Gṛhya Sūtra* which refers to Vaiśaṃpāyana, the narrator, as *mahābhāratācārya*, a teacher of the *Mahābhārata*.[117] Vaiśaṃpāyana as a Later Vedic figure is also mentioned in the *Taittirīya Āraṇyaka* and Pāṇini's *Aṣṭādhyāyī*.[118] This convergence of several sources to a particular time bracket is too rare an event in ancient history to ignore.

Ruth Cecily Katz accepts the existence of several layers in the text but also points out that the text retained a unity of its basic narrative throughout its journey. Its journey possibly began as an oral composition by the *sūtas*. In the second stage it became a tradition recited in the royal courts under royal patronage. The final phase was its transition into a written text with several influences, including that of the Bhārgavas and several *bhakti* groups. The text therefore contains *brāhmaṇa*, *sūta-kṣatriya*, and *bhakti* materials. Katz thinks that all three strands existed in the text at least from the second stage of its composition, represented by Vaiśaṃpāyana's narration to Janamejaya, as the narrator was a *brāhmaṇa* and the patron a *kṣatriya* king directly descended from Arjuna, the ultimate *bhakta*.[119]

There is no reason to disagree with Katz, as her identification—following Sukthankar—of the three stages being represented by the *sūta* Saṃjaya's recitation of the war narrative to Dhṛtarāṣṭra, Vaiśaṃpāyana's narration to Janamejaya, and the *sūta* Ugraśravas's narration to the Bhārgava *kulapati* Śaunaka is compellingly well-structured. A middle ground between the Analytical and Synthetic attitudes seems not just plausible but also necessary. However, whether *bhakti* was really present in the time of Janamejaya and Vaiśaṃpāyana, who are definitely figures of the Later Vedic times, is very much questionable. Similarly, how much Brahmanization of the text happened at the hands of Vaiśaṃpāyana can be questioned, for he received the bardic tradition of Vyāsa and performed it exclusively for a Kuru king.

However, searching for a history of the ninth century BCE in a text which received its final shape more than a thousand years later is problematic. In fact, the task is impossible unless there is some way to find the voice representing the original oral tradition. Thapar has shown that it can be done only with the help of corroborative archaeological, anthropological, and historical evidence. A comparison with other sources indicates a difference between the nature of the narrative and didactic sections of the *Mahābhārata*. The former probably represents the older world of clan chiefships gradually moving towards a state system with monarchy as the norm. Lineage retains its vitality, while the fairly flexible kinship forms revolve around a pastoral-cum-agricultural economy where cattle raids and gift exchanges are very important. Heroism is mainly connected with the defence of territory and clan honour. On the other hand, the didactic sections represent a highly stratified monarchical state society with an agrarian and commercial economy.[120]

In *The Past before Us*, Thapar thoroughly discusses the embedded histories in both Vedic and the epic traditions (as well as the subsequent historical traditions of early India). Here she elaborately shows how the narrative and didactic sections of the *Mahābhārata* serve two distinct roles as historical traditions of two distinct social scenarios. Whereas the narrative section serves the needs of a clan society, the didactic sections, such as the 'Śāntiparvan' and the 'Anuśāsanaparvan', espouse a monarchical state protecting the *varṇa* order.[121] Elsewhere she raises the question whether Kurukṣetra symbolizes the end of the clan society.[122] This also involves a shift in the roles of the storytellers. Whereas the *sūta* bards are the initial tellers of the *Mahābhārata*, they gradually lose their status with the growing Brahmanization of the text. By the time of the *Manu Smṛti*, they are ascribed a very low social status. The *brāhmaṇas* recognized the power involved in capturing and controlling the past and gradually took over the data originally kept by the *sūtas*. When the literate *brāhmaṇas* appropriated and refashioned oral bardic lore in Sanskrit, they also downgraded many of these from whom they purloined their material.[123]

In her PhD thesis, Naina Dayal has shown that the process is more complex. The *sūtas* themselves might not have been a homogenous category. Therefore, while the social status of the *sūtas* in royal employment no doubt decayed, the wandering storytellers called *paurāṇika sūtas* were accepted gradually as *brāhmaṇas*. While the early bards narrated their compositions usually to a patronizing elite audience, the Brahmanization and Vaiṣṇavization of the epics changed their purpose. Therefore, in their later stages, the epics were for dissemination to a larger mass of people. This is particularly true in the *Rāmāyaṇa*'s case, which now acquired the character of a didactic text teaching unqualified goodness and espousing an ideal *varṇa*-ordered society. The *Mahābhārata* also acquired Brahmanical and monarchical sentiments. However, it never lost its basic nature of an *itihāsa*, and therefore its grim, practical mood could never be done away with. It retained the features of a practical text with the representation of a mixed bag of good and evil in the troublesome Kali Age, and thus even the locations of its telling are necessarily the grim surroundings of a serious if not destructive sacrifice.[124]

R.S. Sharma finds some genuine echoes of earlier times in the main narrative of the epic. The practice of *niyoga* and the polyandry of Draupadī are taken as references to an archaic society where matrilineal practices were still important. The king was still a tribal chief, *viśāṃpati* or *janeśvara*, advised mainly by his kinsmen and friends. The didactic sections, however, show a *varṇa*-divided state-based society with a system of taxation, a professional army, and an elaborate administrative apparatus.[125]

Similar observations have been made by Kevin McGrath who thinks that the text of the *Mahābhārata* contains both 'archaic' and 'classical' elements. By 'archaic', he refers to a preliterate and pre-monetary 'late Bronze Age' culture, characterized by the lack of sculptural and architectural reference, scarcity of devotional practice, and the absence of any reference to money, writing, urbanization, commerce, and metallurgy. This aspect is representative of the heroic culture of the *kṣatriya* warriors who excelled in chariot warfare. On the other hand, the classical elements are more representative of Brahmanical values and portray a post–Second Urbanization socio-economic context.[126] Hence, he shows that the nature of kingship represented in the 'Śāntiparvan' and the ensuing books was drastically different from that depicted in the earlier parts of the text.[127] Yudhiṣṭhira's kingship, in the early books, was a 'fraternal kingship' in which he shares his authority with his brothers and elders of the clan, as well as his friend and cousin Kṛṣṇa, and in which the corporate voice of the community (representing the people) was still an active and crucial presence. But what Bhīṣma demonstrates in the 'Śāntiparvan' is a more classical Brahmanical (McGrath calls it 'Hindu') kingship.[128] He also argues that the oldest parts of the text are possibly the four war books narrated by Saṃjaya whose bardic performance banked on a claim of visual reception of knowledge, unlike the later bard Vaiśaṃpāyana whose performance was based on auditory reception of knowledge.[129] The four war books and 'Sauptikaparvan' together, accounting for the entire Bhārata War, contains about twenty-four thousand verses in the Critical Edition, a number curiously similar to the number of verses supposed to have been in the earliest version of the *Bhāratasaṃhitā* composed by Vyāsa (see Vyāsa: I.1.61).[130] On the other hand, there are sections which can easily be identified as works of edition than of inspiration, a product of literacy than of preliteracy. For instance, the 'Ādiparvan' has no simple narrative process or even a singular and uniform time sequence. It is not an immediate composition but *bricolage*, creation from a diverse range of previously fabricated but uncombined elements. There is a confusion of plot in the first few *adhyāyas*, and what results is a comprehensive *imbroglio*.[131] However, he admits that there is no way to recover the *ur-Mahābhārata* text, even though it is possible to hypothetically assume its nature:

> What the Bhārata was, the *ur*-poem which Vyāsa first composed, as opposed to the Mahā-bhārata writ large, is lost to us forever and remains—just like the supposed Peisistratean recension of the Homeric Iliad—only a hypothetical and pre-initial composition.[132]

He further argues that the heroic poem of the *Mahābhārata* ends with the 'Strīparvan'. The last seven books represent a different poetic tradition whose poets tried to 'copy' the heroic model of the earlier tradition but was not totally successful, being much distant from the social context that produced the model. Therefore, Arjuna—the supreme hero of the war books—is nothing but a feeble copy of his former heroic self in the later books.[133]

McGrath's argument about preliteracy and heroic Bronze Age cults follows a framework of looking at the Homeric epics, championed by scholars such as M. Parry, A.B. Lord, and Gregory Nagy, and an overarching structure for looking at the Indo-European society, as proposed by Calvert Watkins and M.L. West.[134] Transposing it to the Indian context has its own problems. The pre-Second Urbanization context that the *Mahābhārata* addresses is still possibly an Iron Age rather than Bronze Age world. As discussed earlier, archaeology attests the existence of the major *Mahābhārata* sites in the period of the Later Vedas, the material context of which is of the Iron Age culture of the PGW users. Similarly, even though the *kṣatriyas* had their own code of valour, which is comparable to that of the Homeric heroic model, whether the two models are as close to each other as McGrath thinks is questionable. That is why the gradual decay in Arjuna's heroism may not necessarily represent a different poetic tradition but can be a tool used by the poets to show how age (both physical age and age in terms of the *yuga* cycle) could affect even the greatest of warriors or how Arjuna's heroism was contingent upon Kṛṣṇa's guidance as a charioteer.

Moreover, even though McGrath grants that the *Mahābhārata* represents a 'repository of historical consciousness', he thinks that the poets touched the audience with their reconstruction of an ideal past—one that bears no relation to any historical reality.[135] Perhaps, the historical reality McGrath talks of is basically a chronologically arranged factual account of authentic events of the past. This, as we have seen earlier, was not the goal of the historical tradition named *itihāsa*. But if we consider a convincingly accurate and comprehensive representation of a historical milieu—social, economic, political, cultural, and spiritual—as a depiction of 'historical reality', then McGrath's own work shows how successfully the poet(s) of the *Mahābhārata* tradition had performed that. That is why, despite centuries of reworking and interpolation, the text still allows a scholar like McGrath to distinguish the 'archaic' historical milieu of the early sections from the 'classical' milieu of the later sections. However, despite these issues, McGrath raises some valuable points—not quite different from the ones raised by Thapar and R.S. Sharma—including the existence of different kinds and levels of bardic performative traditions in the text and the apparent relative lateness of the social context of the 'Śāntiparvan' and the 'Anuśāsanaparvan' in comparison to the earlier books such as the 'Sabhāparvan'.

An interesting attestation to this model comes from the observations of Luis Gonzalez-Reimann. He shows that the famous theory of the four gradually decadent and shortened *yugas*—*kṛta*, *tretā*, *dvāpara*, and *kali*—succeeding one another in a cycle (with the Bhārata War being located at the juncture of the *dvāpara* and the *kali*), which possibly makes its appearance in the *Mahābhārata*, is almost absent from the narrative sections of the text. It appears nine times in the Critical Edition, out of which eight are from didactic sections, mostly from Mārkaṇḍeya's storytelling in the 'Āraṇyakaparvan', Bhīṣma's discourses in the 'Śāntiparvan' and the 'Anuśāsanaparvan', and the portions championing Kṛṣṇa's deification and Vaiṣṇavization of the text. Gonzalez-Reimann thinks that the *yuga* theory, absent in the Vedic corpus, was shaped only in the later strata of the text and superimposed on the narrative to serve three main purposes: providing a rationale (a cosmic explanation) for the unrighteous behaviour of the heroes and the devastating consequences of the war, turning a story of royal succession into a cosmic drama requiring divine intervention to restore a decadent *dharma*, and reflecting the historical reality of the crisis of Brahmanical religion in the later centuries BCE and first centuries CE when the coming of Central Asian ruling groups and growing influence of heterodox movements challenged the Vedic authority and the *varṇa* order. On the other hand, the narrative sections of the *Mahābhārata*, also aware of the momentous transition taking place, had a different concept of time, *kālavāda*, which envisioned Time (*kāla*) as a powerful, unstoppable force driving everything to its conclusion. The author, Vyāsa, is himself described as a *kālavādin*. This was a concept prevalent in the Later Vedic world. The *Atharva Veda* considers *kāla* as the supreme principle, and the *Śvetāśvatara Upaniṣad* mentions *kāla* as an explanation for the cause of things.[136]

Gonzalez-Reimann's arguments are supported by the fact that the earliest reference to the *Mahābhārata* war being located in the juncture of the *dvāpara* and *kali* comes from the *Yuga Purāṇa*, a part of the *Gārgya Jyotiṣa*, composed possibly in the first century BCE,[137] which says:

> Keśava will arise at the end of Dvāpara, in order to destroy horses and elephants, princes and men.
>
> (He will be) four-armed, of great valour, bearing the conch, disc and mace: (and he will be) called Vāsudeva, the strong one dressed in yellow clothes . . .

> The cause (of strife) of these might(y) kings will be Kṛṣṇā, the daughter of Drupada, (and) the earth will go to her destruction.
>
> Then, when the destruction of men had occurred and the circle of the kings has ended, there will be the fourth and final Yuga called Kali.[138]

The narrative sections possibly represent the historical scenario of the Later Vedic period, since independent Later Vedic texts attest Kuru-Pañcāla dominance, their rivalry, and eventual alliance and remember Parikṣit and his descendants as actual rulers. Not only Parikṣit and Janamejaya but also some ancestors of the *Mahābhārata* heroes, mentioned in the epic, are known from other Later Vedic sources. Later sections of the *Ṛg Veda* mention Purūravas Aila, Āyus, Yayāti Nāhuṣya, Pūru, Ṛkṣa, Saṃvaraṇa, and Kuru. The most famous king of the lineage, Bharata Dauṣyanti Saudyumni, is referred to in the ŚB as making sacrifices on the rivers Yamunā, Gaṅgā, and Sarasvatī, attesting his association with the Kuru realm. The ŚB also speaks of Śakuntalā—the mother of Bharata in the epic—as an *apsarā* raised by the sage Kaṇva, corroborating the epic account of Śakuntalā being the daughter of the *apsarā* Menakā and foster-daughter of Kaṇva. The other famous king, Kuru also appears frequently in the *Brāhmaṇa* literature. Among the kings directly featuring in the *Mahābhārata*, Pratīpa appears in the *Atharva Veda*, Bāhlīka Pratīpīya in the ŚB, and Śaṃtanu in Book X of the *Rg Veda*. Dhṛtarāṣṭra Vaicitravīrya appears in the *Kaṭhaka Saṃhitā* as an opponent of Baka Dālbhya who appears in the *Mahābhārata* as a great enemy of Dhṛtarāṣṭra's sons.[139] In Yāska's *Nirukta* it is said that Devāpi acted as domestic priest for his brother Śaṃtanu who had anointed himself king, corresponding to the account of the *Mahābhārata* that Śaṃtanu became king when his elder brother Devāpi became an ascetic.[140] Kṛṣṇa Devakīputra appears in the CU.[141] The ŚB identifies Arjuna with Indra,[142] and the ĀŚS knows him as 'Pārtha'.[143]

More importantly, the *Mahābhārata* characters and events appear across historical traditions. Even in the Buddhist legends, Vāsudeva (Kṛṣṇa) and Baladeva, as rulers of Dvārāvatī, appear in the *Ghaṭa Jātaka*,[144] whereas Vāsudeva's marriage with Jāmbabatī is mentioned in the *Mahāummaga Jātaka*.[145] Both the *Ghaṭa Jātaka* and the *Kaṇha Dīpāyana Jātaka* mention the great sage Kaṇha Dīpāyana (Kṛṣṇa Dvaipāyana).[146]

All five sons of Pāṇḍu are mentioned by names in the *Kuṇāla Jātaka*, as the husbands of Kaṇhā (Kṛṣṇā Draupadī).[147] The *Daśabrāhmaṇa Jātaka* refers to the Kaurava kings of Yudhiṣṭhira's lineage ruling from the Kuru capital Indraprastha.[148] The heroes of the *Mahābhārata* are well known to the Jaina tradition as well.[149]

By the time of Pāṇini, there were already communities who worshipped Kṛṣṇa and Arjuna.[150] Megasthenes also reports about worshippers of Kṛṣṇa (Heracles) in Methora (Mathura) and Cleisobora (Kṛṣṇapura?).[151] The *Arthaśāstra* categorically mentions two *Mahābhārata* characters Nala and Yudhiṣṭhira to illustrate the bad effects of gambling.[152]

In fact the close connection between the *Mahābhārata* and the Later Vedic literature can hardly be denied. Michael Witzel shows how most of the Vedic corpus was composed in the Kuru-Pañcāla region and under Bharata-Kuru patronage.[153] A more or less continuous history of the Bharatas starting from Divodāsa and Sudās can be gleaned from the family books of the *Ṛg Veda*. The last Bharata-Kuru king appearing in the *Ṛg Veda* is Śāṃtanu,[154] from whose reign the main narrative of the *Mahābhārata* unfolds.

Witzel, in his article 'Early Sanskritization: Origin and Development of the Kuru State', argues for recognizing the Kuru kingdom as the first 'state' of northern India. He contends that it is this state under Parikṣit, whose magnificent reign is praised in the *Atharva Veda*, that led to the formation of the Vedic orthodoxy and orthopraxy, by canonizing the Vedic corpus and introducing the *varṇa* order. The Kuru dominance continued for a period of time before the Śālva invasion reduced their power and Pañcāla became the new power centre.[155] In fact, Witzel convincingly shows the correlation between the Vedic and the *Mahābhārata* worlds, even if the *Mahābhārata* events and chief protagonists might have been later inventions.[156]

Though Witzel's studies are very comprehensive and valuable, his focus only on the Vedic corpus makes him overlook the linkages which the *Mahābhārata* provides. The Bhārata War possibly provided the necessary background to the peaceful reign of Parikṣit who used the favourable situation for consolidation. This peace and consolidation could have facilitated the intellectual upsurge that led to the canonization of the Vedic corpus. That this canonization is attributed to Vyāsa, the author of the *Mahābhārata*, is an interesting pointer indeed. The first formalization of Vyāsa's *Mahābhārata* possibly took place under the patronage of Janamejaya, Parikṣit's son. While attributing the decline of the Kuru power to the Śālva invasion, on the basis of Vedic authority, Witzel misses the crucial link that the Hastināpura flood might have provided.

Similarly, Witzel shows the context of the *Mahābhārata* as Vedic, since both the predecessors and successors of the *Mahābhārata* protagonists are Vedic figures. However, he thinks that the intervening generation was invented in a much later non-Vedic context. His proposition is that the Battle of Ten Kings, involving the closely related groups of the Bharatas and Pūrus, was turned into the Bhārata War in later bardic narrative. He points out the absence of the Pāṇḍavas from the Vedic corpus, considers them as representatives of the Śālvas—whose invasion might have destroyed the Kurus—and shows how the actions of the Pāṇḍavas could have been modelled on the Vedic *vrātyas*. Assuming, from various linguistic and historical evidences, that the *Mahābhārata* had been compiled under Śuṅga patronage around 150 BCE, Witzel proposed that the *Mahābhārata*, like Homer's *Iliad*, is a war tale dealing with Bronze Age heroes of the Kuru realm of *c.* 1000 BCE, which was seamlessly put by later bards in an Iron Age setting of *c.* 500–100 BCE. It is unclear which 'Indian Homer' would have put all this together unless one accepted the traditional attribution of that role to Kṛṣṇa Dvaipāyana Vyāsa.[157]

Whereas Witzel's article brilliantly shows how the *Mahābhārata* is very much linked with the Bharata-Pūrus and the Kurus of the Vedic literature, it is difficult to accept the equation between the *dāśarājña* (Battle of Ten Kings) and the Bhārata War. There can very well be two different major wars related to the traditional history of the same clan. Also, though there are interesting genealogical inconsistencies in the *Mahābhārata* (some of which we shall discuss in Chapter 3), they might not necessarily be the result of the refashioning of the Vedic genealogy and the insertion of an intervening generation. There could have been different versions of the genealogy of a clan in different traditions. The bardic tradition from which the *Mahābhārata* originated could have had a very different idea of Kuru genealogy from the Vedic-Brahmanic tradition. When both of them were accommodated in the Brahmanized later version of the text, inconsistencies would naturally arise. Moreover, we shall see in Chapters 2 and 5 how the tradition about the Battle of Ten Kings and the complicated relationship between the Vedic chief Sudās and his two priests (Viśvāmitra and Vasiṣṭha) were reshaped in the *Mahābhārata* and the *Rāmāyaṇa* as a narrative very different from the narrative of the Bhārata War. Thus, there is little room for confusion between the two. The Pāṇḍavas might not have been mentioned separately in the Vedic literature simply because they were also Kurus (like their descendant Parikṣit). It is true that even their personal names do not occur in the Vedic corpus. However, the early Buddhist corpus knew at least Yudhiṣṭhira and Arjuna, whereas both of them were known to Pāṇini as well. On the other hand, there is little evidence to suggest any connection between the Pāṇḍavas and the Śālvas, and the latter are present as a separate community in the *Mahābhārata* as well. Though there are similarities between the Pāṇḍavas and the *vrātyas*, Witzel overlooks the glaring differences. For instance, if polyandrous Draupadī represents the promiscuous women who accompanied the unmarried Vedic *vrātyas*, the formulation would need to overlook that all the Pāṇḍavas are represented as married outside their polyandrous arrangement as well, and at least one of those marriages—the one between Arjuna and Subhadrā—is crucial for both the vital Pāṇḍava-Yādava connection Witzel notes and the establishment of the link between the Pāṇḍavas and Parikṣit.

However, Hiltebeitel carries forward the proposition by arguing that the *Mahābhārata* was the result of the activities of out-of-sorts Pūrvaśikhā *brāhmaṇas* who migrated to South India after the invasions by Indo-Greeks and Śakas in the first century BCE and wanted to recreate their past in the Vedic idioms of the Kuru-Pañcāla territory, which is nothing more than a hypothetical assumption based on little evidence.[158] Why would these *brāhmaṇas* imagine their past in an idiom so separate in time and in a territory not their own, or, more importantly, why would they 'invent' a generation in a Vedic clan, that too a *kṣatriya* one, is hardly explained by Hiltebeitel's model.

Scholars like Thapar, R.S. Sharma, and McGrath provide us with a completely new approach to study the *Mahābhārata*. Still, the narrative-didactic divide seems too simplistic. Even the earlier version might have contained some didactic elements, and even narrative passages could have been interpolated later. Therefore, this study tries to understand the basic events of the narrative section—the struggle between the Kauravas and the Pāṇḍava-Pañcālas—in their historical context. That determines my selection of certain events, each having its own considerable historiography.

The events selected are the major turning points of the Kuru succession struggle, namely the division of the Kuru kingdom followed by the burning of the Khāṇḍava forest and the establishment of Indraprastha, Yudhiṣṭhira's *rājasūya* sacrifice followed by the dice games where Yudhiṣṭhira lost all his wealth, the Kaurava cattle raid in Matsya which revealed the identity of the Pāṇḍavas, and the Bhārata War. But before getting into these, we must start our journey from the Vedic world, where the Vedic poets—particularly Viśvāmitra and Vasiṣṭha—recorded the prehistory of the Bharata-Kurus in their memoirs of the Battle of Ten Kings. Interestingly, with the millennium-long journey of the text, Viśvāmitra and Vasiṣṭha themselves were appropriated within the historical traditions, showing us a classic example of how a historical tradition was reshaped and reinterpreted by changing societies to serve different social functions.

Notes

1. Romila Thapar, *From Lineage to State*, Oxford University Press, New Delhi, 2008a (reprint).
2. See H.C. Raychaudhuri, *Political History of Ancient India*, new edition with a commentary by B.N. Mukherjee, Oxford University Press, New Delhi, 2006, pp. 2–9.
3. F.E. Pargiter, *Ancient Indian Historical Tradition*, Motilal Banarsidass, Delhi, 1997 (reprint), pp. 13–14.
4. Pargiter (1997); F.E. Pargiter, *Dynasties of the Kali Age*, Motilal Banarsidass, Delhi, 1975 (reprint); R. Morton Smith, *Dates and Dynasties in Early India*, Motilal Banarsidass, Delhi, 1973.
5. S.N. Pradhan, *Chronology of Ancient India*, Cosmo Publications, Calcutta, 1927.
6. A.D. Pusalker, *Studies in the Epics and Purāṇas*, Bharatiya Vidya Bhavan, Bombay, 1958; A.D. Pusalker, 'Aryan Settlements in India' in R.C. Majumdar (ed.), *The History and Culture of the Indian People: The Vedic Age*, Bharatiya Vidya Bhavan, Mumbai, 1996 (reprint), pp. 245–267.
7. P.L. Bhargava, *India in the Vedic Age*, D.K. Printworld, Lucknow, 1956.
8. Romila Thapar, 'Society and Historical Consciousness: The *Itihāsa-purāṇa* Tradition' in Romila Thapar, *Cultural Pasts*, Oxford University Press, New Delhi, 2008b (reprint), p. 123.
9. Raychaudhuri (2006), pp. 11–84.
10. The Later Vedic texts, of course, are there, but they are liturgical literature providing very little and incidental historical references.

11. A.A. Macdonell, *History of Sanskrit Literature*, Motilal Banarsidass, Delhi, 1990 (reprint), p. 11.
12. E.J. Rapson (ed.), *The Cambridge History of India* (Vol. I), Cambridge University Press, Cambridge, 1922, p. 57.
13. R.C. Majumdar, 'Ideas of History in Sanskrit Literature' in C.H. Philips (ed.), *Historians of India, Pakistan and Ceylon*, Oxford University Press, London, 1961, p. 13.
14. U.N. Ghoshal, *Studies in Indian History and Culture*, Orient Longman, Calcutta, 1957, pp. 1–242.
15. Burton Stein, 'Early Indian Historiography: A Conspiracy Hypothesis', *Indian Economic and Social History Review*, Vol. 6, No. 1, 1969, pp. 41–60.
16. H. Kulke, 'Historiography in Early Medieval India' in G. Berhman et al., *Exploration in the History of South Asia: In Honour of Dietmar Rothermund*, Manohar, Delhi, 2001, pp. 71–83.
17. Sheldon Pollock, 'Mīmāṃsā and the Problem of History in Traditional India', *Journal of the American Oriental Society*, Vol. 109, No. 4, 1989, pp. 603–610.
18. A. Nandy, 'History's Forgotten Doubles', *History and Theory*, Vol. 44, No. 2, 1995, pp. 44–66.
19. Vinay Lal, *The History of History: Politics and Scholarship in Modern India*, Oxford University Press, Delhi, 2009, pp. 14–16, 58–60.
20. R. Guha, *History at the Limit of World History: An Indian Historiography of India*, Columbia University Press, New York, 2002, p. 33.
21. Jan Huizinga, 'A Definition of the Concept of History' in Ernst Cassirer, R. Klibansky, and H.J. Paton (eds), *Philosophy and History*, Harper and Row, New York, 1963, pp. 8–9.
22. Romila Thapar, *The Past before Us*, Permanent Black, Ranikhet, 2013, pp. 10–14.
23. Thapar (2013), p. 16.
24. Thapar (2013), p. 4.
25. Thapar (2013), p. 4.
26. Thapar (2013), p. 3.
27. Thapar (2013), p. 4.
28. Thapar (2013), p. 5.
29. Thapar (2013), pp. 113–136.
30. Thapar (2013), pp. 130–133.
31. *Hymns of the Atharvaveda* (vols I and II), translated by Ralph T.H. Griffith, Munshiram Manoharlal, New Delhi, 2002, XV.6.11. All references to the AV are from this volume.
32. *Bṛhadāraṇyaka Upaniṣad* in *Upaniṣads*, translated by Patrick Olivelle, Oxford University Press, Oxford, 2008, IV.1.2. All Upaniṣadic references are from this volume.
33. *Chāndogya Upaniṣad*, VII.1.2.
34. Thapar (2013), pp. 56–57.

35. Kauṭilya, *The Arthaśāstra* (vols I–III), edited and translated by R.P. Kangle, University of Bombay, Bombay, 1960, I.5. All references to the *Arthaśāstra* are from this volume.
36. Bharata, *The Nāṭyaśāstra*, I.15.
37. Taranatha Tarkavachaspati, *Vācaspatyam*, Vol. I, Chowkhamba Surbharati, Varanasi, 1990, p. 924.
38. Yāska, *The Nighantu and the Nirukta*, edited by Lakshman Sarup, Motilal Banarsidass, New Delhi, 1962, II.16, XII.1, IV.6, VI.11, XII.10.
39. Thapar (2013), p. 57.
40. Sibesh Chandra Bhattacharya, 'Mahābhārata, Itihāsa, Agency' in Sibesh Chandra Bhattacharya, Vrinda Dalmiya, and Gangeya Mukherji (eds), *Exploring Agency in the Mahabharata: Ethical and Political Dimensions of Dharma*, Routledge, London and New York, 2018, p. 36.
41. The same status has been claimed for the *Rāmāyaṇa* by some Early Medieval literary critics and poets such as Ānandavardhana, Abhinavagupta, and Bhavabhūti. However, the *Rāmāyaṇa* itself does not claim to be an *itihāsa*.
42. Vyāsa, *The Mahābhārata*, I.56.33. Van Buitenen translates *dharma*, *artha*, and *mokṣa* as Law, Profit, and Salvation, respectively. However, their implications are broader, and they can be approximately translated as social morality, political economy, and liberation, respectively. All references to Vyāsa's *Mahābhārata* are from the multivolume Critical Edition prepared under the general editorship of V.S. Sukthankar, published by the Bhandarkar Oriental Research Institute, Poona. The complete details of all the volumes used are given in the Bibliography. The translations which have been followed are: Vyāsa, *The Mahābhārata* (Vol. I), translated by J.A.B. van Buitenen, University of Chicago Press, Chicago, 1973 (for the 'Ādiparvan'); Vyāsa, *The Mahābhārata* (Vol. II), translated by J.A.B. van Buitenen, University of Chicago Press, Chicago, 1975 (for the 'Sabhāparvan' and the 'Āraṇyakaparvan'); Vyāsa, *The Mahābhārata* (Vol. III), translated by J.A.B. van Buitenen, University of Chicago Press, Chicago, 1978 (for the 'Virāṭaparvan' and 'Udyogaparvan'); Vyāsa, *Mahābhārata* (Book Six): Bhishma (Vols 1 and 2), translated by Alex Cherniak, New York University Press, New York, 2008 (for the 'Bhīṣmparvan'); Vyāsa, *Mahābhārata* (Book Nine): Shalya (Vols 1 and 2), translated by Justin Meiland, New York University Press, New York, 2007 (for the 'Śalyaparvan); and Vyāsa, *The Mahābhārata* (Vol. VII), translated by James Fitzgerald, University of Chicago Press, Chicago, 2004 (for the 'Strīparvan' and 'Śāntiparvan' 1–167). For the rest of the text, the translations are mine unless otherwise specified.
43. Vyāsa, *The Mahābhārata*, I.1.24. I have slightly modified van Buitenen's translation here by keeping the word *itihāsa* intact rather than using 'history' as its translation.
44. Vyāsa, *The Mahābhārata*, I.2.9, III.148.37, VI.62.39.
45. Maurice Winternitz, *History of Indian Literature*, Vol. 1, translated by V. Srinivas Sarma, New Delhi, Motilal Banarsidass, 1987, p. 305.

46. Cited in V.S. Sukthankar, *On the Meaning of the Mahābhārata*, The Asiatic Society of Bombay, Bombay, 1957, pp. 2–3.
47. Cited in Sukthankar (1957), p. 5.
48. Cited in John Brockington, *The Sanskrit Epics*, Brill, Leiden, 1998, p. 54.
49. R.N. Dandekar, 'The *Mahābhārata*: Origin and Growth', *University of Ceylon Review*, Vol. 12, No. 4, April 1954, pp. 65–85.
50. Cited in Alf Hiltebeitel, 'Kṛṣṇa and the Mahābhārata', *Annals of the Bhandarakar Oriental Research Institute*, Vol. 60, 1979, p. 95.
51. J. Kennedy, 'The Child Krishna and His Critics', *Journal of Royal Asiatic Society*, 1908, pp. 505–521; J. Kennedy, 'The Child Krishna, Christianity and the Gujars', *Journal of Royal Asiatic Society*, 1907, pp. 951–991.
52. Cited in Sukthankar (1957), pp. 6–8.
53. E. Washburn Hopkins, *The Great Epic of India*, Punthi Pustak, Calcutta, 1969a (reprint).
54. Sukthankar (1957), pp. 18–19.
55. Cited in Brockington (1998), p. 45.
56. Sukthankar (1957), p. 17.
57. Cited in Brockington (1998), p. 45.
58. Cited in Brockington (1998), pp. 53–54.
59. F.E. Pargiter, 'The Nations of India at the Battle between the Pāṇḍavas and Kauravas', *Journal of the Royal Asiatic Society of Great Britain and Ireland*, April 1908, pp. 309–336.
60. George A. Grierson, 'A Note on Mr. Keith's Note on the Battle between the Pāṇḍavas and Kauravas', *Journal of the Royal Asiatic Society of Great Britain and Ireland*, July 1908, pp. 837–844.
61. A. Berriedale Keith, 'The Battle between the Pāṇḍavas and the Kauravas', *Journal of the Royal Asiatic Society of Great Britain and Ireland*, July 1908, pp. 831–836.
62. D.D. Kosambi, 'The Autochthonous Element in *Mahābhārata*', *Journal of the American Oriental Society*, Vol. 84, No. 1, January–March 1964, pp. 31–44.
63. K. Kunjunni Raja, 'Architectonics of the *Mahābhārata* and the Place of Legends in Its Structure' in T.R.S. Sharma (ed.), *Reflections and Variations on the Mahābhārata*, Sahitya Akademi, New Delhi, 2009, pp. 67–68.
64. Cited in Sukthankar (1957), pp. 19–25.
65. Sukthankar (1957), pp. 54–55.
66. Sukthankar (1957), pp. 54–55.
67. Patricia M. Greer, 'Ethical Discourse in Udyogaparvan' in T.S. Rukmani (ed.), *The Mahābhārata: What Is Not Here Is Nowhere Else*, Munshiram Manoharlal, New Delhi, 2005, pp. 211–224.
68. Raja (2009).
69. A.K. Ramanujan, 'Repetition in the Mahābhārata' in Arvind Sharma (ed.), *Essays on the Mahābhārata*, Motilal Banarsidass, Delhi, 2007, pp. 419–443.

70. Radhavallabh Tripathi, 'Aesthetics of the Mahābhārata: Traditional Interpretations' in Arindam Chakrabarti and Sibaji Bandyopadhyay (eds), *Mahābhārata Now*, Routledge, New Delhi, 2014, pp. 85–94.
71. Vishwa Adluri, 'Introduction' in Vishwa Adluri (ed.), *Ways and Reasons for Thinking about the Mahābhārata as a Whole*, Bhandarkar Oriental Research Institute, Pune, 2015a, p. xiv.
72. Adluri (2015a), p. xiv.
73. Adluri (2015a), p. xv.
74. Adluri (2015a), p. xv.
75. Adluri (2015a), p. xxiii.
76. Adluri (2015a), p. xxxii.
77. Simon Brodbeck, 'Some Textological Observations on the Analytic and Synthetic Modes' in Vishwa Adluri (ed.), *Ways and Reasons for Thinking about the Mahābhārata as a Whole*, Bhandarkar Oriental Research Institute, Pune, 2015, pp. 135–154.
78. There can be an inexhaustible bibliography presented in support of this. Even without going into that, for a basic idea of the evolution of historical methodologies, one can see E.H. Carr, *What Is History?*, Penguin, Basingstoke, 1986 (reprint); R.G. Collingwood, *The Idea of History*, Oxford University Press, Oxford, 1994 (reprint); Leon Goldstein, *Historical Knowing*, University of Texas Press, Austin, 1976; Daniel Woolf, *A Global History of History*, Cambridge University Press, Cambridge, 2011; Marc Bloch, *The Historian's Craft*, Knopf, New York, 1953; Lynn Hunt, *Writing History in the Global Era*, Norton, New York, 2014; Ranajit Guha, 'Introduction' in Ranajit Guha (ed.), *Subaltern Studies* (Vol. 1), Oxford University Press, New Delhi, 1982, pp. 1–8.
79. Muneo Tokunaga, 'Bhīṣma's Discourse on *Śokāpanodana*' in Robert P. Goldman and Muneo Tokunaga (eds), *Epic Undertakings*, Motilal Banarsidass, Delhi, 2009, pp. 371–382.
80. Alf Hiltebeitel, *Rethinking the Mahābhārata: A Reader's Guide to the Education of the Dharma King*, University of Chicago Press, Chicago, 2001; Alf Hiltebeitel, 'New Possibilities in Considering the Mahabharata's Intention as "History"' in Vishwa Adluri (ed.), *Ways and Reasons for Thinking about the Mahābhārata as a Whole*, Bhandarkar Oriental Research Institute, Pune, 2015, pp. 29–62.
81. Cited in James L. Fitzgerald, 'Mahābhārata' in Sushil Mittal and Gene Thursby (eds), *The Hindu World*, Routledge, New York, 2004, pp. 52–74.
82. Jan Gonda, 'Some Observations on Dumezil's Views on Indo-European Mythology', *Mnemosyne*, Vol. 4, 1960, pp. 1–15; Jan Gonda, 'Dumezil's Tripartite Ideology: Some Critical Observations', *Journal of Asian Studies*, Vol. 34, 1974, pp. 139–149.
83. F.B.J. Kuiper, 'Some Observations on Dumezil's Theory', *Numen*, 1961, pp. 34–45.
84. Gesta Johnson, 'Varuna and Dhrtarastra', *Indo-Iranian Journal*, Vol. 9, 1965–1966, pp. 245–265.

85. Nick Allen, 'Bhīṣma as Matchmaker' in Simon Brodbeck and Brian Black (eds), *Gender and Narrative in the Mahabharata*, Routledge, London, 2007, pp. 176–188; N.J. Allen, 'Arjuna and Odysseus: A Comparative Approach', *South Asia Library Group Newsletter*, Vol. 40, 1993, pp. 39–42.
86. Julian Baldick, *Homer and the Indo-Europeans: Comparing Mythologies*, I.B. Tauris, London, 1994.
87. Cited in Brockington (1998), pp. 77–78.
88. Cited in Brockington (1998), p. 79.
89. Fernando Alonso Wulff, 'Greek Sources in the Mahābhārata' in Vishwa Adluri (ed.), *Ways and Reasons for Thinking about the Mahābhārata as a Whole*, Bhandarkar Oriental Research Institute, Pune, 2015, p. 155.
90. Wulff (2015), pp. 157–158.
91. Wulff (2015), p. 167.
92. Wulff (2015), pp. 161–166.
93. See Allen (2007).
94. Wulff (2015), pp. 176, 179, 181.
95. Wulff (2015), pp. 174–178.
96. Wulff (2015), p. 173.
97. Wulff (2015), pp. 157–161.
98. Wulff (2015), p. 181.
99. Cited in Brockington (1998), pp. 71–72.
100. Cited in Saroja Bhate, 'Methodology of the Critical Edition of the Mahābhārata' in Arindam Chakrabarti and Sibaji Bandyopadhyay (eds), *Mahābhārata Now*, Routledge, New Delhi, 2014, p. 35.
101. Hiltebeitel (1979).
102. Brockington (1998), pp. 74–75.
103. Buddhadeb Basu, *Mahābhārater Kathā*, M.C. Sarkar and Sons Private Limited, Kolkata, 2001 (reprint).
104. Vishwa Adluri, 'Hermeneutics and Narrative Architecture in the Mahabharata' in Vishwa Adluri (ed.), *Ways and Reasons for Thinking about the Mahābhārata as a Whole*, Bhandarkar Oriental Research Institute, Pune, 2015, pp. 1–28; Joydeep Bagchee, 'Ruru, Etymology from Hell' in Vishwa Adluri (ed.), *Ways and Reasons for Thinking about the Mahābhārata as a Whole*, Bhandarkar Oriental Research Institute, Pune, 2015, pp. 119–134.
105. Fitzgerald (2004a).
106. B.B. Lal, 'The Two Indian Epics vis-à-vis Archaeology', *Antiquity*, Vol. LV, 1981, pp. 27–34.
107. B.D. Chattopadhyaya, 'Indian Archaeology and the Epic Traditions' in *Studying Early India*, Permanent Black, New Delhi, 2003, pp. 29–38.
108. B.B. Lal (1981), p. 30.
109. Pargiter (1997), pp. 175–184.
110. Raychaudhuri (2006), p. 33.
111. AV, XX.127.7.10.

112. *Śatapatha Brāhmaṇa* (Vols I–V), translated by Julius Eggeling, Motilal Banarsidass, New Delhi, 2005 (reprint), XII.5.4.3. All further references to the ŚB are from this volume.
113. *Aitareya Brāhmaṇa* in *Ṛg Veda Brāhmaṇas*, translated by A. Berriedale Keith, Harvard University Press, Cambridge, MA, 1920, VIII. All further references to the AB are from this volume.
114. *Bṛhadāraṇyaka Upaniṣad*, III.3.1.
115. J.A.B. van Buitenen, 'The Mahābhārata: Introduction' in Vyāsa, *The Mahābhārata* (Vol. I), translated by J.A.B. van Buitenen, University of Chicago Press, Chicago, 1973a, p. xxiv.
116. Bhattacharya (2018), p. 34.
117. *Āśvalāyana Gṛhya Sūtra* in *Gṛhya Sūtras* (Part I), translated by Hermann Oldenberg, Motilal Banarsidass, New Delhi, 1964 (reprint), III.4. All further references to the *Āśvalāyana Gṛhya Sūtra* are from this volume.
118. Raychaudhuri (2006), p. 7.
119. Ruth Cecily Katz, *Arjuna in the Mahābārata*, Motilal Banarsidass, Delhi, 1989, pp. 15–20.
120. Romila Thapar, 'The Historian and the Epic' in Romila Thapar, *Cultural Pasts*, Oxford University Press, New Delhi, 2008c, pp. 613–629.
121. Thapar (2013), pp. 146–207.
122. Romila Thapar, *Early India*, Penguin, New Delhi, 2000, p. 102.
123. Romila Thapar, 'Genealogical Pattern as Perceptions of the Past' in Romila Thapar, *Cultural Pasts*, Oxford University Press, New Delhi, 2008d, pp. 718–719.
124. Naina Dayal, 'Tellers of Tales: Paurāṇikas, Ṣūtas, Kuśīlavas, Vyāsa and Vālmīki', PhD thesis submitted to Jawaharlal Nehru University, New Delhi, 2009.
125. R.S. Sharma, *Material Culture and Social Formations in Ancient India*, MacMillan, Delhi, 1983a, pp. 135–152.
126. The model is gradually developed in a series of books such as Kevin McGrath, *The Sanskrit Hero: Karṇa in Epic Mahābhārata*, Brill, Leiden, 2004; Kevin McGrath, *Strī: Women in Epic Mahābhārata*, Orient BlackSwan, New Delhi, 2011a; Kevin McGrath, *Jaya: Performance in Epic Mahābhārata*, Harvard University Press, Cambridge, MA, 2011b; Kevin McGrath, *Heroic Kṛṣṇa: Friendship in Epic Mahābhārata*, Harvard University Press, Cambridge, MA, 2013; Kevin McGrath, *Rājā Yudhiṣṭhira: Kingship in Epic Mahābhārata*, Cornell University Press, Ithaca, 2016a; Kevin McGrath, *Arjuna Pāṇḍava: The Double Hero in Epic Mahābhārata*, Orient BlackSwan, Hyderabad, 2016b; Kevin McGrath, *Bhīṣma Devavrata: Authority in Epic Mahābhārata*, Orient BlackSwan, Hyderabad, 2018.
127. McGrath (2016a).
128. McGrath (2016a), pp. 2–3.
129. McGrath (2011b).
130. McGrath (2016b), p. 190.
131. McGrath (2018), pp. 156–157.

132. McGrath (2018), p. 156.
133. McGrath (2016b), pp. 107–118.
134. M. Parry, 'Studies in the Epic Technique of Oral Versemaking: II, The Homeric Language as the Language of Oral Poetry', *Harvard Studies in Classical Philology*, Vol. 43, 1932, pp. 1–50; A.B. Lord, *The Singer of Tales*, Harvard University Press, Cambridge, MA, 1960; Gregory Nagy, *Homer the Preclassic*, University of California Press, Berkeley, 2010; Gregory Nagy, *The Ancient Greek Hero in Twenty-Four Hours*, Harvard University Press, Cambridge, MA, 2013; Calvert Watkins, *How to Kill a Dragon: Aspects of Indo-European Poetics*, Oxford University Press, Oxford, 1995; M.L. West, *Indo-European Poetry and Myth*, Oxford University Press, Oxford, 2007.
135. McGrath (2016a), p. 4.
136. Luis Gonzalez-Reimann, 'Time in the *Mahābhārata* and the Time of the *Mahābhārata*' in Sheldon Pollock (ed.), *Epic and Argument in Sanskrit Literary History: Essays in Honor of Robert P. Goldman*, Manohar, New Delhi, 2010, pp. 61–73.
137. *The Yuga Purāṇa*, critically edited with an English translation and detailed introduction by John E. Mitchiner, The Asiatic Society, Calcutta, 1986, p. 81.
138. *The Yuga Purāṇa*, verses, 29, 30, 36, and 37.
139. Raychaudhuri (2006), p. 23.
140. Yāska (1962), II.10.
141. CU, III.17.6.
142. ŚB, V.4.3.7.
143. Raychaudhuri (2006), p. 7.
144. *The Jātaka* (Vol. IV), translated by W.H.D. Rouse, Munshiram Manoharlal, New Delhi, 2002, pp. 50–57.
145. *The Jātaka* (Vol. VI), translated by E.B. Cowell and W.H.D. Rouse, Munshiram Manoharlal, New Delhi, 2002, pp. 156–245.
146. *The Jātaka* (Vol. IV), pp. 17–22, 50–57.
147. *The Jātaka* (Vol. V), translated by H.T. Francis, Munshiram Manoharlal, New Delhi, 2002, p. 225.
148. *The Jātaka* (Vol. VI), pp. 227–231.
149. J.N. Sumitra Bai and Robert J. Zydenbos, 'The Jaina Mahābhārata' in Arvind Sharma (ed.), *Essays on the Mahābhārata*, Motilal Banarsidass, Delhi, 2007, pp. 251–273.
150. Pāṇini, *The Ashtadhyayi*, edited by Srisa Chandra Basu, Motilal Banarsidass, New Delhi, 2003, IV.3.98.
151. R.C. Majumdar, *Ancient India*, Motilal Banarsidass, New Delhi, 1987, p. 173. The word 'Kṛṣṇapura' is a phonetic reconstruction. Majumdar assumes that it is Vṛndāvana, but the identity is doubtful.
152. Kauṭilya, VIII.3.43.
153. Michael Witzel, 'On the Localization of Vedic Texts and Schools' in G. Pollet (ed.), *India and the Ancient World: History, Trade and Culture before A.D. 650*,

Department Orientalistiek, Leuven, 1987, pp. 173–213; Michael Witzel, 'The Development of Vedic Canon and Its Schools: The Social and Political Milieu' in Michael Witzel (ed.), *Inside the Text, Beyond the Text: New Approaches to the Study of the Vedas*, Harvard Oriental Series, Opera Minor 2, Cambridge, MA, 1997a, pp. 257–348.

154. *Ṛg Veda Saṃhitā* (Vols I–II), translated by Romesh Chandra Dutt, Haraf, Kolkata, 2000 (reprint), X.98. All further references to the text of the *Ṛg Veda Saṃhitā* are from the text in this book. However, the English translations quoted are from *Hymns of the Ṛgveda* (Vols I and II), translated by Ralph T.H. Griffith, Munshiram Manoharlal, New Delhi, 1999 (reprint).
155. Michel Witzel, 'Early Sanskritization: Origin and Development of the Kuru State' in B. Kolver (ed.), *The State, Law and Administration in Classical India*, R. Oldenbourg, Munich, 1997b, pp. 27–52.
156. Michael Witzel, 'The Vedas and the Epics: Some Comparative Notes on Persons, Lineages, Geography and Grammar' in Petteri Kosikallio (ed.), *Epics, Khilas and Purāṇas: Continuities and Ruptures*, Croatian Academy of Sciences and Arts, Zagreb, 2005, pp. 21–80.
157. Witzel (2005).
158. Hiltebeitel (2015).

2

Bharatas, Pūrus, Kurus, and the Vedas

A Politico-textual History

2.1 The Ṛgvedic Poets and Their World

In the first chapter, we outlined the necessity of situating the origin of the *Mahābhārata* tradition as an *itihāsa* of the Later Vedic Kurus. However, the Kurus came into being through the amalgamation of two Early Vedic tribes: the Bharatas and the Pūrus. Text creation under the patronage of these tribes dates back to the Ṛgvedic times when the Bharata priests Viśvāmitra and Vasiṣṭha valorized the achievements of the Bharata chief Sudās whose successes were attributed to their priestly interventions. This chapter will survey the prehistory of the Kurus from their compositions and find out the linkages between the Vedic and *itihāsa* traditions.

The sages Viśvāmitra and Vasiṣṭha, and their conflict, have been the theme of numerous stories and legends from the Later Vedic literature onwards. In fact, these stories possibly constitute the most well-known cycle of legends about *brāhmaṇa-kṣatriya* conflict. However, both Viśvāmitra and Vasiṣṭha were well-known Vedic poets whose families account for two of the six oldest books of the *Ṛg Veda*. Therefore, both of them belonged to a period when the *varṇa* identities did not even emerge. However, a study of their compositions indicates that their relationship, even in that period, was far from a friendly one.

Our survey of the Vasiṣṭha-Viśvāmitra cycle of legends starts with the *Ṛg Veda* where we try to understand Viśvāmitra and Vasiṣṭha as two poets in their historical context. We shall try to recognize the position of the principal Vedic tribes, both priestly and chiefly. Our study takes us on a journey from the earliest migrations of the Indo-Aryans from Iran through the migration of the Bharata-Pūrus, facilitated by Divodāsa's famous victory over the Dāsa chief Śambara, to ultimately the expansion

From Dāśarājña to Kurukṣetra. Kanad Sinha, Oxford University Press. © Oxford University Press 2021.
DOI: 10.1093/oso/9780190130695.003.0002

of the Bharata power under Sudās. The root of the Vasiṣṭha-Viśvāmitra conflict can be traced in a sacrificial debate in Sudās's *aśvamedha* where Viśvāmitra, the chief priest of Sudās, was almost defeated by the immigrant Vasiṣṭha, before the former was saved by his Bhārgava friend Jamadagni. Comparison between the compositions of Viśvāmitra and Vasiṣṭha reveals how Sudās adopted the immigrant Vasiṣṭha as his priest, who ultimately helped him to a victory over the ten tribes united by Viśvāmitra against him. The victory resulted in Bharata hegemony, as well as the prominence of Vasiṣṭha who reconciled the two cults of Indra and Varuṇa and left some lasting contributions in the field of religion.

However, it seems that the fate of the two priests was reversed after the death of Sudās, when the sons of Sudās brought Viśvāmitra back into prominence and had Vasiṣṭha's sons killed. Vasiṣṭha still remained steadfast to his rituals and ultimately became rich in progeny and cattle. Wary of the power struggles and conflicts, he possibly did not take up the Bharata priesthood again and preferred to work for a minor Vedic tribe—the Ikṣvākus. However, even in this role, Vasiṣṭha could not avoid conflict with Viśvāmitra. The former possibly espoused the pre-classical ritual of human sacrifice in a sacrifice for the Ikṣvāku chief Hariścandra, while the latter saved and adopted the victim Śunaḥśepa.

Understanding the Vasiṣṭha-Viśvāmitra cycle must start from the compositions of these two poets, which needs a thorough understanding of the Ṛgvedic world. The *Ṛg Veda*, as we know, is a collection of hymns composed by several poets mostly between *c.* 1400 and 1000 BCE, while some of the older hymns in the collection may even belong to the early part of the second millennium BCE. The text is divided into ten books out of which the first and last are definitely later additions. Books II–VII are organized according to a certain principle and are considered to be the oldest. These are called the 'family books', since each book is attributed to a family of poets. The initial part of Book VIII also has characteristics of the family books and contains mainly the compositions of the poets of the Kāṇva family. Before studying the books of Viśvāmitra's and Vasiṣṭha's families, a quick survey of the major families of the Vedic poets and their location is in order.

The poets of Book II of the *Ṛg Veda* are the Gṛtsamadas. The major poet in the book is Gṛtsamada, who was the son of the Āṅgirasa Śunahotra but adopted by Bhārgava Śunaka. According to the ĀŚS, the

Gṛtsamadas were expelled from the Āṅgirasa family due to their imprisonment by the Asuras. Then, the Bhārgavas adopted them.[1] Thus, they were a part of the Bhārgava clan, though they had an Āṅgirasa pedigree. Witzel locates the Gṛtsamadas in the extreme west and northwest of the Indian subcontinent.[2] Somāhūti, the son of Gṛtsamada, composed five hymns of the book. There is another poet named Kūrma Gārtsamada. However, his exact location in the family is not known.

Book III belongs to the family of the Kuśikas starting from Kuśika, son of Iṣīratha. However, it is indicated that one of the distant ancestors of the family could have been Jahṇu.[3] Iṣīratha's son is Gāthin; and Viśvāmitra, Gāthin's son, is the most important poet of the family. Viśvāmitra's sons Kata and Ṛṣabha, and Kata's son Utkīla, also composed some of the poems of the book. The family also produced a poet named Prajāpati (III.38, III.54–56, IX.84, IX.101, and X.129), possibly the son of Vāc (X.125). Among the Kuśikas whose poems are found in the other books of the *Ṛg Veda* are Madhuchandas (I.1–10 and IX.1), Reṇu (IX.70 and X.89), and Aṣṭaka (X.104)—the sons of Viśvāmitra; Jetṛ (I.11) and Aghamarṣaṇa (X.190)—sons of Madhuchandas; and Purāṇa (X.160). Witzel locates them in the Panjab, up to the Sarasvatī valley.[4]

Almost the entire Book IV has been composed by Vāmadeva, an Āṅgirasa. Two hymns to the Aśvins are composed by Purumīlha and Ajāmīlha, the sons of Suhotra, whose relationship with Vāmadeva is not clear. Though there is no composition of Vāmadeva's descendants in the book, Books I and VIII contain several Āṅgirasa poets. Rahugaṇa Āṅgirasa (IX.37–38) seems to be Vāmadeva's son. The successors of Rahugaṇa are Gotama Rāhugaṇa (I.74–93 and IX.31), Nodhas Gautama (I.58–64, VIII.88, and IX.93), and Ekādyu Naudhaṣa (VIII.80). They also resided in the northwest and Western Panjab, according to Witzel.[5]

Book V is the composition of the Atris. There are compositions of Atri himself, as well as of several poets with the epithet Ātreya. Śyavāśva is the most prolific of them. There is also a hymn by a female poet, Viśvavārā Ātreyī. The family was more accommodative than most of the others. Therefore, their book includes poetries of the Āṅgirasas Dharuṇa (V.15) and Prabhuvasu (V.35–36), the Vāsiṣṭha Gaurīviti (V.29), the Vaiśvāmitra Saṃvaraṇa (V.33–34), and the Kāśyapa Avatsāra (V.44). Witzel thinks that the Atris covered a wide geographical area, starting from the northwest, covering entire Panjab, up to the banks of the Yamunā.[6]

Three composers of the Book VI—Bharadvāja, Śaṃyu, and Garga—descend from Bṛhaspati (X.71–72). Bharadvāja composed most of the book. Ṛjiśvan and Pāyu are Bharadvāja's sons. There are other poets named Nara, Suhotra, and Śunahotra. Witzel notes that they covered an even wider geographical range, starting from the northwest, covering entire Panjab and Sarasvatī valley, up to the Gaṅgā valley.[7] He suggests that this is also an Āṅgirasa family.[8]

The entire Book VII, except one hymn, is attributed to Vasiṣṭha. However, from the other books, we can identify Śakti (part composer of IX.108) and Citramahas (X.122) as his sons. Śakti had two sons, Gaurīviti (V.29 and X.73–74) and Parāśara (I.65–73). Another Vāsiṣṭha poet can be Dyumnīka, who may be the composer of VIII.87. The family was firmly settled in the Panjab, as Witzel shows, especially in the area between the Sindhu and Sarasvatī valleys. They had knowledge about the Yamunā valley as well.[9]

There are numerous Kāṇvas in Book VIII.1–48. They were also well settled in the northwest, Indus valley, and Panjab, according to Witzel.[10]

The *Ṛg Veda* has many other poets in Books I, IX, and X. As we have already seen, among the seven major families, the Vāmadevas and Bharadvājas were Āṅgirasas, and the Gṛtsamadas had an Āṅgirasa affiliation. Books I, VIII, IX, and X have many other Āṅgirasa poets. Therefore, the Āṅgirasas seem to be the most prominent priestly clan of the age.

A very curious case is that of the Bhṛgus. The Gṛtsamada Śaunakas were Bhārgavas by adoption. But the main line of the Bhṛgus has no family book. The most prominent Bhārgava poet of the text is Jamadagni (III.62.16–18, VIII.101, IX.62, IX.65, IX.67, IX.107, and X.110). There are several references to the clan. But Bhṛgu himself is a shady and mythical figure in the text. Only IX.65, which seems to be Jamadagni's composition, has sometimes been attributed to Bhṛgu. Bhṛgu's son Kavi is the poet of IX.47–49 and IX.75–79. Uśanas (VIII.84 and IX.87–89), son of Kavi, seems to be the most famous poet of his time. Even Vasiṣṭha and Vāmadeva, by no means affiliated to the Bhṛgus, remember him as a great poet.[11] Even in the much later text of the *Bhagavad Gītā*, Kṛṣṇa describes himself as Bhṛgu among the sages and Uśanas among the poets.[12] However, that might have been an effect of 'Bhārgavization' of the *Mahābhārata* (which we shall discuss in detail in Chapter 5). Despite the influence of the Bhārgavas on the contemporary intelligentsia, and the fame of Uśanas, it is strange that the Bhṛgus have so little composition in the text. Possibly, they were not very enthusiastic about the form of religion practised in the Panjab. Jamadagni was a contemporary of Viśvāmitra (the issue of Jamadagni is discussed in detail later). Bhṛgu, Kavi, and Uśanas possibly belonged to a much earlier time.

Witzel thinks that though the *Ṛg Veda* was compiled in the Panjab under the patronage of the five major tribes (the issue is to be discussed later), there was an Indo-Iranian level and a pre–*Ṛg Vedic* level (proto *Atharva Veda mantras*) of Vedic composition.[13] It seems that the compositions of Bhṛgu, Kavi, and Uśanas can fall under the Indo-Iranian level. Weller argues in favour of a pre-Aryan Indic origin of the Bhṛgus.[14] However, several scholars speak in favour of assigning the Bhṛgus an Iranian origin. A. Padmanabhayya and A.J. Karandikar locate the cradle of the Bhṛgus in the western portion of modern Persia, to the north of Kuzistan, as far as the middle of the Trans-Caucasian country.[15] D.D. Kosambi suggests survival of West Asian cultural elements in the Bhṛgu tradition, comparing them with the Phrygians.[16]

An indirect support to locate the early Bhṛgus in Iran can be found in some later tradition. Thus, the most famous Vedic poet—Uśanas (later also known as Śukrācārya)—is astonishingly described as the priest of the Asuras.[17] This may not seem that surprising if Uśanas belonged to Iran where Asura (Ahura) is the name of the Supreme God. The word '*asura*', in fact, retained its positive connotations even in the *Ṛg Veda*. Thus, Prajāpati describes the great power of the deities as '*asuratva*'.[18] This seems a strong possibility, since in tradition the Deva priest, Uśanas's antagonist, is the Āṅgirasa Bṛhaspati. We have seen that the Āṅgirasas were the most notable of the Deva-worshipping Vedic clans. Another factor that the Gṛtsamadas were discarded by the Āṅgirasas, for association with the Asuras, but adopted by the Bhārgavas substantiates our assumption.

The Kuśikas, the Atris, and the Vasiṣṭhas had no Āṅgirasa or Bhārgava affiliation. Among them, the Kuśika Viśvāmitra adopted a Bhārgava as his teacher (to be discussed in detail later). However, the Vasiṣṭhas seem to be immigrants. The great Vasiṣṭha is known to have come crossing the Indus.[19] He was the priest of Sudās, the victor in the Battle of Ten Kings. Witzel thinks that he was an Iranian, drawing parallels between Vasiṣṭha and the Iranian Vahista.[20] The fact that the Iranian Vahista is the spirit of Truth and Righteousness, the two virtues Vasiṣṭha is obsessed with, makes the point stronger. Moreover, while other Vedic poets accepted Manu as the first man, in Vasiṣṭha's book it is Yama.[21] Interestingly, in the Iranian tradition, the first man is Yima, Yama's Iranian counterpart.[22]

From the priests, we can now shift our attention to the Ṛgvedic tribes in general. There are several references to the five famous Vedic tribes—Yadu, Turvaśa, Druhyu, Anu, and Pūru—coming through mountain passes (the routes through Khyber, Bolan, and Gomal?), crossing various rivers, and defeating the Dāsas by storming their forts. Witzel rightly says that it seems that the Yadu, Turvaśa, Druhyu, and Anu migrated earlier.[23] Some poems of the *Ṛg Veda* remember their exploits. In this context also, the Yadus and Turvaśas seem to have moved as a pair, while Druhyus and Anus formed another pair. However, the *Ṛg Veda* was finally compiled when the later migrants, the Pūrus and their associate tribe Bharatas, triumphed over the earlier migrants and settled in the region later named Kurukṣetra.

The Kāṇvas seem to be most favourable to the Yadu-Turvaśas, who formed a clearly more powerful force than the Druhyu-Anus. They relate the four tribes to the Aśvins,[24] celebrate a Turvaśa gift of one hundred horses,[25] and view Indra among the Anus and the Turvaśas.[26] The Āṅgirasas also seem to remember their exploits. Thus, the books of the Vāmadevas, the Gṛtsamadas, and the Bharadvājas record how Indra brought Yadu and Turvaśa from far away[27] and how they crossed narrow passages and rivers.[28] Some of the victories over the local inhabitants seem to have been remembered as how Ṛjiśvan, son of Vidathin, defeated Pipru Mṛgaya by putting down fifty thousand enemies,[29] how Dabhīti overcame thirty thousand Dāsas,[30] and how Nami Sapya killed the Dāsa Namuci.[31] Entering India, they settled themselves in the following order from west to east—Druhyu, Anu, Turvaśa, and Yadu.[32] Witzel assumes that the Druhyus settled in the Gāndhāra region, which seems probable since the next in the line—the Anus—were on the banks of river Pāruṣṇī (Ravi).[33] The *Ṛg Veda* does not clearly say where the Turvaśas were located; but the *Śatapatha Brāhmaṇa* links them with the Pañcāla region of central Uttar Pradesh.[34] The Yadus must have been further east. If their identification with the Yākṣus in the verse VII.18.14 is correct, then they were on the banks of the Yamunā.[35] This seems interesting as even in the *Mahābhārata*, the Yadus are associated with the banks of the Yamunā.

The next stream of migrants had the Bharatas and Pūrus, both of whom initially were associated with the Āyus.[36] Their entry seems to have been led by the Bharata Divodāsa and the Pūru chief Kutsa. The indigenous chief who seems to have staged the biggest resistance to them was Śambara. Only in the fortieth year of his campaign could Divodāsa defeat Śambara.[37]

In fact, the *Ṛg Veda* allows a proper reconstruction of the history of the struggle between Divodāsa and Śambara. H.D. Velankar describes how Śambara, son of Kulītara, a rich Dāsa chief, possessed one hundred strong hill forts.[38] One of them, his residence, was full of treasures. Indra hunted him from fort to fort for forty years. Then he was found in his hundredth fort and pushed down from the lofty mountain peak. His head was battered but not completely smashed. He managed to come down to the plains where he joined hands with his friend Varcin. Divodāsa killed the followers of Varcin. Then he found out both Śambara and Varcin in a water-bounded cow station.[39] He went on to destroy Śambara's forts while Pūrukutsa destroyed autumnal forces of the Dāsas.[40]

However, the earlier settlers did not welcome the new migrants with a warm heart. The Turvaśa chief Vayya and his son Turvīti, along with the Yadus, were well settled. The men of Āyus, Kutsa and Atithtigva (either Divodāsa's father or identical with him), must have faced strong resistance from them and were defeated by another Turvaśa chief, Turvayāna.[41] But the Āyus (Bharata-Pūru migrants) resiliently advanced and ultimately established themselves as the power to reckon with.[42] It was the victory of the Bharata chief Sudās over an alliance of ten kings which sealed the issue. The books of Viśvāmitra (priest of the Bharatas), Atri (pro-Pūru), and Vasiṣṭha (himself an immigrant, and the chief priest of Sudās) record the memory of the victorious Bharata-Pūrus. With this background in mind, we can have a look at the compositions of Viśvāmitra and Vasiṣṭha to understand their role in the Ṛgvedic age.

2.2 Viśvāmitra's Poetry

As discussed in the previous section, the earliest known sources for the history of the Bharatas are the compositions of the priests Viśvāmitra and Vasiṣṭha. Therefore, we begin with a reflection on the contents of

Viśvāmitra's compositions. Viśvāmitra, and his family called the Kuśikas, composed Book III of the *Ṛg Veda*. It contains sixty-two hymns out of which forty-six are attributed to Viśvāmitra. He seems to be a worshipper of Indra and Agni as twenty-one of his hymns are dedicated to Indra, fourteen to Agni, and two to Indra and Agni jointly. He was deeply attached to the sacrificial process and the sacrificial fire. In Hymn III.5, he views Agni as the embodiment of all deities, including Mitra, Sūrya, and Varuṇa. In Hymn III.26, he identifies himself with Agni. He even dedicates a hymn, III.8, to the sacrificial altar. In his Agni hymns, Viśvāmitra often refers to the legend of Mātariśvan who is said to have brought the fire to the Bhṛgus,[43] which indicates that he might have had a close relationship with the Bhṛgus.

Objects of Viśvāmitra's prayers are very materialistic, stereotypical, and traditional, including strength, physical safety, wealth, cattle, male offspring, victory, long life, eradication of sins, grain, horses, power, mastery, knowledge, and the Soma drink. Surprisingly, he also prays for becoming a defender of the people and their king.[44] However, there is no sign that he became a chief in reality, and his priestly office in the *Ṛg Veda* is beyond doubt. Thus, Velankar's suggestion that this verse is the origin of his later *kṣatriya* identity is not totally convincing.[45] He is very antagonistic to Dāsas, Dasyus, Paṇis, and Rākṣasas and celebrates Indra and Agni's exploits over them. One interesting hymn is Hymn III.60 which relates how the Ṛbhus, sons of Sudhanvan, attained godhood by their skill and sacrifices.[46]

Viśvāmitra clearly appears as the priest of the Bharatas. In Hymn III.33, he engages into a conversation with the rivers Beas and Sutlej which the Bharatas wish to control by Indra's grace.[47] More crucial is Hymn III.53 where Viśvāmitra strongly claims patronage for the Kuśikas. In this hymn, composed in the context of Sudās's *aśvamedha* sacrifice officiated by him, he describes himself as a great sage, close to the deities, leader of the people, capable of stopping the river's flow (definitely a reference to his aid to the Bharatas in crossing Śutudri and Vipāś), and the one who popularized Indra among the Kuśikas and the Bharatas.[48] He desires protection for the Bharatas[49] and demands more gifts, including the gifts given to the 'undeserving low-borns'.[50] He invokes Indra for the destruction of his enemies and proclaims his superiority over them. It seems that he overcame his 'rivals' in some ritualistic debate, being aided by Jamadagni's famous speech named *sasarparī*,[51] and received ample rewards which he was carrying on a bullock cart. All the magical attempts of his enemies to harm him were to go in vain, because of their inferiority in performing rituals.[52] In the curse in the concluding *ṛc* of the hymn, he probably identifies his enemies as the Vasiṣṭhas whom he warns of permanent enmity with the Bharatas.[53]

Despite composing a fascinating description of the dawn in a hymn praising Uṣā[54] and praying for the honourable divine radiance (*vareṇyam bhargo devasya*) over the human heart, to Savitṛ, in his famous *gāyatrī*,[55] Viśvāmitra's approach remains utterly materialistic. Several of his hymns conclude with the following prayer:

> Call we on Maghavan, auspicious Indra, best Hero in the fight where spoil is gathered,
> The Strong, who listens, who gives aids in battles, who slays the Vṛtras, wins and gathers riches.[56]

The remaining sixteen hymns of the book are mostly composed by the other Kuśikas. The only exception is the Hymn III.23 composed by two Bhāratas, members of the patron clan of the Kuśikas, named Devaśravas and Devarāta. Of the other fifteen hymns, Hymn III.31 is possibly a composition of Kuśika, the father figure of the clan. Kuśika's son and Viśvāmitra's father, Gāthin, composed four, Viśvāmitra's sons Ṛṣabha and Kata two each, and Kata's son Utkīla two. An interesting poet is Prajāpati, son of Vāc of the same family (or son of Viśvāmitra), who does not conform to the materialistic tendencies of the book. He aspires to comprehend the knowledge of the great ancient sages in III.38. His brilliant Hymn III.55 goes on to proclaim at the end of each *ṛc* that great is the Supreme Power of the gods, which is indeed One (*mahad devānāṃ asuratvam ekam*).[57] He is also probably the composer of the agnostic Creation Hymn in the Tenth Book. Among these sixteen hymns, eleven are dedicated to Agni, three to the Viśvadevas, one to Indra and Varuṇa, and only one to Indra. Thus, Viśvāmitra's claim that he made Indra popular among the Kuśikas seems justified. However, a more complex theology and worldview can be found in the poetry of Viśvāmitra's arch-rival, Vasiṣṭha.

2.3 Thus Spake Vasiṣṭha

Vasiṣṭha is the most prolific and versatile of the Vedic poets. His poetry has similarities as well as striking differences with the compositions of Viśvāmitra, which we discussed in the previous section. Now we need to focus on the much larger and diverse corpus of Vasiṣṭha's compositions. He composed 103 out of the 104 hymns in Book VII of the *Ṛg Veda*. He is also the poet of two hymns of Book IX, which is a collection of all the compositions dedicated to Soma. Almost no Vedic deity, major or minor, failed to capture Vasiṣṭha's imagination. Out of his 105 hymns, 17 invoke Agni, 15 Indra, 8 the Aśvins, 8 the Viśvadevas, 7 Uṣā, 4 Varuṇa, 4 Mitra and Varuṇa, 3 all the Ādityas, 3 Vāyu, 3 the Maruts, 2 Sūrya, Mitra, and Varuṇa, 2 Agni and Indra, 2 Savitṛ, 2 Parjanya, 2 the Āpas, 1 Rudra and the Maruts, 1 Indra, Bhaga, and Uṣā, 1 Dadhikrā, 1 the Ṛbhus, 1 Dyaus and Pṛthivī, 1 Vāstospati, 1 Vāstospati and Indra, 1 Sarasvatī, 1 Sarasvatī and Sarasvān, 1 Indra and Bṛhaspati, 1 Indra, Bṛhaspati, and Brahmaṇspati, 1 Indra and Viṣṇu, 1 Viṣṇu, 1 Agni, Mitra, Varuṇa, and the rivers, and 1 various deities, including Soma, Indra, Deva, Grāvā, the Maruts, Agni, Dyaus, and Pṛthivī. One hymn is curiously dedicated to frogs.

The same versatility can be observed regarding the themes of his poetry. There are hymns of deep philosophical thought; there are hymns of intimate study of the nature; there are hymns for material benefits, including wealth, male offspring, eradication of enemies and diseases, protection from hunger, grain, strength, cattle, horses, rain, happiness, fame, long life, fortune, victory, and gold; there are hymns in praise of and prayer for his patron kings; there are shamanic hymns for snake-charming or rain-bringing. Rahurkar divides his poetry in five different categories—lyrics of nature, religious lyrics, ritualistic hymns, historical war songs, and songs of everyday sentiment.[58]

His hymns to Agni are mainly for material benefit. He invokes Indra mainly as a war hero, the function of rain giver being reserved for the Maruts and Parjanya. Thus, Indra is frequently praised as the destroyer of Dāsas, Dasyus, Paṇis, Rākṣasas, and phallus worshippers. It is Indra, or Indra along with Varuṇa, who is thanked for the military victories of Vasiṣṭha's patron Sudās.

Sudās, son of Pijavan and grandson of Devavat, is said to have been graced by Indra to a victory over the ten chiefs.[59] However, Vasiṣṭha did not personally despise all of Sudās's rivals. The chief Turvaśa has been described by Vasiṣṭha as virtuous,[60] though eager for wealth. He was connected with the Bhṛgus and the Druhyus.[61] We do not know why Sudās's relationship with Turvaśa and the Druhyus became antagonistic. However, the other allies of Turvaśa and the Druhyus, mentioned by Vasiṣṭha, are the Pakthas, Bhalanas, Alinas, Śivas, and Viṣāṇins.[62] Sudās, in his contest against the ten chiefs, was aided by the Tṛtsus.[63] Ludwig identifies the Tṛtsus with the Bharatas, whereas Geldner thinks that they are the royal family of the Bharatas.[64] However, the Tṛtsus are described usually in priestly functions.[65] Therefore, it seems that the scholars like Oldenberg, Hillebrandt, and Witzel are right in considering the Tṛtsus as the Vasiṣṭhas.[66] Among the antagonists of Sudās, the Kavaṣas and the Druhyus were drowned.[67] The sons of Anu and Druhyu were defeated by Sudās.[68] The Tṛtsus captured the house of Anu's sons.[69] Twenty-one people of two Vaikarṇa tribes were also scattered by Sudās.[70] The centre of attention was the river Pāruṣṇī.[71] Sudās achieved an overall victory over the grand alliance and therefore acquired much wealth.[72] More importantly, he gained control over navigable rivers.[73] Sudās donated generously.[74] Vasiṣṭha received two hundred cows, two chariots and four horses from the patron.[75] Therefore, Vasiṣṭha claims to be an owner and allocator of many cows.[76] He continued to pray for the protection of Sudās's house and power[77] and a complete victory over Turvaśa and the Yādavas.[78] The victory over the Pūrus also seems to be incomplete.[79] They seem to have ended up in some alliance with Sudās. Therefore, Vasiṣṭha also prayed for the Pūru chief Kutsa, who had defeated the Dāsas Śuṣṇa and Kuyava, and his son Trasadasyu.[80]

The Battle of Ten Kings was not the only victory of Sudās during Vasiṣṭha's priesthood. On the banks of the Yamunā, Sudās defeated the powerful and wealthy chief Bheda, who led a confederacy of the Ajas, Śigrus, and Yākṣus who brought to Sudās horse heads as tribute.[81]

Rahurkar thinks that another enemy overcome by Vasiṣṭha was Jarūtha whom Vasiṣṭha claims to have slain.[82] Ludwig also identifies Jarūtha as an enemy of Vasiṣṭha, and Karandikar tries to identify him with the Iranian prophet Zarathushtra.[83] However, this Jarūtha-slaying appears only in hymns to Agni. Vasiṣṭha, in another hymn, refers to it in a manner that indicates that he is citing some ancient legend about the fire god.[84] A similar reference has been found in Book X of the text as well.[85] Therefore, it appears that the reference is to an ancient fire myth about burning off some evil spirit. Vasiṣṭha probably had Iranian connections and the fire cult was no doubt popular in ancient Iran. Still, identifying Jarūtha with Zarathushtra is difficult. Firstly, it is doubtful whether Zarathushtra flourished before Vasiṣṭha's time. Even if he did, why Agni, out of all the deities, should destroy the fire-worshipping Zarathushtra is not understandable. If Zarathushtra were the intended enemy, then the likely slayer would be Indra, a deity whom Vasiṣṭha and the Vedic sages adopted, but the Zoroastrians discarded, rather than Agni whose importance was pivotal to the Zoroastrians as well.

However, despite his prolific success as priest of the victorious kings, Vasiṣṭha's mind was thirsty for something beyond the material gains. He was eager to know the types of hymns which previously satisfied the gods.[86] Carried on by the flow of materialism like a cloud carried by wind, desiring for more and more wealth like a man feeling thirsty while standing in water, he prayed for mercy of Varuṇa, a deity to whom he was too emotionally attached to pray for material benefits.[87] In his moving collection of hymns to Varuṇa,[88] he only prayed for the removal of his sins, companionship of the deity, mercy, and freedom from worldly bondage. Thus, Vasiṣṭha's poetry included a germ of what later became devotionalism with a longing for either liberation or unity with the beloved deity, going beyond the world of interests and conflicts. Moreover, two deities, whose subsequent forms would occupy centre stage in later devotionalism, captured Vasiṣṭha's imagination. To Rudra, Vasiṣṭha prayed:

> Tryambaka we worship, sweet augmenter of Prosperity.
>
> As from its stem the cucumber, so may I be released from death, not reft of immortality[89]

This hymn is usually considered a later addition, and Śākalya does not deal with it in his *Padapāṭha*. However, Vasiṣṭha also precedes numerous later poets in describing Viṣṇu as one with a form beyond dimensions and with glory incomprehensible to all beings born and yet to be born, the only knower of the Absolute Abode unknown to all others who know at best the earth and the heaven.[90]

Vasiṣṭha was able to see more than the apparent in the nature. He invoked the grace of the dawn in the seven beautiful hymns to Uṣā.[91] He felt no constraints to devote a hymn to the frogs whose prayer matched his prayer as bringer of rain.[92] He viewed with wonder how the sun rays created rain, how the fire was lit all over the expansive body of the earth decorated with mountains, how the ever-mobile wind blew everywhere, how the milk-producing cows were raised, and how up in the sky—in the sun's vicinity—the clouds shed their rainy springs.[93] Thus, in Hymn III.35, Vasiṣṭha prays only for the peace of everything in the universe. As a contrast to Viśvāmitra's favourite materialistic prayer, most of Vasiṣṭha's hymns end with the prayer '*yuyaṃ pāta svastibhiḥ sadā naḥ*' (Preserve us evermore, ye Gods, with blessings).[94] A firm believer in the idea of sharing prosperity liberally with other members of the society, Vasiṣṭha tried to assert that the gods helped those who helped others. K.R. Potdar notes the similarity of this idea of Vasiṣṭha with the later richer ideal of sacrifice described in the *Gītā*.[95]

However, Vasiṣṭha was not a lenient person who would take Viśvāmitra's curses lightly. In Hymn VII.104, he strongly attacked Viśvāmitra, though he did not name him. He condemned the liars (*mithyācāra*) who brought false allegation of performance of black magic against him and said that he would die if the allegation was proven. Rather, he marked his 'enemies' as performers of black magic, liable to destruction. His obsession with truth becomes apparent in this hymn. He observed the simultaneous existence of truth and untruth but was sure about securing divine favour for the purpose of the propagation of the Truth.[96] The gods were known for striking down falsehood.[97] Thus, Vasiṣṭha vowed that he was not a 'worshipper of falsehood' (*anṛtadeva*).[98] Though clearly a response to Viśvāmitra's Hymn III.53, where he mocked his rival's unsuccessful magic spells, this hymn is curiously juxtaposed with charms for destruction of the Rākṣasas.

An interesting hymn is Hymn VII.33, the only hymn in the book not composed by Vasiṣṭha. It is a hymn dedicated to Vasiṣṭha, composed by his sons. It sounds like an epitaph to assure that Vasiṣṭha was always with them. The sons attributed a divine birth to their father, as a son of Mitra and Varuṇa, and Urvaśī. They celebrated Vasiṣṭha's victory in a sacrificial contest over King Pāśadyumna's priest. Vasiṣṭha himself never claimed to be a son of Mitra and Varuṇa, not even in the hymns to them. Thus, the myth was clearly made for 'deification of mortal par excellence', as Sadashiva A. Dange notes.[99] Moreover, the hymn proceeded to claim continuity of the power of the Great Vasiṣṭha of the divine birth in all the Vasiṣṭhas of his lineage.[100] F. Max Muller thinks that the hymn metaphorically represents Vasiṣṭha as the sun, identifying Mitra and Varuṇa with day and night and Urvaśī with Uṣā, the mother of the sun god.[101]

The world of Vasiṣṭha's compositions is thus quite rich and complex. Ellison Banks Findly attempts a psychohistorical analysis of the book to understand the personality of Vasiṣṭha as a 'religious actualist'. He uses the terminology used by Erik Erikson about Gandhi to understand Vasiṣṭha as a spiritual innovator with a 'precocious and relentless conscience' which, alongside creating a strong emotional need to remain morally unblemished, creates a conviction of one's own superiority bound to the transcendental truth in some extraordinary way. Thus, as the bearer and transmitter of a superior way of life, Vasiṣṭha is certain about the inferiority of the irreligious *dasyus*, and his opponents. He was bound to triumph over his ignorant (*acetas*) opponents, as the upholder of the true order (*ṛta*), with his proper knowledge of the ritual to bring Indra's favour. On the other hand, his opponents lacked judgement and had no hope under an unworthy 'shepherd' (Viśvāmitra).

The victory thus validated Vasiṣṭha's selection as the Bharata priest. Vasiṣṭha then faced a greater spiritual challenge. Acquiring the supreme spiritual portfolio of his time, he had to choose his course of action. On one hand was his old cult of Varuṇa, based on peaceful introspection on truth and righteousness, to which he was emotionally attached. On the other hand was the emerging cult of the militaristic Indra, to which he owed his material successes. Vasiṣṭha's greatest contribution was the reconciliation between the two in a religious conception where Indra conquered and Varuṇa ruled. His involvement in militaristic and materialistic activities troubled his conscience; he trembled in the fear of sin and Varuṇa's displeasure. However, he could retain his moral superiority by reconciling the two orders. This achievement of Vasiṣṭha might have turned him into a spiritual celebrity by the time of his death. Therefore, VII.33 shows how the Vasiṣṭha legacy is preserved as a family tradition, turning Vasiṣṭha into the son of the protectors of *ṛta*, Mitra and Varuṇa, and a special associate of Indra (Potdar also notes Vasiṣṭha's emphasis on virtues of family life and continuity of family line). Ritual enactment of Vasiṣṭha's ordination as a priest, kind of a second birth, transcends his death and continues his legacy in a family tradition which valorizes contemplative lifestyle over active lifestyle.[102]

This analysis of Vasiṣṭha's psychology is immensely important for understanding his role in Indian religious life, which perpetuated his position as the most celebrated sage in legends. He not only espoused the superiority of truth and righteousness over the attainment of ends but also provided a model of two gods performing preserving and destroying activities. Rahurkar also accepts Vasiṣṭha's role as a cultic reconciler and pioneer of the *bhakti* cult.[103] The two different aspects which Vasiṣṭha entrusted on Indra and Varuṇa are quite clear from his hymns where he said that Indra destroyed the Vṛtras while Varuṇa maintained the holy laws, and that Varuṇa held the folks distinct and sundered while Indra slayed resistless foemen.[104] However, the devotee of Varuṇa kept for him the place of a universal sovereign, though he accepted Indra as an earthly monarch.[105] This duality of a preserver and a destroyer would last in Indian religion for a long time. Varuṇa and Indra would be replaced by Viṣṇu and Śiva in these roles (even though their roles would not be limited to these functions in the complex Purāṇic mythology developed around them), and these two deities (or at least Viṣṇu) made their first prominent appearance in his poetry. He also provided the model of personal devotion to reach the gods, which would be a lasting element in Indian religious life. The valorization of the contemplative over the active, the spiritual over the military, is no doubt the factor that would place him as the champion of Brahmanical virtues against the '*kṣatriya*' Viśvāmitra in the legends to be discussed in Chapter 5.

2.4 Sudās and the Ten Tribes: Reflections on the *Dāśarājña*

The earlier discussion shows that Oldenberg's claim that the *Ṛg Veda* does not give any evidence of strife between Vasiṣṭha and Viśvāmitra is totally unfounded.[106] Rather, their antagonism seems to be at the centre of the events leading to the Battle of Ten Kings. In this section, we shall analyse the information found in the poetry of Viśvāmitra and Vasiṣṭha to make certain observations about the history of the Battle of Ten Kings and related issues.

The relationship between the Bharatas and the Pūrus is important for understanding the political milieu before the Battle of Ten Kings. Otherwise, it seems a bit confusing why the Bharata priest Viśvāmitra tormented Sudās, who is also supposed to be a Bharata. The flurry of curses exchanged between Viśvāmitra and Vasiṣṭha shows a clear antagonism between the two priests. Witzel tries to form genealogies of both the Bharatas and the Pūrus from the *Ṛg Veda*. The resultant genealogies are shown here.[107]

Bharatas	**Pūrus**
Pratṛd	
Atithigva	Girikṣit
Divodāsa	Kutsa/Pūrukutsa
Sudās	Trasadasyu
Sons of Sudās	Tṛkṣi
Devaśravas	
Devavat	
Sṛñjaya Daivavāta? (VI.27, IV.15.5)	

The Pūru genealogy can be easily confirmed by the Ātreya book of the *Ṛg Veda*, but the Bharata genealogy is problematic. Velankar has an alternative suggestion that Divodāsa's father was Vadhryaśva whose priests were the Sumitras and whose enemy was Dāsa Bṛṣaya.[108] However, Witzel takes Divodāsa as the son of Atithigva. Vadhryaśva, mentioned in VI.61.3 and X.69, was possibly an ancestor of both Divodāsa and Atithigva. That Vadhryaśva was a person of much older times is also indicated by the obscurity of these Sumitras among the Ṛgvedic poet-seers.[109] By the time of Divodāsa, however, Āṅgirasa Bharadvājas were the priests of the Bharatas, and the priest Pāyu received rich rewards after Divodāsa's victory over Śambara and Varcin. But the genealogy of Divodāsa's successors is complicated. Vasiṣṭha knew Sudās as the son of Pijavan and grandson of Devavat. Thus, Witzel's genealogy is problematic unless there is some decisive proof to support the identification of Atithigva and Devavat, or Divodāsa and Pijavan. Velankar suggests that Divodāsa was succeeded by Pratardana who is mentioned in the *Kaṭhaka Saṃhitā* and *Kauśitakī*

Upaniṣad,[110] who continued with the Āṅgirasa Bharadvajās as his priests.[111] Pratardana is the poet of a Ṛgvedic hymn (IX.96) and a verse (X.179.2). The verse VI.26.8 refers to Kṣatraśrī whom Velankar identifies as Pratardana's son.[112] C. Kunhan Raja, on the other hand, rightly notes that Divodāsa, who is often coupled with Atithigva, could have been identical with him, rather than being his son.[113] It also seems that there were some intervening chiefs between Divodāsa and Pijavan whose son Sudās held the *aśvamedha* where Viśvāmitra officiated as a Bharata priest.[114] However, the time gap between these chiefs was not very long, since all the chiefs from Atithigva/Divodāsa to Sudās were contemporaries of Pūrukutsa whose son Trasadasyu succeeded him only in Sudās's time.

This leads to a really complicated scenario. If Sudās was a Bharata and Viśvamitra was the Bharata priest who officiated at his *aśvamedha*, why did he curse Vasiṣṭha who appears to be Sudās's priest during the battle? Moreover, why did Vasiṣṭha, who prayed for both Sudās and the Pūru chief Trasadasyu,[115] also pray for defeating the Pūrus?[116]

The answer lies possibly in the activities of the Pūrus. The Bharatas and the Pūrus, both being offshoots of the Āyus, migrated together from Iran, defeating Śambara and the other Dāsas and breaking the Yadu-Turvaśa resistance. Viśvāmitra seems to be a priest of this Bharata-Pūru alliance that continued to advance under Sudās.[117] He prayed for a safe crossing of the rivers Beas and Sutlej by the Bharatas, who thus held the Apācya, Dṛṣadvatī, and Sarasvatī valleys.[118] Sudās never moved towards the south which was inhabited by the Kīkaṭas led by Pramaganda.[119] Then Sudās's *aśvamedha* was held. After that, some problems probably occurred between Viśvāmitra and Sudās, and Viśvāmitra assumed the role of the tormentor of Sudās.

How Viśvāmitra tormented Sudās is not clear, but some clue may come from Vasiṣṭha's reference to the Bhṛgus being close allies of the Druhyus and possibly of Turvaśa as well. The close relationship between Viśvāmitra and the Bhṛgus, indicated by Viśvāmitra's espousal of the Mātariśvan myth, interestingly, matches the later legends. Viśvāmitra, in later legends, is the son of Gādhin whose daughter Satyavatī was married to the Bhṛgu sage Ṛcīka. Ṛcīka and Satyavatī had a son, Jamadagni, who was about the same age as Viśvāmitra (the legend is discussed in detail in Chapter 5). More interestingly, there was the Bhṛgu poet Jamadagni whom Viśvāmitra accepted as his teacher. He possibly taught him the formula *sasarparī* with which he overcame the Vasiṣṭhas in the debate at Sudās's *aśvamedha*.[120] In the Book X of the *Ṛg Veda*, there is a hymn to Indra, jointly composed by Viśvāmitra and Jamadagni.[121] Even the *Taittirīya Saṃhitā* remembers Jamadagni as a friend of Viśvāmitra and antagonist of Vasiṣṭha.[122] The later legend thus seems to contain remnants of the actual relationships among the Vedic poets. Viśvāmitra could use his connection with the Bhṛgus to spoil Sudās's relationship with the older tribes.

Pradeep Kant Choudhary says that there is no clear reference to Jamadagni's Bhārgava identity in the *Ṛg Veda*.[123] However, the identification is well attested in the later tradition. John Mitchiner has pointed out that a tradition about the seven principal *ṛṣis* has been prominent in the Vedic literature. These *ṛṣis* are Viśvāmitra, Bharadvāja, Gotama, Atri, Jamadagni, Vasiṣṭha, and Kāśyapa, with Agastya being the eighth (as an attached outsider). This list, a bit later, has been replaced by a list of the seven *gotra* founder *ṛṣis* who are Bhṛgu, Aṅgiras, Atri, Viśvāmitra, Vasiṣṭha, Kāyapa, and Agastya. Here, Mitchiner suspects that the transformation occurred as the Bhṛgus absorbed the Jamadagnis and the Āṅgirasas absorbed the Bharadvājas and the Gautamas. A similar transformation occurred in the later sections of the *Mahābhārata* and the Purāṇas, when the list had been modified into Marīci, Atri, Aṅgiras, Pulastya, Pulaha, Kratu, and Vasiṣṭha (with Bhṛgu sometimes being the eighth).[124] Mitchiner, therefore, also suggests that the absorption of the Jamadagnis within the Bhṛgus has been a later development.

However, the first list of the seven sages had been formed in the *Ṛg Veda* itself which attributes some hymns—such as IX.67 and IX.107—to this group. Therefore, it is interesting to investigate what determined the selection of these seven in the *Ṛg Veda*. It seems that the principle is to pick one representative from each of the chief Vedic families. The six family books of the *Ṛg Veda* belong to the Gṛtsamadas, Viśvāmitras, Gotamas, Atris, Bharadvājas, and Vasiṣṭhas. Each of them, except the Gṛtsamadas, has been represented in the list of the seven sages. Agastya's position as the outsider eighth is also consistent with the text where no family book of the Agastyas exist, but the last twenty-seven hymns of Book I creates a mini-book of Agastya's single-handed creation. The strange inclusion is Kāyapa, and the strange exclusions are the Kāṇvas.

The Kāṇvas, the first part of Book VIII clearly belonging to them, were more likely to have their representative as the seventh sage. On the other hand, Kāyapa has only six hymns attributed to him, and his descendants have little to their credit. However, the Kāśyapas are quite prominent in Book IX, a collection of all the hymns dedicated to Soma. Maybe, this collection was worked out by this family, which earned them a place in the list of the seven sages. A more likely possibility is that the Kāṇvas are themselves Kāśyapas, a suggestion attested by the *Mahābhārata*.[125]

But what about the Gṛtsamadas? Why is a family having a proper family book not represented in the list of the seven sages? The only possible answer lies in the person who takes that place in the list—Jamadagni. It seems that the Gṛtsamadas have been viewed as a part of the Bhārgava family. Therefore, the most prominent Bhārgava sage of the time has been taken as their representative rather than any Gṛtsamada. Thus, Jamadagni's Bhārgava identity seems to be attested by the *Ṛg Veda* as well and can really be a clue in understanding how Viśvāmitra mobilized the ten tribes.

Who were the ten tribes who fought against Sudās? No clear list is provided by the *Ṛg Veda*. However, nine names can easily be found as the Turvaśa chief, the Bhṛgus, the Druhyus, the Anus, and their five allies the Pakthas, the Bhalanas, the Alinas, the Śivas, and the Viṣāṇins. The word '*matsya*' appears in VII.18.6, but whether that refers to the fishes or to the Matsya tribe or to both is doubtful. Two Vaikarṇa tribes, ancient Kavaṣa, and the Pūrus are also mentioned. Verse VII.33 mentions Vasiṣṭha's sacrificial victory over the priest of the chief Pāśadyumna. No direct reference to antagonism with the Yadus is present. However, as we have seen, the Yadus were always associates of the Turvaśas, and Vasiṣṭha continued to pray for a complete victory over these two tribes.

Therefore, the ten tribes are possibly the famous five (Yadu, Turvaśa, Druhyu, Anu, and Pūru) and five minor allies (Pakthas, Bhalanas, Alinas, Śivas, and Viṣāṇins). Whether the Matsyas are referred to as a tribe is highly doubtful. The Bhṛgus were definitely priests aiding the confederacy, not actual fighters. Kosambi, however, thinks that the Bhṛgus were fighters participating in the battle in which they were badly vanquished, and only the priestly Bhṛgus survived.[126] Rahurkar assumes that Turvaśa won them over by wealth, a suggestion that can neither be proved nor disproved.[127] The same could have been the case with the ancient Kavaṣa.[128]

Pāśadyumna is possibly the personal name of the leader of the confederacy, though his tribal identity is unknown. Any two of the five lesser tribes could have been the Vaikarṇas.

Kunhan Raja strongly opposes such identification of the ten tribes, although most of the Vedic scholars accept it. Since the ten chiefs are called *ayajyu* (non-worshippers) by Vasiṣṭha in VII.83.6–7, he thinks that it is unlikely that the famous 'five people', the great patrons of the Vedic religion, would be described as such. Therefore, he thinks that Sudās fought ten invading 'foreign' tribes, and there was hardly any internal feud among the Vedic chiefs.[129]

The argument is not convincing, since evidences of internal feud among the Vedic tribes are too numerous. Moreover, we have already seen that the Vedic tribes were themselves in the process of migrating to the North Indian plains. The career of Sudās was one of crossing one river after another (Vipāś and Śutudrī followed by Pāruṣṇī and finally Yamunā). Repulsion of foreign invasion, in that scenario, makes no sense as an idea. Rather, Indra, Divodāsa, and Pūrukutsa can very well be described as 'foreign aggressors' whom Śambara and Varcin failed to repel.

Still, the word '*ayajyu*' deserves some explanation. No doubt, the opponents of Sudās also followed the Vedic religion. Vasiṣṭha himself praised Turvaśa for that and officiated for the Pūrus. That Pāśadyumna also held a sacrifice has been seen. The guides of Sudās's opponents were the most revered Vedic priests such as the Bhṛgus and Viśvāmitra. Then could the ten *ayajyus* include the five great tribes, even if the other five were non-Vedic? The problem seems to be in interpreting the term too literally. We have already seen how Vasiṣṭha distinguished 'true' worship from 'false' worship and held responsible the trueness of his worship for the victory over the ten chiefs who chose a 'wrong shepherd'. Therefore, guided by Viśvāmitra, the ten chiefs were diverted from the real spirit of Truth and Sacrifice, even if they adhered to the religious rituals. This makes the matter intelligible, since the mention of at least three (Turvaśa, the Druhyus, and the Anus) of the five is too clear cut to dismiss.

However, battle with the Yadu-Turvaśas and Druhyu-Anus was nothing new for the Bharatas. What could be new was the defection of their old allies, the Pūrus, to the other side. Was it Viśvāmitra, with his Bhārgava friends, who effected the famous alliance of the Vedic *pañca jana* by bringing the Pūrus together with the Yadu-Turvaśas and the

Druhyu-Anus?[130] The defection of both his priest and his closest allies must have created a great problem for Sudās. He was facing five powerful tribes, supported by five minor ones, who also received support from all the prominent priestly families—the Kāṇvas, the Āṅgirasas, the Bhṛgus, and the Kuśikas. Therefore, Sudās chose the immigrant Tṛtsu priests—led by the great Vasiṣṭha—for patronage, and Viśvāmitra and the Pūrus were ousted.[131] There was complete victory over the Druhyu-Anus.[132] Sudās's overall victory led to lavish gifts for Vasiṣṭha.[133] The subdued Ajas, Śigras, and Yākṣus (Yadus?) brought horseheads as tribute to Sudās's sacrifice in honour of Indra.[134] Unlike the Druhyus and Anus, the Yadus were not completely vanquished. They remained on the banks of the Yamunā. The testimony of the ŚB shows that the Turvaśas were not vanquished either. Thus, Vasiṣṭha continued to pray for complete victory over the Yadu-Turvaśas.[135] There is no clear reference to support A.D. Pusalker's assumption that Pūrukutsa was killed in this battle.[136] The Pūrus seem to have returned to their old allies. Therefore, Vasiṣṭha and Nodhas[137] prayed for both Sudās and the Pūru chiefs Pūrukutsa and Trasadasyu. This, possibly, is the reason why the Yadus and Pūrus were quite prominent in the later traditions, whereas the Druhyus and Anus were never important again. The Turvaśas were defeated by a later Bharata chief, Sṛñjaya Daivavāta.[138] Though Vasiṣṭha now became the chief priest, Viśvāmitra's family also came to some settlement. Thus, the later Bharatas Devaśravas and Devavāta composed a hymn that was included in the Kuśika book.[139]

2.5 The Kurus and the Later Vedas

As already discussed, the compilation of the *Ṛg Veda* seems to have taken place under Bharata-Pūru patronage in the post-Sudās days. The older poetry of the Kāṇvas, Āṅgirasas, Gṛtsamadas, and the main Bhārgavas also received a place in the text. But the prominent place was occupied by the books of Bharadvāja, Viśvāmitra, and Vasiṣṭha, particularly the last one who has the highest number of hymns in the collection. The Atris seem to have flourished under Bharata-Pūru patronage, under Trasadasyu's son Tṛkṣi, and they describe the Bharata-Pūrus in a glorious manner.

The Bharata-Pūrus, whose victorious journey has been documented in the preceding sections, gradually evolved into the Kurus or the Kuru-Pañcālas. They shifted their geographical centre to the Kurukṣetra region, ranging from modern Eastern Panjab and Haryana up to the Upper Doab of the Yamunā and Gaṅgā.[140] King Kuruśravaṇa, of the Trasadasyu's lineage, is known in the later portions of the *Ṛg Veda*.[141] The last Kuru chief mentioned in the *Ṛg Veda* is Śaṃtanu for whom his brother Devāpi composed a rain-making hymn.[142] The main narrative of the *Mahābhārata* begins with Śāṃtanu. The Kuru king Parikṣit, a prominent figure in the Later Vedic literature, particularly the *Atharva Veda*, is known to the very late *Khila* hymns of the *Ṛg Veda* (ṚV.Khil.5).[143] In this section, we shall try to locate the Kurus in the Later Vedic world.

Witzel's detailed studies on the localization of the Vedic schools and texts reveal that a huge number of the Vedic texts were composed under Kuru, or Kuru-Pañcāla, patronage. Three of the four versions of the Black *Yajur Veda* were definitely composed in the Kuru realm. The KS, and its allied text *Kapiṣṭhala-kaṭha Saṃhitā*, can be located in the Kurukṣetra realm on the basis of the former's knowledge of the rivers flowing westwards most copiously.[144] The KS also records the eastward march of the Kurus for grain.[145] The *Maitrāyaṇī Saṃhitā* traces the march southwards.[146] The KS also refers to the Kuru king Dhṛtarāṣṭra Vaicitravīrya and his troubles with Baka Dālbhya, which is discussed in the *Mahābhārata* as well.[147] The connection between the Kuru region and the Maitrāyaṇīyas can be traced even in the late Vedic text *Mānava Śrauta Sūtra* where Kurukṣetra is present with its complete landscape, including the rivers Sarasvatī, Dṛṣadvatī, and Yamunā, the Plakṣa Prasravana, Kārāpacava, Vyarṇa Naitandhava, Pāriṇah, and Triplakṣa.[148] The Black *Yajur Veda* recension named the *Taittirīya Saṃhitā* is located by Witzel to the Pañcāla region.[149] The *abhiṣeka mantras* in both the TS and the TB specifically mention the Bhāratas, which may signify both the Kurus and the Pañcālas.[150] The affinity with the Kurus is also assumed from the importance given to pilgrimage along the Sarasvatī[151] and suggestion of the use of Sarasvatī water in the *rājasūya* ritual.[152] The Baudhāyana branch of the Taittirīyas shows their affinity to the Madhyadeśa in the *Baudhāyana Śrauta Sūtra*. Not only does the coronation formula refer to the Bhāratas but the Bharata kings are mentioned time and again.[153] The focus, however, is on Pañcāla where the Kurus are described as migrating.

The Pañcāla king Keśin Dālbhya has a prominent position.[154] Among the other Taittirīya texts, the *Āpastamba Śrauta Sūtra* mentions the Kuru-Pañcālas in the coronation formula and suggests the water of Yamunā for the ritual,[155] and *Hiraṇyakeśin Śrauta Sūtra* names the Kurus in the ritual.[156] Thus, the entire corpus of the Black *Yajur Veda* has the Kuru-Pañcālas, particularly the Kurus, at the centre. Above all, the supposed author of *Yajur Veda* is Vaiśaṃpāyana, the person who is known to have narrated the *Mahābhārata* to the Kuru king Janamejaya.[157]

If the Black *Yajur Veda* is essentially a Kuru product, so should be at least one of the two major versions of the *Sāma Veda*, for the Kauṭhumas were closely related with the Kaṭhas.[158] The *Jaiminīya Saṃhitā* is most likely a product of the same location since even the later Jaiminīya texts—despite having a wide geographical knowledge—retain a special sentiment for the Kuru realm. Therefore, the JB remembers the crossing of the Indus by the Bharatas,[159] the fight between the Kurus and the Mahāvṛṣas and Trikartas,[160] the pilgrimage centres along the Sarasvatī,[161] the Khāṇḍava wood,[162] and the ritual adversity between the Kurus and the Pañcālas.[163]

The close affinity between the Kurus and the *Atharva Veda* is even more intriguing. The text is a Bhārgava-Āṅgirasa one created by the Śaunakas, who are a Bhārgava clan of Āṅgirasa pedigree. The other version, the Paippalāda text, in Witzel's opinion, was composed definitely in Kuru territory.[164] He locates the Śaunaka text to Kośala,[165] but the lavish praise of Parikṣit may suggest otherwise.[166] Moreover, a Śaunaka composed the *Aitareya Āraṇyaka*.[167] That the Aitareyas were Kuru people can be determined from the first five books of the AB where the water flows copiously towards the west and the wind blows strongest from the north-west.[168] Though an eastward thrust is noticeable in Books VI–VIII, the Kuru origin of the Śaunaka-Aitareyas can be ascertained.

Witzel locates the *Pañcaviṃśa* and the *Ṣaḍviṃśa Brāhmaṇas* in Videha.[169] However, the *Pañcaviṃśa Brāhmaṇa* has a graphic knowledge of the geography of Kurukṣetra with the Plakṣa Prasravana, Khāṇḍava Forest, Pāriṇah, Kārāpacava, Triplakṣa, Vyarṇa Naitandhava, Sthūlārāma, the Dṛṣadvatī river, the Naimiṣa forest, and the Sarasvatī.[170]

The Kuru-Pañcāla region is prominent even in the White *Yajur Veda* and the early parts of the ŚB. The coronation formula of the Kāṇva version of the White *Yajur Veda* has the Kuru-Pañcāla king as the addressee

(XI.3.3), which is also followed by the same version of the ŚB.[171] The Madhyaṇḍina version of the ŚB also recommends the Sarasvatī water for coronation and mentions the Bharata throne.[172]

The political hegemony of the Kurus did not last forever. The ŚŚS reports their defeat and expulsion from Kurukṣetra.[173] The focus gradually shifted eastwards, at first to Pañcāla—where the king Keśin Dārbhya played a prominent role in the development of the *dīkṣā* ritual of the KB—and then to Kośala and Videha.[174] By the time of the BU,[175] composed in Videha, descendants of Parikṣit were gone, but the Pañcālas were still there.[176] Witzel tries to explain the decline of the Kurus by Śālva invasion.[177] However, a more likely cause would be the flood at Hastināpura around 800 BCE, which forced the main branch of the Kurus to shift to Kauśāmbī. What can be said for sure is that the Kurus, or the Kuru-Pañcālas, dominated the Later Vedic world for a long period of time.

The narrative section of the *Mahābhārata* possibly records the activities of the Kurus and the Pañcālas in the period between Śaṃtanu and Parikṣit. On the other hand, the didactic portions of the *Mahābhārata* reshape the antagonism of Viśvāmitra and Vasiṣṭha in a new mould of *brāhmaṇa-kṣatriya* conflict. The remnants of the old tradition and the new additions would be interesting to explore. However, before that we may have a glimpse at the Later Vedic literature which stands like a threshold between the *Ṛg Veda* and the *Mahābhārata*.

2.6 From Saudāsas to Śunaḥśepa: Viśvāmitra and Vasiṣṭha in the Later Vedic World

As we have ascertained that the Kuru region, ruled by the successors of the Bharata-Pūrus, substantially contributed to the growth of a huge number of Later Vedic texts, it is especially noteworthy how these texts showcased the legendary Bharata priests of the Ṛgvedic age, Viśvāmitra and Vasiṣṭha, and we shall deal with that in this section.

We may take the *Bṛhaddevatā* as the starting point in our survey of Later Vedic literature on Viśvāmitra and Vasiṣṭha. The text, composed around fifth to fourth century BCE, is no doubt a late one, but it is basically a guidebook to the *Ṛg Veda*. Thus, it is an affiliate text of the *Ṛg Veda*, concerned with the Ṛgvedic world. More importantly, it is attributed to the Śaunakas.

As we have already seen, the history of Viśvāmitra and Vasiṣṭha is closely related with the history of the Bhṛgus who were a very old priestly family. Even in the Ṛgvedic times, they were known to be the ones who originated the fire cult. The rich corpus of the Bhārgava myths led scholars to offer diverse opinions about the Bhṛgus. A. Bergagne identified Bhṛgu with Agni.[178] A. Kuhn and A. Barth identified Bhṛgu with the lightning flash.[179] A. Weber seeks relics of primitive Indo-Germanic mythology in the Bhārgava legends.[180] However, we have seen that the Bhṛgus were real priests whose importance may go back to the Indo-Iranian times. The Ṛgvedic poets remember a Bhārgava, Uśanas Kāvya, as a poet par excellence, and this Uśanas appears in the later texts as a highly powerful Asura priest. One branch of the Bhārgavas was the Śaunakas who adopted Gṛtsamada, and this family composed Book II of the *Ṛg Veda*. Another Bhārgava, Jamadagni, did not compose much poetry but was a great support to Viśvāmitra in his struggle against Vasiṣṭha. The two oldest clans of the Vedic priests—the Āṅgirasas and the Bhārgavas—took much interest in magic and sorcery and composed the *Atharva Veda* whose principal *saṃhitā* is a work of the Śaunakas. However, the Bhārgavas did not relinquish their connection with the Ṛgvedic corpus, and a Śaunaka composed the *Bṛhaddevatā*, a Bhṛgu interpretation of the *Ṛg Veda*.

More importantly, the Śaunakas are the link between the Vedic world and the *Mahābhārata*. The *Mahābhārata* is a tradition whose origin would go back to ninth to eighth century BCE. Attributed to Vyāsa, possibly it was preserved by the *sūta* bards who recited it under the patronage of the Kuru kings who—as already seen—dominated the Later Vedic landscape. The first public recitation of the tradition might have taken place at a sacrifice of the Kuru king Janamejaya, but there was definitely a time gap between that and the Brahmanization of the originally *sūta-kṣatriya* text. Scholars such as V.S. Sukthankar and R.P. Goldman have convincingly shown from the internal evidence of the *Mahābhārata* that the Śaunakas were majorly responsible for this Brahmanization.[181] The text indeed records its last recitation before codification in a sacrifice organized by the head of the Śaunakas, and it also remembers the patron's demand for a history of the Bhārgavas—alongside the history of the Kurus—from the bard.[182] It can explain the addition of a huge amount of Bhārgava material, and a short genealogical history of the Bhārgava family,[183] to the *Mahābhārata*. Therefore, the *Bṛhaddevatā* is invaluable in understanding the form the Vasiṣṭha-Viśvāmitra legend would take in the *Mahābhārata*, since the clan which Brahmanized the text was the clan which composed the *Bṛhaddevatā*.

The *Bṛhaddevatā* clearly says that Viśvāmitra was the priest of Sudās and went to the confluence of the Vipāś and the Śutudrī with him.[184] The route of Vasiṣṭha-Viśvāmitra conflict is explained in a story where, in Sudās's sacrifice, Viśvāmitra was rendered unconscious by Śakti, son of Vasiṣṭha. With Jamadagni's help, Viśvāmitra regained consciousness and cursed the Vasiṣṭhas.[185] Therefore, the close connection between Viśvāmitra and the Bhārgava Jamadagni is reiterated and the instrumental role of the Bhṛgus in Viśvāmitra's struggle against Vasiṣṭha indicated.

Vasiṣṭha's divine birth is an established legend in the text.[186] More strikingly, with no Ṛgvedic support, the text describes Viśvāmitra as a king who attained the position of a *brahmarṣi* by penance.[187] The story of Viśvāmitra's erstwhile royal pedigree is thus referred to but not counted as the reason of his conflict with Vasiṣṭha.

A more striking reference in the *Bṛhaddevatā*, however, is that Vasiṣṭha's hundred sons had been slain by the Saudāsas or Sudās who, in consequence of a curse, had been transformed into a Rākṣasa.[188] It seems hardly believable after the cordiality between Sudās and Vasiṣṭha in the *Ṛg Veda*. But the tradition is quite well founded in Later Vedic literature.

The texts still remember Vasiṣṭha as the priest of Sudās Paijavana.[189] The JB shockingly says that Śakti, son of Vasiṣṭha, was cast into the fire by the sons of Sudās.[190] The KB remembers Vasiṣṭha praying after the death of his sons: 'May I be propagated with offspring, with cattle. May I overcome the Saudāsas'. He obtained his objectives by performing the Vasiṣṭha sacrifice on a Phālguna full moon.[191] Similar stories are narrated by the PB[192] and the TS.[193]

The stories clearly indicate that Vasiṣṭha, though highly favoured by Sudās, had a very antagonistic relationship with Sudās's sons. The reason is not clear, but maybe the Saudāsas did not like their father's decision to choose an immigrant priest over Viśvāmitra who possibly shared the Bharata lineage. The indication comes from the AB which calls Viśvāmitra a Bharata.[194] V.G. Rahurkar thinks that the Bharatas were a broad clan with both warrior and priestly groups. The Kuśikas could be the priestly group among the Bharatas.[195] Thus the sons possibly reinstated Viśvāmitra, after Sudās's death, and killed the sons of Vasiṣṭha, including Śakti. They possibly took away Vasiṣṭha's cattle as well and might have given that to Viśvāmitra who made a case for taking away the gifts bestowed on the 'unworthy recipients' and for bestowing that on the worthy Kuśikas.

Herman Lommel takes Śakti's victory over Viśvāmitra in a sacrificial contest as the starting point of the conflict, which might have resulted in Viśvāmitra's dismissal in favour of Śakti's father. The possibility is strong as the conflict most probably originated in Sudās's sacrifice, where Viśvāmitra was defeated by a Vasiṣṭha (may be Śakti) before he recovered to save his day with Jamadagni's help. But that was possibly not enough for saving his office. However, there is no evidence to claim that the killing of Vasiṣṭha's sons took place in Sudās's lifetime, as Lommel thinks.[196]

The Vedic Age was no doubt an age of violent conflicts. Still, cold-bloodedly casting a priest into fire, not even in a battle situation, and slaying other priests would account as very gruesome acts worthy of the Rākṣasas. That might have provoked Vasiṣṭha to compose his answer to Viśvāmitra's allegations and curses within a hymn meant for warding off the Rākṣasas. We will come back to the Rākṣasa act of the Saudāsas later. But Vasiṣṭha also recovered his status and became rich in progeny and cattle. He also overcame the Saudāsas but possibly did not become the Bharata priest again. In later literature, the Vasiṣṭhas invariably appear as the priests of the Ikṣvākus who seem to be a minor Vedic tribe.

Whether Viśvāmitra's Bharata pedigree and his use of political means to reach his goals, whereas Vasiṣṭha always is shown resisting his opponents through typical priestly devices, later on painted him as a *kṣatriya* is not sure. But, already in the PB, ĀŚS, and MŚS, he is known to have been a king who defeated the Vṛcivats.[197] The kingly past of Viśvāmitra is accepted by the *Bṛhaddevatā* and the *Nirukta*.[198] However, an older version also exists in the JB and the PB, which opines that Viśvāmitra helped the Bharatas to defeat the Vṛcivats, Aikṣvākas, and Mahāvṛṣas.[199]

In the general corpus of the Later Vedic literature, Vasiṣṭha, Viśvāmitra, and Jamadagni are remembered mainly because of their priestly capacities. Viśvāmitra and Vasiṣṭha both attained the realm of Indra,[200] and

Vasiṣṭha received revelation from Indra.[201] Jamadagni increased his descendants by a four-day sacrifice.[202]

However, the contest between Vasiṣṭha and the Viśvāmitra-Jamadagni duo is also well attested. We have already mentioned the sacrificial contest referred to in the TS. That both the parties brought accusation against each other is shown by the JB, which demonstrates how Jamadagni defended himself against his enemies (the Māhenas).[203] It also contains a story about how Vasiṣṭha gained deliverance when some sages reproached him for being a *vaiśya*.[204] However, in all these legends, both Vasiṣṭha and Jamadagni use their priestly capacities for both offence and defence. Viśvāmitra's use of militant methods, therefore, can really be a reason of his alleged *kṣatriyahood*.

For a priest, Viśvāmitra seems to be a strange person indeed. The matter may become clearer through a glance at the story of Śunaḥśepa in the AB.[205] The story starts with the Ikṣvāku king Hariścandra who, following an advice from the sage Nārada, prayed to Varuṇa for a son. The childless king promised Varuṇa that if the deity blessed him with a son, he would sacrifice that son to him. But after the birth of the son, Rohita, he started making a series of excuses till Rohita became capable of bearing arms. Then, Rohita, following Indra's advice, left the palace and wandered for six years till he met the family of the Āṅgirasa *brāhmaṇa* Ajīgarta in a miserable condition. The needy *brāhmaṇa* handed over his second son Śunaḥśepa for an amount of hundred (cows?) and himself agreed to bind and execute his son for two hundred more. Śunaḥśepa started to pray to one deity after another and ultimately succeeded in rescuing himself. Viśvāmitra, Jamadagni, Vasiṣṭha, and Ayaśva were the priests officiating in the sacrifice. The impressed Viśvāmitra adopted Śunaḥśepa as his own son. Ajīgarta wanted his son back, but Śunaḥśepa refused to return to the parents who valued 300 pieces of wealth more than his life. Viśvāmitra awarded Śunaḥśepa the position of his eldest son. However, the eldest fifty of Viśvāmitra's one hundred and one sons refused to accept it. Viśvāmitra cursed them to become *dasyus*, and they formed outcast tribes such as the Andhras, Pulindas, Śabaras, Mūtibas, and Puṇḍras.

The story cannot be totally dismissed as a mere Later Vedic legend trying to incorporate the aboriginal tribes within the world of Brahmanical mythology. The second part obviously does that, but the first part is more curious. Śunaḥśepa, the son of Ajīgarta, is a Ṛgvedic poet of eight hymns.[206] The first two of those are clearly the prayers of a man tied to be sacrificed. Therefore, Śunaḥśepa—like Viśvāmitra, Jamadagni, and Vasiṣṭha—was a figure of the Ṛgvedic age. The legend therefore may contain a memory of the sacrifice of a minor Vedic chief, where Viśvāmitra, Vasiṣṭha, and Jamadagni were present (just like Sudās's Aśvamedha) and where Viśvāmitra saved and adopted an unfortunate victim about to be sacrificed. Rahurkar thinks that the AB story has nothing to do with the Ṛgvedic Śunaḥśepa, since the latter does not mention Hariścandra, Ajīgarta, Nārada, or Viśvāmitra in his prayers.[207] However, it is not clear why these figures should be necessarily mentioned in Śunaḥśepa's prayer to different deities for saving his life. What else can explain Śunaḥśepa's composition of the hymns while tied as a victim should also be considered. Therefore, the unorthodox priest who used military means to punish his former patron Sudās and instigated the Saudāsas to kill his rival priest's sons might indeed have also stopped the very sacrifice where he was supposed to officiate. The later author elaborated on this story and added the portion on Viśvāmitra's sons to provide a rationale for the existence of the non-Vedic people. Viśvāmitra, a priest both respected and hated, was the ideal person to become at once the ancestor of the *dasyus* and the one to have cursed them.

An important point raised by Pargiter is the role of Vasiṣṭha in the whole Śunaḥśepa episode, which deserves closer scrutiny. Pargiter thinks that Vasiṣṭha, who always wanted to completely control Ayodhyā, plotted the entire thing. After all, Varuṇa could not have, in reality, come and demanded Rohita as a sacrificial victim, but the message of Varuṇa was likely to be conveyed by the chief priest. Similarly, Indra could not have kept Rohita wandering for six years, and Pargiter views that also as an act of Vasiṣṭha. Therefore, he thinks that Vasiṣṭha wanted to ruin both the king and the prince, which would make him the authority over Ayodhyā.[208] The inadequacy of this interpretation can easily be pointed out. Pargiter also complicates the issue by reading a myth as a historical account at first and considering the physical intervention of the deities (quite common in mythological stories) as practically impossible and, thus, designs of the priest. However, the roles of Vasiṣṭha, Varuṇa, and Indra in the AB legend deserve closer scrutiny.

The special relationship between Varuṇa and Vasiṣṭha has already been discussed. It has also been noted that Vasiṣṭha was possibly acting as a reconciler between the old cult of Varuṇa and the new cult of Indra. The pledge of the Ikṣvāku king, who had Vasiṣṭha as priest, of a human sacrifice to Varuṇa is thus quite interesting. Human sacrifice, after all, is not a very common practice in Vedic literature. However, J.C. Heesterman has brilliantly shown that human sacrifice was definitely practised in preclassical times, though the actual sacrifice was replaced by sacrificial metaphor in 'classical' Vedic sacrifice.[209] The old cult of Varuṇa, therefore, could have contained an element of human sacrifice. Vasiṣṭha, who had a close emotional bonding with that cult, could have thus been instrumental in Hariścandra's pledge, and could have pressurized him to fulfil his vow. The reason for that does not seem to be Vasiṣṭha's material interest to capture power, but the conservative and normative insistence of the Vasiṣṭha family on the virtues of purity of behaviour and truthfulness, as shown by K.R. Potdar.[210] On the other hand, the prevalent Vedic cult centring Indra did not condone human sacrifice. Therefore, we can see Indra repeatedly stopping Rohita from returning to the kingdom to save his life. It is not Vasiṣṭha, as Pargiter argues, but possibly Viśvāmitra who could have represented Indra in the story. Viśvāmitra not only popularized Indra among the Kuśikas but is also well known for his association with Indra in Later Vedic literature. When Viśvāmitra ultimately saves Śunaḥśepa, the element of cultic confrontation in the legend also becomes clear.

The conflict of Vasiṣṭha and Viśvāmitra had been further reshaped in the *Mahābhārata* and the *Rāmāyaṇa*, and we shall return to that in due time. However, what the Vedic compositions of these two poets show are invaluable for the history of the Bharata-Pūrus. We have seen how these two poets, both of whom had served the Bharata chief Sudās as priests, documented the migration of the Bharata-Pūrus, their advancement under Sudās who had performed an *aśvamedha*, the Battle of Ten Kings where Sudās's success established the Bharata hegemony, the coming together of the Bharatas and the Pūrus, and the creation of a new religious order under Vasiṣṭha. We have also seen how the Kuru-Pañcāla region, particularly the Kuru kingdom under Parikṣit, became the epicentre of the creation of the Vedic corpus in the early part of the Later Vedic Age. This process probably included the creation of the Vedic orthodoxy and orthopraxy with the coming of the *varṇa* system. Thus, the massive transition taking place in the Later Vedic Age had much to do with the Kuru kingdom after Śaṃtanu's reign. Is the *Mahābhārata*, telling the story of the Kurus between Śaṃtanu to Parikṣit, a text of this transition? Did the narrative sections of the *Mahābhārata* really represent a Later Vedic context? Even if it did, is that context discernible in a text that had received so many revisions over more than a millennium? We shall seek the answers in the next chapter.

Notes

1. *Āśvalāyana Śrauta Sūtra*, edited by R. Vidyaratna, Bibliotheca Indica, Calcutta, 1874, XII.10.13.
2. Michael Witzel, 'Ṛgvedic History: Poets, Chieftains and Polities' in George Erdosy (ed.), *The Indo-Aryans of Ancient South Asia*, Munshiram Manoharlal, New Delhi, 1995, pp. 307–354.
3. ṚV, III.58.6.
4. Witzel (1995), p. 318.
5. Witzel (1995), p. 318.
6. Witzel (1995), p. 318.
7. Witzel (1995), p. 318.
8. Witzel (1995), p. 314.
9. Witzel (1995), p. 318.
10. Witzel (1995), p. 318.
11. ṚV, IV.16.2, IX.97.7.
12. Vyāsa, VI.32.15, VI.32.37.
13. Witzel (1997a), p. 294.
14. Hermann Weller, 'Who Were the Bhṛguids?', *Annals of the Bhandarkar Oriental Research Institute*, Vol. 18, Part 3, 1936, pp. 296–302.
15. Cited in Pradeep Kant Choudhary, *Rāma with an Axe*, Aakar, New Delhi, 2010, p. 28.
16. D.D. Kosambi, 'The Study of Ancient Indian Tradition', in B.G. Gokhale (ed.), *Indica: The Indian Historical Research Institute Silver Jubilee Commemoration Volume*, St. Xavier's College, Bombay, 1953, pp. 196–214.
17. *The Veda of the Black Yajus School Entitled Taittirīya Saṃhitā*, translated by Arthur Berriadale Keith, Motilal Banarsidass, Delhi, 1967 (reprint), II.5.8.5; *Pañcaviṃśa Brāhmaṇa*, translated by W. Caland, Asiatic Society of Bengal, Calcutta, 1938, VII.5.20; *Śāṅkhāyana Śrauta Sūtra*, translated by W. Caland, Motilal Banarsidass, Delhi, 1980 (reprint), XIV.27.1. All further references to these three texts are from these respective volumes.
18. ṚV, III.55.
19. ṚV, VII.33.3.
20. Witzel (1995), p. 335.

21. ṚV, VII.33.9.
22. Witzel (1995), p. 335.
23. Witzel (1997a), p. 294.
24. ṚV, VIII.10.5.
25. ṚV, VIII.4.19.
26. ṚV, VIII.4.1.
27. ṚV, VI.45.1.
28. ṚV, IV.19.6, IV.30.17, VI.20.12.
29. ṚV, IV.16.13.
30. ṚV, IV.30.21.
31. ṚV, VI.20.6.
32. ṚV, VIII.10.5.
33. Witzel (1995), p. 328.
34. ŚB, XIII.4.5.6.
35. Witzel makes this assumption, and the geographical location seems to support it. But we must accept that there is no concrete evidence in support of this identification.
36. ṚV, VI.18.13.
37. ṚV, II.12.11.
38. H.D. Velankar, 'The Family Hymns in the Family Maṇḍalas', *Journal of the Bombay Branch of the Royal Asiatic Society*, Vol. XVIII, 1942, pp. 9–10.
39. ṚV, II.12.11, II.14.6, II.24.2, IV.26.3, IV.30.14, IV.30.15, VI.26.5, VI.47.2, VI.47.21–25, VII.18.20, VII.99.5.
40. ṚV, VI.20.10.
41. ṚV, I.54.6, II.13.12, VI.18.13.
42. ṚV, X.49.5.
43. ṚV, III.5.10, III.9.5.
44. ṚV, III.43.9.
45. Velankar (1942), p. 3.
46. ṚV, III.60.
47. ṚV, III.33.
48. ṚV, III.53.9.
49. ṚV, III.53.12.
50. ṚV, III.53.14.
51. ṚV, III.53.15–16.
52. ṚV, II.17–20.
53. ṚV, III.53.21–24. These four verses are known as *vasiṣṭhadveṣināḥ*. These curses are probably directed towards the Vasiṣṭhas, since all the commentators unanimously support this interpretation. If we follow Griffith's translation, Vasiṣṭha is not directly named. However, R.C. Dutt, in his translation, names Vasiṣṭha.
54. ṚV, III.61.
55. ṚV, III.62.10.

56. Ṛv, III.30.22, III.32.17, III.34.11, III.35.11, III.36.11, III.39.9, III.43.8, III.48.5, III.49.5, III.50.5.
57. Ṛv, III.55.
58. V.G. Rahurkar, *The Seers of the Ṛgveda*, University of Poona, Poona, 1964, pp. 140–150.
59. Ṛv, VII.18.22, VII.33.3, VII.83.7–9.
60. The term used in Ṛv, VII.18.6, is *puroḍḍāś*, which probably means a person presiding at solemn rites.
61. Ṛv, VII.18.6.
62. Ṛv, VII.18.7.
63. Ṛv, VII.18.15.
64. Cited in A.A. Macdonnell and A.B. Keith, *Vedic Index of Names and Subjects* (Vol. II), Motilal Banarsidass, Delhi, 1922, p. 95.
65. Ṛv, VII.83.8.
66. Cited in Macdonnell and Keith (1922), p. 95; Witzel (1995), p. 334.
67. Ṛv, VII.18.12.
68. Ṛv, VII.18.14.
69. Ṛv, VII.18.13.
70. Ṛv, VII.18.11.
71. Ṛv, VII.18.8–9.
72. Ṛv, VII.18.17.
73. Ṛv, VII.18.5.
74. Ṛv, VII.18.24.
75. Ṛv, VII.18.22–23.
76. Ṛv, VII.8.6.
77. Ṛv, VII.18.25.
78. Ṛv, VII.19.8.
79. Ṛv, VII.18.13.
80. Ṛv, VII.19.2–3.
81. Ṛv, VII.18.18–19.
82. Ṛv, VII.9.6.
83. Cited in Rahurkar (1964), p. 130.
84. Ṛv, VII.1.7.
85. Ṛv, X.80.3.
86. Ṛv, VII.29.3.
87. Ṛv, VII.89.
88. Ṛv, VII.86–89.
89. Ṛv, VII.59.12.
90. Ṛv, VII.99.
91. Ṛv, VII.75–81.
92. Ṛv, VII.103. Scholars have given different interpretations of the hymn dedicated to the frogs. Max Muller views it as a satire on the Vedic priests. Geldner thinks that the satire is directed against Vasiṣṭha's rivals, particularly the Viśvāmitras.

For Deussen, it is a parody on the materialistic attitude of the Vedic poets who always begged something from the deities. On the other hand, Winternitz thinks that the humorous hymn had been turned into a magic spell gradually. Scholars like Gonda, Thomas, and Rahurkar see it as a magico-religious spell for bringing rain (Rahurkar [1964], pp. 134–135). No doubt the hymn has some comic similes, especially regarding the Vedic educational system. However, the overall tone is serious, and the overall message seems to be a praise of the frogs as the real rain-bringing priests. It can or cannot have magical significance, but that does not affect the significance of the poet's sensitivity to the nature.

93. ṚV, VII.36.1–3.
94. ṚV, VII.1.25, VII.3.10, VII.4.10, VII.7.7, VII.8.7, VII.9.6, VII.11.5, VII.12.3, VII.13.3, VII.14.3, VII.19.11, VII.20.10, VII.21.10, VII.22.9, VII.23.6, VII.24.6, VII.25.6, VII.26.5, VII.27.5, VII.28.5, VII.29.5, VII.30.5, VII.34.25, VII.35.15, VII.36.9, VII.37.8, VII.39.7, VII.40.7, VII.41.7, VII.42.6, VII.43.5, VII.45.4, VII.46.4, VII.47.4, VII.48.4, VII.51.3, VII.53.3, VII.54.3, VII.56.25, VII.57.7, VII.58.6, VII.60.12, VII.61.7, VII.62.6, VII.63.6, VII.64.5, VII.65.5, VII.67.10, VII.68.9, VII.69.8, VII.70.7, VII.71.6, VII.72.5, VII.73.5, VII.75.8, VII.76.7, VII.77.6, VII.78.5, VII.79.5, VII.80.3, VII.84.5, VII.85.5, VII.86.8, VII.87.7, VII.88.7, VII.90.7, VII.91.7, VII.92.5, VII.93.8, VII.95.6, VII.97.10, VII.98.7, VII.99.7, VII.100.7, VII.101.6.
95. K.R. Potdar, 'Contribution of the Vasiṣṭha Family', *Oriental Thought*, Vol. V, No. 4, December 1961, pp. 4–5.
96. ṚV, VII.104.12.
97. ṚV, VII.104.13.
98. ṚV, VII.104.14.
99. Sadashiva A. Dange, 'The Birth of Vasiṣṭha', *The Quarterly Journal of the Mythic Society*, Vol. LV, Nos 3–4, October 1964–January 1965, p. 89.
100. Dange (1964–1965), p. 91.
101. Cited in Rahurkar (1964), p. 119.
102. Ellison Banks Findly, 'Vasiṣṭha: Religious Personality and Vedic Culture', *Numen*, Vol. 31, Fasc 1, July 1984, pp. 74–105.
103. Rahurkar (1964), pp. 138–139.
104. ṚV, VII.83.9, VII.85.3.
105. ṚV, VII.82.2.
106. Cited in Macdonnell and Keith (1922), p. 275.
107. Witzel (1995), p. 319.
108. Velankar (1942), pp. 8–9.
109. X.60, X.70, and X.105 are the three surviving compositions of Sumitra.
110. *Kaṭhaka Saṃhitā*, edited by L. von Schroeder, Franzn Steiner Verlag, Wiesbaden, 1971–1972, XI.10; *Kauśītakī Upaniṣad*, III.1.
111. Velankar, (1942), p. 9.
112. Velankar, (1942), p. 12.

113. C. Kunhan Raja, 'Dāśarājña', *Indian Historical Quarterly*, Vol. XXXVII, No. 4, December 1961, pp. 272–273.
114. ṚV, III.53.11–14.
115. ṚV, VII.19.
116. ṚV, VII.18.13.
117. It seems that the nomadic pastoralists moved gradually from west to east. Rivers provided natural frontiers between the areas of movement of different tribes. Thus, river crossings were major events.
118. ṚV, III.23.4.
119. ṚV, III.53.14.
120. ṚV, III.53.15–16, III.62.18.
121. ṚV, X.167.
122. TS, III.1.7.3.
123. Choudhary (2010), p. 35.
124. John E. Mitchiner, *Traditions of the Seven Ṛṣis*, Motilal Banarsidass, Delhi, 1982.
125. Vyāsa, I.64.25.
126. Kosambi (1953), p. 212;D.D. Kosambi, 'Early Stages of the Caste System in North Northern India', *Journal of the Bombay Branch of the Royal Asiatic Society*, New Series, Vol. 22, 1946–1947, p. 41; D.D. Kosambi, 'Origin of the Brahmin Gotras', *Journal of the Bombay Branch of the Royal Asiatic Society*, New Series, Vol. 22, 1950–1951, p. 43.
127. Rahurkar (1964), p. 12.
128. The Kavaṣas are a priestly family of the *Ṛg Veda*. One of their ancestors had been drowned during the Battle of Ten Kings. Another composed Hymns X.30–34. Their descendent, Tura Kāvaṣeya, is a prominent priest in the Later Vedic literature.
129. Kunhan Raja (1961), pp. 261–278.
130. ṚV, I.7.9, I.89.10, I.100.12, II.2.10, V.32.11, VI.11.4, VI.61.12, IX.65.23.
131. ṚV, VII.8.4.
132. ṚV, VII.18.12–14.
133. ṚV, VII.18.22–23.
134. ṚV, VII.18.19.
135. ṚV, VII.19.8.
136. A.D. Pusalker, 'Aryan Settlements in India', in R.C. Majumdar (ed.), *The History and Culture of the Indian People: The Vedic Age*, Bharatiya Vidya Bhavan, Mumbai, 1996, p. 249.
137. ṚV, I.63.7.
138. ṚV, VI.27.7.
139. ṚV, III.23.
140. Witzel (1997a), p. 266.
141. ṚV, X.32.9, X.33.4.
142. ṚV, X.98.
143. Witzel (1997a), p. 263.

144. KS, III.7.1, XXIII.8.
145. KS, XXVI.2.123.17.
146. *Maitrāyaṇī Saṃhitā*, F.A. Brockhaus, Leipzig, 1886, IV.7.9.104.14.
147. KS, X.6; Vyāsa, IX.40.1–25.
148. *Mānava Śrauta Sūtra*, translated by J.M. van Gelder, Śata Piṭaka Series, Delhi, 1961–1963, IX.5.4.1.
149. Witzel (1997a), p. 336.
150. Witzel (1997a), p. 302.
151. TS, VII.2.1.4.
152. TS, I.8.18.
153. *Baudhayana Śrauta Sūtra*, edited by W. Caland, Bibliotheca Indica, Calcutta, 1904–1924, XII.9, XVI.32, XXVI.20.
154. *Baudhayana Śrauta Sūtra* (1904–1924), XVIII.38.18.
155. *Āpastamba Śrauta Sūtra*, edited by R. Garbe, Bibliotheca Indica, Calcutta, 1881–1903, XII.12.12.7.
156. *Hiraṇyakeśin Śrauta Sūtra*, edited by K.B. Agase, Anandasrama Sanskrit Series, Poona, 1907–1932, XIII.5.24.175.
157. Witzel (1997a), p. 334.
158. Witzel (1997a), p. 270.
159. *Jaiminīya Brāhmaṇa*, edited by Raghu Vira, Sarasvati Vihara, Nagpur, 1934, III.238.9.
160. *Jaiminīya Brāhmaṇa* (1934), I.234, II.297.8.
161. *Jaiminīya Brāhmaṇa* (1934), II.207, II.300, III.64, III.168, III.245.
162. *Jaiminīya Brāhmaṇa* (1934), III.168.
163. *Jaiminīya Brāhmaṇa* (1934), I.262.
164. Witzel (1997a), p. 279.
165. Witzel (1997a), p. 336.
166. AV, XX.127.
167. Witzel (1997a), p. 293.
168. AB, I.7.
169. Witzel (1997a), p. 336.
170. PB, XXV–XXVI.
171. Witzel (1987), p. 199.
172. ŚB, V.3.4.3, V.4.4.1.
173. ŚŚS, XV.12–16.
174. *Kauśītakī Brāhmaṇa* in *Ṛg Veda Brāhmaṇas*, VII.4.
175. BU, III.3.1.
176. Witzel (1997a), p. 304.
177. Witzel (1997a), p. 304.

178. V.S. Sukthankar, 'The Bhṛgus and the Bhārata: A Text Historical Study', *Annals of the Bhandarkar Oriental Research Institute*, Vol. 18, 1936–1937, p. 278.
179. Sukthankar (1936–1937), p. 278.
180. Sukthankar (1936–1937), p. 278.
181. Sukthankar (1936–1937); R.P. Goldman, 'Akṛtavarṇa vs Śrīkṛṣṇa as Narrator of the Legend of the Bhārgava Rāma: Apropos Some Observations of Dr. V.S. Sukthankar', *Annals of the Bhandarkar Oriental Research Institute*, Vol. 53, 1972, pp. 161–173; R.P. Goldman, *Gods, Priests and Warriors: The Bhṛgus of the Mahābhārata*, Columbia University Press, New York, 1977.
182. Vyāsa, I.5.3.
183. Vyāsa, I.5–12.
184. Śaunaka, *The Bṛhaddevatā* (Part II), translated by A.A. MacDonell, Motilal Banarsidass, Delhi, 1965 (reprint), IV.106.
185. ṚV, IV.112–114.
186. Śaunaka, V.149–159.
187. Śaunaka, IV.95–96.
188. Śaunaka, VI.28, VI.33–34.
189. AB, VII.34.9, VIII.21.11, ŚŚS, XVI.11.13–15.
190. JB, I.150, II.390, III.26, III.83, III.149, III.204.
191. KB, IV.8.
192. PB, IV.7.3.
193. TS, VII.4.7.
194. In AB, VII.17, Viśvāmitra is addressed as '*bharatarṣabha*'.
195. V.G. Rahurkar, 'Viśvāmitra and the Viśvāmitras in the Ṛgveda', *Oriental Thought*, Vol. V, No. 1, January 1961, p. 28.
196. Herman Lommel, 'Vasiṣṭha und Viśvāmitra', *Oriens 18/19*, 1965/1966, pp. 200–227.
197. PB, XXI.12.2; ĀŚS, XXII.20.2; MŚS, IX.4.2.
198. Śaunaka, IV.95–96; Yāska, II.14.
199. JB, III.183, III.237–38; PB, XIV.3.12–13.
200. AB, VI.20; *Jaiminīya Upaniṣad Brāhmaṇa*, translated by H. Oertel, *Journal of the American Oriental Society*, Vol. 16, 1896, III.3.7–10.
201. TS, III.5.2; PB, XV.5.24; ŚB, XII.6.1; *Gopatha Brāhmaṇa*, edited by R.L. Mitra, Bibliotheca Indica, Delhi, 1972 (reprint), II.2.13.
202. JB, II.285; PB, XXI.10.5–6, XXII.7.2; ĀŚS, XII.18.16; MŚS, IX.4.2.1; ŚŚS, XVI.23.7–8.
203. JB, I.152.
204. JB, III.195.
205. AB, VII.13–18.

206. ṚV, I.24–30, IX.3.
207. Rahurkar (1961), pp. 42–43.
208. F.E. Pargiter, 'Viśvāmitra, Vasiṣṭha, Hariścandra and Śunaḥśepa', *Journal of the Royal Asiatic Society of Great Britain and Ireland*, January 1917, pp. 37–67.
209. J.C. Heesterman, *The Inner Conflict of Tradition: Essays in Indian Ritual, Kingship and Society*, Oxford University Press, New Delhi, 1985.
210. Potdar (1961), pp. 1–8.

3

The Great Saga of the Bharatas

3.1 Searching for a Lost History of 'Time': Layering the *Mahābhārata*

The location of the *Mahābhārata* as an *itihāsa*, and its relationship with the Vedic world, has already been noted in the first two chapters. It is a text about the Kuru-Pañcālas who were the most prominent people in the Later Vedic Age. The *Ṛg Veda* provides almost a continuous history of the Bharata-Pūrus and then the Kurus, up to the time of Śaṃtanu. The *Mahābhārata* takes up the story from Śaṃtanu's time and carries it forward up to the time of Parikṣit. Parikṣit and his son Janamejaya are famous personalities in the Later Vedic texts. It is in Janamejaya's sacrifice that the *Mahābhārata* underwent its first redaction by Vaiśaṃpāyana, another well-known Later Vedic figure. However, the text was gradually 'Brahmanized'. The entire journey of the text could have been a millennium long or even longer, though its main narrative possibly refers to a ninth century BCE context. This is the date which F.E. Pargiter, H.C. Raychaudhuri, and B.B. Lal arrive at, using totally different methodologies. The appearances of Śaṃtanu in Book X of the *Ṛg Veda*, of Dhṛtarāṣṭra Vaicitravīrya in the *Kaṭhaka Saṃhitā*, and of Parikṣit in the *Ṛg Veda Khila* and the *Atharva Veda*, the presence of Janamejaya and Vaiśaṃpāyana in the Later Vedic texts, and the supposed disappearance of the family by the time of the BU would confirm this dating which has also been accepted by J.A.B. van Buitenen.

We have noted that scholars such as Romila Thapar and R.S. Sharma rightly associate the narrative section of the *Mahābhārata* with the period when the Later Vedic texts were composed (*c.* 1000–600 BCE), though much of the didactic portion is definitely later. However, the equation between didactic legends and later interpolation seems too simplistic. Therefore, in this chapter we shall closely inspect some of the major

From Dāśarājña to Kurukṣetra. Kanad Sinha, Oxford University Press. © Oxford University Press 2021.
DOI: 10.1093/oso/9780190130695.003.0003

pointers of the main narrative of the *Mahābhārata*—such as the partition of the kingdom, the burning of the Khāṇḍava forest and establishment of Indraprastha, Yudhiṣṭhira's *rājasūya* and the subsequent dice games, the cattle inspection in the Dvaita forest and the cattle raid in the Matsya kingdom, and the Bhārata War—to determine their context with the help of other contemporary and near-contemporary sources. However, before analysing the *Mahābhārata* narrative in its historical context, we should have a look at its textual context.

The succession struggle between the two branches of the Kuru family, which is the central content of the main narrative, is preceded by a huge volume of legends about preceding generations. There is little in these legends that would stand a test of historical corroboration. The figures appearing in the genealogical lists of the Bharata-Kurus in the text would often betray the evidence given by the Vedic literature. Sometimes, random Vedic names are invoked to substantiate a new story. However, these legends are important to understand the context the text itself creates for the succession struggle of the main narrative. Moreover, at times, deconstructing these legends shows how an old history or legend is loaded with new meanings in a new context in the form of a newly fashioned story.

For instance, we may have a look at the story about the origin of the Pūrus. King Yayāti, son of Nahuṣa, and of Āyus's lineage, was married to Devayānī, the daughter of Śukrācārya, and had two sons (Yadu and Turvaśa) by her. The king also secretly married Śarmiṣṭhā—daughter of the Asura king Vṛṣaparvan—who gave birth to Druhyu, Anu, and Pūru. When the secret marriage got exposed, Devayānī left Yayāti and Śukrācārya cursed him of premature *jarā* (literally, old age, but probably carrying the connotation of frigidity here). The only cure to the curse was exchanging it with someone's youth. Yayāti's first four sons refused to accept the exchange and were banished, while Pūru succeeded his father by accepting it.[1]

The story, if deconstructed, can reveal the faint memory of the early history of the Vedic *pañca jana*, discussed in the preceding chapter. Under the story of Yayāti lies the fact that the Yadu, the Turvaśa, the Druhyu, and the Anu tribes—who shared a common origin with the Pūru tribe—had to leave their original abode in Iran and migrate to India, while the Pūrus still remained there. The close association of Yadu-Turvaśa and Druhyu-Anu is explained by the two pairs being born of Devayānī and

Śarmiṣṭhā, respectively. That the Bhṛgus might have had a role in it is indicated by Śukrācārya's curse. The possibility of locating the early Bhṛgus, including Uśanas (Śukrācārya), who enjoyed a healthy relationship with the 'Asuras', in Iran has been discussed earlier. The *Ṛg Veda* remembers Nahuṣa and his son Yayāti as well.[2] They are part composers of a hymn (IX.101). More importantly, it is the Iranian immigrant Vasiṣṭha who remembers how Nahuṣa's tribe was forced to bring tributes.[3] Are these also remnants of the Indo-Iranian level of the *Ṛg Veda*, memories of some Iranian chiefs of the Āyus tribe, as discussed in the previous chapter? It is highly possible that this is so.

However, Yadu, Turvaśa, Druhyu, Anu, and Pūru, even though they are remembered together in the *Mahābhārata*, are not Vedic tribes but five sons of Yayāti. Therefore, the legend has been shifted from the context of tribal migration to a genealogical context. Similarly, Bharata, the word that is at the root of the name '*Mahābhārata*', is no longer a tribe but a king within the same genealogy. The tribal identity is transformed into a clan identity where genealogy is crucial in unifying the clan on the basis of a perceived lineage from a common ancestor. Thus, to understand the *Mahābhārata*, we must understand its genealogical framework, which we shall attempt in this section.

In the *itihāsa-purāṇa* tradition, almost all royal genealogies are subsumed under two great lineages: the Sūryavaṃśa (Solar Lineage) and the Candravaṃśa (Lunar Lineage). Of course, the names signify mythological descent from the sun god and the moon god, respectively. But, probably, the Candravaṃśa (also known as Somavaṃśa) and the Sūryavaṃśa also stood for two different genealogical conceptions. One kind of genealogy maps out the clan with all its branches, with an account of all the segments represented by different collaterals. The other kind of genealogy follows a line of primogeniture, with only the first-born male being enlisted in each generation. As Romila Thapar has noted, '[T]he listing of all the segments is as essential to the Candravaṃśa as it is absent in the Sūryavaṃśa'.[4] The *Rāmāyaṇa* is a typical Sūryavaṃśa story, tracing the genealogy from the main Sūryavaṃśa line, that of the Ikṣvāku clan, and—naturally—the question of primogeniture, the eldest son succeeding to the throne, is the central political interest of the epic. The idea is encapsulated beautifully in the statement of Vasiṣṭha, the traditional teacher of the Sūryavaṃśa, to Rāma:

ikṣvākūṇāṃ hi sarveṣāṃ rājā bhavati pūrvajaḥ/
purvajenāvarahaḥ putro jyeṣṭho rājye'bhiṣicyate//
sa rāghavāṇāṃ kuladharmam ātmanaḥ sanātanaṃ nādya vihātum arhasi/

(Among all the Ikṣvākus the first-born has always become the king. When the first-born is living, it is not a younger son but only the eldest who is consecrated for kingship. This is the age-old custom of your own house, the house of the Rāghavas, and you must not abandon it now.)[5]

Is the *Mahābhārata* a Sūryavaṃśa story or a Candravaṃśa story? What is the genealogical schema of the Kuru clan? If one goes through the *Mahābhārata* narrative, one would see that the understood lineage of the Kurus was Candravaṃśa. Bhīma identified himself within the Somavaṃśa.[6] Nahuṣa named Soma as his ancestor.[7] A similar identity was invoked for Yayāti.[8] Dhṛtarāṣṭra traced the beginning of his line to Soma Prajāpati.[9] Saṃjaya, while describing the genealogy of the Yādavas, traced the lineage of Yadu, son of Yayāti, from Atri and his son Soma.[10] However, the *Mahābhārata* interestingly presents two genealogical accounts for the Kurus, one in verse (I.70–89) and the other in prose (I.90). It would be easy to see it as a textual discrepancy (particularly when the two genealogies often contradict each other) created by later interpolation of one of the genealogies. Yet, that would not answer why such an interpolation would take place. More interestingly, both the genealogies are placed in the narration of Vaiśaṃpāyana, negating the possibility that the two genealogies are presented for two kinds of audiences (*kṣatriya* first and *brāhmaṇa* later) the text's narrators (represented by Vaiśaṃpāyana and Ugraśravas, respectively) were addressing in two different times. Complicating the matter further, the verse genealogy (*vaṃśa*) follows the Candravaṃśa pattern of naming the collaterals representing all the segments, whereas the prose *vaṃśa* follows the Sūryavaṃśa pattern of a primogenitive single line.

One may wonder if the *Mahābhārata* is a Candravaṃśa story, what is the point of the Sūryavaṃśa-style prose *vaṃśa*? However, despite the firm belief of the characters in their Candravaṃśa origin, the genealogical details indicate otherwise. The prose *vaṃśa*'s primogenitive line is described as Dakṣa—› Aditi—› Vivasvat (Sun)—› Manu—› Ilā—› Purūravas—› Āyus—› Nahuṣa—› Yayāti:

dakṣād aditiḥ. aditer vivasvān. vivasvato manuḥ. manor ilā. ilāyāḥ purūravāḥ. purūravasa āyuḥ. āyuṣo nahuṣaḥ. nahuṣasya yayātiḥ.[11]

Therefore, it is an unqualified Sūryavaṃśa identity. This attribution of the genealogy is not contradicted by the Candravaṃśa-style verse *vaṃśa* as well. It says that Dakṣa Prajāpati, son of Pracetas, had fifty daughters from his wife Vīriṇī. One of them was Dākṣāyaṇī (probably the same as Aditi of the prose *vaṃśa*) who was married to Kaśyapa. Their son was the sun god Vivasvat. His son was Yama Vaivasvata. He was followed by his son Mārtaṇḍa (another solar deity) whose son was Manu. Manu had a daughter named Ilā whose son was Purūravas.[12]

Hence, both the *vaṃśas* attribute the Bharata-Kurus, traced from Yayāti's son Pūru, a Sūryavaṃśa identity. The identity is further crystallized in later narrations. Thus, describing the origin of the beings to the sages assembled at the Naimiṣa forest, Ugraśravas said:

> The great Sun is the son of the sky and soul of the eye, the Resplendent One who is also Savitar, Ṛcīka, Arka, Āśāvaha, the Bringer-of-Hope, and Ravi. Of all the sons of Sun Vivasvant, the last one is Mahya, who had a son that shone like a God, who is hence known as Subhrāj—the Well-Shining One. Subhrāj had three sons of much fame who had abundant offspring, Daśajyoti, Śatajyoti and the self-possessed Sahasrajyoti. The great-spirited Daśajyoti had ten thousand sons. Śatajyoti ten times that number, and Sahasrajyoti again ten times that. From them arose the lineage of the Kurus, those of the Yadus and of Bharata, the lines of Yayāti and Ikṣvāku and of the royal seers in general—many dynasties arose and creations of creatures in their abundant varieties.[13]

We can see that Ugraśravas had a fundamentally different idea about how the Kurus originated from that of Vaiśaṃpāyana. Yet, the point both of them agreed upon was the Sūryavaṃśa origin of the Kurus. Of course, when Ugraśravas was narrating, Sūryavaṃśa seems established as the only possible genealogical pattern, and the Sun the fountainhead of all dynasties. That was not the case with Vaiśaṃpāyana. Yet, his genealogies also trace the origin of the Kurus from Vivasvat.

Then why did the *Mahābhārata* characters unanimously regard themselves as belonging to the Somavaṃśa? Neither the verse nor the prose *vaṃśa* answers the question. However, the *Harivaṃśa* provides a crucial link. It says that Iḍā, Manu's daughter and Ikṣvāku's sister, was born of a ceremony for Mitra and Varuṇa. The two deities made her their daughter and Manu's son. Thus she could be both female and male (named Sudyumna). As Iḍā, she bore Purūravas from Budha, the son of the moon god. As Sudyumna, she gave birth to three sons—Utkala, Gaya, and Vinatāśva.[14]

If we leave the male Sudyumna alone, Manu's daughter Ilā/Iḍā provides the crucial link between the Sūryavaṃśa and the Candravaṃśa. Since she was Manu's daughter, her descendents could be counted in Manu's solar line through her. However, Budha, the son of the moon god, was the biological father of Ilā's son, Purūravas. Hence, Purūravas was Budha's son, and Saṃjaya's Candravaṃśa genealogy of Atri—› Soma—› Budha—› Purūravas—› Āyus—› Nahuṣa—› Yayāti in *Mahabhārata* VII.119 is also justifiable. Commenting on this, Simon Brodbeck rightly suggests that 'the *Mahābhārata* is thus the story of a lunar line becoming solar'.[15]

The *Mahābhārata* therefore begins with a genealogical complication. The text frames out a context where the Kuru dynastic norms could follow both Sūryavaṃśa and Candravaṃśa norms. Thus, primogeniture, the Sūryavaṃśa norm, could be claimed as the model. But the junior branches could also assert their rights on the basis of the Candravaṃśa norms. The implications of such a dual origin myth shall be discussed later. However, before that we must ponder over why between the narrations of the two *sūtas*, Saṃjaya and Ugraśravas, not only the Candravaṃśa origin of the Kurus had to be substituted by Sūryavaṃśa origin but the Sūryavaṃśa came to be regarded as the only possible origin of beings.

Let us go back to Ilā for the answer. Like Yayāti and his sons, Ilā and Purūravas are characters known to the Vedic corpus. In fact, the *Ṛg Veda* knows Purūravas as the son of Ilā.[16] However, what is more important for us is the ŚB account of the Great Deluge, originally a Mesopotamian myth that entered the mythological corpus of several cultures and religions. The story is there in the *Mahābhārata* as well. In the *Mahābhārata*, it is said that when Manu, son of Vivasvat, was practising austerities at

Badarī, a fish in the river Vīriṇī asked for his protection. He placed it in a jar. When it overgrew the jar he placed it successively in a pond, in the Gaṅgā, and at last in the ocean. The fish then predicted the Great Flood and told Manu to build an ark and fill it with the seeds of all the creatures. Following the instructions, Manu survived the flood on his ship. The fish reappeared, and Manu tied the ship to its horn. Pulling the ship for many years, the fish brought it to the highest peak of the Himālaya where Manu moored it. The fish revealed itself as Brahmā and asked Manu to repopulate the Earth with creatures, which Manu did.[17]

The *Mahābhārata* does not say how Manu repopulated the Earth. The ŚB, telling the same story, elaborates on this. It narrates that Manu, desirous of offspring, engaged in worship and austerities. He performed a *pāka* sacrifice, offering clarified butter, sour milk, whey, and curds in the water, which produced a daughter named Iḍā. The daughter was seduced by Mitra and Varuṇa, but she refused them and clung to Manu. Through her Manu generated the humankind.[18]

Therefore, originally the story of Iḍā was a story of father-daughter incest. Naturally, there is no mention of any husband for Ilā in the genealogies, and her son is included in Manu's line. That the myth was not forgotten soon is indicated by the *Harivaṃśa* story cited earlier. There also we see Iḍā (significantly it is the ŚB name, and not the Ilā of the *Mahābhārata*, that is used) being born out of a sacrifice and being offered to Mitra and Varuṇa. However, the incest part is modified. Mitra and Varuṇa adopt Iḍā as a daughter, and Budha becomes the genitor of her son. Significantly, Iḍā is still not married to Budha here. Moreover, turning into a male, she provides offspring for Manu's line too. Hence, the idea that Iḍā's offspring were produced in the reproductive enterprise of her father Manu, and not of any husband, is very much there.

Then why did Budha enter the modified myth? How did the idea of a Candravaṃśa come into being? The answer probably lies in the taboo about incest in the Brahmanical ideology. Origin myths, even in the Buddhist tradition, contain incest. The Iḍā story also looks similar. However, as the society started to become sedentary from the Later Vedic Age, incest was gradually becoming a taboo. If we look at Book X of the *Ṛg Veda*, the latest interpolation in the text, belonging more to the Later Vedic world than to the Ṛgvedic milieu, there is the interesting hymn which is a conversation between Yama, the first mortal in Vedic tradition, and his twin sister Yamī.[19] Yamī approaches Yama sexually, claiming incest as natural, but Yama successfully resists her. Thus, the hymn speaks of an earlier idea of 'natural' incest now being negated as a taboo. Probably, with this taboo, Yama represents a new human order, being the first one in it.

If we look closely at the genealogies discussed earlier, it is not only Manu who was supposed to have obtained descendants through his daughter but also Dakṣa Prajāpati who obtained Vivasvat through her daughter Aditi/Dākṣāyaṇī. This seems to be another incest myth belonging to an earlier world that was negated in Later Vedic literature. Thus, the *Ṛg Veda* contains a vague reference to a divine father-daughter incest through which a deity satisfied his lust.[20] But Prajāpati's incest with his own daughter (probably the sky goddess Aditi) is not just described but also punished by Rudra's arrow in both the AB and the ŚB.[21] The *Mahābhārata*, as shown earlier, brought in Kaśyapa as the husband of Dākṣāyaṇī in the verse *vaṃśa*. Yet, the sons born—most notably Vivasvat—are enlisted within Dakṣa Prajāpati's line, not Kaśyapa's. Budha plays a role similar to Kaśyapa in the modified Ilā legend.

However, in a patrilineal society where the offspring would usually be enlisted within the father's lineage, how did Budha's and Kaśyapa's sons perpetuate the lineage of their mother's father? The replacement of the incest element thus needed another social explanation. This explanation has been pointed out brilliantly by Brodbeck in the notion of a *putrikā* daughter.[22]

We shall return to the importance of the *putrikā* daughter soon. But before that, we must consider the social context which necessitated this idea. We can see that the taboo about incest can be contextualized in the transition from Ṛgvedic to Later Vedic society. The establishment of sedentary agricultural life contains, among various dimensions, a fundamental importance of the transmission of immobile private property, namely land. Inheritance thus acquires a much more nuanced significance than in earlier socio-economic organizations. With the coming of hereditary kingship, inheritance becomes even more crucial for the ruling groups which would be the *kṣatriyas* in the *varṇa*-divided Later Vedic society. When the state society would be established, smooth transmission of office and property from one generation to another would be pivotal.

Thus, primogeniture would be the norm. In Brahmanical tradition, primogeniture was also given a ritual sanction. Thus, Brodbeck notes the ritual of *śrāddha* which was to be performed by the primogenitive heir for assuring his ancestor's stay at heaven.[23] Thapar therefore rightly presumes that in a developed state system the collaterals would be omitted from genealogies and primogeniture emphasized.[24] Thus, we may assume the Sūryavaṃśa as a marker of the well-established state society. The *Rāmāyaṇa*, the archetypal Sūryavaṃśa text, represents the triumph of the state society.[25]

However, the case of the *Mahābhārata* is different. Of course, when the final phase of its transmission was on, when Ugraśravas was narrating the *Mahābhārata* in the Naimiṣa forest, the transition to the state society (and to the Sūryavaṃśa) was complete. But most of the *Mahābhārata* narrative seems to be a story of the period of that transition. Therefore, we may have a look at the nature of the transition that sedentary agricultural life and coming of the state generated.

According to Claude Meillasoux, if an economic cycle extends over a long period and if the survival of the oldest is linked to their control over the younger ones, then the women and the young ones will be at stake. Since pubescent women are not expendable, women of the group have to be protected against capture by rival groups and the captured women must be guarded. Women thus become objects of war. Peace ensues if there is an orderly circulation of pubescent women arranged through chieftains capable of negotiating betrothal and marriage, that is, management of reproduction at a political level. Women are no longer objects of war, but subjects, pledges in alliances or allegiance, kept available through incest prohibition, to build up political networks.[26] Thus what Meillasoux indicates is how men use their socially dominant position (patriarchy) to manage social reproduction (which leads to patriline) and how incest prohibition is the vital first step for it. Of course the resultant patrilineal society, like the clan societies of Later Vedic India, would place immense importance on the idea of kinship.

Starting from Claude Levi-Strauss's idea of kinship being the imposition of culture upon the facts of biological procreation and essence of kinship system being the exchange of women by men (sex oppression), Gayle Rubin points out that kinship system is not just exchanging women but exchanging social access, genealogical statuses, lineage names and ancestors, rights, and people—men, women, and children—in concrete systems of social relationships.[27]

This is a situation where marriage tends to become defined by procreation, since inheritance of title, position, and wealth becomes a paramount concern with the non-producing elite holding political power over the producing classes. This observation is made by Christine Ward Gailey in studying the transition of the Tongan society from kinship to kingship[28] but—as the subsequent discussion would show—can be equally true of the non-producing elite, the *brāhmaṇa* and the *kṣatriya*, of Later Vedic India.

Similarly, commenting upon the transition to agriculture in Mesopotamia, Gerda Lerner shows how the transition led to women's reproductive capacity becoming reified as a resource of a particular kin group. Women's sexual labour was appropriated, sexual autonomy was denied, and they became the first form of property.[29]

Though the socio-economic context of Bronze Age Mesopotamia and Vedic India were considerably different, there are some similarities in the pattern of gender and reproductive relationships discernible from the sources. Uma Chakravarti, after a thorough discussion of the aforementioned positions, comments that two parallel processes can be observed from the Later Vedic texts: ritualization of cohabitation and reproduction with marriage, and regulation of desire and sexual practices for women, since cohabitation is linked to reproduction and birth of children, mainly sons, which ensure patrilineal continuity.[30]

The Later Vedic texts, no doubt, show an anxiety over the continuation and perpetuation of the patriline, possibly for both economic (smooth and uncontested transmission of property) and religious (unbroken performance of the *śrāddha* ritual) reasons. Since the eldest male child continues the patriline in a primogenitive order, the anxiety was centred around the women's wombs as vehicles for male children. The *puṃsavana* ritual, for turning the female foetus into male, itself is an expression of this anxiety, as are the other rituals like *garbhādhāna*, *sīmantonnayana*, and *garbharakṣaṇa*, all designed to protect the embryo from any potential harm. The injunction against *bhrūṇahatyā* (foeticide) is also an expression of the reification of the female womb.[31] The reified womb, of course, had to be protected from all forms of external intrusion so that the woman's reproductive capacity could be the exclusive property of the husband in particular and the husband's clan by extension. This control was so crucial that the wife is required to publicly declare her extramarital affairs (or their absence) during the *cāturmāsya* rite.[32] The *Atharva Veda* contains spells to render the lover of the wife impotent, indicating that the woman having a lover was not as much a threat as the woman's womb being occupied by an outsider's seeds.[33] Indicating the interconnection between agrarian economy and these new reproductive norms, the woman—or her reified womb—was considered a cultivable field (*kṣetra*) of the husband where only his seeds (or seeds from his clan) were supposed to be planted.

If we read the genealogical stories of the *Mahābhārata* with this history in mind, their Later Vedic context becomes clear. The *Mahābhārata* is very much a story of this anxiety about patriline, various reproductive crises faced by the Kurus, various strategies adopted by the Kurus to counter them, and their eventual repercussions. Indeed, in a society where patrilineal succession is so pivotal, what happens to a person or a clan (especially if it is royal) without a successor?

When Pāṇḍu, cursed to sexual inactivity, suffered from this anxiety and eventually requested his wife Kuntī to beget children for him using someone else's seeds, a long debate followed, indicating the reproductive norms of the time. In fact, Pāṇḍu presented an account of how the sexual regulations were supposed to have originated. Women were earlier free to roam and indulge in their desires (*kāmacārav ihāriṇyaḥ*) and were self-willed (*svatantrā*). This was not *adharma* at that time because it was also how animal society functioned. This eternal law (*dharmaḥ sanātanaḥ*) was favourable to women (*strīṇām anugrahakaraḥ*). Yet, once, the sage Śvetaketu, son of Uddālaka, seeing his mother being taken by the hand by a *brāhmaṇa* in front of his father, became angry and laid down restrictions on women's sexual freedom.[34] The rules were:

vyuñcarantyāḥ patiṃ nāryā adya prabhṛti pātakam/
bhrūṇahatyākṛtaṃ pāpaṃ bhaviṣyaty asukhāvaham//
bhāryāṃ tathā vyuñcarataḥ kaumārīṃ brahmacāriṇīm/
pativratām etad eva bhavitā pātakaṃ bhuvi//
patyā niyuktā yā caiva patny apatyārtham eva ca/
na kariṣyati tasyāś ca bhaviṣyaty etad eva hi.

(A woman's faithlessness to her husband shall be a sin equal to aborticide, an evil that shall bring on misery. Seducing a chaste and constant wife who is avowed to her husband shall also be a sin on earth. And a wife who is enjoined by her husband to conceive a child and refuses shall incur the same evil.)[35]

The story not only points out that the restriction on women's sexuality is neither the natural law nor the eternal *dharma* but the product of a historical context, but also shows that context as Later Vedic, since Uddālaka Āruṇi and his son Śvetaketu are well-known Later Vedic figures who play a prominent role in both the CU and the BU. Chakravarti notes how the three laws attributed to Śvetaketu defined the scope of patrilineal monogamy: husband's exclusive ownership over the wife's sexuality, prohibition on other men from violating this monopoly, and the husband's complete ownership over the progeny delivered by her.[36] More interestingly, the sin incurred by the violation of these norms was supposed to be that of aborticide (*bhrūṇahatyā*), indicating that the prime concern was not the wife's emotional fidelity but the control over her reified womb. Therefore, Pāṇḍu—commenting on the story—declared:

ṛtāvṛtau rājaputri striyā bhartā yatavrate/
nātivartavya ity evaṃ dharmaṃ dharmavido viduḥ//
śeṣesv anyeṣu kāleṣu svātantryaṃ strī kilārhati/
dharmam etaṃ janāḥ santaḥ purāṇaṃ paricakṣate//

(Princess so strict in your vows, those who know the Law know this for the Law that at every season the woman may not avoid her husband. At all other times, however, the woman may exercise her own choice. This the strict people expound as the ancient Law.)[37]

Hence, Pāṇḍu also knew that the husband's ownership was over the reproductive capacity of the wife and not over her person. Therefore, the woman was free to exercise her own choice when not at her season, but when her reified womb would be fertile she should be completely under the husband's control. By asking Kuntī to beget children from others, Pāṇḍu was not invoking the eternal *dharma* of women's sexual freedom. He was not even asking her to follow the ancient *dharma* of women's sexual freedom when not fertile. He was outlining the contour of Śvetaketu's injunctions to invoke its third clause which asked the wife to unquestioningly provide her reproductive capacity for begetting children when instructed by the husband. It was because Pāṇḍu's anxiety was the anxiety of a society post Śvetaketu's injunctions, where a male progeny was vital for both succeeding to the throne and acquiring the heaven.[38] Therefore, Pāṇḍu also enlisted the six categories of suitable heirs according to the prevalent custom:

svayaṃjātaḥ praṇītaś ca parikrītaś ca yaḥ sutaḥ/
paunarbhavaś ca kānīnaḥ svairiṇyāṃ yaś ca jāyate//

(The son fathered by oneself, the son presented, the son purchased, the son born by one's widow, the son born by one's wife before her marriage, and the son born by a loose woman.)[39]

Pāṇḍu also pointed out that the son gifted, bartered, born by artifice, come by himself, come with marriage, of unknown seed, or fathered on a lowly womb would not be considered as legitimate heir. A close observation would reveal that the first four of the acceptable categories represent the husband's complete control over the wife's womb as his *kṣetra*, while the fifth and sixth would indicate his claim over the *kṣetra*. The six unacceptable categories are situations in which either the *kṣetra* or the seed or both were out of control. That is why Pāṇḍu could not simply adopt or barter a son but sought a son from his wife, thereby exercising his control over her womb. In fact, had Kuntī not decided to feign the role of a chastity-obsessed devoted wife, claiming that she would not even think of going to any other man but him and telling the awe-inspiring story of Bhadrā Kakṣīvatī who, through her unparalleled devotion to her husband Vyuṣitāśva, made him father her children even after his death,[40] she could have pacified the anxiety of Pāṇḍu at once by telling him that he already had a son of the *kānīna* variety (the son born of one's wife before marriage), fathered by Sūrya. However, probably because she was unaware of the whereabouts of this son whom she had discarded at birth (and who would later enter the narrative as Karṇa), she had to engage in the lengthy discussion about other possible alternatives.

Speaking of the alternatives, the second and third varieties are most noteworthy. If an adopted or bartered son was not acceptable, then what could be the possible meanings of a *praṇīta* (presented) and a *parikrīta* (purchased/hired for) son? Here we must go back to Brodbeck's formulation that a *praṇīta* son was one presented not after birth but before birth, through a *putrikā* daughter.[41] A *putrikā* was a daughter (usually brotherless) who would marry on condition that her offspring would perpetuate her father's lineage. Brodbeck shows that the *Mahābhārata* has numerous such examples and explains how a woman's womb could be an object of contestation between her father's and husband's families. The model in a patriarchal system would definitely be the *pativratā*, one who would relentlessly serve the husband's family, but the *putrikā* would always be a threatening alternative possibility, particularly if the woman was brotherless.[42] Brotherless maidens were considered dishonest even from the Ṛgvedic time.[43] Now, the *putrikā* possibility became crucial in providing offspring to sonless fathers. In case of a *putrikā*, the offspring to be born would be promised to the lineage of the woman's father, making him a potential *praṇīta* son. Since this concept allowed a daughter to perpetuate the father's line without incest, it could facilitate the third stage in the refashioning of the Ilā legend. The original incest story of Manu and Iḍā was initially modified by providing Iḍā a male partner in Budha, which placed the Kurus in the Candravaṃśa. Now, with the state society coming into being, and primogeniture becoming the favoured and established norm, it was again modified by making Ilā a *putrikā* daughter of Manu and eliminating Budha from the *vaṃśa*. Rather, it is said that Ilā became both the mother and father of Purūravas: '*sā vai tasyābhavan mātā pitā ceti hi naḥ śrutam*'.[44]

Similarly, when Arjuna wanted to marry Citrāṅgadā, a princess of Maṇalūra (or Maṇipura), a small matrilineal kingdom somewhere in Kaliṅga, Citravāhana—her father—stated the norms of a *putrikā* marriage:

putro mām eyam iti me bhāvanā puruṣottama/
putrikā hetuvidhinā saṃkṣita bharatarṣabha//
etac chulkaṃ bhavatvasyāḥ kulakṛj jāyatām iha/
etena samayenemāṃ pratigṛhṇīṣva pāṇḍava//

(My fancy is that she is my son, and I have styled her my *putrikā* according to the provisions, bull of the Bharatas. So let her bring forth a son, who shall be the dynast: this son I demand as my price for her. By this covenant you must take her, Pāṇḍava.)[45]

Arjuna's preceding marriage with the Nāga Ulūpī, a widow who begged him for sex,[46] is not precisely stated as a *putrikā* marriage. However, Brodbeck rightly presumes it as one, on the basis of the references that Irāvat, the son of Arjuna and Ulūpī, was forsaken by a wicked *pitṛvya* and grew up in his mother's realm, and he was assisted by his maternal Nāga relatives (*mātṛkā*) in his cameo in the Bhārata War.[47] It is not clear whether the 'wicked paternal uncle' not willing to take responsibility of the *putrikā*'s daughter without any genealogical value was Arjuna's brother, Yudhiṣṭhira, as Brodbeck guesses.[48] Since Yudhiṣṭhira has not been addressed as 'wicked' anywhere else in the *Mahābhārata*, it seems unlikely. Rather, it was probably a brother of Ulūpī's dead husband who was unhappy about the loss of his clan's control over Ulūpī's womb, since he might have expected Ulūpī's son to belong to his lineage as a son of *paunarbhava* (son born to one's widow) category or might have regretted the lost opportunity to impregnate her. We shall see later that it was not unnatural for a brother-in-law to consider it within his right to get the first opportunity to impregnate the childless widow of his brother. Nevertheless, the *putrikā* nature of both Ulūpī and Citrāṅgadā is attested by the fact that neither Irāvat nor Babhruvāhana (son of Arjuna and Citrāṅgadā) are counted in the lists of the eleven sons of the five Pāṇḍavas.[49]

The *putrikā* custom, therefore, was well prevalent, and the woman's womb was often the object of contestation between the lineages of her father and her husband. However, since the contest was over the womb and not the person of the woman, the same woman could act as *putrikā* and *pativratā* at different situations, providing one or more sons to each of the lineages. Therefore, we see that Yayāti, probably after disowning his first four sons and before Pūru obtained any offspring, wanted to have his daughter's sons,[50] and gave away his daughter Mādhavī to a poor *brāhmaṇa* named Gālava who had rented her out to three kings and a sage for one year each. Mādhavī begot four sons—Vasumanas, Pratardana, Śibi, and Aṣṭaka—in this way, and they eventually stopped

Yayāti's fall from heaven.[51] As it is said that Mādhavī's sons saved four royal *vaṃśas*,[52] it would not be wrong to assume that the three royal sons of Mādhavī served their father's lineages, whereas Aṣṭaka—begotten on her by the sage Viśvāmitra—probably offered *śrāddha* to Yayāti's lineage as a *putrikā*'s son.

The contest, therefore, was between two lineages and not merely between the husband and the father. The woman's womb, in a clan society, belonged to the clan, though directly it belonged to the husband. Therefore, we see that when the pregnant Mamatā, the devoted wife of the seer Utathya, was approached by his younger brother Bṛhaspati, the only argument she could present (and so did the child in the womb!) was that Bṛhaspati's seed would be wasted as the womb was already occupied.[53] Thus, it was not the woman's fidelity or choice but the prudent use of the seed in the context of the womb which mattered most. Bṛhaspati, being the younger brother of Utathya, belonging to the same clan and therefore carrying the same seed, could not be resisted with any other logic. The Vedic context of this *Mahābhārata* story is unmistakable as the same story has been narrated in the *Bṛhaddevatā*.[54]

For the same reason, the fraternal polyandry of the Pāṇḍavas, even though startling, was accepted. Being married to five brothers, Draupadī's womb remained the *kṣetra* for the seeds of a single clan. Interestingly, Yudhiṣṭhira justified the act by the precedence of a woman named Jaṭilā who lay with the seven seers.[55] It is not specified which set of seven seers is being spoken of, but I presume it to be the later set of the seven mind-born sons of Brahmā: Vasiṣṭha, Marīci, Atri, Aṅgirā, Pulastya, Pulaha, and Kratu. All being sons of Brahmā, they would have the same lineage and the same seed, making the polyandry of Jaṭilā acceptable.

Sarva Daman Singh has noted the preponderance of polyandry as an institution well known to early Indian texts, despite the later attempts to sanitize such references.[56] Polyandry was an institution quite prevalent among various Indo-European speaking communities.[57] The *Ṛg Veda* contain several references about the prevalence of polyandry, known alike to deities and humans. Thus, Sūryā has been often described as the common wife of the Aśvin twins, while Rodasī was the common wife of the Maruts. The Viśvadevas seem to have followed suit.[58] Some Ṛgvedic prayers clearly refer to a polyandrous situation.[59] The continuity of the tradition is unmistakable in the early part of the Later Vedic period. The AV, in particular, contains numerous references to the custom.[60] The reification of the female womb for begetting progeny for the family, in an agricultural society, as the primary purpose of polyandry, is vividly evident in the Atharvavedic declaration:

> (As) a soulful cultivated field hath this woman come; in her here, O men, scatter ye seed; she shall give birth to progeny for you from her belly, bearing the exuded sperm of the male.[61]

The TS of the *Yajur Veda* also alludes to polyandry.[62] However, the same text also prohibits polyandry, while it allows a man to have two wives.[63] Polyandry is categorically prohibited by the AB.[64] Therefore, it was a known institution in the Vedic period, though preference for monogamy was making it gradually unpopular during the Later Vedic period. This may explain why the polyandry of Draupadī did not trouble the characters much in the *Mahābhārata*, even though it had to be accepted after some deliberation. Smita Sahgal points out that Draupadī, in the *Mahābhārata*, was neither appalled not outraged by the prospect of polyandry as she might have been familiar with the institution of fraternal polyandry. She hailed from the resource crunched region of Pāñcāla where fraternal polyandry might have been common as a way of securing property against division.[65] Even though polyandry was not the usual norm in the society depicted in the narrative sections of the *Mahābhārata*, it was not completely unknown in certain regions. Karṇa mocked at Śalya by referring to the promiscuous sexual practices, including polyandry, prevalent among the women of the latter's native land, Madra, in the northwestern parts of the Indian subcontinent.[66] Sarva Daman Singh rightly notes that the same northwestern regions supplied two queens, Mādrī and Gāndhārī, to the Kuru kingdom.[67] Draupadī's polyandry, therefore, seemed unusual but not blasphemous.

This reification of the womb into a property of the husband's family/clan brings us to the third variety of the acceptable son, the *parikrīta*, possibly the most crucial to the *Mahābhārata* narrative. Van Buitenen has translated *parikrīta* as 'purchased'. However, the translation is problematic. 'Purchased' would have been an apt translation for the *krīta* variety of son, mentioned in the second list of unacceptable heirs, which van Buitenen translates as 'bartered'. However, the second list makes it clear that the adopted and purchased/bartered sons, or the sons who had already been born, were not acceptable as heirs. Then, what does the *parikrīta* son signify? Brodbeck provides a better translation 'hired for', suggesting that it is a son hired for before the birth. In other words, it is the situation when a childless man hires for a genitor to provide him with offspring on his wife.[68] This custom of levirate was known as *niyoga*, and the son born of *niyoga* belonged not to the genitor but to the man who (or whose clan) commissioned it, since the son would be born in the womb (*kṣetra*) of the husband. Hence, the son was also known as *kṣetraja putra*.

There can be no doubt that Brodbeck's interpretation of the *parikrīta* son as a son born of *niyoga* is correct. After all, this is the kind of son Pāṇḍu wanted Kuntī to beget, and therefore this had to be one of the six acceptable varieties he had spoken of. This very custom of *niyoga*, however, would again bring us back to the Later Vedic context of the narrative. A.S. Altekar has mentioned how many scholars connect the genesis of the practice to the recognition of a woman as a species of property which is passed into the husband's family on her marriage. She was married not only to a person but also into his family. So, if the husband died, his brother or any other near relative would either marry his wife or raise children on her. In fact, it was the sacred duty of the brother to see that a son was raised on his sister-in-law to perpetuate his brother's memory and ensure him a seat in heaven. This was also a way of preventing the widow from marrying a stranger and being lost to the family.[69] Sahgal rightly locates the initial institutionalization of this practice amongst the pastoralists and early farmers. It was institutionalized to prevent the loss of the wife's reproductive and productive assets to the family. The link of the system with the coming of agriculture is testified as the entire terminology for those involved in the practice comes from the world of agriculture, wife as field, husband as owner of the field, the son as product of the field, and the inseminator as the seed giver.[70]

Niyoga was a known tradition in the tribal society of the Early Vedic Age. The custom has been mentioned in the family books of the *Ṛg Veda*.[71] However, references are more frequent in the later books. M.B. Emmeneau and B.A. van Nooten have analysed two verses from Book X of the *Ṛg Veda* in this context.[72] Interestingly, the *Ṛg Veda* often does not mention the name of the inseminator or describe some deity as the inseminator. Thus, it is said that Indra and Varuṇa helped Purukutsa's wife beget Trasadasyu, when Purukutsa was held captive.[73] In some other instances, the Aśvin twins helped Vimadā and Vadhrimatī in getting sons.[74] Possibly, in the Vedic society, a childless widow would have been inseminated by some other male member of the tribe, most preferably the husband's brother. However, Sahgal rightly thinks that allusions to gods were often sought to disguise certain relationships which the custodians of the social set-up may not have wanted to reveal or to become public knowledge. The power of women to pray and summon deities, without much social negotiation, may also indicate their wilful participation as partners.[75] However, P.V. Kane points out that the custom became contentious by the end of the Later Vedic Age. The *Gautama Dharma Sūtra* and the *Vasiṣṭha Dharma Sūtra* approved it only as a compassionate and pragmatic allowance after obtaining permission from the elders, whereas the *Āpastamba Dharma Sūtra* condemned it as immoral.[76] Most of the *Dharmaśāstras* of the post-Maurya and Gupta periods, apart from the *Yājñavalkya Smṛti*, are against the practice. Manu discusses it, but condemns it as the way of animals. Nārada is ready to allow it with much restriction. Bṛhaspati forbids it, declares that even a sonless chaste wife goes to the heaven, and associates the practice with the 'other' women, especially the Khasas.[77]

The *niyoga*, thus, was a custom of the Vedic period, becoming more popular from the later part of the Ṛgvedic period, and gradually fell into disuse after the onset of the Common Era. The *Mahābhārata* knows *niyoga* as an old custom.[78] Several precedents of *niyoga* were known to the *Mahābhārata* characters, which were alluded to in deliberations about *niyoga*. Bhīṣma told how the *kṣatriya* women gave birth to *kṣetraja putras*, being inseminated by *brāhmaṇas*, after Jāmadagnya Rāma had killed off all *kṣatriyas* in rage.[79] Similarly, Balin had invited the blind sage Dīrghatamas to impregnate his wife Sudeṣṇā.[80] Pāṇḍu also narrated to Kuntī how Śāradaṇḍāyinī, a *kṣatriya* woman instructed by her elders to bear a child, produced three sons by a *brāhmaṇa* she had picked up from a crossroads where she had stood at night in search of a suitable man.[81] He also referred to the story of Madayantī, the wife of Kalmāṣapāda Saudāsa, who had obtained a son from the sage Vasiṣṭha after being enjoined by her husband to conceive a child.[82] The Pāṇḍavas, during their forest exile, also heard the story of how the *brāhmaṇa* Damana granted a daughter and three sons to the king Bhīma and his wife, being pleased by their hospitality, probably an allusion to a *niyoga*.[83]

However, unlike polyandry, *niyoga* in the *Mahābhārata* is not just an old custom known through ancient lores and practised as an exception. Rather, it was still a well-prevalent practice, at least among the *kṣatriyas*, in case of a genealogical crisis. In fact, *niyoga* gave birth to some of the most important characters of the *Mahābhārata* narrative. Pāṇḍu got his five famous sons from five deities after Kuntī and Mādrī performed *niyoga*, following his instructions.[84] The legitimacy of the birth of the Pāṇḍavas was certified by the *brāhmaṇas*.[85] However, not only the practice of *niyoga* but also its nature indicates a Vedic context for the birth of the Pāṇḍavas, since—following the Vedic model—the inseminators have been identified as deities. Kuntī and Mādrī, like the Vedic women, therefore had some role in choosing their partners. We may safely follow Sahgal in accepting that the gleaming of divinities over human entities was probably to camouflage the actual *niyoga* and to give the Pāṇḍavas a semi-divine status.[86] We have seen earlier that this was a common strategy used in Vedic literature to hide the identity of the inseminators, possibly because the choice by the women might at times be deemed incestuous.

We must remember that even the birth of Pāṇḍu himself was the result of a *niyoga* in a genealogical crisis. After the Kuru king Vicitravīrya died young and childless, the Kuru lineage was faced with extinction. Vicitravīrya's elder half-brother, Bhīṣma, had already taken the vows of not accepting the throne and lifelong celibacy (Bhīṣma's vow and its ramifications shall be discussed in detail later). Satyavatī, Vicitravīrya's mother, requested Bhīṣma to perform *niyoga* on the widows of the deceased king. Bhīṣma refused to break his vow of celibacy but suggested hiring a *brāhmaṇa* as an alternative. Satyavatī then revealed the secret of having a *kānīna* (premarital) son, Vyāsa, from the sage Parāśara. Vyāsa was invited to perform the *niyoga*, and he gave birth to Dhṛtarāṣṭra, Pāṇḍu, and Vidura on the two widows of Vicitravīrya (Ambikā and Ambālikā) and a *dāsī* who had once substituted for Ambikā.[87] Though the practice of invoking *brāhmaṇas* as inseminators does not find much support in Vedic literature, and seems to be a practice developed later, the choice of Vyāsa seems to have more to do with his position as a distant brother-in-law than with his disputable *brāhmaṇa*-hood. After all, when

Satyavatī convinced Ambikā to perform the *niyoga*, she had stated that the inseminator would be a brother-in-law.[88]

Not only the Pāṇḍavas and their father and uncles but also their common wife, Draupadī, probably was born of a *niyoga*. Though the birth of Draupadī and her brother Dhṛṣṭadyumna has been described as resulting from a sacrifice performed by the Pāñcāla king Drupada, Brodbeck rightly notes that the ceremony described is curiously similar to *niyoga*.[89] The narrative says that the righteous *brāhmaṇa* Upayāja had refused to perform the ceremony and referred Drupada to his greedy and impure brother Yāja. Possibly the act was impure because a *niyoga* would be legitimate only in the absence of any biological offspring. Drupada already had children but was motivated to have an outstanding son who would be able to kill Droṇa, the famous martial teacher who had humiliated Drupada.[90] At the end of the offering, Yāja summoned Pṛṣatī, the wife of Drupada, saying: '*praihi māṃ rājñi pṛṣati mithunaṃ tvām upasthitam*' (Stride forward to me, Queen Pṛṣatī! The time for cohabitation has come).[91] Yet, the birth of the twins was declared as a supernatural birth from fire, and not the result of a *niyoga*, probably because the *niyoga*—while Drupada had biological offspring—would not be ritually acceptable. Fire, in Later Vedic literature, is often used as a simile for women's reproductive system. The BU says:

> Prajāpati then thought to himself: 'Now, why don't I prepare a base for that semen?' So he created woman and after creating her, had intercourse with her. A man, therefore, should have intercourse with a woman. Prajāpati stretched out from himself the elongated stone for pressing Soma and impregnated her with it.
>
> Her vulva is the sacrificial ground; her pubic hair is the sacred grass; her labia majora are the Soma-press; and her labia minora are the fire blazing at the centre.[92]

The CU almost echoes it:

> A fire—that's what a woman is, Gautama. Her firewood is the vulva; when she is asked to come close, that is her smoke; her flame is the vagina; when one penetrates her, that is her embers; and her sparks are the

> climax. In that very fire gods offer semen, and from that offering springs the foetus.[93]

Significantly, even though Dhṛṣṭadyumna and Draupadī were proclaimed as born from the sacrificial fire, Pṛṣatī requested Yāja that the children should know her as their mother![94]

Thus, these birth stories point to the social context where *niyoga* was known as an ancient custom and was practised among the *kṣatriya* royal clans where genealogical succession was vital. However, it was supposed to be practised only in the absence of a biological offspring. The brother-in-law still retained the first right to inseminate the widow. Hence, Bhīṣma and Vyāsa were the first and second choices to inseminate the widows of Vicitravīrya. This explains why Mamatā had to use her pregnancy as an argument in her attempt to resist her brother-in-law, Bṛhaspati, and why Ulūpī's brother-in-law was unhappy about her being impregnated by Arjuna. However, the *varṇa* system was established in the Later Vedic society and the *brāhmaṇas*, as the supreme *varṇa* and the providers of ritual legitimacy, also claimed a right to inseminate the *kṣatriya* widows.

Altogether, however, the ritual also presents the complete subjugation of the woman's womb to her husband's clan. The Later Vedic Age had witnessed deterioration in the sexual freedom and social respect of women in many ways. *Niyoga* also was not a matter of the woman's sexual choice. It was commissioned either by the husband or by the husband's kinsmen, and the woman had to only provide her womb as the vehicle for carrying out the order. Hence, Kuntī, despite her reluctance to perform it, ultimately had to give in to Pāṇḍu's demand, as Pāṇḍu declared:

> Those who know the Law also know, princess, that whatever a husband tells his wife, by Law or against Law (*dharmyaṃ vādharmyam eva vā*), she must do it, especially if one, himself deprived of the power of progeny, is hungry for sons, as I am, flawless Kuntī, longing to set eyes on a son.[95]

Kuntī, like some of the women mentioned in Vedic literature, was at least fortunate to have a say in the choice of the men hired. Others faced worse situations. Ambikā, for instance, was befooled by Satyavatī, who had only told her that a brother-in-law was to copulate with her.[96] Knowing Bhīṣma as her only brother-in-law, she was definitely expecting him, and was eventually traumatized by the terrible look and odour of Vyāsa. As a result, she closed her eyes.[97] When her next turn for copulation with Vyāsa came, she avoided it by sending a *dāsī* as a substitute.[98] The less resistant Ambālikā was also frightened by Vyāsa's appearance.[99] Bhīṣma also knew the story of how Sudeṣṇā, enjoined by her husband Balin to copulate with the repulsive, old, and blind *brāhmaṇa* Dīrghatamas, had sent her maid to him. He produced eleven sons on the maid before Sudeṣṇā was finally caught and forced to yield and beget a son from the sage.[100] It seems that even Pṛṣatī was reluctant to copulate with Yāja.[101] But the women, clearly, had no control over their reproductive devices.

In fact, the degenerate position of women implied that the womb was now considered only a vehicle for childbirth, the real reproductive potential being placed in the semen. A seed after all can produce plants at any *kṣetra*. Hence, both the Vedic literature and the *Mahābhārata* also contain stories of parthenogenesis where women are considered totally dispensable even in the domain of mothering. Wendy Doniger O'Flaherty comments on how the myths, where men are capable of unilateral procreation, are a reversal of the medical fact that women can procreate unilaterally, but not men.[102] Already in the *Ṛg Veda* we see the seeds of the myths of parthenogenesis. Indra had an intention to avoid the birth canal, but failed.[103] However, the sages Vasiṣṭha and Agastya are credited with being born from Mitra and Varuṇa's thoughts of Urvaśī.[104] In the *Mahābhārata*, just as *niyoga* was a prevalent custom among the *kṣatriyas*, parthenogenesis seems to have been a marker of the power of the *brāhmaṇas*. Both the teachers of the Kuru princes had such birth. Kṛpa and his sister Kṛpī were born when the sage Śāradvata Gautama ejaculated in a reed forest after watching the *apsarā* Jālapadī.[105] Droṇa was born in a pot where the sage Bharadvāja ejaculated after being turned on by the sight of the *apsarā* Ghṛtācī.[106] As Mary Carroll Smith notes, men can unilaterally procreate in any female receptacle, any container at all, the power of fertility being in the semen alone.[107] Women's womb, therefore, was nothing but one of the possible containers for the semen. As the aforementioned quotation shows, the BU thinks that women were created only as a base for discharging semen.

This subjugation of women's sexuality, particularly in the *kṣatriya* clans, is reflected in the marriage customs as well. The *Mahābhārata* seems to be well aware of all the eight forms of marriage enlisted in the later Dharmaśāstric literature.[108] However, it is abduction, or the *rākṣasa* form of marriage, which is considered the most prestigious for a *kṣatriya*. Manu has described this form of marriage as the forcible capture of a girl, weeping and crying, from a house after injuring and slaying her relatives and breaking the defences.[109]

The narrative shows that Bhīṣma, the epitome of *kṣatriya* virtue, had procured brides for his brother Vicitravīrya by abducting the Kāśī princesses—Ambā, Ambikā, and Ambālikā—from their *svayaṃvara* (bridegroom choice). After discussing various forms of marriage, Bhīṣma declared the supremacy of the *rākṣasa* form.[110]

L. Sternbach believes that the *rākṣasa* marriage showed the remnants of a past when invaders forcibly captured a woman or plundered princesses of their enemy's country as part of their booty.[111] The suggestion seems plausible. However, we get no such celebration of the *rākṣasa* marriage in the *Ṛg Veda* which represents an earlier society. Moreover, the instances of *rākṣasa* marriage we get usually do not show an abduction following a political war between two erstwhile enemies. The abductions seem to be ends in themselves. Hence, it seems to be a practice popularized by the *kṣatriya* code of valour and subjugation of women in the Later Vedic Age. Minoru Hara thinks that the popularity of *rākṣasa* marriage can be explained by the *kṣatriya* code of not accepting a gift. Thus, it was preferable than the *kanyādāna* forms of marriage. Moreover, the *kṣatriya* was supposed to conquer the Earth by force, defeating and—if necessary—killing its previous holders. Since the Earth also was conceived as a maiden, the *rākṣasa* form of forcibly taking a maiden by injuring or killing her relatives would appeal to a *kṣatriya*.[112] Duryodhana, a firm believer in the *kṣatriya* code of valour, also abducted a Kaliṅga princess from a *svayaṃvara*.[113]

However, another reason why the *rākṣasa* form was more preferable than even the *gāndharva* (where the bride and the groom chose each other out of love) or *svayaṃvara*—none of which was a *kanyādāna* marriage—is visible in an episode of the *Mahābhārata* narrative. Arjuna, after seeing Kṛṣṇa's sister Subhadrā, wanted to marry her.[114] Understanding his friend's intention, Kṛṣṇa suggested:

svayaṃvara kṣatriyāṇāṃ vivāhaḥ puruṣarṣabha/
sa ca saṃśayitaḥ pārtha svabhāvasyānimittataḥ//
prasahya haraṇaṃ cāpi kṣatriyāṇāṃ praśasyate/
vivāhahetoḥ śūrāṇām iti dharmavido viduḥ//
sa tvam arjuna kalyāṇīṃ prasahya bhaginīṃ mama/
hara svayaṃvare hy asyāḥ ko vai veda cikīrṣatam.

(The *kṣatriya*'s marriage is the bridegroom choice, bull of men. But that is dubious, Pārtha, since one's own sentiments have no influence on the outcome. Forcible abduction is also approved as a ground of marriage for *kṣatriyas* who are champions, as the Law-wise know. Abduct my beautiful sister by force, for who would know her designs at a bridegroom choice?)[115]

Therefore, the difference between *svayaṃvara/gāndharva* marriage and *rākṣasa* marriage was the woman's choice and agency. Arjuna was advised to abduct Subhadrā because she might not choose him at a *svayaṃvara*, possibly because Arjuna was her cousin or because he already had many wives. The *rākṣasa* marriage could eliminate the woman's choice from the equation and therefore completely subjugate her to the abductor's clan. That is why Bhīṣma had complete authority over the women he had abducted, and he decided to give them in marriage to his brother Vicitravīrya who had no role in their abduction.

The discussion so far presents to us the Later Vedic *kṣatriya* clan society as one moving towards state formation. Alongside the process of state formation was the establishment of hereditary monarchy which necessitated a smooth machinery of transmission of office and property from one generation to the next. This was achieved by a new concept of genealogical succession based on primogeniture—the genealogical model of the Sūryavaṃśa—which was established by the complete subjugation of the woman and her reproductive capacity to the husband and his clan.

However, the *Mahābhārata* is not the story of unilinear triumph of an idea but the *itihāsa* of a time of transition, a time of contradiction and clashes between competing ideas. Hence, amidst this picture of the subjugation of women, alternative voices of women's freedom in choosing their partners can also be heard. Women's free sexuality was not only described by Pāṇḍu as the eternal law favourable to women, but it was supposed to have been still prevalent in Uttarakuru.[116] Uttarakuru, of course, was the utopia in the *Mahābhārata* imagination, where no agricultural labour, private property, conflict of interest, punishment, meat-eating, or sexual restrictions existed,[117] but the sexual promiscuity of the women of the northwestern regions of Madra and Bāhlīka was also well known.[118] If the *rākṣasa* form of marriage and the complete denial of women's agency seem to be a norm, there was the *gāndharva* marriage as a counter-norm. The *Mahābhārata* recalls several women who freely chose their husbands, including Devayānī,[119] Śarmiṣṭhā,[120] Śakuntalā,[121] Gaṅgā,[122] Śivā,[123] Hiḍimbā,[124]and Sāvitrī,[125] even if we leave aside the *putrikā* Ulūpī. That there was no prejudice against these marriages is testified by the fact that one of these marriages, that of Śakuntalā, produced the archetypal good ruler Bharata, while another woman who chose her husband, Sāvitrī, is regarded as the ideal wife. In contrast to Bhīṣma's opinion, the sage Kaṇva thought that *gāndharva* was the best form of marriage for the *kṣatriyas*.[126] Between *gāndharva* and *rākṣasa* lay the custom of *svayaṃvara* which could either be a *gāndharva*-type free choice in the presence of the parents (as in the case of Damayantī)[127] or a liquidated *rākṣasa* marriage with the bride being a prize of a martial contest which could be followed by a real confrontation with the failed suitors (as in the case of Draupadī).[128] That the woman's choice could not totally be ignored even in a *rākṣasa* marriage is indicated when Bhīṣma, even after abducting the three princesses of Kāśī, had to let Ambā go when she confessed that she wanted to marry Śālva.[129] In fact, at times the *rākṣasa* marriage could also be an act of the woman's choice. Thus, in an episode alluded to in the *Mahābhārata* and elaborated in the *Harivaṃśa*, Rukmiṇī, the princess of Vidarbha, loved Kṛṣṇa but was forcibly betrothed by her family to Śiśupāla. Hence, Kṛṣṇa had to abduct her, fighting her kinsmen.[130] Uma Chakravarti rightly notes that the *Mahābhārata* narrative represents a historical context when there was considerable tension in forging *kṣatriya* marriages, even though both *svayaṃvara* and *rākṣasa* forms—as well as *gāndharva*—were providing brides for various lineages and were described as lawful. The *rākṣasa* form of marriage was a matter of conflict, but the woman's recognition as a prize for her reproductive potential—the reification of her womb—was final. Therefore, even though Bhīṣma showed nominal respect towards Ambā's choice to marry Śālva, she eventually got rejected by Śālva, Vicitravīrya, and Bhīṣma for the temerity to believe that she could choose who she wanted to be with.[131] The defeated and humiliated Śālva refused to accept her as she was already Bhīṣma's lawfully conquered chattel, while, to Bhīṣma, Ambā's claim to sexual autonomy and choice had made her unfit to be incorporated to the house of her abductors.[132] Suicide swearing revenge on her abductor, Bhīṣma, was the only option left to her. Thus, despite the lip-service to the woman's choice in case of Ambā, Chakravarti thinks that all three Kāśī princesses were reproductive potentials violently obtained before their choice could be asserted. Reified as wombs, all three had a tragic history of thwarted sexual autonomy, Ambā becoming a social non-entity and her sisters being eventually forced into sexual unions against their will, 'virtual rapes', from which they produced faulty children.[133] Yet, the very concept of women's sexual autonomy was still not an unheard of thing.

Similarly, despite the conversion of the Kuru *vaṃśa* into a Sūryavaṃśa and an attempt to present a single genealogical line in the prose *vaṃśa*, the Candravaṃśa characteristics could not be totally smoothed out. The notion of primogeniture is very often challenged by the collaterals, and there are numerous examples of what Brodbeck calls 'junior branch takeover'. After all, if we go back to the refashioned Yayāti legend, it is the youngest son Pūru, and not the eldest Yadu, who succeeded the king. The verse *vaṃśa* says that Pūru was succeeded by his eldest son Pravīra and Pravīra by his son Manasyu. However, it also records the line of Pūru's youngest son Raudrāśva. Raudrāśva's son Ṛcepu and his brothers are said to have performed *rājasūya* and *aśvamedha*, rituals signifying royal sovereignty. Ṛcepu's grandson Taṃsu is described as holding sovereignty, and then the line continued from Taṃsu's son Ilina.[134] The Sūryavaṃśa-type prose *vaṃśa* omits this takeover by a junior line and, bringing in many intermediate figures, places Ilina in a direct line from Pūru.[135]

However, a more serious pointer is the succession after Bharata, the son of Duḥṣanta and Śakuntalā. Bharata is the archetypal great ruler in the text. His name has provided the name to the dynasty concerned, the war centring the dynasty, the text about the war, and—by extension—the Purāṇic name for the entire Indian subcontinent. However, if we take the text seriously, the Bharata bloodline seems to have ended with Bharata himself. It says that

> Bharata begot nine sons on his three wives, but the king did not approve any one of them, for they were not of his stature. Thereupon Bharata offered up grand sacrifices and received a son from Bharadvāja by the name of Bhūmanyu, O Bhārata. The scion of the Pauravas deemed himself Bhūmanyu's father and consecrated him Young King, O best of Bhāratas. Then the king himself had a little son, Vitatha, and this Vitatha became a son of Bhūmanyu.[136]

In the prose *vaṃśa*, Bhūmanyu is the biological son of Bharata, born of his wife Sunandā.[137] But what the verse *vaṃśa* account implies is quite significant, and the exact nature of obtaining a son from Bharadvāja is not clear. Brodbeck thinks that Bharadvāja was an elder brother of Bharata and Bhūmanyu his son.[138] The story is very similar to the birth of Dhṛṣṭadyumna and Draupadī and can very well be the story of a *niyoga* for a competent heir while the king had living biological offspring. Whatever it may be, the implication of the story is interesting. It shows that Bharata, of all kings, did not regard primogeniture or even royal blood necessary for kingship. He discarded his own sons because of their lack of ability to rule. Hence, the Bharatas are not really Bharata's descendants by bloodline but the descendants of Bharata's legacy, a legacy that rated ability over heredity, a legacy suiting the Candravaṃśa much more than the Sūryavaṃśa. If we read the main narrative of the *Mahābhārata* with this context in mind, the problematic of the text can be understood in a more nuanced way and the link between the *Mahābhārata* and the Vedic world better appreciated.

The main narrative of the *Mahābhārata* begins with the Kuru king Śaṃtanu. However, Śaṃtanu is also the latest Kuru chief to be named in the *Ṛg Veda*, in Book X. There, the sage Devāpi prays for rain in the realm of Śaṃtanu.[139] Explaining this hymn, the *Bṛhaddevatā* says that the Kuru prince Devāpi, affected by a skin disease, abdicated his throne in favour of his brother Śaṃtanu and became an ascetic. This violation of the law of primogeniture brought twelve rainless years in Śaṃtanu's kingdom, to end which Devāpi performed the rain-making charm.[140] The *Mahābhārata* also supports the story of Devāpi's abdication in favour of his brother for becoming an ascetic, in both the *vaṃśas*.[141] Though no other reason for the abdication is specified in the *vaṃśas*, elsewhere Dhṛtarāṣṭra showed that he was aware of the story about Devāpi's skin disease.[142] This is a classic case where the law of primogeniture was not followed because of a physical problem in the eldest son making him unfit to be a ruler. The *Mahābhārata* unconditionally accepts this triumph of ability over primogeniture. However, the Brahmanical texts like the *Ṛg Veda* or the *Bṛhaddevatā* view it as a transgression from norm, which was punished by twelve rainless years. Therefore, two ideas were clearly at loggerheads in the Later Vedic time. The fact that Devāpi himself performed the rain-making rite for Śaṃtanu brought a happy resolution of the conflict in this case, indicating that the abdication was willing and Śaṃtanu was no transgressor. However, what happened if the unfit elder did not abdicate willingly? The Vedas do not engage with the problem; the *Mahābhārata* does.

The Vedas do not show much interest in the life of Śaṃtanu after his rule was legitimized by Devāpi's rite. This is where the main narrative of the *Mahābhārata* begins. Śaṃtanu had a competent son, Devavrata, from his unsuccessful first marriage with Gaṅgā who had left him but returned to him his son in due time. Later, he was attracted towards Satyavatī, the adopted daughter of a fisherman. When he wanted to marry her, the fisherman wanted a pledge that the son born to Satyavatī would inherit the kingdom. Śaṃtanu could not grant this unfair demand, though he suffered a lot because of it. Eventually Devavrata came to know of it and satisfied the fisherman by taking two vows of renouncing kingship in favour of Satyavatī's unborn son and lifelong celibacy (so that his offspring would not challenge Satyavatī's son). These terrible vows were much appreciated, earning Devavrata the epithet 'Bhīṣma', and he guarded these vows throughout his life like a model *kṣatriya*.[143]

Gautam Chatterjee has argued that Bhīṣma's vows, though remarkable, are not justifiable either on deontological or teleological ground, for they betrayed the legacy of Bharata by promising the kingdom to an unborn child whose merits were unknown. This vow virtually changed the rule of succession to primogeniture and disregarded Bharata's principles.[144] We may more or less agree with Chatterjee's position except the fact that Bhīṣma's vows would not be acceptable even according to the law of primogeniture. The conundrum these vows had created was that it disregarded both the Sūryavaṃśa norm of primogeniture (since Bhīṣma was Śaṃtanu's eldest surviving son) and the Candravaṃśa norm of succession on merit (since Bhīṣma was competent whereas the merits of the unborn children of Satyavatī were yet to be tested). This triggered a series of events eventually leading to the Bhārata War.

Neither of Satyavatī's two sons—Citrāṅgada and Vicitravīrya—proved suitable to rule. Yet, the kingship was conferred on them one by one. Both died young and heirless, threatening the existence of the Kuru line. As discussed earlier, Satyavatī and Bhīṣma tried to solve the problem through *niyoga*, and Vyāsa was invited to beget children on the two widows of Vicitravīrya. However, Dhṛtarāṣṭra, the eldest of the *kṣetraja putras*, was born blind, and hence the kingdom went to the younger Pāṇḍu.[145] But Dhṛtarāṣṭra did not have the magnanimity of Devāpi and was not happy with the loss. Thus the question of whether to follow the Sūryavaṃśa pattern of primogeniture or the Candravaṃśa pattern of succession on merit loomed large a generation after both the competing principles were disregarded by Bhīṣma's unique vow. The situation became further complicated when Yudhiṣṭhira, the first *kṣetraja putra* of the younger Pāṇḍu, was born before Dhṛtarāṣṭra's eldest son, Duryodhana.[146] Now, was Yudhiṣṭhira, being the eldest in the generation, the rightful successor according to primogeniture? The question was too complicated to answer because in a Sūryavaṃśa-style primogeniture, where collaterals were not even counted, Yudhiṣṭhira would not even be mentioned in the genealogy. Duryodhana would have been the rightful claimant as the eldest son of the eldest son and Yudhiṣṭhira a potential interloper. On the other hand, there was also the legacy of Bharata to consider, especially after Dhṛtarāṣṭra was deprived of kingship in favour of Pāṇḍu on the basis of merit. The narrative presents Yudhiṣṭhira as the more meritorious and popular of the two. Yet, merit was subjective, and Duryodhana would probably score over Yudhiṣṭhira if the code of *kṣatriya* heroism was the standard. The subsequent narrative up to the Bhārata War revolved around these complications.

Therefore, the central problematic of the *Mahābhārata* narrative, though located in the dynastic issues of the Kuru royal family, was not just a feud between two branches of the same clan. What the *Mahābhārata* represents is the *itihāsa* of a time of transition, when an old world was giving way to a new world, when sedentary life was gradually leading towards state formation, when new genealogical norms were being established and challenged, when *varṇa* emerged as the sanctifier of a new hereditary social organization but there was constant questioning from a counter-normativity based on ability, and when women were losing their sexual and social freedom but voices in favour of women's agency and choice could also be heard. In the subsequent chapters, we shall go through some key episodes of the *Mahābhārata* narrative to see whether they can be understood better in their original Later Vedic context before returning to the question of how the *Mahābhārata* responds to this transition. To recover and appreciate the lost history of a time, documented by the *itihāsa* named *Mahābhārata*, one has to first see whether it is possible to identify the different layers of the text's long journey over more than a millennium. We shall try exactly that in the following sections by inspecting some key episodes of the *Mahābhārata* narrative, starting with the burning of the Khāṇḍava forest.

3.2 Heroes, Forest, and the Vedic Deities: Revisiting the *Khāṇḍavadāhana*

> Goddess of wild and forest who seemest to vanish from the sight.
> How is it that thou seekest not the village? Art thou not afraid?
> What time the grasshopper replies and swells the shrill cicala's voice,
> Seeming to sound with tinkling bells, the Lady of the Wood exults.
> And, yonder, cattle seem to graze, what seems a dwelling-place appears:
> Or else at the eve the Lady of the Forest seems to free the wains.
> Here one is calling to his cow, another there hath felled a tree:
> At the eve the dweller in the wood fancies that somebody hath screamed.
> The Goddess never slays, unless some murderous enemy approach.
> Man eats of savoury fruit and then takes, even as he wills, his rest.
> Now have I praised the Forest Queen, sweet-scented, redolent of balm,
> The Mother of all sylvan things, who tills not but hath stores of food.[147]
>
> —Hymn to the Forest, *Ṛg Veda*

The primary concern of early Indian literature rests in the settled society. Still, the forest (*vana*/*araṇya*) has occupied a pivotal place in its domain. It has featured as early as in the Ṛgvedic hymn to the *araṇyānī*. The Āraṇyakas and the Upaniṣads are known to have been composed in the forest hermitages of the world renouncers. Often, the forest plays the role of a fantasy world, a world of utopian harmony in hermitages, monstrous demons with supernatural power, and spectacular natural beauty. Like the 'wine-dark sea' in Homer's *Odyssey*, it often constitutes the 'unknown other' in the imagination of the poets. However, it will be wrong to assume that there is no realistic portraiture of the actual life in the forest or its relationship with the settled society. In fact, often this relationship is expressed through a language of massive violence. Especially striking, in this regard, is the ruthless violence displayed in the episode of the burning of the Khāṇḍava forest in the *Mahābhārata*. After our analysis of the birth and marriage stories of the *Mahābhārata* in the previous section, which outlined the Later Vedic layout of the *Mahābhārata* narrative, here we shall try to locate the *khāṇḍavadāhana* episode—that kind of marked the rise of the Pāṇḍavas as a political force and thus was instrumental in bringing out the narrative's central conflict—in its context, using its internal references as well as other contemporary sources. In the process, we shall need to focus on the issues of forest and forest clearance in early India.

In the *Mahābhārata* narrative, the burning of the Khāṇḍava forest and the establishment of Indraprastha are the first major episodes after the Kuru succession struggle reached a point of no return and the junior branch (the Pāṇḍavas) were maritally allied with the Pāñcālas (because of their polyandrous marriage with Draupadī). The Kuru realm was partitioned, and the Pāṇḍavas were assigned the forest tract of Khāṇḍavaprastha, whereas the sons of Dhṛtarāṣṭra received Hastināpura proper. The Pāṇḍavas, however, went on expanding their circle of allies, and their alliance with the Vṛṣṇis was cemented when Arjuna married Subhadrā, the half-sister of the Vṛṣṇi chief Kṛṣṇa. The birth of Abhimanyu, the son of Subhadrā, was thus an event of joyful celebration. The Pāṇḍavas, their wives, and Kṛṣṇa were enjoying themselves in a pleasure trip. There the fire god Agni approached Kṛṣṇa and Arjuna and asked them to burn down the Khāṇḍava forest. He also pointed out the problems involved in the process:

idam indraḥ sadā dāvaṃ khāṇḍavaṃ parirakṣati/
taṃ na śaknomy ahaṃ dagdhuṃ rakṣyamāṇaṃ mahātmanā//
vasaty atra sakhā tasya takṣakaḥ pannagaḥ sadā/
sagaṇas tat kṛte dāvaṃ parirakṣati vajrabhṛt.

(Indra always protects this Khāṇḍava Forest from conflagration, and as long as the good-spirited God protects it, I cannot burn it. His friend lives there with his people, the Snake Takṣaka, and for his sake the Thunderbolt-wielder protects it from burning.)[148]

On the request of Agni, the water god Varuṇa provided Kṛṣṇa and Arjuna with some extraordinary weapons necessary to meet the challenge. Kṛṣṇa and Arjuna then burnt the forest with a massive carnage, defeating Indra and his forces:

> Standing on their chariots at both ends of the forest, the two tigerlike men started a vast massacre of the creatures on every side. Indeed, whenever the heroes saw live creatures escaping, such as lived in the Khāṇḍava, they chased them down. They saw no hole to escape, because of the vigorous speed of the chariots—both the grand chariots and their warriors seemed to be strung together. As the Khāṇḍava was burning, the creatures in their thousands leaped up in all ten directions, screeching their terrifying screams. Many were burning in one spot, others were scorched—they were shattered and scattered mindlessly, their eyes abursting. Some embraced their sons, others their fathers and mothers, unable to abandon them, and thus went to their perdition. Still others jumped up by the thousands, faces distorted, and darting hither and thither fell into the Fire. All over, the souls were seen writhing on the ground, with burning wings, eyes, and paws, until they perished. As all watery places came to a boil, Bhārata, the turtles and fish were found dead by the thousands. With their burning bodies the creatures in that forest appeared like living torches until they breathed their last. When they jumped out, the Pārtha cut them to pieces with his arrows and, laughing, threw them back into the blazing Fire. Their bodies covered with arrows and screeching fiercely, they leaped upward nimbly and fell back into the Fire. The noise of the forest animals, as they were hit by the arrows and left to burn, was like the ocean's when it was being churned.[149]

The ruthless violence of the enterprise is described in vivid details:

> The Khāṇḍava creatures, Dānavas, Rākṣasas, Snakes, hyenas, bears and other forest beasts, rutting elephants, tigers, full-maned lions, deer and buffalo, and hundreds of birds were frightened by the falling mountain,

> and, much perturbed, they and the other races of beings crawled away. They saw the conflagration raging and the two Kṛṣṇas with their weapons ready; and the roaring sound of the upheaval brought them to terror. Janārdana let loose his discus, which shone with its own light, and the humble creatures as well as the Dānavas and the Stalkers of the Night were cut down by the hundreds, and they all fell instantly into the Fire. Rent by Kṛṣṇa's discus, the Rākṣasas were seen besmirched with fat and blood like clouds at twilight. The Vārṣṇeya went about like Time, killing off Piśācas, birds, Snakes, animals by the thousands, O Bhārata. And whenever that discus of enemy-slaying Kṛṣṇa was thrown, it came back to his hand after killing numbers of creatures.[150]

However, they spared Maya, an Asura architect, who—on return—built a magnificent palace for the king Yudhiṣṭhira. The burning of the forest increased the habitable and cultivable territory of Khāṇḍavaprastha to a great extent, and gradually Khāṇḍavaprastha became the great city of Indraprastha.[151]

The episode has been interpreted by scholars in various ways. M. Biardeau interprets it as a mythical representation of the theme of *pralaya* and re-creation.[152] She bases her argument on a story about King Śvetakī who held an unusually long sacrifice—on the advice of Śiva and officiated by the sage Durvāsas, a part-incarnation of Śiva—which caused a sickness in Agni. The remedy to Agni's sickness was the devouring of the Khāṇḍava forest. Thus, it was Śiva—the lord of *pralaya*—who pushed Śvetakī to an excessive and 'unethical' sacrifice. Agni's sickness represented the pitiful situation of *dharma*, on the verge of destruction, when restoration was possible only through a great disaster. The survivors of *pralaya* were only those who were indispensable for re-creation after destruction, such as Maya, representing illusion (*māyā*), which permitted the empirical world to be re-created and to subsist, and the four Śārṅgaka birds, representing the four Vedas.

However, the whole hypothesis is based on a legend mentioned only in some Northern Recension manuscripts and not included in the narrative of the Critical Edition. Therefore, this story of Śvetakī—and Biardeau's subsequent theory—has little value in our search for the original content of the tradition.

Alf Hiltebeitel views in the story the initiation of Arjuna by defeating Indra—his father and the king of the Devas—whose opposition is actually a test and treats it as a parallel to the initiation of the Buddha by defeating Māra, the lord of this world. He notices the similarities between Arjuna and the Buddha by showing that both got married by drawing a great bow in a *svayaṃvara*. The Buddha's wife was named Gopā or Yaśodharā whose son Rāhula kept his lineage. One of Arjuna's wives, Subhadrā, was often called *yaśasvinī* and was once dressed as a *gopa* lady, and it was her son—Abhimanyu—who kept the Pāṇḍava lineage.[153]

The parallelism is too weak to be taken seriously. It stretches the adjective *yaśasvinī* to make it a counterpart to Yaśodharā, and equating a *gopī*'s costume with the name Gopā is even more far-fetched. Most importantly, Subhadrā was not the woman whom Arjuna had married at the *svayaṃvara*. While Abhimanyu had actually maintained the Kuru lineage, through his son Parikṣit, Rāhula took *pravrajyā* before begetting a son. However, initiation may be a subplot in the episode, as Buddhadeb Basu has noted that here—at the end of the 'Ādiparvan'—Arjuna received his Gāṇḍīva bow by passing the test of defeating his father, Indra, just like Yudhiṣṭhira who got initiated at the end of the 'Āraṇyakaparvan' by passing the test of defeating his father Dharma.[154] But initiation is not the main theme of the narrative and definitely not in the manner Hiltebeitel presents it.

The section, in fact, clearly corresponds to the practice of burning forests to establish new agrarian settlements. Clearing of forests to establish agrarian settlements was no doubt a major factor behind the rise of the *mahājanapadas* and state formation. Though Shereen Ratnagar has pointed out that large-scale deforestation began in the Gaṅgā valley only when the British understood the utility of the *sal*, it is undeniable that a great portion of the forests had been cleared to establish settlements.[155] R.S. Sharma takes the introduction of iron tools for productive purposes—*c.* 700 BCE onwards—as the pivotal break, arguing that the clearance of forest with iron axe and wet rice cultivation aided by iron ploughshare had helped to generate enough surplus for state formation and urbanization.[156] D.P. Agrawal also argues that iron technology addressed the task of land clearance for agriculture and settlement in the Gaṅgā-Yamunā Doab and Mid-Gangetic valley, marked by monsoon forests, swampy jungles, and *kankry* lands.[157] M.D.N. Sahi traces the iron-aided changes in the PGW phase and tries to show the existence of an agricultural base, new cereals, subsistence production, existence of full-time specialists, social stratification, proliferation of artisanal production, and beginning of urbanization in that period.[158] B.B. Lal also credits the PGW users for introducing iron-aided large-scale agriculture in the Gaṅgā-Yamunā Doab.[159] The technological determinism of the thesis has undergone much criticism. However, the fact of forest clearance remains. A. Ghosh, a major critique of Sharma's thesis, points out that fire, not iron axe, was the popular instrument of forest clearance.[160] That fire had a major role in Aryanization and occupation of new areas in the Later Vedic Age is shown in the ŚB which says how the hero Videgha Maṭhava and his priest Gotama Rāhugaṇa stopped at the bank of the river Sadānīrā, before entering Videha, as Agni Vaiśvānara cleared the other bank for them.[161] The role of Agni Vaiśvānara, in both the colonization of Videha and the burning of the Khāṇḍava forest, may mean both the clearance of forest by fire and the process of Aryanization represented by the sacrificial fire. C.V. Vaidya sees *khāṇḍavadāhana* as a marker of the slash-and-burn form of land cultivation, interpreted as a dedication to Agni.[162] Thapar also views it as an instance of forest clearance by burning.[163]

The burning of the Khāṇḍava forest, as an instance of forest clearance, is integrally linked with perceptions of the forest in early India. Forest (*araṇya*) in ancient India was conceptualized as an antithesis to the settled society (*grāma/kṣetra*). Therefore, the idea of forest was more about its cultural location than its landscape. The idea of different landscapes in ancient India has received some attention in Francis Zimmermann's book *Jungle and the Aroma of Meat*. Here, Zimmermann discusses the Āyurvedic concept of different *caras* (eco-zones). Thus, uncultivated unsettled land (*araṇya*) could be of two distinct ecological natures—*jaṅgala* (dry) and *ānūpa* (marshy). While the former was usually associated with the west, the latter was associated with the east. The *jaṅgala* is supposed to be an area of dry climate which leads to excesses of the Āyurvedic humours wind (*vāta*) and bile (*pitta*), whereas the unctuous climate of the *ānūpa* leads to dominance of phlegm (*kapha*) and wind. No inherent superiority of one of the *cara* over the other is implied. However, in other places it is reiterated that *jaṅgala* is better, since the meat of the *jaṅgala* creatures and the water of the westward flowing rivers are dry, salty, light, and beneficial, whereas the meat of the *ānūpa* creatures and the water of the eastward flowing rivers are heavy and unhealthy. Therefore, Manu and Yājñavalkya instruct the kings to clear forest and settle in the *jaṅgala* regions. However, the best eco-zone lies in between the two, in the Delhi Doab, called the *sādhāraṇadeśa* or *madhyadeśa*, which provides the ideal balance of the three humours.[164]

Though these concepts are found in the Āyurvedic texts composed in a period much later than the period of our concern, the dominance of the Madhyadeśa, the Kuru-Pañcāla region, is quite interesting. As forest clearance and establishment of settlements is suggested mainly for the *sādhāraṇadeśa* and the *jaṅgala* regions, the Khāṇḍava forest seems to be an ideal forest for clearance. It was located in the *sādhāraṇadeśa* which also had certain *jaṅgala* characteristics implied in the name Kurujāṅgāla for the region. Moreover, Zimmermann also shows the assumed medical potential of the 'light' and 'heavy' *jaṅgala* meat, which may have had some role in shaping the later northern legend about the Khāṇḍava animals being prescribed as remedial diet for the diseased Agni.

The forest-burning episode concerns not only the forest but also the forest dwellers. Aloka Parasher-Sen minutely surveys the relationship between the settled society and the forest tribes in ancient India and notices a flexible social environment. She quotes Andre Beteille to note that the tribes for centuries and millennia continued to exist in the lap of civilization and that the real issue is thus 'not not identifying the evolutionary stage to which the tribal type of organization corresponds but in coming to terms with the co-existence of the tribal and other types of social organization within the same social and historical context'.[165] She notices the distinction between subordinate and marginal groups from the *Amarakośa* of Amarasiṃha (*c.* fifth century CE), where the lower *varṇas* within the *varṇa*-ordered society (*śūdra*, *pāmara*, *jalma*, *prākṛta*, *kṣudra*, *nihīna*, *itara*), the untouchables subordinate to it (*kiṅkara*, *dāsa*, *bhṛtya*, *bhujiṣya*, *preṣya*, *paricāraka*, *caṇḍāla*, *mātaṅga*, *jaṅgama*, *pukkasa*, *śvapāca*), and the hunting tribes outside it (*kirāta*, *śabara*, *pulinda*) are categorically distinguished.[166] The forest tribes are therefore marked by exclusion rather than subordination. Thus, the forest tribes are invariably bracketed with the *foreign*, being outside the *varṇa* order, as *mleccha*. This tendency is not exclusive to the Brahmanical tradition since similar categorization can be found in the Jaina *Prajñāpana* and the writings of the Buddhist scholar Buddhaghoṣa, both datable around the fifth to sixth centuries CE.[167]

However, exclusion does not necessarily mean antagonism. Instances of both cooperation and conflict between the *ārya* and the *mleccha* can be found in early Brahmanical literature. The Niṣādas had a prominent role in the *viśvajit* sacrifice in which the sacrificer had to temporarily reside among the Niṣādas and the *iṣṭi* was to be performed by a Niṣāda chieftain.[168] In Yāska's *Nirukta*, the Niṣādas, along with the four *varṇas*, form the *pañca jana*. On the other hand, the AB describes the Niṣādas as evildoers and thieves who rob wealthy men in the forest. Both the attitudes are combined beautifully in the *Mahābhārata* legend where the Niṣāda shares common ancestry with the first king Pṛthu, both being born of the evil king Veṇa's body, but is excluded from the latter's dominion. Here the *Mahābhārata* enlists some other forest tribes alongside the Niṣādas, which are the Karṇapravaras, the Kālamukhas, and the Rākṣasas.[169]

Like the Niṣādas, the Kirātas were another prominent forest tribe mostly associated with the hilly tracts of the Himalayas and the Vindhyas. The *Rāmāyaṇa* describes them as wearing thick topknots and subsisting on raw flesh.[170] In the *Mahābhārata*, they are shown as Himalayan tribals attired in skins and eating roots and fruits. Their hunting characteristic is shown in the *kirātārjunīya* story in both the *Mahābhārata* and Bhāravi's later long poem on the theme. Later on, their conflicts with the rulers of the Vindhyan region have been recorded in the Śrāvaṇa Belgolā inscription of Narasiṃha II who claims to have broken their power, and the claim of the Western Gaṅga king Satyavākya Koṅganivarman to be the destroyer of the Kirātas.[171]

Less prominent forest tribes living in primitive condition were the Śabaras and the Pulindas. The *Arthaśāstra* mentions them among the hunters, trappers, and forest dwellers, who were to guard the frontiers. Greek writers mention them as Sabarai and Poulindai. They were included as a target of Aśoka's *dhamma*.[172] They are also quite prominent in the *Kathāsaritsāgara*. Other tribes such as the Puṇḍras and the Andhras got gradually incorporated into the mainstream.

However, the line between the subordinated and excluded groups was not always rigid. Therefore, Manu tried to include both the Niṣādas and the Kirātas within the *varṇa-jāti* fold. The *niṣāda* became an *anuloma jāti* born of a *brāhmaṇa* father and a *śūdra* mother, whereas the *kirāta* was designated a *vrātya kṣatriya* status.[173] Amarasiṃha categorized the

Niṣādas among the untouchables like the *caṇḍālas*. Thus, the system was flexible and varied in different sociopolitical conditions.[174]

Parasher-Sen's study provides us valuable insight about the forest tribes and their position vis-à-vis the mainstream society. However, it does not go into much detail about the actual lifestyle and activities of these tribes, focusing more on their status in the normative texts. Moreover, the tribes prominent in the epic tradition—such as the Rākṣasas, the Vānaras, and the Nāgas—are left out of the study. A closer scrutiny of these tribes would provide us clearer ideas about the representation of the 'other'.

In her essay 'Of Tribes, Hunters and Barbarians: Forest Dwellers in the Mauryan Period' Parasher-Sen underscores the settled society's tendency to exclude the tribal communities from their cultural landscape, be it in the different Brahmanical concepts of Āryāvarta or in the Buddhist idea of Majjhimadeśa. However, the forest had its importance as well, as a supplier of fuel, timber, fodder, game, and edible produce. Thus, the forest's importance as a resource base coexisted with the apprehension about the 'barbarian' *āṭavīkas*. In the Mauryan period, forest gained more attention, and Kauṭilya, with his typical emphasis on resources, categorizes the forests according to their resource potential, giving special importance to elephant forest (*nāgavana*) and material forest (*dravyavana*). He also suggests special storehouses for forest products and appointment of special officers for tapping forest produce. Forbidding clearance of the elephant forests and encouraging planting of the *dravyavanas*, he welcomes the possibility of clearing other kinds of forests for establishing new settlements (*janapadaniveśa*). However, he shares the earlier apprehension about the forest tribes. Thus, *aṭavībala* or force of the forest tribes is to him less desirable than a force of the aliens led by an *ārya*, and the former is recommended only in an emergency, like attack by a force consisting of forest tribes. The *Arthaśāstra* also recommends different ways of breaking up free and armed forest tribes. That even Aśoka was not free of this apprehension is clear in his Rock Edict XIII where he gives an oblique warning to the forest tribes that his lenient policy only means 'patience as far it is possible to exercise'. Still, sensitively enough, he strictly prohibited burning down of forests, and his Fifth Pillar Edict enlists a complete ban on killing of certain creatures and restriction on killing of some others, although this might not have been a pleasing measure for the hunters and fishermen.[175] In this antagonism and cooperation between the settled society and forest in ancient India, though important as a source of resources, the forest was the realm of the 'other', and the state practised as much non-interference as possible, being happy with the extraction of certain resources.

That the forest attained more focus in the Mauryan period is not surprising: Candragupta Maurya possibly hailed from a forest tribe of Pipphalīvana. In many legends, he meets his mentor Cāṇakya in a forest and undergoes a series of miracles in forest regions. However, for us, the Aśokan decrees are more significant. The prohibition on burning down forests is an indication of prevalence of such practice in pre-Mauryan time. The restriction and prohibition on killing of several creatures also is a happy contrast with the massive slaughter and cruelty involved in the burning of the Khāṇḍava forest.

Thapar's essay 'Perceiving the Forest: Early India' discusses the dichotomous as well as complementary relationship between the forest and the settled society and the threefold role of the forest as the site of hunting, hermitage, and exile. Hunting, with almost the entire army in action, often took the form of a 'surrogate raid on nature'. The violent and massive hunting of Duḥṣanta or the great carnage involved in the burning of the Khāṇḍava forest, both in the *Mahābhārata*, seem more to be necessary precondition for power rather than used in a symbolic sense. The burning of the Khāṇḍava appears to be a claim on the land as territory and differs in mood from the *Śatapatha Brāhmaṇa* story of Videgha Maṭhava where fire plays a more legitimizing role. The hunt could also be a mechanism of asserting control over the grazing ground. Thus, the Kurus seem to have extended their control over Dvaitavana where they established a pastoral settlement. Inspection of cattle becomes an excuse for hunt and display of power. However, the resistance of the forest dwellers to this infringement of the forest comes in the form of the Gandharvas of Dvaitavana. The Gandharvas are counted also as one of the forest tribes resisting the burning of the Khāṇḍava.

The most frequent imagery of the forest people in the epics, however, is that of the Rākṣasas, appearing as the unfamiliar forest dwellers who obstruct hunting expeditions and harass those establishing settlements in the forest, such as the *ṛṣis* setting up their *āśramas*. The hermitage of the renouncer, in fact, is to be located outside the settled society whose norms he renounces. But for the forest tribes, it remains an infringement of the forest by the settled society, and the hermitage indeed played the role of a mediator between the two. As the realm of the unknown, the forest is also the place of exile in both the epics, where the most fantastic incidents of the epics unfold.

The equation changed a bit with the appearance of the state machinery. In the Mauryan period, Kauṭilya views the forest as a source of resources and also discusses the diplomatic possibilities of alliances with the forest people. That the forest dwellers still had a dichotomous relationship with the state is indicated in the warning in Aśoka's Rock Edict XIII. In the Gupta period, Samudra Gupta is known to have brought the *āṭavīka* chiefs to servitude. Closer contacts between the two worlds were facilitated by the grant of *agrahāra* lands in the forest regions in the subsequent periods. Thus, the distinction remained, but the antagonism became less ferocious. In Kālidāsa's *Abhijñānaśākuntalam*, Duḥṣanta's hunt loses its *Mahābhārata* ferocity. In Bāṇabhaṭṭa's *Harṣacarita*, the picture of the forest is quite close to that of a village. The description of the nephew of the Śabara chief matches the stereotypes of the Niṣāda or the Rākṣasa, but he is no longer feared or fantasized. Rather, Bāṇabhaṭṭa acknowledges him as someone who knows every leaf of the forest.[176]

The antagonistic relationship between the forest-dwelling Rākṣasas and the settled society is reflected in the two exiles of the Pāṇḍavas. Whenever the Pāṇḍavas entered the forest as exiles, this infringement was resisted by the Rākṣasa chiefs such as Hiḍimba and Kirmīra.[177] On the other hand, when Baka, a Rākṣasa chief, tried to impose his authority on the settled society of Ekacakrā, by demanding the sacrifice of one human from one family of the village every day, he was slain by Bhīma, his body becoming a public spectacle.[178]

The dichotomy of the village and the forest, in ritual and actual context, is also an object of interest in Charles Malamoud's *Cooking the World*. Malamoud shows how *araṇya* constituted the 'other' to the 'self' of the settled village and could include all kinds of landscapes other than the cultivated village, ranging from forest to desert. The village was the settled society governed by social norms (*dharma*) observed by the householder (*gṛhastha*), while the forest was the 'other' world of wilderness. Therefore, forest animals were not to be used for sacrifice to prevent the householder becoming a part of the other landscape. Yet, as the sacrifice implied human authority over both the realms, the forest had to be absorbed into the village. In the horse sacrifice, forest animals were tied to the posts between the posts where village animals were tied. But they were then set free while the latter were sacrificed. Forest was therefore both within and without the village: within, as the realm inferior to that ruled by *dharma* and subjected to those worshipping Agni, the god of the sacrificial fire; without, as the realm of unknown wilderness that might account for the Absolute Reality. It is the forest where, in contrast to the *gṛhastha*, the renouncer (*sannyāsin*) sought the Absolute, transcending the normative reach of *dharma*. Ascetics would sometimes use only the hollow of their hand as dish for eating, while some others would directly eat with their mouth like animals. Man could be a part of both the worlds. He was the village animal par excellence, the ideal object of sacrifice, and the only animal who could also be a sacrificer. But he was also considered among the forest animals in many cases, including the list of sacrifices in the horse sacrifice. The secret lay in the contrast of the *gṛhastha* and the *sannyāsin*, though each could be a stage in the same man's life. However, the ancient Indian thinkers also tried to juxtapose the two in the stage of *vānaprastha*, a utopia according to Malamoud. It is a stage when the householder entered a forest establishment, permitted only to take his wife and his fire. However, the sacrifice would be of wild rice, not of anything cultivated. Thus, the natural harmony remained undisturbed, and that harmony of nature in the hermitage attained fantastic proportion in Kālidāsa's picturesque language.[179] Malamoud also agrees that the relationship between the forest and the village in ancient India was both dichotomous and complementary. Whether his description of *vānaprastha* as a utopia can be accepted is, however, questionable. *Vānaprastha* abounds in early Indian literature. Whereas the complete harmony of nature in the hermitages, described by poets like Kālidāsa, might have utopian elements in it, the existence of *vānaprasthaāśrama* as a social reality cannot altogether be denied as utopic.[180]

From the state's perspective, perceiving the forest as a place of both antagonism and complement to the complex society could not be enough. Though the forest space was otherized, it was to be subordinated to the complex society over which the king ruled. B.D. Chattopadhyaya notes that the mystique of forest with transcendental as well as evil characteristics can be traced as early as in the Ṛgvedic hymn to the *araṇyānī* and the *Āraṇyaka* texts. However, the complex society could not treat the forest by complete separateness, since the forest was an important source of resources and often pivotal to the security strategies. Therefore, forest was to be brought within the moral-cultural authority of the complex society, though as a marginal area. The forest dwellers were to provide services to the complex society but as marginal untouchables or outcastes. The attempt to culturally hegemonize the forest space and the resistance of the forest dwellers to it created a certain tension between the two. This led to the repeated references to the forest-dwelling Rākṣasas spoiling the sacrifices. We have already seen that even the usually lenient Emperor Aśoka spoke apprehensively of the forest dwellers and issued veiled threats to make them adhere to the moral order. These attempts of hegemony became widespread from the Gupta Age onwards. Samudra Gupta vanquished many forest chiefs, and the practice of granting lands in forest areas gradually led to the transformation of many forest areas into settled villages or towns. The forest chiefs, with this incorporation, often acquired symbols and substance of political authority of the contemporary complex society as well. Sanskritization became a major tool for that, as Chattopadhyaya shows from the inscriptions of Samkṣobha, a *parivrājaka mahārāja* subordinate to the Gupta kings, and of the Hoysalas. He also notes elements of Sanskritization on the forest hunter Kālaketu of the *Caṇḍīmaṅgala*, a sixteenth-century Bengali text by Mukundarāma Cakravartī. Conversely, those chiefs who did not take part in the transformation remained forest chiefs, rather than becoming monarchs matching the requirements of a complex state society, even up to the twentieth century, as Chattopadhyaya shows from the instance of the forest *rājā* in the *Āraṇyaka*, a Bengali novel by Bibhutibhushan Bandyopadhyaya.[181]

We can sum up from this rich historiography that, at least in the pre-Gupta days, the state's attempt to hegemonize the forest space often took the form of violent confrontations. The forest dwellers could have been violent in spoiling sacrifices, as the state could be violent in imposing its order on the forest. With this background in mind, we may proceed to the most comprehensive study of the concerned episode in Ruth Katz's *Arjuna in the Mahābhārata*. Katz does not accept Biardeau's description of the event as a representation of *pralaya*, arguing that the *pralaya* imagery is nothing but a descriptive tool. In fact, one major methodological contribution of Katz is pointing out the formulaic nature of various literary imageries used by the poet, which are mostly descriptive tools rather than serious mythical or historical pointers. Indeed, there is hardly any thematic possibility of the Khāṇḍava burning being conceived as dissolution, since mythically the *Mahābhārata* represents the end of Dvāpara and beginning of Kali, not the time of dissolution at the end of Kali.

The principal interest of Katz lies in understanding Arjuna at three levels of his personality: heroic, human, and devotee. However, the violent massacre in the Khāṇḍava forest becomes problematic at the heroic level. It not only offends modern sensibilities (both Hindu and Western) but also hurts the moralities of non-violence (emphasized in the didactic sections of the very text as well as in classical Hinduism) and rightful warfare (in which, according to the text itself, innocent bystanders were not to be slain). More surprising is the lack of attempt to justify the act anywhere in the text. To understand this aspect, Katz explores several possibilities. One is that a battle against cosmic forces might not have been bound by the moral dilemmas that battle with human enemies would entail. Therefore, the code of warfare might not have been adhered to in this case. To prove that the battle was actually conceived as one between cosmic forces, Katz draws a parallel with the *Iliad* where Achilles fights the river Skamandros. There Achilles, aided by Poseidon and Athena, could ultimately overcome the combined strength of the river and its tributary Simoeis only when he was helped by fire brought by the smith Hephaistos. This duality of fire and water in Indo-European myth is represented in the fight between Agni and Indra in the Khāṇḍava episode as well. Moreover, this violent cosmic duel can actually have a positive overtone if it is conceived in a sacrificial nature which the presence of the fire god indicates. Katz refers to other such instances of massive positive cosmic destruction in sacrificial cause in the epic mythology, most notably the churning of the ocean by the Devas and the Asuras. She also compares the companionship of Arjuna and Kṛṣṇa in the event with that of Gilgamesh and Enkidu in the *Epic of Gilgamesh* where the two heroes fight the forest guardian Humbaba. There Humbaba had both fiery and watery characteristics which Gilgamesh could overcome with the force of the winds sent to his aid by the sun god Shamash.

This episode leads to the maturation of Arjuna and Kṛṣṇa as warriors. Therefore, the two display an amoral and premature martial ecstasy which was to be refined later on. That Arjuna was to mature into an ethical warrior, rather than to become a brutal ecstatic killer like Bhīma, is indicated in his brief spell of chivalry to save the architect Maya.[182]

Finally, at the level of Arjuna's devotion, Katz notes that Kṛṣṇa was still not a deity. He needed Varuṇa's aid to face Indra as badly as Arjuna did. However, the duo is described as the incarnations of the sages Nara and Nārāyaṇa at the end of the narrative. These two brilliant sages, believed to be upholders of *dharma* incarnated in every epoch, would gradually be deified in the Pañcarātra Vaiṣṇava tradition of *bhakti*. There Nārāyaṇa would be identified with Viṣṇu, and Nara conceived as the Human Universal. Thus the indication to the Nara-Nārāyaṇa characters of Arjuna and Kṛṣṇa can also be an indication to Arjuna's identification as a devotee of Kṛṣṇa. This devotion and companionship would also lead to Arjuna's deification as early as in the time of Pāṇini.[183]

The hypothesis of Katz is well argued. However, while she dismisses the dissolution imagery as a descriptive tool, why the sacrificial imagery could not be treated in the same way is not clear. The sacrificial imagery is definitely there, as is the antagonism between water and fire. However, the biggest problem in viewing the event as a sacrifice is the presence of Indra in the antagonistic side, a problem Katz herself notes but prefers to ignore. Moreover, while in the Achilles-Skamandros story, it is the power of fire that defeats the water, here the ultimate fight was not between Indra and Agni, as the two human heroes dominated the scene. Buddhadeb Basu notes the uniqueness of the episode not only in the overwhelming importance of the human heroes vis-à-vis the deities but also in the treatment where the narrative dealing with the eternal opposition of fire and water curiously shows the necessity of the conjunction of these two forces as well, since the victory of the force of fire is accomplished only with the help of the weapons supplied by the water god Varuṇa.[184]

The comparison with the Gilgamesh-Enkidu story seems too far-fetched. It is true that the Indo-European and Semitic traditions may not be as separate as is usually believed, and there are reasons to claim some mythical connections between the Gilgamesh tradition and Indian mythology. But in this case, companionship of two heroes and the fiery stormy nature of heroic battles are too general commonalities to argue for something substantial. Moreover, in the Gilgamesh-Enkidu story, both fire and water are on the side of Humbaba, and the forces those help Gilgamesh are wind and sun which are not very substantial in the Khāṇḍava episode or in the *Iliad* story.

Therefore, Katz also accepts that it is probable that the episode represents a historical forest burning for the purpose of conquest or land clearing, wiping out the wild tribes. In that case, the violent nature of the massacre becomes understandable. In fact, in both the Indian epics, it seems that the codes of warfare were observed only in the cases of battle between the *kṣatriya* warriors, whereas ruthlessness is well approved in the contest with forest tribes. We have already discussed the killing of Vālin in the *Rāmāyaṇa* which makes the matter clearer. The case of Kṛṣṇa and Arjuna may be similar here.

Holtzmann (the younger) views the forest as a retreat for Natives (Asuras) against Aryan onslaught.[185] But, in this case, the Nāgas rather than the Asuras are at the centre stage. Irawati Karve thinks that the Nāgas and Birds were forest clans whom the Aryan 'conquering settlers'—Kṛṣṇa and Arjuna—liquidated.[186]

The description also points to a human, rather than beastly, nature of the victims. The fact that the Nāgas were an ancient community, who appeared frequently in Indian history, is well known. They were a powerful group, who were sometimes allies or antagonists of the *kṣatriya* rulers. Thus, even in the Gupta period, while Samudra Gupta fought several battles against them,[187] Candra Gupta II married a Nāga princess.[188] Similarly, in the *Mahābhārata*, marital alliance between the Kurus and the Nāgas is mentioned (like Arjuna's aforementioned marriage with Ulūpī). Kosambi notes the importance of the Nāga cycle in the epic, reflected in the Nāga aid to Bhīma, Nahuṣa's conversion into a Nāga, Balarāma's transformation into a Nāga, and Dhṛtarāṣṭra's assumed Nāga characteristic.[189] The Nāgas were also antagonistic to the Kuru heroes and their associates. Legends hold that Kṛṣṇa subdued Kālīya Nāga on the banks of the Yamunā. Arjuna and Kṛṣṇa butchered the Nāgas of Takṣaka's lineage in the Khāṇḍava forest. A Takṣaka later killed Parikṣit, the grandson of Arjuna. Janamejaya resolved to kill all Nāgas to avenge his father's death.

The poet(s) of the *Mahābhārata* represents these forest-dwelling tribes with all their characteristics with much sensitivity probably derived from better first-hand knowledge of them than the poet of the *Rāmāyaṇa*. Vālmīki, whose geography starts faltering the moment it moves beyond the North Indian plains, perceives the forest tribes as cannibalistic monstrous Rākṣasas or animal-like Vānaras, adorns them with fantastic qualities, and punishes the open display of sexual desire of their females by mutilation of their organs. Devoid of much first-hand knowledge about these communities, he also attributes Sanskritized names—like Kumbhakarṇa, Vibhīṣaṇa,. Sugrīva, and Śūrpaṇakhā—to them. But the case is different in the *Mahābhārata*. Here we notice the possibility of a greater contact with these people whose names (Hiḍimba, Baka, Kirmīra, Ghaṭotkaca) bear clear non-Sanskritic origins. The ways in which the settled society and forest dwellers tried to preserve their own spheres, and resisted any infringement by the other, are shown in the Hiḍimba and Baka episodes mentioned earlier. The open sexual advances of the Rākṣasa and Nāga women have been accepted in most cases and not punished by mutilation.

The difference between the Brahmanical society and that of the Nāgas, the forest-dwelling Rākṣasas, and the non-Aryan tribes of the northeast is made clearer by the instances of matrilineal succession among the latter groups. Thus, Ghaṭotkaca, the son of Bhīma by the Rākṣasī Hiḍimbā, remained with his mother and became a chief. Similarly, Irāvat, Arjuna's son by the Nāga princess Ulūpī, also remained with his mother. Citrāṅgadā, the classic *putrikā*, kept her son Babhruvāhana with her as her successor. The aggressive nature of the conflict is also made clear by the fact that Arjuna killed Takṣaka's wife when she tried to save her son.

But describing the episode as an outright Aryan/non-Aryan conflict is difficult. Rather, the forest dwellers—in this case—seem to be Vedicized people who worshipped Indra. Kṛṣṇa and Arjuna reportedly fought against a full army of the Vedic deities, excluding Agni. However, they were aided by two Vedic deities, Agni and Varuṇa, as well. The army they faced was a mixture of opposites as the deities fought alongside the Rākṣasas, Dānavas, and Daityas. More surprisingly, it was not only the Nāgas who resisted Kṛṣṇa and Arjuna but also the Garuḍas—the traditional adversaries of the Nāgas. The fact that the Nāgas and Garuḍas might have been closely related—despite their antagonism—is indicated in the myth which shows them as born of the same father—Kāśyapa—and different mothers—Kadrū and Vinatā—who were sisters.[190] Therefore, it was a combined resistance of all the residents of the forest, who set aside their internal conflicts to protect their abode. The account seems to represent not an Aryan/non-Aryan conflict but a conflict of two ideas—the old idea of the Early Vedic nomads of association with nature and forest, and the rising idea of settlement and proto-urbanization through forest clearance. That even the Aryan elites were divided on this issue is indicated by the presence of Indra and Agni as opponents and of Varuṇa on both the sides. The setting is still Vedic, and not later, as shown by the list of the deities involved—Agni, Indra, Varuṇa, Yama, the Aśvins, Dhātṛ, Jaya, Tvastṛ, Aṃśa, Aryaman, Mitra, Puṣan, Bhaga, and Savitṛ. Śiva was present but only as a participant in Indra's army and nothing more.

That the Khāṇḍava forest suddenly disappeared from the geography of Kurukṣetra sometime in the Later Vedic Period is indirectly attested by Later Vedic literature as well. Therefore, the concerned forest is a part of the geography of Kurukṣetra in both the JB[191] and the PB[192] but not in the slightly later text MŚS.[193] All the materials surveyed, therefore, strongly indicate that the *khāṇḍavadāhana* episode is not a mere mythological metaphor but is representative of a real process of forest clearance for the establishment of settlements in Later Vedic Kuru kingdom, a process that might have faced stiff resistance leading to violent repercussion.

After these analyses, a natural question arises: why did the forest have to be burnt when so much opposition was involved? Apart from the fact that it occupied a substantial section of Khāṇḍavaprastha, assigned to the Pāṇḍavas, there might have been some geopolitical reasons as well, as J.A.B. van Buitenen writes:

> The oval figure beginning at Hastināpura, continued through Ahicchatra and Kāmpilya, and reversed through Mathurā of the Vṛṣṇis, must if it is to return to its source, once more intersect the river Yamunā. It is at this approximate spot that we find Indraprastha, the city founded by the Pāṇḍavas in the Khāṇḍava Tract given them by Hastināpura after the alliance with Pañcāla. It is surely Kuru country, but it is Vṛṣṇi riverside, and it is the Vṛṣṇi diplomat Kṛṣṇa who helps them to clear the area and establish themselves. A triangle of alliance has been forced by Kṛṣṇa, from Indraprastha to Mathurā to Kāmpilya, and the security of Mathurā secured by the marriage bond of Indraprastha and Kāmpilya. In the process Kṛṣṇa has also wound up with the balance of power: If war is to break out, Indraprastha, Mathurā and Kāmpilya can jointly converge on Hastināpura.[194]

Kṛṣṇa's engagement in burning the forest may become more meaningful in this light if we remember that the Vṛṣṇis were also trying to regain Mathurā from the Magadha chief Jarāsaṃdha who had driven them out to Dvārakā.

Thus, the burning of the Khāṇḍava forest can be safely contextualized in the period of the later Vedas as an instance of forest clearance by fire for establishing a new settlement of economic as well as geopolitical advantage. The pantheon involved in the legend is essentially Vedic, and the episode is a remarkable instance of different antagonistic Vedic forest tribes fighting together to defend their abode. The legend also shows the beginning of the rise of Kṛṣṇa and Arjuna as heroes, and the former's assault on the old religious system centring Indra, though his deification was yet to mature. Indraprastha, the resultant settlement, survived for a considerable period. While Hastināpura was deserted for Kauśāmbī around 800 BCE, Indraprastha remained a centre of the Kuru power at least till the time of the Buddha, since even the *Daśabrāhmaṇa Jātaka* remembers it as the capital of the Kuru *mahājanapada* where the people of Yudhiṣṭhira's lineage were ruling.[195] However, Yudhiṣṭhira's own days in Indraprastha is represented as quite eventful. His reign reached its climax with the grand celebration of the *rājasūya* in his new capital, which was not long before he staked and lost everything in two consecutive games of dice. What do we make of these episodes, so crucial to the narrative of the *Mahābhārata*? We shall look into that in the next section.

3.3 Dice, Duel, and *Dharma*: Contextualizing Yudhiṣṭhira's *Rājasūya*

The burning of the Khāṇḍava forest and the establishment of Indraprastha—which we tried to contextualize within the Later Vedic scenario, in the previous section—marked the beginning of the rise of the Pāṇḍavas as a formidable power, which culminated in Yudhiṣṭhira's *rājasūya*. However, the magnificence of the sacrifice generated envy in Duryodhana. Śakuni, his maternal uncle, thus advised him:

dyūtapriyaś ca kaunteyo na ca jānāti devitum/
samāhūtaś ca rājendro na śakṣyati nivārtitum/
devane kuśalaś cāhaṃ na me'sti sadṛśo bhuvi/

triṣu lokeṣu kaunteyaṃ taṃ tvaṃ dyūte samāhvaya//
tasyākṣakuśalo rājan nādāsye'ham asaṃśayam/
rājyaṃ śriyaṃ ca tāṃ dīptāṃ tvad arthaṃ puruṣarṣabha/
idaṃ tu sarvaṃ tvaṃ rājñe duryodhana nivedaya/
anujñātas tu te pitrā vijeṣye taṃ na saṃśaya//

(The Kaunteya loves to gamble but does not know how to play. If the lordly king is challenged, he will not be able to resist. And I am a shrewd gambler. I don't have my match on earth or in all three worlds. Challenge the Kaunteya to a game of dice—with my skill with the dice, king, I am certain to take from him his kingdom and his radiant fortune, in your behalf, bull among men.)[196]

Śakuni and Duryodhana persuaded the reluctant Dhṛtarāṣṭra to give consent for the match, against the advices of his favourite counsellor Vidura. Similarly Yudhiṣṭhira—though reluctant—came to play the match, saying that he could not turn down a request of Dhṛtarāṣṭra, and he had sworn not to refuse a challenge in the game. He lost all his property, his brothers, his own self, and finally Draupadī in the game. Ecstatic in victory, the victorious side ordered Pratikāmī—an usher—to bring the newly won slave Draupadī to the hall. Draupadī raised a technical question whether Yudhiṣṭhira lost himself before staking Draupadī, since a man who lost his own self could not stake anything. Without answering it, Duryodhana ordered his brother Duḥśāsana to bring Draupadī forcibly to the hall, which he did. In her monthly period and wearing a single piece of cloth, Draupadī came to the court and raised the same issue. The hall was stormed by Vidura's constant condemnation of the game, Vikarṇa's support to Draupadī, Bhīṣma's avoidance of a direct answer, Karṇa's brutal rebuttal to Vikarṇa, silence of the Pāṇḍavas except Bhīma, Duḥśāsana's failed attempt to disrobe Draupadī, Duryodhana's vulgar gestures to her, and Bhīma's violent vows against Duḥśāsana and Duryodhana. A scared Dhṛtarāṣṭra freed Draupadī and offered her boons, which she used to free her husbands, who were also given back the lost property. But as soon as the Pāṇḍavas left, Dhṛtarāṣṭra again succumbed to Duryodhana's demands and recalled the Pāṇḍavas for a sequel to the game. Strangely enough, Yudhiṣṭhira consented to play again. Losing again, the Pāṇḍavas had to accept an exile of thirteen years.[197]

The dice-game episode is remarkable by itself, because of Yudhiṣṭhira's obsessive gambling—staking even his brothers and wife—and the brutality of the Kauravas. But more striking is the seriousness a game of dice assumed. Therefore, contextualizing the incidents seems very important.

Dice was a popular game right from the Vedic period, if not from Harappan times. The prevalence of the game in the time and space with which we are concerned is confirmed by the unearthing of dice pieces from the PGW layer of Hastināpura.[198] The fact that succession could actually be decided by a game of dice among kinsmen clearly points to a clan society and would be unimaginable in a well-developed state society. It may well have represented a potlatch competition between two phratries for redistribution and destruction of wealth, as G.J. Held opines, following Marcel Mauss who views the *Mahābhārata* as a story of a tremendous potlatch.[199] Van Buitenen sees a ritual significance in it, linking it with Yudhiṣṭhira's *rājasūya*, as the sacrifice was necessarily followed by a dice match.[200] R.S. Sharma also thinks that the *rājasūya* sacrifice shows the tribal character of gift exchange followed by redistribution of the wealth by the chief.[201]

Romila Thapar argues that a closer scrutiny of the list of gifts brought by the guests in Yudhiṣṭhira's *rājasūya* shows a clear lack of commodity production and trade, since none but the Central Asians brought finished products and no ruler's party consisted of traders. The only craft products found in the list are pottery items and textiles. The thrust was on gold and gems, animals, slaves, and textiles, indicating a society where animal wealth and raw materials were more important than landed property, grain, and finished products. Similarly, a survey of Yudhiṣṭhira's stakes in the dice match shows pearls set in gold, hundred jars containing gold pieces, chariots, elephants, cow elephants, slaves, horses, cattle, sheep, and gold. It shows in a clearer manner the picture of a society where wealth primarily consisted of gold, animals, and slaves.[202]

The presence of the Chinese and the Central Asians among the tribute payers can raise a suspicion about the dating of the passage. However, Thapar's argument seems convincing that these people and the items brought by them were later additions to the passage which is an early one, as can be seen in the structure of relationships represented.

R.S. Sharma, in his *Aspects of Political Ideas and Institutions in Ancient India*, throws considerable light on the Later Vedic political structure, especially the *rājasūya* ceremony. Significantly, he notes that the ceremony continued to exist until the end of the Vedic period. The *rājasūya* is an essentially Yajurvedic ceremony that was initiated in the land of the Kuru-Pañcālas, since the people to be ruled by the would-be king are described as Bhāratas, Kurus, and Pañcālas in the concerned texts, namely the TS, the MS, the KS, the TB, and the ŚB. Therefore, the time and space of Yudhiṣṭhira's *rājasūya* can be contextualized in the Later Vedic Kuru realm.[203]

Sharma places emphasis on the *ratnahaviṃśi* ceremony in which the sacrificing king went to the houses of his '*ratnins*' (jewel holders) and offered oblations there. These *ratnins* are identified by Sharma, following K.P. Jayaswal, as a rudimentary body of high functionaries of the state.[204] U.N. Ghoshal's far-fetched description of the *ratnins* as constitutional positions has been logically refuted, since the use of the term 'constitution', as we understand it now, for the Later Vedic polity defies logic.[205] Even the concept of 'state' appears to be problematic. However, the Later Vedic Kuru polity can claim to be at least an emerging state or proto-state where a rudimentary bureaucracy had been conceived in the form of the *ratnins*. We have already discussed how Witzel argues that Kurukṣetra witnessed the rise of the first state in India, with a strong kingship—going beyond the common chieftainship—helped by a rudimentary administrative apparatus maintained by distribution of booty as well as collection of tax or tribute, which received ideological legitimacy from the newly emerging Vedic orthopraxy and orthodoxy based on the setting up of complicated *śrauta* rituals.[206]

A glance at the list of the *ratnins* therefore can give us an insight into the administrative apparatus of the Kuru-Pañcāla kings. The traditional number of *ratnins* is eleven or twelve, which Sharma conceives as a number of the members of the king's council, following the older Indo-European tradition. Councils of twelve members existed even among the ancient Saxons, Swedish, Frisians, and Celts.[207]

Among the twelve, those who appear in almost every list, and in an almost identical sequence, are the *brāhmaṇa* (priest), *rājanya* (warrior), *mahiṣī* (chief queen), *parivṛkti* (discarded barren queen), and *senānī* (commander-in-chief). Six other designations are also quite frequent. They are the *sūta* (chronicler/charioteer), *grāmaṇī* (supervisor of a village or a band), *kṣatṛ* (chamberlain), *saṃgrahītṛ* (master of treasury/

charioteer), *bhāgadugha* (tax collector), and *akṣavāpa* (dice thrower). While these eleven *ratnins* are present in almost all the lists, some other designations appear in one list or the other—*vāvātā* (the king's favourite wife), *govikarta/govikartana/govyaccha* (gamekeeper), *takṣana* (carpenter), *rathakāra* (chariot maker), and *pālagāla* (messenger).[208]

Sharma's theory of a twelve-member council seems a bit far-fetched. Firstly, the number of the *ratnins* is not invariably twelve in all the lists. It is eleven in the TS and fourteen in the MS. Moreover, all the mentioned *ratnins* might not be present in all the cases. For instance, a king might not necessarily have a discarded barren wife. Even if he had one, it is difficult to imagine a discarded barren queen being a member of the king's council. Moreover, it is likely that the *mahiṣī*, in many cases, would also be the king's favourite wife. However, Sharma rightly notes that on the one hand some features of a state become visible in indications to tax collection (*bhāgadugha*) and a standing army (*senānī*), but remnants of the tribal order are also evident in the prominence of a functionary like the *akṣavāpa*. As the *ratnins* are time and again described as the givers and takers of the kingdom (TB, I.7.3) or consecrators and sustainers of kingship (PB, XIX.1.4), the indication is clear that the dice thrower still had the power to make and unmake a king. The importance of this indication in the *Mahābhārata* context is quite clear.

Sharma also points out the several tribal elements present in the various stages in the performance of the *rājasūya* and *vājapeya* ceremonies. The presence of ceremonies involving a cattle raid, game of dice, and chariot race, where the king had to overcome one or more of his tribesmen (*sajāta*) in a mock contest, definitely retained elements of a tribal polity where victory in actual contests would be necessary for obtaining leadership.[209] However, Sharma thinks that gradually the tribal elements lost importance. Thus, in a comparatively late text—the ŚB—women (*vāvātā* and *parivṛkti*) and lower castes (*takṣaṇa* and *rathakāra*) were no more considered as *ratnins*.[210]

A completely different understanding of the *rājasūya* is presented in J.C. Heesterman's *The Ancient Indian Royal Consecration*. He views the *rājasūya* as an abridged representation of the unending cyclical process of decay and regeneration and discusses the various rituals involved in the ceremony to mark out the metaphors supporting his thesis. He argues that the *rājasūya* is not a royal consecration, performed once and for all, to bestow royal power on a king. It did not have the pomp and prestige of the *aśvamedha*. It consecrated, and not inaugurated, the king. Rather, it is like the other yearly festivals to regenerate the active powers in the universe. The king is treated as a common sacrificer, *yajamāna*. Thus, just like a common sacrifice, the *rājasūya* was basically concerned with the two poles of cosmic life: birth and death, integration and disintegration, ascension and descent. The fact that the crucial moment of the unction was preceded by a year-long preparation by the *cāturmāsya* ceremonies, and followed by another year of *dīkṣā*, points to an original pattern of yearly repeated unction and regeneration ceremonies. The entire system starts with the *prāyanīya* ceremony which indicates the introduction to a sacrificial session as well as the ascent to heaven and concludes with the *udayanīya* or *kṣatrasya dhṛti* symbolizing the descent to the Earth. The intervening rituals supposedly seem to be full of metaphors of impregnation, birth, fertility, and rebirth, the benevolent (*anumati*) and malevolent (*nirṛti*) aspects of the coverings of the womb being an issue of major concern. To Heesterman, thus, the *ratnin* offerings had hardly anything to do with the functioning of the royal apparatus, the royal consorts, governmental and household dignitaries, and artisans being incoherently mixed up. The king's tour of the residences of the *ratnins* is thus viewed in comparison with the sun's visit to various parts of the universe. Heesterman thinks that it implies the idea of marriage and entering the womb of the priest (whose relationship with the king is frequently conceived as a marital union) and the royal consorts. The charioteers (*sūta*, *grāmaṇī*, *ksattṛ*, *saṃgrahītṛ*, *takṣa*, *rathakāra*) are connected with the idea of embryonic covers. The following sacrifices to Mitra and Bṛhaspati are seen as the growth of the embryonic royalty in its *brāhmaṇa* womb, while in the royal unction the ultimate birth is proclaimed. The fertility and revitalizing potential of the new king is represented in the mounting of different quarters, the chariot drive, and the game of dice. The same motif is also represented in the recitation of the Śunaḥśepa legend, originating in the *rājasūya* context, which also has the theme of sacrifice and rebirth.[211]

The interpretation of Heesterman is not improbable, but it is not the only possible interpretation. Actually, Heesterman, to support his hypothesis, often overlooks the surface implications in search of metaphors. On the surface, the *rājasūya* rituals can also be seen as a series of ceremonies providing a king with some legitimacy. He prepares himself by invoking the positive permissive aspect (*anumati*) and warding off the evil aspect (*nirṛti*) of his function. After that, he has to procure the assurance of goodwill from the important elements of his ruling apparatus. The unction is followed by the declaration of the legitimacy of his kingship by the priest to the people (Bhāratas/Kurus/Pañcālas/Kuru-Pañcālas). He has to prove his mettle as the ablest person among his tribesmen through various contests such as the cattle raid and dice game, which gradually lose their competitive edge and become ritual obligations. Throughout the process, the king tries to absorb the kingly elements of different divinities such as Indra, Soma, Varuṇa, Agni, Mitra, Sūrya, Prajāpati, and Savitṛ. Since all of these divinities have a cosmic nature and fertility connection, it is quite possible to discover a fertility overtone in all the rituals involved. But other interpretations are equally possible.

In fact, in some instances Heesterman stretches his point too far or contradicts himself. About the *ratnins*, he fails to recognize the nature of tribal polity where civil and political offices are not always distinct. His theory of entering wombs through the ceremony also seems to be a bit far-fetched. His characterization of the swelling belly of king Hariścandra in the Śunaḥśepa legend as a marker of pregnancy with the sacrificer's own rebirth is difficult to accept, since the swelling in the story is the result of breaking a vow rather than of a creative context symbolizing fertility. About the *daśapeya* ceremony, he once argues that an older concept of a ten-monthly year is at large, but then contradicts it by taking the gift of twelve cows as representative of twelve months in a year. Too engrossed with his idea of cosmic imageries, Heesterman also fails to realize the historical significance of the *ratnin* ceremony, chariot race, or dice game in a clan/tribal polity as a means of acquiring the status of the best among equals. Sharma explores this aspect brilliantly, with adequate examples drawn from other early societies. The need for establishing this kind of legitimacy becomes more relevant in the case of the *rājasūya*, which, unlike the simple *abhiṣeka*, is not just the inauguration of a new king but the consecration of an already inaugurated king who felt the necessity to ritually legitimize his kingship.

Having a glance at Yudhiṣṭhira's *rājasūya*, occurring much after his inauguration to kingship, in this light, can be very interesting. A disputed kingship in the Later Vedic Kuru polity seems to be the perfect background for a *rājasūya*. Whether we can demarcate some of the *ratnins* in Yudhiṣṭhira's performance of this typical Later Vedic Kuru ritual is a question that needs an answer. It is evident that Dhaumya was the priest of the Pāṇḍavas, Yudhiṣṭhira the king, Draupadī the chief queen, and Arjuna the *senānī*. That Draupadī played a major role in the ritual as the *mahiṣī* is also shown in the statement that Duḥśāsana defiled the hair of Draupadī, which had been recently bathed in the sacred water of the *rājasūya*. Yudhiṣṭhira had another wife, Devikā, but she was neither his favourite wife nor a discarded barren one. The *sūtas* play a very important part throughout the *Mahābhārata*, and Saṃjaya seems to be the most important *sūta* of the Kurus. Yudhiṣṭhira's personal charioteer—Indrasena—must have also been present in the sacrifice. All the four brothers of Yudhiṣṭhira played the part of the *bhāgadugha*, before the sacrifice. In the *rājasūya*, Yudhiṣṭhira assigned his cousin Duryodhana the role of the *saṃgrahītṛ*, the receiver of gifts and tributes.

However, what takes centre stage in the *Mahābhārata* is the game of dice. As J.A.B. van Buitenen has rightly pointed out, the dice game in the *Mahābhārata* was probably not an isolated incident but a supplement to Yudhiṣṭhira's *rājasūya*.[212] The ritual obligation of accepting a challenge in a dice game with a *sajāta* made the game unavoidable. However, it should be pointed out that these contests were meant to be mock contests. But textual prescriptions are not always bound to be followed in practice. At least the mock contest had the potential of becoming a real one if both the *sajāta* contestants had a claim over kingship and each considered himself the rightful claimant to the throne.

That the Vedic sacrifices bear the remnants of a more primitive prehistory of an actual and often violent contest has also been pointed out by Heesterman in his *The Inner Conflict of Tradition: Essays in Indian Ritual, Kingship and Society*. He thinks that the Vedic rituals—representing the triumph of life over death—bear the remnants of some preclassical agonistic rituals. The original rituals might have contained real contest and resulted in death. Thus, the *śrauta* rituals require placing of three sticks for *yajña* (sacrifice), *yajamāna* (sacrifice), and *bhrātṛvya* (rival).[213] Many Vedic rituals contain allusions to contests, such as the *sadyaṣkrā*, involving a chariot race, by winning which, against the Āṅgirasas, the Ādityas are said to have attained heaven. Similarly, Keśin Dārbhya is said to have assumed the kingship of the Pañcālas by defeating Khaṇḍikā in a *parikrī* ritual.[214] Remnants of the real contests may be sought in a ritual dice game in the *rājasūya*, the chariot race in the *vājapeya*, and a series of martial and verbal contests in the *mahāvrata*.

Kumkum Roy has also described the *rājasūya* as a status-conferring enterprise for attaining kingship, suzerainty, and overlordship (*ādhipatya*), where the dice game was as integral a part as chariot racing was to *vājapeya*. Both the rituals possibly incorporated popular practices within new ritualized contexts.[215]

Therefore, the dice game can be—and probably should be—perceived as a part of the *rājasūya*. This may be the reason why Yudhiṣṭhira could not turn down a challenge to a friendly dice match by a kinsman, despite knowing that it would not remain a friendly one, since he was the one who had involved the entire Kuru clan in his *rājasūya*. While the partition of the kingdom was a temporary solution to the disputed succession, probably both the sides were dissatisfied with the arrangements. Yudhiṣṭhira, by organizing a *rājasūya* where other Kurus, including Duryodhana, were assigned subsidiary portfolios suiting the *ratnins*, virtually asserted his legitimacy as the sole Kuru chief, which was validated by the presence of and gift exchanges with the other contemporary kings. In that case, Duryodhana's jealousy had more serious causes than Yudhiṣṭhira's wealth. But in such a scenario, Yudhiṣṭhira would have been bound to participate in the subsequent dice game against his *bhrātṛvya* Duryodhana to complete the ritual of his legitimization.

Of course, the texts prescribe a mock contest. But in case of a seriously disputed succession, the prescription might not have been followed to the letter. In fact, the *Mahābhārata* perception of the *rājasūya* indicates that the contest was likely to be real in most cases. After all, the context of the *rājasūya* was usually a succession dispute which was to be solved for good; hence the rule that two living people from the same *kula* (clan) could not perform the *rājasūya*.[216] The *rājasūya* performer had to legitimize his kingship both internally and externally. That is why he needed the sanction of his *ratnins*, as well as the support of the other *kṣatriyas*.[217] This support had to be demonstrated at the event.[218] Probably the possibility of a real contest in most cases was the reason why it was assumed that the *rājasūya* usually triggered destruction.[219] Even the mythology around *rājasūya* was dominated by an overtone of conflict. It was believed that when Soma performed a *rājasūya*, it was followed by the battle between the Devas and Asuras, in which Skanda killed the Asura

Tāraka.[220] Varuṇa's *rājasūya* was preceded by a battle between Varuṇa and the other Devas and accompanied by a battle between the Devas and the Asuras.[221] These myths are quite interesting, given that the Devas and Asuras are not just divine and demonic archrivals, but also members of the same *kula*, having a common father while their mothers are sisters, who fight over wealth and the kingdom of heaven. Moreover, Soma—one of the two divine performers of the *rājasūya*—is also the mythological originator of the Candravaṃśa to which the Bharata-Kuru clan traced its identity.

Therefore, if the *akṣavāpa* Śakuni played the game as a real one and won the contest in Duryodhana's favour, the Pāṇḍavas—despite their allegations about betrayal and foul play—had to respect the result. That is why when Yudhiṣṭhira complained about Śakuni defeating him by *trick*, Śakuni could silence him by saying that a gamester had every right to defeat his opponents by superior skill just like a scholar had the right to win a debate with superior knowledge:

> *śrotriyo'śrotriyam uta nikṛtyaiva yudhiṣṭhira/*
> *vidvān aviduṣo'bhyeti nāhustāṃ nikṛtiṃ janāḥ//*
> *evaṃ tvaṃ mām ihābhyetva nikṛti yadi manyase/*
> *devanād vinivartasva yadi te vidyate bhayam//*
>
> (A scholar surpasses a nonscholar only through his trick, Yudhiṣṭhira, so does a wise man surpass a fool; but people don't call that a trick. You have come to me: if you think it is trickery, desist from the game if that is your fear!)[222]

That may explain why, in the great debate initiated in the hall by Draupadī, none except Vidura questioned the rationale of the game, rather than scrutinizing its technicalities. Karve criticizes Draupadi for 'arguing about legal technicalities when what was happening to her was so hideous that she should only have cried out for decency and pity in the name of Kshatriya code'.[223] Instead of suggesting what Draupadi should have done, Karve could have done better by utilizing her anthropological knowledge to understand why the call for decency and pity would not work but technical questions could.

Neither Dhṛtarāṣṭra nor Yudhiṣṭhira willingly consented to the game but seemed to have had no choice but to consent when the proposal came. Thus, Dhṛtarāṣṭra declared:

aśubhaṃ vā śubhaṃ vāpi hitaṃ vā yadi vāhitam/
pravartatāṃ suhṛd dyūtaṃ dviṣṭam etan na saṃśayaḥ//

(Holy or unholy, beneficient or maleficent, the family game of dice should proceed, for certainly it is so destined.)[224]

He tells Vidura:

neha kṣattaḥ kalahastapsyate māṃ na cehaivaṃ pratilomaṃ bhaviṣyat/
dhātrā tu diṣṭasya vaśe kiledaṃ sarvaṃ jagad veṣṭati na svatantram//

(No quarrel bothers me, steward, here
For otherwise fate would run counter to dicing.
This world submits to the Placer's design
And thus does the world run, not by itself.)[225]

Strangely, same argument comes from Yudhiṣṭhira as well:

mahābhayāḥ kitavāḥ saṃniviṣṭā māyopadhā devitāro'tra santi/
dhātrā tu diṣṭasya vaśe kiledaṃ nādevānāṃ kitavair adya tair me//

(Most dangerous gamblers have been collected,
Who are sure to play with wizard tricks.
But this world obeys the Placer's design—
I do not refuse now to play with those gamblers.)[226]

In fact, this behaviour of both Dhṛtarāṣṭra and Yudhiṣṭhira—their determination to participate in the dice game despite their prior knowledge of its evil effects, passing all responsibility to the Placer (*dhātṛ*)—baffled the scholars and the ordinary readers of the *Mahābhārata* alike. Even the various redactors of the *Mahābhārata* seem puzzled with the paradoxical behaviour of the otherwise nearly infallible Yudhiṣṭhira, who suddenly acted like an obsessive gambler, and the text itself provides at least four different and contradictory interpretations of the episode: the preordained will of the Placer (already discussed), Yudhiṣṭhira's 'duty' to play the game (II.56.16; probably referring to the *rājasūya* context of dicing), Yudhiṣṭhira's greed to win the wealth of the Kauravas (III.35.2; probably a reference to his rash decision of organizing the *rājasūya* and involving all the Kurus in it, claiming the status of the only legitimate Kuru sovereign and therefore making the dice game inevitable); and Yudhiṣṭhira's folly brought forth by his addiction to dicing (III.35.16; where Yudhiṣṭhira therefore said that Bhīma should have stopped him from committing this mistake). We cannot also rule out the possibility proposed by Buddhadeb Basu that Yudhiṣṭhira, always uncomfortable with kingship and the materialism and violence associated with it, used gambling as a way out from the mechanical affluence of palace politics to the open, liberal natural world of the forest where he would happily roam around and quench his intellectual curiosity by listening to various sages throughout the 'Āraṇyakaparvan'.[227] Yet, his particular fascination for dicing demands a closer scrutiny.

Dicing, though extremely popular from the Vedic (or perhaps pre-Vedic) times, has not been perceived very positively in ancient Indian tradition. The lure and the danger of gambling have been noticed right from the Ṛgvedic times. Thus, the *Ṛg Veda* records the laments of a poet, Kavaṣa Ailuṣa, who seems to be a compulsive gambler:

> Sprung from tall trees on windy heights, these rollers transport me as they turn upon the table.
> Dearer to me the die that never slumbers than the deep draught of Mūjavān's own Soma.
> She never vexed me nor was angry with me, but to my friends and me was ever gracious.
> For the die's sake, whose single point is final, mine own devoted wife I alienated.
> My wife holds me aloof, her mother hates me: the wretched man finds none to give me comfort.
> As of a costly horse grown old and feeble, I find not any profit of the gamester.
> Others caress the wife of him whose riches the die hath coveted, that rapid courser:

Of him speak father, mother, brothers saying, We know him not: bind him and take him with you.

When I resolve to play with these no longer, my friends depart from me and leave me lonely.

When the brown dice thrown on the board, have rattled, like a fond girl I seek the place of meeting.

The gamester seeks the gambling-house, and wonders, his body all afire, Shall I be lucky?

Still do the dice extend his eager longing, staking his gains against his adversary.

Dice, verily, are armed with goads and driving hooks, deceiving and tormenting, causing grievous woe.

They give frail gifts and then destroy the man who wins, thickly anointed with the player's fairest good.

Merrily sports their troop, the three-and-fifty, like Savitar the God whose ways are faithful.

They bend not even to the mighty's anger: the King himself pays homage and reveres them.

Downward they roll, and then spring quickly upward, and, handless, force the man with hands to serve them.

Cast on the board, like lumps of magic charcoal, though cold themselves they burn the heart to ashes.

The gambler's wife is left forlorn and wretched: the mother mourns the son who wanders homeless.

In constant fear, in debt, and seeking riches, he goes by night unto the home of others.

Sad is the gambler when he sees a matron, another's wife, and his well-ordered dwelling.

He yokes the brown steeds in the early morning, and when the fire is cold sinks down an outcast.

To the great captain of your mighty army, who hath become the host's imperial leader,

To him I show my ten extended fingers: I speak the truth. No wealth am I withholding.

Play not with dice: no, cultivate thy corn-land. Enjoy the gain, and deem that wealth sufficient.

There are thy cattle, there thy wife, O gambler. So this good Savitar himself hath told me.
Make me your friend: show us some little mercy. Assail us not with your terrific fierceness.
Appeased by your malignity and anger, and let the brown dice snare some other captive.[228]

The supposed author of the hymn 'Kavaṣa Ailuṣa' is well known in the Vedic tradition both as a great sage and as an infamous gambler. The AB narrates an episode where the other sages decided to ostracize Kavaṣa for his low birth (son of a *dāsī*) and addiction to gambling.[229] Kavaṣa's merit was established ultimately by the grace of the river goddess Sarasvatī; but the episode also indicates the sage's ill-reputation as a gambler. The quoted hymn, coming from the latest portion (Book X) of the ṚV, therefore, can be a true representation of the gambler-sage's personal experience reflecting the nature of dicing in the Later Vedic society. Here we can see dicing as a popular and attractive game which can be dangerous to the addict. The compulsive gamester loses everything, resolves not to play again, yet repeatedly succumbs to the temptation of the game. Kavaṣa's situation—wandering homeless, whose wife is wretched and fondled by others (probably being lost as a stake), but who repeatedly returns to the game—is structurally quite similar to that of Yudhiṣṭhira. After all, Yudhiṣṭhira played the game despite knowing its harmful consequences, lost everything including his self and his wife, and agreed to play again even after the disastrous first game. Not only that, despite being turned into a pauper from a mighty king and witnessing the utter humiliation of Draupadī, Yudhiṣṭhira retained his passion for dicing; and when the time came to decide his masquerade during the thirteenth year of the exile, he decided to take up the gamester's post in the court of Matsya:

When I come to King Virāṭa, the bull among men, I shall be Royal Dicing Master of the great spirited king, and pose as a brahmin by the name of Kaṅka, one who knows the dice and is an ardent gambler. I shall roll out the fascinating dice, those made of beryl and gold and ivory, the phosphorescent nuts, and the black and red dice.[230]

This aspect of Yudhiṣṭhira's character is indeed difficult to explain, especially after dicing was being perceived with a growing negativity in the Later Vedic and the post-Vedic times. Kauṭilya considers gambling as one of the four cardinal sins to be avoided by a king, and Manu recommends that a king should avoid dicing.[231] Not only that; Kauṭilya cites two *Mahābhārata* examples—of Yudhiṣṭhira and Nala—to show the vice of dicing.[232]

Nala, therefore, is an interesting point of reference to understand Yudhiṣṭhira's position as a gambler. The romance of Nala and Damayantī is one of the most well known of the *Mahābhārata* stories, worthy of a respectable place in the history of Sanskrit literature as an independent story. The story is narrated in the 'Āraṇyakaparvan' by a sage called Bṛhadaśva who also gives Yudhiṣṭhira a lesson in dicing. The 'Āraṇyakaparvan' of the *Mahābhārata* contains several such legends and stories, probably incorporated in the text during its Bhārgava refashioning. However, the Nala story might not have been a Bhārgava invention. Van Buitenen appears to have been right in assuming that it was an independent folktale incorporated within the *Mahābhārata*.[233] However, since the context of the incorporation is the issue of Yudhiṣṭhira's dicing, the story must have been refashioned in a manner that suited the contextual need.

The story is based on the theme of love between Nala, the king of Niṣadha, and Damayantī, the princess of Vidarbha. The beautiful Damayantī was sought after even by the deities who played several tricks to make her choose one of them as her husband but ultimately succumbed to the power of Damayantī's love for Nala. While the benevolent deities—Indra, Agni, Yama, and Varuṇa—were gracious in defeat, and appreciated the couple's love by bestowing on Nala many supernatural qualities, the malevolent Kali sought revenge. With the help of his ally Dvāpara, Kali planned the downfall of Nala in a game of dice where Nala, possessed by Kali, hastily staked everything he possessed against his brother Puṣkara who won every round thanks to the rigged dice possessed by Dvāpara. However, when Puṣkara goaded Nala to stake Damayantī, Nala stopped and left his kingdom, accompanied by Damayantī. Still behaving crazily due to the possession by Kali, Nala left the sleeping Damayantī in the middle of a forest, clad in half a garment whose other half he sliced off. This pathetic separation was followed by a series of adventures by both

Damayantī and Nala at the end of which both found each other, primarily due to Damayantī's prudence. By that time, Nala had freed himself from the possession of Kali and mastered the game of dice from a champion gamester, King Ṛtuparṇa of Ayodhyā. The story ended in happy reunion of the couple, after which Nala won his kingdom back by defeating Puṣkara in a decisive game of dice.[234]

The structural similarity of the Nala story with Yudhiṣṭhira's case can hardly be overlooked. Nala lost his kingdom in a game of dice—against his brother and because of an envious grudge—just like Yudhiṣṭhira. Both the heroes were exiled to the forest. Both Draupadī and Damayantī were nearly disrobed. Both the ladies saved the situation through their prudence. Nala, accompanied by the qualities of four different deities, can be taken as a counterpart of the five Pāṇḍavas together. Therefore, the incorporation of the Nala story in the *Mahābhārata* is largely a face-saving justification for the situation of Yudhiṣṭhira, the *dharmarāja* who seemed highly susceptible to one of the four cardinal sins which a king should avoid. The post-Vedic Bhārgava redactors, unable to understand Yudhiṣṭhira's insane gambling, sought parallel in a popular folktale that indicated the possibility of a happy ending in Yudhiṣṭhira's case. Kavaṣa Ailuṣa could establish himself as a great sage despite his addiction to gambling. Nala could get his kingdom back after gambling it away. Then why should Yudhiṣṭhira not be suitable to rule just for this one mistake? What he needed was to master the skill of the game he had a passion for. Therefore, Bṛhadaśva provided him the training which Ṛtuparṇa provided to Nala. As indicated earlier, it was Śakuni's superior skill in dicing that had overpowered Yudhiṣṭhira. Learning the tricks of the game properly would, therefore, bring one out of the clutches of the malevolent Dvāpara and Kali (which are not just the names of two deities personifying the two least virtuous ages within the time cycle but also the two losing scores in the game of dice).

Despite all these justifications, what the Nala story fails to explain is Yudhiṣṭhira's compulsion to play. After all, Nala played only when he was possessed by Kali and not out of his own sensible judgement. Yudhiṣṭhira, on the other hand, consciously decided to play, though he knew that the results would be disastrous. Dhṛtarāṣṭra also consented to the game even after knowing its evil effects; and both Yudhiṣṭhira and Dhṛtarāṣṭra backed their decisions with curiously similar fatalistic arguments.

Sibaji Bandyopadhyay tries to provide a psychological explanation for this, arguing that both Yudhiṣṭhira and Dhṛtarāṣrra represent a special case of obsessive compulsive disorder, which he called the '*Yudhiṣthira*-complex'. Bandyopadhyay explains *Yudhiṣṭhira*-complex as a simultaneous adherence to 'deterministic chaos' and 'deterministic order', a combination of *precipitous* afforded by retrospective and *sagacity* buttressed by the prospective, a combination which gambling provides. Thus, a compulsive insatiate gambler, fitting this model, is psychologically programmed to court 'determinism' and predisposed to capitulate without bothering about its upshot *and* seek solace for his capitulation by passing on the responsibility to 'Destiny'.[235]

Dicing, indeed, is often used in ancient Indian tradition as a metaphor for deterministic chaos rather than pure chance. That is why the cosmic series of creation and destruction is often represented as a series of dice games between Śiva and the Devī.[236] The connection between deterministic chaos and dicing is perhaps testified best by the naming of the four ages of the time cycle as *kṛta*, *tretā*, *dvāpara*, and *kali*, the four possible scores in the traditional game of dice. Yet, Bandyopadhyay's argument seems a bit overstretched. It is difficult to assume from a study of the *Mahābhārata* that Dhṛtarāṣṭra and Yudhiṣṭhira represent the same psychological condition. Whereas Yudhiṣṭhira's motive for playing the game of dice is confusing (which led to so many different interpretations), Dhṛtarāṣṭra's indulgence of Duryodhana's wish is quite clear. Except in this case, where there was a clear assurance of winning the Pāṇḍava kingdom for Duryodhana, Dhṛtarāṣṭra hardly does anything that would qualify him as a compulsive gambler. Even in Yudhiṣṭhira's case, though his passion for gambling is well documented, assuming an obsessive compulsive disorder is hardly tenable. After all, Yudhiṣṭhira—after these two disastrous games of dice—never returned to play dice, unlike the Ṛgvedic Kavaṣa Ailuṣa. His assumption of the position of a gamester in the Matsya court might have been an indulgence to his passion but hardly had any serious consequence. Moreover, before he assumed that position, he had protected himself from a further disaster in dicing by acquiring the tricks of the game from Bṛhadaśva. The fatalistic sentiment and words shared by Yudhiṣṭhira and Dhṛtarāṣṭra therefore seem to be not a result of the same psychological condition but the same unpleasant context. The context, most plausibly, would be Yudhiṣṭhira's *rājasūya* which rendered him unable to refuse a challenge to a dice game from the other contender Duryodhana. Entangled by his own decision to transgress the earlier partition of the kingdom by holding a *rājasūya* where Duryodhana was assigned a subordinate position (as the receiver of gifts, which was virtually the role of *saṃgrahitṛ*, a *ratnin*), Yudhiṣṭhira had to accept the challenge and Dhṛtarāṣṭra had to sanction the game. Therefore, Yudhiṣṭhira was as much helpless as the possessed Nala to play the game. However, what Yudhiṣṭhira was not compelled to do was to stake Draupadī, and that was what differentiated him from Nala. Even under the possession of Kali, Nala refused to stake Damayantī, whereas Yudhiṣṭhira agreed to play Draupadī as his final bet. Thus, more than the game, it is this final bet that makes the episode very intriguing.

Possibly a ritual obligation in a clan-based polity was what made the dice game so providential. That can also justify the role played by the *sabhā*, as an assembly of kinsmen, during the dice game. Thapar assumes that the association of the *sabhā* with gambling may have had antecedents in the division of grazing lands and arable lands by lot. The *sabhā* not only witnessed the dice match but also seriously debated and discussed the question raised by Draupadī.[237] Therefore, when Draupadī argued her case, she knew that her best chance lay in technically proving that she was not won. Whether a man who had lost his own self still retained his rights over his wife was a question subtle enough to unsettle Bhīṣma who by-passed it to Yudhiṣṭhira. Bhīma, who angrily admonished Yudhiṣṭhira for staking his wife, also admitted that Yudhiṣṭhira did not play for his own cause. Arjuna supported Yudhiṣṭhira by saying:

> *na sakāmāḥ pare kāryā dharmam evācarottamam/*
> *bhrātaraṃ dhārmikaṃ jyeṣṭhaṃ nātikramitum arhati//*
> *āhūto hi parai rājā kṣātradharmam anusmaran/*
> *dīpyate parakāmena tatra kīrtikaraṃ mahat//*
>
> (The king was challenged by his foes, and, remembering the *kṣātradharma*, he played at the enemy's wish. That is our great glory.)[238]

When Vikarṇa, a younger brother of Duryodhana, raised his voice in Draupadī's support, he also banked on technical specificities:

tad ayaṃ pāṇḍuputreṇa vyasane vartatā bhṛśam/
samāhūtena kitavair āsthito draupadīpaṇaḥ//
sādhāraṇī ca sarveṣāṃ pāṇḍavānām aninditā/
jitena pūrva cānena pāṇḍavena kṛtaḥ paṇaḥ//
iyaṃ ca kīrtitā kṛṣṇā saubalena paṇārthinā/
etat sarvaṃ vicāryāhaṃ manye na vijitām imām//

(The Pāṇḍava was under the sway of his vice when the gamblers challenged him and he staked Draupadī. The innocent woman is held in common by all the Pāṇḍavas, and the Pāṇḍava staked her when he already had gambled away his own freedom. It was Saubala who mentioned Kṛṣṇā when he wanted a stake. Considering all this I do not think she has been won.)[239]

When Karṇa refuted this argument he, on the other hand, stressed on the fact that Yudhiṣṭhira had staked everything he owned, which also included Draupadī. Moreover, when Draupadī was staked, all of her other husbands gave silent consent.[240] That is why Shalini Shah observes that Vikarṇa's defence of Draupadī was not a defence but a debate with Karṇa about technicalities. His arguments did not contradict that the wife was the husband's property.[241]

Sharma, in his *Perspectives in Social and Economic History of Early India*, points out that women are often treated as property in the epic Purāṇic literature. Women and property are often referred to jointly, and the necessity to protect both is emphasized. It is declared that the vice of anarchy is that property cannot be retained and the wife is not under control (*Rāmāyaṇa* II.67.11). In fact, kingship emerged to ensure the security of property and women, while the first king accepted this duty in return for a share of the property and women of his subjects (*Mahābhārata* XII.68.15–24).

Women are not only conceived as desirable possession bestowed by the wish-fulfilling tree (*Harivaṃśa* I.86.56) but they are often bracketed with animal wealth, probably being considered movable property. Like any property, they could be sold, mortgaged, or given away. According to the *Garuḍa Purāna* 109.1, a man should defend himself at the cost of his wealth and wife. Having a similar idea, King Hariścandra gives away his wife to appease Viśvāmitra, in the *Mārkaṇḍeya Purāṇa* (VII.24). The *Agni*

Purāṇa (253.63.4) also mentions an interest rate of one-seventieth of the original value for the pledged women and animal.[242]

If that was the scenario, then there would be no room for debate regarding Yudhiṣṭhira's authority in staking Draupadī. However, Sharma notes that the picture is different in the Vedic texts where women are not necessarily treated as property. The tendency becomes stronger from the Gupta period and thus is reflected mainly in the Purāṇas and a very late book—the 'Śāntiparvan'—of the *Mahābhārata*. The *rājasūya* and the dice game, referring to a much earlier context, therefore represented a social condition where the women's status as property was not taken for granted and could generate a heated debate. More importantly, the debate ended in the favour of the woman's claim to freedom.

Vijay Nath has different views regarding women's status as property. She notices an apparent dichotomy between women's social status and economic competence. In the Ṛgvedic age, women enjoyed a relatively good social status, including post-puberty marriage, freedom to choose consorts, possibility of remarriage, access to Vedic education, and right to participate in the Vedic rites, chariot races, the deliberations of the *sabhā*, and even tribal warfare. In the Later Vedic texts, preference for the male child is visible, and women's participation in the *sabhā* stops. Still, women's access to the *upanayana*, Vedic education, and religious rites continued till the time of the *Dharmasūtras*. Even the *Atharva Veda* permitted widow remarriage, though the preferred candidate now was the husband's brother. Nath connects this relatively good social status of women with women's productive role in a tribal order. Women also acted as weavers, embroiderers, dyers, bamboo splitters, and corn grinders.

However, right from the NBPW period (*c*. 600 BCE onwards), intensive field agriculture started, with the help of slave and hired labour. The need to associate women with economic production was thus reduced. Craft specialization also separated the home and the workplace. The role of the family as a social unit became immensely important to maintain the patrilineal inheritance of landed property. Therefore, there was a greater restriction on the social and sexual freedom of the women. Early marriage, before puberty, was advocated by the *Dharmasūtras*. Girls thus were now seen as liabilities to be married off as soon as possible. Early marriage reduced the scope of education for women. They had to be kept under constant control of the male members of the family, such as the father, husband, or son. Widow remarriage was also discouraged. However, most of these restrictions pertained to the upper class women and mainly to the rural agriculture-oriented social milieu. The lower class women and the women in the urban commerce-oriented social milieu, represented more in the Pali texts, could still live as weavers, dyers, basket makers, flower sellers, nuns, and courtesans.

However, women's economic condition apparently contradicted their social status. In the patriarchal tribal tradition of the Vedic Age, women were considered property. The Vedic literature, the narrative sections of the *Mahābhārata*, and the Pali texts have instances where women could be kept as pledge in dicing or given away. There was also the concept of *kṣetraja putra*, where a woman was clearly seen as her husband's field where, even if the seed was sown by another man, the resultant fruit must belong to the owner.

In the stratified class society based on individual households, on the other hand, the importance of the individual family members increased. The need to preserve patrilineal ownership of land created an intense concern about the chastity of the women and their fidelity to their husbands. Therefore, lawgivers such as Āpastamba, Manu, and Yājñavalkya declared that family members could not be gifted, sold, or pledged. Manu clearly differentiates the wife, obtained from God, from cattle or gold, obtainable in the market. The Pali texts show that the urban milieu offered women immense scope of earning their own livelihood and courtesans like Āmbapālī or Sāmā possessed huge amounts of private property. Thus, the Brahmanical lawgivers also gave women a right to own some non-landed movable property as *strīdhana*. As the state was emerging as a powerful element, and as there was the threat of the family lands of an heirless man being escheated by the state, lawgivers like Yājñavalkya and Bṛhaspati allowed the widows and daughters of a sonless man some right to inherit landed property as well. However, this right was never full property right, including the authority to sell or mortgage land, but only a custodial right for the protection of family land.[243]

In his article, Nath does not give much importance to the Purāṇic texts where women are frequently seen as chattel. However, as we are concerned more with the earlier period, the important point noted by Nath is the contradiction between women's freedom and their social status in the Vedic period. Whereas women had a considerable amount of social, educational, religious, and sexual freedom, at large she was a property in a patriarchal tribal order. However, still it was the tribal patriarch, rather than the husband, who had the ultimate authority over her. The system of begetting *kṣetraja putra* is quite common in the narrative section of the *Mahābhārata.* The sexual freedom of the woman involved varied from case to case, as we have seen in the first section of this chapter. Thus, in the case of Ambikā and Ambālikā, the sexual partner was chosen by the elders and enforced upon them, whereas Kuntī and Madrī exercised a greater freedom in choosing partners. When the Ṛgvedic tribal order was gradually breaking up towards more complex social institutions, these ideas were also being questioned and contested. Therefore, Draupadī's case created a huge debate in the clan assembly (*sabhā*) where women were no longer members but still had the right to raise a question. Though the final decision went in favour of Draupadī, the case was not simply a rejection of the husband's ownership over the wife. Rather, various factors—such as the right of a person to stake something after losing his own self, the psychological condition of Yudhiṣṭhira while staking, and the joint ownership of the five Pāṇḍavas over Draupadī—were also pointed out. It was Bhīma who criticized the staking of a woman as a property. But his criticism was more on moral grounds than on legal technicality. His outbursts could generate nothing more than a fear factor and sentimental appeal in the *sabhā* which had to judge the matter on the basis of legal technicalities following the ritual norms of the *rājasūya.*

Thus, even Duryodhana showed his respect for ritual correctness by declaring that Draupadī would be freed if Yudhiṣṭhira declared he did not own her, or if one of the other Pāṇḍavas challenged his ownership over them. Indeed, Draupadī was freed just after Arjuna questioned Yudhiṣṭhira's ownership:

īśo rājā pūrvam āsīd gṛhe na/
kuntīputro dharmarājo mahātmā//
īśastv ayaṃ kasya parājitātmā/
tajjānīdhvaṃ kuravaḥ sarva eva//

(The king was our master when first he played us,
Great-spirited Dharma, the son of Kuntī:
But whose master is he who has lost himself?
That you should decide, ye Kurus assembled.)[244]

Reflecting on this decisive intervention of Arjuna, M.A. Mehendale comments that Arjuna had (befitting his fame as an archer) 'hit the bull's eye'.[245]

Therefore, the point initially raised by Draupadī, whether a man who lost himself could stake her, contributed—alongside Bhīma's threats—to her freedom, which brought freedom for her husbands as well, and the verdict of the clan patriarch Dhṛtarāṣṭra was accepted as the final word on the matter. Not without reason did Karṇa comment that Draupadī had been the salvation of the Pāṇḍavas and brought their boat to the shore.[246] Kṛṣṇa echoed the sentiment in saying that Kṛṣṇā (Draupadī) lifted up both the Pāṇḍavas and herself like a ship from a swell in the ocean.[247] These may answer Karve's question why Draupadī acted like a 'lady pundit'.

The question raised by Draupadī, therefore, was a very personal and contextual one. Though Alf Hiltebeitel thinks that she acted as an 'ambivalent feminist' filing a 'class action suit' on behalf of the daughters and daughters-in-law,[248] what made Draupadī's question potent seems to be the way it addressed the technical specificities involved in the post-*rājasūya* dice game. Uma Chakravarti shows that Draupadī spoke only for herself, raising the question if a queen could be reduced to slavery after the king had become a slave and his mastery over her as king/husband had ceased, or if she was enslaved/reduced to servitude with him.[249] Though the attempt to strip Draupadī of her upper garment and her sexual humiliations, including the pulling of her hair and Duryodhana's display of his left thigh (which was considered a phallic symbol), were part and parcel of the usual denial of honour, virtue, and modesty to the slaves, Draupadī failed to address the issue of either the women or the slaves in general.[250] However, again a contextual explanation of the episode would reveal why a technical question about ritual specificity would be appreciated much more in a Later Vedic clan *sabhā* witnessing a post-*rājasūya* dicing contest than a discourse on human rights or a feminist manifesto against the humiliation of women. Draupadī would perform her duty in the latter role as well, again contextually, in the 'Virāṭaparvan', when she would be disguised as a servant woman and would resist the sexual advances of the powerful royal kinsman Kīcaka, showing a clear conviction that even a servile woman should not be molested at will.

However, the technical problem raised by Draupadī disqualified only the last stake, not the entire match. Thus, a rematch—with a clear stake of thirteen years of exile—was necessary to complete the ritual. Therefore, Yudhiṣṭhira returned to play again, when Dhṛtarāṣṭra called him back, voicing the same argument:

> *dhātur niyogād bhūtani prāpnuvanti śubhāśubham/*
> *na nivṛttis tayor asti devitavyaṃ punar yadi//*
> *akṣadyūte samāhvānaṃ niyogāt sthavirasya ca/*
> *jānann api kṣayakaraṃ nātikramitum utsahe//*
>
> (It is at the disposal of the Placer that creatures find good or ill. There is no averting of either. If we must play again, although I know that the challenge to the dicing at the old man's behest will bring ruin, I cannot disobey his word.)[251]

The argument thus gets back to the square one. Draupadī's question might have nullified her slavery alongside that of the Pāṇḍavas. However, Yudhiṣṭhira, by organizing a *rājasūya* which was a claim to establish himself as the only legitimate ruler in the context of a disputed Later Vedic Kuru succession, had been entangled in a vicious ritual obligation to prove his mettle in a dice game against his *bhrātṛvya* (rival/cousin) Duryodhana. As the *akṣavāpa* Śakuni clearly favoured Duryodhana, and Yudhiṣṭhira lacked the skill necessary to defeat him, he knew that the game could only bring further misery. Yet, Yudhiṣṭhira had no choice, not because he was a 'compulsive gambler', not even because it had been preordained by the Placer (the view Yudhiṣṭhira himself preferred to chose), but because of the ritual consequences of a *rājasūya* in the Later Vedic Kuru polity, which he could not avert even if he disliked or dreaded that.

3.4 When the *Bhūpati* Sought the *Gopati*'s Wealth: Locating the *Mahābhārata* Economy

As we have seen in the previous section, the *rājasūya* of Yudhiṣṭhira and the subsequent dice games, which constitute the core of the 'Sabhāparvan', were probably interrelated events and should be understood in the context of the Later Vedic polity of the Kuru clan. However, the present text of the *Mahābhārata* becomes more multilayered after the Pāṇḍavas are exiled to the forest for twelve years followed by a year of disguised disappearance. The Pāṇḍava exile provided the later redactors a useful opening to interpolate didactic sections within the narrative. While the Pāṇḍavas spend their time listening to these numerous legends from different sages, we may analyse the economic data in the narrative sections of the *Mahābhārata*.

We have already discussed how the *rājasūya* and the dice game represent a Later Vedic context. The wealth, as indicated by the gifts delivered in Yudhiṣṭhira's *rājasūya* and the stakes made in the dice game, consisted mainly of gold, gems, animals, slaves, and textiles, indicating a society where animal wealth and raw materials were more important than landed wealth, grain, and finished products. It was an economy where gold, animals, and slaves were the most prized possessions. A similar picture arises from the list of Draupadī's marital gifts which included chariots, horses, elephants, young slave women, and ornamented clothes.[252] The importance of animals as a major form of wealth can actually be extremely significant in contextualizing various episodes from the narrative section of the *Mahābhārata*.

Animals, especially cattle, were the chief forms of wealth in the Ṛgvedic age. A wealthy person was called *gomat*. Prayers were made for increase of cattle. The sacrificial priest was rewarded with cattle. Cattle raid was often the cause of intertribal war or *gaviṣṭi*. The tribal chief was primarily a *gopati* or *gojit*, protector and winner of cattle. Settled agrarian life and the idea of territorial kingship expanded in the subsequent period. R.S. Sharma shows how the *gopati* was turning into a *bhūpati* claiming overlordship over a demarcated territory and collecting a share of the produce of the land as tax.[253] Still, for a considerable period of time, cattle retained immense economic importance.

Ranabir Chakravarti, in his book *Warfare for Wealth*, points out the association of cattle lifting with the Vedic milieu. He notes that cattle constituted the chief form of wealth and cattle raid was the commonest form of warfare in the tribal politics of the Ṛgvedic age. However, he also accepts that agriculture facilitated by irrigation was not unimportant, and the most famous Ṛgvedic battle, the Battle of Ten Kings, was possibly fought for control over certain rivers. Still, instances of battles, both offensive and defensive, for cattle are too frequent to doubt the importance of cattle. Moreover, the terms for a rich person (*gomat*), battle (*gaviṣṭi*), and a chief (*gopati*) indicate the predominance of cattle as a component of wealth and object of warfare.

The Later Vedic Age definitely witnessed a transformation in this scenario. Sedentary cultivation replaced pastoralism as the most important economic activity. Territorial kingship emerged. However, that does not mean that the importance of cattle disappeared. Therefore, in the *Atharva Veda*, a king desires villages as well as horses and cattle. In the *vājapeya* sacrifice described in the ŚB, the king prayed for acquisition of cattle wealth. Thus, the propensity to lift cattle stayed throughout the Vedic period, though the importance of cattle reduced a little in the later part of it.[254]

In fact, one of the major reasons for the economic importance of cattle till the very end of the Vedic period was probably its role as a medium of exchange. There is no definite evidence of the regular production and circulation of metal currency before *c.* sixth century BCE when the silver and copper punch-marked coins appeared. Cattle probably remained one of the chief mediums of exchange, and a prized possession, till the time of the early Upaniṣads at the end of the Vedic period. Therefore, the BU records the great sacrifice organized by Janaka, the philosopher king of Videha, who decided to reward the most learned *brāhmaṇa* with a thousand cows each having ten pieces of gold tied to their horns.[255] When Yājñavalkya, the ultimate champion in the competition, impressed Janaka with his philosophical mastery, Janaka exclaimed: 'I'll give you a thousand cows together with bulls and elephants!'[256] Similarly, the KU begins with a sacrifice held by Uśan, son of Vājaśravas, where the chief wealth distributed was cattle. Naciketas, the son of the sacrificer, was concerned about the issue that his father, who had vowed to give away all his possessions, was actually gifting sick and barren cows:

> They have drunk all their water, eaten all their fodder,
> They have been milked dry, they are totally barren—
> "Joyless" are those worlds called, to which a man goes, who gives them as gifts.[257]

If this was the situation even during the period of the early Upaniṣads, the importance of cattle as wealth can easily be assumed in the early part of Later Vedic period, even though settled agricultural life was becoming the norm. Thus, the *Atharva Veda* contains numerous charms and benedictions to protect cattle. The following charm is an example:

> First, O Arundhatī, protect our oxen and milky kine:
> Protect each one that is infirm, each quadruped that yields no milk.
> Let the Plant give us sheltering aid, Arundhatī allied with Gods;
> Avert Consumption from our men and make our cow-pen rich in milk.
> I welcome the auspicious Plant, life-giving, wearing every hue.
> Far from our cattle may it turn the deadly dart that Rudra casts.[258]

With this background in mind, two *Mahābhārata* episodes related to cattle can provide us interesting insight into the economic context. The first is the *ghoṣayātrā* in the Āraṇyakaparvan. Here the Kaurava princes themselves went to inspect cattle and brand the calves, leading to a temporary cattle fair in Dvaitavana, distribution of presents and gifts to the cattle herders, and a probable cattle raid by the Gandharvas. As the raid was on the wealth of the Kurus, the Pāṇḍavas—who were in exile—came to the aid of Duryodhana, despite the fact that Duryodhana's motive was to humiliate them. Clearly, in this case clan honour became more important than personal issues.

The intention of the episode, of course, was not to highlight the importance of cattle as a form of wealth but the Kaurava family feud. It began with Karṇa urging Duryodhana to undertake a journey to Dvaitavana where the exiled Pāṇḍavas were living, assuming that a full-scale display of Duryodhana's wealth would add to the humiliation of the Pāṇḍavas. But a cattle expedition was used as the pretext, when a cowherd named Samaṅga—already manipulated by Duryodhana—informed Dhṛtarāṣṭra about the necessity of the inspection. The purpose cited was primarily the counting of the cattle and branding of the calves, while hunting was mentioned as an added incentive. The Kaurava party went in full grandeur, with chariots and elephants, infantry and cavalry, traders and bards, wives and prostitutes.[259] Duryodhana camped in the cowherd station, inspected the cattle, marked them with signs and figures, branded the calves, and had the number of cows tallied with the number of young calves. He also enjoyed his stay at the cowherd camp with much singing, dancing, hunting, and frivolity.[260] Subsequently, the narrative moves into Duryodhana's conflict with the Gandharvas and his ultimate rescue by the Pāṇḍavas.[261] However, the episode also signifies that the Kurus, though ruling over an agrarian kingdom, still had some interest in cattle wealth. The cowherd camp of Dvaitavana was located inside a forest in the fringe of the Kuru realm. Yet, the king tried to exert some control over the herds, through periodical inspection, counting, and branding. If the Gandharvas were some local forest tribes with whom the Kurus got entangled in a skirmish, the role of the Pāṇḍavas becomes clearer. Despite their enmity with Duryodhana and his party, the Pāṇḍavas had a huge stake in protecting the clan honour of the Kurus (since they claimed to be a part of the clan) and the cattle wealth of the Kuru king (which was a part of the resources of the kingdom they were competing for).

The Kuru king's interest in the cattle wealth of the cowherds living in the fringe of his kingdom,[262] however, does not help us much in contextualizing the episode. Kings have shown passing interest in cattle wealth not only in the Vedic period but also later. Thus, *vraja* (pasture) is considered one of the seven sources of revenue in Kauṭīlya's *Arthaśāstra*. The Mauryan emperor Aśoka appointed *vacabhūmika mahāmātras* definitely to exert some control on the herdsmen. However, though the king's interest and claim over cattle wealth continued, his active role as a cattle lifter and cattle raider did not continue after the Vedic period. In this context, the cattle lifting in the 'Virāṭaparvan' becomes even more interesting.

After the twelve years of exile, the Pāṇḍavas spent their last year of disguise in the Matsya realm. There, Bhīma killed Kīcaka, the brother-in-law of King Virāṭa and the mainstay of the Matsya army, who had assaulted Draupadī. The death of Kīcaka triggered a series of incidents, including the Kurus and Trigartas considering it a great opportunity to lift the immense cattle wealth of the king of Matsya. There followed two successive cattle raids on Matsya. While the disguised Yudhiṣṭhira, Bhīma, Nakula, and Sahadeva helped Virāṭa in repelling the invasion by the Trigarta king Suśarman, Arjuna came to the rescue of the cattle when the Kurus led the second raid.[263]

In this episode, the proposal of the cattle raid came from Suśarman, the king of Trigarta. But Duryodhana readily agreed, particularly being interested in the cattle:

> *te yātvā sahasā tatra virāṭanagaraṃ prati/*
> *kṣipraṃ gopān samāsādya gṛhṇantu vipulaṃ dhanam//*
> *gavāṃ śatasahasrāṇi śrīmanti guṇavanti ca/*
> *vayam api nigṛhṇīmo dvidhā kṛtvā varuthinīm//*
>
> (Arriving suddenly at Virāṭa's city we should immediately subdue the cowherds and take their ample wealth. We shall divide our army into two and rob his hundreds of thousands of glossy-coated and excellent cattle.)[264]

The immediate acceptance of the proposal by the Kurus, followed by a full-scale raid where great heroes such as Bhīṣma and Droṇa participated, indicates that cattle lifting was far from being considered unworthy of a king or a hero. Treating the 'Virāṭaparvan' as a late book, as van Buitenen does,[265] without considering its economic context, can therefore be misleading.

The Kuru kingdom—in the fertile Gaṅgā-Yamunā Doab—was primarily an agrarian kingdom. Thus, cattle wealth, despite its importance, was kept in the marginal region of Dvaitavana where the cowherds lived in relative freedom except for some occasional inspection. The picture was different in the Matsya kingdom in the arid region of Rajasthan, a place where pastoralism has always been more important than agriculture. The cattle wealth of King Virāṭa was a reason of envy for other rulers, and the wealth was safe only because of the might of the Matsya commander Kīcaka. As van Buitenen observes, Virāṭa was a 'cattle baron'.[266] Therefore, his cowherds lived very much within the kingdom of Matsya, and a raid on his cattle had to be an invasion of the kingdom itself. The rudimentary government of Virāṭa included a post of supervisor of his herdsmen and cattle, the post which Sahadeva was holding in disguise.[267] Kīcaka's death generated enthusiasm among other kings, and the Kurus made a combined plan with Suśarman to rob the cattle. The might of the disguised Pāṇḍavas, particularly Arjuna, saved the cattle. But the fact that even the Kurus of the *Mahābhārata* represented a polity where the king, despite assuming settled territorial rulership, still did not shed off the status of a Vedic *gojit* becomes clear from the incident. This aspect becomes even clearer from the praise of Yudhiṣṭhira as a ruler by Droṇa, coming from the same book, where the markers of the Kuru kingdom's prosperity seem to be agrarian wealth combined with cattle wealth. Droṇa says:

> *sadā ca tatra parjanyaḥ samyag varṣīṃ na saṃśayaḥ/*
> *sampannasasyā ca mahī nirītīkā bhaviṣyati//*
> *rasavanti ca dhānyāni guṇavanti phalāni ca/*
> *gandhavanti ca mālyāni śubhaśabdā ca bhāratī//*
> *vāyuś ca sukhasaṃsparśo niṣpratīpaṃ ca darśanam/*
> *bhayaṃ nābhyābiśet tatra yatra rājā yudhiṣṭhiraḥ//*
> *gāvaś ca bahulas tatra na kṛśā na ca durduhāḥ/*
> *payāṃsi dadhisarpīṣi rasavanti hitāni ca//*
>
> (There, no doubt, God Parjanya will rain in the proper season, and the earth will bear rich crops and be free from plagues. The rice will be fine, the fruit juicy, the garlands fragrant, speech gentle, the wind pleasant to feel, visits agreeable, and no fear will enter where King Yudhiṣṭhira lives. Cows will be teeming, none of them lean or poor milk-givers; the milk, curds and butter will be tasty and wholesome.)[268]

That the economic context of the earliest strata of the narrative section of the *Mahābhārata*, including the 'Virāṭaparvan', represents the Later Vedic Kuru polity becomes apparent if we compare this passage with a similar passage from a Later Vedic text. The praise of the Kuru king Parikṣit, who was the immediate successor of Yudhiṣṭhira in the *Mahābhārata*, in the *Atharva Veda* echoes the economic aspirations reflected in the praise of Yudhiṣṭhira mentioned earlier, the aspirations of a kingdom rich in crops but also full of milk, butter, and curds, a kingdom where both land and cattle were protected, in other words, a kingdom where the king was a well-settled *bhūpati* retaining the traces of a potent *gopati* as well:

> 'Mounting his throne, Parikshit, best of all, hath given us peace and rest'
> Saith a Kauravya to his wife as he is ordering his house.

'Which shall I set before thee, curds, gruel or milk, or barley-brew?'
Thus the wife asks her husband in the realm which King Parikshit rules.
Up as it were to heavenly lights springs the ripe corn above the cleft.
Happily thrive the people in land where King Parikshit reigns.
Indra hath waked the bard and said, Rise, wander singing here and there.
Praise me, the strong: each pious man will give thee riches in return,
Here, cows! Increase and multiply, here ye, O horses, here, O men.
Here, with a thousand rich rewards, doth Pushan also set himself.
O Indra, let these cows be safe, their master free from injury.
Let not the hostile-hearted or the robber have control of them.[269]

Therefore, we can safely assume the location of Duryodhana and Yudhiṣṭhira in the narrative section of the *Mahābhārata* as Later Vedic clan chiefs, who ruled over an agricultural kingdom but had to protect/lift cattle as well, just like their successor Parikṣit in the *Atharva Veda*, and not full-fledged monarchs of a state society.

3.5 Cousins, Clans, and Kingdoms: Studying the Kurukṣetra War

After locating the substantial portion of the central narrative of the *Mahābhārata*—including the birth and marriage legends, the partition of the kingdom, the burning of the Khāṇḍava forest, establishment of Indraprastha, Yudhiṣṭhira's *rājasūya*, the dice games, and the cattle raids—in their original Later Vedic context, we shall now look at the great Bhārata War. As the culminating event of the narrative, it must have been there from the earliest telling. However, the present text represents it as not just a war among the Bhāratas (the descendents of Bharata, i.e., the Kurus and the Pañcālas, or the Kauravas and the Pāṇḍavas) but a war involving the entire area called 'Bhāratavarṣa'. Troops from all over the subcontinent are shown as participants in either side. Taking the list of participants seriously, F.E. Pargiter tried to understand the formation of the two sides and the diplomatic reasons for the alliances.[270] Nrisinha Prasad Bhaduri conceives a battle between the dominant regions of Northern and Western India against the subdued regions of the South and the East.[271] However, there can hardly be any doubt that the list became longer over the years, as every new Brahmanized region wanted to see that their rulers played a part in the most famous event of India's traditional history.

R.S. Sharma has pointed out that the kingship depicted in the narrative section of the *Mahābhārata* was primarily a tribal chiefship. The king was a clan chief, *viśaṃpati*, or *janeśvara*. His chief advisors were his kinsmen and friends.[272] For example, Dhṛtarāṣṭra was advised mainly by his brother Vidura and uncle Bhīṣma. Yudhiṣṭhira's chief advisors were his brothers and his friend, Kṛṣṇa, who was also a relative from his mother's side. Duryodhana's principal counsellors were his maternal uncle Śakuni, brother Duḥśāsana, and friend Karṇa. However, the *brāhmaṇa* teachers and priests—like Droṇa, Kṛpa, Dhaumya, and the priest of Drupada—were patronized and accepted as important counsellors by the rulers. Otherwise, the royal administrative apparatus was quite rudimentary and primarily formed by kinsmen except for some *sūtas* such as Adhiratha and Saṃjaya. So informal and rudimentary was the administrative machinery that a *brāhmaṇa*, whose property was stolen, could immediately reach Arjuna personally and compel him to find it out, despite the fact that Arjuna had to risk an exile in order to accomplish the task.[273]

McGrath's discussion on the nature of kingship in the *Mahābhārata* brings out the nature of the polity depicted in the epic in vivid details. He shows how the narrative section of the *Mahābhārata* depicts a clan polity with 'corporate kingship' in which the institution of the clan (*kula/saṃgha*) assumed far greater importance than the office of the king. Power was shared by the king with his kinsmen, often leading to a situation in which more than one person could be addressed as the king. The kingdom of Yudhiṣṭhira, for instance, was a 'brotherly chiefdom'.[274] Even on the verge of his victory in the Bhārata War, therefore, Yudhiṣṭhira declared to Kṛṣṇa that he had become the king of the Earth along with his brothers (*adya rājāsmi govinda pṛthivyāṃ bhrātṛbhiḥ saha*).[275] In fact, when Yudhiṣṭhira became the king, he did not have much of a paid apparatus of government servants but had appointed Bhīma as the crown prince, Vidura as the counselor, Nakula as the controller of the forces, Arjuna as the commander-in-chief, and Sahadeva as his personal guard. The only non-kin office-bearers were the *sūta* Saṃjaya, the *brāhmaṇa* priest Dhaumya, and the *guru* Kṛpa.[276] Moreover, despite being the father of Yudhiṣṭhira's rival, Dhṛtarāṣṭra retained a position of authority as the head of the clan. Thus, Yudhiṣṭira had described him as a father-figure worthy of respect like a god (*pitā no daivataṃ param*) and considered it his duty to serve him.[277] The Pāṇḍavas consulted that 'king' (Dhṛtarāṣṭra) for all tasks.[278] One may rightly read these as instances of the magnaminity of Yudhiṣṭhira. However, sharing of the royal power was not unique to him in the text. Before Yudhiṣṭhira regained his kingdom, both Dhṛtarāṣṭra and Duryodhana have been called kings throughout the text, with no clarity over who actually held the office. Similarly, when Yudhiṣṭhira finally renounced the kingdom, he anointed Parikṣit the king but also bestowed the kingdom on Yuyutsu. Throughout the main narrative, the clan becomes the centre of political identity. When Duryodhana was captured during the cattle inspection in the 'Āraṇyakaparvan', Yudhiṣṭhira rescued him because kinship was crucial to him.[279] He shows the same sentiment when Bhīma kicks the dying Duryodhana, because, even if defeated, a king, a kinsman, must not be insulted.[280] In fact, the laws of kinship were respected by both the parties. We have seen earlier that kinship laws were crucial in Yudhiṣṭhira's *rājasūya*, since Duryodhana's participation in it as a *ratnin* assured Yudhiṣṭira's position as the sole legitimate king of the clan. On the other hand, the same rules ensured that Yudhiṣṭhira could not refuse the invitation to a dice game following the *rājasūya*, when invited by a kinsman. However, despite winning the kingdom, Duryodhana was not permitted to perform the *rājasūya* as long as Yudhiṣṭhira, a performer of the sacrifice from the same clan, lived.[281] He performed a different sacrifice, named *vaiṣṇava yajña*, instead.[282] Yudhiṣṭhira prudently refused the invitation to participate in this sacrifice,[283] which ensured that nominally he did not become a subordinate of Duryodhana but remained the sole successful *rājasūya* performer of the clan (even if he lost his kingdom because of the ritual obligations of the same sacrifice).

McGrath also notices that, in the clan polity of the *Mahābhārata*, it was not only the members of the royal family but also the common members of the clan who had a significant part. Therefore, the kings in the *Mahābhārata* narrative had to respect popular opinion. Yayāti was questioned by the people about his decision to ignore Yadu and choose Pūru as his successor.[284] He could anoint Pūru only after satisfying the urban and the countryfolk (*paurajānapadais tuṣṭaiḥ*).[285] Duḥṣanta, despite recognizing Śakuntalā as the woman he had secretly married, rejected her initially, fearing the suspicion of the people.[286] The subjects could request Bhīṣma to become the king when faced with a crisis of succession.[287] Similarly, both Pāṇḍu and Dhṛtarāṣṭra could become kings as they were accepted by the people.[288] The citizens (*paurāḥ*), angry with Dhṛtarāṣṭra's treatment of the Pāṇḍavas, could become dissident and wanted to anoint Yudhiṣṭhira.[289] When the Pāṇḍavas were exiled, they censured Duryodhana as a 'bad king' and wanted to follow Yudhiṣṭhira.[290] However, after Duryodhana ruled successfully and performed the *vaiṣṇava* sacrifice, the people had also praised him as a great king.[291] When Dhṛtarāṣṭra decided to retire from active life and to become a forest hermit, he had to ask the people to dismiss him.[292] The Pāṇḍavas had to do the same when they decided to renounce the world.[293] Janamejaya was pronounced king by the assembled urbanfolk (*sametya sarve puravāsino janāḥ*).[294] McGrath thinks that the familiarity of kingship, its immediacy of clan orientation, and its reliance on the informal institution of a *saṃgha* are phenomena specific to premonetary and pre-urban society.[295] It was a clan system where the king was still more of an oligarchic chief.[296] Thus, McGrath sums up:

> There is no solitary autocratic ruler, and what exists in this poetry is the rule of a clan where a fraternity—and a powerful wife and her mother-in-law—dominate, with the eldest of the brothers as its leading figure, the one who bears the title. This fraternal company ... is itself intrinsically founded upon the consensus and approbation of popular society; a presence that is voiced in and out of the poetry as a constant steady refrain, but only and in reference to the kingly office.[297]

Therefore, kingship in the *Mahābhārata* narrative does not imply a full-fledged monarchy. We may not totally agree with McGrath's characterization of the Kuru polity as a *saṃgha* because of the ritual prestige of the royal office, the emphasis on hereditary succession, and the heated political contest for becoming the king. *Saṃgha* or *gaṇa-saṃgha*, in early India, represented a different kind of polity which was akin to an oligarchy or a republic and in which the singular ritual prestige of the kingly office was absent. The *Mahābhārata* rightly portrays the Yādava-Vṛṣṇis as such a polity in which Kṛṣṇa could assume political pre-eminence without even a nominal or ritual claim to the kingly office. That was not the case of the Later Vedic Kurus, as both the *Mahābhārata* and the Later Vedic texts would indicate. Rather, the fraternal clan-based kingship was more in tune with the office of a clan chief than with that of a monarch.

Understanding of this specific character of the political context will help us realize the character of the Bhārata War. Sharma shows that the arrangement of the two sides was mainly based on clan solidarity and kinship relations rather than on the *maṇḍala* theory of Kauṭiliyan diplomacy.[298] It would be natural in a pre-monetary economy that kinsmen and friends tied by blood ties and codes of honour, rather than paid retainers, would dominate the battle scene. Though, later on, the list of the participants reached gigantic proportion, those who played some important role were all kinsmen and friends—Bhīṣma (Kuru clan head), Droṇa (teacher), Kṛpa (teacher), Karṇa (Duryodhana's friend), Śalya (maritally related to the Kurus), Aśvatthāman (Droṇa's son), Dhṛṣṭadyumna and Śikhaṇḍin (Pañcāla princes), Drupada (Pañcāla king), Duryodhana, Duḥśāsana, Yudhiṣṭhira, Bhīma, Arjuna, Nakula and Sahadeva (all Kuru princes), Abhimanyu (Arjuna's son), Ghaṭotkaca (Bhīma's son), Jayadratha (Duryodhana's brother-in-law), Bhuriśravas (belonging to a junior branch of the Kurus), Virāṭa (Abhimanyu's father-in-law), Kṛṣṇa (cousin and friend of the Pāṇḍavas, Arjuna's brother-in-law), and Sātyaki and Kṛtavarman (Kṛṣṇa's kinsmen). Battling against kinsmen was the precise objection which Arjuna raised at the start of the *Bhagavad Gītā*.

What we may still glean from this highly inflated list of combatants is that the Kauravas—being the main branch of the clan—probably had a larger army than their opponents. The Pāṇḍavas, the offshoots, sided with the Pañcālas, which might have forced Bhīṣma, the Kuru clan head, to fight for his own clan, despite his sympathy for the Pāṇḍavas. The only exceptions to this pattern of kinship-based formation—among the warriors who left some mark on the battle—were the Trigartas who had launched a suicidal attack to keep Arjuna away from the main duels.[299] The reason for the participation of the Trigartas, an old ally of the Kurus and vanquished by the Pāṇḍavas during their cattle raid in Matsya, in the Kaurava side is clear.[300]

Not only the list of the participants but also the mechanism of warfare point towards a Later Vedic context. Sarva Daman Singh inspects the various components of army, arms and armours, forts and fortifications, military organization, and ethics of warfare in ancient India, starting from the Stone Ages through the Harappan, the Ṛgvedic, and the Later Vedic Age, up to the period of the composition of the Buddhist *Nikāyas* and the *Vinaya Piṭaka*, as well as the early parts of the two epics. The state of warfare in the *Mahābhārata* is thus thoroughly surveyed. Singh dates the Bhārata War around 1000–900 BCE, though he dates the composition of the epics to a later period (*c.* 600–400 BCE). The work can be highly useful to us in comparing the state of warfare in the *Mahābhārata* with that in the Ṛgvedic, Later Vedic and Post-Vedic texts, to contextualize the Bhārata War.

Warfare in ancient India depended on an army with four wings: infantry, chariots, cavalry, and elephantry. However, the relative importance of the four wings varied in different periods. Moreover, the ethics of warfare varied from one period to another. Therefore, we can have a look at the military details gleaned by Singh from the texts representing the respective periods.

The chariots were the most important component of warfare in the Ṛgvedic period, and they usually had two wheels and were drawn by horses (in some cases, asses). The vehicle was so important to the Vedic Aryans that the powerful priestly family of the Bhṛgus is described as chariot builders. The warrior fought from the chariot with bow and arrow, using spears, swords, and daggers if necessary. He wore armour, breastplate, helmet, armlet, and wreaths. Indra, in his warrior form, is the charioteer par excellence. Some of the Maruts, members of Indra's army, also fight from chariots. The charioteer stood on the right to guide the car.[301]

While the famed warrior fought from the chariot, common soldiers formed the infantry that followed it. Infantry, no doubt, was the most numerous arm of the force, though its role was subordinated to the chariots in battle. Frequent references to banners and flags suggest a marching order. The Maruts, forming Indra's infantry, move in fixed formations, with golden mantles, helmets, and armlets. The chief weapon of the infantry was also bow and arrow, though foot soldiers also used lances, spears, swords, axes, and slingstones. Not many infantrymen could afford armours, but they at least used a hand guard. Some infantrymen carried musical instruments. However, infantry was no match for chariots and often suffered heavy casualties. Still, Singh thinks, they must have been useful in hilly and difficult terrains, inaccessible to the chariots, and in siege warfare.[302]

The use of cavalry and elephantry was quite limited in the Ṛgvedic age. However, there is no doubt that horse riding was known to the Vedic Aryans. Singh quotes some verses about the Maruts which definitely show them as cavalrymen and uses some other passages to claim that the role of horses in Ṛgvedic warfare was not limited to drawing chariots. The Ṛgvedic cavalrymen fought mainly with lances and swords. However, cavalry, without stirrup and saddle, was by no means a regular or effective arm of the Ṛgvedic army.[303] There is no definitive evidence in favour of the use of elephants in the Ṛgvedic warfare, though Singh suggests that their use was not impossible.[304]

The Ṛgvedic chief commanded the army, though the decisions regarding war and peace could have been taken by the *vidatha*. There was a profound belief in the magical power of the priests to affect the outcome of a battle. The chief was assisted by his general (*senānī*), the commandant of a fighting group (*grāmaṇī*), and the commander of a garrison (*purpati*). There were spies and envoys as well.[305]

The period *c.* 1000–600 BCE witnessed a similar military organization in a more elaborate and developed form. The chariot warrior still dominated the battlefield. The office of the charioteer gained immense importance during the period and was considered as one of the kingmakers (*ratnins*). The principal charioteer (*saṃgrahitṛ* or *sārathi*) was often assisted by others, such as *anukṣattṛ* (attendant), *puraḥ sarau* (forerunners), and *pariskanda* (footmen running beside the chariot).[306] The Bharata charioteer could even receive as much as one-fourth of the booty, according to the AB.[307] The chariot maker was still an important person.

The common people still constituted the rank and file. The TS describes the Maruts organized in seven troops,[308] while the AB refers to the Asura army organized in three columns.[309] Bow and arrow were still the most celebrated weapons. The infantrymen also used swords, axes, spears, snares, nets, and traps.[310] However, the *Atharva Veda* considers the infantry as inferior to the chariot.[311]

The cavalry was still an irregular force of war. It was existent, as indicated by the *Sāma Veda*'s description of the Maruts as horsemen.[312] There are numerous references to horse riding. References to its usage in war are less frequent but not absent. The fourfold classification of the army occurs in the *Sāma Vidhāna Brāhmaṇa*.[313] The *Chāndogya Upaniṣad* alludes to the leader of a cavalry or *aśvanāya*.[314] The Vedic cavalry was possibly a light irregular force used mainly for skirmishes and cattle raids.[315] The fourfold classification of the army indicates towards some use of elephants in war as well.

The military apparatus of the king was extending. The belief in priestly magic continued to exist. The *senānī* or *senāpati* was one of the king-makers, as was the charioteer (*sūta*). The latter, apart from running the chariot, also acted as a herald, bard, and envoy. The extended usage of horses and elephants in warfare is indicated by the existence of the posts of horse and elephant keepers. The *grāmaṇī* still commanded the smallest unit. Spies and envoys were well in usage. The deliberative role of the *vidatha* as a war council was taken over by the *samiti*.[316]

The post-Vedic period saw a transition from the Vedic warfare. The chariot lost its absolute superiority, and cavalry and infantry gained in importance. Chariots were still important, and the chariot warrior fought with bow and sword. But the emphasis now shifted to a balance between the four wings than on chariots alone.[317] Therefore, the Kuru king Rāṭṭhapāla of the *Majjhima Nikāya* had to master all the four modes of warfare (II.69).[318] All the four divisions of the army had a role to play in the battle between Ajātasatru and Pasenadi, as described in the *Samyutta Nikāya*.[319] Cavalry and elephantry were now integral parts of the armed force. The *Vinaya Piṭaka* clearly shows their existence as separate units.[320] The elephant is a favourite royal mount as well as beast of war in Buddhist scriptures.[321] That the infantry was also gaining a role more meaningful than inflating the list of casualties caused by the great chariot warriors is indicated by King Pasenadi's dialogue with the Buddha, in the *Samyutta Nikāya*, where the former accepted that he would prefer a foot soldier with requisite qualities than one with the requisite caste status.[322]

Still, the king commanded the army in person, assisted by the *senāpati*. The priests were substituted by chief ministers who occasionally marched with the army. The *Samyutta Nikāya* indicates that all the four divisions of the army were now organized with hereditary professionals, and each had its separate head. These headmen were *yodhajīva gāmanī*, *hatthāroha gāmanī*, *assāroha gāmanī*, and *asibandhakaputta*.[323] With the emergence of full-fledged towns, *dovārika* or gatekeeper became an important official whose duty was to defend a fort. Standard bearers (*celaka*), billeting officers (*cālaka*), suppliers (*piṇḍadāyika*), storm troopers (*pakkhandino*), warriors in cuirasses (*cammayodhino*), and home-born slaves (*dāsakaputta*) also had some role to play in warfare. Spies were extensively used. This fourfold organization of the army continued till the Nanda and the Maurya periods, as can be seen in the descriptions of the other three wings of the army.[324]

With this backdrop in mind, we can now focus on Singh's depiction of warfare in the *Mahābhārata* and try to contextualize it. In the *Mahābhārata*, the chariot was the supreme apparatus of warfare, and the war chariot was usually the Vedic chariot. Some large four-wheeled chariots have also been mentioned. The only notable improvement of the chariot was a seat for the charioteer. Every hero had his own symbol on the flagstaff. The chariots were small arsenals and were followed by carts and other vehicles for further supplies. The horses yoked to the chariots were often protected with armours including chain armours, leather robes, and wooden breastplates. Sometimes, mules were also used for carrying chariots. The charioteer was a very important person. Though the 'Udyogaparvan' tells us that each chariot had three drivers (V.152.11), Sarva Daman Singh provides numerous examples to rightly show that most of the *Mahābhārata* heroes had only one charioteer on their chariots. So important was the charioteer's role that great heroes and princes such as Kṛṣṇa, Śalya, and Uttara assumed the role of a charioteer when needed. However, his status was still lower than that of a warrior. Thus, the stigma of being a charioteer's son haunted Karṇa's life. Śalya burst into anger before accepting the role of Karṇa's charioteer. Apart from driving the chariot, a charioteer also acted as a herald, ambassador, reporter, and bard. The hero was accompanied by junior chariot warriors who acted as his wheel guards. Moving with such elaborate paraphernalia, the famed chariot warriors encountered each other, usually with bow and arrow. These duels decided the fate of the battle.[325]

However, the numerically superior wing was the infantry whose role was that of fodder for the chariot warriors. Still, fighting on foot could not be neglected and had to be learnt by even the famous warriors. After all, despite the dominance of chariot archery throughout the Bhārata War, the decisive battle was a duel with the mace between Bhīma and Duryodhana. Even in the regular course of chariot warfare, a warrior, deprived of his chariot, could escape only with his skill as a foot soldier holding sword and shield. Nakula is praised as a consummate swordsman (III.255.10). Moreover, wrestling was a popular form of duel, with quite a high standard. Bhīma's excellence in this field was shown in his marathon duel with Jarāsaṃdha, and his application of the ancient equivalents of modern wrestling techniques such as 'bow-and-arrow hold' and 'aeroplane spin' in killing different Rākṣasas. Dhṛtarāṣṭra's care in maintaining the standard of his infantry (VI.72) indicates a significant military role of the unit, overlooked by the poets whose imagination was captured by greater heroes. The infantrymen used bows and arrows, swords and shields, javelins and lances, axes and pikes, clubs and maces. Careful formation of battle arrays, ranking of the troops, and award of names and badges indicate that the infantry had some say in the battles. But, in most cases, the infantrymen were nothing but men for slaughter by great warriors shooting their arrows from chariots. Still, fighting on foot was a prized skill, since it was the skill to which one had to resort when everything else failed.[326]

Cavalry was an integral component of the *Mahābhārata* warfare. Cavalrymen performed some gallant feats in the battle, and a hero—deprived of his chariot—could escape on horseback. Some kings, like the king of Gāndhāra, relied on their cavalrymen carrying lances (IX.22.29). However, the cavalry could not make a decisive contribution to victory or defeat. Without a proper saddle or stirrup, the role of the cavalry could hardly be a very prominent one.[327]

Elephants played a limited role in the *Mahābhārata*. Some kings, such as Bhagadatta and Śaibya, preferred to use them as their mounts in war. Some others, such as Bhīma, used them as an occasional mount. The epic actually provides clear signs of use of elephants in war. Each elephant could carry seven warriors, two carrying hooks, two archers, two swordsmen, and one with a lance and a banner.[328]

In fact, the location of the elephants in warfare can provide crucial clues to contextualize the narrative sections of the *Mahābhārata* in the Later Vedic Period when the transition from the clan polity to the monarchical state was occurring. Thomas R. Trautmann's *Elephants and Kings* has clearly shown the growing importance of the elephant in the Indian armies with the coming of the monarchical state.[329] He identifies the use of elephants in warfare as a Later Vedic invention which started around 1000 BCE, alongside the emergence of rudimentary kingship, which became normative and significant by 500 BCE when the monarchical state was well established in the Gaṅgā valley.[330]

War elephants were never mentioned in the battle scenes of the *Ṛg Veda*, and elephants were not part of the gifts given by the Ṛgvedic chiefs to their priests. Indra, the chief of the Ṛgvedic Devas, rides a chariot.[331] The situation started to change during the Later Vedic period, and the elephant was gradually being associated with the emerging kingship. The elephant Airāvata became Indra's mount in Later Vedic literature.[332] The AB mentions gifts of elephants.[333] Yet, the role of the elephants remained marginal, and the elephantry has no significant role to play in any of the battle scenes in Later Vedic literature.[334]

With the establishment of the monarchical state, elephants became a crucial component of the fourfold royal army. The *Rāmāyaṇa* indicates the presence of the *caturaṅga* army in both Daśaratha's Kosala and Rāvaṇa's Laṅkā.[335] That the elephant attained symbolic association with monarchy is shown when Bharata, deciding to rule as the regent of the exiled Rāma, placed Rāma's sandals on the royal elephant's head.[336] By the fourth century BCE, when Alexander invaded the northwestern parts of India, the elephant was the established royal mount. Nearchus described it as the most preferred royal mount.[337] The coins of Alexander show him mounted on his horse Bucephelas, while the Indian king Porus sits on an elephant.[338] According to the figures given by Arrian, Porus's fourfold army consisted of thirty thousand foot soldiers, four thousand horses, three hundred chariots, and two hundred elephants.[339] That the other contemporary kings also maintained war elephants is indicated by the various references to the Indian kings gifting elephants to Alexander. The king of Taxila is said to have gifted twenty-five elephants initially, and thirty more subsequently, to the Macedonian conqueror. Abisares gifted him forty elephants at first and thirty more later. King Mousikanos presented all his elephants to Alexander. Elephants were captured from the two sacked cities of King Oxykenos's realm.[340] However, while elephants became a regular feature in the monarchical forces, the republics seem to have had no or a small number of elephants in their armies. Thus, Diodorus and Curtius mentioned no elephant when they enlisted the numerical strength of the Malloi, Oxydrakai, and Sabaracae forces, while the Assakenoi army is said to have contained thirty elephants alongside thirty thousand infantrymen and twenty thousand cavalrymen.[341] In light of this, Strabo's solitary reference to a republican force with five thousand elephants cannot be taken seriously.[342]

The easy availability of war elephants seems to have facilitated the rise of Magadha as the supreme power in the North Indian plains under the Nandas and Mauryas in the fourth century BCE. Trautmann, comparing the figures given by Diodorus, Curtius, Plutarch, and Pliny, shows that the strength of the Nanda army ranged between two hundred thousand and six hundred thousand foot soldiers, twenty thousand and eighty thousand horses, three thousand and nine thousand elephants, and two thousand and eight thousand chariots.[343] That the Mauryas continued to possess a large number of elephants is attested by Candragupta's gift of five hundred elephants to Seleucus.[344] Megasthenes described Candragupta's army as one containing the traditional four wings alongside two extra wings for admiralty and transport and commissariat.[345] Similarly, the *Arthaśāstra* presumes a fourfold army and considers the chariot and the elephant as of equivalent status and value as a royal mount.[346] However, the chariot gradually became obsolete in warfare by the first century of the Common Era.[347] Rise of Magadha, rich in elephant forests, as an imperial power, and the successful use of elephants in battles,[348] must have elevated the position of the elephant as a part of the royal army and paraphernalia. The cavalry became more effective from the post-Maurya period when the Central Asian rulers, such as the Kuṣāṇas, replaced bareback horseriding with the introduction of saddle and stirrups. Naturally, the chariot lost its earlier importance and effectiveness with the growth of these mightier and faster wings.

If we look at the position of the elephant in the *Mahābhārata* with this background in mind, the context of the narrative becomes clear. The *Mahābhārata* is aware of the presence of the war elephant and the fourfold division of the royal army. Yudhiṣṭhira received elephants as gift during his *rājasūya*.[349] Arjuna was trained in all four kinds of fighting.[350] The *Mahābhārata* armies were commanded by the kings who chose their chief commanders and consecrated them on the model of almost a royal consecration. There were *balamukhyas* or captains under the commander. The post of muster-master is mentioned only in the Śāntiparvan (XII.41.11) which is definitely a later book. Spies and envoys were also used in war.[351] The *caturaṅga* concept was outlined in the depiction of warfare where chariots engaged chariots, infantrymen other infantrymen, cavalrymen engaged cavalrymen, and elephants other massive elephants:

rathāḥ rathaiḥ samājagmuḥ padātaiś ca padātayaḥ/
sādibhiḥ sādinaś caiva gajaiś cāpi mahāgajāḥ.[352]

The location of the war elephants as an integral part of the royal army has also been described:

bhīmaś ca mattamātaṅgāḥ prabhinnakaraṭāmukhāḥ/
kṣaranta iva jīmūtāḥ sudantāḥ ṣaṣṭihāyanāḥ/
svārūḍhāḥ yuddhakuśalaiḥ śikṣitair hastisādibhiḥ/
rājānam anvayuḥ paścāc calanta iva parvatāḥ.

(Terrifying rutting elephants with riven temples, well-tusked sixty-year olds like gliding clouds, well-mounted by trained elephant-riders skilled in fighting, followed behind the king like moving mountains.)[353]

Yet, elephants played a marginal role in the war. Most of the elephant riders came from the eastern lands outside the domain of the Later Vedic *madhyadeśa*—the Kuru-Pañcāla realm—which was at the centre of the *Mahābhārata* narrative. For instance, Bhagadatta of Prāgjyotiṣa (Assam) fought the king of Daśārṇa on elephant back.[354] Aṅga (eastern Bihar) provided several skilled elephant riders,[355] while the *mleccha* chief of Aṅga (clearly different from Karṇa, the Kuru regent of the region) was killed along with his elephant by Nakula.[356] A *mleccha* force of thirteen hundred elephants attacked Arjuna.[357] The Kulindas were also capable elephant fighters.[358] The list of elephant riders includes mainly eastern and southern tribes such as the Prācyas, Dākṣiṇātyas, Aṅgas, Vaṅgas, Puṇḍras, Magadhas, Tāmraliptakas, Mekalas, Kośalas, Madras, Daśārṇas, Niṣādas, and Kaliṅgas.[359] Therefore, the use of elephants in warfare was known to the Kuru-Pañcālas of the *Mahābhārata*, though it played a marginal role in their forces where the chariot remained the most important component. However, they knew that the elephant was essential to the military operations of the eastern powers, including Magadha where the Nanda and the Maurya empires would emerge in the fourth century BCE, with their fourfold army containing a significant elephantry. But the *Mahābhārata* depicts a context where the Kuru-Pañcālas were still at large. The eastern powers were marginal, and so was the importance of the war elephant.[360]

The depiction of warfare in the *Mahābhārata* definitely points to a period later than the Ṛgvedic age and earlier than the earliest Buddhist texts. As we have seen, warfare in the Ṛgvedic age was mainly based on chariots and infantry, whereas cavalry and elephantry had some role to play in the Bhārata War. However, the overall dominance of chariot warfare predates the period of the Buddha when the other wings of the army also became quite prominent. The *Mahābhārata* represents a context where the fourfold classification of the army became known, and all four modes became a part of the military training of the princes, but chariot archery overshadowed all others. Elephantry had limited significance, cavalry started to gain its feet, and infantry had only numerical superiority. Thus, it reinforces the idea that the *Mahābhārata* represents the Later Vedic context, a period of transition from the Ṛgvedic age to the age of the Buddha. The fact that kinsmen and friends, rather than paid soldiers, decided the outcome of the battle also points to a clan-tribal society.

Finally, we should have a look at the ethics of warfare to understand the context of the *Mahābhārata* war better. War and aggression were part and parcel of the Ṛgvedic world, which hardly needed any justification. Prayers for victory and material benefits were routinely uttered without shame, and destruction and devastation of the enemy was celebrated without embarrassment. Use of poisoned arrows or any other weapon was not prohibited. The occasional justification for warfare was always sectarian, as in the case of the clashes against the Dāsas, Dasyus, or phallus worshippers. Even in the Later Vedic texts, turning prisoners of wars into slaves was quite usual. Though the idea of contracts and treaties existed, Indra retained his position despite deceitfully killing his friend Namuci.[361] But the Later Vedic sensibilities show a gradual development in moral consciousness which culminated in the Upaniṣads where non-violence appeared as a great virtue. The glorification of violence finally gave way to the teachings of the Buddha and Mahāvīra, who passionately pleaded for non-violence and peace.

The morality of warfare in the *Mahābhārata* lies between these two attitudes. The ethos of a heroic age was still vibrant, but unrighteous conquest was discouraged. The evils of war were pointed out repeatedly to Duryodhana, the champion of the heroic virtue of the *kṣatriyas*. When war could not be averted, a lofty moral standard was set where only equals should fight equals, one should fight one on one, non-combatants should remain unharmed, and the fatigued and frightened should be spared. Ambassadors and *brāhmaṇas* were declared unslayable, and so were the spectators.[362]

The reality of war was much different from the ideas of the time. Therefore, when fighting started, much of these promises were forgotten by both the parties. Great heroes slaughtered ordinary soldiers, and charioteers were mercilessly killed.[363] But that the rules were conceived, a good deal of them were followed, and the aberrations were criticized and debated indicate an age of transition from a period of unrestrained violence to the period when non-violence would be valued.

This assumption is largely supported by Kaushik Roy and Torkel Brekke, both of whom have analysed the peculiarity of the military ethics of the *Mahābhārata* (*dharmayuddha*) and contrasted it with the realpolitik (*kūṭayuddha*) advocated in the *Arthaśāstra*.[364] Roy's book *Hinduism and the Ethics of Warfare in South Asia* brackets the Vedic and 'epic' periods together in its analysis of the evolution of military ethics in ancient India. The labelling of an 'epic period' is definitely problematic, so is its merger with the Vedic period. Moreover, the work is heavily reliant on secondary literature and contains many mistakes in minute details as a result.[365] However, a survey of the information cited by Roy easily explains why he chose to see the representation of warfare in the epics alongside the Vedic texts. Roy shows that the Ṛgvedic forces comprised primarily *paṭṭis* (infantry) and *rathins* (chariot warriors). The Ṛgvedic chariot was a two-wheeled vehicle with a light body, consisting of a wooden framework fixed on an axle tree and fastened by cowhide thongs. The value system in the *Ṛg Veda* was primarily heroic, where the dead warrior was supposed to have gained the merit of donating one thousand cows.[366] The concept of a fourfold army emerged in the Later Vedic period, and clear references to taming of elephants come from the *Yajur Veda*.[367] The *Mahābhārata* also indicates the introduction of the elephant and horses in the army, though not on a massive scale. It also has the knowledge that the people of Magadha were good elephant fighters, while the Kambojas of the northwest were better cavalrymen. Yet, the outcome of the battle was primarily decided by a series of individual combats between chariot warriors, that being the dominant mode of warfare in the Doab.[368] The chariots used are mainly Ṛgvedic chariots, but some big chariots pulled by four horses are also mentioned.[369] Similarly, the Ṛgvedic heroic values are not totally gone, as Duryodhana is said to have attained heaven on the basis of his death on the battlefield. Yet, the ethical issues are dealt with in a more complex manner. There are long discussions on the ethics of war and peace in both the 'Udyogaparvan' and the *Bhagavad Gītā*. The 'Bhīṣmaparvan' also provides an elaborate list of military ethics to be followed in a 'just war'. War is accepted not as something heroic by itself, but as the last option when all other paths are closed. Heroism is supplanted by an emphasis on *dharma* with multiple dimensions. Even in warfare, a distinction is made between *dharmayuddha* and *asurayuddha*, just and unjust warfare.[370] All these taken together would point towards the context of a period after the Ṛgvedic period, before the advent of Buddhism and Jainism (when non-violence became the celebrated virtue), and definitely before the time of Kauṭilya who saw nothing unjust in perceiving warfare in a diplomatic manner (*kūṭayuddha*).

In fact, the Bhārata War is described as a *dharmayuddha*, a war in the cause of righteousness. The most persistent slogan in the *Mahābhārata* is: '*yato dharmas tato jayaḥ*' (where there is *dharma*, there is victory). Ruth Cecily Katz notes how the poet represented the war in the metaphor of a sacrifice to create an order.[371] However, the trickeries resorted to by the victorious Pāṇḍavas pose a challenge to this formulation. Not just were the means used by the Pāṇḍavas unfair but also the end—upholding Yudhiṣṭhira's claim to the throne—was not clearly justified, since the complicated genealogies of the *Mahābhārata* made the issue of succession really disputable. Therefore, the argument that one has to use unfair means to attain fair ends in the Kali Age is not also fully satisfying.[372]

Katz finds the explanation to this dilemma in the theory of divine play (*līlā*). The war was nothing but a game of God, and here the God was the great trickster Kṛṣṇa. Even before the commencement of the war, Kṛṣṇa told Arjuna that he had already killed the warriors to be killed. The war was caused by a game of dice which was caused by a 'palace of illusion' built by a demon architect. All these imageries turn the war into nothing but the God's game. Therefore, the Pāṇḍavas were the rightful victors, not because their claim was fair or they fought fairly but because they were the true devotees of Kṛṣṇa. The slogan 'where there is *dharma*, there is victory' became in an altered version 'where there is *dharma*, there is Kṛṣṇa; where there is Kṛṣṇa, there is victory' or '*yato dharmas tato kṛṣṇaḥ yato kṛṣṇas tato jayaḥ*'.[373]

Similar arguments have been made by Brekke who thinks that the epics primarily espouse a heroic ideal, and there is a lack of clearly laid out rules for conducting just wars. There was no unequivocal definition of the conditions which could make a war just. No distinction was made between violence against internal and external enemies. The war was ultimately a conglomeration of heroic duels.[374] Even if there was a set of rules, they were violated throughout the war and completely shattered when Bhīma attained the decisive victory by hitting Duryodhana below the belt. This incident was defended by Kṛṣṇa and Bhīma with consequentialist moral reasoning where the end justified the means. The end of Pāṇḍava victory was not legitimized on any legal or technical ground, but due to their association with the divine Kṛṣṇa. Therefore, Brekke thinks that the Kurukṣetra war is called a *dharmayuddha* not because it was a 'just war' but because it was a 'holy war' where God fought on one side.[375]

To accept what Katz and Brekke argue, one has to admit that from the earliest version—which could have been just the battle reports narrated by Saṃjaya to Dhṛtarāṣṭra—*kṛṣṇabhakti* was the most dominant theme of the text. This seems improbable, though Katz is inclined towards such a formulation. Therefore, it is better to look at the ground realities of the battle than on the *kṛṣṇabhakti* which possibly entered the narrative in a later redaction. Moreover, Kaushik Roy has rightly argued that unlike the concepts of *jihād* or crusade, the Brahmanical texts do not offer any justification of a *dharmayuddha* against 'foreigners' or the people of other faiths.[376] Surya P. Subedi also states that *dharmayuddha* has to be directed against evil, be it internal or alien.[377] If one sees the codes of *dharmayuddha*—including not using poisoned weapons, not slaying a man standing on ground or begging for mercy, not striking an unarmed man or a non-combatant, not hitting a frightened or seriously wounded man—they do not seem to be comparable to that of a 'holy war'. Rather, it seems that Manoj Kumar Sinha has been right in assuming that the proponents of *dharmayuddha* generated laws of armed conflict based on humanitarian considerations in order to limit the suffering caused by war.[378]

M.A. Mehendale attempted to understand why the Bhārata War has been called a *dharmayuddha*, war in the cause of righteousness. He thinks that it means that either the war was fought for righteous ends or by righteous means. In the latter case, the concerned war does not deserve the tag. He enlists the several codes of ethical warfare from the text and shows that while certain rules such as issuing of challenge before a contest, answering a verbal abuse verbally, not attacking unconscious ones, not attacking one without arms or one fleeing from the battlefield, not killing the suppliers or musicians, and leaving war reporters unharmed were observed by both sides, many other rules were violated. Common soldiers were killed by the heroes of both the parties, even while fleeing, disregarding the rule of fight among equals. Heroes of both the sides killed the charioteers of their opponents. Arjuna cut off Bhuriśravas's hand while he was busy in a duel with Sātyaki. Droṇa was killed by Dhṛṣṭadyumna while not fighting and inattentive. Though one could legitimately intervene in a duel to help a comrade in distress, Abhimanyu was killed by multiple interventions which were possibly beyond the tolerable limit. Duryodhana was killed by Bhīma by an illegal blow below the belt. Aśvatthāman, Kṛpācārya, and Kṛtavarman killed sleeping, inattentive warriors in the Pāṇḍava camp. Thus, no side could claim the war to be a *dharmayuddha*.

Therefore, Mehendale views the war as a war fought and decided by strategy rather than righteousness. Thus, he understands Kṛṣṇa's epithet *yogeśvara* in *Gītā* (XVIII.78) as 'the master of expedient means of war stratagems', though in other places of the *Gītā* the same word means a master of *yogaśāstra* (XVIII.76) or a master of great power (XI.9, XI.4). He brought the Pāṇḍava victory as their chief strategist and brought the downfall of Droṇa, Karṇa, Duryodhana, and possibly Śalya. The Kauravas also had their *yogeśvaras* in Śakuni, who had won them the kingdom in a dice game and had also suggested some less successful strategies in the war; Droṇa, the most successful and instrumental general of the Kauravas; Śalya, not as a general, but while acting as the charioteer of Karṇa; and an owl, from whom Aśvatthāman had got the idea of a night attack.[379]

Describing the war as one of strategy rather than ethics is quite correct. However, Mehendale's argument that no code was broken in Karṇa's killing, since not attacking one in difficulty was not an agreed upon rule, is not convincing. When Karṇa was killed, he was unarmed and inattentive. Therefore, it was definitely a violation of the code of warfare. Mehendale's demarcation of the owl as a *yogeśvara* is also quite amusing, since it is not the owl but Aśvatthāman—who turned the owl's acts into a battle strategy—who is really worthy of that epithet.[380]

However, a more serious issue is Mehendale's condemnation of the heroes of both the sides for killing multitudes of common soldiers who were certainly not their equals. Surely, some common soldiers were killed. But the number of the slain soldiers described in the text seems to be a case of poetic exaggeration rather than a ground reality. T.A. Heathcote rightly observes: 'Battle was considered to be merely a series of individual combats with the courage and morale of the mass depending upon the visible performance of their leaders'.[381]

If the Bhārata War cannot be accepted as a *dharmayuddha*, then its nature remains to be explained. The nature of the Bhārata War has been interpreted variously by scholars. Recently, McGrath tried to portray it as a conflict between Kaurava patriline and Pāṇḍava matriline, in which the Yādavas emerged triumphant through the Pāṇḍava successor Parikṣit, the son of Abhimanyu born of the Yādava Subhadrā. Yādava *jaya* (victory) in the Bhārata War, which was an engagement to death between the Yādava allies and the Kurus, is the essential subtext in McGrath's opinion.[382] However, it is difficult to accept this proposition. It is true that the Pāṇḍavas had no blood relation with the Kurus, as they had with the Yādava-born mother Kuntī. However, their common identity was the result of the supposed paternity of Pāṇḍu. It was not Kuntī's blood but Pāṇḍu's name that created a unit in them, which included even the two sons of Mādrī. These sons, born of levirate, might not have any blood relation with the Kurus. But, as we have seen earlier, the institution of *niyoga* was integral to the idea of patrilineal succession, and the mother's womb was nothing but a property of the clan to ensure the lineage. Parikṣit succeeded the Pāṇḍavas because of patriline, not because of his matriline. Therefore, when the Pāṇḍavas retired at the end of the text and handed over the kingdom to Parikṣit, Yuyutsu (the son of Dhṛtarāṣṭra and a *dāsī*), the only remaining bearer of Dhṛtarāṣṭra's bloodline, was appointed the custodian of the kingdom alongside him.[383] Vajra, a Yādava, was appointed the ruler of a part of the kingdom at Indraprastha. But it was clearly a position subordinate to Parikṣit. Thus, Subhadrā, the Yādava queen of the Pāṇḍavas, was warned not to set her mind on *adharma* (possibly referring to any design to supplant Kuru kingship in favour of her Yādava relatives).[384] Thus, as we have seen earlier, the Buddhist texts know of the rulers of Yudhiṣṭhira's lineage ruling at Indraprastha, whereas Megasthenes found the Śūrasena followers of the Kṛṣṇa cult in and around Mathurā. The *Mahābhārata*, despite Kṛṣṇa's immense importance, is a Kuru text, not a Yādava one.

George A. Grierson sees an underlining *brāhmaṇa-kṣatriya* rivalry behind the Kuru-Pañcāla battle. He thinks that the Pañcāla *kṣatriyas* were unorthodox in nature, as shown in the CU which mentions that Pravahana Jāvāli, a Pañcāla *kṣatriya* who silenced the *brāhmaṇas*, gave instructions to the *brāhmaṇa* Gautama and claimed that true knowledge did not belong to the *brāhmaṇas* but to the *kṣatriyas* alone. Similarly, the unorthodox Drupada, who was a party to his daughter's polyandrous marriage, insulted a *brāhmaṇa*, Droṇa, who took shelter in the Kuru realm for revenge. His revenge through the Kuru princes renewed the Kuru-Pañcāla conflict which ultimately manifested itself in the great encounter at Kurukṣetra.[385]

Arthur Berriedale Keith challenges this formulation arguing that Later Vedic literature hardly contains any account of Kuru-Pañcāla rivalry, and refers more to their proximity in sharing the Madhyadeśa. The battle was, therefore, a battle between the Kauravas and the Pāṇḍavas who were a 'northern', perhaps 'semi-Mongolian', tribe who succeeded in winning the leading position among the Bhāratas.[386] Keith is right in pointing out that the Pañcālas shared the Madhyadeśa with the Kurus and were as Brahmanical as them. The ŚB celebrates the language and rituals of the Kuru-Pañcālas.[387] Thus stretching the point of the personal conflict between Droṇa and Drupada to a general *brāhmaṇa-kṣatriya* conflict would be to stretch the point a bit far.

However, Grierson seems to be right in marking the war as a Kuru-Pañcāla fight. H.C. Raychaudhuri has shown that an antagonism between the Kurus and the Sṛñjayas (Pañcālas) is indicated in the ŚB.[388] The togetherness of the Kuru-Pañcālas, mentioned by Keith, could well be a result of the war where the Pāṇḍava-Pañcala unit triumphed. Assuming the Pāṇḍavas to be 'outsiders', because they are not mentioned in the Vedic literature, is not very logical, since the Pāṇḍavas were no separate people but members of the Bharata-Kuru clan. We have already mentioned how even Buddhist literature remembers the rulers of Yudhiṣṭhira's lineage, ruling in Indraprastha, as Kauravas. Therefore, we may conclude that the battle of Kurukṣetra was fought between the Kurus and the Pāñcālas—commanded by their respective clan heads Bhīsma and Dhṛṣṭadyumna, where a junior branch of the Kurus joined the Pāñcālas and eventually succeeded to the throne. The first two Kaurava generals, Bhīṣma and Droṇa, were killed by two Pāñcālas, Śikhaṇḍin and Dhṛṣṭadyumna, respectively. Moreover, the war ended with the death of all the Pāñcālas—Dhṛṣṭadyumna, Śikhaṇḍin, and the five sons of Draupadī—at the hands of Aśvatthāman.

Ruth Katz, in her essay 'The *Sauptika* Episode in the Structure of the *Mahābhārata*', points out how the epic theme culminated in this event, making the story of a Pañcāla victory into a story of Pāṇḍava survival. The heroine of the epic, the Pañcāla princess Draupadī, also lost her importance in the royal lineage with the death of all her children. The story became a story of the succession to the Kuru-Pañcāla throne by the survivor Parikṣit, grandson of Subhadrā and blessed by Kṛṣṇa, the ruler celebrated in the *Atharva Veda*. This made peace, order, and cultural development in the reign of Parikṣit possible. It made the story suitable for the audience in the sacrifice of Janamejaya, son and successor of Parikṣit, by Vaiśaṃpāyana.[389] Indeed, the journey of Vaiśaṃpāyana's narration through ages, till it reached the shape of the present *Mahābhārata*, has been long and eventful and has attracted much historiographical attention. But it probably originated as the story of the Later Vedic Kurus who survived the calamitous war in which their senior branch was overpowered by the Pāñcālas, an ideal story to remember in a Kuru sacrifice, an ideal *itihāsa* to be presented to a later Kuru king mourning Parikṣit, Janamejaya.

3.6 Constituting the 'Fifth Veda': The Voice of Vyāsa

In the previous sections of this chapter, we have contextualized the *Mahābhārata* as a text representative of the transition taking place in the period of the Later Vedas. Now, in this concluding section, we may have a look at how the text itself perceives this transition. However, to do so, it is necessary to interrogate the question of the authorship of the text. Who is the author of the *Mahābhārata*? The traditional answer is Vyāsa. However, as David Shulman and Madeleine Biardeau have argued, 'Vyāsa' is not a name but an epithet which means an 'arranger' or 'divider' or 'diffuser'.[390] The proper name of the poet is supposed to be Kṛṣṇa Dvaipāyana. What did Kṛṣṇa Dvaipāyana arrange or divide or diffuse? Primarily, he is supposed to be the arranger or the divider of the Vedic corpus in three/four Vedas and hence called '*vedavyāsa*'. However, as Biardeau notes, he is also regarded as the diffuser of the epic-Purāṇic tradition, the primary symbol of the authoritativeness of the epic and Purāṇic texts.[391] Therefore, he is not only the supposed author of the *Mahābhārata* but also the supposed author of all the major Purāṇas (and many Upapurāṇas) composed in the first two Christian millennia.

Interestingly, though Vyāsa is not just the supposed author but a principal character in the *Mahābhārata*, the story is not told in his voice. As already discussed, the *Mahābhārata* contains two frames of storytelling. In the inner frame, it is Vaiśaṃpāyana, a disciple of Vyāsa, who tells the story to the Kuru chief Janamejaya. In the outer frame, the story of Vaiśaṃpāyana's telling is retold by the *sūta* bard Ugraśravas to the assembled sages at the Naimiṣa forest for a twelve-year-long *satra* organized by the Bhārgava Kulapati Śaunaka. Apart from these two principal frames, there are instances when the authorial role is transferred to others. Thus, the *sūta* Sanṃjaya narrates the war to Dhṛtarāṣṭra, and Bhīṣma gives long discourses to Yudhiṣṭhira in the 'Śāntiparvan' and the 'Anuśāsanaparvan'. Therefore, when we speak of the authorial voice in the *Mahābhārata*, we must be careful about which author we are talking about or which voice. What do the author figures of Vyāsa, Vaiśaṃpāyana, and Ugraśravas represent? Is the text a poetic account or a bardic narrative for the Kuru court or a refashioning of that narrative suitable for a primarily *brāhmaṇa* audience? The text probably contains all of these elements if we are to believe in the various layers in its creation.

However, Alf Hiltebeitel has come up with an ingenious suggestion that 'the *Mahābhārata* was composed between the mid-second century (BCE) and the year zero'[392] by a group/committee/syndicate/symposium.[393] A major factor behind this conviction of Hiltebeitel is his belief that the *Mahābhārata* had originated as a written text. Contrary to the general idea of several scholars, recently well synthesized by John Brockington, that the origin of the *Mahābhārata* lies in bardic oral tradition that went through a Brahmanical takeover before its commitment to writing,[394] Hiltebeitel dismisses the possibility of a preliterate oral epic and argues for a kind of 'literate orality' with the composition done by a group of *brāhmaṇa* scholars proud of their knowledge of grammar and their ability to possess a written text of what they perform orally.[395] He identifies this group of scholars with the *satra*-performing *brāmaṇas* of the epic's outer frame, who he considers more likely to provide a key to its composition than Janamejaya and Vaiśaṃpāyana of the inner frame.[396] Vyāsa, Vaiśaṃpāyana, and Ugraśravas are fictional characters created by these authors—a fictional author and two 'unreliable narrators' who act as oral performers.[397] Taking a cue from Michel Foucault's idea of an 'author function',[398] Hiltebeitel shows how the fiction of Vyāsa, a time-travelling intergalactic *ṛṣi* located in otherworldly hermitages accessible only by thought,[399] plays a crucial role in the proliferation of meaning through a new literary technique in which the 'author' plays the role of the regulator of the fictive by suddenly entering the story in crucial junctures to mark his significant role in controlling the narrative and regulating the characters.[400] Therefore, outside the inner (genealogical/historical) and outer (cosmological) frames, the fiction of Vyāsa provides an outermost authorial frame also defining the ontology of the text.[401] However, it is the 'cosmological' outer frame which to Hiltebeitel is most pivotal in outlining the 'chronotope' through which the *Mahābhārata* fuses its spatial and temporal indicators[402] and in recognizing the real authors of the text. The *brāhmaṇas* who represent themselves as situated in the 'Naimiṣa Forest' (a word derived from *nimeṣa* or *nimiṣa*, meaning a moment and a wink, respectively), the 'Momentous Forest', or the 'Forest of Literary Imagination', where ancient *purāṇa* is absorbed into a new stream that connects past, present, and future in the twinkling of an eye, where bards like the 'hair-raising' Lomaharṣaṇa and his 'frightful-to-hear' son Ugraśravas can enchant the *ṛṣis*,[403] are the ones really in charge of the composition and not the bards.[404] These *brāhmaṇas* might have named the various processes and roles in the making of the text by the fictions of Śaunaka and his co-*satrins*, Ugraśravas, Vyāsa, and his disciples, and the Naimiṣa *satra* itself.[405] But the work is a product of a committee (*satrins*) whose inner core contained a philosopher, a *dharmaśāstra* connoisseur, possibly a retired *brāhmaṇa* general, and of course the master of the house (*kulapati*) who kept them all to a common purpose. The emplotment might have been done by an author in three years (as *Mbh* I.56.32 says that Vyāsa composed the *Mahābhārata* in three years), and the bard might represent the narrative skill, but the rest of the committee would have been *brāhmaṇas*.[406] These *brāhmaṇa* authors had ghost-written the

Mahābhārata in collaboration with the fictional Vyāsa under the cover of the Naimiṣeya *ṛṣis*.[407] Their voice can be glimpsed through at certain places, for instance, where Śaunaka laughs out in amusement after Ugraśravas ingeniously invents an etymology of the name Jaratkārū and comments that 'it fits' (I.36.3–5) even though the interpretation would not fit any etymological test. Who narrates this conversation and Śaunaka's laughter? Who praises such a daring sense of 'fit'? There Hiltebeitel traces the *brāhmaṇa* ghost-writers of the *Mahābhārata*.[408]

Of course, if we accept Hiltebeitel's proposition, then there is no possibility of placing the *Mahābhārata* in a Later Vedic context of the oral bardic traditions. Hiltebeitel finds nothing to support the idea that the *Mahābhārata* grew in three different stages often associated with the names *Jaya*, *Bhārata*, and *Mahābhārata*, respectively. The text uses these three names synonymously, and any contrast between the last two names is by no way supported by the text.[409] Hiltebeitel contextualizes the *Mahābhārata* with the backdrop of the low-born rulers of Magadha, particularly the Mauryas, who had patronized the heterodox religions but had often acted as despots and patricides, engendering a hostile response from the *brāhmaṇas*.[410] It is in the ambience of the pro-Brahmanical rule of the Śuṅgas and the Kānvas, though not necessarily under their patronage, that such a text would be created by the *brāhmaṇas*, speaking about the ideal situation where rulership would be *kṣatriya* and also depicting the demise of the old *kṣatriya* order represented by figures such as Duryodhana, Jarāsaṃdha, Bhīṣma, and Vṛddhakṣatra.[411] Hiltebeitel notes that the *Mahābhārata* characters are not known to the Vedic corpus and that Pāṇini is the only author to mention the *Mahābhārata* and some of its characters (Vāsudeva, Arjuna, Yudhiṣṭhira) before the date he postulates for the text (mid-second century BCE to the year zero) and claims that 'by *Mahābhārata* he (Pāṇini) probably refers to a story known in one or more genres, though he could mean an otherwise unknown personal name, and with Arjuna and Vāsudeva he probably alludes to a local cult'.[412] Thus, the Vedic connections of the text are explained away as recalling of an older order by the authors through their knowledge of the Vedas. The *brāhmaṇa* authors modelled the old *kṣatriya* order, which it envisions as well as loathes, on 'India's first state', the Kuru-Pāñcāla kingdom of the 'early post-Ṛgvedic period'.[413] Janamejaya, the king of the inner frame, is no more than a great king from the past, idealized as a royal audience.[414]

But the problems in Hiltebeitel's proposition are several. None of the three frames spoken of by Hiltebeitel represents the *Mahābhārata* as a written text. Why the *Mahābhārata* necessarily has to be a written text to begin with, when the entire Vedic corpus could be composed and transmitted orally, and the *itihāsa-purāṇa* is a tradition as old as the Vedic tradition (as shown in Chapter 1) is not understandable. The contrary seems much more plausible, since the discussion in the previous sections clearly show how the context for the main narrative of the *Mahābhārata* is the Later Vedic clan society. Why Pāṇini should refer to an otherwise unknown personal name by *Mahābhārata* has not been explained. The reference to Vāsudeva and Arjuna can very well be about a local cult, but the characters needed to be well known for such a cult to develop. Apart from the *Mahābhārata*, do we know of any other tradition that may account for a cult of Vāsudeva and Arjuna together? Moreover, such an explanation cannot be given to the name 'Yudhiṣṭhira'. The argument that apart from Pāṇini, no pre-Maurya author refers to the *Mahābhārata* characters of the main narrative is also grounded weakly. Parikṣit and Janamejaya, so famous in Later Vedic literature, and Vaiśaṃpāyana himself (mentioned in the *Āśvalāyana Gṛhya Sūtra* as *mahābhāratācārya*) are as important *Mahābhārata* characters as any. Same can be said about Śaṃtanu of the Tenth Book of the *Ṛg Veda* and Kṛṣṇa Devakīputra of the CU. Certain *Mahābhārata* characters also feature quite prominently in the Buddhist and the Jaina cannons, parts of which are possibly pre-Maurya.[415] Hiltebeitel himself discusses the occurrence of Dhṛtarāṣṭra Vaicitravīrya in the KS 10.6.[416]

Similarly, to argue that the Vedic context of the *Mahābhārata* is maintained through the knowledge of the Vedas that the authors of the *Mahābhārata* possessed demands the poets to be extremely efficient as historians, an overbearing expectation from the poets of a preliterate society in the assumed absence of an older bardic tradition to at least colour their historical imagination. Moreover, if the authors were deliberately placing the events at a Vedic past of clan societies, why did they succeed in doing that in some sections but not in some others, such as the 'Śāntiparvan' and the 'Anuśāsanaparvan', where the context becomes a well-organized state society, cannot be explained.

Moreover, assuming the *Mahābhārata* to be a Brahmanical reaction against the Maurya heterodoxy from the period of the Brahmanical

Śuṅgas also seems to be overrating both Maurya heterodoxy and Śuṅga orthodoxy. There is enough evidence of the Mauryas patronizing the heterodox religions, but none to suggest that they showed any less favour to the *brāhmaṇas*. The *brāhmaṇas* and Śramaṇas got equal mention and respect throughout the Aśokan edicts. If we have to believe in the legends that Candragupta became a Jaina, we cannot ignore the influential legends about his being mentored by the *brāhmaṇa* Cāṇakya as well. The *Arthaśāstra*, at least parts of which were probably composed during the Maurya period and possibly under Maurya patronage,[417] is as Brahmanical a text as any. Thus, there is no strongly grounded historical evidence to suggest that the Mauryas were antagonistic to the Brahmanical religion. Rather, they probably followed an eclectic religious policy patronizing different religions.

Similarly, the Śuṅgas might not have been as anti-Buddhist as they are believed to be, given that many famous Buddhist sites such as Bharhut and Sanchi thrived under them. Moreover, the Śuṅgas did not command an empire as large as the Mauryas did. They succeeded a disintegrated Maurya Empire in the Magadha region and parts of Central India. However, there is no reason to definitely assume that the *Mahābhārata* was composed in the territories controlled by the Śuṅgas and the Kāṇvas. A large part of North India, including the regions where the *Mahābhārata* events are located, was ruled in the post-Maurya period initially by the king Khāravela of Kaliṅga, who was a devout Jaina, and then the Kuṣāṇas, a power of Central Asian origin, whose coins show a highly eclectic religious ambience in which several religions, including both the Brahmanical religion and Buddhism, were granted patronage.

With this background in mind, Hiltebeitel's idea of a symposium of angry *brāhmaṇas* writing down the *Mahābhārata* in response to the memory of Maurya heterodoxy, reflecting upon the Later Vedic *kṣatriya* clans of whom no bardic tradition existed, seems to have little credibility. One wonders why Śaunaka and his twelve-year *satra*, which Hiltebeitel himself shows to be highly metaphorical and symbolic, will be taken with such historical seriousness, when all other characters and events (many of whom are present in other texts and traditions as well) are regarded as fictitious. It is also strange that everything about Vyāsa and his authorship is considered as fiction of the outermost frame, but the stray reference to his composition of the text in three years is taken seriously as the time span for the emplotment of the text. In fact, if we follow C.Z. Minkowski in defining a frame story as a story about the telling of another story,[418] it is doubtful if we can consider the authorial interventions of Vyāsa—fictional, actual, or mythological—as the outermost frame. The Vyāsa frame does not definitely answer the question who tells the story of Ugraśravas of the outer frame the way the outer frame answers the question who tells the story of Vaiśaṃpāyana of the inner frame. Rather, if Vyāsa represents any frame at all as the author or a character or both, that is the innermost frame whose story Vaiśaṃpāyana tells in the inner frame. It is a frame because it possibly encompasses a bardic war narrative represented in the temporary transfer of authorial power to the *sūta* Saṃjaya during the war.

Of course, the author-character Vyāsa emboxes Saṃjaya's telling in a frame where Saṃjaya's war report is a result of the special divine vision and immunity granted to him by Vyāsa who also appears in the text to secure it when the immunity is threatened. However, that Saṃjaya's vision aiding him as a war reporter might also have been grounded in his capacity as a professional *sūta* is also indicated in places that show him as capable of a special vision irrespective of Vyāsa's boon. Thus, he was one of the five viewers of Kṛṣṇa's theophany at the Kuru court[419] and the one to know and reveal the real supernatural selves of Kṛṣṇa and Arjuna.[420] He could predict that Śikhaṇḍin would fell Bhīṣma even before anybody knew the secret behind it.[421] He could view the Pāṇḍava forces in a trance even before being gifted the divine vision.[422] However, around Saṃjaya's war narrative, the innermost Vyāsa frame builds the ontology of the text *Mahābhārata*, the story that Vaiśaṃpāyana tells Janamejaya.

McGrath has clearly pointed out the difference between the poetic-performative traditions represented by Saṃjaya and Vyāsa on the one hand and Vaiśaṃpāyana and Ugraśravas on the other. He takes a cue from Gregory Nagy's distinction between the *adoidos*, who composes his verse during performance, and the *rhapsoidos*, who recites from memory what he has previously heard from the other poets. Therefore, the *adoidos* necessarily precedes the *rhapsoidos* in time.[423] The source of the *adoidos* is spontaneous creativity, or poetic vision, while the *rhapsoidos* develops on what he had heard and rehearsed. In the *Mahābhārata*, Vaiśaṃpāyana and Ugraśravas perform as the *rhapsoidos*, narrating what they had heard from other poets and performers. Vyāsa and Saṃjaya, on the other hand, bank completely on their poetic vision. In other words, Vyāsa and Saṃjaya are visually or experientially inspired, while Vaiśaṃpāyana and Ugraśravas are merely audially inspired.[424] Thus, Vyāsa's comprehension was based on his powerful vision to directly experience the past, present, and future (*pratyakṣadarśī* ... *bhūtabhavyabhaviṣyavit*).[425] Saṃjaya, even before Vyāsa transferred his power to him before the war, claims to have a similar poetic vision (*ahaṃ ca jānāmi bhaviṣyarūpam/ paśyāmi buddhyā svayam apramattaḥ/ dṛṣṭiś ca me na vyathate purāṇī*).[426] Though Vyāsa's performance is not directly recorded in the *Mahābhārata*, the text develops Saṃjaya's character as a powerful bard and still presents the war books—around which the text was probably composed—as Saṃjaya's performance in the Kuru court of Dhṛtarāṣṭra. The later poets paid their tribute to Saṃjaya as well, nearly imparting on him the 'immortality' accorded to the eternal poet Vyāsa, since Saṃjaya was said to have escaped the forest fire that had killed his patron Dhṛtarāṣṭra and undertaken a journey towards the Himalayas which often symbolizes eternity in Indian tradition.[427]

The outer frame, as Minkowski says, is brief and insubstantial, much less carefully elaborated and much less organically connected with the main story.[428] Bruce M. Sullivan has also noted how these sections narrated by Ugraśravas do not concern the Bhārata War directly and seem to be self-consciously later than the parts narrated by Vaiśaṃpāyana.[429] Therefore, historicizing the outer frame of the text, deliberately ignoring the multiple other frames from Saṃjaya through Vyāsa and Vaiśaṃpāyana up to Ugraśravas, is methodologically problematic. If we add to that the way Hiltebeitel goes on to imagine the composition of the committee that wrote the *Mahābhārata*, with a philosopher, a *dharmaśāstra* connoisseur, a retired *brāhmaṇa* general, and so on again taking the representation of some characters and elements in the text with seriousness and arbitrarily ignoring the others, without any evidence whatsoever, we may come to the conclusion that Hiltebeitel, in his attempt to bring out the fiction of Vyāsa serving the 'author function' of the *Mahābhārata*, ended up creating a new fiction of his own.

Therefore, we may return to the question of the authorship of the *Mahābhārata*, whose main narrative clearly addresses the context of the Later Vedic clan societies, particularly of the Kuru-Pañcāla realm. E. Washburn Hopkins says:

There was no one author of the great epic, though with a not unknown confusion of editor with author, an author was recognized, called Vyāsa. Modern scholarship calls him the Unknown, or Vyāsa for convenience.[430] The fact that the present text of the *Mahābhārata* is not the work of a single author, but contains multiple layers of authorship, is well established within the text itself. However, the attribution of the authorship to the figure of Vyāsa is not a simple confusion. 'Vyāsa' cannot be the author-figure created just for convenience because the implications of the attribution of the authorship to him could be highly inconvenient for the group that controlled the text for the longest period of time.

The *Mahābhārata*, at times called the 'fifth Veda', has entered the Brahmanical corpus and undergone thorough Brahmanization. The most natural attribution of such a text would be a divine '*apauruṣeya*' origin. But that has not been the case. The *brāhmaṇas* could not attribute the text to any divinity or even a 'purely' *brāhmaṇa* author. Rather, it has been attributed to an author-character born of a premarital union between a *brāhmaṇa* and an outcaste fisherwoman. What could have been the reason for such a highly uncomfortable attribution? The answer probably lies in the popularity of such attribution in public perception which did not allow the *brāhmaṇa* redactors to revise that bit.

However, there are more issues with the figure of Vyāsa. He is celebrated as the author of the *Mahābhārata* and the editor-compiler of the three/four Vedas, author of the *Harivaṃśa* and the Purāṇas, and possibly the philosopher of the *Brahmasūtra*. These are texts composed over at least a time span of two millennia if not more. As a result, Vyāsa—to most scholars—has become a mythical eternal author rather than a real author working in a real historical context.[431] Sullivan views Vyāsa—the creator of the epic, editor of the Vedas, and grandfather of the epic heroes—as equivalent to Brahmā—the Universal Creator, Grandfather, and the author of the Vedas.[432] He cites the *Vāyu Purāṇa* (II.15.74–75) to show that Vyāsa has been identified as a quarter portion of Brahmā[433] and shows a lot of parallelism between the two.[434] However, Hiltebeitel rightly points out that though the parallelism succeeds, Sullivan strains to find out an incarnational relationship between them.[435] J.L. Mehta views Vyāsa as a prototype of an author. He is a strange absentee author of 'being and becoming', whose work carries no signature, 'worthy of the deconstructive lucubrations of a Derrida!'[436] Mastering the art of *pratismṛti*, he views how the future unfolds, being—as indicated in the *Viṣṇu Purāṇa*—indeed no other than lord Nārāyaṇa himself.[437] But, again, the Purāṇic reference to an incarnational relationship is very difficult to establish from the text.

Many scholars have tried to view Vyāsa as a symbol. For J.A.B. van Buitenen, he is 'a kind of a universal uncle' whose contributions to Vedic, epic, and Purāṇic texts are intended as a 'symbolic authorship'.[438] Mangels views him as the 'spokesman' of the *epiker* in the text.[439] Sullivan also understands Vyāsa as 'the symbolic representation of all the epic poets, the Ṛṣis of the fifth *veda*, who perceived the correspondence between the epic they were composing and the myths and rituals of their heritage'.[440]

Robert P. Goldman notes the interesting contradiction of accepting Vālmīki—traditionally known as the author of the *Rāmāyaṇa*—as a historical personage, but not Vyāsa. He says that there is no real evidence to contradict the fact that the central portion of the *Rāmāyaṇa* had a single author and no reason to doubt the unanimous tradition that the name of the author is Vālmīki. But, similarly, there is no inherent reason to argue against the single authorship of the presumed Bharata nucleus of the *Mahābhārata* and the name of that single author being Kṛṣṇa Dvaipāyana[441] who has in fact, by appearing as a principal character in the narrative, made a greater claim to contemporaneity with his work than Vālmīki did.[442]

In fact, the *Mahābhārata* represents Vyāsa as the poet of that nucleus only and not as symbolic of all the poets contributing to the tradition. The text says the Vyāsa had created the *Bhārata* collection without the minor stories.[443] It was promulgated by his disciples Sumantu, Jaimini, Paila, Śuka, and Vaiśaṃpāyana in their own ways.[444] In the *Āśvalāyana Gṛhya Sūtra*, four of these—except Śuka, Vyāsa's son—appear together, and Jaimini and Vaiśampāyana are described as the teachers of *Bhārata/Mahābhārata*.[445] Incidentally, an alternative version of the story, or at least the 'Āśvamedhikaparvan', attributed to Jaimini, is still extant.[446] In support of the idea that the story can be followed in many layers, the text declares that there are *brāhmaṇas* who learn the *Bhārata* from Manu onwards, others from the tale of Āstīka onwards, and still others again from the tale of Uparicara onwards.[447]

Moreover, Vyāsa is also a figure known from the Later Vedic times and even outside the texts attributed to him. He is known as a teacher of Jaimini in the *Sāmavidhāna Brāhmaṇa* as well.[448] In the GB, he makes the comment that one who knows the *Atharva Veda*—incidentally it is the text that praises the Kuru king Parikṣit as a contemporary—knows all.[449] Most intriguingly, Vyāsa Pārāśarya, in the TĀ, says that one without desire does not die,[450] a teaching very close to the maxims of the *Bhagavad Gītā*. More interestingly, a figure called Dīpāyana or Kaṇha Dīpāyana is quite well known in the Buddhist and the Jaina canons as well. In fact, in the *Kaṇha Dīpāyana Jātaka*, he appears in the context of the story of Aṇīmāṇḍavya, a sage who was mistaken as a thief and partially impaled, that appears in the *Mahābhārata* as well and is identified as a Bodhisattva which in the *Jātaka* tales means a previous incarnation of the Buddha.[451] There is an interesting story about the killing of the sage Kaṇha Dīpāyana by the Andhaka-venhus (Andhaka-Vṛṣṇis) in the *Ghaṭa Jātaka* and the *Saṃkicca Jātaka*.[452] The Jaina tradition also makes the rage of the sage Dīpāyana (Dvaipāyana) responsible for their destruction, after he was stoned to death by some Yādavas.[453] The suggestion is interesting. Of course, Vyāsa is traditionally regarded immortal in the Brahmanical tradition. But that seems to be homage to the immortality of his literary creation, because even the *Arthaśāstra* says that the Vṛṣṇis perished because they had maltreated Dvaipāyana.[454] We shall deal with this legend further when we discuss the Vṛṣṇis in Chapter 4. But these examples would suffice to argue that Kṛṣṇadvaipāyana Vyāsa was already a well-established figure across traditions from the Later Vedic period onwards up to the Maurya period, and some connection was already established between the *Mahābhārata* tradition and Vyāsa and his disciples. By the early Christian centuries, the Buddhist Aśvaghoṣa, who also tells an otherwise unknown story of Vyāsa being kicked by the prostitute Kāśisundarī,[455] was well aware of the tradition of Vyāsa's arrangement of the Vedas in four groups.[456] Therefore, by the time the *Mahābhārata* finally underwent Brahmanization, Vyāsa's position as the composer of the nucleus of the text and arranger of the Vedas was probably too well established across traditions to alter.

Probably, Vyāsa was already regarded as the towering intellectual figure of the Later Vedic period when the initial bardic recording of the Bhārata War tradition, the arrangement of the Vedas, a systematization of the *itihāsa-purāṇa* tradition, and the emergence of the Vedāntic-Upaniṣadic philosophy all took place. Therefore, the principal scholarly contributions attributed to Vyāsa may not be as distant in time from each other as it appears, if we consider that Vyāsa is credited with the origin of these texts and not with the final shape they attained. In this context, it will be highly interesting to note what the nucleus of the *Mahābhārata* narrative, located in the Later Vedic Kuru realm where the Vedic-Brahmanical orthodoxy and orthopraxy were taking shape with the emergence of the *varṇa* system, may imply, being attributed to a person who, by the notion of *varṇa*, would not be a *brāhmaṇa* but the result of a socially unacceptable union between a *brāhmaṇa* and an outcast.

In fact, while Sullivan has taken Vyāsa as an epitome of a *dhārmika brāhmaṇa*,[457] Fitzgerald is right in treating this conclusion as hasty and incomplete.[458] Vyāsa's birth was not of a pure *brāhmaṇa*, and he avoids one of the principal duties of a *dharma*-abiding *brāhmaṇa*—taking a wife and leading a householder's life. Hiltebeitel has noted the ambiguity about Vyāsa's relation with the Vedic-Brahmanic tradition. He is the divider of the Vedas, the foremost Vedic authority of his time, composer of the 'Fifth Veda', and teacher of both the *Mahābhārata* and the Vedas. But he is not a Vedic seer. He is known to some Later Vedic texts, but no verse of any Vedic text is attributed to him. It is not even told in the *Mahābhārata* how and when he learnt the Vedas.[459] Thus, Vyāsa represents both a close correspondence with and a difference from the Vedic tradition. His work and the Vedas were recited on the same occasions, but the *brāhmaṇas* told stories based on the Vedas, while his disciple—who could also be a bard like Ugraśravas—told the tale of the *Mahābhārata*.[460] In fact, Vyāsa himself seems to be more of a bard than a *brāhmaṇa*. The *Mahābhārata* describes him as a composer of epic-Purāṇic tales under the patronage of the Kuru king after the Bhārata War:

> *vyāsaś ca bhagavān nityaṃ vāsaṃ cakre nṛpeṇa ha/*
> *kathāḥ kurvān purāṇarṣir devarṣinṛparākṣasām//*
>
> (The resourceful Vyāsa always made a home with the king, and made epics about the seers of the old days, divine sages, kings, and Rākṣasas.)[461]

These were tales recited alongside the Vedic stories in a Vedic ritual but not absorbed in them. Thus, Vyāsa's reflections on the Vedic society came not only along with the *Mahābhārata*, but—as Hiltebeitel puts it nicely—'through it'.[462] Vyāsa, the arranger of the Vedas, might not be the one who followed them thoroughly. Rather, he created a Veda of his own, the 'Veda of Kṛṣṇa(dvaipāyana)',[463] the 'fifth Veda'.[464]

The sociopolitical landscape of Later Vedic India was complex. On the one hand, the first institutionalization of the *varṇa* system was taking place, while on the other, the ritualistic Vedic sacrificial religion was facing the first voice of dissent from the Upaniṣadic *ṛṣis*. The Upaniṣadic tradition allowed itself to be incorporated into the Vedic corpus as its fourth subdivision, but it questioned the infallibility of the Vedas and pointed out the futility of sacrificial ritualism. On the political plain, rudimentary Kuru-Pañcāla kingships were seeking legitimacy from the *brāhmaṇas* who were demanding hereditary monopoly of spirituality for themselves and hereditary kingship for their patrons. But the *gaṇasaṃghas*—like the Yādava-Vṛṣṇis—were carrying forward the tradition of tribal egalitarianism. The conflict of the two orders is represented in the conflict of the Vṛṣṇi chief Kṛṣṇa with the Magadha king Jarāsaṃdha (discussed in details later), but still the *gaṇasaṃgha* was strong enough to emerge victorious and its chief important enough to be venerated in the most important ritual of kingship—Yudhiṣṭhira's *rājasūya*. Thus it was a two-way struggle between Vedic-Brahmanical order based on heredity and the older order (also supported by a large section of the Upaniṣadic thinkers) based on ability. In this situation, fraught with possibilities, we can locate Vyāsa, the poet born outside the *varṇa* order and who seems to have been much allied with the Upaniṣadic way of thinking. Not only has Vyāsa been associated with the *Brahmasūtra* later but the CU celebrates his tradition as the 'fifth Veda' and refers to his hero Kṛṣṇa Devakīputra—who is known to have synthesized the Upaniṣadic philosophy in the *Gītā*—as a student of the Upaniṣadic scholar Ghora Āṅgirasa.[465]

Thus, Vyāsa tells not just the story of a Kuru-Pañcāla political clash where the Pāñcālas were aided by a branch of the Kurus but also the story of a clash between hereditary succession claimed by Duryodhana (the eldest son of the king Dhṛtarāṣṭra) and succession by ability claimed by Yudhiṣṭhira (a son of queen Kuntī by 'Dharma') who had no blood relation with the Kuru clan. As discussed in the section titled 'Searching for a Lost History of 'Time': Layering the *Mahābhārata*' of this chapter, in the mythological framework of the text, we can see it as a clash between Sūryavaṃśa and Candravaṃśa principals. Simon Brodbeck and

Brian Black rightly describe the main issue of the text as the conflict of primogenitive birthright and behavioural fitness.[466] Primogeniture appears to be a new idea in kingship, not yet completely established. The tribal notion of selecting the ablest as the chief was still present, by virtue of which the great king Bharata chose Bhūmanyu—son of Bharadvāja—as his successor, neglecting all his own sons.[467] The system continued up to the period of Śaṃtanu in whose favour his elder brother, Devāpi, abdicated the throne.[468] However, Śaṃtanu's passion for the fisherwoman Satyavatī brought a disjuncture. Devavrata (Bhīṣma), who was the fittest to succeed to the throne, made a vow to Satyavatī's father, assuring the unborn children of Satyavatī the throne.[469] Bhīṣma's famous vow unfolded into a crisis, as both the sons of Satyavatī died young.[470] Born of *niyoga*, Dhṛtarāṣṭra—the eldest of the next generation princes—was denied the throne on account of his blindness, and the younger Pāṇḍu became the king. However, this choice of the abler over the legitimacy of primogeniture frustrated Dhṛtarāṣṭra whose son Duryodhana fought hard to establish his claim to the throne.

Duryodhana, despite his degradation to the status of a 'villain' in public perception, contains elements of a tragic anti-hero who wanted his birthright and stood steadfast in his *kṣātradharma* (virtues of a good *kṣatriya*). At the very moment preceding his death, after being fatally wounded by Bhīma in an unlawful manner, Duryodhana thus summarized his life and virtues in an extremely heroic manner:

> I have studied the Vedas, bestowed gifts according to ordinance, ruled the earth with its oceans and stood at the head of my enemies. Who is more fortunate than me? What *kṣatriyas* regard as our desired *dharma* I have won by meeting my destruction in battle. Who is more fortunate than me? I have won human pleasure worthy of gods, and hard for kings to come by. I have reached the ultimate wealth and majesty. Who is more fortunate than me? Unshakable Kṛṣṇa! I am bound for heaven with my friends and kin. You will live on to grieve, all your purposes destroyed.[471]

The poet's respect for the virtues of his anti-hero is reflected in the shower of flowers from heaven, after Duryodhana's statement, bringing shame to Kṛṣṇa and the Pāṇḍavas.[472] Even in his very last moments, Duryodhana remained steadfast in his dignity of a great king and warrior in addressing his surviving followers—Aśvatthāman, Kṛpa, and Kṛtavarman:

> Having protected the earth I now approach this conclusion! How fortunate that I never turned back from combat, no matter what happened! How fortunate that I was slain by sinners, and that, too, using the worst trickery! How fortunate that I always fought with courage and perseverance! How fortunate that I see you escaped from that destruction and come to me safe and sound—that is the best thing to me! Do not grieve at my death out of friendship! If the Vedas are authoritative, I have conquered imperishable worlds.[473]

Duryodhana, in the *Mahābhārata*, is often the champion of the Vedic Brahmanical order, often even displaying supernatural abilities. In a strange passage, he claimed to possess matchless celestial energy:

> Supreme indeed is the fiery might the celestials possess, but my own the Gods cannot match, know it, Bhārata. While the world looks on, I shall with my incantations steady the earth's mountains and peaks if they are shattered. The terrifying, thundering gale and avalanche of rocks that spell the destruction of the sentient and insentient, the standing and moving—I shall slay them any time, before the eyes of the world, out of sheer compassion for the creatures. Chariots and foot soldiers will march over water that I have frozen, any time at all: I am the sole mover of the affairs of Gods and Asuras! Whatever may be the country in which I have business with my grand-armies, the waters will speed me there, wherever I want.[474]

Duryodhana's death has been described as a moment when the entire cosmos reacted with heavy wind and seismic movements, meteors and showers of dust, sounds of drums, conches, and animals, and rivers flowing backwards.[475] What were all these about? Was Duryodhana a repository of pre-Vedic shamanic powers, of unearthly forces the Brahmanical world abhorred, as indicated by the eerie incident of the Dānavas of the underworld reassuring him when he felt low after his humiliation at the Dvaita forest?[476] McGrath thinks so.[477] However, a completely opposite interpretation also seems plausible. Was Duryodhana, in a way, the ideal

Vedic king who could, thus, represent the orderliness of the cosmic forces? Angelika Malinar has shown such a possibility, explaining Duryodhana's strange claims as the ones of a 'spellbinder of royal power' comparable to Pṛthu Vainya, the ideal Vedic king who had instituted the earthly order and had stabilized the waters.[478] In fact, Duryodhana backs up his claim of supernatural power with a statement of his good governance:

> In my domain, no danger lurks from snakes and such, king; because of me, no fearful things beset the sleeping creatures. Parjanya rains when they wish for those who dwell in my domain. All my subjects are most law-abiding and there is nothing that plagues them.[479]

Duryodhana's magical power was perceived by Yudhiṣṭhira as divine (*daivī māyā*) and not demonic.[480] This would explain the cosmic reaction at Duryodhana's fall, followed by *gandharvas*, *siddhas*, and *apsarases* singing in the sky while fragrant breezes moved and a great shower of auspiciously smelling flowers fell on the dying hero.[481] The *Mahābhārata* asserts that Duryodhana had rightfully earned his place in the heaven by following *kṣātradharma*.[482]

David Gitomer rightly notes the importance of the plays of Bhāsa in this context.[483] Bhāsa, who possibly composed his plays in the second century CE, flourished in a period before the traditionally accepted date of the final Brahmanical redaction of the *Mahābhārata*. The source of his six plays on the plots derived from the *Mahābhārata* thus was either an oral tradition or an older version of the *Mahābhārata*. In his plays, Duryodhana appears in the full grandeur of a righteous and legitimate king. In *Dūtavākya*, he stands steadfast for *kṣatriya* virtue, against the harbinger of the alternative idea, Kṛṣṇa:

> Kingship is enjoyed by great princes by conquering their foes in battle. It cannot be had by begging, nor is it conferred by the poor upon this world. If they (Pāṇḍavas) desire to become kings, let them venture forth on the battlefield, or else let them at their will enter a hermitage.[484]

In *Pañcarātra*, Bhāsa almost reverses the *Mahābhārata* to make Duryodhana an epitome of virtue and a great patron of Vedic Brahmanism, praised by Bhīṣma for his righteousness, who gives away half of his kingdom to the Pāṇḍavas to fulfil a pledge to Droṇa! The greatest celebration of Duryodhana, however, comes in the *Urubhaṅga* where Duryodhana lives and dies a king who performed the Vedic rites, supported his kinsmen, showered favours on even the foes, never cheated his dependents, and bowed his head only in front of his father.[485] Thus Bhāsa adopted the Duryodhana of Vyāsa, who was a tragic victim of changing times, aware of the power of the preacher of that change—Kṛṣṇa, but still ready to contest him:

> I am mindful of the power of Kṛṣṇa, whose *tejas* is immeasurable, but he has not shaken me from following the *kṣātradharma*. I have entirely won him. I am not to be grieved for at all.[486]

No wonder that despite the *Mahābhārata*'s overall presumption that Yudhiṣṭhira was the ruler desired by the subjects, it also records how all the people of Hastināpura wailed in grief when they received the news of Duryodhana's death.[487] Even long after his death, a *brāhmaṇa* remembered in the Kuru court that the people were maintained well by King Duryodhana (*duryodhanenāpi rājñā suparipālitāḥ*), which is not a little achievement for a king.[488]

However, what Vyāsa celebrates in his work is not the tragedy of the Brahmanical virtue of Duryodhana but the *jaya* of a new virtue, epitomized by the heroes of a new kind. In the very beginning of the political turmoil, the poet himself entered the politics to copulate with the widowed wives and a *dāsī* of the childless king Vicitravīrya. Out of the three sons born, the author's favourite was the son of the *dāsī* who copulated with the dark and ugly sage willingly. With a hurt male ego, the poet attributed the physical deformities of the two royal princes to the reluctance of the queens to copulate with him.[489] The *dāsīputra* Vidura still could not get the throne, but became a powerful minister to champion the cause of the Pāṇḍavas and was often helped by another *dāsīputra*, Yuyutsu (a son of Dhṛtarāṣṭra by a *dāsī*), in this project.

As the story unfolded, a certain Ekalavya lost his thumb for daring to surpass the *kṣatriya* princes in archery.[490] But unlike the poet of the 'Uttarakāṇḍa' of the *Rāmāyaṇa*, who celebrated the assassination of the *śūdra* ascetic Śambūka, Vyāsa did not celebrate the *brāhmaṇa guru* who preserved the order but the '*gurubhakti*' of the outcast disciple:

> Forever devoted to the truth, with happy face and unburdened mind, he cut off his thumb without a moment's hesitation, and gave it to Droṇa.[491]

Droṇa, Kṛpa, and Aśvatthāman—despite being *brāhmaṇas*—chose their martial ability as means of livelihood. However, the life that typically characterized this contest between birth and ability, so crucial to the world Vyāsa represented, was Karṇa.

According to McGrath, Karṇa is the most typical Indo-European 'hero' in the *Mahābhārata*.[492] He understands the hero as 'a martially and verbally gifted figure with some kind of divine genealogy who is separated or isolated from his community and returned to that community only after death, via the medium of praise and lament'.[493] McGrath finds Karṇa's heroism in his lineage, his divine and intrinsic armour, and his adherence to the *kṣatriya* code of valour.[494] Moreover, his character seems not to have been overlaid by 'later' doctrinal considerations of Vaiṣṇavism, making him an 'unalloyed' and 'original' version of an 'epic hero'. Much like Achilles, Karṇa had power but lacked status. Like an archetypal *kṣatriya* hero, he banked on his code of valour (*tejas*) to acquire the heroic laments and remembrance in an 'epic' (*kathā*) of his own, which would render him immortal fame (*kīrti*). 'Karṇa's epic', which McGrath thinks to have been subsumed under the more Vaiṣṇavized 'Arjuna's epic', is considered by him as the best representative of the heroic model of *kṣatriya* behaviour in a 'bronze-age society'.[495] Karṇa, in McGrath's opinion, represents a 'heroic model neither overtly Vedic (exemplified by Indra) nor excessively Hindu (exemplified by Kṛṣṇa) in its orientation'.[496] Thus, Karṇa is neither a basic and elementary hero as Bhīma nor a supernaturally and devotionally endowed hero as Arjuna but a typical 'bronze age martial hero' whose death immortalized him through praises and laments.

McGrath's thesis raises some valid points, such as the role of narrative epic (*kathā*) in rendering the mortal hero an immortal fame—*kīrti*—different from the more materially based 'glory' (*yaśas*). His characterization of Karṇa as a transitional hero between the Vedic and the Purāṇic also makes perfect sense. However, as discussed earlier, McGrath's entire understanding of an Indo-European hero is coloured by the model of the Greek heroes. As a result, many of his ideas do not fit in the Indian context. More importantly, though Karṇa was obsessed with the 'fame' or *kīrti* attainable by martial valour on which the *kṣatriya* code was based, an attempt to consider him as an archetypal *kṣatriya* hero would overlook the crucial point that he was denied *kṣatriya* identity throughout his life. The crucial question around Karṇa's life was not if he was an ideal *kṣatriya* but whether one became a *kṣatriya* by his birth or social status or by his ability. Being the first-born son of Kuntī, Karṇa had a rightful claim to the throne, at least a more rightful claim than Yudhiṣṭhira. Yet, that remained unknown to the world during his lifetime and even to him for the greater part of his life. Therefore, Karṇa's life was about questioning the convention in which status was based on supposed heredity and not on ability. Karṇa, therefore, stood not so much between the Vedic heroism of Indra and Purāṇic heroism of Kṛṣṇa but between the hereditary *kṣatriya* heroism of Duryodhana and the *varṇa*-neutral alternative heroism of Yudhiṣṭhira. Karṇa belonged to both the worlds, had both the heredity and the ability needed for being the king, but was denied his claim to both. There lies the irony of Karṇa's character, especially of his *kṣatriya*-hood.

In his early years, he tried to show his martial ability against the celebrated prince Arjuna but was denied the opportunity because of his supposed low birth by two *brāhmaṇas* (Kṛpa and Droṇa).[497] Throughout his life, Karṇa struggled for a chance to receive the recognition of his valour which was denied to him because of his supposed *sūtaputra* status. But he was never disrespectful to that identity. Rather, even after Duryodhana crowned him a king, he bent his head at the feet of his foster father, the *sūta* Adhiratha.[498] Before the war started, he gave away his only inherited aid—his divine armour and earrings—to the deceitful Indra, an event highly celebrated in Bhāsa's *Karṇabhāram*. Then, suddenly, Kṛṣṇa and Kuntī opened up a world of success and prosperity to him by revealing his true identity as the son of Sūrya and Kuntī. This, of course, would mean that Karṇa, not Yudhiṣṭhira, would be the claimant to the throne as the eldest son of Kuntī (since he—as a son of the *kānīna* type—would be considered a legitimate son of Pāṇḍu). Moreover, Karṇa's position would be virtually unchallengeable, given that few would be able to stand against the combined military ability of Karṇa and Arjuna. It would also entitle Karṇa to a share in the polyandrous arrangements with Draupadī. But Karṇa rejected this golden way to luxury and preferred to die for his loyalty to the man who had valued him for his ability rather than his birth,

Duryodhana. He rejected his divine and princely parentage for the love displayed to him by his selfless foster parents:

> Adhiratha, a sūta, no sooner did he see me
> Than he carried me to his home, Madhusūdana,
> And proffered me to Rādhā, with love!
> Out of love for me the milk of Rādhā's breasts
> Poured forth at once, and she accepted my piss and shit.
> How could a man like me deny her the ancestral offering?[499]

Aditya Adarkar notes how the epic poet praises him as a 'proud and splendid man' whose mind did not falter, who stood fast by truth.[500]

Of course, the life of Karṇa signifies much more than just steadfastness in truth. Uma Chakravarti thinks that Karṇa (as well as Vidura) represents a figure at the margins of the *kṣatriya* household in a text where power was the restricted privilege of the *brāhmaṇas* and the *kṣatriyas*. Cast away at his birth, Karṇa lost his native *kṣatriya* status and acquired a *sūta* status from his adoptive parents. Being a *sūtaputra*, he could only be a 'hanger on' at the margins of a *kṣatriya* household and not a serious contender for *śrī* (neither the fortune of royalty nor its titular goddess in her earthly incarnation of Draupadī). Even though Duryodhana supported Karṇa's bid to 'acquired *kṣatriya*-ness' through martial valour, the bid would fail. When Karṇa rejected the offer of switching over to the Pāṇḍava side, the text assured that the royal power would remain out of the *sūtaputra*'s reach. Even at the moment of his death, Karṇa was remembered primarily as a *sūtaputra*.[501] Uma Chakravarti comments:

> In the final analysis, Karṇa's life and his death is that of a warrior who tried to rise to the status of a *kshatriya* through heroic skills but could not make it. Not content to sing the praises of the heroes as a *suta*, or drive their chariots, even as he refused to give up his adoptive *suta* identity he could not live his life as a *kshatriya* warrior in a royal household—the earth drank his blood as a *suta* and was quenched.[502]

However, did Karṇa really fail to make it? After all, both Kṛṣṇa and Kuntī had offered Karṇa *kṣatriya* status, and Kṛṣṇa's proposal clearly acknowledged his entitlement to the throne (and to the Śrī-incarnate

Draupadī). The poet of the *Mahābhārata* did not really represent Karṇa as unworthy of either. But the offer was unworthy of acceptance to him. Karṇa was respectful to his adoptive *sūta* parents through mutual love and never let go of that identity. But, in his action, he was a *kṣatriya*, a hero, and not a *sūta* who would sing the glories of the heroes and drive their chariots. Karṇa stood up for *kṣatriya*-hood as a status acquired through skill, not inherited. Hence, he refused his entitlement to the throne as a born *kṣatriya* and preferred to die in commitment to his (acquired) *kṣatriya dharma* on the battlefield. Karṇa made it to *kṣatriya*-hood not on the basis of his *kṣatriya* birth but by virtue of his heroic death, without surrendering his *sūta* identity. Thus, at the moment of Karṇa's death, while the Pāṇḍavas rejoiced at the death of the '*sūtaputra*', the *sūta* composers of the *Mahābhārata* noted with pride that a blazing luminosity left Karṇa's body and entered the sky (*dehāt tu karṇasya nipātitasya tejo dīptaṃ khaṃ vigāhyācireṇa*).[503] Karṇa did not rule. But his death established him as a real hero of eternal glory, uniting him in splendour and luminosity with the sun god, his supposed biological father and favourite deity. Though he was denied his *kṣatriya*—honour for his supposed *sūta* identity, he died a *kṣatriya* hero, not because the secrets of his birth were revealed but because of his actions and choices. The recognition, though in secret, came even from Bhīṣma, the typical *kṣatriya* hero who always derided Karṇa, during the fag end of his life, when he blessed him with the achievement of the worlds attainable by *kṣatriya dharma*: '*kṣatradharmajitān lokān saṃprāpsyasi na saṃśayaḥ*'.[504]

Karṇa did not rule, but Yudhiṣṭhira did. And the biggest challenge to the notion of hereditary *varṇa* in the text comes from him. Vyāsa's dubious birth possibly provides a background to what T.R.S. Sharma marks as his obsession with the question of true *brāhmaṇa*-hood.[505] Yudhiṣṭhira, Vyāsa's hero, thus opined that the notions of caste could hardly stand a test, since

jātir atra mahāsarpa manuṣyatve mahāmate/
saṃkarāt sarvavarṇānāṃ duṣparīkṣyeti me matiḥ//
sarve sarvāsvāpatyāni janayanti yadā naraḥ/
vāṅ maithunam atho janma maraṇaṃ ca samaṃ nṛṇāṃ.

(I think, great and wise Serpent, birth is hard to ascertain among humankind, because of the confusion of classes when any man begets children on any woman: language, intercourse, birth and death are common lot of all men).[506]

Yudhiṣṭhira asserted that *varṇa* was determined by observance of task, and, hence, a *brāhmaṇa* was one in whom cultured conduct was postulated.[507] Yudhiṣṭhira, thus, was a complete contrast to Duryodhana. He was doubtful about *varṇāśrama*, more given to pacifism and renunciation than to his inherent *kṣātradharma*, always questioning the rationale of warfare, and fundamentally Upaniṣadic rather than Vedic in his ideas. Therefore, we see that after a long discourse about the relative merits of *dharma*, *artha*, and *kāma* among the Pāṇḍavas and Vidura—where Vidura, Nakula, and Sahadeva extolled *dharma*, Arjuna spoke in favour of *artha*, and Bhīma in defence of *kāma*—Yudhiṣṭhira subordinated all these values to the Upaniṣadic ideal of *mokṣa*.[508]

In fact, Yudhiṣṭhira, the *dharmarāja*, was definitely not a follower of the traditional *varṇāśrama*-based notion of *dharma*. However, despite his Upaniṣadic leanings, he was not a renunciant either. Did he then represent a new notion of *dharma*? Mukund Lath has identified this new notion in a concept called *ānṛśaṃsya* (non-cruelty).[509] He thinks that this was an ideal of the *pravṛttimārga* (path of action) espoused by the *Mahābhārata*, in contrast to the better-known ideal of *ahiṃsā* (non-violence) which was more suitable for the *nivṛttimārga* (path of renunciation).[510] Of course, *ahiṃsā* had been a cardinal virtue in non-Brahmanical Śramaṇic religions, such as Jainism and Buddhism, which also espoused renunciation. Following Lath, Hiltebeitel has also noted that *ānṛśaṃsya* has been celebrated as the highest *dharma* nine times in the *Mahābhārata* (III.67.15, III.203–41, III.297.55, III.297.71, V.32.11, XII.220.109, XII.316.12, XIII.47.2, XIII.159.6), more than any other ideal, including *ahiṃsā* which is called the greatest *dharma* four times (I.11.12–14, III.198.69, XIII.116.1, XIII.117.37–41).[511] He also connects the idea as a response to the fact that the Magadha kings (including Aśoka), who patronized the heterodox religions celebrating *ahiṃsā*, had been absolutist despots and murderers of their fathers and brothers.[512]

Sibaji Bandyopadhyay takes a cue from Lath and Hiltebeitel and maintains this contrastive framework between *ahiṃsā* and *ānṛśaṃsya*, considering *ānṛśaṃsya* as a critique of non-violence.[513] Is *ānṛśaṃsya* then an alternative to *ahiṃsā*, a response to the Śramaṇic religions such as

Jainism and Buddhism, with little connection with the Later Vedic context of the *Mahābhārata* narrative? It would seem so if one were to focus on the long discourse on *ānṛśaṃsya* delivered to a proud *brāhmaṇa* by Dharmavyādha, a righteous meat-seller of Mithilā, who practised an 'impure' profession for livelihood but lived according to the tenets of *dharma* in his personal life. Here, Dharmavyādha strongly pointed out the impossibility of adhering to complete *ahiṃsā* and extolled *ānṛśaṃsya* as an alternative.[514] Much of Bandyopadhyay's discussion on *ānṛśaṃsya* is based on this particular episode.

However, if we look beyond this highly didactic and late section,[515] we may see that the concept of *ānṛśaṃsya* has a gradual development in the central narrative of the text, and it plays a crucial part in what Hiltebeitel calls 'the education of the Dharma-king'. In fact, if the central narrative of the *Mahābhārata* has something to do with the establishment of Yudhiṣṭhira as a new kind of hero, the role of *ānṛśaṃsya* is crucial in the process.

Hiltebeitel has also noticed that the term '*ānṛśaṃsya*' appears for the first time in the *Mahābhārata* not in the context of Yudhiṣṭhira but as advice to Vyāsa himself. When Vyāsa agreed to beget children on the widows of Vicitravīrya, Satyavatī asked him to perform the act with *ānṛśaṃsya* and *anukrośa*.[516] In fact, both Lath and Hiltebeitel note that *anukrośa* is an ideal crucial for understanding the nature of *ānṛśaṃsya*.[517] *Anukrośa*, translated as 'commiseriat' by Hiltebeitel, literally means 'crying with another', a kind of consideration or empathy for beings. However, Vyāsa does not seem to have succeeded in performing the task with *ānṛśaṃsya* and *anukrośa* then. It seems not. Vyāsa got angry inconsiderately when Ambikā and Ambālikā were repulsed by his appearance and smell. Rather than dealing with their revulsion with empathy, Vyāsa ended up holding them responsible for the physical deformities of their sons. The *Mahābhārata* narrative thus starts with the failure of its author to fulfil an ideal set in front of him by his mother. Subsequently, the author celebrates the story of a hero, Yudhiṣṭhira, who did not fail.

In fact, the birth of the Pāṇḍavas themselves has been set in the context of a failure to practise *ānṛśaṃsya*. The curse that had caused Pāṇḍu's impotence was brought forth by his killing of a sage and his wife who were copulating in the disguise of deer.[518] The killing itself was not condemned, for it was normal for a *kṣatriya* king to hunt deer. The act was lacking in *ānṛśaṃsya* because Pāṇḍu did not have the consideration to wait until the deer finished making love.[519] Yudhiṣṭhira, the eldest surrogate son of Pāṇḍu, therefore undertook a difficult journey to establish an ideal his father and grandfather had failed to live up to.

We hear Yudhiṣṭhira speak of *ānṛśaṃsya* for the first time in a very unusual context—as one of the qualities of Draupadī before staking her at the dice game.[520] We shall see later that Yudhiṣṭhira's assumption about Draupadī was not right in this case. *Ānṛśaṃsya* might have been a virtue Yudhiṣṭhira had already started to regard in high esteem and expected in his wife, but it was certainly not something that Draupadī had much respect for. However, that Yudhiṣṭhira's regard for *ānṛśaṃsya* had gradually increased would be evident when he would declare it to be the highest *dharma* to Dharma disguised as a heron-Yakṣa in the 'Āraṇyakaparvan'.[521] That he was now ready to live his ideal could be seen when, given the option of saving the life of only one of his brothers, he chose to save Nakula (and not Bhīma or Arjuna without whose valour he would never get his kingdom back) out of consideration for his already deceased stepmother Mādrī.[522] Of course, Dharma was pleased with Yudhiṣṭhira's *ānṛśaṃsya*, and he passed the test convincingly.[523] Gradually, *ānṛśaṃsya* became the cardinal value of Yudhiṣṭhira's life, which he kept on preaching and practising.[524] When Yudhiṣṭhira seemed to have lost his composure temporarily, after the death of Ghaṭotkaca in the war, the author himself intervened to remind him of his virtues, including *ānṛśaṃsya*.[525] Even after the battle, he continued to rule with *ānṛśaṃsya*, being empathetic to the war widows and the mothers who lost their sons, as well as to the poor, blind, and helpless.[526] Such was the extent of his *ānṛśaṃsya* that he was considerate and empathetic even to Dhṛtarāṣṭra who, along with his sons, had been the cause of all his sufferings.[527] In the final journey of his life, the *mahāprasthāna*, Yudhiṣṭhira's *ānṛśaṃsya* faced its final test, which he had also passed with distinction by not agreeing to choose heaven if it meant leaving out the dog that had accompanied him throughout his journey.[528] The poet, of course, is emphatic about the view that the journey of Yudhiṣṭhira's *ānṛśaṃsya* did not end with his mortal life, nor did the multiple tests that such a virtue needed to undergo end with his life on earth. Therefore, reaching the heaven in his earthly body, and seeing his brothers and Draupadī suffering in hell, Yudhiṣṭhira decided to forego heavenly pleasure at once, to share the torment of hell with his lifelong companions,[529] for he declared that where his brothers and his dear Draupadī were, that was his heaven.[530] Finally, Yudhiṣṭhira earned another round of praise from his father Dharma for not swerving from his heart even after reaching heaven.[531]

Ānṛśaṃsya, therefore, is a philosophy of non-cruelty and considerate empathy for all beings, including low borns or former foes, half-rākṣasas or the lowly and the destitute, a dead woman (Mādrī) or even a dog, as Hiltebeitel has noted.[532] Moreover, it is a value to be practised by the capable who undergo multiple tests in life and beyond and has nothing to do with the *varṇa* assigned by birth. Hence, it is stated that *ānṛśaṃsya* can be found among the people of all *varṇas*.[533]

It is worth noting that nowhere in the referred instances is *ānṛśaṃsya* presented as a counterpoint to *ahiṃsā*. Rather, we see the gradual establishment of Yudhiṣṭhira as a counterpoint to Duryodhana, the strict adherent of his prescribed *varṇadharma*, the violent *kṣātradharma* (for following which he won the promised reward of heaven). In fact, Hiltebeitel's list of the various acts considered *nṛśaṃsa* (cruel) in the *Mahābhārata*—including Purocana's attempt to burn alive the Pāṇḍavas in the lacquer house (I.36.3), Śiśupāla's verbal attack on Kṛṣṇa, Bhīṣma, and the Pāṇḍavas during the *rājasūya* of Yudhiṣṭhira (II.42.6–11), Kaikeyī's intrigue to send her stepson Rāma into exile (III.261.32), Kīcaka's attempts to molest the helpless Draupadī (IV.29.5), the Pāṇḍavas' conspiracy to disarm Droṇa by deceit and killing him unarmed (VII.166.19), and Jayadratha's role in killing the young Abhimanyu (XIV.77.38)[534]—clearly shows that what *ānṛśaṃsya* opposed was not the *ahiṃsā* of the Śramaṇic religions but the cruelty inherent in the violent conflicts in *kṣatriya* clan society. Therefore, Yudhiṣṭhira faced most of the counterarguments not from any non-violent ascetic but from his own mother and wife, Kuntī and Draupadī, both firm believers in the *kṣātradharma*.

McGrath rightly notes that 'women in epic *Mahābhārata*, more than male heroes, speak what is considered to be social truth: what is right for *kṣatriyas* and what constitutes good behaviour'.[535] It is the action of the women that 'weaves the tissue of *kula* clan', and the women's speeches sustain and refine the values of both kin and *varṇa*.[536] Thus, placed in the context of a clan society, Vyāsa's heroines are quite vocal and assertive, particularly in the defence of *kṣātradharma*. Devayānī compelled King Yayāti to marry her and left him at her will.[537] Śakuntalā fiercely criticized her husband Duḥṣanta in an open court, when he refused to accept her and her child.[538] Gaṅgā continued to kill one child after another and left her husband the moment she was questioned.[539] Satyavatī instructed her premarital son and her daughters-in-law to cohabit for offspring.[540] Bhīṣma's abduction of Ambā, for his brother Vicitravīrya, led to Ambā's violent attack on Bhīṣma and the ultimate vow to avenge her insult by killing him.[541] Though both Satyavatī and Kuntī abandoned their premarital children, Vyāsa and Karṇa, respectively, the mother's right over the child was considered equal to the father's in both the cases.[542] Gāndhārī not only berated both Dhṛtarāṣṭra and Duryodhana for not following the path of *dharma*[543] but also admonished Bhīma for his unlawful blow to kill Duryodhana and the indecent act of drinking Duḥśāsana's blood.[544] She even did not spare Kṛṣṇa for his lapses.[545]

Kuntī, who controlled her five sons throughout her life, appears to have been an even stauncher adherent of *kṣātradharma*. In the 'Udyogaparvan', she tried to instigate the pacifist Yudhiṣṭhira to fight by praising *kṣatriya* virility.[546] Criticizing the notion of *ānṛśaṃsya*, she said:

> *na hi vaiklavyasaṃsṛṣṭa ānṛśaṃsye vyavasthitaḥ/*
> *prajāpālanasaṃbhūtaṃ kiṃ cit prāpa phalaṃ nṛpaḥ//*
>
> (A king infected by cowardice, who does not act ruthlessly, does not win the reward that results from the protection of his subjects.)[547]

She would rather see Yudhiṣṭhira deliver his patrimony by any kind of stratagem:

> *pitryam aṃśaṃ mahāvāho nimagnaṃ punar uddhara/*
> *sāmnā dānena bhedena daṇḍenātha nayena ca//*
>
> (Unearth your ancestral share that lies buried, strong-armed son! Do it with persuasion, bribery, subversion, punishment, or policy.)[548]

Kuntī had no respect for Yudhiṣṭhira's considerate policies which, she thought, would only drown his ancestors if he did not fight.[549] To inspire him, she also narrated the story of another aggressive mother, Vidurā, who had urged her lazy son Saṃjaya to fight for and recover his lost patrimony.[550]

However, the most striking female character in the epic was no doubt the principal heroine, the polyandrous Draupadī. Sally J. Sutherland Goldman contrasts the outward expression of Draupadī's aggression with the inward aggressive masochism of Sītā in the *Rāmāyaṇa*.[551] Whenever there was a need to protect herself, Draupadī was not reluctant to be aggressive. We have already discussed how her questions perturbed the Kuru court during the dice match and how she rescued not only herself but also her husbands. She was also continuously critical of Yudhiṣṭhira's passivity. In the 'Āraṇyakaparvan', she lamented to Kṛṣṇa:

garhaye pāṇḍavāṃs tv eva yudhi śreṣṭhān mahābalān/
ye kliśyamānāṃ prekṣante dharmapatnīṃ yaśasvinīm//
dhig balaṃ bhīmasenasya dhik pārthasya dhanuṣmatām/
yau māṃ viprakṛtāṃ kṣudrair marṣayetāṃ janārdana//

(I *detest* the Pāṇḍavas, those grand strongmen in war, who looked on while their glorious consort in Law was molested! A plague on the strength of Bhīmasena! A plague on the bowmanship of the Pārtha! Both stood by, Janārdana, when churls manhandled me.)[552]

She also complained:

naiva me patayaḥ santi na putrā madhusūdana/
na bhrātaro na ca pitā naiva tvaṃ na ca bāndhavāḥ//
ye māṃ viprakṛtāṃ kṣudrair upekṣadhvaṃ viśokavat//

(I have got no husbands, no sons, Madhusūdana, not a brother nor a father, nor you, nor friends, if you mercilessly ignored me when I was plagued by the vulgar.)[553]

When Jayadratha tried to assault Draupadi, she physically resisted him and then wanted to avenge her insult by killing him. Infuriated by Yudhiṣṭhira's passivity, she urged Bhīma and Arjuna:

kartavyaṃ cet priyaṃ mahyaṃ vadhyaḥ sa puruṣādhamaḥ/
saindhavāpasadaḥ pāpo durmatiḥ kulapāṃsanaḥ//

(If you want to do me a kindness, kill off that wretched abortion of the Saindhavas, the evil, ill-minded defiler of his race.)[554]

Similarly, when in disguise in the Matsya realm, she was sexually assaulted by Kīcaka, the king's brother-in-law, in front of the passive Yudhiṣṭhira, she became vocal in rage against her husbands and even admonished King Virāṭa and his court, despite being in the disguise of a mere maidservant:

> Where on Earth are the great warriors roaming in disguise, they who were the refuge of those who sought shelter? How can those powerful, boundlessly august men like castrates suffer that their beloved and faithful wife is kicked by a *sūta*'s son? Where has their intransigence gone, where their virility and splendor, if they choose not to defend their wife who is being kicked by a blackguard? What am I to do with Virāṭa here who sees the Law violated, an innocent woman kicked, and allows it? King, you do not act like a king at all in the matter of Kīcaka, for your Law is the Law of Dasyus and does not shine in the assembly! Neither Kīcaka nor the Matsya abide in any way by their own Law. I don't blame you, King Virāṭa, in the assembly of the people, but it is not right that I am struck in your presence, Matsya! Let the courtiers bear witness to the crime of Kīcaka.[555]

She vented out her disgust about Yudhiṣṭhira to Bhīma, her only husband who tried to protect her:

> *ahaṃ sairandhriveśeṇa carantī rājaveśmani/*
> *śaucadāsmi sudeṣṇāyā akṣadhūrtasya kāraṇāt//*
>
> (Because of that gamester I run about in the royal palace in the guise of a chambermaid, cleaning up after Sudeṣṇā.)[556]

Draupadī would not undergo a fire ordeal like Sītā to prove her chastity. Rather, it was the abusers who, according to her, deserved the vengeance of her *kṣatriya* husbands. Thus, she had no remorse in asking Bhīma to crack Kīcaka like a pot upon a stone (*bhindhi kumbham ivāśmani*)[557] or tear him out as an elephant tears out a reed.[558] Clearly, she was not in agreement with Yudhiṣṭhira's perception of *ānṛśaṃsya* and detested such an idea. She would not consider a *kṣatriya* without righteous anger a valid entity (*na nirmanyuḥ kṣatriyo'sti loke*)[559] and berated weakness.[560] In the series of debates she had on such topics with Yudhiṣṭhira in the forest, she not only praised the path of rightful action (*svakarma kuru mā glāsīḥ karmaṇā bhava daṃśitaḥ*),[561] which probably meant performing prescribed *varṇa* duties, but also openly proclaimed violence:

> *yo na darśayate tejaḥ kṣatriyaḥ kāla āgate/*
> *sarvabhūtāni taṃ pārtha sadā paribhavanty uta//*
> *tat tvayā na kṣamā kāryā śatrun prati kathañcana/*
> *tejasaiva hi te śakyā nihantuṃ nātra saṃśayaḥ/*
>
> (A *kṣatriya* who does not show his authority when the moment comes all creatures will despise forever after. Pārtha! Don't show patience to your enemies under any conditions, for with authority alone you can cut them down, no doubt about that!)[562]

In fact, the poet describes the character of Draupadī as one who is perpetually offended particularly with Yudhiṣṭhira (*abhimānavatī nityaṃ viśeṣeṇa yudhiṣṭhire*),[563] which is testified by Draupadī's comment, '*aśocyaṃ nu kutas tasyā yasyā bhartā yudhiṣṭhiraḥ*' (What pity doesn't a woman deserve who has Yudhiṣṭhira for her husband?).[564] Repeatedly complaining about Yudhiṣṭhira's lack of anger,[565] she forcefully argued why neither extreme vengefulnss nor extreme forgiveness was desirable and one had to maintain a balance of both in his dealings.[566] She went to the extent of arguing that gentleness, patience, uprightness, and tenderness—the cornerstones of Yudhiṣṭhira's cherished *dharma*—were futile.[567]

However, even these persistent complaints could not swerve Yudhiṣṭhira from the ideal of *ānṛśaṃsya*. Dismissing Draupadī's allegation that righteousness did not produce any result, he emphatically claimed that he performed *dharma* not because of its rewards but because it was the right conduct and his inherent nature.[568] Delivering a long discourse on the problematic nature of anger and why forgiveness was preferable to cruelty,[569] he declared that anger was the slayer of human beings (*krodho hantā manuṣyāṇāṃ*)[570] and should be forsaken (*tyajet krodhaṃ puruṣaḥ*).[571] The birth of creatures was rooted in peace.[572] Arguing that patience and forgiveness were markers of a superior virtue, he pointed out the difference between himself and Duryodhana:

> Suyodhana is not capable of patience, and therefore can find none: I am capable of it, and therefore patience has found me. This is the way of those who have mastered themselves, this their eternal Law, to be patient and gentle, and thus shall I act.[573]

He did not succeed in convincing Draupadī who mocked the Divine Ordainer for bestowing on Yudhiṣṭhira what she considered nothing but delusion (*mohaṃ*).[574] Bhīma had joined her in calling Yudhiṣṭhira's pacifism impotent (*klība*)[575] and urged him on to follow the path of cruelty and violence.[576] However, Yudhiṣṭhira remained unmoved.

Yudhiṣṭhira's *ānṛśaṃsya* therefore seems to be an alternative to the ideal of martial heroism, which celebrated violence and cruelty of the *kṣatriya* clan society rather than a critique of heterodox non-violence. The opposition to the ideal was located not in the heterodox religions but in his surroundings, particularly in his cousin Duryodhana, his mother Kuntī, and—most vocally—his wife Draupadī. Yudhiṣṭhira never accepted that violence could ever be righteous, though he could be persuaded to fight a war for the sake of his rightful claim when all attempts at peace failed. However, the worst sufferer of this battle was Draupadī, the most vocal advocate for the battle. She lost her father in the battle, and the night attack by Aśvatthāman on the Pāṇḍava camp—probably the most *nṛśaṃsa* of all the incidents in the *Mahābhārata* narrative—took away the lives of her brothers and all her five sons. This was the pivotal moment that showed the vagary of violence, since a war to avenge the humiliation of Draupadī produced the worst consequences for Draupadī herself. Given her natural inclination, she initially wanted a violent revenge, the death of Aśvatthāman. However, eventually, she settled for the gemstone on Aśvatthāman's head and placed it on Yudhiṣṭhira's head.[577] Thus, the cycle of cruelty and violence ended when the crown gem of the *nṛśaṃsa* Aśvatthāman was passed on to the *anṛśaṃsa* Yudhiṣṭhira, and the irony that this transfer was prompted by Draupadī herself, who was hardly in agreement with Yudhiṣṭhira's idealism till then and who had lost all her children as a result of her cherished belief in martial heroism, probably marked the final establishment of *ānṛśaṃsya* as a new form of heroism in the text.[578]

Shirshendu Chakrabarti, in a different context, points out how Yudhiṣṭhira, often accused of irresolution, represents a new idea of 'agency' or 'freedom' in the predominantly deterministic world of the *Mahābhārata*. Chakrabarti compares Yudhiṣṭhira's heroic agency with Hamlet, to understand him through the Renaissance idea of self-interrogation as the freedom specific to man. Yudhiṣṭhira was always aware of ethical alternatives. He was plunged into moral dilemma out of deliberate choice and not because of circumstances. He interrogated accepted codes and dwelt on the margins. He remained suspended in self-questioning between the code of the *kṣatriya* and that of the *brāhmaṇa*, extending thereby the margins of either. He did not subscribe to any received code, order, or coterie. He listened to all the sages but chose none as his *guru*. He ultimately reflected and acted on his own: he was the true agent, his agency anchored in self-questioning selfhood.[579] While agreeing with Chakrabarti's premise, we must note that the ideal of *ānṛśaṃsya* was the guiding principle in Yudhiṣṭhira's unique reflection and action and, therefore, the foundation of his alternative heroism.

Vyāsa was the poet of a new time, a new ideal, the end of an era. His poetry represents not only the transition from the age of clan society to an age of well-developed polity but also a transition in which the attempts to organize polity and society according to birth was not much effective, except in theory. Pande broadly notes the transition depicted in the *Mahābhārata*:

> The traditional Varna system was becoming unreal in practice, and attempts were being made to define and question the social order even as technology was changing tools and weapons, trade and towns were emerging as a factor in social and cultural consciousness, smaller Janapada states were leading to larger empires, the Vedic religious tradition was being subjected to scepticism and criticism, the doctrines of Karman, Samsara and Nivrtti posed a challenge to the ritualistic order, new types of spirituality were emerging, and attempts were being made of new philosophical syntheses.[580]

Though this description is too simplistic, the days when kingship would be a monopoly of the *kṣatriya* clan chiefs, bound by a code of valour and depending on the ritual support of the *brāhmaṇas*, was indeed coming to an end. Within roughly five centuries of the date we have surmised for the origin of the *Mahābhārata* narrative, the throne of Magadha, the most illustrious kingdom of India, would not remain beyond the reach of a barber, Mahāpadma Nanda. In fact, post-Nanda India would hardly see *kṣatriya* kingship, at least not till the Early Medieval period when the Rajput clans would emerge with a claim to *kṣatriya* status. New channels of legitimization and patronage would be provided by the heterodox religions which would question the very basis of the caste system. Almost ignored by the Vedic tradition, the low-born Vyāsa was the *ṛṣi* of this fifth Veda, a Veda for the women and the *śūdras*, greater than the combined weight of the four Vedas,[581] a text which, rendering the Vedas insignificant, claims to contain everything conceivable about all the four quarters of life: *dharma* (social order), *artha* (power and resources), *kāma* (material pleasure), and *mokṣa* (salvation):

> *dharme cārthe ca kāme ca mokṣe ca bharatarṣabha/*
> *yad ihāsti tad anyatra yan nehāsti na tat kvacit.*[582]

Standing on this crossroads of ages, Vyāsa provides a new *dharma*, not of *varṇa* duties or martial violence but of non-cruelty, empathy, and consideration. As the *ṛṣi* of the fifth Veda, Vyāsa proclaims:

> *mātāpitṛsahasrāṇi putradāraśatāni ca/*
> *saṃsāreṣv anubhūtāni yānti yāsyanti cāpare//*
> *harṣasthānasahasrāṇi bhayasthānaśatāni ca/*
> *divase divase mūḍham āviśanti na paṇḍitam//*
> *ūrdhvavāhur viraumy eṣa na ca kaś cic chṛṇoti me/*
> *dharmād arthaś ca kāmaś ca sa kim arthaṃ na sevyate//*
> *na jātu kāmān na bhayān na lobhād dharmaṃ tyajej jīvitasyāpi hetoḥ/*
> *nityo dharmaḥ sukhaduḥkhe tv anitye jīvo nityo hetur asya tv anityaḥ//*
>
> (Thousands of mothers and fathers, and hundreds of sons and wives, experiencing world (or *saṃsāra*) have gone. And others will go. There are a thousand situations of joy and a hundred situations of fear. They affect the ignorant daily, but not the wise. With uplifted arms I cry this aloud, but no one hears me. *Artha* and *kāma* are from *dharma*. For what purpose is it not served? For the sake of neither desire nor fear nor greed should one ever abandon *dharma*, even for the sake of living. *Dharma* is eternal, but happiness and suffering are not eternal; the soul is eternal but its cause is not eternal.)[583]

The *Mahābhārata* was the ideal story to be recited in Janamejaya's Snake Sacrifice by Vaiśampāyana. Minkowski describes the Snake Sacrifice as an artfully chosen frame story that appropriately foreshadows the wider theme of the epic that it introduces.[584] The *sarpasatra* itself, of course, has Vedic precedents, and Janamejaya is a well-known Later Vedic figure. However, rather than being a rite to exterminate all Nāgas, it seems to be a Vedic rite practised by many communities, including the Nāgas. The rite is known to various Vedic texts.[585] Interestingly, some of them mention among the previous performers of the rite Janamejaya as well as his principal adversary Takṣaka.[586] Why this Vedic rite had been refashioned by the authors of the outer frame to locate the narration of the inner frame is a question worth some consideration.

The *sarpasatra* in the *Mahābhārata* is not a stray incident but is located within a chain of events depicting the clashes between the Kurus and the Nāgas. Of course, in the *sarpasatra* narrative the Nāgas appear like real snakes. However, that they were an ancient community, well-documented historically till at least the Gupta Age, has been discussed earlier.[587] Some of the major Nāga figures, such as Dhṛtarāṣṭra Airāvata,[588] Takṣaka,[589] and Arbuda Kādraveya[590] are well-known characters in Vedic literature. One of them, Arbuda Kādraveya, is also considered the poet of *Ṛg Veda* X.94, while Takṣaka seems to be a Later Vedic figure, well known to the *Atharva Veda*. Minkowski rightly says that

> [t]he *sarpasattra* is nothing new. It is not the invention of a late redactor of the epic. In fact it has more Vedic precedent than the *Bhārata* story itself.[591]

Interestingly, the *Baudhāyana Śrauta Sūtra* locates the original *sarpasatra* at Khāṇḍavaprastha, not only a part of the Kuru kingdom but also the original abode of Takṣaka in the *Mahābhārata*.[592] Even more interestingly, the *sarpasatra* of Janamejaya took place at Takṣaśīlā,[593] the place where the Khāṇḍava Nāgas might have shifted their base after they were driven away from the Khāṇḍava forest. This assumption is strengthened by the experience of Onesikritas, a companion of Alexander to India in the fourth century BCE, who encountered a community of huge number of snakes and snake worshippers at Taxila.[594]

In the *Mahābhārata*, the Nāgas had an overall troubled relationship with the Kurus, despite Arjuna's marriage with Ulūpī.[595] The animosity started with the eviction of Takṣaka's family from the Khāṇḍava forest by Arjuna and Kṛṣṇa, including the killing of Takṣaka's wife by Arjuna.[596] Aśvasena, Takṣaka's son, wanted to avenge the death of his mother by aiding Karṇa in killing Arjuna, but Karṇa refused the aid.[597] Takṣaka, however, killed Arjuna's grandson, Parikṣit.[598] Janamejaya's vow was to kill Takṣaka and exterminate all the Nāgas. Thus, it became a series of seemingly endless violence that culminated in the *sarpasatra* of Janamejaya. However, the *satra* was halted midway by Āstīka, a half-*brāhmaṇa* half-Nāga.[599] This became the occasion for Vaiśaṃpāyana's narration of the *Mahābhārata*.

Therefore, an ongoing feud with a chain of violence, halted midway by a neutral person, is the best occasion for the recitation of an epic of *ānṛśaṃsya* which shows how violence and vengeance fail to bring any resolution and lead to catastrophe, whereas non-cruelty and empathy establish *dharma*. Vyāsa had woven his *itihāsa* around the clash between primogenitive birthright and behavioural fitness in the Kuru kingdom and came up with the new ideal of *ānṛśaṃsya*. Now, Vaiśaṃpāyana narrated the epic of *ānṛśaṃsya* to a Kuru king committed to vengeance, with a number of background stories of vengeful and violent feuds between the Nāgas and the Garuḍas, the Devas and the Asuras, Rāhu and the Sun and the Moon, and culminating in the fraternal feud between the Pāṇḍavas and the Kauravas. It seems that Vaiśaṃpāyana had succeeded in conveying the message of his teacher. When his narrative ended, the rites of the *sarpasatra* were stopped.[600] The message of *ānṛśaṃsya*, the voice of Vyāsa, triumphed over the code of *kṣātradharma* and the bloodthirst of vengeance.

However, it would be wrong to assume that the *Mahābhārata* is just an epic of *ānṛśaṃsya*. Rather, *ānṛśaṃsya* seems to be a vital component in a new understanding of *dharma* that Vyāsa propounded. To explore the grand design of that *dharma*, let us return to Vyāsa at the moment of his first significant intervention in the *Mahābhārata* narrative. We have noticed earlier how Vyāsa had failed in the task of impregnating Ambikā and Ambālikā with *ānṛśaṃsya* and ended up cursing the unborn children with deformities because of the repulsion their mothers had shown in cohabiting with the ugly, smelly sage. These curses would seem to have far-reaching consequences since it was Dhṛtarāṣṭra's blindness that had deprived him of his throne and created all the complexities leading to the Kuru family feud. Is the *Mahābhārata* then as much a story of Vyāsa's failure as it is of Yudhiṣṭhira's success? Or is there any other meaning to the episode that caused Dhṛtarāṣṭra's blindness?

Arti Dhand emphasizes the crucial role that Vyāsa plays in the *Mahābhārata*. He is much more than an author function. He is the virtual creator of the *Mahābhārata* in all its three senses—the text, the Bharata clan, and the Bhārata War. In fact, Vyāsa created the *Mahābhārata* world: materially (by biologically saving the Bharata clan from extinction), efficiently (by instigating the conflict leading to the Bhārata War, by his curse), and transcendentally (as the author of the text), and almost assumed the role of God for its textual universe.[601] In such a scenario, what is the significance of Vyāsa's cruelty towards Ambikā and Ambālikā?

Dhand considers misogyny to be a possible explanation. Vyāsa, after all, is not just the narrator who reports or the poet who imagines the *Mahābhārata*, he is also a major character in the text with a unique pattern of action. Vyāsa the author shows Vyāsa the character as extremely distant from women. Not only was Vyāsa curiously unmarried, but he had spent the minimal time in the womb and did not need any rearing from his mother.[602] While his only moment of being seduced, by the Apsarā Ghṛtācī, led to the birth of a son, Śuka,[603] that son had become famous for his abstinent asceticism triggered by Vyāsa's discourses against familial and sexual life.[604] Though Vyāsa impregnated Ambikā and Ambālikā, they failed to produce what the *niyoga* was planned for: good, flawless heirs. Though he had blessed Gāndhārī with one hundred sons,[605] her prolonged pregnancy assured that Duryodhana would be born after Yudhiṣṭhira (complicating his chances of succession) and she had to witness the death of all the one hundred sons (the daughter, Duḥśalā, not part of Vyāsa's blessing of one hundred sons, survived). In his actions as a character, Vyāsa had little consideration for the sentiments of the Pāṇḍava women when he allowed Aśvatthāman to direct his missile to their wombs.[606] He even did not hesitate to urge the Kaurava widows to commit suicide by drowning themselves.[607] Then, was Vyāsa a misogynist and his treatment of Ambikā and Ambālikā a result of that?[608] That would be a hasty conclusion about a poet whose work displays an unequalled focus on women's sentiments and agency in ancient Indian literature.

After all, a closer scrutiny of the episode would reflect that Vyāsa's seeming cruelty was not extended to all women. As Dhand points out, it is the *dāsī* Ambikā had sent as her surrogate, the mother of Vidura, who emerged as the real hero of the episode. Intervening in the long-standing debate in Indian philosophy between *pravṛtti* (action) and *nivṛtti* (renunciation), Vyāsa advocated a bold middle ground which persuaded people to perform necessary action but without desire or attachment.[609] Such action needed mental firmness and commitment to duties irrespective of situations. Therefore, Vyāsa wanted Ambikā and Ambālikā to undergo a year of self-purification and preparation, the time Satyavatī could not grant.[610] Then Vyāsa had forewarned Satyavatī that the princesses would have to bear with his ugliness.[611] The two princesses failed in their tests of detachment and commitment to duty. After all, the *niyoga* was a duty they were supposed to perform in an emergency and not exactly an occasion of sexual gratification. The children suffered not a curse but the consequences of this failure. On the other hand, the low-born *dāsī* passed the test with complete detachment, and the resulting pleasure led to the birth of a perfect offspring.[612] Here, even if the context was of patrilineal and genealogical necessities, the women of high birth were defeated in their test of detachment and mental purity to the low-born *dāsī*. This victory was celebrated by Vyāsa, a *dāsīputra*.

Of course, even the poet could not transcend his time. The *dāsīputra* Vidura, though the most competent and the poet's favourite, could not be the king.[613] But Vyāsa told the *itihāsa* of a transition that would change the social scenario. At the end of the *Mahābhārata*, the situation would change. Yudhiṣṭhira would be able to at least consider the *dāsīputra* Yuyutsu as his successor.[614]

The emergence of Yudhiṣṭhira as a hero of a new age is thus part of a process that dictates the ontology of Vyāsa's work. Yudhiṣṭhira himself needed training in that ontology, the training of complete commitment to duty and detachment from results. That was what made him fight a war while retaining his pacifism, to show *ānṛśaṃsya* even to his erstwhile enemies, to ignore the lure of heaven for the sake of his loved ones or a loyal dog.

Yet, the question remains about who oversaw this training of Yudhiṣṭhira? Vyāsa, no doubt, intervened in crucial junctures. But his job was primarily to record or reflect on the transition than to direct its courses. Yudhiṣṭhira exemplified *ānṛśaṃsya*, an extremely useful value to match the standards required by a new ideal of *dharma* which encouraged action with detachment. But who set the standards? If Yudhiṣṭhira was the protagonist of *ānṛśaṃsya*, who was the protagonist of the greater ideal of performing actions with complete detachment, *niṣkāma karma*, which—if the TĀ is to be believed—Vyāsa earmarked as the way to immortality?

Answering this question will make us ponder if the primary concern of the narrative was the Kuru-Pañcāla clash over succession issues in the Kuru kingdom, what was its involvement with a person who was neither a Kuru nor a Pañcāla, and if neither was concerned with monarchical succession nor was a great champion of *ānṛśaṃsya*. In other words, what role does Vāsudeva Kṛṣṇa play as a hero (if not 'the hero') of the *Mahābhārata* narrative? How would the charioteer who allegedly led a reluctant warrior towards violence in the *Bhagavad Gītā* become so important in the text so insistent on the importance of *ānṛśaṃsya*? Did he also have a new ideal, a new message, to contribute to a new epoch? We seek the answer in the next chapter.

Notes

1. Vyāsa, I.70–80.
2. ṚV, I.31.7, VIII.46.27, X.63.1.
3. ṚV, VII.6.5.
4. Romila Thapar, *Exile and the Kingdom*, The Mythic Society, Bangalore, 1978, p. 11.
5. Vālmīki, *The Rāmāyaṇa*, Vol. II, translated by Sheldon Pollock, New York University Press, New York, 2007, II.102.30–31.
6. Vyāsa, III.147.3.
7. Vyāsa, III.177.6.
8. Vyāsa, V.112.6.
9. Vyāsa, V.147.3.
10. Vyāsa, VII.119.
11. Vyāsa, I.90.7.
12. Vyāsa, I.70.1–16.
13. Vyāsa, I.1.40–44.

14. *Harivaṃśa*, edited by P.L. Vaidya, Bhandarkar Oriental Research Institute, Poona, 1969 (reprint), IX.1–20.
15. Simon Brodbeck, 'Solar and Lunar Lines in the Mahābhārata', *Religions of South Asia*, Vol. 5, Nos 1–2, 2011, p. 136.
16. ṚV, X.95.18. Purūravas is called Aila, which may mean son of Ilā or son of a male named Ilā.
17. Vyāsa, III.185.
18. ŚB, I.8.1.7–11.
19. ṚV, X.10.
20. ṚV, I.71.5.
21. AB, III.33; ŚB, I.7.4.1–17.
22. Brodbeck (2011), p. 138; Simon Brodbeck, *The Mahābhārata Patriline*, Ashgate, Surrey, 2009, pp. 48–56.
23. Brodbeck (2009), pp. 31–40.
24. Thapar (1978), p. 11; see also Thapar (2008d).
25. See Thapar (1978).
26. Cited in Uma Chakravarti, *Of Meta-narratives and 'Master' Paradigms: Sexuality and the Reification of Women in Early India*, Centre for Women's Development Studies, Delhi, 2009.
27. Gayle Rubin, 'The Traffic in Women: Notes on the Political Economy of Sex' in Joan Wallach Scott (ed.), *Feminism in History*, Oxford University Press, Oxford, 1996, pp. 105–151.
28. Christine Ward Gailey, *Kinship to Kingship: Gender Hierarchy and State Formation in the Tongan Islands*, University of Texas Press, Austin, 1987.
29. Gerda Lerner, *The Creation of Patriarchy*, Oxford University Press, New York, 1986.
30. Chakravarti (2009), p. 16.
31. Chakravarti (2009), pp. 19–20.
32. Chakravarti (2009), p. 19.
33. AV, VI.138.7–9.
34. Vyāsa, I.113.3–16.
35. Vyāsa, I.113.17–19.
36. Chakravarti (2009), p. 26.
37. Vyāsa, I.113.25–26.
38. Vyāsa, I.110.26.
39. Vyāsa, I.111.28.
40. Vyāsa, I.112.5–30.
41. Brodbeck (2009), pp. 63–64.
42. Brodbeck (2009), p. 52.
43. ṚV, IV.5.5.
44. Vyāsa, I.70.1–16.
45. Vyāsa, I.207.21–22. The translation has been slightly modified, since van Buitenen's translation of *putrikā* as 'puppet' seemed unacceptable to me.

46. Vyāsa, I.206.29, VI.86.7–9.
47. Brodbeck (2009), p. 185.
48. Brodbeck (2009), p. 186.
49. Vyāsa, I.57.100–103, I.90.82–89, I.213.
50. Vyāsa, V.113.12–14.
51. Vyāsa, I.81.3–I.88.10.
52. Vyāsa, V.120.17.
53. Vyāsa, I.98.6–15.
54. Śaunaka, IV.11–15, 21–25.
55. Vyāsa, I.188.14.
56. Sarva Daman Singh, *Polyandry in Ancient India*, Motilal Banarsidass, Delhi, 1978.
57. Singh (1978), pp. 70–75.
58. Singh (1978), pp. 46–50.
59. Ṛ V, X.85.37.
60. AV, XIV.1.44, XIV.1.46, XIV.1.61, XIV.1.62, XIV.2.1, XIV.2.17, XIV.2.18, XIV.2.27, XIV.2.38.
61. AV, XIV.2.14.
62. TS, III.5.6, VI.1.6.
63. TS, VI.4.3.
64. AB, XII.2.
65. Smita Sahgal, 'Locating Female Sexuality: A Study of Polyandrous Representation', *Social Science Probings*, Vol. 18, No. 2, December 2006, pp. 33–52.
66. Vyāsa, VIII.27.75–78.
67. Singh (1978), p. 80.
68. Brodbeck (2009), pp. 63–64.
69. A.S. Altekar, *The Position of Women in Hindu Civilization: From Prehistoric Times to the Present Day*, Motilal Banarssidas, 2005, p. 144.
70. Smita Sahgal, *Niyoga*, Primus, Delhi, 2017, pp. 13–14.
71. Ṛ V, II.3.9, III.4.9.
72. M.B. Emmeneau and B.A. van Nooten, 'The Young Wife and Her Husband's Brother: Ṛgveda 10.40.2 and 10.85.44', *Journal of the American Oriental Society*, Vol. 111, No. 3, 1991, pp. 481–494.
73. Ṛ V, IV.42.8–9.
74. Ṛ V, I.111.19, I.116.13, I.117.20, X.39.7, X.65.12.
75. Sahgal (2017), p. 30.
76. Cited in Arti Dhand, 'The Subversive Nature of Virtue in the *Mahābhārata*: A Tale about Women, Smelly Ascetics and God', *Journal of the American Academy of Religion*, Vol. 72, No. 1, March 2004, pp. 38–39; Sahgal (2017), pp. 35–37.
77. Sahgal (2017), pp. 61–63, 84–85.
78. Vyāsa, I.99.37.
79. Vyāsa, I.98.4–6.
80. Vyāsa, I.98.17–32.
81. Vyāsa, I.111.33–35.

82. Vyāsa, I.113.21.
83. Vyāsa, III.50.5–10.
84. Vyāsa, I.113–115.
85. Vyāsa, I.117.
86. Sahgal (2017), p. 52.
87. Vyāsa, I.97–100.
88. Vyāsa, I.99.
89. Brodbeck (2009), p. 66.
90. Vyāsa, I.155.
91. Vyāsa, I.155.34.
92. BU, VI.4.2–3.
93. CU, V.8.1–2.
94. Vyāsa, I.155.47–48.
95. Vyāsa, I.113.27–28.
96. Vyāsa, I.100.2.
97. Vyāsa, I.100.5.
98. Vyāsa, I.100.23.
99. Vyāsa, I.100.15.
100. Vyāsa, I.98.22–32.
101. Vyāsa, I.155.35–36.
102. Wendy Doniger O' Flaherty, *Women, Androgynes and Other Mythical Beasts*, University of Chicago Press, Chicago, 1980, p. 50.
103. ṚV, IV.18.1–3.
104. Vyāsa, VII.33.9–13.
105. Vyāsa, I.120.
106. Vyāsa, I.121.
107. Mary Carroll Smith, 'Epic Parthenogenesis' in Arvind Sharma (ed.), *Essays on the Mahābhārata*, Motilal Banarsidass, Delhi, 2011.
108. See Manu, *The Ordinances of Manu*, translated by Arthur Coke Burnell and Edward W. Hopkins, Oriental Books Reprint Corporation, New Delhi, 1971, III.28–35, for example. All further references to the *Manu Smṛti* are from this volume.
109. Manu, III.33.
110. Vyāsa, I.96.11.
111. L. Sternbach, *Judicial Studies in Ancient Indian Law*, Part I, Motilal Banarsidass, Delhi, 1965, pp. 348–350.
112. Minoru Hara, 'A Note on the Rākṣasa Form of Marriage', *Journal of the American Oriental Society*, Vol. 94, No. 3, 1974, pp. 296–306.
113. Vyāsa, XII.4.10–13.
114. Vyāsa, I.211.15.
115. Vyāsa, I.211.21–23. Translation slightly modified, since van Buitenen's translation of *kṣatriya* as baron is completely unacceptable.
116. Vyāsa, I.113.4–8.

117. Vyāsa, II.25.8–12, VI.8.2–11, XIII.105.25–28.
118. Vyāsa, VIII.27.71–90, VIII.30.7–81. Brodbeck notes that the promiscuity of Bāhlīka women was well known even during the time of the *Kāma Sūtra* (II.6.45–47). See Brodbeck (2009), p. 18. One must also remember that the sexual appeal and appetite of Pāṇḍu's northwestern wife Mādrī was partially responsible for his death. Even before that, Mādrī, given a chance to choose her divine partner in *niyoga*, chose both the Aśvins together. See Vyāsa, I.115–116.
119. Vyāsa, I.72.5, I.76.16.
120. Vyāsa, I.77.19.
121. Vyāsa, I.69.31.
122. Vyāsa, I.92.5.
123. Vyāsa, III.214.6.
124. Vyāsa, I.143.9.
125. Vyāsa, III.279.
126. Vyāsa, I.67.26.
127. Vyāsa, III.53.
128. Vyāsa, I.178–181.
129. Vyāsa, V.60.178.
130. The episode is discussed in details in Chapter 4.
131. Uma Chakravarti, 'Textual-Sexual Transitions: The Reification of Women in the Mahābhārata' in Sibesh Chandra Bhattacharya, Vrinda Dalmiya, and Gangeya Mukherji (eds), *Exploring Agency in the Mahābhārata: Ethical and Political Dimensions of Dharma*, London and New York, Routledge, 2018, pp. 174–175.
132. Vyāsa, V.60.178.
133. Chakravarti (2018), p. 175.
134. Vyāsa, I.89.5–13.
135. Vyāsa, I.90.11–28.
136. Vyāsa, I. 89.17–20.
137. Vyāsa, I.90.34–35.
138. Brodbeck (2009), p. 138.
139. ṚV, X.98.
140. *Bṛhaddevatā*, VII.153–VIII.6.
141. Vyāsa, I.89.53, I.90.47.
142. Vyāsa, V.147.14–18.
143. Vyāsa, I.92–94.
144. Gautam Chatterjee, 'The Ethical Foundations of Bhīṣma's Promises and Dilemma' in T.S. Rukmani (ed.), *The Mahābhārata: What Is Not Here Is Nowhere Else*, Munshiram Manoharlal, New Delhi, 2005, pp. 145–162.
145. Vyāsa, I.102.23.
146. Vyāsa, I.107.24–33.
147. ṚV, X.146.
148. Vyāsa, I.215.6–7.
149. Vyāsa, I.217.1–13.

150. Vyāsa, I.219.1–7.
151. Vyāsa, I.214–220.
152. Cited in Alf Hiltebeitel, 'The Burning of the Forest Myth' in Bardwell L. Smith (ed.), *Hinduism: New Essays in the History of Religion*, E.J. Brill, Leiden, 1982, p. 218.
153. Hiltebeitel (1982), pp. 17–18.
154. Buddhadeb Basu, *Mahābhārater Kathā*, M.C. Sarkar and Sons, Kolkata, 2004 (reprint), p. 64.
155. Shereen Ratnagar, 'Archaeology and the State' in B.P. Sahu (ed.), *Iron and Social Change in Early India*, Oxford University Press, New Delhi, 2006, pp. 179–190.
156. R.S. Sharma, 'Material Background of the Origin of Buddhism' in B.P. Sahu (ed.), *Iron and Social Change in Early India*, Oxford University Press, New Delhi, 2006, pp. 42–48; R.S. Sharma, 'Material Background of the Genesis of the State and Complex Society in the Middle Gangetic Plains' in B.P. Sahu (ed.), *Iron and Social Change in Early India*, Oxford University Press, New Delhi, 2006, pp. 150–168.
157. D.P. Agrawal, 'Protohistoric Chronology and Technology and Ecological Factors: A Synthesis' in B.P. Sahu (ed.), *Iron and Social Change in Early India*, Oxford University Press, New Delhi, 2006, pp. 49–59.
158. M.D.N. Sahi, 'Agricultural Production during the Early Iron Age in Northern India' in B.P. Sahu (ed.), *Iron and Social Change in Early India*, Oxford University Press, New Delhi, 2006, pp. 191–197.
159. Irfan Habib, 'Unreason and Archaeology: Painted Grey Ware and Beyond' in K.M. Shrimali (ed.), *Reason and Archaeology*, Association for the Study of History and Archaeology, Delhi, 2007, pp. 17–27.
160. A. Ghosh, 'City in Early Historical India' in B.P. Sahu (ed.), *Iron and Social Change in Early India*, Oxford University Press, New Delhi, 2006, pp. 100–113.
161. ŚB, I.4.1.14–17.
162. Hiltebeitel (1982), p. 214.
163. Thapar (2008a), p. 68.
164. Francis Zimmermann, *Jungle and the Aroma of Meat*, Motilal Banarsidass, New Delhi, 1999.
165. Aloka Parasher-Sen, '"Foreigner" and "Tribe" as Barbarian (Mleccha)' in Aloka Parasher-Sen (ed.), *Subordinate and Marginal Groups in Early India*, Oxford University Press, New Delhi, 2004a, p. 292.
166. Aloka Parasher-Sen, 'Introduction' in Aloka Parasher-Sen (ed.), *Subordinate and Marginal Groups in Early India*, Oxford University Press, New Delhi, 2004b, p. 17.
167. Parasher-Sen (2004b), pp. 20–21.
168. Parasher-Sen (2004a), p. 297.
169. Parasher-Sen (2004a), p. 299.
170. Parasher-Sen (2004a), p. 298.
171. Parasher-Sen (2004a), p. 297.

172. Parasher-Sen (2004a), p. 299.
173. Parasher-Sen (2004a), p. 298.
174. Parasher-Sen (2004b), p. 19.
175. Aloka Parasher-Sen, 'On Tribes, Hunters and Barbarians: Forest Dwellers in the Mauryan Period', *Studies in History*, Vol. 14, No. 2, 1998, pp. 173–191.
176. Romila Thapar, 'Perceiving the Forest: Early India', *Studies in History*, Vol. 17, No. 1, 2001, pp. 173–191.
177. See Vyāsa, I.139–143, III.12.
178. See Vyāsa, I.145–152.
179. Charles Malamoud, *Cooking the World*, Oxford University Press, New Delhi, 1996, pp. 91–94.
180. For a detailed discussion about hermitages in early Indian history, see Kanad Sinha, 'Envisioning a No-Man's Land: Hermitage as a Site of Exemption in Ancient and Early Medieval Indian Literature', *Medieval Worlds*, No. 6, 2017, pp. 20–39.
181. B.D. Chattopadhyaya, 'State's Perception of the Forest and the "Forest" as State in Early India' in B.B. Chaudhuri and Arun Bandyopadhyaya (eds), *Tribes, Forest and Social Formation in Indian History*, Manohar, New Delhi, 2004, pp. 23–37.
182. Katz (1989), pp. 71–84.
183. Katz (1989), pp. 213–221.
184. Buddhadeb Basu (2004), pp. 64–70.
185. Hiltebeitel (1982), p. 214.
186. Irawati Karve, *Yuganta*, Orient Longman, Hyderabad, 2007, pp. 93–108.
187. 'Allahabad Pillar Inscription of Samudragupta' in *Corpus Inscriptionum Indicanum*, Vol. 3, edited by J.F. Fleet, The Superintendent of Government Printing, Calcutta, 1888, pp. 203–220.
188. Raychaudhuri (2006), p. 489.
189. Kosambi (1964), p. 39.
190. Vyāsa, I.18.
191. JB, III.168.
192. PB, XXV–XXVI.
193. MŚS, IX.5.4.1.
194. J.A.B. van Buitenen, 'Introduction' in Vyāsa, *The Mahābhārata* (Vol. I), translated by J.A.B. van Buitenen, University of Chicago Press, Chicago, 1973b, pp. 10–11.
195. *The Jātaka* (Vol. IV), pp. 227–231.
196. Vyāsa, II.44.18–20.
197. Vyāsa, II.43–72.
198. Lal (1981), p. 30.
199. G.J. Held, *Mahabharata: An Ethnological Study*, Kegan, Paul, Trench, Trubner and Co., London, 1935; Marcel Mauss, *Forms and Functions of Exchange in Archaic Societies*, Norton, New York, 1967, p. 54; Marcel Mauss, *The Gift*, Routledge, London, 2002, first published in 1950, p. 71.

200. J.A.B. van Buitenen, 'Introduction to the Book of the Assembly Hall' in Vyāsa, *The Mahābhārata* (Vol. II), translated by J.A.B. van Buitenen, University of Chicago Press, Chicago, 1975a, pp. 27–30.
201. R.S. Sharma (1983a), pp. 143–144.
202. Thapar (2008c), pp. 613–629; Romila Thapa, 'Some Aspects of the Economic Data in the *Mahābhārata*' in Romila Thapar, *Cultural Pasts*, Oxford University Press, New Delhi, 2008e (reprint), pp. 630–646.
203. R.S. Sharma, *Aspects of Political Ideas and Institutions in Ancient India*, Motilal Banarsidass, Delhi, 1996 (reprint), p. 105.
204. R.S. Sharma (1996), p. 114.
205. R.S. Sharma (1996), p. 114.
206. Witzel (1997a), pp. 27–52.
207. R.S. Sharma (1996), p. 115.
208. R.S. Sharma (1996), pp. 103–112.
209. R.S. Sharma (1996), pp. 119–129.
210. R.S. Sharma (1996), p. 112.
211. J.C. Heesterman, *The Ancient Indian Royal Consecration*, Mouton and Co., The Hague, 1957.
212. Van Buitenen (1975a), pp. 27–30.
213. Heesterman (1985), p. 28.
214. Heesterman (1985), p. 29.
215. Kumkum Roy, *The Emergence of Monarchy in North India: Eighth to Fourth Century BC*, Oxford University Press, New Delhi, 1994, pp. 27, 83, 107, 201, 205, 285.
216. Vyāsa, III.241.26–27.
217. Vyāsa, II.18.11, II.22.35–36.
218. Vyāsa, II.31, II.42.35–37, II.42.46–48.
219. Vyāsa, II.11.68–69.
220. Vyāsa, IX.42.38–41, IX.50–51.
221. Vyāsa, IX.48.11–14.
222. Vyāsa, II.53.11–12.
223. Karve (2007), p. 90.
224. Vyāsa, II.45.53.
225. Vyāsa, II.51.25.
226. Vyāsa, II.52.14.
227. Buddhadeb Basu (2004), p. 38.
228. ṚV, X.35.
229. AB, II.19–20.
230. Vyāsa, IV.1.19–22.
231. Kauṭilya, VIII.3.44; Manu, VII.47.50.
232. Kauṭilya, VIII.3.43.
233. J.A.B. van Buitenen, 'Introduction to The Book of the Forest' in Vyāsa, *The Mahābhārata* (Vol. II), translated by J.A.B. van Buitenen, University of Chicago Press, Chicago, 1975b, pp. 182–185.

234. Vyāsa, III.55–77.
235. Sibaji Bandyopadhyay, 'Of Gambling: A Few Lessons from the *Mahābhārata*' in Arindam Chakrabarti and Sibaji Bandyopadhyay (eds), *Mahābhārata Now*, Routledge, New Delhi, 2012, p. 21.
236. For detailed discussion on the game of dice in early India, see Kanad Sinha, 'Sporting with *Kāma*: Amusements, Games, Sports and Festivities in Early Indian Urban Culture', *Journal of the Asiatic Society*, Vol. LV, Nos 1–2, 2013, pp. 73–120.
237. Thapar (2008a), p. 56.
238. Vyāsa, II.61.8–9. Translation slightly modified, since van Buitenen's translation of *kṣātradharma* as baronial law seems misleading.
239. Vyāsa, II.61.22–24
240. Vyāsa, II.61.30–34.
241. Shalini Shah, *The Making of Womanhood (Gender Relations in the Mahābhārata)*, Manohar, Delhi, 1995, p. 31.
242. R.S. Sharma, *Perspectives in Social and Economic History of Early India*, Munshiram Manoharlal, New Delhi, 1983b, pp. 39–44.
243. Vijay Nath, 'Women as Property and Their Right to Inherit Property up to the Gupta Period', *Indian Historical Review*, Vol. 20, Nos 1–2, 1993–1994, pp. 1–15.
244. Vyāsa, II.63.21.
245. M.A. Mehendale, 'Draupadi's Question', *Journal of the Oriental Institute, Baroda*, Vol. 35, Nos 3–4, 1985, p. 192.
246. Vyāsa, II.64.1–3.
247. Vyāsa, V.29.35.
248. Alf Hiltebeitel, 'Draupadī's Question' in Kathleen Erndl and Alf Hilebeitel (eds), *Is the Goddess a Feminist? The Politics of South Asian Goddesses*, New York University Press, New York, 2000, pp. 113–122.
249. Uma Chakravarti, 'Who Speaks for Whom? The Queen, The Dāsī and Sexual Politics in the Sabhāparvan' in Arindam Chakrabarti and Shibaji Bandyopadhyay (eds), *Mahābhārata Now*, Routledge, New Delhi, 2012, p. 147.
250. Chakravarti (2012), pp. 132–152.
251. Vyāsa, II.67.3–4.
252. Vyāsa, I.190.15–17.
253. R.S. Sharma (1996), pp. 85–95.
254. Ranabir Chakravarti, *Warfare for Wealth*, Firma KLM Private Limited, Calcutta, 1986, pp. 7–26.
255. BU, III.1.1.
256. BU, IV.1.
257. KU, I.3.
258. AV, VI.59.
259. Vyāsa, III.226–228.
260. Vyāsa, III.229.1–13.
261. Vyāsa, III.229–235.

262. We have already discussed the liminal location of the forest vis-à-vis the settled society in ancient India. The location of Dvaitavana is no exception. Since the Kuru king had the power to inspect and brand the cattle, the forest seems to be within the Kuru kingdom. Yet, the Pāṇḍavas—who were exiled from the Kuru kingdom—were living there. So, the forest was located at the margin of the Kuru realm, not quite within the kingdom, though technically part of it.
263. Vyāsa, IV.24–62.
264. Vyāsa, IV.29.25–26.
265. J.A.B. van Buitenen, 'Introduction to the Book of Virāṭa' in Vyāsa, *The Mahābhārata* (Vol. III), University of Chicago Press, Chicago, 1978a, pp. 16–17.
266. Van Buitenen (1978a), p. 10.
267. Vyāsa, IV.9.8–14.
268. Vyāsa, IV.27.15–18.
269. AV, XX.127.8–13.
270. Pargiter (1908), pp. 309–336.
271. Nrisinha Prasad Bhaduri, *Mahabharater Bhāratyuddha o Kṛṣṇa*, Ananda Publishers, Kolkata, 2004.
272. R.S. Sharma (1983a), p. 142.
273. Vyāsa, I.205.
274. McGrath (2018), p. 108.
275. Vyāsa, VIII.69.31.
276. Vyāsa, XII.41.
277. Vyāsa, XII.41.2.
278. Vyāsa, XV.1.6.
279. Vyāsa, III.32.2.
280. Vyāsa, IX.58.15.
281. Vyāsa, III.241.226–227.
282. Vyāsa, III.241–242.
283. Vyāsa, III.242.11.
284. Vyāsa, I.80.12.
285. Vyāsa, I.80.24.
286. Vyāsa, I.69.36.
287. Vyāsa, V.145.25.
288. Vyāsa, V.146.7.
289. Vyāsa, I.129.18.
290. Vyāsa, III.1.11–20.
291. Vyāsa, III.243.1.
292. Vyāsa, XV.5.
293. Vyāsa, XVII.1.16.
294. Vyāsa, I.40.6.
295. McGrath (2016a), p. 141.
296. McGrath (2016a), p. 9.
297. McGrath (2016a), p. 164.

298. R.S. Sharma (1983a), pp. 135–152.
299. This force was called the *saṃśaptakas*. For their role in the war, see Vyāsa, VII.16–31.
300. See the preceding section for detailed discussion.
301. Sarva Daman Singh, *Ancient Indian Warfare with Special Reference to the Vedic Period*, E.J. Brill, Leiden, 1965, pp. 26–32.
302. Singh (1965), pp. 8–11.
303. Singh (1965), pp. 56–66.
304. Singh (1965), pp. 74–76.
305. Singh (1965), pp. 135–144.
306. Singh (1965), pp. 32–35.
307. AB, II.25.
308. TS, V.4.7.7, IV.3.13.7.
309. AB, VI.4.
310. Singh (1965), pp. 11–15.
311. AV, VII.62.1.
312. *Sāma Veda Saṃhitā*, I.2.3.1, edited and translated by Paritosh Thakur, Haraf, Kolkata, 1975.
313. *Sama Vidhana Brahmana with Commentary of Sayana*, critically edited by B.R. Sharma, Rashtriya Sanskrit Vidyapeetha, Tirupati, 2004, III.6.11.
314. CU, VI.8.3–5.
315. Singh (1965), pp. 56–66.
316. Singh (1965), pp. 135–144.
317. Singh (1965), pp. 35–36.
318. *The Middle Length Discourses of the Buddha*, translated by Bhikkhu Ñāṇamoli and edited by Bhikkhu Bodhi, Wisdom Publications, Boston, 2009, II.69.
319. *The Connected Discourses of the Buddha*, translated by Bhikkhu Bodhi, Wisdom Publications, 2009, Boston, I.83–84.
320. *The Vinaya Texts*, translated by T.W. Rhys Davids and Hermann Oldenberg, The Clarendon Press, Oxford, 1881, IV.107–108.
321. Singh (1965), pp. 66–67, 78–80.
322. *The Connected Discourses of the Buddha*, I.98.
323. *The Connected Discourses of the Buddha*, IV.308–312.
324. Singh (1965), pp. 144–146.
325. Singh (1965), pp. 36–52.
326. Singh (1965), pp. 17–22.
327. Singh (1965), pp. 67–71.
328. Singh (1965), pp. 80–84.
329. Thomas R. Trautmann, *Elephants and Kings*, Permanent Black, Ranikhet, 2015.
330. Trautmann (2015), pp. 68–69.
331. Trautmann (2015), p. 98.
332. Trautmann (2015), p. 100.

333. The King Aṅga gifted his priests 88,000 horses, 10,000 slave girls, 2,000,000 cows, and 10,000 elephants in the AB, VIII.22. AB also refers to the gift of 107,000 elephants by Bharata Dauḥṣanti, the celebrated predecessor of the Kuru-Pañcālas.
334. Trautmann (2015), p. 101.
335. Vālmīki, *The Rāmāyaṇa* (Vol. I), 'Bālakāṇḍa', translated by Robert P. Goldman, Princeton University Press, Princeton, 1984, I.6.19–21; Vālmīki, *The Rāmāyaṇa* (Vol. VI), 'Yuddhakāṇḍa', translated by Robert P. Goldman, Sally J. Sutherland Goldman, and Barend A. van Nooten, Motilal Banarsidass, Delhi, 2010, VI.28.4.
336. Vālmīki, II.104.23.
337. Trautmann (2015), p. 121.
338. Trautmann (2015), p. 123.
339. Trautmann (2015), p. 193.
340. Trautmann (2015), pp. 194–195.
341. Trautmann (2015), pp. 193–194.
342. Trautmann (2015), p. 195.
343. Trautmann (2015), p. 192.
344. Trautmann (2015), p. 196.
345. Trautmann (2015), p. 111.
346. Kauṭilya, X.3.4–45.
347. Trautmann (2015), pp. 112–114.
348. The small number of elephants held by Porus had posed a great threat to Alexander's cavalry, and this might have been one of the reasons why the force of Alexander did not want to face the might of the enormous Nanda elephantry. That Indian war elephants were of much attraction to the Hellenistic forces is testified by the fact that Seleucus surrendered three provinces to Candragupta in exchange for five hundred elephants.
349. Vyāsa, II.49.7.
350. Vyāsa, I.123.7.
351. Trautmann (2015), pp. 146–152.
352. Vyāsa, III.31.8.
353. Vyāsa, IV.30.26–27.
354. Vyāsa, VII.25.28.
355. Vyāsa, VII.68.31.
356. Vyāsa, VIII.17.17–20.
357. Vyāsa, VIII.59.10.
358. Vyāsa, VIII.62.35–37.
359. Vyāsa, VIII.171.4.
360. The significance of the eastern regions—particularly Magadha, Cedī, Puṇḍra, and Prāgjyotiṣa—in the *Mahābhārata* narrative and their relationship with the *madhyadeśa* shall be discussed in detail in Chapter 4.
361. MS, IV.3.4; TB, I.7.1.6; ŚB, XII.7.1.1–10, XII.7.3.1.
362. Vyāsa, VI.1.26–32.

363. Singh (1965), pp. 153–167.
364. Kaushik Roy, *Hinduism and the Ethics of Warfare in South Asia*, Cambridge University Press, New Delhi, 2012; Torkel Brekke, 'Breaking the Thigh and the Warrior Code' in Raziuddin Aquil and Kaushik Roy (eds), *Warfare, Religion and Society in Indian History*, Manohar, Delhi, 2012, pp. 43–61.
365. For example, the book declares—without cross-checking—that Arjuna had killed Droṇa, when verification from the primary text would easily reveal that the act was performed by Dhṛṣṭadyumna. See Kaushik Roy (2012), p. 40.
366. Kaushik Roy (2012), pp. 20, 23, 31.
367. Kaushik Roy (2012), pp. 20, 24.
368. Kaushik Roy (2012), pp. 19, 24.
369. Kaushik Roy (2012), p. 23.
370. Kaushik Roy (2012), pp. 28–32.
371. Katz (1989), pp. 105–118.
372. Katz (1989), pp. 155–186.
373. Katz (1989), pp. 239–245.
374. Torkel Brekke, 'Between Prudence and Heroism: Ethics of War in the Hindu Tradition' in Torkel Brekke (ed.), *Ethics of War in Asian Civilizations*, Taylor and Francis, London, 2005a, pp. 113, 115, 119; Torkel Brekke, 'The Ethics of War and the Concept of War in Asia and Europe', *Numen*, Vol. 52, 2005b, pp. 72–73.
375. Brekke (2012), pp. 55–57.
376. Kaushik Roy (2012), p. 5.
377. Surya P. Subedi, 'The Concept in Hinduism of Just War', *Journal of Conflict and Security Law*, Vol. 8, No. 2, 2003, pp. 342–343.
378. Manoj Kumar Sinha, 'Hinduism and International Humanitarian Law', *International Review of the Red Cross*, Vol. 87, Part 858, 2005, pp. 285–286.
379. M.A. Mehendale, *Reflections on the Mahābhārata War*, Indian Institute of Advanced Study, Shimla, 1995.
380. As the narrative goes, after Duryodhana was struck below the belt by Bhīma, Aśvatthāman took a vow—as the last Kaurava general—in front of his dying king to avenge his unlawful killing. However, he could not initially think of any strategy to combat the victorious Pāṇḍava force with only Kṛpa and Kṛtavarman left on his side. During the sleepless night he spent, he observed how just one owl attacked and killed a flock of sleeping crows in their nest, taking advantage of their slumber and its nocturnal vision. Aśvatthāman decided to attack the Pāṇḍava camp at night and kill the unprepared, sleeping enemies. The plan was executed successfully, wiping out the greater part of the Pāṇḍava force, excluding the five Pāṇḍavas, Kṛṣṇa, and Sātyaki. See Vyāsa, X.1–7.
381. T.A. Heathcote, *The Military in British India: The Development of British Land Forces in South Asia 1600–1947*, Manchester University Press, Manchester, 1995, p. 3.
382. McGrath (2016a), p. 1.
383. Vyāsa, XVII.1.6.

384. Vyāsa, XVII.1.9.
385. Grierson (1908), pp. 837–844.
386. Keith (1908).
387. ŚB, III.2.3.15.
388. Vyāsa, XII.9.3.
389. Ruth Katz, 'The *Sauptika* Episode in the Structure of the *Mahābhārata*' in Arvind Sharma (ed.), *Essays on the Mahābhārata*, Motilal Banarsidass, Delhi, 2007, pp. 130–149.
390. David Shulman, 'Towards a Historical Poetics of the Sanskrit Epics', *International Folklore Review*, Vol. 11, 1991, pp. 9–17; Madeleine Biardeau, 'Some More Considerations about Textual Criticism', *Purāṇa*, Vol. 10, No. 2, 1968, p. 119.
391. Biardeau (1968), p. 119.
392. Alf Hiltebeitel, *Rethinking the Mahābhārata: A Reader's Guide to the Education of the Dharma King*, University of Chicago Press, Chicago, 2001, p. 18.
393. Hiltebeitel (2001), pp. 166–167.
394. Brockington (1998), pp. 21–22.
395. Hiltebeitel (2001), pp. 22–23.
396. Hiltebeitel (2001), p. 178.
397. Hiltebeitel (2001), p. 101.
398. Michel Foucault, 'What Is an Author?' in Josue V. Harari (ed.), *Textual Strategies: Perspectives in Post-Structuralist Criticism*, Cornell University Press, Ithaca, 1979, pp. 141–160.
399. Hitebeitel (2001), p. 45.
400. Hiltebeitel (2001), pp. 33–35.
401. Hiltebeitel (2001), p. 92.
402. Hiltebeitel (2001), p. 92.
403. Hiltebeitel (2001), p. 96.
404. Hiltebeitel (2001), p. 101.
405. Hiltebeitel (2001), p. 165.
406. Hiltebeitel (2001), p. 169.
407. Hiltebeitel (2001), p. 176.
408. Hiltebeitel (2001), pp. 174–176.
409. Hiltebeitel (2001), p. 108.
410. Hiltebeitel (2001), pp. 17, 177–179.
411. Hiltebeitel (2001), p. 181.
412. Hiltebeitel (2001), p. 18.
413. Hiltebeitel (2001), p. 180.
414. Hiltebeitel (2001), p. 178.
415. For detailed discussion on these references, see Chapter 1.
416. Hiltebeitel (2001), pp. 125–126.
417. For some recent discussions on the date of the *Arthaśāstra*, see Thomas R. Trautmann, *Kauṭilya and the Arthaśāstra: A Statistical Investigation*

of the Authorship and Evolution of the Text*, Brill, Leiden, 1971; and S.K. Mital, *Kauṭilīya Arthaśāstra Revisited*, Centre for Studies in Civilization, Delhi, 2000.

418. C.Z. Minkowski, 'Janamejaya's *Sattra* and Ritual Structure', *Journal of the American Oriental Society*, Vol. 109, No. 3, 1989, p. 402.
419. Vyāsa, V.129.13.
420. Vyāsa, V.65–66.
421. Vyāsa, V.47.35.
422. Vyāsa, V.49.9–14.
423. Gregory Nagy, *Homeric Questions*, University of Texas Press, Austin, 1996, chapter 2; Gregory Nagy, *Homeric Responses*, University of Texas Press, Austin, 2003, p. 2.
424. McGrath (2011), pp. 11–17.
425. Vyāsa, VI.2.2.
426. Vyāsa, V.47.95.
427. Vyāsa, XV.45.33.
428. Minkowski (1989), pp. 405–407.
429. Bruce M. Sullivan, *Kṛṣṇa Dvaipāyana Vyāsa and the Mahābhārata: A New Interpretation*, E.J. Brill, Leiden, 1990, p. 9.
430. Hopkins (1969a), p. 58.
431. For example, see R.G. Bhandarkar, 'Inaugural Address at Bhandarkar Oriental Research Institute, delivered on December 15, 1918' in Narayan Bapuji Utgikar and Vasudev Gopal Paranjpe (eds), *Collected Works of Sir R.G. Bhandarkar* (Vol. 1), Bhandarkar Oriental Research Institute, Poona, 1933, p. 519; and V.S. Sukthankar's 'Prolegomena' in the first volume of the Critical Edition of the *Mahābhārata*, p. ciii.
432. Bruce M. Sullivan, 'The Epic's Two Grandfathers, Bhīṣma and Vyāsa' in Arvind Sharma (ed.), *Essays on the Mahābhārata*, Motilal Banarsidass, Delhi, 2007, pp. 204–211.
433. Sullivan (1990), p. 100.
434. Sullivan (1990), pp. 80–101.
435. Hiltebeitel (2001), p. 41.
436. J.L. Mehta, 'Dvaipāyana, Poet of Being and Becoming' in T.R.S. Sharma (ed.), *Reflections and Variations on the Mahābhārata*, Sahitya Akademi, New Delhi, 2009, pp. 70–80.
437. Mehta (2009).
438. Van Buitenen (1973b), p. xxiii.
439. Cited in Hiltebeitel (2001), p. 32.
440. Sullivan (1990), p. 24.
441. Vālmīki (Vol. I), pp. 29–31.
442. Of course, such a claim for Vālmīki has also been made by the 'Uttarakāṇḍa' of the *Rāmāyaṇa*, but that book seems to be a later addition. For details, see Kanad Sinha, 'A Tale of the Three Couples and Their Poet: *Rāmakathā*, Love and

Vālmīki in South Asian Tradition', *Studies in Humanities in Social Sciences*, Vol. XVIII, Nos 1–2, 2011, pp. 43–80.

443. Vyāsa, I.1.61.
444. Vyāsa, I.57.74–75.
445. Sullivan (1990), p. 7.
446. See the detailed discussion in R.D. Karmakar's 'Introduction' to the 'Āśvamedhikaparvan' volume of the Critical Edition of the *Mahābhārata*, p. xxiv–xliv.
447. Vyāsa, I.1,50.
448. SVB, III.9.8.
449. GB, I.9.2.
450. *Taittirīya Āraṇyaka*, edited by R.L. Mitra, Bibliotheca Indica, Calcutta, 1872, I.9.2.
451. *The Jātaka* (Vol. IV), pp. 17–22.
452. *The Jātaka* (Vol. IV), pp. 50–57; *The Jātaka* (Vol. V), translated by E.B. Cowell and W.H.D. Rouse, Motilal Banarsidass, Delhi, 2002 (reprint), p. 138.
453. J.N. Sumitra Bai and Robert J. Zydenbos, 'The Jaina Mahābhārata' in Arvind Sharma (ed.), *Essays on the Mahābhārata*, Motilal Banarsidass, Delhi, 2007, pp. 251–273.
454. Kauṭilya, I.6.10.
455. Aśvaghoṣa, *Buddhacarita*, edited and translated by E.H. Johnston, Munshiram Manoharlal, 1995 (reprint), IV.16.
456. Vyāsa, I.42.
457. Sullivan (1990), p. 27.
458. Cited in Hiltebeitel (2001), p. 41.
459. Hiltebeitel (2001), p. 42.
460. Vyāsa, I.53.31.
461. Vyāsa, XV.1.12.
462. Hiltebeitel (2001), p. 42.
463. Vyāsa, I.1.205, I.56.17.
464. Vyāsa, I.1.19, I.57.74, XII.327.18.
465. CU, III.17.6.
466. Simon Brodbeck and Brian Black, 'Introduction' in Simon Brodbeck and Brian Black (eds), *Gender and Narrative in the Mahābhārata*, Routledge, London, 2007, p. 3.
467. Vyāsa, I.89.17–20.
468. Vyāsa, I.89.53, I.90.47.
469. Vyāsa, I.94.
470. Vyāsa, I.95–96.
471. Vyāsa, IX.60.47–50.
472. Vyāsa, IX.60.51–55.
473. Vyāsa, IX.64.22–27.
474. Vyāsa, V.60.10–14.

475. Vyāsa, IX.57.46–59.
476. Vyāsa, III.240.1–24.
477. McGrath (2016a), p. 78.
478. Angelika Malinar, 'Duryodhana's Truths: Kingship and Divinity in *Mahābhārata* 5.60' in J.L. Brockington (ed.), *Battle, Bards and Brahmins*, Motilal Banarsidass, Delhi, 2012, pp. 63–68.
479. Vyāsa, V.60.15–17.
480. Vyāsa, IX.30.3.
481. Vyāsa, IX.60.51.
482. Vyāsa, XVIII.1.13.
483. David Gitomer, 'King Duryodhana: The *Mahābhārata* Discourse of Sinning and Virtue in Epic and Drama', *Journal of the American Oriental Society*, Vol. 112, 1992, pp. 222–232.
484. Bhāsa, *Dūtavākya*, translated by C.R. Devadhar, Oriental Book Agency, Poona, 1957, I.24.
485. Bhāsa, *Urubhaṅga*, translated by C.R. Devadhar, Oriental Book Agency, Poona, 1957, I.47–52.
486. Vyāsa, IX.64.28–29.
487. Vyāsa, IX.1.18.
488. Vyāsa, XV.15.20.
489. Vyāsa, I.100.
490. Vyāsa, I.123.1–39.
491. Vyāsa, I.123.36–37.
492. Kevin McGrath, 'The Sanskrit Hero: Karṇa in Epic Mahābhārata', a thesis presented to the Department of Sanskrit and Indian Studies, Harvard University, Cambridge, Massachusetts, February 2001 (later published from Brill, Leiden, 2004).
493. McGrath (2001), p. 1.
494. McGrath (2001), p. 4.
495. McGrath (2001), pp. 9–10.
496. McGrath (2001), p. 299.
497. Vyāsa, I.126.
498. Vyāsa, I.127.1–5.
499. Vyāsa, V.139.5–7.
500. Aditya Adarkar, 'Karna's Choice: Courage and Character in the Face of an Ethical Dilemma' in T.S. Rukmani, *The Mahābhārata: What Is Not Here Is Nowhere Else*, Munshiram Manoharlal, New Delhi, 2005, pp. 117–130.
501. Uma Chakravarti, 'A Sutaputra in a Royal Household: The *Kshatriya* World of Power and Its Margins' in Kumkum Roy (ed.), *Looking within and Looking without: Exploring Households in the Subcontinent through Time*, Primus, New Delhi, 2015, pp. 173–201.
502. Chakravarti (2015), p. 196.
503. Vyāsa, VIII.67.27.

504. Vyāsa, VI.117.31.
505. T.R.S. Sharma, 'Introduction: Many Makers, Many Texts/Contexts' in T.R.S. Sharma (ed.), *Reflections and Variations on The Mahabharata*, Sahitya Akademi, New Delhi, 2009, p. 19.
506. Vyāsa, III.177.26.
507. Vyāsa, III.177.30–35.
508. Vyāsa, XII.161.
509. Mukund Lath, 'The Concept of *Anrshamsya* in the *Mahabharata*' in T.R.S. Sharma (ed.), *Reflections and Variations on the Mahabharata*, Sahitya Akademi, New Delhi, 2009, pp. 82–89.
510. Lath (2009), p. 89.
511. Hiltebeitel (2001), p. 207.
512. Hiltebeitel (2001), pp. 205–206.
513. Sibaji Bandyopadhyay, 'A Critique of Non-violence' in *Three Essays on the Mahābhārata: Exercises in Literary Hermeneutics*, Orient BlackSwan, Hyderabad, 2016a, pp. 267–307.
514. Vyāsa, III.197–206.
515. The lateness of the 'Śāntiparvan' shall be discussed in Chapter 5.
516. Vyāsa, I.99.33.
517. Lath (2009), pp. 84–85; Hitebeitel (2001), p. 212.
518. Vyāsa, I.109.5–31.
519. See Hiltebeitel (2001), pp. 109–200.
520. Vyāsa, II.58.33–37.
521. Vyāsa, III.297.55.
522. Vyāsa, III.297.71.
523. Vyāsa, III.298.10.
524. Vyāsa, V.30.38, V.32.11, V.52.10.
525. Vyāsa, VII.158.53–62.
526. Vyāsa, XII.42.10–11.
527. Vyāsa, XV.2.3.
528. Vyāsa, XVII.3.1–15.
529. Vyāsa, XVII.3.36.
530. Vyāsa, XVIII.1.20–XVIII.2.12.
531. Vyāsa, XVIII.3.28–30.
532. Hiltebeitel (2001), p. 213.
533. Vyāsa, III.117.8.
534. Hiltebeitel (2001), p. 211.
535. McGrath (2011a), p. 154.
536. McGrath (2011a), p. 158.
537. Vyāsa, I.73–80.
538. Vyāsa, I.68–69.
539. Vyāsa, I.92–93.
540. Vyāsa, I.99.

541. Vyāsa, V.170–197.
542. Vyāsa, I.99.29, V.138.9–10.
543. Vyāsa, V.127, V.146.
544. Vyāsa, XI.13.19, XI.14.12–13.
545. Vyāsa, XI.25.
546. Vyāsa, V.130.7.
547. Vyāsa, V.130.20.
548. Vyāsa, V.130.30.
549. Vyāsa, V.130.32.
550. Vyāsa, V.131–134.
551. Sally J. Sutherland, 'Sītā and Draupadī: Aggressive Behaviour and Female Role-Models in the Sanskrit Epics', *Journal of the American Oriental Society*, Vol. 109, No. 1, January–March 1989, pp. 63–79.
552. Vyāsa, III.13.58–59.
553. Vyāsa, III.13.112–113.
554. Vyāsa, III.255.45.
555. Vyāsa, IV.15.20–36.
556. Vyāsa, IV.19.1.
557. Vyāsa, IV.20.32.
558. Vyāsa, IV.21.38.
559. Vyāsa, III.28.34.
560. Vyāsa, III.31.42.
561. Vyāsa, III.33.8.
562. Vyāsa, III.28.35–36; translation slightly modified.
563. Vyāsa, XII.14.4.
564. Vyāsa, IV.17.1.
565. Vyāsa, III.28.
566. Vyāsa, III.29.
567. Vyāsa, III.31.4.
568. Vyāsa, III.32.4–5. These ideas almost echo the general framework of desireless action based on *svabhāva*, propounded by Kṛṣṇa in the *Bhagavad Gītā*, which we shall discuss in Chapter 4.
569. Vyāsa, III.30.
570. Vyāsa, III.30.1.
571. Vyāsa, III.30.23.
572. Vyāsa, III.30.30.
573. Vyāsa, III.30.50.
574. Vyāsa, III.31.1.
575. Vyāsa, III.34.13.
576. Vyāsa, III.34.52.
577. Vyāsa, X.10–16.
578. This discussion on *ānṛśaṃsya* is developed from my previously published essay. See Kanad Sinha, 'Redefining *Dharma* in a Time of Transition: *Ānṛśaṃsya* in

the *Mahābhārata* as an Alternative End of Human Life', *Studies in History*, Vol. 35, No. 2, 2019, pp. 147–161.

579. Shirshendu Chakrabarti, 'Irresolution and Agency: The Case of Yudhiṣṭhira' in Sibesh Chandra Bhattacharya, Vrinda Dalmiya, and Gangeya Mukherji (eds), *Exploring Agency in the Mahabharata: Ethical and Political Dimensions of Dharma*, Routledge, London and New York, 2018, pp. 133–141.
580. G.C. Pande, 'The Socio-cultural Milieu of the Mahabharata: An Age of Change' in T.R.S. Sharma (ed.), *Reflections and Variations on the Mahabharata*, Sahitya Akademi, New Delhi, 2009, pp. 60–61.
581. Vyāsa, I.1.208–209.
582. Vyāsa, I.56.33.
583. Vyāsa, XVIII.5.47–50.
584. Christopher Minkowski, 'Snakes, Sattras and the *Mahābhārata*' in Arvind Sharma (ed.), *Essays on the Mahābhārata*, Motilal Banarsidass, Delhi, 2011, p. 385.
585. PB, 25.15.2–4; MŚS, 9.5.5.39; *Āpastamba Śrauta Sūtra*, 23.14.8; BŚS, 17–18; BGS, 3.10.
586. PB, 25.15.3; BŚS, 17–18; BGS, 3.10.
587. See Section 2.
588. AV, VIII.10.22; JUB, IV.26.15.
589. AV, IV.6, V.13, VI.12, VIII.10.29, VIII.14.14; JB, II.284.
590. ṚV, II.11.20, II.14.4, VIII.3.19, VIII.32.3, VIII.32.26; AB, VI.1; KB, 29.1; ŚB, XIII.4.3.9; JB, I.345, II.222, III.374; ĀŚS, 10.7.
591. Minkowski (2011), p. 386.
592. Minkowski (2011), p. 390.
593. Vyāsa, XVIII.5.29.
594. J. Fergusson, *Tree and Serpent Worshippers*, India Museum, London, 1868, pp. 44–47.
595. Vyāsa, I.206.
596. Vyāsa, I.218.1–11.
597. Vyāsa, VIII.66.1–24.
598. Vyāsa, I.45.6.
599. Vyāsa, I.51.16–I.53.14.
600. Vyāsa, XVIIII.5.26–27.
601. Arti Dhand, 'The Subversive Nature of Virtue in the *Mahābhārata*: A Tale about Women, Smelly Ascetics and God', *Journal of the American Academy of Religion*, Vol. 72, No. 1, March 2004, pp. 33–58.
602. Vyāsa, I.54.2–4.
603. Vyāsa, XII.311.1–10.
604. Vyāsa, XII.309.
605. Vyāsa, I.107.7–8.
606. Vyāsa, X.15.32.
607. Vyāsa, XV.41.7.

608. In this context, it may be useful to remember that Aśvaghoṣa knew of a story of Vyāsa being kicked by a prostitute named Kāśisundari. Though this tradition is not known anywhere else, curiously Ambikā and Ambālikā are also the princesses of Kāśī. Did their repulsion at Vyāsa's looks and smell remind him of a similar repulsion of a prostitute of the native kingdom of the princesses and the insult he had faced from a Kāśī woman, leading to the curses? Is it another version of the same story? This also makes us ponder if Vyāsa was primarily imagining or reporting. The *Mahābhārata*, after all, is an *itihāsa* and not a historical chronicle. Hence, the focus was probably on the depiction of a time of great transition and the various conflicting ideas contending with each other, rather than an authentic record of facts and events. Therefore, the fine line between the report of the *aitihāsika* and the imagination of the *kavi* is often blurred, more so when the poet himself appears as a character.
609. Dhand (2004), pp. 46–49.
610. Vyāsa, I.99.38–41.
611. Vyāsa, I.99.42–43.
612. Vyāsa, I.100.25.
613. Vyāsa, I.102.23.
614. Vyāsa, XV.6–7.

4

New Text, New Era, New Hero: Vāsudeva Kṛṣṇa and His *Svadharma*

4.1 Kṛṣṇa or the Kṛṣṇas?: Questioning a Deified Hero

> A bizarre figure, a Yādava chieftain who looks and acts not uncommonly like a mortal—and a very ordinary mortal at that and who has the incredible effrontery to say that he is God, a cynic who preaches the highest morality and stoops to practice the lowest tricks, in order to achieve his mean ends. An opportunist who teaches an honest man to tell a lie, the only he had told in his life! A charlatan who declares himself to be the god of gods, descended from the highest heaven for establishing righteousness on earth, and advises a hesitating archer to strike down a foe who is defenceless and crying for mercy![1]
>
> He was Krishna Vasudeva, the resplendent one, the one who lacked nothing, the one who gave magnificently.[2]

The two totally contradictory statements quoted here incidentally refer to the same person—Vāsudeva Kṛṣṇa—and interestingly are equally well grounded in their sources. More surprisingly, even that source is the same text called the *Mahābhārata*. Who was this Vāsudeva Kṛṣṇa, the hero of the *Mahābhārata* or a successful deceiver? A charlatan or a messiah? 'A great statesman' or a 'slippery opportunist'? One can hardly decide. Moreover, this figure did not remain just an enigmatic epic hero or a paradoxical historical/mythical figure but became one of the most popular divinities in the subcontinent. However, even as a deity, his hagiography portrays him as a butter thief in childhood, an adulterous playboy in adolescence, a ruthless killer in youth, and a shrewd trickster in mature

From Dāśarājña to Kurukṣetra. Kanad Sinha, Oxford University Press. © Oxford University Press 2021.
DOI: 10.1093/oso/9780190130695.003.0004

age. But to the same person is attributed the most celebrated discourse in Indian philosophy and the most celebrated political victory in his contemporary world. Moreover, his apparent contradictions hardly matter to his followers, and a devotee could easily perceive the spiritual excellence of his Lord as a continuation of his seemingly unscrupulous activities:

vraje prasiddhaṃ navanītacauraṃ
gopāṅgaṇānāṃ dūkulacauram//
bahujanmaparamārjitapāpacauraṃ/
caurāgragaṇyaṃ satataṃ namāmi//

(I always salute the greatest of thieves—the famous butter thief of Vraja, the one who stole the clothes of the milkmaids, the one who steals away the sins accumulated in numerous births.)

Kṛṣṇa's elusive life, and even more elusive claim to divinity, indeed remained a paradox to even his contemporaries, if we are to rely on the *Mahābhārata*. There we find Bhīṣma saying about Kṛṣṇa:

Of Brahmins he is the elder in knowledge, of *kṣatriyas* the superior in strength, and both these grounds to honor Govinda are found firm. Knowledge of the Vedas and their branches, and boundless might as well—who in the world of men possesses these so distinguishedly if not Keśava?

Liberality, dexterity, learning, gallantry, modesty, fame, a supreme resolve, luster, pentinacity, contentment, and prosperity are forever in Acyuta. All of you must agree that he, fully accomplished teacher, father, and guru, is to be honored and worthy of honor.[3]

But the same section of the text contains Śiśupāla's pointed reply:

[I]s it not a great wonder that he killed Kaṃsa, the mighty prince, whose food he had eaten? ... Strict, honest, law-abiding people have always instructed us in the world not to raise weapons against women, cows, brahmins, him whose food one has eaten, and him who seeks mercy with you ... You talk me of praising Kṛṣṇa as ancient, old and superior, as if I knew nothing? But how does a cow-killer and woman-killer deserve praise, Bhīṣma?

Even though upon your word that 'he is the wisest of all, he is the lord of the world', Janārdana believes it is all true, surely it remains all a lie![4]

Therefore Kṛṣṇa always remained a paradox, a mixture of opposites, someone whom one could love or hate or behold in wonder but never ignore. No wonder that he has been deified, because—even without the magic vision bestowed on Arjuna—we can behold Kṛṣṇa in the way Arjuna viewed him in the eleventh chapter of the *Gītā*, as a cocktail of everything in the universe, the *viśvarūpa*.

But who is this Vāsudeva Kṛṣṇa: A man, or a god, or an incarnation, or an epic hero, or a historical figure, or just an idea? Moreover, why is this Vāsudeva Kṛṣṇa so important in the *Mahābhārata*? In the first three chapters, we have identified the origin of the *Mahābhārata* tradition as an *itihāsa* of the Later Vedic Kurus, traced how the rise of the Bharata-Pūrus and eventually of the Kurus was integrated with the process of Vedic text creation, and inspected the key elements of the *Mahābhārata* narrative to identify how it was a document of transition in a period when the principles of ability and heredity were being fiercely debated over and how it professed a new kind of philosophy that could be followed irrespective of one's birth and could offer a middle ground between the obligations of an active, violent life and the absurdity of complete renunciatory non-violence. But if this text is all about the affairs of the Kurus (and, at best, of their Pāñcāla neighbours), then the figure of Vāsudeva Kṛṣṇa appears to be a misfit. Yet, entering the family feud of the Kurus in a sudden and abrupt manner, Kṛṣṇa rises to the position of the principal guiding force of the chain of events to the degree that enabled him to claim godhood. Therefore, it is worth having a look into the life of the enigmatic figure who, born in confinement and bred in a pastoral village, grew up to be the most revered diplomat of his time; who—starting his career as a cowherd—ended up herding the complex movements of an epoch; who was never a king but had the crowns of all the kings placed under his feet; who was not a sage but the idol of the greatest of sages; whose fingers were as brilliant in playing the flute as in wielding the *cakra*; who, after living as the greatest kingmaker, died on a poor hunter's breast in a forest; whose cheerful flirting with the milkmaids transcended his life and whose immortal sermon preached on a battlefield claimed to transcend death; who was a wonder to his contemporaries and a greater wonder to those who followed; a character of such complexity for whom deification seems too meagre and obvious a homage.

We can start our survey of the character by locating Kṛṣṇa in the *Mahābhārata*. As noted already, Kṛṣṇa had no direct link with the two major kingdoms involved in the central conflict. Stationed in faraway Dvārakā, he was an important leader of the Yādava-Vṛṣṇi *gaṇasaṃgha* but got involved in the problems of the faraway Kuru realm only because the Pāṇḍavas were his cousins (and possibly because of the geopolitical reasons discussed in Chapter 3). He suddenly appeared during the *svayaṃvara* of Draupadī, as a spectator, and met his cousins who married the Pañcāla princess. From then on, he appeared time and again as a counsellor of the Pāṇḍavas. He cemented his alliance with them by facilitating his sister Subhadrā's marriage with Arjuna, his closest friend among the Pāṇḍavas. Then, he joined Arjuna in burning the Khāṇḍava forest to clear the land for the establishment of the Pāṇḍava capital Indraprastha. Kṛṣṇa's political life got entangled with that of the Pāṇḍavas when Yudhiṣṭhira sought his counsel before deciding to organize a *rājasūya*. Kṛṣṇa narrated to the Pāṇḍavas how he had killed the tyrannical Kaṃsa to free the Yādava-Bhojas of Mathura and, in the process, made an enemy of the powerful Magadha chief Jarāsaṃdha. In fear of Jarāsaṃdha, the Yādavas deserted Mathurā and settled in Dvārakā. We see the first application of Kṛṣṇa's trickery in getting Jarāsaṃdha killed in a wrestling bout with Bhīma. In the *rājasūya* of Yudhiṣṭhira, Kṛṣṇa was honoured as the best among all dignitaries, and the first claim to his divinity was made. Both these claims were denounced by Śiśupāla who eventually died in a duel with Kṛṣṇa. Thus the *rājasūya* marked Kṛṣṇa's rise to political power. After this, the Pāṇḍavas gradually lost their track, lost everything in a dice game, and were exiled. Kṛṣṇa constantly expressed his solidarity with them and was instrumental in the marriage of Abhimanyu, the son of Subhadrā and Arjuna, and Uttarā, the Matsya princess. Before the war, both Duryodhana and Arjuna sought his help. Kṛṣṇa gave Duryodhana his formidable Nārayaṇīya regiment and personally joined the Pāṇḍava camp as the non-combating charioteer of Arjuna. He made a last attempt at peace as a messenger to the Kaurava camp but in vain. When Arjuna was depressed by the possibility of a war where all his kinsmen were fighting each other, Kṛṣṇa inspired him with rich philosophical arguments and sanctioned his own divinity in the process. Through Kṛṣṇa's guidance and tricks, the Pāṇḍava-Pañcāla force won the war. Kṛṣṇa spent the next thirty-six years of his life mostly in

Dvārakā, trying in vain to control his proud and rowdy clan. He failed. The Yādavas killed each other in a drunken brawl. Kṛṣṇa entered a forest where a hunter accidentally killed him.

However, just as the *Mahābhārata* is not only about Kṛṣṇa, Kṛṣṇa is not just a *Mahābhārata* character. Since the *Mahābhārata* provides only scanty information about his early life, numerous texts have been composed to fill that gap, the *Harivaṃśa* (known as a sequel to the *Mahābhārata*) being the most important of those and the very late *Bhāgavata Purāṇa* the most popular. These texts, namely the *Harivaṃśa*, the *Viṣṇu Purāṇa*, the *Brahma Purāṇa*, the *Bhāgavata Purāṇa*, and the *Brahmavaivarta Purāṇa*, are the ones which provide fascinating accounts of Kṛṣṇa's picturesque childhood in the cowherds' village, the moving motherly affection of his foster-mother Yaśodā, his killing of the several demons sent by Kaṃsa, his childhood pranks, including butter stealing, his fight with Indra, his subjugation of the Nāga Kālīya, his dalliance with the milkmaids, and his special fondness for one of them named Rādhā. More than the *Mahābhārata* hero, this Kṛṣṇa has been the favourite of the poets, mystics, devotees, and artists. Apart from these stories, the Purāṇas also provide legends about his contest with many other antagonists (mostly the allies of Jarāsaṃdha), his abduction of Rukmiṇī, his thrilling search for the jewel Syamantaka which led to two more marriages, his expedition against the Assamese chief Narakāsura from whom he would rescue sixteen thousand abducted women, and so on.

These legends raise more questions. Whether this cowherd boy had anything to do with the *Mahābhārata* hero and the chief of Dvārakā is a question that has troubled scholars. Kṛṣṇa the cowherd, Kṛṣṇa the Lord of Dvārakā, Kṛṣṇa the enemy of Jarāsaṃdha, Kṛṣṇa of the *Mahābhārata*, Kṛṣṇa the philosopher of the *Gītā*—are they all the same person or different persons? Is Kṛṣṇa somehow related to the original narrative of the *Mahābhārata*, or is he a folk hero who had been slipped into the text at a later stage? Even if he was there, is he the same Kṛṣṇa who was the cowherd of Vṛndāvana? Is the chief of Dvārakā identical with the hero of Mathurā? Even if there was a Kṛṣṇa in the *Mahābhārata*, still is not the *Gītā* a didactic and, therefore, later section? A volley of questions arises, and scholars tried to answer them in different manners.

Christian Lassen views two layers in the Kṛṣṇa tradition. He thinks that the tradition about the pastoral Kṛṣṇa is more ancient than that about the warrior. The pre-Buddhist pastoral Yādava hero was deified in post-Buddhist times and entered the *Mahābhārata* which was initially a tale of Kuru-Pāñcāla war. The didactic sections, including the *Bhagavad Gītā*, are undoubtedly later interpolations.[5]

Walter Ruben is possibly the biggest propounder of a Kṛṣṇaless *Mahābhārata*. He separates the three cycles of legends about Kṛṣṇa: the Mathurā-Braj cycle, the Dvārakā cycle, and the Hastināpura cycle. He considers Kṛṣṇa's contest with Jarāsaṃdha a historical event, since the weakness of Kṛṣṇa showed in it could not be the product of the imagination of the pro-Kṛṣṇa poets. However, he thinks that this historical account has been overlaid by many local legends. On the other hand, the Kuru-Pāṇḍava conflict is another historical tradition in which Kṛṣṇa initially had no role to play. For Ruben, Kṛṣṇa is an inessential absentee hero in the *Mahābhārata*, who does not have any prominent role to play in the epic. In Draupadī's *svayaṃvara*, he was not a participant but a spectator. In the war, he was not a combatant but a mere charioteer, and so on. The Dvārakā cycle, Ruben thinks, was initially about some different hero but has been grafted onto the story through the presumed link of Kṛṣṇa's historical flight in fear of Jarāsaṃdha.[6]

Therefore, Lassen and Ruben believe in a historical Kṛṣṇa, probably a pastoral tribal hero cum demigod, who had no connection with the *Mahābhārata* originally. Hermann Jacobi also considers Kṛṣṇa as the tribal hero of a lost epic poem of the Yādavas.[7] However, some other supporters of a Kṛṣṇaless *Mahābhārata* question that historicity as well.

R.G. Bhandarkar thinks that an Upaniṣadic scholar named Kṛṣṇa, disciple of Ghora Āṅgirasa, had been later equated with a Sātvata-Vṛṣṇi deity called 'Vāsudeva'.[8] He thinks that the childhood legends of Kṛṣṇa evolved from the legends about Christ, brought to India by the Ābhīras who had come from Asia Minor.[9]

A similar view is harboured by D.D. Kosambi who thinks that Kṛṣṇa was initially nothing but a demigod of the Mathurā saga and the stories about his killing of Jarāsaṃdha and Kaṃsa are nothing but fabrications. The Jarāsaṃdha legend represents nothing but the westward scattering of the people who worshipped Kṛṣṇa as a patron deity. This Kṛṣṇa entered the *Mahābhārata* at a very late stage.[10]

However, some other scholars speak of a historical Kṛṣṇa in the *Mahābhārata* whose exact role is difficult to determine. Adolf Holtzmann propounded an 'inversion theory' which claimed that the Kauravas were the initial heroes of the *Mahābhārata* and the Pāṇḍavas and Kṛṣṇa were on the 'other' side. Thus, he considered Kṛṣṇa as a deified tribal hero of a non-Brahmanical people with a taste for drunkenness and sensuality. He was a propounder of immoral advices as seen in the war. The original *Gītā*, thus, was not said by Kṛṣṇa but by Droṇa whose counsel Duryodhana asked at the start of the *Gītā*![11]

Washburn Hopkins does not rule out the possibility of Kṛṣṇa being present in the original epic but at best as a 'demigod chieftain' who gradually assumed the position of the supreme divinity. The epic contains many instances where his original human nature is shown, including his cowboy manners before Jarāsaṃdha, his occasional ignorance on the battlefield, his 'unreasonable rage' when Arjuna fails to kill Bhīṣma and a possibility of breaking his promise, his occasional worshipping of Umā and Śiva, his reception of power from gods to kill Naraka, his occasional admissions of powerlessness, Śiśupāla's condemnation of his deceitful and cowardly nature, his weakness and despair in front of his rowdy kin, and his fear of Jarāsaṃdha.[12] According to Hopkins, Kṛṣṇa's demigod status was not acquired before 400–200 BCE. His emergence as an all-god is dated between 200 BCE and 200 CE.[13]

On the other hand, there are scholars who tried to show that Kṛṣṇa is essentially linked with the *Mahābhārata*. Sylvain Levi speaks of the central importance of Kṛṣṇa in the epic. He shows how many of the books of the epic start with the benediction praising Nārāyaṇa and Nara who are incarnated as Kṛṣṇa and Arjuna, respectively, in the epic. Levi thinks that the *Mahābhārata* is primarily a *kṣatriya* tract that preaches the cult of Kṛṣṇa, and therefore Kṛṣṇa's propagation of the *kṣatriya* code in the *Gītā* is the kernel of the epic. The benediction he cites does not appear in many manuscripts and has been discarded by the Critical Edition, but Levi is quite right about the recurrence of the formula 'wherever is *dharma*, there is Kṛṣṇa, wherever is Kṛṣṇa, there is victory'.[14]

V.S. Sukthankar views the epic on three planes: mundane, ethical and spiritual, and revolving around the *Gītā*. Therefore, the *Gītā* is the heart of the *Mahābhārata* even to the chief editor of its Critical Edition.[15]

The famous Bengali novelist and essayist Bankim Chandra Chattopadhyay picked up the historical Kṛṣṇa as a figure to be idolized to foster Indian nationalism. His *Kṛṣṇacaritra* remains one of the earliest and most extensive works in search of the historical personality of the *Mahābhārata* hero Kṛṣṇa by selecting the original legends and separating the later interpolations.[16]

H.C. Raychaudhuri has methodically shown how the Upaniṣadic Kṛṣṇa, disciple of Ghora Āṅgirasa, is no different from the *Mahābhārata* Kṛṣṇa who echoes the same teachings in the *Gītā*. He uses several historical sources to reconstruct the life of the philosopher-teacher Vāsudeva Kṛṣṇa. However, he dismisses the Purāṇic stories of Kṛṣṇa's childhood as later fabrications.[17] Madhav M. Deshpande has shown how the *Gītā* is contextually interlinked with the rest of the *Mahābhārata* and therefore is an integral part of the epic.[18]

Stig Wikander, Georges Dumezil, Madeleine Biardeau, Heino Gehrts, and Alf Hiltebeitel, focusing on the religious and mythical narrative of the epic, emphasize the integral importance of Kṛṣṇa in the text. They view Kṛṣṇa's importance not as a historical figure but as integral to the eschatological myth that the *Mahābhārata* represents.[19]

However, some other scholars have also tried to understand the historical personality of Kṛṣṇa. The anthropologist Irawati Karve tried to understand the various *Mahābhārata* characters, and, to her, Vāsudeva Kṛṣṇa is a historical personality later deified by the Ābhīras. She thinks that the *Mahābhārata* Kṛṣṇa is historical, whereas the legends about his childhood are later fabrications.[20]

J.A.B. van Buitenen views Kṛṣṇa as a Bhoja-Vṛṣṇi chieftain whose gradual prominence in the politics of the famous kingdoms creates a surprise which, he thinks, can be explained by his role in eliminating Jarāsaṃdha.[21] In his Bengali essay on Kṛṣṇa, the Sanskritist Nrisinha Prasad Bhaduri tries to establish collaboration between the several sources referring to Kṛṣṇa to understand his historical position.[22] With all these diverse opinions in mind, we can proceed to understand the historical role of Vāsudeva Kṛṣṇa in various kinds of sources in the following sections.

4.2 'There Is No Song without Kānu': Sourcing Vāsudeva Kṛṣṇa

Though we have extensively discussed the historical context of the *Mahābhārata* in the previous chapter, it does not clearly indicate the historicity of Kṛṣṇa, since the *Mahābhārata* is the source of only a part of the Kṛṣṇa legend and whether Kṛṣṇa was originally a part of the *Mahābhārata* has also been questioned. The Kṛṣṇa of Mathurā, the Kṛṣṇa of Dvārakā, the Kṛṣṇa of the *Mahābhārata*—whether they are the same or different, if same then whether he is a historical personality, if different then whether any of the Kṛṣṇas has some historicity, all these questions cannot be addressed on the basis of the *Mahābhārata* alone. Therefore, in this section, we shall discuss the various sources which can be useful in studying the character of Vāsudeva Kṛṣṇa.

In the previous section, we discussed the information about Kṛṣṇa that the *Mahābhārata* provides, but that contains very little material on Kṛṣṇa's early life. Therefore, the *Harivaṃśa* took up the task of filling this gap. This text is known as a supplement to the *Mahābhārata* and is attributed to the author of the *Mahābhārata*, Vyāsa. However, a serious reader of the text can easily identify the text as much later than that of the *Mahābhārata*, though that does not challenge its position as a supplement.

The fact that the *Mahābhārata* says little about Kṛṣṇa's early life is quite striking. It contains birth legends and stories about the early lives, though mostly fabulous, of even minor characters such as Kṛpa or Aśvatthāman. It cannot be argued that the text does not do so in Kṛṣṇa's case because Kṛṣṇa was not part of the original text, since the text provides birth legends of even Jarāsaṃdha and Śiśupāla, who are present in the text only as the antagonists of Kṛṣṇa. In fact, the attempts to conceive a Kṛṣṇaless *Mahābhārata* have not given any fruitful result. Ruben's idea that Kṛṣṇa plays no essential role in the major events is not very well grounded. The very narration of the *Mahābhārata* and the continuity of the Kuru race are directly related with Kṛṣṇa. It was he who helped Arjuna marry his sister Subhadrā. This couple produced the child Abhimanyu whose son was the famous Parikṣit who preserved the Kuru line. As we have seen already, it may not be an overstretching to say that without Parikṣit and Janamejaya there might not have been any propagation of the *Mahābhārata*. Apart from this crucial connection, Kṛṣṇa fought along with Arjuna to burn down the Khāṇḍava forest to establish Indraprastha. Kṛṣṇa's counsel created the background of Yudhiṣṭhira's *rājasūya* and assured its safety with the killing of Jarāsaṃdha. Again, Kṛṣṇa occupied the centre stage in that *rājasūya* and killed Śiśupāla. He raised Abhimanyu during the Pāṇḍava exile and was instrumental in his marriage to the Matsya princess Uttarā. He was the final messenger of peace before the war. He disclosed to Karṇa, the mainstay of the Kaurava force, that the Pāṇḍavas were his brothers, and thus partly predetermined the outcome of the battle. He counselled Arjuna when he was reluctant to fight. He was instrumental in the downfalls of Bhīṣma, Droṇa, Bhuriśravas, Jayadratha, Karṇa, and Duryodhana. Ruben, in a bid to sustain his thesis, goes to the extreme of claiming that the battle between Yudhiṣṭhira and Śalya, where the Kaurava commander fell without Kṛṣṇa's intervention, was the single decisive battle in the original *Mahābhārata*.[23] However, it is not comprehensible how the killing of a person who was neither a Kaurava nor a Pāṇḍava nor even a Pāñcāla, and who was the least celebrated of the commanders in the Kaurava camp, could decide the fate of the battle. If Kṛṣṇa is inessential in the *Mahābhārata* after all his feats, how is Śalya so essential?

Therefore, Kṛṣṇa being an integral part of the *Mahābhārata*, it is surprising why nothing about his early life appears in the text. The only reason can be that the poet(s) assumed the tales of Kṛṣṇa's early life to be already known to the audience. That can be possible only if the *Mahābhārata* Kṛṣṇa is the same as the Kṛṣṇa of folk legends, that is, the Kṛṣṇa of Mathurā-Vṛndāvana. However, in a later period, with Kṛṣṇa becoming more and more important as a deity, a codified hagiography was needed, and the *Harivaṃśa* came up to serve that purpose. The text does not have the grandeur or brilliance of its prequel *itihāsa* and contains many features of the Vaiṣṇavite Purāṇas. But, nevertheless, it does not pretend to be a Purāṇa and prefers to be seen as a supplement to the *itihāsa*. Its purpose is not the famous five *lakṣmaṇas* of a Purāṇa but telling the tale of Kṛṣṇa. Thus it stands as an intermediary between the *itihāsa* and the *purāṇa* traditions. Since the earliest of the extant Purāṇas, like the *Viṣṇu Purāṇa* and the *Vāyu Purāṇa* , were codified possibly in the early Gupta period (fourth century CE), the *Harivaṃśa* can be safely dated sometime in the first three Christian centuries and remains very important as the first canonical collection of the oral tradition about Kṛṣṇa. The *Viṣṇu Purāṇa* also takes up the Kṛṣṇa legends but follows mainly the *Harivaṃśa* structure. The *Brahma Purāṇa* repeats the *Viṣṇu Purāṇa* story. The most famous biography of Kṛṣṇa is no doubt the *Bhāgavata Purāṇa*. But the text is quite late, variously dated between the seventh and ninth centuries. We will return to these accounts later, but whether the legends contained even by the *Harivaṃśa* and the *Viṣṇu Purāṇa*, even if we leave the *Bhāgavata Purāṇa* alone, have any historical validity to know about a person who belonged to tenth to ninth centuries BCE if ever has to be decided.

The only way to come to that decision is to look for Vāsudeva Kṛṣṇa in older sources and alternative traditions, and Kṛṣṇa does not disappoint us in either case. It is quite understandable that searching for Kṛṣṇa in the *Ṛg Veda* would be futile, since the text was composed before the Later Vedic Age. However, his appearance in some late passage is not quite impossible. In fact, the Kṛṣṇa who fought Indra in *Ṛg Veda* VIII.96.13–15 seems to be Vāsudeva Kṛṣṇa himself. He was a leader who was resisting Indra on the bank of the river Aṃśumatī (which is another name of the Yamunā). The significance of this passage, and the reason for the identification made, will be discussed later. But, before that, let us proceed to clearer references.

The TĀ identifies Vāsudeva with the Vedic deity Viṣṇu in the prayer '*nārayaṇāya vidmahe vāsudevāya dhīmahi tanno viṣṇuh pracodayāt*'.[24] Bhandarkar has identified this Vāsudeva as a Sātvata-Vṛṣṇi deity later equated with Kṛṣṇa, as already mentioned. But there is not a single reference to any Sātvata-Vṛṣṇi Vāsudeva different from Kṛṣṇa in any source, which makes this assumption totally untenable. A.B. Keith rightly says, 'The separation of Vāsudeva and Kṛṣṇa as two entities, it is impossible to justify'.[25]

An even clearer and much more discussed reference comes from the CU. The passage says:

After Ghora Āṅgirasa had taught the same thing to Kṛṣṇa the son of Devakī, he continued—he was then altogether free from desires and at the point of death: 'One should turn to these three for protection: You are undecaying! You are the imperishable! You are fortified by breath'.[26]

Here, not only Kṛṣṇa the son of Devakī appeared in person but he was taught the doctrine of the undecaying, imperishable, deathless soul that he would teach Arjuna: a small passage linking the Kṛṣṇa of Mathurā and the Kṛṣṇa of Kurukṣetra.

Another teacher named Gobala Vārṣṇa is mentioned in the TS and the JUB.[27] It is not improbable that this Gobala Vārṣṇa is none but Gopāla Vārṣṇeya—Gopāla Kṛṣṇa, of the Vṛṣṇi clan. Therefore, in the Later Vedic literature itself, Kṛṣṇa the son of Vāsudeva and Devakī was known as an

Upaniṣadic intellectual, a deity equivalent to Viṣṇu, and possibly a warrior who had resisted Indra in the Yamunā valley.

More crucial is a formula of the grammarian Panini (*c.* fifth century BCE)—'*vāsudevārjunābhyāṃ buñ*'.[28] The formula means that the worshippers of Vāsudeva and Arjuna were termed '*vāsudevaka*' and '*arjunaka*'. The passage clearly shows that there was a community worshipping Vāsudeva in Pāṇini's time. This Vāsudeva was not a limited Sātvata-Vṛṣṇi deity of Mathurā but one closely associated with the *Mahābhārata* hero Arjuna, and he was possibly superior to Arjuna (otherwise the formula would have been *arjunavāsudevābhyāṃ buñ*).[29] The *Baudhāyana Dharma Sūtra* (II.5.24) knows very well the identification of Viṣṇu with Kṛṣṇa and calls Viṣṇu Govinda, Dāmodara and Keśava, names associated with Kṛṣṇa's activities.[30] There are reasons to believe that Kṛṣṇa legends were well known to Yāska, the author of *Nirukta*, who was born in Pāṇini's time or a little earlier. The issue will be discussed later. Kosambi also notes a Mirzapur cave painting, datable to the early centuries of the first millennium BCE, showing a hero hurling a discus, Kṛṣṇa's special weapon.[31]

In the fourth century BCE, the Greek envoy Megasthenes had noticed the prevalence of the worship of a deity whom he confused with Heracles. That he was none other than Vāsudeva Kṛṣṇa is testified by his worship among the Sourasenoi (Śūrasenas) of Methora (Mathurā) and Cleisobora (Kṛṣṇapura?) on the banks of the river Iobares (Aṃśuvatī/Yamunā).[32] However, again, the worship of this deity was not limited among the Śūrasenas of Mathurā. The Roman historian Curtius writes about the army of king Porus of Punjab:

> An image of Hercules was borne in front of the line of infantry, and this acted as the strongest of all incentives to make the soldiers fight well. To desert the bearers of this image was reckoned a disgraceful military offence.[33]

Patañjali, a grammarian of the second century BCE, was well aware of the Kṛṣṇa legends, particularly his killing of Kaṃsa. He knows of a drama which used to be performed, based on this theme, where black-masked actors sided with Kaṃsa and red-masked actors with Kṛṣṇa. He describes Kṛṣṇa's killing of Kaṃsa in historical past—'*jaghāna kaṃsam kila vāsudevah*'—and explains the word 'Vāsudeva' as a name of the God—'*sanjñaiṣā tatra bhavataḥ*' (III.2.111). He also makes an interesting statement—'*asādhur mātule kṛṣṇaḥ*' (Kṛṣṇa had behaved inappropriately with his maternal uncle), indicating that Patañjali did not approve of Kṛṣṇa's killing of Kaṃsa. More interesting is the Garuḍa Pillar in Vidiśā. Heliodorus, an envoy of the Greek king Antialchidas, sent to the court of Kāśīputra Bhagabhadra, became a devotee of *devadeva* Vāsudeva whom he mentions on his votive pillar.[34] Thus, Heliodorus, a figure of the second century BCE, not just knew Vāsudeva but was well aware of his identification with Viṣṇu whose vehicle was Garuḍa. Another Garuḍa pillar, donated by another Bhāgavata named Gotamīputra, has been found from the same region, datable to *c.* 100 BCE.[35]

A coin found from Ai-Khanoum, minted during the reign of Agathokles (*c.* 180–165 BCE), shows Kṛṣṇa with his brother Saṃkarṣaṇa (Balarāma).[36] The Ghoṣūṇḍī and Hathibāḍā inscriptions of King Gājāyana Pārāśarīputra (*c.* third to first century BCE) mention worship of Vāsudeva and Saṃkarṣaṇa in a Nārāyaṇa-vāṭaka, indicating Kṛṣṇa's identification with Nārāyaṇa.[37] The two brothers are also mentioned in the Nānāghat Cave Inscription of the Sātavāhana queen Nayanikā (first century BCE).[38] The Koṭhī Inscription of the Śaka Mahākṣatrapa Ṣoḍaśa mentions the construction of a Vāsudeva temple near Mathurā.[39]

That the Kṛṣṇa legends were quite popular by the beginning of the first millennium CE is well attested by the dramas of Bhāsa (*c.* second to third centuries CE). His *Bālacarita* is based on the childhood exploits of Kṛṣṇa and could have been composed before the *Harivaṃśa*. But he also deals with the *Mahābhārata* Kṛṣṇa in dramas like *Dūtavākyam* and *Urubhaṅga*. Thus, the two Kṛṣṇas were quite well known to Bhāsa and that too as the same person. Bhāsa's dramas are invaluable in our search for the original Kṛṣṇa legend, possibly being the earliest available collection of those.

If Vāsudeva Kṛṣṇa was quite well known to the various Brahmanical texts, Greek travellers, and secular literature, even the alternative traditions are quite well aware of the character. The Buddhists were well aware of the Kṛṣṇa legends. The *Mahāniddesa* (I.4.25), a commentary on the *Khuddaka Nikāya*, mentions Vāsudeva and Baladeva.[40] The Buddhist version of the Kṛṣṇa legend comes from the *Ghaṭa Jātaka*, and he is mentioned in the *Mahāummaga Jātaka* as well.

The *Ghaṭa Jātaka* story has its similarities and differences with the *Harivaṃśa* and *Bālacarita* accounts. The Kṛṣṇa story in the *Harivaṃśa* and the Purāṇas is about the Yādava-Vṛṣṇi confederacy. The Yādavas had a *gaṇasaṃgha* polity with many small clans such as the Vṛṣṇis,

Andhakas, and Bhojas. This Vṛṣṇi *saṃgha* was in fact known to the *Arhaśāstra* as well.[41] The main story starts with the Bhoja Ugrasena as the chief of the confederacy and the Vṛṣṇi Vāsudeva as an important leader. This Vāsudeva was married to Devakī, the daughter of Ugrasena's elder brother Devaka. However, a prophecy declared that the eighth child of this union would kill Kaṃsa, the son of Ugrasena. The scared Kaṃsa wanted to kill Devakī, but at last came to a settlement that every child born of the marriage would be handed over to him. He kept the couple, as well as his father, virtually captivated. The *gaṇasaṃgha* became a kingship. Kaṃsa killed six children born of Vāsudeva and Devakī. After Devakī became pregnant for the seventh time, the embryo got magically transported to the womb of Vāsudeva's other wife, Rohiṇī, who was living in a village of the cowherds, in the care of Vāsudeva's friend Nanda. This child was Balarāma. Kṛṣṇa was the eighth child of the couple. After his birth at night, Vāsudeva somehow escaped the guards and, with many supernatural favours, succeeded in giving his child to Nanda in return for the latter's newborn daughter. Kaṃsa tried to kill the baby girl, but in vain. The girl declared that Kaṃsa's would-be killer was being raised in the village of the cowherds, Gokula. Kaṃsa sent several demons to kill the infant Kṛṣṇa in Gokula and Vṛndāvana. But all of them were killed by Kṛṣṇa. In the meanwhile, Kṛṣṇa also did some other magical feats. He criticized the way the cowherds spent lavishly for a sacrifice in honour of Indra and persuaded them to spend the amount for better purposes. Angry Indra tried to drown Vṛndāvana, but Kṛṣṇa saved it by lifting the Mount Govardhana for a week. He also subdued the Nāga Kālīya. He had also been known for romantic dalliance with the cowherd women. Akrura came from Mathurā with Kaṃsa's invitation for a sacrifice. Kaṃsa made many secret designs for killing him on the way, but all failed. Kṛṣṇa and Balarāma entered the sacrificial arena where they defeated and killed Cāṇūra and Muṣṭika, Kaṃsa's appointed wrestlers, before killing Kaṃsa. They freed Vāsudeva and Devakī and restored Ugrasena to power.

Kaṃsa's death involved Kṛṣṇa in a bigger political turmoil. Kaṃsa's father-in-law was the powerful Magadha king Jarāsaṃdha who attacked Mathurā several times. Unable to face his mighty army, Kṛṣṇa decided to leave Mathurā and establish a new settlement in faraway Dvārakā. He killed Jarāsaṃdha's Greek ally Kālayavana as well. Jarāsaṃdha wanted to strengthen the bond between his allies by arranging the marriage of

Śiśupāla, the king of Cedī, and Rukmiṇī, the princess of Vidarbha. But Kṛṣṇa abducted Rukmiṇī and married her. After getting Jarāsaṃdha killed by Bhīma and killing Śiśupāla in Yudhiṣṭhira's *rājasūya*, Kṛṣṇa gradually killed off the other allies of Jarāsaṃdha, including the king of Puṇḍra who also adopted the title 'Vāsudeva'. Getting involved in an intra-clan conflict over a jewel called Syamantaka, Kṛṣṇa resolved it after a prolonged turmoil, which led to his marriage with Jāmbavatī, the daughter of a forest chief he defeated, and Satyabhāmā, the daughter of Satrājit whose jewel he recovered. Requested by the deities, he led expeditions against the Assamese plunderers Mura and Naraka and recovered sixteen thousand women abducted by the latter. He married all of them. There are various legends about Balarāma, Pradyumna (Kṛṣṇa's son), and Aniruddha (Pradyumna's son) as well.

With this background, we may have a look at the *Ghaṭa Jātaka* account. It also speaks of Kaṃsa and the prophecy. In this account, the lady Devagabbhā was the uterine sister of Kaṃsa, the king of Asitāñjana, and Upakaṃsa. Because of the prophecy, Kaṃsa kept Devagabbhā locked up in a tower so that she stayed unmarried. But Devagabbhā's serving woman Nandagopā helped her to copulate with Upasāgara, the prince of upper Mathurā and a friend of Upakaṃsa, and she gave birth to a daughter named Añjanā. Kaṃsa felt no threat from the daughter and raised her with great care. Devagabbhā was married off to Upasāgara, and they settled in the village Govaddhamana (clearly a village of the cowherds, literally meaning 'a village where cattle are increased'). Gradually ten sons were born to Devagabbhā and ten daughters to Nandagopā. But they exchanged their children, since Kaṃsa felt threatened only by the sons of Devagabbhā. Thus, Devagabbhā's children were raised by Nandagopā and her husband Andhakabenhu. Vāsudeva Kaṇha (Vāsudeva Kṛṣṇa) was the eldest of these ten sons. Among the brothers of Vāsudeva (Kṛṣṇa), we find Baladeva, Arjuna, Ghaṭapaṇḍita, and Aṅkura alongside the moon god, the sun god, the fire god, and the deities Varuṇa and Parjanya. These children grew up as competent wrestlers who plundered even the presents meant for the king. Gradually the secret got revealed, and Kaṃsa planned to kill the ten children in a wrestling bout with two famous wrestlers Cāṇūra and Muṭṭhika (Muṣṭika). Baladeva killed both the wrestlers, and Vāsudeva slayed Kaṃsa and Upakaṃsa with his famous *cakra*. Led by Vāsudeva, the brothers conquered various areas, with their metropolis in Dvārāvatī which they conquered following the advice of the sage Kaṇhadīpāyana (Kṛṣṇa Dvaipāyana). Vāsudeva killed many kings with his *cakra*. The brothers divided their kingdom in ten parts, each ruling one while Aṅkura gave his share to the sister Añjanā and chose trading as his profession. However, Vāsudeva mentally broke down after the death of one of his sons, and Ghaṭapaṇḍita—the Bodhisatttva—consoled him, teaching him the transitory nature of beings. Vāsudeva ruled for a long period of time, before his clansmen killed each other in a drunken brawl, following a curse by the sage Kaṇhadīpāyana whom the sons of the ten brothers killed. Baladeva was killed by the reincarnated Muṣṭika. Vāsudeva was killed by an arrow shot by a hunter named Jarā. Their sister, Añjanādevī, was the lone survivor.[42] The *Mahāummaga Jātaka* knows about the marriage between this Vāsudeva of Dvārāvatī and a *caṇḍālī* named Jāmbavatī.[43]

Therefore, the Buddhist legends also know about the childhood exploits of the Mathurā Kṛṣṇa and connect the same person with Dvārāvatī. However, as the reason of his migration to Dvārāvatī, Jarāsaṃdha is not mentioned. Even an element of the *Mahābhārata* Kṛṣṇa is found in the story of the destruction of the Yādavas and the presence of Kaṇhadīpāyana (Kṛṣṇa Dvaipāyana), though the Pāṇḍava-Kaurava story is not linked with Kṛṣṇa except in the presence of Arjuna among Kṛṣṇa's brothers.

Kṛṣṇa is present even in the Jaina tradition. However, there his story is linked with that of the twenty-second *tirthankara* Ariṣṭanemi or Neminātha. The fundamental framework of Jaina mythology is based on the listing of sixty-three *śalākāpuruṣas*. That includes twenty-four *tīrthaṅkaras*, twelve *cakravartins*, nine *vāsudevas*, nine *baladevas*, and nine *prativāsudevas*. The *tīrthaṅkaras* are the highest propagators of Jainism, and the *cakravartins* are the world rulers. However, the naming of the twenty-seven others clearly shows the influence of Vāsudeva Kṛṣṇa even on Jaina mythology. These twenty-seven are the men of action, the action on which Kṛṣṇa emphasizes so much in the *Gītā*. A '*vāsudeva*' is a ruler of great valour, splendour, and of the seven most precious things in the world, and the lord of the most beautiful woman. He lacks nothing, he finds something good in everything, and he never fights standing on the ground. *Baladeva* is the brother of *vāsudeva*, known for his devotion to him. The *prativāsudeva* is the main antagonist of the *vāsudeva*.

Kṛṣṇa, Balarāma, and Jarāsaṃdha are known as the last set of *vāsudeva*, *baladeva*, and *prativāsudeva*, just like Lakṣmaṇa, Rāma, and Rāvaṇa were an earlier set.[44] However, the very designations indicate that the categories were created around Vāsudeva Kṛṣṇa, his brother, and chief antagonist, and eight other legendary sets were just fitted into the model.

The Jaina account of the *Harivaṃśa* also revolves around the Vṛṣṇis. Andhaka Vṛṣṇi of Śauripura had ten sons, Samudravijaya being the eldest and Vasudeva the youngest. They had two sisters—Kuntī and Mādrī. On the other side, Bhojaka Vṛṣṇi had three sons—Ugrasena, Mahāsena, and Devasena. Kaṃsa was Ugrasena's son and Devakī Devasena's daughter. The adventurous Vasudeva married many damsels and won over Rohiṇī in a *svayaṃvara* where he faced his own brother Samudravijaya in a battle. Vasudeva and Rohiṇī had a son named Rāma. Kaṃsa was forsaken as soon as he was born, but Vasudeva taught him. In the meanwhile, Jarāsaṃdha of Magadha declared that anybody who could defeat his antagonist Siṃharatha could marry his daughter. Kaṃsa achieved that feat with Vasudeva's guidance. He overthrew his father with Jarāsaṃdha's help and married off Devakī to Vasudeva. But on learning from the sage Atimuktaka that Devakī's son would turn into an enemy who would kill him, he kept Devakī in his palace and planned to kill all her sons. Devakī thrice gave birth to twins who were saved by the deity Harinaigamesi and became monks. The fourth time, she gave birth to Kṛṣṇa who was exchanged for Nanda's daughter. Kaṃsa did not kill the girl but damaged her nose so that no powerful man would marry her. Kṛṣṇa did many spectacular things in Nanda's village. Kaṃsa tried several methods to kill him, but failed. Finally, he invited Rāma and Kṛṣṇa to Mathurā to duel with the famous wrestlers Cāṇūra and Muṣṭika. After the wrestlers were killed, Kṛṣṇa killed Kaṃsa. The enraged Jarāsaṃdha attacked Mathurā, and the Vṛṣṇis migrated to Dvārāvatī. There Samudravijaya and Śivadevī gave birth to Ariṣṭanemi. Kṛṣṇa married eight princesses, and his chief wife Rukmiṇī gave birth to Pradyumna who also did marvellous things. In the meanwhile, the Pāṇḍavas—children of Kuntī—had a prolonged quarrel with their Kuru cousins. They were cheated at a game of dice and exiled. After a lot of adventures, including Draupadī's marriage with the five brothers, they found refuge in Dvārāvatī. Kṛṣṇa, aided by the Pāṇḍavas and others, met Jarāsaṃdha aided by the Kurus and the others, at Kurukṣetra, in a decisive battle. Here Kṛṣṇa killed Jarāsaṃdha, became the master of half of Bhārata, and cemented his position as *vāsudeva/nārāyaṇa*.

Draupadī was abducted by Padmanābha. Kṛṣṇa defeated him and returned her to the Pāṇḍavas. However, on the way home, Bhīma's practical joke infuriated Kṛṣṇa, and Kṛṣṇa ordered the Pāṇḍavas to leave Dvārakā. They went to the south and established a kingdom. In a test to decide who was the best among the Yādavas, Kṛṣṇa failed to even move a finger of Nemi's. Seeing the latter's passion raised in a feast at Mount Raivataka, Kṛṣṇa arranged for his marriage with Rajimatī. However, seeing animals tied to be killed for the marriage feast, Nemi felt disgusted with material pleasure and renounced the world. After becoming the twenty-second *tīrthaṅkara*, he made a prophecy that the Yādavas would destroy themselves because of drinking and Dīpāyana's curse, and Kṛṣṇa would be killed by his brother Jaratkumāra. Hearing this, Jaratkumāra left Dvārakā and entered a forest, and Dīpāyana renounced the world. Kṛṣṇa banned drinking in Dvārakā. All wine was poured into a stonepit outside the city. Still, after twelve years, some Yādavas drank from that stonepit, and, while drunk, stoned Dīpāyana to death. The sage died uttering a curse which burned the city. All except Kṛṣṇa and Rāma died. Kṛṣṇa was killed by Jaratkumāra's arrow in a forest, while going to the Pāṇḍavas. Rāma refused to accept Kṛṣṇa's death and carried the body for six months before becoming a monk. The Pāṇḍavas learnt the secrets of their lives from Nemi and also became Jaina ascetics. Kṛṣṇa was born in the third hell after death, since being a *vāsudeva* tied him to his *karma*.[45]

The Jaina account is even closer to the *Mahābhārata* and *Harivaṃśa* than the Buddhist one. It matches with the Brahmanical version more or less, except in the material added about Nemi. There Kṛṣṇa is a single person connected to Mathurā, Dvārakā, and the Pāṇḍavas. However, the Pāṇḍava-Kaurava conflict is shown as marginal, with the conflict of Kṛṣṇa and Jarāsaṃdha at the centre, and both are joined together in a decisive battle at Kurukṣetra.

It is difficult to determine the dates of the Buddhist and Jaina accounts. The Jātakas are known to be folk traditions canonized by the Buddhists. That canonization might have occurred in the first millennium BCE itself, since some of the stories have been represented on the panels of Bharhut and Sanchi, but the final codification took place sometime in the first millennium CE. Similarly, the Jaina tradition may go back to the time of Mahāvīra but was codified in the Council of Valabhī in the sixth century CE. The Jaina epics from which the Jaina version of the Kṛṣṇa legends have been reconstructed are even more later, though they are based on the older tradition. Therefore, the three traditions had a parallel period of growth, with the *Mahābhārata* (but not the *Harivaṃśa*) possibly being a bit earlier than the others, and the Jaina version a bit later. They probably derived their material from a common pool of orally transmitted tradition which might have been utilized even by the dramatist Bhāsa.

In fact, Bhāsa is not the only literary figure of the time to refer to that tradition. The *Gāthāsatsai*, a collection of Prakrit folk poems made by the Sātavahana king Hāla, which contains poems composed roughly between the third century BCE and third century CE, has three verses referring to Kṛṣṇa's life in Vṛndāvana. Many other such poems might have been composed and lost in the first millennium BCE.

Even in the South Indian Tamil tradition, Kṛṣṇa was not unknown. Kṛṣṇa's connection with South India is not only indicated by the migration of the Pāṇḍavas to the south in the Jaina version but the Greeks also heard about some confused South Indian tradition regarding Kṛṣṇa and the Pāṇḍavas.[46] In the Sangam literature, much of which was again composed in the first millennium BCE, he appears as Mayavan/Māyon, the lord of the cowherds. He, along with his brother Balarāma and consort Pinnāi, appear in the Tamil epic *Cilappaṭikāram* (*c.* fifth century CE) which knows of his dance in the cowherd camp and the killing of Kaṃsa.

Therefore, we can see that Kṛṣṇa has been present in materials throughout the first millennium BCE. Be it in the Vedic tradition or in the *itihāsa*, be it in the Buddhist tradition or in the Jaina, be it in grammatical treatises or in secular literature, be it in Greek accounts or in South Indian tradition, there is hardly any tradition in early India which could overlook Kṛṣṇa. Moreover, his position as a deity was more or less established quite early. There is hardly any other historical personality in the first millennium BCE, except Gautama Buddha and Candragupta Maurya, who appears so universally in so many traditions. What made Kṛṣṇa so important?

Perhaps the answer lies in his life and teaching. Therefore, we now proceed to explore the life of this great figure (as we have already seen, he is a single figure) about whom we can find an astonishing profusion of sources. There have been numerous writings on his childhood legends, but the story of Kṛṣṇa's political rise is usually overlooked. This chapter intends to understand that bit of Kṛṣṇa's life. His position in the first millennium BCE itself shows clearly that any history of that period without the history of Kṛṣṇa would be incomplete. For, as a Vaiṣṇava poet of medieval Bengal would put it, 'without Kānu (Kṛṣṇa) there is no song'.

4.3 'I Am Born as Thy Friend': Kṛṣṇa the Cowherd

As we have noted the proliferation of ancient Indian sources referring to Vāsudeva Kṛṣṇa, we can now proceed to analyse the various accounts to understand what the character signified in a Later Vedic Kuru *itihāsa*. However, as already discussed, the *Mahābhārata* provides little information about the early days of Kṛṣṇa's life, possibly with an assumption that the audience of the text would be familiar with those utterly popular legends. Therefore, we have to depend on much later and unreliable sources that shaped those legends to supplement the *Mahābhārata*, starting with the *Harivaṃśa* and the *Viṣṇu Purāṇa*. Fortunately, we can also take account of a variety of older and parallel narratives, including the Buddhist and Jaina accounts, stray Vedic and Upaniṣadic references, the plays of Bhāsa, and the popular legends in Tamil and Prakrit about the early life of the hero, and our reconstruction in this section shall take all of these into account.

Kṛṣṇa, across traditions, has been located in the clan of the Vṛṣṇis, a branch of the Yadus. We have seen in Chapter 2 that the Ṛgvedic Yadus were vanquished but not exterminated by the Bharata-Pūru chief Sudās in the Battle of Ten Kings.[47] If Michael Witzel is right in his identification of the Yadus with the Yākṣus, then they were defeated in one more battle with Sudās, that too in their own stronghold—the Yamunā valley—and brought horseheads as tributes in Sudās's horse sacrifice.[48] Their power and prestige in the Vedic world was nothing compared to that of the Kuru-Pañcāla kingdoms. But their existence in the Vedic period cannot be doubted. Not only are the Yadus known to the *Ṛg Veda* but the Sātvatas and Vṛṣṇis, who were the major people in the confederacy in which Kṛṣṇa was born, are also well known in the Later Vedic literature.[49] That the Vṛṣṇis were a *gaṇasaṃgha* is known to the *Arthaśāstra* as well.[50]

However, Kṛṣṇa's birth was preceded by a trouble in such a polity. As we can see in all the accounts, Kaṃsa was at the centre of the problem. Married to the daughters of Jarāsaṃdha of Magadha, Kaṃsa considered himself quite powerful and tried to turn the *gaṇasaṃgha* into a kingship. Jarāsaṃdha, the rising Magadha chief, was possibly contemplating an ultimate showdown with the powerful Kurus and Pāñcālas. However, irrespective of his power, it was impossible for a Magadha chief of tenth to ninth century BCE to lead a sustainable military operation from faraway Magadha into the heart of the Gaṅgā-Yamunā Doab, that too against the stronger kingdoms. Therefore, he chose softer targets. He entered the politics of Mathurā through a marriage alliance and slowly used his son-in-law to turn the *gaṇasaṃgha* into a kingship loyal to him. Such an attempt must have faced some opposition within the *gaṇasaṃgha*, and Kaṃsa's father Ugrasena and his brother-in-law Vasudeva seem to be the faces of that opposition.

None of the accounts before the *Bhāgavata Purāṇa* speaks of an outright imprisonment of Vasudeva, Devakī, or Ugrasena. In the *Harivaṃśa* in particular, Vasudeva and Devakī are not imprisoned, and Vasudeva takes part in the clan assembly. However, it can be assumed that Kaṃsa suspected his opponent Vasudeva very much and kept him under strict scrutiny. That is the idea in the Jaina account as well as in the *Viṣṇu Purāṇa*. The latter clearly says that Kaṃsa kept Vasudeva and Devakī in secret confinement—'*guptāvadhārayat*'.[51] To assure the safety of his wives and children, Vasudeva thus kept them away from Kaṃsa's grasp in the cowherd camp at Gokula. Interestingly, neither the Buddhist nor the Jaina account speaks of Kaṃsa killing all the children of Vasudeva and Devakī. Rather, in the Buddhist legends, all of them were raised in the cowherd village. Even the highly pro-Kṛṣṇa and very late *Bhāgavata Purāṇa* says that Kaṃsa decided to spare the first-born child of Vasudeva and Devakī and returned the child to its parents before Nārada's warning caused him to kill the child and imprison Vasudeva, Devakī, and Ugrasena.[52] The *Viṣṇu Purāṇa*, which speaks of Kaṃsa's killing of the six children born to Vasudeva and Devakī, interestingly, says that after Kṛṣṇa's birth, Kaṃsa assured the safety of the children to be born further to the couple:

tad alaṃ paritāpena nūnaṃ tad bhāvito hi te/
arthakā yuvayor doṣāc cāyuṣo yad viyojitaḥ//

(The children, who shall be born to you, after this, may enjoy life till its natural course; no one shall cut it short.)[53]

In the Jaina account, Kaṃsa carefully raised the daughter born to Devakī and the daughters of Nandagopā presented to him as Devakī's daughters. Therefore, it seems that Kaṃsa's role as a serial child killer is not sanctioned by the early tradition, and it should be noted that the Buddhist account shows Kṛṣṇa as the first son of the couple.

All the accounts seem to agree on the tradition that Kṛṣṇa was raised with the cowherds, as Vasudeva left him in the charge of Nanda and his wife. The selection of this cowherd camp has to be explained. As we have seen in Chapter 3, pastoralism was the chief source of livelihood of the Ṛgvedic people. However, with the gradual rise of agriculture in the Gaṅgā-Yamunā Doab, it receded to the background. Now, in these settled agrarian societies, agriculture was given the prime importance. Thus, as shown in Chapter 3, in the agrarian Kuru kingdom, the cattle herders settled in the fringe area of Dvaitavana. They lived almost a free life without much intervention except for an occasional royal tour for inspection and tribute collection. Still, the royal hold was so weak in such an area that we see the Kuru princes in trouble in their tour of inspection, when faced with a raid by the forest dwellers. The situation was of course different in the arid kingdom of Matsya where pastoralism was the chief form of livelihood. The king there had an enviable stock of cattle, and the cow pen was a part of the royal establishment. As Mathurā was an agrarian territory, the herdsmen lived in fringe areas such as Gokula and Vṛndāvana and kept on shifting their habitat. The royal control would not be very firm there. That might have led to Vasudeva's choice of such a refuge for his wives and children.

His friendship with Nanda may also have wider implications. In the Buddhist legends, Nanda and Yaśodā are named Andhakabenhu and Nandagopā, respectively. Nandagopā may mean Nanda Gopa's wife. But Andhakabenhu was certainly the tribal name Andhaka Vṛṣṇi. Therefore, even these cowherds were considered a part of the clan and might have had some role to play in the clan politics. In the Buddhist legend, Nandagopā was instrumental in Devagabbhā's marriage and conception. Thus, Balarāma and Kṛṣṇa, in Nanda's house, were relatively safe from Kaṃsa but within the ambit of Yādava-Vṛṣṇi politics. The entire process, therefore, seems to be a political design to dismount Kaṃsa, and the prophecy story seems to be nothing but a later fabrication. In fact, in Bhāsa's *Bālacarita*, there is neither any prophecy nor any supernatural intervention for saving Kṛṣṇa. Vasudeva just seeks a refuge for his child in the cowherd village, which Nanda provides.

We will return to the realm of the Yādava politics for killing Kaṃsa, but before that we will have a brief survey of Kṛṣṇa's colourful life at Gokula and Vṛndāvana. The early life of the great hero and deity, spent among the simple cowherds, gave ample scope of emotional expression to the later mystics and poets. Kṛṣṇa's childhood exploits have been dismissed as later legends by Bankim Chandra Chattopadhyay in his bid to show him as an ideal iron-man. Raychaudhuri also dismisses these legends culled from the later Purāṇas and opines:

We have practically no authentic information as to the way in which the childhood of Kṛṣṇa was spent. The most probable view is that he lived with his preceptor Ghora Āṅgirasa and returned to Mathurā on arriving at adolescence.[54]

But we have already seen that Kṛṣṇa's life in the cowherd camp is not mentioned by the Purāṇic poets alone but is known to the Brahmanical, Buddhist, and Jaina sources as well as to Bhāsa and the Saṅgam literature. The cowherd Kṛṣṇa is the Kṛṣṇa who appears in the *Gāthāsaptaśatī*. We will see later how this life is not just mentioned but also mocked at in the *Mahābhārata*. The *Baudhāyana Dharma Sūtra* knows Viṣṇu as 'Govinda', 'Dāmodara', and 'Keśava', and all three epithets are connected with Kṛṣṇa's cowherd life. No doubt much of the descriptions concerning this phase of Kṛṣṇa's life are fanciful and fantastic poetry. But the weight of source materials will be highly tilted against dismissing this phase altogether. We can also notice that the three fundamental tenets of Kṛṣṇa's character started sprouting among the cowherds: his propagation of a new philosophy, his rise as a great warrior, and his emergence as a fascinating lover.

In fact, the most remarkable feature of Kṛṣṇa's life in Vṛndāvana seems to be his critique of the contemporary religious system. His sharp and critical mind questioned it in a simple and straightforward way. However, after his Upaniṣadic training under Ghora Āṅgirasa, this simple criticism would take a rich, sophisticated shape in the *Gītā*. To simplify the matter, we can see the young Kṛṣṇa raise his voice against three important aspects of his contemporary religion—vegetational rites, Vedic sacrifices, and the Nāga cults.

The first of the three is indicated by the story of Kṛṣṇa breaking up the two *arjuna* trees after being tied to them by his foster mother. The *Bālacarita* and the *Harivaṃśa* make it quite clear that these trees were centres of worship. The Purāṇas make these the cursed spirits of two sons of Kuvera, the Yakṣa chief, freed by Kṛṣṇa. As vegetational rites were often connected with popular cults of the Yakṣas, their freeing seems to be the statement of Kṛṣṇa ending those cults.

Another important cult of the time was that of the Nāgas, a community whose prominence in the *Mahābhārata* has already been noted. These aboriginal people, using serpent totems, had an ambiguous relationship with the rulers throughout early Indian history. They adopted the Vedic religion and were supporters of the Indra cult. They would establish a marital tie with Arjuna but would also kill Parikṣit and face a threat of large-scale destruction by Janamejaya. Even in a much later period, the Brahmanized Nāgas such as the Bhāraśiva-Nāgas would assume rulership, but many Nāga chiefs would also be vanquished by Samudra Gupta.

Kṛṣṇa's highly mythologized conflict with the Nāga chief Kālīya possibly represents such a clash. The myth says that the venomous snake Kālīya was making the Yamunā poisonous and uninhabitable. At last, Kṛṣṇa subdued him and danced on his hood before making him leave the Yamunā with an understanding of mutual non-interference.[55] It seems to be a conflict over territory in which the cowherds succeeded against the Nāga chief, due to Kṛṣṇa's leadership. The dancing on the hood is no doubt a symbol of subduing Kālīya.

The more important factor, however, is Kṛṣṇa's conflict with Indra. Here, for a moment, we have to go back to the Ṛgvedic hymn which we suspect to be a later one alluding to Vāsudeva Kṛṣṇa:

> The Black Drop sank in Aṃśumatī's bosom, advancing with ten thousand rounds about it.
> Indra with might longed for it as it panted: the hero-hearted laid aside his weapons.
> I saw the drop in the far distance moving on the slope bank of Aṃśumatī's river,

Like a black cloud that sank into the water. Heroes, I send you forth. Go, fight in battle.
And then the drop in Aṃśumatī's bosom, splendid with light, assumed its proper body;
And Indra, with Bṛhaspati to aid him, conquered the godless tribes that came against him.[56]

The black (*kṛṣṇa*) foe facing Indra on the bank of Aṃśumatī (Yamunā) with ten thousand followers was probably no non-Aryan antagonist. The Ṛgvedic poet would hardly compare a non-Aryan antagonist with the sun, especially when the major Ṛgvedic deities were virtually the solar deities—the Ādityas. Moreover, when he left the battlefield, his army became '*adevī*' (godless; without a *deva*). This term '*deva*' would never be used for a non-Aryan hero who would be a *dasyu* or *dāsa*. Therefore, this Kṛṣṇa seems to be a leader of some Aryan tribe of the Yamunā valley, who was considered a solar deity. The only suggestion that comes to our mind is Vāsudeva Kṛṣṇa who was possibly equated with the Vedic solar deity Viṣṇu by his followers. Though Indra triumphed, the acceptance of Kṛṣṇa as a *deva* shows certain compromise.

Let us now see what the *Harivaṃśa* and *Viṣṇu Purāṇa* have to say on the matter. There we see that the cowherds used to organize a sacrifice in Indra's honour. When Kṛṣṇa wanted to know the rationale behind it, an old herdsman almost echoed the Ṛgvedic praises of Indra:

Indra is the lord of the celestials and clouds. This is his great festival. The clouds, inspired by him, strengthened by his arms, increase the crops by raining new water. They are his servants. They receive their water from him. That Indra, lord of the three worlds, pleases the entire universe when pleased. The crop which is thus produced, we and the other beings are sustained by that and we please the deities also by that. When the deity becomes pleased and provides rain, crops are produced again. When the earth is satisfied, the entire world seems to be full of nectar. These cows provide milk and calves. There is no land barren of crops or grasses, where the clouds rain. Therefore, the people are not tormented by hunger. Indra creates the clouds by sucking the sap through the sunrays. From that cloud is secreted the pure sweet water. That water roars as clouds while travelling through the wind. It is because the cloud, with the wind, carries it, the massive sound like the mountain-shattering thunder is heard. Indra rains by directing the thunderous clouds, his servants. The clouds sometimes create a disaster, sometimes are scattered, sometimes assume the colour of dark cohl, sometimes rain, sometimes are without water. It is because of Devendra that the sky is thus ornamented by the clouds and the water acquired by the sunrays thus fertilises the earth for the welfare of all the beings. It is because Indra creates the monsoon in the sky that the kings delightfully organise the Great Festival of Indra. We also organise the festival following that.[57]

A similar statement is made by Nanda in the *Viṣṇu Purāṇa*:

meghānāṃ payasām ceśo devarāja śatakratuḥ/
tena saṃ codita megha varṣaty ambumayaṃ rasaṃ//
tad vṛṣṭijanitaṃ sasyaṃ vayaṃ anye ca dehinaḥ/
vartayāmopayuñjānās tarpayāmaś ca devatāḥ//
kṣīravatyā imā gāvo vatsavatyāṃ ca nirvṛtaḥ/
tena saṃvardhitair sasyais tuṣṭāḥ puṣṭā bhavanti vai//
nāsasyā nātṛṇā bhumir na bubhukṣārdito janaḥ/
dṛśyate yātrā dṛśyante vṛṣṭimanto balāhakāḥ//
bhaumame tat payo dugdhaṃ gobhiṃ suryasya vāridaiḥ/
pārjanyas sarvalokasyodbhavāya bhuvi varṣati//
tasyāt prāvṛṣi rājānas sarve śakraṃ mudā yutāḥ/
makhais sureśam arcanti vayam anye ca mānavāḥ//

(Śatakratu . . ., the king of the celestials, is the lord of the clouds and waters; ordered by him the clouds pour down water on earth, by which the grain is produced, on which we and other embodied beings live and by which we please the gods.

By this too these cows bear calves and give milk and are happy and well-nourished.

Wherever the clouds pour waters, the earth is neither barren of corn, nor bare of verdure, nor is man stricken with hunger.

Having drunk the milk of the earth by means of the rays of the sun, Indra, the giver of water, pours it again on earth for the sustenance of all the worlds.

For this reason all sovereign princes offer, with delight, sacrifices to Indra at the end of the rainy season, and so also do we and so do the other people.)[58]

Here, we can see the cult of Indra in its classical Vedic form. But the reply Kṛṣṇa gives shows a complete novelty of idea, totally unknown to the Vedic world:

na vayaṃ kṛṣikartāro vāṇijyājīvano na ca/
Gāvo'smad daivataṃ tāta vayaṃ vanacarā yataḥ//
ānviikṣikī trayī vārtā daṇḍanītis tathā parā/
vidyā catuṣṭayaṃ caitad vārtāmātraṃ śṛṇusva me//
kṛṣir vaṇijyā tad vac ca tṛtīyaṃ paśupālanaṃ/
vidyā hy ekā mahābhāga vārtā vṛttitrayāśrayā//
karṣakāṇāṃ kṛṣir vṛttiḥ paṇyaṃ vipaṇijīvināṃ/
asmākaṃ gauḥ parāvṛttir vārtābhedair iyaṃ tribhiḥ//
vidyayā yo yayā yuktas tasya sā daivataṃ mahat/
saiva pujyārcaniyā ca saiva tasyopakārikā.

(We, father, are neither cultivators of the soil, nor merchants—we are sojourners in the forest, and cows are our gods.

There are four divisions of knowledge—logical, spiritual, practical, and political. Hear from me, what is the practical science.

Agriculture, commerce, and tending the cattle—the knowledge of these three professions, o noble Sire, is the practical science.

Agriculture is the means of subsistence to the cultivators, buying and selling to the traders, and tending of cattle is our subsistence.

The practical science has thus been divided into three branches. The object that is cultivated by anyone, should be to him, his chief deity—he must worship that, for that is his benefactor.)[59]

Kṛṣṇa's response in the *Harivaṃśa* echoes the same spirit.[60]

Thus, Kṛṣṇa's opposition to the cult of Indra was on the ground of practicality. Already he perceived a unique *svadharma* for each profession and that *dharma* was based on practical action rather than on birth. Therefore, it was not *varṇa* or *jāti*, but *vṛtti* that Kṛṣṇa was emphasizing on. And he declared his conclusion which sounded like the modern slogan of 'work is worship':

mantrayajñaparā viprāsmīrayajñāś ca karṣakāḥ/
girigoyajñaśīlāś ca vayam adrivanāśrayāḥ//

(*Brāhmaṇas* offer worship with prayer; cultivators of the earth worship their landmarks; but we, who tend our cattle in the forests and mountains, should worship them and our kine.)[61]

Therefore, Kṛṣṇa opined that the herdsmen would do better by worshipping their cattle and mountains and feeding the *brāhmaṇas* and all others who wanted to partake of the food.[62] The angry Indra started showering heavily on Vṛndāvana, causing massive disaster. Kṛṣṇa then lifted the Mount Govardhana to protect his folk. After that, a compromise was reached, with both Indra and Kṛṣṇa dividing the seasons for their worship. However, Indra's upper hand in the compromise is clear in even the pro-Kṛṣṇa account. Indra retained his position as the great king of the gods (Indra/Mahendra), with Kṛṣṇa being recognized as a deity, but a minor, junior one, lord of the cowherds (Govinda/Upendra).[63] The account, thus, does not differ much from the pro-Indra Ṛgvedic one. The term '*upendra*' also marks out Kṛṣṇa's identification with the Vedic Viṣṇu, an Āditya junior to and associate of Indra in the Vedas.

It was a limited success. However, even this limited success had a military dimension. The Ṛgvedic hymn speaks of Kṛṣṇa hiding in a secret place. The lifting of Mount Govardhana may be a supernatural representation of hiding behind the mountain, or in its passes and caves, to avoid a direct face-to-face combat, and directing skirmishes from there. We will see Kṛṣṇa use this guerrilla strategy again and again, when faced with a larger army, be it of Kālayavana or of Jarāsaṃdha. Thus, the episode was immensely important, marking Kṛṣṇa's first major challenge to the prevalent religion, first significant military operation, and first step to his status as a demigod of the pastoralists (Govinda). However, this limited success would not please Kṛṣṇa at all, and we will see him returning to settle the scores with the supporters of the Indra cult.

Therefore, Kṛṣṇa gradually established himself as the lord of the cowherds. He was becoming the propagator of a new religious outlook, a very effective military leader, and a demigod. However, Kṛṣṇa had to use his fighting abilities to defend himself as well. Another important aspect, here, was the beginning of Kṛṣṇa's deification. We have already seen that Kṛṣṇa was mainly a deity of the Mathurā region and one associated with the cowherds for a long time. The incidents mentioned earlier raised him to the position of a tribal demigod already, and the cowherds started wondering about his real identity. However, Kṛṣṇa did not relish his new deified form at all. Rather, he admonished the cowherds for such attitude:

mat saṃbandhena vo gopā yadi lajjā na jāyate/
ślāghyo vāhaṃ tataḥ kiṃ vo vicāreṇa prayojanam//
yadi vo'smi mayi prītiḥ ślāghyo'haṃ bhavatām yadi/
tad ātmabandhusadṛśī buddhir vaḥ kriyatāṃ mayi//
nāhaṃ devo na gandharvo na yakṣo na ca dānavaḥ/
ahaṃ vo bāndhavaḥ jāto naitac cityam ito'nyathā//

(Herdsmen, if you are not ashamed of my relationship, if I have deserved your praise, then what necessity have you to discuss thus concerning me?

If you have any love for me, if I merit your praise, then consider me your friend.

I am neither a god, nor a Gandharva nor a Yakṣa nor a demon. I am born as thy friend and you should not think otherwise of me.)[64]

The news of Kṛṣṇa's gradual rise must have reached Kaṃsa at a certain point of time, and he made some efforts to kill Kṛṣṇa. But these efforts failed. The myths turned these agents of Kaṃsa into demons, and the *Bhāgavata Purāṇa* is full of them. However, some are mentioned in the *Mahābhārata* as well, in the course of Siśupāla's mocking at the achievements of Kṛṣṇa.[65]

Among these, the first was the killing of Pūtanā, a demoness who tried to kill Kṛṣṇa with poisonous milk of her breast, but the infant Kṛṣṇa sucked the life out of her. Kosambi views it as the killing of a mother goddess.[66] However, in this case, Bankim Chandra Chattopadhyay's allegorical interpretation seems more logical. The word '*pūtanā*' means a disease of infants which gets cured if the baby suckles with force.[67] Even in the *Viṣṇu Purāṇa*, we see Yaśodā waving over Kṛṣṇa a cowtail while Nanda placed dried and powdered cow dung on his forehead and gave him an amulet, after Pūtanā's death,[68] mechanisms which would suit the precautions for a child who just survived a disease in a herdmen's village than for a divine kid who had just killed a mighty demoness.

Similarly, the overturning of a cart by the playful kick of a powerful baby was nothing very surprising, though many hagiographers turned that into the killing of Śakaṭāsura (the cart demon) and Śiśupāla precisely made this hyperbole a point in his mockery. However, Śiśupāla also spoke of Kṛṣṇa's killing of Aśva and Bṛṣabha, alluding possibly to Keśin and Ariṣṭa, respectively. The frequent use of the name 'Keśava' for Kṛṣṇa in the *Mahābhārata* certainly testifies to the former's case. However, these feats seem to be nothing better than killing a dangerous bull and a mad horse. The only human agent of Kaṃsa present in most of the sources is Pralamba. However, he was killed not by Kṛṣṇa, but by Balarāma. These are the feats which possibly spread the fame of Balarāma and Kṛṣṇa as wrestlers and led Kaṃsa to decide for a final showdown between his choicest wrestlers and the sons of Vasudeva. But before that account, we will have a glimpse at another aspect of Kṛṣṇa's life in Vṛndāvana, probably the most popular of all his aspects.

It is needless to repeat that the most popular facets of Kṛṣṇa as a divinity are his roles as a butter thief and as the flute-playing lover of Rādhā and other milkmaids. Whether a boy brought up in a village of cowherds used to steal butter or not is not within the scope of a historical enquiry. But there is no doubt that the charismatic figure of Kṛṣṇa, already blooming in Vṛndāvana, might have attracted many women. However, in most of the sources, Kṛṣṇa's romance with the milkmaids comes in the form of a dance. This dance is called *hallīśaka* in the *Bālacarita*, *halliśakrīḍā* in the *Harivaṃśa*, and *rāsa* in the Purāṇas. It seems that in the tribal village of the cowherds, this ecstatic group dance was part of a seasonal festival observed on the autumn full moon, and the free mixing of the men and women in it was not forbidden. In fact, in the *Bālacarita*, we see a rather festive atmosphere where the old cowherd called out the girls to dance with Kṛṣṇa. Thus, Bhāsa did not find anything offensive in it, and there is absolutely no scope of viewing the dance as adulterous. However, with Kṛṣṇa rising as a charismatic and handsome adolescent boy, he could naturally be the chief attraction for the girls in that dance. The feeling is beautifully expressed in a verse of the *Gāthāsaptaśatī*:

nartanaślāghananibhena pārśvaparisaṃsthitā nipuṇagopī/
sadṛśagopikānāṃ cumbati kapolapratimāgataṃ kṛṣṇaṃ//

(The clever cowherdess, standing nearby, kisses the image of Kṛṣṇa reflected on the cheeks of her fellow cowherdesses, under the guise of praising their dances.)[69]

The nature of the dance is beautifully reflected in the Tamil epic *Cilappaṭikāram*. There, a cowherd woman named Mātari remembers it as a festive dance of the cowherds:

To rid the cows and calves of their pain, we shall perform the round dance in the presence of Kannakī, that jewel among the daughters of the earth. It is one of the boyhood dances of Mayavan and Balarāma with Pinnāi of the wide, spearlike eyes performed in the open courtyard of the village of the cowherds.[70]

The *Harivaṃśa* and the *Viṣṇu Purāṇa* also portray the dance in the simple way of a festival in a cowherd camp. In the *Harivaṃśa*, the women use nothing but dried cow dung as their cosmetic (*karīṣapāṃśudigdhāṅgāḥ*).[71] The *Viṣṇu Purāṇa* shows the eagerness of the youthful girls for Kṛṣṇa's company and how the young Kṛṣṇa tackled them to get the dance going:

> *tataḥ kāṃ cit priyālāpaiḥ kaś cid bhrubhaṅga-vīkṣaṇaiḥ/*
> *ninye'nunayamanyāṃ ca karasparśena mādhavaḥ//*
> *tābhiḥ prasannacittabhir gopībhis saha sādaram/*
> *rarāsa-rāsagoṣṭhībhir udāracarito hariḥ//*
> *rāsamaṇḍalabandho'pi kṛṣṇapārśvam anujjhatā/*
> *gopījanena naivābhud ekasthān asthirātmanā//*
> *hastena āgṛhya caikaikāṃ gopīnāṃ rāsamaṇḍale/*
> *cakāra tat karasparśanimīlitadṛśaṃ hariḥ//*
>
> (Thereupon coming amongst them Mādhava conciliated some with soft words, some with gentle looks and some he took by the hand and the illustrious Hari sported with them in the stations of the dance, after all the damsels had been propitiated.
> As each of the damsels attempted to remain in one place close to the side of Kṛṣṇa, the circle of the dance could not be constructed.
> Thereupon taking each by the hand and when their eyelids were closed by the effects of such touch Hari formed the circle.)[72]

In the *Cilappaṭikāraṃ*, the dance is associated with a contest of taming some powerful bulls by the virtue of which seven cowherd girls could be won over. Mayavan succeeded in that and won over the girls who were already impressed by his flute playing. Interestingly, even in the *Harivaṃśa*, it was during this dance that Kṛṣṇa tamed the bull named Ariṣṭa.

Of course this dance of youthful ecstasy turned amorous at times, as the poet describes:

parivṛttiśramenaikā calad valayālāpinīm/
dadau bāhulatā skandhe gopī madhunighātinaḥ//
kācit pravilasadbāhuṃ parirabhya cucumba tam/
gopīgītastutivyājānnipuṇā madhusūdanam//
gopikapolasaṃśleṣam abhigamya harer bhujau/
pulakodgamasasyāya svedāmbughanatāṃ gatau//

(At times, one of them exhausted by the revolving dance, threw her arms, adorned with the tinkling bracelets round the neck of the slayer of Madhu; another proficient in singing his praises embraced him.

The drops of perspiration from the arms of Hari were like fertilizing rain which produced a drop of dew upon the temples of the damsels of cowherds.)[73]

The amorosity is even more explicit in the *Harivaṃśa*:

mukham asyāparā vīkṣya tṛṣitā gopakanyakāḥ/
ratyantaragatā rātrau pivanti ratilālasāḥ//
hāheti kurvatas tasya prahṛṣṭās tā varāṅganāḥ/
jagṛhur niḥsṛtāṃ vāṇīṃ sāmnā dāmodarer itam//
tāsāṃ grathitasīmantā ratiśrānty ākulikṛtāḥ/
cāru viśrāṃ śire keśāḥ kucāgre gopayoṣitāṃ//

(Thirsty with the desire of sporting, the cowherd girls, being involved in the sport at night, started to drink the lotus-like face of Kṛṣṇa.

When Kṛṣṇa exclaimed saying 'ha ha' the beautiful damsels received those words with delight.

The hair of those cowherd girls, well-tied in buns, became scattered in the exhaustion of the sport and fell on the top of their breasts.)[74]

However, this amorosity was freely accepted in the freer society of the village of cowherds. Thus, though we see that some cowherdesses were so eager for Kṛṣṇa's company at night that they went to him even after being forbidden by their parents and brothers, in the *Harivaṃśa*, that led to no serious problem:

> *tā vāryamānā pitṛbhir bhrātṛvir mātṛvis tathā/*
> *kṛṣṇaṃ gopāṅgaṇā rātrau mṛgayante ratipriyāḥ//*
>
> (Despite being resisted by their fathers, brothers, and mothers, the cowherd girls went to sport with Kṛṣṇa at night.)[75]

Rather, the amorous love play at night led to exchange of tender signals in the morning, in the poetry of the *Gāthāsaptaśatī*:

> *adya api bālaḥ dāmodaraḥ iti iti japite yaśodayā/*
> *kṛṣṇamukhapreṣitākṣaṃ nibhṛtaṃ hasitaṃ vrajabadhūbhiḥ.*
>
> (Even to this day Dāmodara seems (to me) a child'—when this was spoken by Yaśodā, the women of the Vraja (cowherds' village) smiled covertly casting their look towards Kṛṣṇa's face.)[76]

Here, the reference to the *vrajabadhūs* suggests that the poet imagines even the married women of Vraja among Kṛṣṇa's amorous playmates. The *Viṣṇu Purāṇa* changes the *Harivaṃśa* verse a bit to add the husbands among the ones forbidding the women to go to Kṛṣṇa.[77] However, irrespective of the marital status of the women, Kṛṣṇa's love play was basically an amorous festive dance in the earlier sources. The *Bhāgavata Purāṇa*, however, stretches the matter much beyond a simple festive dance in a society with lesser taboos and makes Kṛṣṇa steal the clothes of the bathing cowherdesses and satisfy all kinds of demands of these women who are portrayed as selfless devotees.

The *Brahmavaivarta Purāṇa* goes further in providing Kṛṣṇa a principal consort in Rādhā and making the union of Kṛṣṇa and Rādhā the most important cosmic secret. These are the texts which portrayed Kṛṣṇa as a hypersexual adulterer, and some scholars have even tried to seek the mystery of Kṛṣṇa's hypersexuality in psychoanalytical impact of the excessive physical affection provided by the cowherdesses in his childhood.[78]

However, a survey of the earlier sources provide us nothing more than an amorous festive dance where men and women participated and mixed freely, where Kṛṣṇa was the star attraction for the women, and where the adolescent Kṛṣṇa also enjoyed the attention he received. Kṛṣṇa might also have a personal favourite, as indicated by Pinnāi of the Tamil tradition and a verse of the *Gāthāsaptaśatī*:

> *mukhamārutena tvaṃ kṛṣṇa gorajaḥ radhikāyāḥ apanayan//*
> *etāsāṃ ballabhīnām anyāsām api gauravaṃ (or gauratāṃ) harasi//*
>
> (O Kṛṣṇa! By removing particles of earthly dust or dust raised by the cows, with blows of your mouth-breeze, from (the eyes of) Rādhikā, you have removed the pride or favour or fairness of complexion of the other Ballabhīs.)[79]

If we look at the legend of the stealing of clothes in the *Cilappaṭikāram*, the story has a different and much practical shape. Here it was only Pinnāi whose clothes Kṛṣṇa stole in the playfulness of their lovemaking, rather than stealing the clothes of all the cowherd girls during a festival for granting all of them their secret wishes. The Tamil epic tells about Pinnāi and Mayavan:

> How can we describe his presence who hid
> The clothes of the girl with a waist so thin
> It might have snapped had she bent?
> How can we describe the sweet, tender face
> Of the girl who fainted when he hid her clothes?
> How can we describe the beauty of the girl
> Who stole the heart of the lord
> Who tricked her in the waters of the Yamuna?
> How can we describe his presence who cheated
> The girl, who stole his heart, of her virtue and bangles?
> How can we describe the face of the girl who covered
> Herself with her hands when she lost her clothes and bangles?
> How can we describe his presence who burns with love,
> And is troubled on seeing the face of the girl
> Who covered herself with her hands?[80]

But the Rādhā we know is not this Pinnāi or the Rādhikā of the *Gāthāsaptaśatī* verse but a creation of much later times. She was the chief female consort of Kṛṣṇa in Jayadeva's twelfth-century romance the *Gītagovinda* and became the central divinity of the very late *Brahmavaivarta Purāṇa*. Numerous Vaiṣṇava poets, including the adherents of later forms of Vaiṣṇava Tantra, centred their poetry and theology around Rādhā, her selfless adulterous love for Kṛṣṇa, her readiness to forsake all worldly objects (including social morality and reputation) for her beloved (and worshipped), and her silent suffering after Kṛṣṇa went to Mathurā, leaving her alone. But this Rādhā, as important as Kṛṣṇa (or more) in her own sphere, is a medieval character who came into prominence from the time of Jayadeva and has little to do with the period we are trying to explore.

However, Kṛṣṇa did not have much time for dalliance with his personal favourite, be it Rādhikā or Pinnāi, since Akrura arrived in Vṛndāvana to fetch him for Kaṃsa's sacrifice. It is difficult to believe that Kṛṣṇa and Balarāma were totally unaware of the plot that was going on against Kaṃsa, since we have already indicated Nanda's part in it. Therefore, the two boys left their childhood in the village of the cowherds, leaving numerous cowherdesses and many more subsequent poets in tears.

Making all of Kaṃsa's plots futile, they reached his sacrificial arena, plundering his clothes, flowers, and cosmetics on their way. Their plundering of royal possessions is mentioned in the Buddhist account as well. Possibly, these activities were a signal of their purpose of establishing the fact that royalty meant nothing in a *gaṇasaṃgha* and Kṛṣṇa and Balarāma had equal right over what Kaṃsa enjoyed. The story of their wrestling with Cāṇūra and Muṣṭika, and the ultimate killing of Kaṃsa, is shared by all the traditions.

However, the way Kṛṣṇa killed Kaṃsa in the latter's own court is quite astonishing. Therefore, the idea of a conspiracy, as indicated by Bhaduri, seems acceptable. In the *Mahābhārata*, Kṛṣṇa himself says that

> *bhojarājanyavṛddhaiś ca pīḍyamānair durātmana/*
> *jñātitrāṇam abhīpsād bhir asmat sabhavanā kṛtā//*
>
> (When thereafter the evil man molested the elders of the Bhoja barons, the latter concluded an accord with us: for they sought to save their kin.)[81]

Therefore, he was indeed not unaware of the situation in Mathurā and was part of a conspiracy hatched up by the Bhoja elders. The *Harivaṃśa* clearly shows that Kaṃsa was not unaware of the situation either. In *Harivaṃśa*, we see him complaining against Vasudeva for intriguing against him:

> Just like a crow plucks out the eyes of that very man, with its claws and beak, on whose head it sits, Vasudeva is living on my food, but is trying to destroy me along with his friends. One can be saved even after committing sins like killing a cow, or a woman, or a foetus; but one cannot be saved whose friend tries to harm his benefactor . . . That sinful person who commits sins against faultless people has to go to the polluted paths of the hells. Irrespective of whether I am a praiseworthy relative or your son is more praiseworthy, both had to be appeased to maintain friendship . . .
>
> Vasudeva, when you caused this conflict in the clan because of jealousy, treachery, and bad interests, then I am certain that your end is approaching. It is because of you that the Yādavas are in a pitiable state. I have uselessly kept you near me, considering you experienced, till now. One does not become experienced only because one's hair is white or one is hundred years old. One whose intelligence has matured is the real experienced man. Your character is very harsh and knowledge is little . . .
>
> You have thought that your son will enjoy Mathurā if Kaṃsa dies! ...
>
> In great folly you have undertaken the task of destroying me; but I will resist that desire of the two sons of yours in front of you. I never killed a *brāhmaṇa*, a woman, or an old man, and will not kill one now; I will never commit an offence against a friend in particular. You have been born here and brought up by my father's care . . .
>
> Still you behave like this? Irrespective of my victory or death in the conflict, will not the Yādavas have to cover their faces with clothes in shame if it is mentioned that 'the intrigue of Vasudeva caused it'? You have acted like an unfaithful person in trying to destroy me in battle, and the Yādavas are also to be blamed. The conflict between me and Kṛṣṇa is inevitable, and the Yādavas have no respite unless a mediating party is created.[82]

It not only shows that Vasudeva remained an influential member of the assembly despite Kaṃsa's suspicion but also indicates Kaṃsa's awareness about the plot that was being made to destroy him. In *Harivaṃśa* II.23.1–7, we see a strong defence of Vasudeva from the leader of the Andhaka clan. If this man stated what he felt flatly on Kaṃsa's face, most of the others conspired behind his back. And these others might not have excluded even his parents. We have seen that the Jaina account describes Kaṃsa as a forsaken child. Even the *Harivaṃśa* does not provide a better picture:

> *mātāpitṛbhayāṃ santyaktaḥ sthāpitaḥ svena tejasā/*
> *ubhabhyām api vidviṣṭo bāndhavaiś ca viśeṣataḥ//*
>
> (Deserted by my parents, established only because of my own power,
> I am disliked by both the parties, particularly by my friends.)[83]

Thus Kaṃsa knew very well that he was a self-made man who had neither his parents nor any reliable friend on his side. It was his power and Jarāsaṃdha's favour that had kept him going. He knew that all the Yādavas had deserted him and went to the side of Kṛṣṇa—'*śeṣāś ca me parityakta yādavāḥ kṛṣṇapakṣiṇaḥ*'.[84]

So, he decided to again rely on his power and meet Kṛṣṇa face to face. He deputed the only man on whom he had some trust left—Akrura. With suspicion in his voice, he requested Akrura:

> *akrura kuru me prītiṃ etāṃ paramadurlabhām/*
> *yadi vā nopajupto'si vasudevena suvrata//*
>
> (If you have not already been brainwashed by Vasudeva, O Akrura of noble vows, do me this rare favour.)[85]

However, as Kaṃsa suspected, Akrura was confused between the two sides, and Kṛṣṇa solved this confusion with a masterstroke. As he says in the *Mahābhārata*, he arranged the marriage of Akrura with Sutanu, the daughter of Āhuka.[86] Bhaduri rightly notes that here the daughter of Āhuka means the daughter of Āhuka's house, the daughter of Ugrasena, known as Ugrasena Sugātrī in the *Harivaṃśa* and Sutanu Ugrasenatanujā in the *Viṣṇu Purāṇa*.[87] With this marriage, and Ugrasena's disfavour to him, Kaṃsa lost Akrura, his last possible ally in Mathurā.

But one thing to note is that Kaṃsa, even being aware of the great conspiracy hatched up by Vasudeva against him, did not kill him, and limited himself to condemning Vasudeva in the open assembly. In such a scenario, killing of six infants is quite unlikely. Thus it seems to be a fabrication of the Purāṇic poets to heighten the emotion before the birth of Kṛṣṇa, which is not supported by the Buddhist and Jaina traditions. There is no reference to the killing of the children by Kaṃsa in the *Mahābhārata* as well, though the killing of Kaṃsa is mentioned many times. The Buddhist tradition understands the situation better and says that Kaṃsa could not kill his own sister in fear of an upsurge against him.

While Kaṃsa lost all his allies in Mathurā, Kṛṣṇa came with his own. Kṛṣṇa knew that the slippery Yādava politicians would never be stable allies, and his suspicion would be proven right in the later stages of his life. But he had his own band, those who saw him as a deity, those whom he had considered as his real friends, those who were behind him in facing the supporters of the Indra cult, those who backed him in his fight against Kālīya—the cowherds. This seems to be Kṛṣṇa's personal army that accompanied him to Mathurā. This was the people with whom Kṛṣṇa and Balarāma celebrated their victory in the wrestling arena:

> *vavalgatus tato raṅge kṛṣṇasaṃkarṣaṇāvubhau/*
> *samānavayaso gopān balād ākṛṣya harṣitau//*
>
> (Kṛṣṇa and Saṃkarṣaṇa danced victorious on the arena, dragging along with them by force the cowherds of their own age.)[88]

At a later stage of his life, in the *Mahābhārata*, Kṛṣṇa would reveal this secret of his special Nārāyaṇīya army which he would hand over to Duryodhana as the great force of the *gopas* (*gopāṇāṃ arbudaṃ mahat*).[89] Before his death, Kaṃsa understood the secret and frantically cried for banishing all the *gopas* from his kingdom—'*gopāṇām api me rājye na kaś cit sthātum arhati*'.[90] In the *Viṣṇu Purāṇa* he is even harsher:

> *valganti gopāḥ kṛṣṇena ye ceme sahitāḥ puraḥ/*
> *gāvo nigṛhya tāṃ eṣāṃ yac cāsti vasu kiṃcana//*
>
> ([A]nd lay hands upon the cattle, and whatever else belongs to those cowherds who are the associates of Kṛṣṇa.)[91]

But his realization was too late. Kṛṣṇa killed Kaṃsa in his own court, without being resisted by a single person. The wife of Ugrasena, who was restored to power, herself disclosed in the *Harivaṃśa* the real reason of Kaṃsa's death:

> *tathaiva jñātilubdhasya mama putrasya dhīmataḥ/*
> *jñātibhyo bhayam utpannam śarīrāntakaraṃ mahat//*
>
> (Thus, the kinsmen were greedy about my intelligent son. The threat from the kinsmen is great, which can lead to death.)[92]

Thus, the killing of Kaṃsa was not universally regarded as the cleanest of incidents. In Bhāsa's drama '*Dūtavākyaṃ*', Duryodhana strongly condemned Kṛṣṇa for this murder:

> You had no pity for king Kaṃsa, the brother-in-law of your own father ... Kaṃsa was wholly betrayed by you. There is no need for self-praise. It was not a brave deed.[93]

By the time of Bhāsa, Kṛṣṇa had a suitable reply:

> That was not my fault. He invited death by imprisoning his old father and making my mother suffer the loss of successive sons.[94]

But, we have seen that the killing of children was possibly not a part of the original account. In the *Mahābhārata*, Kṛṣṇa's defence in the Kuru court was not that but Kaṃsa's tyranny and his attempt to turn the *gaṇasaṃgha* into despotic kingship:

> *bhojarājasya vṛddhasya durācāro hy anātmavān/*
> *jīvataḥ pitur aiśvaryaṃ hṛtvā manyuvaśaṃ gataḥ//*
> *ugrasenasutaḥ kaṃsaḥ parityaktaḥ sa bāndhavaiḥ/*
> *jñatīnaṃ hitakāmena mayā śasto mahāmṛdhe//*
>
> (The wicked and uncontrolled son of king Bhoja in a fit of anger seized power while his father was still alive. This Kaṃsa, the son of Ugrasena, deserted by his relatives, I punished in a great battle for the good of his kinsmen.)[95]

Kaṃsa had been a tyrant who tried to turn a *gaṇasaṃgha* into a kingdom, that too to suit the interest of another tyrant at Magadha. Kṛṣṇa freed Mathurā by killing him. But he could do it so smoothly not just because of the goodwill of the Mathurān diplomats, but also because of their greed and jealousy of the self-made fortune of Kaṃsa to destroy whom they all conspired. Through this conspiracy was facilitated Kṛṣṇa's entrance in the opportunistic politics of Mathurā. But was it the best way to start such a glorious political career? Was it the only way Kṛṣṇa could deal with his maternal uncle who—despite knowing about the conspiracy against him—spared the lives of Kṛṣṇa's parents? Was it appropriate behaviour? One wonders. Our answer may be different, but Patañjali had stated his—'*asādhur mātule kṛṣṇah*'.

4.4 Vāsudeva, *Prativāsudeva*, and the False *Vāsudeva*: Tracing the Rise of a Legend

> I do not need a kingdom. That is not my desire. I have not killed Kaṃsa for his kingdom. I only wanted to help the others and attain glory, and that is why I killed Kaṃsa, a blot on his family, with his lieutenants. I will again go to the forest with my cattle, and roam around with the cowherds like a free-willed elephant.[96]

If we follow the *Harivaṃśa*, this was the desire expressed by Kṛṣṇa while restoring Ugrasena as the chief of the Yādavas. However, this desire would never be satisfied. Kṛṣṇa would never return to the life of a free-willed cowherd which he lived in his early years, as discussed in the previous section. We would never again see him express such a sentiment either. All of these were because of the turn his political career would take, which would show him that the killing of Kaṃsa was not his ultimate task but the very first step in a world where he had much to offer. That Kṛṣṇa ended that career with immense success is a belief about which all the accounts agree. He was the king of all the kings in the *Harivaṃśa* and the Purāṇas. He was the decisive figure in the Bhārata War, in both the *Mahābhārata* and in Bhāsa's dramas. He killed numerous kings to establish his power all over India in the *Ghaṭa Jātaka*. He was the *cakravartin* of half of the Indian subcontinent in the Jaina legends. But he was not a mere *cakravartin* ruler. As in the *Mahābhārata*, *Harivaṃśa*, and the Purāṇas, he was not a king, but the ultimate kingmaker, and so in the Jaina account, he was not a mere king, not even just a *cakravartin*, but a '*vāsudeva*'.

We have seen that the epithet '*vāsudeva*' had been synonymous with Kṛṣṇa from a very early period. It is the king Vāsudeva whom the Buddhist Jātakas remember. However, he is not a different person, but Vāsudeva the Kaṇha. It is Vāsudeva who has been equated with Viṣṇu in the TĀ. It was Vāsudeva whose followers, alongside the followers of Arjuna, were known to Pāṇini. It was the *devadeva* Vāsudeva to whom Heliodorus paid his homage. In Jaina mythology, Kṛṣṇa is the ninth, though the most important, in the series of the *vāsudevas*. Thus, in this section, we shall look into this concept of a *vāsudeva* and try to account for Kṛṣṇa's attainment of that status.

The Jaina idea of a *vāsudeva* has already been discussed. In that concept, the epithet had nothing to do with Kṛṣṇa being the son of Vasudeva. Rather, it is the epithet of someone who attained the supreme position in the realm of action and success. Jaina philosophy does not condone that way very much but cannot ignore it. That the brother of the *vāsudeva* is entitled *baladeva* in the Jaina mythology makes it clear that the concept evolved around Kṛṣṇa and Balarāma, though eight other sets of *vāsudevas* and *baladevas* are perceived. Therefore, Kṛṣṇa seems to be the only person to have historically attained the position of a Vāsudeva.

The idea is actually supported by the Brahmanical tradition as well. The grammarian Patañjali, well aware of Kṛṣṇa being synonymous with Vāsudeva, also says that the word '*vāsudeva*' refers to God. Even in the *Mahābhārata*, Kṛṣṇa is not called 'Vāsudeva' always after his father's name. The word has been explained in two ways. In the 'Śāntiparvan', Kṛṣṇa himself says:

> *chādayāmi jagat viśvaṃ bhūtvā sūrya ivāṃśubhiḥ/*
> *sarvabhutādhivāsaś ca vāsudevas tato hy aham//*
>
> (I cover the entire universe being like the sun or the moon. Since all the beings are situated in me, I am *vāsudeva*.)[97]

The exact relationship between the word '*vāsudeva*' and this definition is not clear. It seems to be a Vaiṣṇavized glorification of Kṛṣṇa's epithet in the 'Śāntiparvan' which is a very late addition to the *Mahābhārata*.

However, another definition is given in the 'Udyogaparvan', which is etymologically more correct and matches with the Jaina concept:

> *vasanāt sarvabhutānāṃ vasutvād devayonitaḥ/*
> *vāsudevas tato vedyo vṛṣatvād viṣṇur ucyate//*
>
> (He is called *vāsudeva* in consequence of his enveloping all creatures, his glorious splendor, or of his being the support and resting place of the gods. Because of his massivity he is called *viṣṇu*.)[98]

In this single couplet, Kṛṣṇa's attaining of both the statuses of '*vāsudeva*' and '*viṣṇu*' are mentioned. From both the Jaina and the *Mahābhārata* descriptions, it is clear that *vāsudeva* is an epithet attainable by one of glorious splendour, one who raises himself to a semi-divine level. The *Mahābhārata*, the *Harivaṃśa*, and the *Viṣṇu Purāṇa* supply us more interesting information that Kṛṣṇa was not the only person in his lifetime to seek that epithet, but there was another *vāsudeva*, the chief of Puṇḍra. The showdown between the 'real' and the 'false' *vāsudevas* will be discussed later. But before that, we have to understand how Kṛṣṇa became the *vāsudeva*, and what made the person—who had once admonished the cowherds for deifying him—accept, relish, and defend this semi-divine status?

In Jaina tradition, it is the victory over Jarāsaṃdha that established Kṛṣṇa in the position of the *vāsudeva*/*nārāyaṇa*. Jarāsaṃdha, not Kaṃsa or Duryodhana, is the *prativāsudeva* in the Jaina legends. In the *Mahābhārata* and the *Harivaṃśa* also, a closer scrutiny will show Jarāsaṃdha as the real opponent of Kṛṣṇa. The Buddhist account, however, is silent about Jarāsaṃdha. But it is the Jarāsaṃdha episode that integrates the three Kṛṣṇas together. The Kṛṣṇa-Jarāsaṃdha conflict is caused by Kṛṣṇa's activities in Mathurā. He leaves Mathurā and resettles in Dvārakā out of fear of Jarāsaṃdha. The killing of Jarāsaṃdha is ultimately accomplished in the *Mahābhārata* with the help of the Pāṇḍavas. Therefore, this legend is immensely important in establishing and understanding the historical personality of Kṛṣṇa.

Let us look at the Jarāsaṃdha episode, as Kṛṣṇa narrated to Yudhiṣṭhira in the *Mahābhārata*. Kṛṣṇa said that Jarāsaṃdha of Magadha was a very powerful, possibly the most powerful, chief aided by many others. Among his allies were mentioned Śiśupāla of Cedī, Vakra the chief of the Karuṣas, two great warriors named Haṃsa and Ḍibhaka, the Vāsudeva of Puṇḍra, Bhagadatta of Prāgjyotiṣa, and Bhīṣmaka of Vidarbha. His daughters Asti and Prāpti were married to Kaṃsa, and that boosted Kaṃsa's power. After Kaṃsa was killed by Kṛṣṇa, Jarāsaṃdha attacked Mathurā, and the Yādava council decided that they had no chance against Jarāsaṃdha's mighty army commanded by Haṃsa and Ḍibhaka. However, due to some confusion, which seems to be Yādava trickery, both Haṃsa and Ḍibhaka committed suicide, and Jarāsaṃdha retreated. But Jarāsaṃdha was continuously being urged on by his daughters to avenge their husband's death. So, the Yādavas fled to Dvārakā and settled down there. Kṛṣṇa also reported that Jarāsaṃdha captured every king he defeated and kept them in bondage for offering them as victims in a great sacrifice in honour of Śiva.[99]

The story is not much different in the *Harivaṃśa* and the Purāṇas, except that much more details are added to it, possibly to salvage Kṛṣṇa's prestige. Kṛṣṇa's marriage with Rukmiṇī, Bhīṣmaka's daughter, alluded to in the *Mahābhārata*, is elaborately discussed. Kṛṣṇa is also made to resist numerous invasions of Jarāsaṃdha before shifting to Dvārakā.

Ultimately, in the *Mahābhārata*, Kṛṣṇa overcame Jarāsaṃdha with Pāṇḍava help. He slipped into Magadha in disguise with Bhīma and Arjuna. Jarāsaṃdha showed great hospitality to them. At night, Kṛṣṇa challenged Jarāsaṃdha to a duel with any one of them. The chivalrous chief chose Bhīma, the strongest. He was killed after a great fight. Kṛṣṇa freed the captive kings, and restored Magadha to Jarāsaṃdha's son Sahadeva.[100]

Various views and interpretations have been offered by the scholars on this episode. As we have already mentioned, Ruben considered the Kṛṣṇa-Jarāsaṃdha episode as a historical encounter, though unconnected with the Pāṇḍava-Kaurava story initially, especially because of Kṛṣṇa's utterly human nature and acknowledged weakness. But many scholars have opined otherwise.

Adolf Holtzmann views Jarāsaṃdha as a symbol of third century BCE Buddhism blended with Śaiva elements. Jarl Charpentier also traces links between Buddhism and Śaivism in Jarāsaṃdha's person. He says that veneration of Śiva was predominant in Magadha, and that included human sacrifice. Jarāsaṃdha was a Śaiva who united fellow believers in a great war against the Vaiṣṇavas for the Śaiva faith. Alf Hiltebeitel also thinks that Jarāsaṃdha's Śaiva affiliations and Kṛṣṇa's undisguised hostility to him reflect relatively late Vaiṣṇava-Śaiva opposition and also connect Jarāsaṃdha's name with the Buddhist concept of *saṃsāramaṇḍala* where old age (*jarā*) and death play a key role.[101]

D.D. Kosambi thinks that the Jarāsaṃdha legend probably represents a real westward scattering of the tribes for whom the pastoral demigod Kṛṣṇa of Mathurā was a patron deity. Kṛṣṇa was not part of the original *Mahābhārata*, and his main action in the text—the killing of Śiśupāla—is inconsequential.[102] Kṛṣṇa's position in the *Mahābhārata* has already been discussed, and it is needless to say that he has many other things to do in the *Mahābhārata*, apart from slaying Śiśupāla, unless action means killing alone.

A. Parpola argues that the Pāṇḍus are a new wave of Aryans arriving in Northern and Western India around ninth to eighth centuries BCE, distinguishable by their Black and Red Ware (BRW). They were pushed southwards through Gujarat by the expansion of Magadha around the fifth century BCE and might have introduced megalithic culture into the Deccan.[103] Parpola's thesis is too overstretched, since there is hardly any textual ground for associating the Pāṇḍus with the BRW. The rise of Magadha around sixth to fifth century BCE is an acknowledged factor, but that does not necessarily prove that the people scattered because of that have to be the initiators of the 'Iron Age' megalithic culture in the Deccan. The fairly early dating of the Hallur iron certainly suggests that an iron-using culture flourished in the Deccan much before the traditional date of the rise of Magadha.

However, many other scholars also relate the Kṛṣṇa-Jarāsaṃdha conflict with the rise of Magadha. Ulrich Schneider links it with the final attempts by the western tribal communities to resist the domination of Magadha in the fourth century BCE.[104]

Madeleine Biardeau interprets the Jarāsaṃdha legend as a myth about cosmic time and its cycles, *jarā* and *sandhi* representing end of the world and twilight period between two cosmic periods.[105] However, the very humane nature of the conflict makes such interpretations unconvincing.

John Brockington argues that the Jarāsaṃdha episode is an anticipatory doublet of the Śiśupāla episode, intended only to underline the latter's significance. He thinks that the Śiśupāla episode is integral to the *Mahābhārata*, and therefore the Jarāsaṃdha episode is a later addition. Jarāsaṃdha is referred to very rarely in the later parts of the *Mahābhārata*. The behaviour of Jarāsaṃdha's sons and of Śiśupāla to Bhīma, when he came to collect tribute before the *rājasūya*, hardly shows that Jarāsaṃdha had been deceitfully killed before that. Brockington dates the Jarāsaṃdha episode to second to first century BCE, after the decline of the Mauryas, because it would be hardly possible to show the Magadha emperor vanquished by the Kuru prince during the Maurya reign.[106]

If we closely examine the views, we can see that there is little ground to consider the Kṛṣṇa-Jarāsaṃdha conflict in a religious light. Though Jarāsaṃdha was a Magadha chief, and Magadha kings often patronized Buddhism between the sixth and the third century BCE, there was absolutely no link shown between Jarāsaṃdha and Buddhism. Jarāsaṃdha's eagerness to hold a sacrifice, that too with human blood, and his liberality towards the *brāhmaṇas* cannot sustain any equation with Buddhism. He has been shown as a worshipper of Śiva, no doubt. But that does not make the issue an outright Śaiva-Vaiṣṇava conflict. Kṛṣṇa's antagonism to Jarāsaṃdha was not because of his Śaivite affiliation but because of his intended human sacrifice, a practice not very well accepted in mainstream Śaivism as well. As a design to undermine Śaivism and glorify Vaiṣṇavism, it is unlikely that the later Vaiṣṇava poets would compose a legend where Kṛṣṇa would have been defeated by a Śaiva chief, would return to face him treacherously, and would be unable to kill him with his own power.

Similarly, it is difficult to see the legend as a reflection of the rise of Magadha and scattering of the western tribes in the fourth to third centuries BCE. In the fourth to third centuries BCE, the Magadhan rise was centred on the great city of Pāṭaliputra, and that city is totally unknown in Jarāsaṃdha's Magadha. In fact, it is on this ground that the legend seems to be a quite old one. It is difficult to conceive a Magadha without Pāṭaliputra after the fourth century BCE. More interestingly, as van Buitenen has noted, the epicentre of Jarāsaṃdha's Magadha was not even Rājagṛha, which was the capital of the Magadha kings Bimbisāra and Ajātaśatru in sixth to fifth centuries BCE, but a mountain fastness in its vicinity, named Girivraja, which has also been excavated.[107]

There are also other reasons to believe that Jarāsaṃdha represents a pre-Buddha and not Maurya or post-Maurya Magadha. Brockington's own arguments also work against his conclusion in this regard. As he thinks that it would be difficult to conceive the Magadha emperor vanquished by a Kuru in the Mauryan period, the case would not be less unlikely in the post-Maurya period also. Never ever after their defeat at the hands of Mahāpadma Nanda, possibly in early fourth century BCE, were the Kurus in a position to vanquish Magadha. Moreover, Yudhiṣṭhira has been called '*ajātaśatru*' (one without enemies) in the *Mahābhārata*.[108] It is highly unlikely that the great Brahmanical hero would be turned into a namesake of one of the greatest Magadha patrons of Buddhism had it been composed after Ajātaśatru's reign (early fifth century BCE). A close review of the Śiśupāla episode, which we will undertake later, can also reveal that the Jarāsaṃdha episode cannot be its anticipatory doublet. Rather, it was the Kṛṣṇa-Jarāsaṃdha conflict that had sown the seeds of the Kṛṣṇa-Śiśupāla showdown.

Therefore, we have to understand the Jarāsaṃdha episode in its original *Mahābhārata* context, and, for that, it is vital to understand the position of Magadha in the tenth to ninth centuries BCE. It has already been discussed that the Kurus and the Pāñcālas are the most important people in the Later Vedic literature. Magadha has no place of importance in the Later Vedic texts. The region and its people were not unknown but were generally not considered a part of the orthodox Vedic landscape. That Magadha was a known yet disliked 'other' to the Later Vedic 'self' is best illustrated by a charm in the *Atharva Veda* for expelling away a fever, because the magician of the *Atharva Veda* was not satisfied with driving away the disease from his land (probably the Kuru kingdom of Parikṣit) but wanted to transfer it to the people of Magadha.[109] However, Magadha, with its unorthodox population, which had a good amount of non-Vedic people such as the Kirātas and the Kīkaṭas, might not have been a negligible power. We have to remember that the two most important bardic groups of the Later Vedic world were the *sūtas* and the *māgadhas*. The *sūtas* were the bards associated with the Kuru-Pāñcāla *kṣatriyas* and had possibly created the *Mahābhārata* tradition. But who were the *māgadhas*? There name suggests a clear link with Magadha. If there were bards to celebrate the glories of the Magadha chiefs, there must have been chiefs powerful enough to be celebrated. It was the bards of Magadha who had a tradition parallel to that of the Kuru bards. It seems that the semi-Vedic and non-Vedic people of Magadha were the biggest challenge to the orthodox Vedic world of the Kuru-Pañcālas. The *sūtas* have left behind the *Mahābhārata* and the Purāṇas. The *māgadhas* left no literature of their own. But the liberality, power, and chivalry of Jarāsaṃdha bear some features which were unmistakably of a hero and not of a demonic figure. Moreover, the tremendous rise of Magadha that started from Bimbisāra's time must have been preceded by a formative period. Jarāsaṃdha of Girivraja seems to be a significant landmark in that formation.

However, there is a huge difference between the material context of the Magadha of tenth century BCE and sixth century BCE. Jarāsaṃdha sitting in his mountain base could not have dreamt of an empire which Ajātaśatru, Mahāpadma Nanda, or Candragupta Maurya could. But he could think of Magadha hegemony. Magadha, even then, had the numerous material advantages which it would utilize later to establish the largest empire of early India. But the resource base was not what could sustain a regular imperial establishment or a long-term military operation outside its vicinity. Therefore, Jarāsaṃdha put his trust on alliances. He gave his daughters in marriage to Kaṃsa through whom he dreamt of controlling the Yādava-Vṛṣṇi confederacy in Mathurā. That would have given him a base to operate in the Gaṅgā-Yamunā Doab. Śiśupāla, his trusted ally, was also related to the Yādavas.

Jarāsaṃdha's Magadha was probably not yet a completely settled agrarian economy. The name of the capital having a suffix such as *vraja* strongly indicates the importance of pasture. Therefore, these semi-Vedic and non-Vedic eastern tribes mainly depended on pastoralism and plundering and raiding. Their mode of warfare was different from that of the mainstream Vedic world. Thus, in his bid for hegemony, Jarāsaṃdha captured the defeated kings. He sought legitimacy, just like the Vedic chief who performed the *aśvamedha* or *rājasūya*. However, leading a mixed group of people, Jarāsaṃdha sought legitimacy from both the Vedic and the non-Vedic worlds. He continued the non-Vedic blood sacrifice (to Śiva who was not a Vedic deity) but also was eager to invite the learned *brāhmaṇas* to his territory. Standing between the Vedic and non-Vedic worlds, he was banking on support of other eastern plundering-raiding tribes as well as of the marginal powers of the Vedic world.

The grand design of Jarāsaṃdha received an early blow from Kṛṣṇa's killing of Kaṃsa. That was what brought Kṛṣṇa and Jarāsaṃdha face to face. Two worlds, two ideas, were at loggerheads. Probably that was the contest of the *vāsudeva* and the *prativāsudeva*, which the Jaina account refers to. No doubt, the winner would attain the ultimate splendour. And it was Jarāsaṃdha who triumphed in the first round.

The pro-Kṛṣṇa poet of the *Harivaṃśa* and the Purāṇas try to salvage some prestige for Kṛṣṇa by making him repel Jarāsaṃdha's repeated invasions. But if the *Mahābhārata* is to be believed, then it was decided in the Yādava assembly right after Jarāsaṃdha's first invasion that they had no chance in the battle. Actually, the impossibility of leading a long invasion in a faraway area, with the limited resource base, would make Jarāsaṃdha withdraw every time. But the huge force, aided by some of the kinsmen of the Yādavas, could never be matched by the small Yādava-Vṛṣṇi army. The result would be repeated invasions leading to repeated stalemates. That might be of advantage for a plundering-raiding band, but the continuous loss of manpower and repeated disrupture of normalcy would certainly be a great trouble for Mathurā.

In the *Harivaṃśa*, when Jarāsaṃdha attacked Mathurā for the first time, Kṛṣṇa rightly described him as the testing stone of his and Balarāma's fighting skills and the first guest of their military career (*āvayor yuddhanikaṣaḥ prathamaḥ samarātithiḥ*),[110] and the *Harivaṃśa* shows Kṛṣṇa and Balarāma defeating the huge army. However, according to the *Mahābhārata*, the first invasion was repelled by spreading a rumour about Haṃsa's death, which led to the suicide of Ḍibhaka, which in turn led to the suicide of Haṃsa. Here, though it is not clearly stated, probably we get to see Kṛṣṇa use his famous tricks against a stronger foe for the first time. The same trick, of spreading rumour about a person's death, would be openly recommended by Kṛṣṇa in the Bhārata War for killing Droṇa. The poet of the *Harivaṃśa* composes a huge story, which is nothing but a classical story of Śaiva-Vaiṣṇava conflict, around the death of Haṃsa and Ḍibhaka. The story is apparently a later exaggeration of the *Mahābhārata* reference, and therefore we are not going into that.

The *Mahābhārata* is clear about the fact that the Yādava assembly was not interested in fighting Jarāsaṃdha after that. Had that been the condition since Kaṃsa's death, there is no reason to believe in its statement that Mathurā withstood eighteen sieges by Jarāsaṃdha. Kṛṣṇa's position was possibly not a very stable one in Yādava politics. Vasudeva's intrigues against Kaṃsa might not have been appreciated by everybody, and there could be some people who preferred the security of Kaṃsa's might than the relative freedom offered by Kṛṣṇa. In the *Mahābhārata*, Kṛṣṇa says that:

> O king, we ran separately and, with our treasures, kinsmen, and relations, we fled in fear of him.[111]

That the story of Kṛṣṇa-Balarāma defeating Jarāsaṃdha is quite late is testified by Bhāsa's '*Dūtavākyam*' as well. There also, Duryodhana asks Kṛṣṇa:

> Where was your bravery when you fled terrified, from the king of Magadha who was enraged at his son-in-law's murder?[112]

Kṛṣṇa's reply has no allusion to any resistance shown to Jarāsaṃdha but a sense of practicality fitting a great political figure like Kṛṣṇa:

> Suyodhana, the wise man's bravery accords with the time, the place and the situation.[113]

However, selection of Dvārakā, settling there, and preparing the necessary defensive and economic arrangements must have taken some time.

The *Harivaṃśa* shows Kṛṣṇa gaining that time in a masterly way. He accepted a self-imposed exile on himself and Balarāma and left Mathurā, knowing that it was he whom Jarāsaṃdha wanted. Here Kṛṣṇa felt no shame in flying away from his enemy and declared that a wise person did not stay near a stronger foe. One must fight when capable and go away if not. The Critical Edition of the *Harivaṃśa* does not include the story of how Kṛṣṇa and Balarāma took refuge in the Mount Gomanta which Jarāsaṃdha besieged and how they survived in that battle. However, this account (Appendix 18 of the Critical Edition) was present in all but one (S1) manuscript, and the fighting strategy was not unfamiliar to us. It was the very strategy Kṛṣṇa used in his fight against the supporters of the Indra cult, taking the Mount Govardhana as his base.

In the meantime, Jarāsaṃdha thought of strengthening his alliances by another marital tie. Therefore, the *svayaṃvara* of Bhīṣmaka's daughter Rukmiṇī, whose brother Rukmin was a trusted supporter of Jarāsaṃdha, was organized with all the pro-Jarāsaṃdha kings. However, Kṛṣṇa—though uninvited—entered Vidarbha, and the kings—unwilling to engage into a battle—postponed the *svayaṃvara*. The reason cited for not inviting Kṛṣṇa was possibly that Kṛṣṇa was not a king. The poet of the *Harivaṃśa*, being a later poet, could not be satisfied with the idea of a *gaṇasaṃgha*. Therefore, he organized a supernatural royal consecration of Kṛṣṇa in Vidarbha about which we need not worry.

The *Harivaṃśa* and the Purāṇas add one more legend here. The legend is about a Greek king named Kālayavana. In a grand assembly of Jarāsaṃdha's camp in Bhīṣmaka's court, the Śālva chief proposed to seek help of this mighty chief for killing Kṛṣṇa. As Jarāsaṃdha, though reluctant to seek another man's help, ultimately consented, Śālva went to the court of the Greek king and requested him to attack Mathurā. Kṛṣṇa again decided not to fight the massive army with the tiny Yādava force and fled from the battlefield. Kālayavana chased Kṛṣṇa till they reached a cave where the royal sage Mucukunda was sleeping since ages. This sage had a divine blessing that anybody who woke him up would be burnt in his rage. The Greek king mistook him for Kṛṣṇa and woke him up, only to be burnt into ashes by his rage.

The story is fabulous and could not have been composed before the Greek kingdoms emerged in the northwest. Norvin Hein views Kālayavana as a representative of the collective memory of earlier invasions.[114] Usually the Kālayavana episode is dated to the post-Maurya period when the Indo-Greek kings settled themselves in the northwest. However, Greek settlements were there in Northwest India even in much earlier periods. Kālayavana has been shown as a worshipper of Śiva. Interestingly, the historians of Alexander mention a Greek settlement in Nysa in the northwestern part of the subcontinent that worshipped Dionysus/Śiva.

Whenever be its composition, the Kālayavana legend seems to be a superimposition on some other legend. Very surprisingly, the Greek king is not Greek by birth. He is the son of Gārgya Śiśirāyaṇa, the priest of the

Andhaka-Vṛṣṇis, and Gopālī, a cowherd woman. The close relationship between the Andhaka-Vṛṣṇis and the cowherds can be seen in Kṛṣṇa's life as well. The birth of Kālayavana indicates a possibility that Jarāsaṃdha and Śālva sought an ally not in a Greek king but among Kṛṣṇa's own kinsmen (as they did in the cases of Kaṃsa and Śiśupāla), before the character was Hellenized in post-Greek invasions period. Kṛṣṇa somehow managed to kill that person by trickery.

Thus, Kṛṣṇa's political career was in no good shape at this point. He had killed Kaṃsa alright. But he had been forced to leave Mathurā for good and resettle in Dvārakā, which gave him some safety but dragged him far away from the politics of the Gaṅgā-Yamunā Doab. Even all of his kinsmen were not on his side. To penetrate into the solidarity of Jarāsaṃdha's camp, he wanted to marry Rukmiṇī. The *Harivaṃśa* says that Rukmiṇī was also fond of Kṛṣṇa. But the proposal was bluntly turned down by Rukmin. Rather, Jarāsaṃdha chose Śiśupāla, his trusted supporter and Kṛṣṇa's cousin, as the groom for Rukmiṇī. However, on the verge of the marriage, Kṛṣṇa abducted Rukmiṇī.

Abduction was not an uncommon practice among the *kṣatriyas* of that period, though the bride might have a say before the marriage, as has already been discussed in Chapter 3. The later Vaiṣṇava devotee-poet of the *Bhāgavata Purāṇa* could not accept Kṛṣṇa as a mere abductor. Thus, he made Rukmiṇī write a long love letter to Kṛṣṇa for saving her from Śiśupāla. But the earlier sources do not say anything like that. In the *Harivaṃśa*, it is only said that Rukmiṇī had developed a fondness for Kṛṣṇa and had told her friends that she would not marry anybody but Kṛṣṇa. But Kṛṣṇa was not much motivated by these factors. The text says:

> That beautiful damsel was going towards the temple with offerings when Keśava saw him. She was as beautiful as Lakṣmī herself. She had the ultimate grace like burning fire. It was as if the Earth-goddess herself has taken a human figure and appeared on the earth, as if the beams of the moon have come to the earth in a female form, as if she was now without her seat on a lotus but would soon become the main companion of Lakṣmī. Her complexion was dusky, her eyes were long and expansive, her corners of the eyes, lips, and nails were copper-coloured, her eyebrows were very pleasant, hair curly and blue, buttocks and breasts quite heavy, teeth equally fine and bright white, face like a full moon.

There was no other woman comparable to her in either beauty or fortune. Looking at Rukmiṇī, clothed in white, Keśava's passion was highly inflamed like fuelled fire. Then he discussed with Baladeva, and decided to abduct her. Hence, the moment Rukmiṇī was out of the temple after worship, Kṛṣṇa took her in his own chariot.[115]

The *Viṣṇu Purāṇa* agrees with the *Harivaṃśa* in its shorter narrative that Kṛṣṇa fell in love with Rukmiṇī and solicited her in marriage, but Rukmin refused. When Bhīṣmaka betrothed her daughter to Śiśupāla, following Jarāsaṃdha's suggestion, Kṛṣṇa abducted her—'*tāṃ kanyāṃ hatavān hari*'[116]

The fact that Kṛṣṇa's marriage with Rukmiṇī was nothing but a case of abduction is clearly revealed by his closest friend, Arjuna, in the *Mahābhārata*:

He devastated the realm of the kings,
And in one chariot abducted alone
The glorious Rukmiṇī of the Bhojas
Who bore the great-spirited Raukmineya.[117]

No doubt, this is the incident that antagonized Śiśupāla to the extreme against Kṛṣṇa. Thus, in the 'Sabhāparvan' of the *Mahābhārata*, Kṛṣṇa says about Śiśupāla:

rukmiṇyām asya mūḍhasya prārthanāsīn mumūrṣataḥ/
na ca tāṃ prāptavān mūḍhaḥ śūdro vedastutiṃ yathā//

(This fool, who must want to die, once proposed himself for Rukmiṇī, but the fool no more obtained her than a *śūdra* a hearing of the Veda.)[118]

And Śiśupāla jeered in reply:

mat pūrvāṃ rukmniṇīṃ kṛṣṇa saṃsatsu parikīrtayan/
viśeṣataḥ pārthiveṣu vrīḍāṃ na kuruṣe katham//
manyamāno hi kaḥ satsu puruṣaḥ parikīrtayat/
anyapūrvāṃ striyaṃ jātuṃ tvad anyo madhusūdana//

> (Have you no shame, at all, Kṛṣṇa, that you broadcast in assemblies, particularly before these kings, that your Rukmiṇī was another man's first? For what self-respecting man but you would broadcast to the street that his wife had belonged to another, Madhusūdana?)[119]

Kṛṣṇa's abduction of the already betrothed Rukmiṇī seems to be as much an outcome of passion as of a political design. But that design was unsuccessful. Kṛṣṇa defeated Rukmin and the others who chased him after the abduction. But contrary to his expectations, Bhīṣmaka and Rukmin did not shift their allegiance but remained loyal to Jarāsaṃdha. Kṛṣṇa sadly said to Yudhiṣṭhira in the *Mahābhārata*:

> Bhīṣmaka ... a slayer of enemy heroes, is loyal to the Magadhan king and holds no loyalty for us who, as his relations, bow to him and loyally do him favors that he returns with disfavor. Without recognition of his own lineage and power he has chosen Jarāsaṃdha, just on seeing his blazing fame.[120]

Thus Kṛṣṇa's first attempt to recover his political foothold was utterly unsuccessful. From this position, how he ended up as the *vāsudeva* is really an interesting development.

We have, thus, charted out Kṛṣṇa's political situation before he made his entry into *Mahābhārata*'s central narrative during Draupadī's bridegroom choice and found his biggest allies in the Pāṇḍavas. The succession struggle in the Kuru kingdom must not have been unknown to him, and the junior branch was in a despicable condition. The Pāṇḍavas, who had hardly any blood relationship with the Kurus, were not only deprived of any share in the kingdom but were almost murdered in the lacquer house. Escaping, they were roaming around in disguise and looking for an opening. That opening came in the form of Draupadī's bridegroom choice. The Pāñcālas were the only kingdom capable of challenging the Kurus. Making the Pāñcāla princess their common wife tied the Pāṇḍavas in a very strong alliance with them, after Arjuna won her in the competition of archery. Drupada, though reluctant at first to give her daughter away in such an unusual marriage, at last agreed. Vyāsa's persuasion, and probably the political advantage of making the breach in the Kuru clan permanent, made him do so. And in this alliance, Kṛṣṇa also found the political opening he was seeking.

Kṛṣṇa did not do much in the *svayaṃvara* except identifying the disguised Pāṇḍavas and persuading other kings to understand that Arjuna had won Draupadī lawfully. But this was the first time we saw him extending his friendship to his Pāṇḍava cousins. The Pāṇḍavas, though enjoying a prestigious lineage, had no power or territory. Kṛṣṇa had a territory and a powerful clan but hardly any prestige. Both of them, joined in an alliance with the Pāñcālas—who had both prestige and power—would definitely make a formidable force. Kṛṣṇa, sending wedding gifts to the Pāṇḍavas, was initiating this alliance.

However, Kṛṣṇa's position in this alliance was still marginal. The Pāñcāla support to the Pāṇḍavas threatened the Kurus, and Dhṛtarāṣṭra gave the Pāṇḍavas a share in the kingdom though in the forested Khāṇḍavaprastha. In this situation, Kṛṣṇa could not remain in the alliance only as a friend of the Pāṇḍavas but needed to cement his position. This he accomplished by marrying off his sister Subhadrā to his closest friend among the Pāṇḍavas, Arjuna. Therefore, when Arjuna expressed to Kṛṣṇa his passion for Subhadrā, Kṛṣṇa himself refused to risk a *svayaṃvara* and advised him to abduct her, suggesting the same course he had adopted for Rukmiṇī:

> Abduct my beautiful sister by force, for who would know her designs at a bridegroom choice?[121]

Thus when the infuriated Yādavas, headed by Balarāma, decided to punish Arjuna after he forcibly abducted Subhadrā, Kṛṣṇa made them realize the importance of the subsequent alliance:

> The Pārtha knows that you Sātvatas are not greedy for riches, and he also judged that he could not win at a bridegroom choice. Who would approve giving the girl away, as though she were cattle? And what man on earth would barter his offspring? I believe that Arjuna saw all these difficulties, and hence abducted the girl lawfully. The alliance is a proper one. Subhadrā is famous, and an equally famous Pārtha took her by force. Who would not want Arjuna, the son of the daughter of Kuntībhoja, born in the lineage of Bharata and the great-spirited

Śaṃtanu? Nor do I see one who could vanquish the Pārtha with gallantry, my worthy, in any of the worlds with their Indras and Rudras. That kind of chariot and my own horses! The Pārtha is a nimble archer; who would match him? Rather run after Dhanaṃjaya and cheerfully make him return with the politest diplomacy.[122]

The Yādavas of course understood the design, and we see them engaged in ecstatic celebrations with the Pāṇḍavas for Subhadrā's marriage which cemented the alliance. When Draupadī angrily told Arjuna, 'Go where that Sātvata woman is, Kaunteya! It is the first knot that comes loose first on a load, however well tied!' Arjuna made Subhadrā change into a simple cow maid's dress. In that simple attire Subhadrā approached Draupadī and greeted her, saying, 'I am Bhadrā, your serving maid', which appeased Draupadī.[123] The narrative is nice and sweet. But why should Subhadrā, never connected with the cowherds, be dressed like a cow maid, unless it was to assert her connection with Kṛṣṇa who had once been a cowherd? It is highly unlikely for Arjuna to know the appeal of simplicity a cowherd's attire would make, unless it had been suggested by someone who still considered the cowherds as his real friends. Though many scholars have tried hard to separate the *Mahābhārata* Kṛṣṇa from the rowdy cowherd, Kṛṣṇa's cowherd past often resurfaces like this in the *Mahābhārata*.

With the alliance with the Pāṇḍavas well established and even more strengthened after the birth of Subhadrā's son, Abhimanyu, Kṛṣṇa concentrated on facilitating the rise of the Pāṇḍavas to power. The first step in that direction was the clearance of the Khāṇḍava forest and establishment of Indraprastha, providing the Pāṇḍavas with a substantial territory and agrarian resource base. The episode, and its geopolitical significance in Kṛṣṇa's political design, has been discussed in detail in Chapter 2.

The burning of the Khāṇḍava forest was a turning point in Kṛṣṇa's career. With this achievement he established his Pāṇḍava friends in a powerful position in which he also now could claim a share. It was the beginning of his real comradeship with Arjuna. Geographically, now he had a base to attempt to regain Mathurā. But, more importantly, after a long engagement in securing his position, Kṛṣṇa again appeared in his full form, the form of not just a diplomat and warrior but of a reformer. The boy who, in his early adolescence, had challenged the cults of the

Nāgas and of Indra, again came up in a violent conflict with them, and this time met with greater success. He was no god yet. But, as a competent diplomat, capable warrior, and harbinger of intellectual novelty, Kṛṣṇa's journey to become a *vāsudeva* had begun. It is in the Khāṇḍava-burning episode that Kṛṣṇa and Arjuna were first identified with Nārāyaṇa and Nara (a non-Vedic deity later identified with Viṣṇu and his companion representing the Human Universal, respectively). The fact that, in the Jaina tradition, the words '*vāsudeva*' and '*nārāyaṇa*' are often synonymous indicates the importance of this identification.

The most significant task accomplished by Kṛṣṇa in this journey, at least from the military point of view, was his success against the plundering-raiding tribes from whom he protected the settled agrarian society. His opponents were centred round Jarāsaṃdha of Magadha but were numerous. To name the most important few, who are present in most of the sources, we must mention Naraka of Prāgjyotiṣa, the other 'Vāsudeva' of Puṇḍra, and the Śālva chief.

Naraka is a very interesting character. He has been described as a demon chief of Prāgjyotiṣa (Assam) and a notorious plunderer. His list of plunders, according to the *Viṣṇu Purāṇa*, included the umbrella of Varuṇa, the jewel mountain crest of Mandāra, and the earrings of Aditi, the mother of the Devas. He was demanding Indra's Airāvata. Moreover, he carried off the maidens of the celestials, sages, demons, and kings and shut them up in his own palace.[124] The list of the *Harivaṃśa* is more or less similar, though Viśvakarman's fourteen-year-old daughter is mentioned specifically among the plundered women. The *Mahābhārata*, however, mentions only Aditi's earrings.[125] Kṛṣṇa killed Naraka after being specifically requested to do so by Indra. Kṛṣṇa won a huge amount of booty as well as the sixteen thousand women abducted by Naraka.

Whether a plunderer from faraway Assam could really create so much trouble in the Gaṅgā-Yamunā Doab is really questionable. But the legend bears an unmistakable sign of the advances of a non-Vedic eastern chief who, like a typical tribal plunderer, captured the wealth and women of the people of the settled society. Kṛṣṇa saved the settled society from this menace.

However, we must remember that these chieftains, though portrayed as demons by the society where they raided in, played an immensely significant role in the early political organization of their own people. Jarāsaṃdha played that role in Magadha and was probably celebrated by the *māgadha* bards for that. Whether Naraka had such bards is not known. But even after a long period of time, Assam remembered Naraka in a very different light. Right from the seventh century CE, when Sanskritized Assam started looking back at its own past, Naraka is remembered as the builder of Kāmarūpa/Prāgjyotiṣa, as a highly pious and benevolent ruler. Just like the inscriptions of Assam, the *Harivaṃśa* and the *Viṣṇu Purāṇa* describe Naraka as the son of the Earth Goddess by the Varāha incarnation of Viṣṇu, a birth suitable for a hero, and definitely not for a demon. The name 'Naraka' is probably the tampered Sanskritization of some aboriginal name. That Naraka is remembered as a grand patron of the local Tāntric fertility cult of Kāmākhyā also sheds some light on his religious affiliation.

However, an outstanding step undertaken by Kṛṣṇa in the legend was marrying the women captured by Naraka. The figure sixteen thousand is immaterial here. The poet of the *Harivaṃśa* could not accept the spirit of Kṛṣṇa marrying the women already enjoyed by others. So, he declared that Naraka did not enjoy any of his plunders and he plundered for the sake of collection only. The women were awaiting their marriage with Kṛṣṇa, remaining steadfast in their vow of 'chastity'. We do not find any reason for believing in such vows and, more importantly, the women being allowed a choice of such vows by their plunderers. It is not their virginity preserved for Kṛṣṇa, but Kṛṣṇa's disregard for that condition in marrying the women who would otherwise be discarded by the society without any fault of their own,[126] which is remarkable in the episode.

Killing Naraka was a breakthrough for Kṛṣṇa, which enriched him in booty and earned him a lot of fame. However, it would never be possible for him to establish himself as a *vāsudeva* as long as Jarāsaṃdha was alive. When Yudhiṣṭhira sought Kṛṣṇa's advice before organizing his *rājasūya*, Kṛṣṇa therefore revealed his fear of Jarāsaṃdha.

We have discussed the implication of the *rājasūya* as a Later Vedic ritual for settling succession disputes in the Kuru-Pañcāla regions in Chapter 2. Though the scale of the sacrifice had been magnified by the later poets, the goal was not suzerainty but legitimacy. What the Pāṇḍavas collected from the other kings was not tributes of subordination but token gifts in acceptance of Yudhiṣṭhira's kingship. There was hardly any reason for any non-Kuru chief not to accept that. However, if Yudhiṣṭhira's power was closely linked with that of Kṛṣṇa, and if the clearance of the Khāṇḍava forest and the establishment of Indraprastha were integrally connected with Kṛṣṇa's bid to regain Mathurā, Jarāsaṃdha must have had a strong case against Yudhiṣṭhira. That is why Kṛṣṇa warned Yudhiṣṭhira about Jarāsaṃdha and told him in detail the history of Jarāsaṃdha's conflict with the Yādavas. However, as we have seen in all the actions of Kṛṣṇa so far, his political designs were always accompanied by some effort towards his reform of the prevalent ethico-religious system. Here also, Kṛṣṇa raised the point that eighty-six kings had been captured by Jarāsaṃdha for a great human sacrifice:

> What joy of life is left to the kings who are sprinkled and cleansed in the house of Paśupati as sacrificial animals, bull of the Bharatas? When a *kṣatriya* dies by the sword, he is honored—should we all not then beat back the Magadhan? Eighty-six kings, king, have been led to their jail by Jarāsandha; king, fourteen are left, and then he will begin his atrocity.[127]

The Kṛṣṇa we have seen so far was not a person to engage in a war, irrespective of the ethical value of the cause, where success would be hard to attain. Attacking a chief as powerful as Jarāsaṃdha on his own territory would have been imprudent for Kṛṣṇa. Therefore, Kṛṣṇa again adopted a strategy to avoid a full-scale battle. He entered Magadha with Bhīma and Arjuna in disguise of *brāhmaṇa snātakas* (who just concluded their studies). As mentioned earlier, Jarāsaṃdha—eager for legitimacy—was showing great favour towards *brāhmaṇas*, and they received the same treatment. However, they made their enmity apparent by breaking up the peak of the Caityaka hill—a place of worship for the Magadhans—plundered garlands to decorate themselves, and did not accept Jarāsaṃdha's hospitality. These events were a clear assertion of their aversion to the popular religion of Magadha (which included human sacrifice) and paralleled Kṛṣṇa's entrance to Mathurā for killing Kaṃsa. They revealed their identities to Jarāsaṃdha, and Kṛṣṇa made it clear that it was not the enmity with the Vṛṣṇis but the plan of sacrificing the kings that prompted this drastic measure.[128] Then Kṛṣṇa challenged Jarāsaṃdha in a duel with any one of the three. As a shrewd diplomat, Kṛṣṇa knew his enemy well and banked on his chivalry. The proud chivalrous king accepted the challenge and chose the strongest—Bhīma—as his opponent. Bhīma killed Jarāsaṃdha. Kṛṣṇa thus finally succeeded in getting Jarāsaṃdha killed, without a battle, without much bloodshed, in a one-to-one duel. The kings were set free. Jarāsaṃdha's son was consecrated as the new king of Magadha.

The *prativāsudeva* died in this manner and it paved the way for Kṛṣṇa's *vāsudeva*-ship. That is probably why the poet suddenly brought in Garuḍa, the vehicle of Viṣṇu, to the scene after Jarāsaṃdha's death. The freed kings celebrated Kṛṣṇa as Viṣṇu.[129] However, this was what a group of kings, saved from imminent death by Kṛṣṇa, felt. The view of the other side would be heard soon. The killing of Jarāsaṃdha had definitely raised Yudhiṣṭhira's prestige much more than ever and made his *rājasūya* easier. But Yudhiṣṭhira's *rājasūya* would not just be an assembly to decide his kingship but also one where Kṛṣṇa's *vāsudeva*-ship would be publicly proclaimed and debated for the first time. Śiśupāla, the most trusted ally of Jarāsaṃdha, would be the central character in that debate. Thus, Jarāsaṃdha's death would not be his end.

As we have seen, the *rājasūya* is primarily a ritual to legitimize the king, and the king should be the person at the centre of the rite. However, during the ceremony, it was Bhīṣma who suggested that Yudhiṣṭhira offer the gifts of honour to the deserving guests—the teachers, priests, relatives, *snātakas*, friends, and kings.[130] This had to be started by choosing one as the most deserving of honour. This selection was not a part of the Yajurvedic ritual of *rājasūya*. Therefore, it must have had some other purpose. Was Bhīṣma speaking of the choice of a *vāsudeva* in an open assembly? The following development makes it seem so.

It was Bhīṣma who chose Kṛṣṇa, and the reasons cited were his glory, strength, and prowess.[131] These are the very criteria which defined *vāsudeva*-ship, according to both Jaina mythology and the *Mahābhārata*. It was precisely at this point that Śiśupāla rose in protest, his main argument being that Kṛṣṇa, not being a king, did not deserve the honour. The first part of Śiśupāla's speech was, in fact, quite well argued:

> How can the Dāśārha, who is no king, merit precedence over all the kings of the earth so that he should be honoured by you? If you consider Kṛṣṇa the elder, bull of the Bharatas, how can the son merit it while the old Vasudeva, his father, stands by? Vāsudeva may favour you and be compliant, but how can a Mādhava merit the honour when a Drupada

> is present? Or if you deem Kṛṣṇa your teacher, bull of the Kurus, why do you honour the Vārṣṇeya while Droṇa stands by? Or if you regard Kṛṣṇa as a priest, scion of Kuru, how can you honour him when Dvaipāyana is present? This killer of Madhu is neither a priest, nor a teacher, nor a king: is he not honoured, best of the Kurus, but out of favoritism? If you must honor Madhusūdana, why bring these kings here—to insult them, Bhārata?[132]

Śiśupāla's argument was not ill-suited for an assembly whose main purpose was to receive the consent of the kings for Yudhiṣṭhira's kingship. He also raised the point that Kṛṣṇa, himself not a king, once slew a king.[133] Thus Yudhiṣṭhira tried to appease him while Bhīṣma rose to defend his decision. The early part of the argument given by Bhīṣma was the statement of Kṛṣṇa's achievements of vanquishing many *kṣatriyas* in battles, his various wonderful achievements from childhood, his knowledge, and his might. Very precisely Bhīṣma described him as 'of *brāhmaṇas* he is the elder in knowledge, of *kṣatriyas* the superior in strength' (*jñānavṛddho dvijātīnāṃ kṣatriyāṇāṃ balādhikaḥ*). He also enumerated among Kṛṣṇa's qualities his liberality, dexterity, learning, gallantry, modesty, fame, resolve, humility, lustre, pertinacity, contentment, and prosperity.[134] The following passage is suddenly a celebration of Kṛṣṇa as the Supreme Deity,[135] not well connected with the earlier portions or the response it generated, which seems to be the result of a later Vaiṣṇavite revision of the episode. In general, Bhīṣma's argument showed that basically Kṛṣṇa had earned a name as a person who combined immense spiritual-ethical knowledge with sound skill in fighting. That was what made him special in the eyes of many, including Bhīṣma and Sahadeva who arrogantly declared that he would place his foot on the head of anyone opposed to honouring Kṛṣṇa.[136]

But there were others like Śiśupāla for whom these qualities were not enough. Śiśupāla had good support, particularly after Sahadeva's insulting statement. Encouraged, Śiśupāla started to slander against both Bhīṣma and Kṛṣṇa, and Kṛṣṇa's early life became the centre of attack. Śiśupāla pointed out how vague was the glorification of Kṛṣṇa's early achievements, including the triumph over Pūtanā, overturning of a cart, killing of some harmful animals, and the Govardhana episode. He also criticized Kṛṣṇa for killing Kaṃsa whose food he had eaten, an incident which had many other critics apart from Śiśupāla. Then he came to the killing of Jarāsaṃdha, which he strongly condemned. He also implied that Kṛṣṇa could not accept Jarāsaṃdha's hospitality because of his lowly birth.[137]

This section of the 'Sabhāparvan' had certainly undergone a Vaiṣṇavite revision, since we suddenly find Bhīṣma telling an absurd story about Śiśupāla's birth and early life to Bhīma, before assuring him of Kṛṣṇa's divinity.[138] But, after that, the situation gradually went out of control, and after Bhīṣma's proud comment that he did not count all the assembled kings any better than straw, Śiśupāla found huge support in his bid to disrupt the sacrifice.

Till then, when it was being debated whether he was a great *vāsudeva* or a mean and useless cowherd, Kṛṣṇa was not interfering at all. However, when a serious threat to the sacrifice was created, he rose to the occasion by enlisting Śiśupāla's crimes that he had forgiven:

> Knowing that we had gone to Prāgjyotiṣa, this fiend, who is our cousin, burned down Dvārakā, kings. While the barons of the Bhojas were at play on Mount Raivataka, he slew and captured them, then returned to his city. Malevolently, he stole the horse that was set free at the Horse Sacrifice and surrounded by guards to disrupt my father's sacrifice. When she was journeying to the country of the Sauvīras to be given in marriage, the misguided fool abducted the unwilling wife-to-be of the glorious Babhru. Hiding beneath his wizardry, the fiendish offender of his uncle abducted Bhadrā of Viśālā, the intended bride of Karuṣa.[139]

After that, both Kṛṣṇa and Śiśupāla complained against each other about the Rukmiṇī episode, and ultimately Kṛṣṇa killed Śiśupāla in a duel. The narration of the duel is brief, as Kṛṣṇa is described to have killed Śiśupāla with his divine discus. But the *cakra* was a commonly used weapon in early India, as the paintings in the Mirzapur caves and the Buddhist text *Avadānaśataka* testify (in this text, king Ajātaśatru—who certainly had no supernatural power—killed a devotee of the Buddha, named Śrīmatī, with his discus). In the 'Udyogaparvan', Dhṛtarāṣṭra recalled Śiśupāla's death in a real duel. It frightened the other kings who did not risk a fight, and the rest of Yudhiṣṭhira's *rājasūya* was a success.[140]

This episode was highly important both in the context of Yudhiṣṭhira's rise to power and Kṛṣṇa's rise to *vāsudeva*-ship. With the killing of Jarāsaṃdha, Kṛṣṇa now became a person who could not be ignored in North Indian politics. Opinions about him were largely divided. If one group—consisting of the Pāṇḍavas, Bhīṣma, Vidura, the kings set free by him from Jarāsaṃdha's prison, and definitely his own people—raised him to the status of a supreme personality who was a brilliant thinker as well as an unparallelled fighter, the other group—former allies of Jarāsaṃdha—considered him nothing more than a lowly cowherd who unlawfully killed Kaṃsa and Jarāsaṃdha. The other group, including Śiśupāla, had nothing personal against Yudhiṣṭhira, and probably respected the prestigious family of the Kurus. Therefore, they consented to Yudhiṣṭhira's *rājasūya* without hesitation. So, it will be too far-fetched to agree with Brockington that Śiśupāla's hospitality to Bhīma shows that the Jarāsaṃdha-episode is an interpolation. Jarāsaṃdha's chief enemy was Kṛṣṇa, and it was the elevation of Kṛṣṇa against which Śiśupāla protested. Much of his personal grudge was expressed in his comments about the killing of Jarāsaṃdha and the abduction of his betrothed Rukmiṇī, both the incidents closely linked with the Kṛṣṇa-Jarāsaṃdha conflict. The list of Śiśupāla's atrocities against his Yādava kinsmen probably indicates that, aided by Jarāsaṃdha, he wanted to take the place of Kaṃsa, a bid in which he failed.

Thus, Kṛṣṇa had still to deal with a band hostile to him. He eradicated most of his opponents. One such opponent would have been the Śālvas. The Śālva chief has been described as one who rode on an ever-mobile chariot that could go anywhere, named Saubha. He attacked and ravaged Dvārakā to avenge Śiśupāla's death, in Kṛṣṇa's absence. Kṛṣṇa chased him down and killed him. This episode is narrated in *Mahābhārata* (III.15). However, this short account did not satisfy the later poets who made Yudhiṣṭhira ask for an elaboration of the episode. That elaboration (III.16–23) has become what van Buitenen called 'an early instance of science fiction'.[141] The poet took all his liberties to describe Śālva's well-furnished spaceship spewing flames, missiles, and illusions on the chariot-bound Kṛṣṇa.

Leaving aside the science fiction, if we concentrate on the shorter account, different observations can be made. The Śālvas were a well-known nomadic people of the Vedic times, whose raids created a great hazard in the Kuru realm. Witzel, in fact, considers the Śālva invasions the main factor behind the decline of the Kurus around 800 BCE.[142] The *Mahābhārata*, however, shows that the nuisance was there but could not become so fatal for the Kurus. Ambā was the betrothed of a Śālva whom Bhīṣma had defeated. The Śālvas, like other plundering-raiding tribes, were ultimately crushed by Kṛṣṇa. The moving fort Saubha possibly represents the nomadic character of the Śālvas. Kṛṣṇa's victory over the Śālvas has been referred to in other places of the *Mahābhārata* as well.[143]

Kṛṣṇa, thus, gradually established himself in a very powerful position by crushing most of the allies of Jarāsaṃdha, including many plundering-raiding tribes. However, Jarāsaṃdha's camp must have had an ideologue as well. That was the last obstacle in Kṛṣṇa's unquestioned position as a *vāsudeva*. The rival *vāsudeva*, the Vāsudeva of Puṇḍra, is a shadowy figure in the *Mahābhārata*. Kṛṣṇa himself describes him to Yudhiṣṭhira as 'the one known as the Supreme Person, who claims that he is the Supreme Person in this world and in his folly always assumes my title—a king powerful among the Vaṅgas, Puṇḍras, and Kirātas, known in the world as the Vāsudeva of Puṇḍra'.[144] Vaṅga and Puṇḍra are regions of Bengal, and his association with the Kirātas shows his non-Aryan identity. Thus, this Vāsudeva was another eastern non-Aryan chief. However, he not only entitled himself '*vāsudeva*' but also claimed his own divinity. Therefore, Kṛṣṇa's position as a *vāsudeva* could not be secured before a final showdown with this man. The *Mahābhārata* sheds no light on this encounter. Vāsudeva of Puṇḍra was present at Draupadī's bridegroom choice, he was enlisted as an ally of Jarāsaṃdha, he was subdued by Bhīma as part of Bhīma's eastward journey for tribute-collection, and he was present in Yudhiṣṭhira's *rājasūya*, but never after that. The killing of this Vāsudeva must have been accomplished shortly after the killings of Śiśupāla and Śālva.

The *Viṣṇu Purāṇa* says that the Vāsudeva of Puṇḍra adopted all the emblems of Viṣṇu and was flattered by the ignorant people as the descendant deity. As his self-esteem grew, he asked Kṛṣṇa to surrender his insignia, weapons, and title of *vāsudeva* and to pay him homage. Kṛṣṇa attacked his territory and killed him.[145]

We do not have any idea about what doctrine the false Vāsudeva taught. His claim of being a *vāsudeva* indicates that he was a special member of the anti-Kṛṣṇa camp. However, the rallying point of that camp was not this Vāsudeva, but Jarāsaṃdha. At least till Yudhiṣṭhira's *rājasūya*, it was the Jarāsaṃdha-Kṛṣṇa conflict that dominated the political scene. The political position Kṛṣṇa attained was mainly a result of his military, intellectual, and diplomatic triumph over Jarāsaṃdha and his allies. Starting with nothing, Kṛṣṇa ended up as the *vāsudeva*, and he had to ally himself with the Pāṇḍavas to accomplish that. Naturally, in his subsequent career, he would have to engage in the Pāṇḍava-Kaurava conflict which, at least from Kṛṣṇa's point of view, was nothing but an offshoot of his struggle against Jarāsaṃdha.

Some other kings and chiefs were probably defeated by Kṛṣṇa. Arjuna mentioned some of these victories in the 'Udyogaparvan':

> Impetuously he churned up Gāndhāra,
> And having defeated all Nagnajit's sons,
> He freed from his fetters by force that friend
> Of the Gods whose name is Sudarśanīya.
> At Kavāṭa he smote the king of the Pāṇḍyas,
> And smashed the Kaliṅgas at Dantakura;
> The city Vārāṇasī, burned by him,
> Stayed many a year without a protector.[146]

Some of these may be just some names to swell Kṛṣṇa's list of conquests. Some of them may be episodes forgotten by the time of the composition of the *Harivaṃśa* and the *Viṣṇu Purāṇa*. Kaliṅga could be a natural enemy of Kṛṣṇa, given his conflict with the eastern powers such as Magadha, Puṇḍra, and Prāgjyotiṣa. The burning of Vārāṇasī is mentioned in the *Viṣṇu Purāṇa* but as a sequel to Kṛṣṇa's victory over the false Vāsudeva. The story is a miraculous one of Śaiva-Vaiṣṇava conflict and should not be given much importance. A more likely possibility is that Kṛṣṇa entered some internal conflict in Vārāṇasī and backed a party led by a man named Babhru, as suggested by Yudhiṣṭhira's statement:

> Obtaining Kṛṣṇa as brother and guide,
> The Kāśī king Babhru, on whom Vāsudeva
> Has showered his wishes, as after the summer
> The cloud on the creatures, has found good fortune.[147]

Another tribal opponent of Kṛṣṇa was probably the Vānara chief Dvivida. The *Viṣṇu Purāṇa* portrays him as a typical non-Aryan forest dweller antagonistic to the settled society and its religion:

> Blinded by ignorance therefore, he interrupted all religious practices, put down all righteous observances, and brought about the death of living creatures; he set fire to forests, to villages and towns: sometimes he deluged cities and villages with a downpour of rocks or lifting up mountains in the waters he cast them into the ocean; then placing himself in the midst of the deep, he agitated the waves until the foaming sea rose above its confines and swept away the villages and cities situated upon its shores. Dvivida, who was capable of assuming shapes as he liked, enlarged his bulk to an immense proportion, and rolling and tumbling and trampling amidst the corn-fields, he crushed and spoiled the harvest.[148]

The Vānaras were probably a non-Aryan tribe living in the forests and mountains of Central India. These people have a tremendously important role in the *Rāmāyaṇa* where also they fight primarily with rocks and trees. It seems that this Dvivida created much nuisance to the settled society by disrupting religious observances, killing people, destroying agricultural products, and setting fire to houses. Balarāma killed this Dvivida. In the *Viṣṇu Purāṇa*, he is an ally of the Vāsudeva of Puṇḍra. However, in the *Mahābhārata*, Vidura refers to him as an ally of Śālva, who attacked Kṛṣṇa with a mighty avalanche of rocks but in vain.[149] All these chiefs had to be defeated by Kṛṣṇa, since these non-Aryan chiefs continued Jarāsaṃdha's legacy.

Thus, if Kṛṣṇa was the *vāsudeva*, it was neither Kaṃsa nor Duryodhana but Jarāsaṃdha alone who could be the *prativāsudeva*. The Jaina authors clearly displayed Kṛṣṇa's *vāsudeva*-ship as a result of his triumph against Jarāsaṃdha, the Pāṇḍavas and Kauravas being the mere supporters of the two opposite camps. The *Harivaṃśa* comes close to that by showing Duryodhana as a minor ally of Jarāsaṃdha. Fighting Jarāsaṃdha was the biggest challenge of Kṛṣṇa's political career. Killing Jarāsaṃdha brought him to the political limelight. Even after that, his position was continuously questioned by the allies of Jarāsaṃdha. Killing Śiśupāla ended the first challenge to his *vāsudeva*-ship. Killing the Puṇḍra chief eradicated the last. He used all kinds of stratagems from burning down a forest to arranging the abduction of his own sister to survive in that struggle. But his political success was always accompanied by his reforming zeal—his denouncing of the Nāga cults, challenge to the Vedic Indra cult, crusade against human sacrifice, or showing the futility of the overemphasis on female virginity.

Kṛṣṇa was really a *vāsudeva*, one of incomparable splendour, knowledge, and power, an unmatched person in the realm of action. It is noteworthy in his rise that his attainment of the demigod status was an earned deification rather than an inherited one. Even though Vaiṣṇavization of the texts has portrayed Kṛṣṇa as the Supreme Divinity roaming around among mere mortals, a close inspection shows him as one of the most 'human' characters of the early days of the *Mahābhārata* tradition, born of two human parents (unlike the Pāṇḍavas, Karṇa, Bhīṣma, and Droṇa) and without any supernatural mechanisms (unlike Duryodhana and his brothers, Draupadī, Dhṛṣṭadyumna, and Jarāsaṃdha). He was brought up in less glamorous surroundings than most *Mahābhārata* heroes and was operating from a minor power in which his position was not that of a king. His attainment of *vāsudeva*-ship was thus well contested as it was the journey of the seemingly ordinary to extraordinary heights. However, it was only Jarāsaṃdha who could be his worthy opponent, the *prativāsudeva*. The 'false' Vāsudeva of Puṇḍra, just like the Pāṇḍavas, was hardly anything but a pawn in the struggle of these two illustrious personalities. With Jarāsaṃdha gone, Kṛṣṇa's rise was smooth but not without repercussions in his own surroundings, among the fellow Yādava diplomats who still knew him to be the cowherd boy they had brought in the forefront in their jealous conspiracy to overthrow Kaṃsa.

4.5 From Butter Thief to Jewel Thief: Kṛṣṇa the Vṛṣṇi Diplomat

The Caitrakas, the Śinis and Andhakas,
The Kaukuras, Sṛñjayas, Vṛṣṇis and Bhojas
All wait on the counsel of Vāsudeva
And subduing their foes they gladden their friends.
Ugrasena and all other Andhaka-Vṛṣṇis

All Indra-like men and guided by Kṛṣṇa,
The spirited men have the valor of truth,
The powerful Yādavas take their pleasure.

— Yudhiṣṭhira [150]

So far we have discussed Kṛṣṇa's journey starting as an insignificant cowherd and culminating in becoming a *vāsudeva*. No doubt, as the *vāsudeva*, Kṛṣṇa had a much more significant role to play. As a widely celebrated diplomat, he would have many more political engagements, and we have already noted how Kṛṣṇa's political activities were integrated with his propagation of a new ethical-spiritual ideology. But understanding Kṛṣṇa's diplomatic role has to start from its base, because, technically speaking, he was primarily a Vṛṣṇi leader. Kṛṣṇa's rise must have benefitted his own people, the Yādava-Vṛṣṇis, and raised their prestige. But how did they react to Kṛṣṇa is an interesting question to ask.

We have seen how Kṛṣṇa's entrance to the opportunistic politics of the Yādava leaders was in the middle of a conspiracy against Kaṃsa. With Ugrasena and Akrura as his allies, Kṛṣṇa succeeded in his struggle against Kaṃsa. However, Vikadru's speech during Jarāsaṃdha's invasion clearly showed that Kṛṣṇa's leadership was initially not unquestionable. With his growing political importance, the scenario must have changed. But whether Kṛṣṇa's unquestionable supremacy pleased all the Yādavas is doubtful. The leaders who were jealous to see the rise in the power and wealth of Kaṃsa might not have been too pleased with Kṛṣṇa's rise as well. But where Kṛṣṇa differed from Kaṃsa was in sharing the benefits with his kinsmen, as Yudhiṣṭhira noted in the statement earlier.

Among Kṛṣṇa's kinsmen, some—such as Śiśupāla and Kālayavana—were clearly against him. But even the ones in Kṛṣṇa's camp had their internal rivalries and personal ambitions. One very significant legend makes the scenario quite clear. That is the legend about the jewel named Syamantaka. This costly jewel was the possession of a Yādava named Satrājit. Kṛṣṇa and many other Yādavas coveted this jewel. One day, Prasena—Satrājit's brother—while carrying the jewel, went missing, and the people suspected Kṛṣṇa of murder and theft. Kṛṣṇa attempted to solve the mystery and found out that Prasena was killed by a lion in a forest. The lion had been killed by a Ṛkṣa chief named Jāmbavān who gave the jewel to his son. Kṛṣṇa defeated Jāmbavān in a long duel and won the jewel back. The impressed Jāmbavān gave his daughter Jāmbavatī in marriage to Kṛṣṇa. When Kṛṣṇa returned the jewel to Satrājit, he married off his daughter Satyabhāmā to Kṛṣṇa as well.

Satyabhāmā was a woman desired by many Yādava chiefs. One of them, Śatadhanvan, murdered Satrājit in Kṛṣṇa's absence. When Kṛṣṇa returned, he banked on the support of Akrura and Kṛtavarman who denied him any help. Śatadhanvan fled but was chased down by Kṛṣṇa. Kṛṣṇa killed him but could not find the jewel which Śatadhanvan had given to Akrura to hide. However, Balarāma did not trust Kṛṣṇa and suspected him of hiding the jewel. He angrily left Dvārakā and settled in Mithilā where Duryodhana learned the art of mace wielding from him. Later, some Yādavas convinced him to return to Dvārakā. Finally, Kṛṣṇa found out that Akrura was the main culprit and pacified Balarāma by revealing the truth. However, Akrura was allowed to keep the jewel.

Some scholars, such as Bankim Chandra Chattopadhyay and Raychaudhuri, have dismissed it as a later Purāṇic tale, since the legend is available only in the *Harivaṃśa* and the Purāṇas and not in the *Mahābhārata*. However, this legend is connected with Kṛṣṇa's two major marriages—with Jāmbavatī and Satyabhāmā. Bankim would denounce these two characters as interpolated later in Kṛṣṇa's monogamous life. However, there is not a single source that calls Kṛṣṇa monogamous, and Satyabhāmā was the most active among the wives of Kṛṣṇa in the *Mahābhārata*. Sāmba—the son of Jāmbavatī—also appears in the Pāṇḍava-Yādava gatherings and has a role to play in the destruction of the Yādavas. Jāmbavatī is the only wife of Kṛṣṇa named in the Buddhist legends and the first among Kṛṣṇa's wives to be mentioned in an epigraphic source.

We will return to Jāmbavatī and Satyabhāmā later. Before that, the antiquity of the legend has to be verified. Bhaduri, following Jogendranath Basu, has pointed out that the tale cannot be dismissed as a later creation of the Purāṇic poets. The Later Vedic etymologist Yāska (*c.* seventh to sixth century BCE) mentions in his *Nirukta*, to explain a rare usage of the root *dā* (to give) in the sense of *dhāraṇa* (to adorn), the following sentence—'*akrura dadate maṇim iti abhibhāṣante*' (they say that Akrura had adorned himself with the jewel).[151] The reference is unmistakable, and the *Harivaṃśa* retains the original flavour by using the term '*dhārayāt*' in the context of Akrura.[152] However, the *Viṣṇu Purāṇa* misunderstands the root *dā* and uses the word *jagrāha* (had taken).[153]

So, the Syamantaka episode was well known by the time of Yāska, and, even then, it was known as an ancient incident about which people spoke—*iti abhibhāṣante*. Basu also notes that the incident, in both the *Harivaṃśa* and the Purāṇas, occurs not in the biography of Kṛṣṇa but in the general genealogical history (*vaṃśānucarita*) of the Vṛṣṇis. Therefore, Basu thinks that the legend might have formed a part of the family ballad or the *gāthā* of the Vṛṣṇis which used to be sung on ceremonial occasions.[154]

However, this ancient episode of the Vṛṣṇi history reveals a quite slippery ground on which Kṛṣṇa stood. It is said in the *Viṣṇu Purāṇa* that Kṛṣṇa desired the jewel for the sake of Ugrasena. The *Brahma Purāṇa* says that Kṛṣṇa himself had an eye on the jewel.[155] But he did not take it in fear of causing some disturbance in the clan—'*gotrabhedabhayād*'.[156] However, despite Kṛṣṇa's perfect care to protect his clan from internal conflict, it was he who was suspected of killing Prasena. Though they did not say it to Kṛṣṇa's face, they began to whisper their suspicion to each other—'*yadulokāḥ parasparaṃ karṇākarṇy akathayat*'.[157]

Here we can see Kṛṣṇa's effectiveness as a clan leader. Knowing of the whispers, he could ignore it or subdue it using his power and authority. But that would suit a tyrant like Kaṃsa. Rather, Kṛṣṇa adopted all necessary steps to eradicate the doubt from the minds of his clansmen.

Even then Kṛṣṇa's political journey in Dvārakā was not smooth. As most of the Yādava leaders coveted the jewel as well as Satyabhāmā, they again conspired behind his back. The *Viṣṇu Purāṇa* says that Akrura, Kṛtavarman, and Śatadhanvan were all admirers of Satyabhāmā. The *Harivaṃśa* presents Śatadhanvan as a suitor for her hand, while Akrura desired the jewel. The shrewd politician Akrura, however, inflamed the jealousy in the young Śatadhanvan to accomplish his revenge on Satrājit and to get the jewel without any risk. He and Kṛtavarman had promised to help Śatadhanvan against Kṛṣṇa when the latter was inspired to kill Satrājit. Akrura, according to the *Brahma Purāṇa*, even boasted of his political position in comparison to Kṛṣṇa's—'If you are attacked by Kṛṣṇa, we will come to your support. Undoubtedly the whole of Dvārakā abides by me today'.[158] But they refused to fulfil that promise after the murder.[159] The cunning Akrura, once Kaṃsa's trusted friend who betrayed him, was ready to plot the murder of Kṛṣṇa's father-in-law and betrayed Śatadhanvan as well. In result, Śatadhanvan got killed for the murder, and Akrura received the jewel without suspicion.

Even more shocking, however, was the reaction of Balarāma. That this simple man, always loyal to his younger brother, though rarely in agreement with him, could suspect Kṛṣṇa was the strangest turn. Possibly, with Kṛṣṇa's rise, the distance between Kṛṣṇa and Balarāma, who was once Kṛṣṇa's companion in all his struggles but was subsequently reduced to nothing more than his insignificant brother, grew. The incident seems not to be a later fabrication, since Duryodhana's discipleship of Balarāma is attested by the *Mahābhārata*. Interestingly, it was Akrura who strengthened Balarāma's belief that Kṛṣṇa had stolen the jewel.[160]

However, being the master diplomat that Kṛṣṇa was, he found out the real culprit by Akrura's sudden flurry of religious activities.[161] Still, he allowed Akrura to keep the jewel, after revealing his crime in front of all, to avoid another conflict, for the jewel was coveted by both Balarāma and Satyabhāmā.[162]

The jewel was coveted by Kṛṣṇa as well, and thus the *Viṣṇu Purāṇa* says that he was internally happy (*parituṣṭāntaḥkaraṇa*) to know the news of Satrājit's death.[163] But, as a true leader, he gave priority to the unity and interest of the clan than to his personal desire. In the course, he must have consolidated his position further in the Yādava politics and gained two of his three principal wives.

These two marriages of Kṛṣṇa are quite significant. We have seen that Kṛṣṇa had to contend with many non-Aryan tribes. However, his marriage with Jāmbavatī testifies that he was not in an Aryan versus non-Aryan crusade. The Ṛkṣas were probably a very lowly non-Aryan tribe who possibly resided in the Ṛkṣavān range. They were marginal associates of the Vānaras in the *Rāmāyaṇa*. The name of their leader is Jāmbavān in the *Rāmāyaṇa* as well. There is no reason to identify the two Jāmbavāns, and possibly Jāmbavān was the epithet of their chief. However, that Jāmbavatī's real identity is more complicated is indicated by the *Mahāummaga Jātaka* which says:

> The mother of the king Śivi is named Jāmbavatī, and she was the beloved queen consort of Vāsudeva the Kaṇha...

> Now the king of Śivi's mother, Jāmbavatī, was of the *caṇḍāla* caste, and she was the beloved queen consort of Vāsudeva, one of the Kaṇhagaṇa clan, the eldest of ten brothers.... He one day went out from Dvāravatī into the park; and on his way he espied a very beautiful girl, standing by the way, as he journeyed on some business from her *caṇḍāla* village to town. He fell in love, and asked her birth, and after hearing that she was a *caṇḍālī*, he was distressed. Finding that she was unmarried, he turned back at once and took her home, surrounded her with precious things, and made her his chief queen. She brought forth a son Śivi who ruled in Dvāravatī at his father's death.[164]

This story indicates that the real identity of the monkey and bear chiefs of the *Rāmāyaṇa* could have been nothing but outcasts like the *caṇḍālas*. However, Kṛṣṇa accepted Jāmbavatī as his wife, and even in the *Mahābhārata*, it was only Sāmba—the son of Jāmbavatī—who survived the destruction of the Yādavas. Thus, the marriage was a significant one, and the very first inscriptional reference to a wife of Kṛṣṇa, in the Tusam Inscription (fourth century CE), was about Jāmbavatī. It describes Kṛṣṇa as the bee who drinks the honey of the lotus-face of Jāmbavatī—'*jitam abhikṣaṇam eva jāmbavatī-badanāravindorjitalīna*'.[165]

If the marriage with Jāmbavatī was important for understanding Kṛṣṇa as a person, his marriage with Satyabhāmā was more significant politically. As we have seen, the marriage with Rukmiṇī was a politically motivated abduction which was not quite successful in obtaining its diplomatic objective. Though Rukmiṇī is Kṛṣṇa's principal wife in most of the later legends, we hardly see her perform any of the roles of a real consort. Jāmbavatī, Kṛṣṇa's second wife, came from a different cultural background. Though she seems to be a beloved wife of Kṛṣṇa and the mother of an important personality, she hardly had any political role to play. The real consort of Kṛṣṇa was Satyabhāmā, a lady from his own clan, and one desired by many Yādava leaders. Kṛṣṇa did not possibly expect to marry her. When he got her, she naturally became his real companion. Though Satyabhāmā produced no famous son like Pradyumna or Sāmba, she remained Kṛṣṇa's favourite wife. It was she who accompanied Kṛṣṇa in his campaign against Naraka; and it was she who went with him to meet the exiled Pāṇḍavas. When her father was killed, she could go alone to meet Kṛṣṇa and tell him about the incident. Almost all the legends of Kṛṣṇa's conjugal love revolve around Satyabhāmā. The *Harivaṃśa* tells of Kṛṣṇa's marriage with two of Satyabhāmā's sisters—Vratinī and Prasvāpinī. But this is not supported by any other account, and these characters have no significant role to play in Kṛṣṇa's life even in the *Harivaṃśa*.

There are several legends about Kṛṣṇa's love for Satyabhāmā, which we do not need to go into right now. However, one of these legends has some additional significance. The legend has been described differently by the *Harivaṃśa* and the *Viṣṇu Purāṇa*. It is a legend about how Kṛṣṇa gifted Satyabhāmā the famous *pārijāta* tree which he took away from the heaven by defeating Indra. The legend seems to be an old one, since Vidura alludes to it in the *Mahābhārata*.[166] The *Viṣṇu Purāṇa* account places the event right after Kṛṣṇa's killing of Naraka. The legend says that when Kṛṣṇa and Satyabhāmā went to heaven to return the divine riches plundered by Naraka, Satyabhāmā saw the *pārijāta* flower and wanted it. The reason was clearly to establish herself as the prime wife of Kṛṣṇa and to make the co-wives jealous:

yadi cetad vacaḥ satyaṃ tvam aty arthaṃ priyeti me/
mad gehaniṣkṛṭārthāya tad ayaṃ nīyatāṃ taruḥ//
na me jāmbavatī tādṛg abhīṣṭā na ca rukmiṇī/
satye yathā tvam ity uktaṃ tvayā kṛṣṇāsakṛt priyaṃ//
satyaṃ tad yadi govinda nopacārakṛtaṃ mama/
tad astu pārijāto'yaṃ mama gehāvibhuṣaṇaṃ//
vibhrati pārijātasya keśapakṣeṇamañjiarīm/
sapatnīnām ahaṃ madhye śobheyam iti kāmaye.

(If what you always say is true that I am really dear to you then take this tree from here for the gardens of my dwelling.

O Kṛṣṇa, you always say, 'O Satyā, neither Rukmiṇī nor Jāmbavatī is beloved unto me like thee'. If this is true and not mere flattery then let this Pārijāta be the ornament of my dwelling. Wearing the flowers of this tree in the braids of my hair I wish to appear graceful amidst my co-wives.)[167]

However, Indra was not ready to allow Kṛṣṇa to take the tree which was a special favourite of his wife Śacī. And here we see Satyabhāmā in a commanding position, rather than being just a nagging wife, in making the logic of her desire clear:

sāmānyas sarvalokasya yady eṣo'mṛtamaṃthane/
samutpannas taruḥ kasmād eko gṛhṇāti vāsava//
yathā surā yathaiveṃdur yathā śrīr vanarakṣiṇaḥ/
sāmānyas sarvalokasya pārijātas tathā drumaḥ//
bhartṛbāhumahāgarvād unaddhyenam atho śacī/
tat kathyatām alaṃ kṣāntyā satyā harayati drumam//
kathyatāṃ ca drutaṃ gatvā paulamyā vacanaṃ mama/
satyabhāmā badaty etad itigarvoddhatākṣaram//
yadi tvaṃ dayitā bhartur yadi vaśyaḥ patis tava/
mad bhartur harato vṛkṣaṃ tat kāraya nivāraṇam//
jānāmi te patiṃ śakraṃ jānāmi tridaśeśvaram/
pārijātaṃ tathapy enaṃ mānuṣī harayami te//

(If this had been produced when the ocean was churned by the celestials then all have equal right over it—why shall Vāsava alone possess it? O ye wardens of the garden, ambrosia, the moon and Lakṣmī are the common properties of all; so is the *pārijāta* tree.

If Śacī has taken possession of it forcibly by the valour of her husband, do ye go and communicate unto her that Satyabhāmā is taking it away and let not Śacī forgive her.

Do ye soon go to her and according to my instructions tell her that Satyabhāmā has given vent to these proud words.

'If thou art dear unto thy husband, if he is under thine control then let him take back the *pārijāta* tree which my husband is taking away.

I know thy husband Śakra is the master of the three worlds. Still being a mortal I take away this *pārijāta* tree.')[168]

Therefore, here we see Satyabhāmā as a wife who was a partner and comrade in Kṛṣṇa's mission. Though she wanted to show her superiority to her co-wives, she also had a larger purpose in mind. Just like she accompanied Kṛṣṇa in his battle with Naraka, she was fighting to establish a point which Kṛṣṇa would like to fight for. Her objection was to the special privilege of a deity about something which should be a common property. With authority in her voice, the mortal woman challenged a deity, with full confidence on the capability of the man who broke any such infringement of common right for personal aggrandizement, be it by Kaṃsa or Jarāsandha or Indra himself. Amazingly, after Kṛṣṇa established the point by defeating Indra, Satyabhāmā disinterestedly dropped the matter and said that she hardly had any interest in the flower itself.

We see a much twisted account of this beautiful legend in the *Harivaṃśa*. There the whole story revolves around the jealousy of Satyabhāmā. It says that Kṛṣṇa gifted Rukmiṇī a *pārijāta* flower which he got from Nārada. This made Satyabhāmā jealous and angry. To appease her, Kṛṣṇa promised to bring the tree for her and asked Indra to send it for the observation of a vow by Satyabhāmā. Indra refused it, arguing that the tree had supernatural and magical properties, and gifting it to a human being would diminish the prestige of the celestials. The matter led to a fierce battle between Indra and Kṛṣṇa, which ended in a stalemate. At last the divine parents, Kaśyapa and Aditi, intervened to convince Indra to allow Kṛṣṇa to take the tree.[169]

This legend, however, seems to be a clear interpolation in the *Harivaṃśa* text. Even in the *Harivaṃśa*, the first reference to the stealing of the *pārijāta* comes at the end of the Naraka episode. Then suddenly this whole episode is inserted without any connection with its initial setting. This version has all the typical markers of later interpolations and poor poetry. The *pārijāta*, nothing but a beautiful flower in the *Viṣṇu Purāṇa*, is suddenly given all kinds of magical properties. The story is also tied up with the *māhātmya* of a pilgrimage centre named Vilvodakeśvara and the celebration of certain vows, indicating its lateness. The earlier flavour of Satyabhāmā's character is thus lost in the legend, and she is portrayed as a nagging, demanding, and jealous wife.

However, the *Viṣṇu Purāṇa* account of the legend has many interesting aspects in it. Not only does it show Satyabhāmā as a wife to please whom Kṛṣṇa could risk fighting the celestials, but it also portrays the Yādava lady as the true partner in Kṛṣṇa's life mission. She was not at all jealous. Nor was she actually greedy for the tree. She only wanted to emphasize the point that her husband always preached. In this way, Satyabhāmā appeared as Kṛṣṇa's only wife who fought alongside him in the latter's lifelong crusade against the Vedic cult of Indra and its special privileges. That true *dharma* did not lie in any special privilege but in equality, and the performance of one's own duties was what Kṛṣṇa tried to emphasize.

Satyabhāmā, in this legend, appears to be the only wife of Kṛṣṇa who understood and fought for the teachings of her husband.

However, there is no point in claiming any historical basis for the legend, except that the poet of the *Viṣṇu Purāṇa* understood the spirit of Kṛṣṇa's character in the ideal narratives and portrayed Satyabhāmā as his real consort. Kṛṣṇa's conjugal life and its chemistry are not what we are looking at. Therefore, we should move on to the next stage in Kṛṣṇa's diplomatic career. We have seen that he had to work really hard to keep his position intact within the Yādava-Vṛṣṇis and that was where his marriage with Satyabhāmā had a crucial role to play. On the other hand, with Jarāsaṃdha and Śiśupāla dead, the false Vāsudeva out of the way, and the Pāṇḍavas and a good number of Kuru-Pañcālas as his followers, Kṛṣṇa was now a much more important figure than a mere Yādava leader. He was a *vāsudeva* whose political and socio-ethical vision mattered to many people. Soon he had to show his ability in that arena, when the family feud of the Kurus went to an unmanageable proportion. The Pāṇḍavas, Kṛṣṇa's biggest allies, lost everything in a game of dice and were exiled to the forest. Before that, Draupadī was publicly humiliated in the Kuru court. After twelve years of exile and a year in disguise, the Pāṇḍavas were to decide their next course of action. This is the scenario where the 'Udyogaparvan' of the *Mahābhārata* unfolded in heated debates about war and peace, ethics and diplomacy, with Kṛṣṇa as the central actor.

4.6 Leader, Teacher, and Envoy: Kṛṣṇa in the 'Udyogaparvan'

In the preceding sections of this chapter, we have outlined the rise of Kṛṣṇa from a cowherd boy to a powerful diplomat with a demigod status, mostly on the basis of sources outside the *Mahābhārata* as well as stray references in the text itself. However, Kṛṣṇa emerges as the central diplomatic figure, with the authority expected of a *vāsudeva*, in the *Mahābhārata* narrative in the fifth book, the 'Udyogaparvan'. The book deals with the deliberations over the upcoming war in the Kuru and the Pāṇḍava-Pāñcāla camps, which encompass larger debates regarding militant and pacifist ways of life. Kṛṣṇa, no longer concerned only with the issues of the Yādava-Vṛṣṇi *gaṇasaṃgha*, came up with the most esteemed voice in those debates, showing the rise of his stature both as a diplomat and as an ideologue. The new philosophy propounded by Kṛṣṇa, merely indicated by some of the episodes discussed earlier and eventually crystallizing in the philosophy of the *Bhagavad Gītā*, also had their first thorough and mature exposition in the 'Udyogaparvan'. In this section, we shall focus on this particular book, immensely important for understanding the position the *itihāsa* takes in a time of transition.

The 'Udyogaparvan' began in a festive atmosphere, but the mood of the book is hardly festive. The Pāṇḍavas finished their exile and masquerade and revealed their identities to Virāṭa, the king of Matsya. In the cattle raid that unveiled the identities of the Pāṇḍavas, Arjuna proved in an open skirmish that he was capable enough to take on the mighty Kuru army. Virāṭa decided to go for an alliance with the Pāṇḍavas, which he ensured by marrying off his daughter Uttarā to Abhimanyu. However, the marriage gathering soon turned into a diplomatic conference where the Pāṇḍavas, the Pāñcālas, the Matsyas, and the Yādavas sat down to decide their next course of action.

Right from this initial assembly, the 'Udyogaparvan' presents several ethical dilemmas. After fulfilling their commitment about the exile, what should the Pāṇḍavas do? Did they not deserve their share of the kingdom back? What if Duryodhana refused to return it? One solution was war. But that would involve killing of numerous people, including own kinsmen. So, which one was better between war and peace? Peace and non-violence were eternal virtues. It was a *kṣatriya*'s duty to fight for his property. Which one between one's caste duty and the eternal *dharma* was to be followed? Then there was another aspect to the problem. The conflict was not only about a share in the kingdom. Even if the Pāṇḍavas sacrificed their political interest, what about the humiliation of Draupadī? Should it not be avenged? But should a wrong necessarily be avenged by violence? Was a crime by the opponent enough justification for initiating a war that would endanger the existence of the entire clan? Draupadī's humiliation was wrong. But how right was a war that pitted a noble-hearted grandfather against his dear grandchildren, a famous teacher against his favourite student, and cousins against their equally capable cousins?

In this huge conundrum of ethical questions, everybody would provide an answer and add some more questions. Yudhiṣṭhira and Duryodhana, Arjuna and Karṇa, Vidura and Saṃjaya, Drupada and Dhṛtarāṣṭra, Kuntī and Gāndhārī—everyone would have a say in the matter. But the final solution had to be provided by Kṛṣṇa, no more the rowdy cowherd who had killed Kaṃsa, no more the mere spectator in Draupadī's *svayaṃvara*, no more the capable leader who was fighting hard against the much stronger Jarāsaṃdha , no more the enigmatic hero the validity of whose position was fiercely debated between Śiśupāla and Bhīṣma, not even the *vāsudeva* whose *vāsudeva*-ship could be challenged by another leader, but Vāsudeva Kṛṣṇa—whose charisma was now equally accepted by both the parties and whose divinity was now a heated speculation.

In the very first meeting, Kṛṣṇa made his stand crystal clear:

> This being the case, think of what will profit
> The Dharma's son and Duryodhana,
> And profit the Kurus and Pāṇḍavas,
> Consistent with Law, correct, earning fame.
> King Dharma is not one to covet the realm
> Of even the Gods, if it were under Unlaw,
> He would strive for lordship even in some village
> If it were consistent with Law and Profit.[170]

Therefore, we can see that Kṛṣṇa's primary ambition was a combination of law (*dharma*) and profit (*artha*), the first representing the eternal virtue while the second represented the practical and material interest. However, while deciding on this ground, Kṛṣṇa no more intervened as an ally of the Pāṇḍavas but reminded a totally pro-Pāṇḍava gathering the need to think of a solution benefitting both the parties. His sympathy for Yudhiṣṭhira was not for their friendship and alliance but because of the latter's dedication in performing the *dharma*. That *dharma*, according to Kṛṣṇa, focused on the defence of a right rather than on personal gain. Therefore, even the rulership of heaven was not to be coveted unrighteously, but the rightful lordship over even a village had to be carefully defended.

Thus, Kṛṣṇa indicated that Yudhiṣṭhira should defend his right to the share in the kingdom but did not advocate war as the means yet. He, rather, emphasized the interest of both the parties and wanted to know Duryodhana's stance before taking any decision. Therefore, he suggested the sending of an ambassador for the purpose.[171] Kṛṣṇa's idea was supported by Balarāma who also reminded the gathering that Yudhiṣṭhira's mindless dicing had a huge role to play behind the crisis.[172]

However, a pro-Pāṇḍava gathering hardly showed any patience for such a neutral stance. The following speeches by Sātyaki and Drupada attacked Balarāma and strongly advocated for an outright war. Drupada's stance seemed particularly interesting, since he was not just Draupadī's father but also the king of the Pāñcālas who were the arch-enemies of the Kurus. Kṛṣṇa no doubt understood that if a war broke out, it would turn out to be a Kuru-Pāñcāla clash. Therefore, he remained civil to Drupada but did not hide his disapproval of the bloodthirst. The following statement of Kṛṣṇa is very much significant in understanding his stance, which is often misrepresented as that of a pro-Pāṇḍava warmonger:

> We ourselves owe the Kurus and the Pāṇḍus the same loyalty, no matter how the Pāṇḍavas and the others see fit to behave. We all, like you, have been fetched here for the wedding, and now the wedding is over we shall return happily to our houses. You yourself are the eldest of the kings in age and learning, and we are like pupils to you, no doubt of that. Dhṛtarāṣṭra has always thought highly of you, and you are friendly with both the teachers, Droṇa and Kṛpa. You are the one to send them word in the Pāṇḍava's interest, and whatever word you send will surely be all right with all of us. If then the bull of the Kurus makes peace as he rightly should, there will be no great loss of brotherly feeling on the part of the Pāṇḍus. But if Dhṛtarāṣṭra's son out of arrogance and folly does not make peace, then, after you have sent for the others, summon us too.[173]

Here we see Kṛṣṇa making his stand clear that while Drupada was to be the leader of the Pāñcāla-Pāṇḍava force, the Yādava-Vṛṣṇis were still neutral outsiders. However, as a friend and well-wisher of the Pāṇḍavas, he also expressed his reluctance towards war before trying hard for peace. He also, through his reference to Drupada's friendship (which turned out to be an enmity disguised as friendship) with Droṇa, alluded to Drupada's responsibility for the upcoming war. Only if all efforts of peace failed, and all other allies were summoned, was he ready to participate in a war.

However, Kṛṣṇa's advice could not overpower Drupada's warmongering, and both the parties were sure that a war was imminent. Though

Kṛṣṇa expressed his willingness to be the last party to be approached for the war, he was now too important a figure to be left out like that. Thus we see both Duryodhana and Arjuna approaching Kṛṣṇa, almost at the same time. Still, Kṛṣṇa did not leave his stand of neutrality and satisfied both. While he himself was chosen by Arjuna as an unarmed participant in the Pāṇḍava camp, Duryodhana was provided with his Nārāyaṇīya army—his biggest support since the killing of Kaṃsa and his only link with his childhood among the cowherds.[174] Balarāma, stressing his neutrality, remained out of the war.[175] Sātyaki, a disciple of Arjuna, joined the Pāṇḍava camp.[176] However, a large chunk of the Yādavas, under Kṛtavarman's leadership, joined Duryodhana.[177] Thus, again we see that Kṛṣṇa, even when his importance was recognized equally by both the warring parties, hardly had a complete control over the faction-ridden Yādavas.

While we see Kṛṣṇa's importance recognized by all, that importance was often accompanied by speculations over his divinity. When Arjuna chose unarmed Kṛṣṇa over an entire army, he had Kṛṣṇa's glory (and not his assumed divinity) in mind:

> There is no doubt that you are able to kill them alone, and I too can kill them alone, best of men. You are famous throughout the world, and the glory of this war will go to you. I too aspire glory, therefore I have chosen you.[178]

Similarly, Arjuna recounted Kṛṣṇa's military achievements without referring to his divinity in a subsequent meeting.[179] Similar statements were made by Yudhiṣṭhira also, without reference to anything divine in Kṛṣṇa.[180] However, if Kṛṣṇa's closest friends and his comrade in the *khāṇḍavadāhana* were satisfied with his remarkable achievements and did not think much about deifying him, there were others who speculated more. A leading person in this issue seems to be Saṃjaya, the *sūta*, whose professional skill was glorifying the heroes. It was he who repeatedly introduced Kṛṣṇa's divinity to Dhṛtarāṣṭra who was overawed by the mystery. Saṃjaya said:

> Janārdana Mādhava has, as though in play, defeated Naraka, Śambara, Kaṃsa and the king of Cedī, all of gruesome aspect. This Supreme Person, whose soul is superior, has, by a mere act of will, brought earth,

> atmosphere and heaven into his power ... Put the entire world on one side and Janārdana on the other, and Janārdana exceeds the entire world in substance. Janārdana could reduce this world to ashes with a thought, but not the entire universe could render Janārdana ashes. Wherever there is truth, wherever Law, wherever modesty and honesty, there is Govinda. Where Kṛṣṇa stands there is victory. As though in play, Janārdana, Supreme Person, soul of the creatures, keep earth, atmosphere and heaven running... The blessed Keśava by his own Yoga makes go around and around, ceaselessly, the Wheel of the World, The Wheel of the Eons. In truth, I tell you, the blessed Lord alone governs time and death, the standing and moving creatures. Hari, the great Yogin, though he rules the world, yet undertakes acts like any powerless peasant.[181]

Dhṛtarāṣṭra, the patron of the bard Saṃjaya, seemed to be unaware of Kṛṣṇa's divine aspect. In answer to his surprise on the issue, Saṃjaya replied:

> Sire, you do not have the knowledge, but my knowledge is not wanting. Devoid of the knowledge and obfuscated by darkness, you do not recognize Keśava. By this knowledge, my friend, I know Madhusūdana of the three Eons as the God who is the unmade Maker, beginning and end of the creatures (*vidyayā tāta jānāmi triyugaṃ madhusūdanaṃ/ kartāram akṛtaṃ devaṃ bhutānāṃ prabhavapy ayam*).[182]

He explained to Dhṛtarāṣṭra the different names of Kṛṣṇa[183] and ultimately indoctrinated him in his belief.[184] He also explained to him that the way to reach Kṛṣṇa involved complete control of the senses:

> Be consistently and unwearyingly in control of your senses, king, let your spirit not stray, but check it hither and yon. This mastering of the senses the Brahmins know as constant wisdom. This is the wisdom and the path by which the wise go forth. Men cannot reach Keśava with unbridled senses, king. The self-controlled man who is learned in the scriptures finds, by virtue of Yoga, serenity in the truth.[185]

With Saṃjaya, possibly the earliest bard to have narrated the events of the Bhārata War, as the main protagonist of Kṛṣṇa's divinity, it is hardly surprising that we find Kṛṣṇa as already deified in the TĀ or in the *Aṣṭādhyāyī*.

Some allusion to Kṛṣṇa's divinity is made also by Vidura while enlisting Kṛṣṇa's achievements, since he counted some of the achievements of Viṣṇu among Kṛṣṇa's achievements in the previous births.[186] Thus, surprisingly enough, Kṛṣṇa's divinity seems to have been a more popular theory in the Kuru court (with people like Saṃjaya, Bhīṣma, Vidura, and Dhṛtarāṣṭra himself believing in it) than among the Pāṇḍavas who still respected and loved him as a dear friend and their best advisor.

Therefore, Kṛṣṇa still had to logically resolve the doubts about war and peace in the Pāṇḍava camp to establish his viewpoint. The doubts were bound to be there, particularly with Yudhiṣṭhira's obsession in observing the *dharma*. Even the Kuru court knew it well and tried to bank on it. Therefore, Dhṛtarāṣṭra's message in reply to the demand of a share of the kingdom for Yudhiṣṭhira, by Drupada's ambassador, turned out to be an ethical quiz. Saṃjaya, the envoy of Dhṛtarāṣṭra, presented war as an evil, a cause of total devastation, infernal and destructive. A victory in such a war would be equivalent to defeat according to him.[187] The imminent war was shown as even more evil, since it involved the death of the kinsmen:

> If you, Pārthas, continue to chastise the Kurus,
> Bring down all your foes and subjugate them,
> Your life would be the same as death,
> For to live with your kinfolk dead is not right.[188]

He pointed out that a victory in the war could only come at the cost of the lives of many near and dear ones, including Bhīṣma, Droṇa, and the Kaurava cousins:

> Now who would desire what leads but to evil
> (Forgiving is better than hugging your comforts)
> Where Bhīṣma Śāntanava is to succumb
> And Droṇa is slain along with his son.
> Kṛpa, Śalya, Vikarṇa, the son of Somadatta,
> Viviṃśati, Karṇa, Duryodhana:
> Having killed all those, what will be the pleasure
> You will find in it, Pāṇḍava, tell me that![189]

Saṃjaya also suggested that begging in the realms of the Andhaka-Vṛṣṇis would be better than reigning by undertaking such a war.[190] Here, the choice of the realm of the Andhaka-Vṛṣṇis was certainly a dig at the position of the Pāṇḍavas as the sidekicks of Kṛṣṇa.

However, the ploy did not work. Yudhiṣṭhira made it clear that he did not covet any wealth through *adharma*[191] but referred the matter to Kṛṣṇa to decide what *dharma* was at that moment. Kṛṣṇa readily pointed out how empty the peace proposal was. He expressed his equal care for both the parties again, which could come only through peace.[192] However, he noted that the Kurus were recommending to the Pāṇḍavas the path of peace without themselves undertaking any effort for the matter. In his long reply to Dhṛtarāṣṭra's message, we find the first clear exposition of Kṛṣṇa's teachings in the *Mahābhārata*. And there, Kṛṣṇa emphasized on the concept, just like he once did in Vṛndāvana to oppose the Indra cult, that *dharma* lay in performing one's own duties properly and nothing else:

It is only such knowledge as brings about acts
That is found to bear fruit and not other knowledge.
And the act itself bears visibly fruit.
One's thirst is appeased by the drinking of water.

The rite is enjoined by virtue of action,
The act is contained in it, Saṃjaya.
I do not hold anything higher than acting;
To prate otherwise is feeble and vain.

By their acts do the Gods in the other world shine,
By his act does the Wind blow here on earth;
Ordaining the days and nights by his acts,
The Sun rises daily unwearyingly.

Unwearied the Moon goes through fortnights and months,
Through constellations and asterisms;
Indefatigably does the kindled Fire
By his act blaze forth for the good of the creatures.

Untiringly does the Goddess Earth
With her own strength carry her heavy load;
Unwearyingly do the rivers carry
Their water and sustain all the creatures that be.

Untiringly does the Slayer of Vala
Of opulent splendor shower his rains,
Making noisy the skies, and he practices *Brahman*,
Desiring the chieftainship of the Gods.

Abandoning pleasure and heart's desires
Has Śakra by acting become the chief,
Protecting the truth and the Law undistracted;
By cultivating the virtues all

Of self-control, patience, equity, pleasure,
Has Maghavat reached the high rule of the Gods.

Bṛhaspati practices diligently,
With his spirit honed, the life of the *Brahman*,
Abandoning happiness, mastering senses,
And so he became the guru of the Gods.

By their act do the constellations shine,
The Rudras, Ādityas, the Vasus and All-Gods,
King Yama, Kubera Vaiśravaṇa,
Gandharvas and Yakṣas and Apsarās bright;
Observing the *Brahman*, the Vedas and rites
The hermits shine forth in yonder world.[193]

Then, he extended this natural law of action to the fourfold *varṇa* system which he understood in terms of action rather than birth:

A Brahmin should study and sacrifice
And give and visit the sacred fords
And teach and officiate for those deserving,
And accept such gifts as are known to him.

A kṣatriya should offer the subjects protection,
Act under Law, make gifts, be alert,
Perform oblations and learn all the Vedas,
Take a wife and virtuously govern his household.

The Vaiśya should study undistracted
Earn wealth with farming, cow-herding, and trade
And save it, do favours for brahmins and *kṣatriyas*
And by Law and with virtue govern his household.

As the ancient Law of the Śūdra is known
That he serve and pay honour to brahmin folk;
Both study and sacrifice are forbidden;
Untiring he always should strive for his welfare.[194]

Since he understood the *varṇa* system in terms of action, Kṛṣṇa envisioned a separate set of duties for the king, beyond the fourfold order:

A king should protect all classes without
Distractions and yoke them each to his task,
Be not given to lusts and be fair to the subjects
And not comply with lawless desires.[195]

Therefore, a king who failed to perform these actions must be considered guilty of *adharma*. Working out of lawless desire for the Pāṇḍava property, Duryodhana thus committed such a sin which needed to be punished:

When one cruelly covets the land of another
And, angering destiny, seizes power
Then this shall be a cause of war among the kings;

Where a thief steals property without witness,
Whether another steals it by force and in public,
They both are guilty of crime:
What sets Dhṛtarāṣṭra's sons apart?[196]

Then he reminded Saṃjaya of the humiliation of Draupadī.[197] The entire speech gives us a clear idea of the philosophy Kṛṣṇa was propagating. He believed in action. It was the proper performance of one's own duty—which we can call *svadharma*—that sustained the Cosmic Order. Even the significance of the *varṇa* order was viewed in this light. The king's duty was in assuring that everybody could perform his own duties. Moreover, the king had his duties as well. A king who failed to do that, coveted the wealth of the others, and was driven by desire was no better than a thief. Only the thief stole secretly, while the powerful seized what he wanted openly. The nature of the crimes was same. Action was to be performed as the Cosmic Duty, not out of any desire. A king who was guilty of crime was to be punished.

Based on this ideology, Kṛṣṇa ripped apart Dhṛtarāṣṭra's empty peace proposal that advised the Pāṇḍavas about the evils of war without promising anything for avoiding war. Duryodhana was guilty of theft, but there was no promise to rectify that. Draupadī was publicly humiliated, no punishment or apology was promised for that. In such a scenario, it became the kingly duty of the Pāṇḍavas to punish the sinners. However, Kṛṣṇa did not deny the essence of the message that war was an evil. Therefore, he took the most crucial decision of himself going to the Kuru court for a final attempt at peace. But that peace was possible only when both the parties were ready to do their duties to avoid war. However, even before going, Kṛṣṇa knew that he would fail. Still, he decided to undertake the role of an unsuccessful envoy. There lay the secret of Kṛṣṇa's philosophy—performing a duty for the duty's sake, not desiring success, not thinking of the end result. The war was inevitable. Kṛṣṇa knew it. But it was his duty to try his best to stop a war, and that he had to do. When Vidura would suggest to him later that his coming as an envoy was unwise, futile, and risky, Kṛṣṇa would again expound the same philosophy:

> Even if a man, while trying to the best of his ability, cannot accomplish a task of Law, he still—and I have no doubt of that—gains the merit of the Law … So I too shall attempt to make peace without dissembling, Steward, to stop a war between the Kurus and Sṛñjayas, who are doomed to perish.
>
> The wise know that he who does not run to the rescue of a friend who is plagued by troubles and does not try to help him as far as he can is guilty of cruelty. Go as far as grabbing him by the hair to keep

a friend from committing a crime, and no one can blame you, for you tried your best.

No, I have come to help the cause of both parties, and having made the attempt I shall be without blame before all men.

If I can make peace between Kurus and Pāṇḍus
Without hurting the cause of the Pāṇḍavas,
I shall have earned outstanding merit
And set free the Kurus from certain death.
And if Dhṛtarāṣṭra's sons will heed
The sage and apposite words I speak
For their Law and Profit, which save their health,
The Kurus shall praise me for having come.[198]

With this decision to go as an envoy to the Kuru court, Kṛṣṇa entered the centre stage in the debate between war and peace. And the debate was intense. As we can see, there were two polar opposites at work. At one hand was Yudhiṣṭhira, an ardent pacifist who wanted to avoid war at any cost. The *dharma* he propounded was the *dharma* of *ānṛśaṃsya*. On the other hand stood Duryodhana, with his staunch belief in the caste duties of a *kṣatriya*, who insisted on fighting. Making the situation more complex, the mothers of the two main contenders propagated doctrines quite opposite to what their sons believed in. Gāndhārī consistently advised Duryodhana to follow the eternal *dharma* for the greater good, while Kuntī fiercely urged Yudhiṣṭhira to leave his obsession with peace and perform the duty expected of a *kṣatriya* warrior. Kṛṣṇa stood in the middle. He had made his stand clear that he preferred peace but not at the cost of tolerating criminal offences. As an envoy, he had the task of persuading the haughty Duryodhana to accept peace. On the other hand, the ambassador of peace had to keep the peace-loving Pāṇḍavas prepared for the war which he knew as inevitable.

As we have seen, Kṛṣṇa had encountered the stereotypical Vedic religion as a chronic challenge. As an envoy going to Duryodhana, he again had to encounter the idea of a *kṣatriya*'s caste duty being relentless fighting. We have seen that Kṛṣṇa's idea of the *varṇa* system was based on action rather than on birth. Moreover, that action would be necessarily without desire. On the other hand, Duryodhana believed in the classical Later Vedic *varṇa* order where the hereditary *varṇa* duty was to be followed like a ritual and the aim was the desire for heaven. That ideology explained a *kṣatriya*'s task as fighting heroically. In military capability lay a *kṣatriya*'s worth and importance.

Therefore, Yudhiṣṭhira's pacifism was unrighteous in Duryodhana's eyes, as his love for fighting was in the eyes of Yudhiṣṭhira. Just as the Pāṇḍavas tried hard to make Duryodhana abide by the ethics they followed, so did Duryodhana try to turn his cousins into 'true' *kṣatriyas*. The sufferings of the Pāṇḍavas, to him, were the punishment for failing to perform their *dharma*:

> I called you barren sesame seeds, and rightly so! For in the city of Virāṭa the Pārtha wore a braid and Bhīmasena served as a cook in Virāṭa's kitchen. That was my doing! That is the way *kṣatriyas* punish a *kṣatriya* who runs from a battle: they condemn him to a gambler's row, to the kitchen, to the braid![199]

Therefore, on the verge of the war, after all attempts at peace failed, Duryodhana's message to the Pāṇḍavas would be:

> *amarṣaṃ rājyaharaṇaṃ vanavāsaṃ ca pāṇḍava/*
> *draupadyāś ca parikleśaṃ saṃsmaran puruṣo bhava//*
>
> (Be a man, remember your banishment from the kingdom, your hardships, your forest exile, the molestation of Draupadī, Pāṇḍava!)[200]

War was the purpose for which, Duryodhana thought, a *kṣatriya* lady gave birth. Surprisingly, the same thought was shared by the lady who actually gave birth to the pacifist Yudhiṣṭhira, Kuntī:

> *aṅgāvekṣasva dharmaṃ tvaṃ yathā sṛṣṭaḥ svayambhuvā/*
> *urastaḥ kṣatriyaḥ sṛṣṭo bāhuvīryopajīvitā//*
>
> (Come, heed the Law that was created by the Self-existent; the *kṣatriya* was created from his chest, to live by the strength of his arms, to act always mercilessly for the protection of his subjects.)[201]

Yudhiṣṭhira's deviation from the *kṣātradharma* was an irritant to Kuntī as it was to Duryodhana:

> Look to the kingly Laws that befits your heritage, for the conduct by which you wish to stand was not that of the royal seers. A king infected by cowardice, who does not act ruthlessly, does not win the reward that results from the protection of his subjects. Neither Pāṇḍu nor I nor Grandfather has ever prayed that you be blessed with the wisdom you live by; the blessings I asked were sacrifice, generosity, austerity, heroism, offspring, greatness of spirit, and the enjoyment of strength forever.
>
> Whether it be Law or not, you are born to it by the very fact of birth … A brahmin should live on alms, a *kṣatriya* should protect, the *vaiśya* should acquire wealth, the *śūdra* should serve them all. Begging is forbidden you, farming is unseemly—you are a *kṣatriya*, the savior from wounds, living by the strength of your arms.[202]

To inspire Yudhiṣṭhira to the code of conduct of a *kṣatriya*, Kuntī told him the story of the lady named Vidurā who had forcibly sent her reluctant son Saṃjaya to a war. Through the mouth of Vidurā, Kuntī sends Yudhiṣṭhira her message:

> Where did you come from? … Too cowardly for anger, barely hanging on to a low branch, you are a man with the tools of a eunuch.[203]

To her, manhood meant truculence and unforgivingness. The meek, forgiving man was neither man nor woman. Contentment, compassion, sloth, and fear only killed off good fortune.[204] While Kṛṣṇa would describe a greedy king's self-aggrandizement as theft, the exact opposite view would come from Vidurā and Kuntī:

> *yo hi tejo yathāśakti na darśayati vikramāt/*
> *kṣatriyo jīvitākāṅkṣī stena ity eva taṃ viduḥ//*
>
> (A *kṣatriya* who clings to life without displaying to the highest degree possible his talent by his feats, him they know for a thief.)[205]

Life and death did not matter to a *kṣatriya*. It was better for him to flame briefly than to smoke long.[206] Irrespective of victory or defeat, a wise person should go ahead with his task—'*alabdhvā yadi vā labdhvā nānuśocanti paṇḍitāḥ*'.[207] The heart of *kṣatriyahood* (*kṣatrahṛdaya*), as described by Vidurā and Kuntī, is expressed in terms identical to those used by Duryodhana. Vidurā is quoted as saying:

> I indeed know the eternal heart of the kṣatriyahood as proclaimed by our forbears and theirs, and our descendents and theirs. No one born a *kṣatriya* here, and knowing the law of the *kṣatriyas*, will either out of fear or hope for a living bow to anyone else. 'Hold up your head and do not bow.' Standing tall means manhood (*pauruṣa*)—rather break in the middle than bend.[208]

However, irrespective of what his mother thought, Yudhiṣṭhira was equally steadfast in his allegiance to *dharma*. Challenging the rationale of the *varṇa* system time and again, he had hardly any regard for the notion of *kṣātradharma*. He clearly stated his disapproval of the idea that a person had to be violent and unforgiving just because he belonged to a certain caste by birth. War to him was evil by all means and so was the *kṣātradharma* that endorsed it:

> What is pretty in war? It is the evil Law of the *kṣatriyas* ... *kṣatriya* kills *kṣatriya*, fish lives on fish, dog kills dog.[209]

Therefore, the power struggle of the *kṣatriyas* is as abominous to Yudhiṣṭhira as a brute fight between dogs:

> The wise have noticed that it is the same as in a mess of dogs. It starts with a wagging of tails, then a bark, a bark in reply, backing off, baring the teeth, loud barking, and then the fight; and the stronger one wins and eats the meat, Kṛṣṇa—it is the same with people, there is no difference at all. It is always the same thing that the stronger does to the weaker: disregard and aggressiveness—and the weak man surrenders. Father, king, and elder always deserve respect, and therefore Dhṛtarāṣṭra deserves our respect and homage, Janārdana.[210]

Ernestly thinking in this line, Yudhiṣṭhira provided us with one of the earliest and strongest statements against war and violence, standing in an era when heroism was the most respected manly virtue:

> War is evil in any form. What killer is not killed in return? To the killed victory and defeat are the same, Hṛṣikeśa (*sarvathā vṛjinaṃ yuddhaṃ ko ghnana na pratihanyate/ hatasya ca hṛṣikeśa samau jayaparājayau*). The victor too is surely diminished: In the end some others will kill a loved one of his; and behold, when he has lost his strength and no longer sees his sons and brothers a loathing for life will engulf him completely, Kṛṣṇa . . . There is always remorse after the killing of others, Janārdana. Victory breeds feuds, for the defeated rest uneasy. But easy sleeps the man who serenely has given up both victory and defeat (*jayo vairaṃ prasṛjati duḥkham āste parājayam/ sukhaṃ praśāntaḥ svapīti hitvā jayaparājayau*).[211]

Thus, Yudhiṣṭhira viewed heroism as a 'powerful disease that eats up the heart'. There were only two ways to end a feud—total eradication (*mūlaghāta*) of the enemy or giving it up. Since the former was a cruel thing, the second was preferable.[212] Yudhiṣṭhira, therefore, would prefer peace by subjugation (*praṇipāta*) than either renouncing the kingdom or ruining the family.[213] His message to Kṛṣṇa was thus:

> Our first course of action, Mādhava, is to assure that we and they may enjoy our common fortune at peace with one another and on equal footing.
>
> The stage beyond that will cause gruesome disaster and ruin, when we regain our realms by killing the Kauravas. However unrelated and ignoble an enemy is, Kṛṣṇa, he does not deserve to be killed, let alone men such as they, for they are kinsmen mostly, friends and gurus, and to kill them is a most evil thing.[214]

Yudhiṣṭhira's teachings seem to have an impact on his brothers as well, for the usually violent Bhīma also requested Kṛṣṇa to try for peace at any cost. Even he would prefer bowing before Duryodhana than causing a disaster in the Kuru family, and he claimed that Arjuna thought the same.[215] Arjuna himself said nothing conclusive except his desire for peace and faith in Kṛṣṇa's ability to achieve that,[216] while Nakula hoped for success of the peace mission.[217]

This entire atmosphere of anti-war sentiment would obviously delight our modern sensibilities. However, in this grand debate about the sharing of the kingdom, the issue of Draupadī's humiliation was almost lost. Only the youngest of the Pāṇḍavas, Sahadeva, spoke in a different voice:

> What the king has said is the sempiternal Law, but see to it that there be war, enemy-tamer! Even if the Kurus should want peace with the Pāṇḍavas, you should still provoke war with them, Daśārha! How could my rage with Suyodhana subside after seeing the Princess of Pāñcāla manhandled in the hall? If Bhīma, Arjuna and King Dharma stick with the Law, I want to fight him in battle, and begone with the law (*yadi bhīmārjunau kṛṣṇa dharmarājaś ca dhārmikāḥ/ dharmam utsṛjya tenāhaṃ yoddhum icchāmi saṃyuge*).[218]

It is for this reason precisely that Kuntī urged her sons to go for a war:

> Not the rape of the kingdom, not the defeat at dice, not the banishment of my sons to the forest grieves me, as it grieves me that that great dark woman, weeping in the hall, had to listen to insults.[219]

Above all, there was Draupadī herself, itching for a war that would avenge her humiliation:

> A curse on Bhīmasena's strength, a curse on the Pārtha's bowmanship, if Duryodhana stays alive for another hour, Kṛṣṇa! If you find favour in me, if you have pity on me, direct your entire fury at the Dhārtarāṣṭras, Kṛṣṇa.
>
> This hair was pulled by Duḥśāsana's hands, lotus-eyed Lord; remember it at all times when you seek peace with the enemies! If Bhīma and Arjuna pitifully hanker after peace, my ancient father will fight, and his warrior sons, Kṛṣṇa! My five valiant sons will, led by Abhimanyu, fight with the Kurus, Madhusūdana! What peace will my heart know unless I see Duḥśāsana's swarthy arm cut off and covered with dust! Thirteen years have gone by while I waited, hiding my rage in my heart

like a blazing fire. Pierced by the thorn of Bhīma's words, my heart is rent asunder, for now that strong-armed man has eyes for the Law only.[220]

Again, in seeking this revenge, Draupadī put stress on the *kṣātradharma* which Yudhiṣṭhira disregarded and Duryodhana held in high esteem:

> For a *kṣatriya*, if he follows his own Law, should kill a *kṣatriya* who has become greedy, and a non-*kṣatriya* too … Those who know the Law know that just as it is sin to kill one who does not deserve it, so a sin is found in not killing one who does deserve it. So see to it, Kṛṣṇa, that this sin does not touch you, the Pāṇḍavas, and the Sṛñjayas with their troops, Dāśārha.[221]

In such a heated environment, Kṛṣṇa had to perform his duty of an envoy. His very decision to go as a messenger of peace was an acceptance of Yudhiṣṭhira's pacifism. However, he was almost sure of the failure of his mission. Therefore, he had to make his stand clear about the subsequent action. Thus, he also quoted the clichéd terms of *kṣātradharma* to persuade Yudhiṣṭhira:

> Mendicancy is not a *kṣatriya*'s business, lord of the people. All those who observe the life stages have said what a *kṣatriya* should beg: victory, or death on the battlefield (*jayo vadho vā saṃgrāme*), as the Placer has ordained for eternity. That is the *kṣtriya*'s law, and cowardice is not extolled. For livelihood is impossible by giving in to cowardice, Yudhiṣṭhira. Stride wide, strong-armed king! Kill the foe, enemy-tamer (*jahi śatrun ariṃdama*)![222]

As a response to Yudhiṣṭhira's hesitation to kill the kinsmen, Kṛṣṇa argued that Duryodhana had already been killed by his sins. However, interestingly, after the stereotypical exposition of *kṣātradharma*, Kṛṣṇa accepted that Yudhiṣṭhira's understanding of the *dharma* was what actually pleased him:

> That very moment, king, when he stood condemned for his shamelessness before all the kings on earth, he was dead, Mahārāja! … He should be killed like a snake, that evil-minded man ignoble to all the world. Kill

him, enemy-tamer! Don't hesitate, king! But, in any case it is worthy of you, and pleasing to me, prince sans blame, that you are ready to prostrate yourself before your father and Bhīṣma.[223]

However, Kṛṣṇa treated Bhīma's pacifism in a totally different manner. If he had respectful admiration for Yudhiṣṭhira's righteousness, he knew that pacifism was not what suited Bhīma. Therefore, he provoked Bhīma to bring out his real self:

> Aho! Has panic at last found you, Bhīma, because now that war is at hand you seem to see signs that point this way or that way? Aho! Do you see unfavourable portents, Pārtha, in dreams or while awake, and that is why you want peace? Aho! Are you a eunuch that you dare not hope for manhood in yourself? You are attacked by cowardice, that is why your mind is awry! Your heart is palpitating, your mind despairs, your thighs are paralyzed, that is why you want peace!
>
> Look at your own feats, Bhārata, and your birth in high family. Rise up. Do not despair, hero, be firm! This is not like you, this weariness, enemy-tamer! A *kṣatriya* does not obtain what he does not grab by force.[224]

The provocation had the desired result, as Bhīma's anger flared up. But it would be wrong to assume Kṛṣṇa as a champion of the *kṣātradharma* on the basis of his advice to Yudhiṣṭhira and Bhīma. Kṛṣṇa, rather, appeared in a totally different light in Hastināpura. Dhṛtarāṣṭra decided to arrange many luxuries and lodges for Kṛṣṇa and thought of offering him a wide variety of gifts, including chariots, elephants, slave girls, sheepskins, yak hides, gems, food, and courtesans. While the nature of the gift items no doubt represents a premonetary economic system, indicating the antiquity of the passage, the typical non-attachment of Kṛṣṇa was also displayed in his complete ignoring of these gifts.[225] Vidura, whose house Kṛṣṇa would ultimately choose as his residence in Hastināpura, possibly understood Kṛṣṇa better than Dhṛtarāṣṭra and clearly told the latter that Kṛṣṇa could not be tempted by wealth. He said:

> Janārdana will want from you no more than a full jar of water, no more than water to wash his feet, no more than an enquiry after his health. So

> offer the great-spirited man, who deserves it, true hospitality, king, for Janārdana is worthy of honor. Keśava is coming to the Kurus hoping for one benefit: so give him that for which he is coming, king. The Dāśārha wants peace between you and Duryodhana and the Pāṇḍavas, Indra of kings. Do as he says.[226]

Vidura understood Kṛṣṇa not as a champion of *kṣātradharma*, which would delight Duryodhana, but as a serious messenger of peace. Kṛṣṇa also fulfilled Vidura's expectations by refusing Duryodhana's homage, saying:

> Envoys eat and accept homage when they have succeeded. When I have succeeded, you and your councilors shall honor me, Bhārata.[227]

Pressed further for having a meal with Duryodhana, Kṛṣṇa refused him in a sterner language and bolder logic that would immediately remind one of his refusal to accept the homage from Jarāsaṃdha:

> I would not transgress the Law out of love, fury, hatred, self-interest, argument or greed. Food is to be accepted either out of affection, or because of need. But neither do I have affection for you, king, nor am I in need.[228]

Therefore, Kṛṣṇa's message to Duryodhana had nothing to do with the latter's favourite *kṣātradharma*. Rather, it placed the eternal *dharma* over any pursuit for material benefit around which a *kṣatriya*'s life was expected to revolve:

> The undertakings of the wise are consistent with the Three Pursuits, Bharata bull, but when all three are impossible to carry out at the same time, men follow Law and Profit. If those two cannot be reconciled, a sagacious person follows the Law, a middling person prefers Profit, a fool the Pleasure of discord. If a man, driven by his senses, abandons Law out of greed, and strives after Profit and Pleasure by foul means, he perishes. Even if he strives for Profit and Pleasure he should still practice the Law from the start, for neither Profit nor Pleasure ever part company with Law.[229]

Kṛṣṇa's message was accompanied by a long speech by Gāndhārī who tried to persuade her son to the path of the eternal *dharma* that depended on control over senses, particularly lust, anger, and greed.[230]

However, the speeches on *dharma* hardly had any effect on Duryodhana who decided to bank on his power and keep Kṛṣṇa as a prisoner.[231] The ploy was discovered by Sātyaki who was accompanying Kṛṣṇa. He informed Kṛtavarman, who had already joined the Kuru camp but was accompanying Kṛṣṇa as a Yādava, and asked him to wait at the gate of the hall in full armour. However, Kṛṣṇa's display of extreme anger, along with Vidura's spirited speech about the power of Kṛṣṇa, spoiled the plan. Kṛṣṇa left the court as an angry, unsuccessful envoy, with Sātyaki and Kṛtavarman. Suddenly a display of Kṛṣṇa's Cosmic Form is inserted in the episode, which seems to be an extremely late interpolation, at least later than even the later sections of *Bhagavad Gītā* which claims that Kṛṣṇa never showed his Cosmic Form to anybody before he showed it to Arjuna at Kurukṣetra. There was hardly any necessity for the supernatural event here, and it would be very unnatural for the original poets to make the mission unsuccessful even after Kṛṣṇa displayed to all that he was the Supreme God. Before coming for the mission, Kṛṣṇa told Arjuna:

> *ahaṃ hi tat kariṣyāmi paraṃ puruṣakārataḥ/*
> *daivaṃ tu na mayā śakyaṃ karma kartuṃ kathaṃcana//*
>
> (I myself shall do the utmost that human agency allows, but I am unable in any way to take care of fate.)[232]

Kṛṣṇa tried for peace to the best of his human ability. He failed to alter the inevitable. There is hardly any reason to turn him suddenly into the Creator and Controller of the fate over which he accepted to have no control. Kṛṣṇa's divinity, by this time, was a popular theme of Saṃjaya's narration in the Kuru court. However, the Pāṇḍavas did not know him yet as a deity, nor did Kṛṣṇa himself.

Leaving his deification aside, we may notice an interesting aspect of Kṛṣṇa's teaching in the entire episode. To Yudhiṣṭhira and Bhima, he valorized war and *kṣātradharma*. To the warmonger Duryodhana, he spoke of the eternal ethics and peace. What was Kṛṣṇa's own stand then? To understand the matter, we have to go back to his exposition of his ideas to

Saṃjaya. He placed action above all. A man's *varṇa* was to be based on his action. Therefore, a man chose his own *svadharma*. What Kṛṣṇa did was to persuade everyone to the performance of his own *svadharma* after offering them several alternatives to choose. The terrible Bhīma, a hard-core warrior, could not be a pacifist, he knew. So he instigated Bhīma to his *svadharma* of an unflinching warrior. He knew that Duryodhana's *svadharma* was the *kṣātradharma*, and he ultimately let him have the war he wanted, but only after an exposition of the other faces of *dharma* in front of him. Yudhiṣṭhira was given his choice as well. Kṛṣṇa extolled the *kṣātradharma* in front of him, but could hardly move him. At the end, he happily went off as Yudhiṣṭhira's messenger of peace.

Why did Kṛṣṇa take up this act of balancing? There lay his own *svadharma*, the *dharma* of performing his duties irrespective of the results and without any attachment. He had to try his best for peace, though in vain. He had to keep Yudhiṣṭhira ready for the war, equally in vain. For the same reason, he had to offer another person a scope to choose his *svadharma*. Before leaving Hastināpura, he took Karṇa on his own chariot for a private discussion.

Karṇa, known to be the son of a *sūta* named Adhiratha, was the closest friend of Duryodhana and the main antagonist of Arjuna. Right from his childhood, he was insulted several times because of his low pedigree. It was only Duryodhana who honoured him for his valour and ability. Tied to Duryodhana by gratefulness, the noble Karṇa participated in all his deeds and misdeeds many of which he personally might have disapproved of. It was mainly because of Karṇa's skill as an archer that Duryodhana was dreaming of a Kuru victory.

Suddenly, Kṛṣṇa disclosed to Karṇa the secret of his birth. He revealed that Karṇa was not the son of the lowly Adhiratha but a premarital abandoned son of Kuntī. As the first-born son of Kuntī, he was the one entitled to kingship if the Pāṇḍavas won. It is understandable that had Karṇa been the projected king, Duryodhana might not have objected to share the kingdom. So, this incident was probably Kṛṣṇa's last attempt at peace.

Karṇa had a choice to make, a choice with his real queen-mother and princely brothers, a respectable pedigree, and the most coveted throne on the one hand, and the lowly but loving foster parents and a benefactor but unrighteous friend on the other. Karṇa made his choice. He chose the humble *sūta* couple who adopted and loved him for no apparent interest and the friend who accepted him on his merit over the princely connections and future prosperity on offer. However, he also knew that Duryodhana and his side would probably end up losing and that would serve the cause of righteousness. Therefore, Karṇa chose death for his benefactor rather than an unrighteous peace through himself, for he knew that such a peace would mean something ethically undesirable:

> So you should suppress word of our taking counsel here, best of men; that would be best, I think, joy of all the Yādavas. If the Law-spirited king of strict vows knows that I am Kuntī's first-born son, he will not accept the kingdom: and if I were then to obtain this large, prosperous kingdom, I would hand it over to Duryodhana, Madhusūdana, enemy-tamer! Let the Law-spirited Yudhiṣṭhira be king forever.[233]

Karṇa's choice decided the fate of the war. Kṛṣṇa, the failed envoy, returned to the Pāṇḍavas. The ethical debate over war and peace was over. It was now time for the real war. However, Kṛṣṇa's discourse on war and peace still awaited its culmination. Karṇa had made his choice. His chief antagonist, Arjuna, was yet to make his. Standing between the two armies ready for battle, with Kṛṣṇa as his charioteer, Arjuna would have to make the choice. And that would bring forth the logical culmination of Kṛṣṇa's teachings. The speculations of the 'Udyogaparvan' would melt into the action of the 'Bhīṣmaparvan'.

4.7 *Svadharma*, *Karman*, and Kṛṣṇa: (Re)reading the *Bhagavad Gītā*

> Kṛṣṇa, at the sight of my own kin standing here ready to fight, my limbs feel tired and my mouth has gone dry, my body is trembling and my hair is standing on end. Gāṇḍīva is slipping from my hand, and my skin is burning all over. I can't stand up, and my mind seems to whirl. I see evil portents, Keśava, and I see no good in killing my own family in war. I don't desire victory, Kṛṣṇa, nor kingdom, nor pleasure. What use is kingdom to us, Govinda, or enjoyments, or life itself?
>
> Those for whose sake we want kingdom, enjoyments and pleasures are drawn up here for battle, ready to give up their lives and

> wealth: teachers, fathers, uncles, fathers-in-law, grandsons, brothers-in-law and other relatives. Though they would kill me, slayer of Madhu, I would not want to kill them even for the sovereignty of the triple world; how much less, then, for the sake of the earth! What joy could there be for us, Janārdana, were we to kill Dhṛtarāṣṭra's sons, our kinsmen. For how could we be happy having killed our family, Mādhava?
>
> —Arjuna[234]

This expression is known as Arjuna's 'depression' (*viṣāda*) which in a way begins the *Bhagavad Gītā*, one of the most powerful philosophical treatises composed ever. The *Gītā* is studied, translated, interpreted, and celebrated often as an independent text, but it occurs in a *Mahābhārata* context. The text unfolds when Arjuna felt depressed, standing between the two armies lined up for battle. He was terrified of the prospect of fighting his own kinsmen for mere kingdom and refused to fight. Kṛṣṇa, now Arjuna's charioteer, criticized Arjuna's attitude and gave a large philosophical lecture that cleared Arjuna's confusions. As a result, Arjuna decided to fight.

The *Gītā* is no doubt the fullest exposition of Kṛṣṇa's philosophy. But before we enter into its analysis, we have to understand the nature of the text. We have so far surveyed the life of Vāsudeva Kṛṣṇa as a leader-cum-teacher of the Later Vedic Age. The *Mahābhārata* has been identified as our primary source, and the issues about its dating have been discussed. Reconstruction of any kind of reliable history, on the basis of the *Mahābhārata*, has to deal with the problem of later interpolations. Therefore, to use the *Gītā* for understanding Kṛṣṇa's teaching, we have to first decide whether the text contains what was initially thought of as Kṛṣṇa's teachings or is a later interpolation built around the deity Kṛṣṇa. Our survey so far has revealed that Kṛṣṇa's outright divinity was not established in the very early layers of the *Mahābhārata*. Rather, his deification was a gradual process. Kṛṣṇa began his journey as the leader of a cowherd community and then of the Vṛṣṇis. He was attaining a semi-divine status among his followers. Gradually, he established himself as the '*vāsudeva*' by defeating Jarāsaṃdha, Śiśupāla, and many other antagonists. Before the Bhārata War, his divinity was a popular theory, especially in the Kuru court. The Kuru bard Saṃjaya was one of its chief propounders. However, to his Pāṇḍava and Pāñcāla friends, he was still a trusted and revered human. The sudden spurt of Kṛṣṇa's divinity in the *Bhagavad Gītā*, therefore, made the antiquity of the text doubtful.

Moreover, the *Gītā* is a didactic text. We have already discussed that scholars such as Thapar and R.S. Sharma consider the narrative sections of the *Mahābhārata* as earlier and the didactic sections as later. Though we are following the general premise of their analysis, the division seems too simplistic. After all, many narrative passages have been added later. Similarly, some didactic passages could have been part of the original text, since there is no reason to assert that the earlier bard-poet(s) had no didactic framework in their minds. Thus, the nature and the location of the *Gītā* have been vigorously debated among the scholars. Before coming to our understanding of the matter, a brief survey of the existing literature is essential.

For many of the scholars, the *Gītā* is a *bhakti* scripture inserted in the *Mahābhārata* to promote Bhāgavatism (a religion with Kṛṣṇa as the Supreme God) or Vaiṣṇavism (a religion with Viṣṇu as the Supreme God) or both. E. Washburn Hopkins, for example, treats it as a Kṛṣṇaite version of an older Viṣṇuite poem which, in turn, was first an unsectarian work, probably a late Upaniṣad.[235] H. Jacobi takes the *Gītā* as a 'textbook of the Bhāgavatas'.[236] H. Oldenberg treats the text as a result of a sudden vision of the poet.[237] Douglas Hill thinks that the *Gītā* is a unified text preaching theism with monistic tendencies.[238] F. Edgerton treats the epic context of the *Gītā* as a 'dramatic absurdity', since such a long discourse when the war was about to begin would disrupt the flow of the bardic narrative. To him, it is an independent text to inspire and exalt, not to instruct or train the intellect.[239] M. Marcovich considers the *Gītā* as a text composed independent of the epic and interpolated in the *Mahābhārata* between the fifth and third centuries BCE.[240]

Another group of scholars, mainly Marxists, think that the *Gītā* was interpolated later in the *Mahābhārata* to represent the interests of the ruling class. D.D. Kosambi takes the *Gītā* as a 'review synthesis' of contradictory positions that was incorporated shortly before the Gupta Era. It shows the antagonism between Aryan pastoralism and pre-Aryan agriculture. The doctrine of *bhakti* suits the structure of a feudal society based on loyalty and hierarchical subordination.[241] Walter Ruben tried hard to show the doctrine of 'disinterested action' as an exposition of 'healthy materialism'.[242] However, G.M. Bailey has shown the fallacious nature of such arguments, since the antagonism negotiated in the *Gītā* is primarily religious, not economic.[243] S.C. Roy thinks that the *Gītā* was composed as an Upaniṣad and interpolated later in the epic. All passages referring to the epic situation are therefore interpolated.[244]

Opinions are heavily divided even among the scholars who consider the *Gītā* as an integral part of the epic, regarding the date, unity, and nature of the epic itself. Therefore, there are scholars who argue for the synthetic unity of the text and others who argue for separating its different layers.

V.S. Sukthankar treats the *Gītā* as the kernel of the *Mahābhārata*, especially on its metaphysical plane where the unity of *jīvātman* and *paramātman* is the essential theme.[245] R.C. Zaehner considers the *Gītā*, a post-Buddhist treatise, as a genuine part of the epic, combining salvation with devotion.[246] G. von Simson thinks that the *Gītā* was incorporated in the epic for apologetic reasons, that is, to justify the 'mean tricks' that brought about the victory of the Pāṇḍavas.[247] M. Biardeau conceives for the *Gītā* a central place in the epic in reconciliating ascetic doctrines with the householder's *dharma* of the king. All activity is transformed into a sacrifice for the sake of maintaining the world. Complete devotion is demanded for the divine *avatāra* Kṛṣṇa who combines the values of the renouncer and the values of the world of *dharma*.[248] J.A.B. van Buitenen thinks that the *Gītā* has been conceived in the context of the *Mahābhārata* where the dilemma of a war which is both just and pernicious is dealt with.[249] Nick Sutton understands the pivotal role of the *Gītā* in the general *Mahābhārata* context of a triangular debate among *svadharma*, general morality, and ascetic tradition. The *Gītā* rejects general morality propounded by Arjuna in its reconciliation between ascetic and ritual tradition. In the *Gītā*, *mokṣa* is thesis, *svadharma* antithesis, and *bhakti* the synthesis.[250]

On the other hand, certain scholars try to separate the layers within the text itself. The *Bhagavad Gītā* consists of eighteen chapters (*Mahābhārata* VI.23–40). The first chapter of the *Gītā* deals with Arjuna's depression and almost half of the second chapter addresses it directly. The first six chapters together preach a doctrine similar to Upaniṣadic monism. In chapters 7–11, suddenly Kṛṣṇa himself appears as the Supreme God who demands absolute devotion. The culmination of this new theistic wave is Kṛṣṇa's display of his Cosmic Form to Arjuna in chapter eleven. Chapter twelve reasserts the importance of *bhakti*. The last six chapters disparately discuss different philosophical themes mentioned in the first eleven chapters. On the basis of this, various analytical methods have been adopted.

W. von Humboldt opines that the first eleven chapters are original and the last six are later. In the first eleven, Kṛṣṇa declares that separation of body and mind, and indifference towards the result of one's action, is the precondition for salvation.[251] This view has been followed by R.N. Minor[252] and P. Schreiner.[253]

Adolf Holtzmann thinks that the chapters one and two were parts of the original epic. Chapter four onwards, a tension arose between 'pantheistic' and 'theistic' teachings. Holtzmann thinks that the theistic parts belong to a more recent layer, a 'Viṣṇuistic revision' of an original 'pantheistic' text, for countering Buddhism by reconciling polytheism with folk belief.[254] A similar view is professed by Jacobi who thinks that the ur-text must have been the one concerning Arjuna's dilemma directly, rather than a long treatise disrupting the war narrative. His ur-text contains *Bhagavad Gītā* II.1–12, 18, 25–27, 30–37, XVIII.73.[255] Charpentier reduces the size of the ur-text further, arguing that what follows II.38 cannot belong to the epic ur-text and discarding even II.12–30 on the ground that these passages contain quotations from other texts such as the *Viṣṇu Smṛti*. The Bhāgavata layer is the latest, its core being chapter eleven.[256] R. Otto also thinks that the older passages are where Arjuna's problem is directly addressed. However, he extends the number of such passages, arguing that the purpose is to make Arjuna understand that he is merely an instrument of God's will. These passages are I.1–II.13, II.20, 22, 29–37, X.1–8, XI.1–51, XVIII.58–61.[257] A similar view has been expressed by M. Jezic who thinks that a 'hymnic layer' was added to an older 'epic layer' later supplemented by didactic passages. The 'hymnic layer' was added when *bhakti* doctrine was added to the text.[258]

On the other hand, R. Garbe thinks that the theistic doctrines are the essence of the *Gītā* and older than the 'pantheistic' teachings. The *Gītā* is a didactic text preaching Kṛṣṇaism around Kṛṣṇa, a deified hero turned into clan deity of the Bhāgavatas who professed 'an ethical *kṣatriya* religion' rejecting Brahmanic ritualism. The theistic text belonged to the older epic. Both the epic and the *Gītā* were revised with the Vedānta philosophy around second century BCE.[259]

Other scholars have argued for the priority of the monistic layer. P. Deussen thinks that a theistic doctrine was superimposed on older monistic teachings. However, the present text has a textual unity. The first six chapters deal with ethics (altruistic fulfillment of one's duties), the next six with metaphysics (transition from the idealistic doctrine of absolute *Brahman* to theism by subordinating the immortal self under the god Kṛṣṇa), and the last six with psychology (obstacles on the path to liberation based on *sāṃkhya* and *yoga*).[260] G.S. Khair thinks that the first six chapters are the oldest and deals with Yoga. A second author added another six chapters (13–18). The third author, the prophet of a new faith—the Bhāgavata religion, composed the six devotional chapters (7–12).[261] Irawati Karve opines that Kṛṣṇa's teaching is contained in the first six chapters of the *Bhagavad Gītā*, and about half of the verses in these chapters are also added later. In the original chapters, Kṛṣṇa talks as a man to his friend who is caught in a terrible mental crisis and needs guidance. But it is a guidance given to an equal and not to a devotee.[262]

A.L. Basham, in his thorough analysis of the possible chronology of the *Gītā*, argues that there are three layers of authorship in the text, and both the monistic and theistic layers are interpolated by two different authors in the original *Gītā* (Chapter I and II.1–37) where Arjuna's doubt was raised and Kṛṣṇa resolved it by reminding him of the duties of a *kṣatriya*. Basham dates this layer at a time when the glory of righteous warfare and martial virtues were being questioned, and—hence—thinks that this layer was later than the rise of Buddhism and Jainism and, possibly, the pacifist policies of Aśoka. The second layer, according to Basham, consists of the chapters II (39 to the end), III, V, VI, VIII, XIII, XIV.7–25, XVI, XVII, and XVIII.1–53. Here Kṛṣṇa's divinity was occasionally referred to, but the basic tenor was philosophical, in which the state of Brahman was the highest one. The third layer is theistic in which Kṛṣṇa appears as the Supreme Deity and even Brahman is subordinated to him. This doctrine is philosophically contradictory with the doctrine of the second layer, and—thus—the intervention of multiple authors is a certainty. Basham includes the chapters IV, VII, IX, X, XI, XIV.1–6, 26, XV, XVII (54 to the end) in this layer and assumes that, given the evidence of the organized Bhāgavatism (with Vāsudeva) as the Supreme God in the second to first centuries BCE, the text's composition was completed by the first century BCE.[263] Basham's analysis is essential as it points out clearly how the *Gītā* contains too much self-contradiction to be the work of a single author. However, his datings remain questionable. For instance, the date for the first layer, which Basham considers a part of the original *Mahābhārata* narrative, seems to be too late, not only because we consider the original *Mahābhārata* narrative emerging out of the Later Vedic context but also because questioning of martial heroism and its resolution by reference to *kṣātradharma* would make more sense in the context of the *kṣatriya* clan society which adhered to such ideals (as we discussed in Chapter 3) than in the post-Aśokan times when nonviolence was regarded as a cardinal virtue across traditions. Moreover, Basham's own admission that the first layer was produced when the doctrine of transmigration of the soul was not fully understood would definitely point towards a pre-Buddhistic scenario.[264] Similarly, while the theistic layer is definitely interpolated later, Basham's reference to the proliferation of Vāsudeva worship in the second to first millennium BCE ignores the definite presence of the cult in the times of Pāṇini and Megasthenes as well. Finally, whereas the separation between the monistic and theistic layers is definite, whether the first two chapters can be so clearly separated from the monistic ones is doubtful. As we shall see later, Arjuna's doubts were not so much about war and peace as it was about his understanding of the Brahmanical system of *kuladharma*, and Kṛṣṇa's championing of a new philosophical system based on action (which, as we have discussed already, had clear antecedents in the *Mahābhārata*) was as essential to resolve them as was the assertion of a *kṣatriya*'s responsibility to fight.

Angelika Malinar follows the analytical method and treats the first six chapters as the oldest. However, though she separates older and later verses, she also tries to understand the significance of the *Gītā* in reconciliating the two ideas of ascetic detachment and royal engagement. Using J. Assman's concept of 'cosmological monotheism', she traces a monotheistic framework with Kṛṣṇa as 'the God'. Ascetic practices are interpreted in terms of sacrificial activity as a detached performance of duty (*karmayoga*) for the sake of 'holding the world together' (*lokasaṃgraha*), equating own activity with those of the cosmic cause of all activity—*Brahman/prakṛti*. Anyone who manages to substitute his own agency with 'cosmic' agency for the sake of 'the welfare of all beings' can be liberated, whether he is a king or an ascetic. In this way, the king can be liberated despite performing his violent worldly duties by being subordinated and devoted to the highest god.[265]

As we can see, the opinions about the *Gītā* are so divided that one has to be very cautious in deciding its historical location. If we look closely at the debates in the 'Udyogaparvan', it becomes quite clear that the *Gītā* comes as an extension of these. Both Malinar and Madhav M. Deshpande take note of the matter.[266] While Malinar has shown that the debate about war and peace was going on in the 'Udyogaparvan', Deshpande shows that several issues picked up by the *Gītā*—including Kṛṣṇa's divinity, doubts about Pāṇḍava victory, lack of will to fight, moral dilemma, and Kṛṣṇa's special relationship with Arjuna—emerge from the epic context. Therefore, it is hardly possible to separate the *Gītā* from its *Mahābhārata* context.

In fact, Kevin McGrath considers the *Gītā* the most crucial ontological element of the *Mahābhārata*. Pointing out Arjuna's role as a 'double-hero' marked by the importance of duality in a heroic culture, he showed how Arjuna's character is marked by various kinds of dualism, including his dual existence in the supernatural and the mortal planes, his dilemma between ethical inhibitions and practical necessities (which is the immediate context of the *Gītā*), the apparent dualism of the two antagonistic armies, and the various relationships of duality the hero develops with his king (Yudhiṣṭhira), charioteer (Kṛṣṇa), and arch-enemy or *bhāga* (Karṇa). Through the monistic metaphysics of the *Gītā*, Kṛṣṇa dissolved all these dualities in a doctrine of Unity, an initiation needed to morally enable Arjuna to kill his elder Bhīṣma and half-brother Karṇa and to facilitate the destruction of his teacher Droṇa, without being troubled by remorse. That way, the *Gītā* is nothing but an exalted charioteer's song which the *sūta* (both charioteer and bard) was supposed to perform to raise the martial spirit and ardour of the warrior before a war. However, the *Gītā* also surpasses this ritualistic role by rejecting the prevalent system of ritual efficacy in favour of a new mode of worship based on personal commitment and dedication (*pūjā*) which promised an affective and practical spiritual transcendence rather than the intellectual transcendence a warrior expected from his fame (*kīrti*) preserved in poetic traditions. McGrath attributes this contrast to the hybrid nature of the *Gītā* in synthesizing 'archaic' (those representing a pre-literate and pre-monetary Bronze Age culture) and 'classical' (post–Second

Urbanization) values.[267] Though McGrath's formulation of the 'archaic' in the *Mahābhārata* as a Bronze Age heroic culture, modelled on a framework to understand Homeric epics, is seemingly out of context, the *Gītā* definitely appears to have contained the values of two different worlds and, in all probability, two different poets.

Therefore, the question remains whether the *Gītā* is a part of the original epic tradition or a later interpolation. For that, dating the *Gītā* is very important. Suvira Jaiswal points out that a Chinese version of the Tripiṭaka quotes passages from the *Bhagavad Gītā*. A heretic called Māthara proclaims:

> I created all things, I am the supreme among all living beings. I gave birth to all living things and produce all non-living things in all worlds. I am the king of the mountain Mahā Sumeru among all mountains. I am the greatest sea of all rivers. I am the grain of all medicines. I am Kapila Muni of all ... If a man offers me wholeheartedly water, herbs, flowers, and fruits, I will not miss him and he will not miss me.[268]

The quotations are very easily identifiable from the *Bhagavad Gītā*:

> *ahaṃ sarvasya prabhavo mattaḥ sarvaṃ pravartate*
> (I am the origin of all... and everything comes from me.)[269]
>
> *meru śikharinām ahaṃ*
> (Of mountains I am Meru.)[270]
>
> .....*sarasām asmi sāgaraḥ*
> (Of lakes I am the sea.)[271]
>
> *siddhānāṃ kapilo muniḥ*
> (Of the *siddhas*, [I am] the sage Kapila.)[272]
>
> *patraṃ puṣpaṃ phalaṃ toyaṃ yo me bhaktyā prayacchati*
> *tad ahaṃ bhakty upahṛtam aśnāmi prayatātmanaḥ.*
>
> (A leaf, a flower, a fruit, water: I accept whatever devotional offering is made by a devout person.)[273]

This heretic Māthara has been identified by Jaiswal as the famous minister of Kaṇiṣka II, who flourished in the second century CE. By this time, the *Bhagavad Gītā* must have been quite popular in the Bhāgavata circle. Therefore, Kosambi's dating of the text in the Gupta Period does not have much ground, and most scholars date the text prior to that. Sarvepalli Radhakrishnan has noted that that the *Baudhāyana Gṛhya Sūtra* (II.22.9) quotes as the 'Lord's statement' the aforementioned verse (*Gītā* IX.26 = *Mahābhārata* VI.31.26).[274] This text is usually dated not later than fifth century BCE. Occurrence of a *Gītā* passage is not a direct evidence of quotation from the *Gītā*. There can even be parallel passages in two texts. The *Gītā* actually has many passages parallel to Upaniṣadic passages. But its occurrence as the 'Lord's statement' indicates its being quoted from a structured *Gītā* where Kṛṣṇa's statements follow the phrase 'thus spoke the Lord' (*śrī bhagavān uvāca*). Moreover, our analysis here will indicate that the ninth chapter of the *Gītā* is one of its latest sections, being a part of the theistic chapters. Therefore, the earlier chapters of the *Gītā* possibly were composed much earlier than the fifth century BCE. Thus, it is highly plausible that the *Gītā*, in some form, formed a part of the earliest *Mahābhārata*.

While discussing about Kṛṣṇa's position in other contemporary texts, we have already discussed Paṇini's statement '*vāsudevārjunābhyaṃ buñ*' and its implications. The statement certainly points out the communities worshipping Vāsudeva and Arjuna, and their close association, as well as the primacy of Vāsudeva over Arjuna. This religious identity closely associating Kṛṣṇa and Arjuna, and making the former superior, can be best explained only through the *Gītā*. It, therefore, seems that at least the earliest chapters of the *Gītā* possibly originated with the *Mahābhārata* tradition itself.

Now, it does not mean that we can take the *Gītā* as an exact description of a dialogue between Kṛṣṇa and Arjuna on a battlefield. Rather, the poet possibly used it as a scene for giving a full exposition of the teachings of his hero. The device of introducing the outlook and philosophy of the central characters of a time through dialogues, discourses, and speeches was not unknown in classical Greek history writing as well. In his *History of the Peloponnesian War*, Thucydides introduces many such speeches to clarify the positions of Athens, Sparta, and Corinth, or of the different Athenian leaders such as Pericles, Cleon, and Diodotus. However, even in that history, a speech that stands out is Pericles's famous 'Funeral Oration'. The speech was definitely not recorded word by word by Thucydides.

Rather, the historian took it as a chance to expound everything Pericles stood for. The *Gītā* seems to be similar, a juncture to expound in detail everything Vāsudeva Kṛṣṇa stood for.

The location of the *Gītā* inside the *Mahābhārata* context also shows such a possibility. We have already discussed how the *Mahābhārata* emerged out of a tradition of the *sūtas*. Even before the composition of the earliest version by Vyāsa, the nucleus of the epic probably lay in the narrations of the Kuru bard Saṃjaya who retold the events of the war to Dhṛtarāṣṭra after the fall of every Kaurava general. This earliest tradition is represented in the five battle books, and the *Gītā* occurs in the very first of them. The *Gītā* is not presented directly by the poet, but through its retelling by Saṃjaya to Dhṛtarāṣṭra. Interestingly, it was Saṃjaya who was not just the earliest narrator of the battle events but also the propounder of Kṛṣṇa's divinity in the Kuru court.

Moreover, the *Gītā* is introduced in a context when Kṛṣṇa was performing the duty of a charioteer, the traditional role of the *sūta*. It was a duty of the charioteer-bard to boost the morale of his warrior by verbal performances of inspiring speeches and praises. Such speech-acts would be of immense importance in a preliterate society not just to increase the warrior's confidence but also to provide himself the assurance that his victory should be celebrated and death mourned in style, to preserve the memory of his glorious achievements (*kīrti*), by his competent charioteer-bard. That the highest exposition of Kṛṣṇa's philosophy shall be introduced in a context when he acted as neither a warrior nor a diplomat nor even a philosopher, but as a charioteer on the battlefield, even at the risk of breaking the flow of the war narrative, strongly suggests the authorship of the *sūtas* for whom the *Gītā* signified not only the best synthesis of Kṛṣṇa's teachings but also the best illustration of the importance of their craft.

However, this does not mean that there is no need of an analytical understanding of the text. Like every other portion of the *Mahābhārata*, the *Gītā* also has undergone revisions, alterations, additions, and interpolations, and finding them out is important. It seems conclusive that the theistic doctrines contained in chapters VII–XII and some parts of the last six chapters were definitely the result of a later Vaiṣṇavized revision of the text. However, a substantial part of the first six chapters was possibly a part of the original *Mahābhārata* narrative, though there are theistic interpolations in these chapters as well, and there are early materials in some of the last six chapters as well. Kṛṣṇa's teachings found in the other parts of the *Mahābhārata* can help us in verifying this working hypothesis and understanding the text.

The earliest layer of the *Gītā*, then, has to be understood in its context, the context in which we are locating the *Mahābhārata*. It is the period when proto-states were emerging on the North Indian plains, in forms of both the kingdoms and the *gaṇasaṃghas*. The formation of territorial and hereditary kingship, possibly with the Kuru state as the centre, was accompanied by a new social organization based on *varṇa*. The hereditary *varṇa* classification of the society no doubt legitimized the hereditary kingship of the *kṣatriya* clans, as well as the hereditary religious leadership of the *brāhmaṇas*. However, this new organization was subject to intense internal and external criticism. The renouncers were trying to bypass this ordered structure, and the Vedic ritualism was subjected to constant scrutiny. Right from Book X of the *Ṛg Veda*, doubts and confusions over the prevalent socio-religious structure were present. From the intellectual whirlpool debating and discussing these issues, gradually would emerge the Upaniṣads (ultimately leading to the Vedānta philosophical system), the Sāṃkhya philosophy (possibly deriving much material from the pre-Vedic fertility cults which focused on the duality of the male principle and the female principle), Cārvāka materialism, and the heterodox religions such as Buddhism and Jainism. Vāsudeva Kṛṣṇa—a member of a *gaṇasaṃgha* like the Buddha and Mahāvīra—seems to be a product of this intellectual climate. The close proximity of his teachings with the Upaniṣads will be discussed later. We also have to remember that Kṛṣṇa Devakīputra, who had anyway questioned the Vedic ritualism as a young cowherd, had some Upaniṣadic training under Ghora Āṅgirasa, a sage mentioned in the CU. The direct influence of Ghora's teachings on the *Gītā* has been meticulously analysed by H.C. Raychaudhuri, and we will also have to get into that to understand the implications of the *Gītā*. Kṛṣṇa used the words '*sāṃkhya*' for knowledge and '*yoga*' for action in the *Gītā*. However, he was not referring to the philosophical systems of Sāṃkhya and Yoga. Many of his teachings closely follow the Sāṃkhya philosophy but not in its classical form. Rather, Kṛṣṇa's Sāṃkhya—with its understanding of *puruṣa* and *prakṛti*, analysis of *buddhi* and *ahaṃkāra*—was still in a rudimentary state where it could be presented as not drastically different from Vedānta. Our dating of the *Gītā* indicates of its pre-Buddhistic nature. Though many scholars have argued that the *Gītā* emerged as a response to Buddhism, we will see how Kṛṣṇa and the Buddha derived their ideas from a common intellectual pool and agreed on certain points while disagreeing on certain others.

In fact, the *Gītā*, like the philosophy of *ānṛśaṃsya* discussed in Chapter 3, seems to be an attempt to create a middle ground between the philosophical extremities of its contemporary world. The *varṇa*-ordered Vedic ritualism had its direct opposite in the philosophy of complete renunciation (*nivṛtti*) which culminated later in the Śramaṇic religions, most prominently Jainism. However, there were philosophical antagonists within the Brahmanical fold who questioned the supremacy of ritual action and highlighted the importance of knowledge. The most prominent strand of such ideas got crystallized in the Upaniṣadic idea of monism, precursor of the Vedāntic philosophy, which spoke of the singular Supreme Reality, the *Brahman* or *Paramātman*, which is manifest in every being. The living beings also contain the same element in the form of the *jīvātman* encased in the material body, and the attainment of the knowledge of one's true self as inseparable from the *Brahman* liberates the self from the painful but unreal world of birth, death, and transmigration. However, there were other philosophical ideals rooted deep in the belief system of the pre-Vedic fertility cults. Such cults were popular all over the ancient world and emphasized the magical power in the productive power of land and reproductive power of women, represented in the form of goddesses symbolizing both, who were worshipped either in the form of female sexual organs or in anthropomorphic forms with highlighted reproductive organs. Gradually, with a better understanding of the role of men in sexual reproduction, fertility cults developed a belief system where the unity of the passive Male Principle with the active Female Principle was conceived as the secret behind the creation of the cosmos, and magico-religious performances (often including sexual acts or symbols) were supposed to generate the effect of that Primeval and Eternal union. Whereas the tantric rites, institutionalized in the Gupta and post-Gupta period, most prominently bear the remnants of these prehistoric cults, the philosophical school of Sāṃkhya seems to have derived ideas from them and presented them in a sanitized Brahmanized form. Thus, the cosmos was conceived in Sāṃkhya as the result of the union of the duo *puruṣa* and *prakṛti*, and the material world had been conceived of as the result of the properties or *guṇas*—*sattva*, *rajas*, and *tamas*—emerging out of the active *prakṛti*, but the predominance of the Female Principle was replaced by the importance given to the passive *puruṣa*. On the other hand, the idea that the body was the universe in miniature, and could be an active vehicle to channelize the cosmic energy, had been the cornerstone of the philosophical school of Yoga but without the preponderance of sexual rites. Kṛṣṇa's philosophy, while highlighting the need of an active (*pravṛtti*) mode of life had attempted a synthesis of these multiple philosophical positions. Thus, the *Gītā* used the word '*sāṃkhya*' to signify knowledge (and not a fully institutionalized philosophical school) which included the understanding of the three *guṇas* of *prakṛti*. However, the real knowledge would help one to transcend the duality of *puruṣa* and *prakṛti*, which bound the soul to the cycle of transmigrations, and attain the singularity of the *Brahman* signifying liberation. However, this stage could be attained through a dutiful and active life, involving intense mental and physical discipline, which the *Gītā* understands as *yoga*. Vedic ritual action, though of little value in this philosophical scheme, was not dismissed altogether, as Kṛṣṇa—in an Upaniṣadic style—understood life through the imagery of a great sacrifice, as his teacher Ghora Āṅgirasa had taught him.[275] Therefore, as the Buddha, emerging out of the same intellectual milieu, had sought to work out a 'middle path' between Vedic ritual action and Jaina renunciation and self-mortification, to attain liberation (*nirvāṇa*) from the painful world of transmigration, Kṛṣṇa tried to organize the several competing strands of philosophy in one philosophical system of desireless action. The result, *brahmanirvāṇa*, resonates equally of the Buddhist ideal of *nirvāṇa* and the Upaniṣadic concept of the *Brahman*. Perhaps, it can be understood better when seen as coming out of the same intellectual milieu shared by the Buddha and the Upaniṣadic sages, rather than as a borrowing from Buddhism. As we shall see later, there were ideas shared by Kṛṣṇa and the Buddha, while there were contradictory ideas in their teachings as well, but the *Gītā* had a similar relationship with the Upaniṣadic philosophy as well.

Locating the *Gītā* in this manner makes it clear that its introduction in the *Mahābhārata* was neither out of context nor a 'dramatic absurdity'. Rather, it was the most opportune moment for the poet to give a full exposition of Kṛṣṇa's philosophy—at the start of the battle books, at a juncture when Kṛṣṇa's divinity itself became a well-known discourse, at the zenith of Kṛṣṇa's career, before the outbreak of the massive violence and destruction, with Saṃjaya as the narrator, and with Kṛṣṇa assuming the *sūta*'s function. The scene of the battlefield is the most ideal metaphor for the problem of human existence the *Gītā* addresses. On this great battlefield of life, every person reaches a juncture when a decision is to be made, a stand is to be taken. In that battle, the person stands alone, between the two antagonistic forces both of which may contain his near and dear ones. Beyond the idea of Self and the Other, transcending the concepts of friend and foe, a person has to make a choice all alone. What does he do? Should he lament over the pitiable condition and leave the battlefield? Or should he fight the battle, perform the duty? But what incentive is there to perform the duties in a life which is so full of sorrow and misery, where friend can become foe and the foe to be slaughtered may be a friend? This eternal dilemma crushes the human soul standing all alone. Or is he alone? The agnostic Buddha would have said so. But, in the *Gītā*, the lonely human's lonely chariot has God as its charioteer, as the only guide to take him through. Arjuna's dilemma represents this eternal crisis. Let us now try to understand what solution Kṛṣṇa provides.

Interpretation of the *Gītā* is often accompanied by two gross misunderstandings. The first of these is that the *Gītā* is an endorsement of war and violence. It persuades a man who is reluctant to commit violence to kill. In this way, the *Gītā* can be a stark contrast to the Buddhist and Jaina philosophies which emphasize non-violence. However, a thorough reading of the *Gītā* does not support this conclusion. As we have already said, the battle scene is possibly metaphorical. Moreover, Arjuna's crisis—unlike the crisis of Yudhiṣṭhira in the 'Udyogaparvan'—had hardly anything to do with violence and non-violence. Arjuna had been a warrior throughout his life. He fought many wars and killed many people. It was not war and violence, but something else, that troubled him. Philosophically, what Kṛṣṇa encouraged is the performance of one's own duty, however unpleasant it may be.

This leads to a more serious misunderstanding. What duty was being endorsed by Kṛṣṇa? Several scholars take it to be one's stipulated caste duty. Since Arjuna was a *kṣatriya*, and he was being encouraged to fight, this simplistic conclusion is reached. However, a closer scrutiny will reveal that the *Gītā*'s concept of duty goes much beyond the hereditary caste order, and Kṛṣṇa's interpretation of the *varṇa* system differs much from the way it was usually understood. We will take up this issue in detail, because the central theme of Kṛṣṇa's teaching seems to be his concept of one's own duty—*svadharma*.

To begin with, what constituted Arjuna's crisis is essential for understanding the solution. According to Holtzmann, it is the fear of death.[276] For A. Hejib and K. Young, it is a crisis of identity, since Arjuna was yet to recover from his camouflage of a eunuch in the Matsya court.[277] For Biardeau, it was the clash of the violence of *kṣatriyadharma* and the teachings of salvation.[278] To van Buitenen, it was the clash of legitimate claims and illegitimate means.[279] Some scholars also try to understand it in terms of the ascetic religions such as Buddhism and Jainism. Bimal Krishna Matilal, for instance, thinks that Arjuna's preference for *bhaikṣa* (begging) over war refers directly to the tradition of the Buddhist mendicants (*bhikṣu*).[280]

Many of these elements were constituents of Arjuna's crisis. Fear of death was definitely there—fear of his own death as well as of the death of the dear ones. He was not very sure about the outcome of the battle either (*yad vā jayema yadi vā no jayeyuḥ*).[281] Similarly, a crisis of identity cannot be denied. However, that seems to have hardly anything to do with Arjuna's eunuch disguise. Even in that disguise, Arjuna fought and won a war against the very people he was to face at Kurukṣetra. Rather, it seems a crisis of identity where a self was lost in confusion over who was a friend and who a foe, who was to be killed and who to be protected. Liberation was not something Arjuna himself was worried about. Rather, it was a new dimension that Kṛṣṇa would reveal to him. Renunciation of the active world for overcoming its misery was no doubt at the heart of Buddhism. However, the ascetic tradition is pre-Buddhistic, and the Buddha chose only one of the prevalent solutions. Therefore, what Arjuna spoke might not necessarily be a representation of the Buddhist doctrine, especially when the Pāṇḍavas themselves had enough experience of living in the forest and practising *bhaikṣa*. That Arjuna stood on the battlefield to get rid of such life was because he thought that his claims were legitimate. But now he wanted to revert to the previous state, shocked by the illegitimacy of the means.

What made the means so illegitimate to Arjuna? War itself could not be illegitimate to an ardent warrior. Rather, it was the prospect of fighting the kinsmen. As we look at Arjuna's depression, it becomes apparent that he felt disturbed by the prospect of killing his own kinsmen (not by the act of killing itself) for wealth, since people sought wealth for the kinsmen. Moreover, killing of kinsmen also disturbed his traditional understanding of *dharma* based on the purity-pollution paradigm of hereditary *varṇa*:

> *kulakṣaye praṇaśyanti kuladharmāḥ sanātanāḥ/*
> *dharme naṣṭe kulaṃ kṛtsnam adharmo'bhibhabaty uta//*
> *adharmābhibhavat kṛṣṇa praduṣyanti kulastriyaḥ/*
> *strīṣu duṣṭāsu vārṣṇeya jāyate varṇasaṃkaraḥ//*
> *saṃkaro narakāyaiva kulaghnānāṃ kulasya ca/*
> *patanti pitaro hy eṣāṃ luptapiṇḍodakakriyā//*
> *doṣair etaiḥ kulaghnānāṃ varṇasaṃkarakārakaiḥ/*
> *utsādyante jātidharmāḥ kuladharmāś ca śāśvatāḥ//*
> *utsannakuladharmāṇāṃ manuṣyāṇāṃ janārdana/*
> *narake niyataṃ vāso bhavatīty anuśuśruma//*
>
> (When a family is destroyed the ancient family customs die and when virtue has been lost, vice prevails over the whole family. When vice prevails the family's women become corrupt; and from the corruption of women comes the mixing of social classes, Vārṣṇeya. Such mixing leads the family's destroyers and the family itself to hell, for the ancestors fall if the offerings of rice and water aren't made. The sins of the family-destroyers cause the mixing of classes and bring the eternal caste traditions and family rites to ruin. We have heard, Janārdana, that people whose family rites have been ruined are doomed to dwell in hell for certain.)[282]

Therefore, Arjuna's crisis was very closely related with the socially and ritually prescribed duties and the maintenance of the *varṇa* order as well and not really of Buddhist orientation.

Kṛṣṇa started by denouncing Arjuna's crisis as a miserable cowardice (*klaibya*) and weakness (*kṣudraṃ hṛdayadaurbalyaṃ*).[283] His teaching begins with the Upaniṣadic concept of an immortal soul:

> *na tv evāhaṃ jātu nāsaṃ na tvaṃ neme janādhipāḥ/*
> *na caiva na bhaviṣyāmaḥ sarve vayam ataḥparam//*

(There wasn't a time when you and I and these lords of men didn't exist; and none of us will cease to exist hereafter.)[284]

As the Upaniṣads describe, Kṛṣṇa differentiated the perishable body from the immortal soul and described the latter as the real self. He pointed out that the body did not remain the same even in childhood, youth, and old age, but those changes would not torment a wise person.[285] Similarly, the change of body should not be something to be distressed about, since it was, for the Self, like changing over from an old cloth to a new one.[286] On the other hand, the soul remained indestructible, imperishable:

nāsato vidyate bhāvo nābhāvo vidyate sataḥ/
ubhayor api dṛṣṭo'ntas tv anayos tattvadarśibhiḥ//
avināśī tu tad viddhi yena sarvam idaṃ tatam/
vināśam avyasyāsya na kaś cit kartum arhati//
antavanta ime dehā nityasyoktāḥ śarīriṇaḥ/
anāśino' prameyasya tasmād yuddhasva bhārata//

(The non-existent can't come into being, and the existent can't cease to be. Those who see the truth see the boundary between these two. So you should know that that by which all this is pervaded is indestructible; no one can bring about the destruction of the imperishable. It is only bodies that are said to come to an end—the bodies of the eternal, indestructible, immeasurable embodied soul. So fight, Bhārata!)[287]

The soul could not be cut by weapons, burnt by fire, made wet by water, or dried by wind. It was uncuttable (*acchedyaḥ*), unburnable (*adāhyaḥ*), unwettable (*akledyaḥ*), and undryable (*aśoṣyaḥ*); it was also unmanifest (*avyaktaḥ*), inconceivable (*acintyaḥ*), and immutable (*avikāryaḥ*). The soul was eternal (*nityaḥ*), all-pervading (*sarvagataḥ*), fixed (*sthāṇūḥ*), immovable (*acalaḥ*), and everlasting (*sanātanaḥ*).[288] Therefore, it could neither kill nor be killed:

ya enaṃ vetti hantāraṃ yaś cainaṃ manyate hatam/
ubhau tau na vijānīto nāyaṃ hanti na hanyate//
na jāyate mṛyate vā kadācin nāyaṃ bhūtvā bhavitā vā na bhuyaḥ/

ajo nityaḥ śāśvato'yaṃ purāṇo na hanyate hanyamāne śarīre//
vedāvināśinaṃ nityaṃ ya enam ajam avyayam/
kaṭhaṃ saḥ puruṣaḥ pārtha kaṃ ghātayati hanti kam//

(Whoever thinks that the soul can kill or be killed, doesn't understand. It neither kills, nor is it killed. It isn't born; it never dies; it isn't something that comes into existence and then ceases to be. It is unborn, eternal, permanent, and primordial; it is not killed when the body is killed. If a man knows it to be indestructible, eternal, unborn, and imperishable, Pārtha, how can he be made to kill? Whom can he kill?)[289]

Since both birth and death were inevitable and impermanent states of the soul, there was hardly any reason to grieve over death. The self was permanent, only unmanifest (*avyakta*) at first, manifest (*vyakta*) in the middle, and again unmanifest at the end.[290]

This entire doctrine of the soul is essentially an Upaniṣadic one. It is the foundation of the Vedānta philosophy, whereas Sāṃkhya also acknowledges the self as the unmanifest *puruṣa*, a term Kṛṣṇa uses often interchangeably for *ātman*. This character of the soul has been identically described in the KU:

hantā cen manyate hantuṃ hataś cet manyate hatam/
ubhau tau na vijānīto nāyaṃ hanti na hanyate//
na jāyate mṛyate vā vipaścin nāyaṃ kutas cin na babhūva kaś cit/
ajo nityaḥ sāśvato'ṃ purāṇo na hanyate hanyamāne śarīre//

(The wise one—
He is not born, he does not die;
He has not come from anywhere;
He has not become anyone.
He is unborn and eternal, primeval, and everlasting.
And he is not killed, when the body is killed.
If the killer thinks that he kills;
If the killed thinks that he is killed;
Both of them fail to understand
He neither kills, nor is he killed.)[291]

G.V. Devasthali thinks that the *Bhagavad Gītā* borrowed these passages from the KU.[292] A. Hillebrandt and Malinar think the other way round.[293] F. Weller thinks that both the texts got the idea from the same unknown source.[294] Indeed, as we have argued earlier, the *Gītā* and the Upaniṣads share their origin from a common pool of ideas from which the Sāṃkhya and the Buddha also derived some concepts. The concept of the soul is pivotal to that pool of ideas. The BU also speaks of the soul that is not affected by good or bad deeds.[295]

The Buddha criticized the Upaniṣadic idea that the world and the Self are the same, and after death one will be permanent, enduring, and eternal, not liable to change.[296] But even Buddhist philosophy derived inspiration from the separation of the self from the body and its pain and pleasure. The great Buddhist scholar Sāriputta says in the *Samyutta Nikāya*:

> Here the uninformed, ordinary person . . . looks on the physical form as the self, or the self as something that possesses physical form, or physical form as in the self, or the self as in physical form. He becomes fixated on the idea that he is physical form, that physical form is his. And then the physical form of this person who is fixated on the idea that he is physical form, the idea that physical form is his, changes and alters. As a result of that change and alteration in physical form grief, lamentation, pain, sorrow, and despair come into being for him.[297]

Therefore, Kṛṣṇa used the generally accepted premise of his contemporary intellectual world to eradicate the fear of death in Arjuna. It established the ground for arguing that fear of death could be no reason for not performing one's duty. Then he identified the upcoming war as Arjuna's duty. He advised Arjuna to follow his *svadharma*, and for a *kṣatriya* the *svadharma* was fighting. Therefore, it should be a happy situation for a *kṣatriya* to find a war where he could fight for a righteous cause. If Arjuna avoided this opportunity, he would have committed a sin and would be disgraced. Everybody would think that he withdrew out of fear.[298] On the other hand, fighting would be a win-win situation:

> *hato vā prāpsyasi svargaṃ jitvā vā bhokṣyase mahīṃ/*
> *tasmāt uttiṣṭha kaunteya yuddhāya kṛtaniścayaḥ//*
> *sukhaduḥkhe same kṛtvā lābhālābhau jayājayau/*

tato yuddhāya yujyasva naivaṃ pāpam avāpsyasi//

(Get up, son of Kuntī, and resolve to fight! For you will either be killed and attain heaven, or you will prevail and enjoy the earth. Make yourself indifferent to pleasure and pain, profit and loss, victory and defeat, and so gird yourself for battle. In this way, you will incur no evil.)[299]

Based on this section, the *Gītā* is often portrayed as an espousal of the *kṣātradharma*. However, such propagations of *kṣātradharma* have already come from Duryodhana and Kuntī. In fact, it was Duryodhana who epitomized this version of *dharma*. If Kṛṣṇa's teaching ended here, as some scholars such as Holtzmann and Charpentier thought, he would have carried the reins of Duryodhana's chariot, rather than Arjuna's.

Rather, it seems to be the beginning of Kṛṣṇa's explanation of duty, which was also needed logically. After all, the encouraging statements discussed this far would have fulfilled Kṛṣṇa's role as a *sūta* to encourage his *kṣatriya* warrior before a war but would hardly resolve Arjuna's principal sphere of doubt about the necessity to preserve *kuladharma*. Arjuna's immediate worry was that he could incur a sin of *kulakṣaya* by fighting the war and be sent to hell. Therefore, Kṛṣṇa explained that even Arjuna's notion of *dharma* assured him heaven rather than hell for fighting the war. The prevalent Vedic religion and *varṇa*-ordered society definitely focused on material benefits in this world and the next. This war provided Arjuna an opportunity for both—kingship in this world and heaven in the next. But would that logic not work for Duryodhana equally? Was war then an amoral affair and mindless violence the ideal way as it could secure material benefits either in this world or in the world beyond? Kṛṣṇa revealed his own opinion which ruthlessly attacked such a conception of *dharma*:

yām imāṃ puṣpitāṃ vācaṃ pravadanty avipaścitaḥ/
vedavādaratāḥ pārtha nānyād astītivādinaḥ//
kāmātmanaḥ svargaparā janmakarmaphalapradām/
kriyāviśeṣabahulān bhog aiśvaryagatiṃ prati//
bhog aiśvarya prasaktānāṃ tayāpahṛtacetasāṃ/
vyavasāyātmikā buddhiḥ samādhau na vidhīyate//

(Delighting in the words of the Veda and claiming there is nothing else, undiscerning men, full of desire and bent on heaven, speak flowery words accompanied by particular rites, Pārtha, for the acquisition of pleasure and power; but these cause rebirth as the fruit of the acts. The resolute understanding, when settled, isn't disturbed by the word of the mindless who cling to pleasure and power.)[300]

Thus Kṛṣṇa advised Arjuna to go beyond his Vedic understanding:

traiguṇyaviṣayā vedā nistraiguṇyo bhavārjuna/
nir dvandvo nityasattvastho nir yogakṣema ātmavān//

(The Vedas have the three modes as their scope. Be free of the three modes, Arjuna, free of dualities, always established in purity, beyond acquisition and preservation, and self-possessed.)[301]

From hereon, we can get a grasp on what Kṛṣṇa preached. He espoused the doctrine of the immortal soul as the real self and negated the possibility of death. However, the doctrine could not be a free mandate to kill at will, just because nobody killed and nobody could be killed in theory. For understanding the doctrine properly, one has to go beyond the realm of personal material interest. However, the entire Vedic religion was based on the pursuit of wealth in this world and heaven in the other. Therefore, Kṛṣṇa denounced that. Just like the soul could not kill or be killed, it could not have any pleasure or pain, interest or passion. According to the Sāṃkhya philosophy, this unmanifest, immobile *puruṣa* remains active due to its union with *prakṛti*. *Prakṛti* keeps the self tied and attached to the body through its three modes—*sattva* (pure and noble), *rajas* (active and passionate), and *tamas* (inert). To understand the soul, one needs to go beyond the three modes, which cannot be achieved by following the materially oriented Vedas.

This is again the Upaniṣadic spirit. In the KU, when Yama, the lord of death, offers Naciketas worldly and heavenly wealth instead of Eternal Knowledge, Naciketas replies:

Since the passing days of a mortal, O Death, sap here the energy of all the senses;
And even a full life is but a trifle; so keep your horses, your songs and dances!

With wealth you cannot make a man content
Will we get to keep wealth, when we have seen you?
And we get to live only as long as you will allow!
So, this alone is the wish that I'd like to choose.

What mortal man with insight, who has met those that do not die or grow old,
Himself growing old in this wretched and lowly place, looking at its beauties, its pleasures and joys,
Would delight in a long life?[302]

Similar sentiment has been uttered by Maitreyī in the BU:

> If I were to possess the entire world filled with wealth, sir, would it make me immortal? ... What is the point in getting something that will not make me immortal?[303]

The realization that material wealth was not the ultimate goal was what formed the quest for salvific knowledge in the Upaniṣads and Vedānta, in the Sāṃkhya, and in Buddhism. Kṛṣṇa, standing in such a philosophical milieu, advised Arjuna to go beyond the three modes of *prakṛti*, a bid in which the Vedas were of no help.

Therefore, Kṛṣṇa suggested his unique and exclusive solution:

karmaṇy evādhikāras te mā phaleṣu kadācana/
mā karmaphalahetur bhur mā te saṅgo'stv akarmaṇi//
yogasthaḥ kuru karmāṇi saṅgaṃ tyaktvā dhanaṃjaya/
siddhy asiddhyoḥ samo bhūtvā samatvaṃ yoga ucyate//

(You have a right to the action alone, never to its fruits. Don't let the action's fruits be your motivation, and don't be attached to inactivity. Perform actions while established in yoga, Dhanaṃjaya, having abandoned attachment, having become even-minded towards success and failure; for yoga is said to be evenness of mind.)[304]

This is the doctrine of 'desireless action' (*niṣkāma karman*), the most important of the *Gītā*'s doctrines, at least the most celebrated one in the past two centuries. In fact, the first line of the verse VI.24.47 (*Gītā* II.47)—*karmaṇy evādhikāras te mā phaleṣu kadācana*—has often been celebrated as the central statement of the text. Sibaji Bandyopadhyay has meticulously analysed the biography of this particular verse to show how its meaning changed over time with shifting trends in translation and interpretation.[305] The way Cherniak translated the verse, as given earlier, is typical of the present trend in translating it, with *karman* translated as 'action', *adhikāra* translated as 'right', and *mā* translated as a negative particle. However, Bandyopadhyay has shown that this standardized translation of the verse was a product of a process to reconstruct this verse as a national motto in the past two centuries.

In the pre-modern commentaries on the *Gītā*, the verse II.47 was hardly given any special importance. However, the situation started to change when the *Gītā* reached Europe with Charles Wilkins's English translation published in 1785. Several other translations, appropriations, interpretations, and commentaries followed. Bandyopadhyay identifies three 'moments' in the Occidental reception of the *Gītā*: the 'moment of jubilation' (starting with Warren Hastings, the governor general of India, who was delighted to find in the text translated by Wilkins many parallels with Christian maxims and values), 'moment of ridicule' (typically represented by Franz Lorinser's German translation of 1869, which tried to represent the *Gītā* as a paltry and pale duplicate of the *New Testament*), and the 'moment of progressivist communion' (best exemplified by J.N. Farquhar's *Gītā and Gospel* published in 1903, which argued that the *Gītā* anticipated the richness of the spirituality which culminated in the Gospel).[306] However, alongside these continuous comparisons with the Bible was a process privileging the doctrine of *niṣkāma karman* propagated in II.47. While Śaṅkara, the great master of Vedāntic monism (*advaitavāda*), dismissed this verse (as well as many others such as II.18, II.31, II.33, IV.15) as void of material value as regards the *Gītā*'s kernel message,[307] Johann Gottfried von Herder's *Zersteute Blätter* (1792) included the verse among the samples representing the philosophy of the *Gītā* (other verses chosen were II.11–15, II.63, II.48, III.10–16, IV.19–24).[308] Wilhelm von Humboldt, who considered the *Gītā* as the 'only real philosophical poem of all known literatures', delineated in 1825–1826 its two leading thoughts as the distinction of mind and body (probably a reference to the distinction between the perishable *deha* and the imperishable *dehin*, or *kṣetra* and *kṣetrajña*) and the performance of duty without the least regard to its consequences.[309] In 1849, Henry David Thoreau included II.47 among the collage of verses representing the *Gītā*'s ideal of the 'forsaking of *karman*'.[310] The verse gained the status of an independent proverb in George Lukacs's essay 'On Poverty of Spirit: A Conversation and a Letter': 'Why should Goodness care about and concern itself with consequences? "Our duty is to do the work, not to try win its fruits", states a Hindu saying'.[311] William Quan Judge, the Theosophist leader writing in 1887–1888, also located the principal message of the *Gītā* in its chapter II.[312] On the other hand, Hegel's vehement dismissal of the philosophy of the *Bhagavad Gītā* was also based on his argument—clearly assuming II.47 as representative of the central argument of the text—that the fruit is inseparable from the performance of any act, and the indifference towards success is a marker of senselessness and stupidity in the performance.[313]

Following the pattern of the *Gītā*'s Occidental reception, modern Indian scholars often highlighted the doctrine propounded in II.47. Bankim Chandra Chattopadhyay considered it as the '*mahāvākya*' (great sentence) of the *Gītā*, without any parallel in the world.[314] Aurobindo Ghosh, the firebrand ideologue of extremist nationalism in Bengal, declared in his famous speech at Uttarpara on 30 May 1909 that the Lord demanded his devotees to do work for him without the demand for fruit, and this line contained the central truth of the Hindu religion.[315] Verse II.47 was celebrated as the central one of the *Gītā* by Bal Gangadhar Tilak, the popular extremist leader of Maharashtra.[316] His contemporary in Punjab, Lala Lajpat Rai, also treated II.47 as the 'master-key' for understanding the *Gītā*.[317] The same verse, so much appropriated by the extremist and revolutionary terrorist leadership, as an inspiration for selfless political violence, also—with an ingenious alteration—had become foundational to Gandhi's philosophy of non-violence.[318] Gradually, through a process of 'abbreviation', the verse not only came to be established as the most representative of the *Gītā*'s teaching (and the *Gītā* as the stand-alone scripture of Vedāntic philosophy, at the cost of Bādarāyaṇa's *Brahmasūtra*) but is now quoted often as a readily available one-liner—divorced from its original context—for different purposes, sometimes leading to extremely problematic implications.

Bandyopadhya thinks that this is a result of certain developments in the history of the translation of the verse. All premodern commentators, except Rāmānuja, had considered the particle *mā* in the first line of the verse as prohibitive rather than negative.[319] Even in modern times, its prohibitive sense has been pointed out in the translation of Judge[320] or in the teachings of the Bengali saint Ramakrishna Paramahansa.[321] However, gradually, the translation of *mā* in the verse as a negative particle got standardized. Similarly, the increasing tendency to standardize the translation of the word '*adhikāra*' in the verse with the liberal legal term 'right' does not have unequivocal support from either the premodern tradition or the initial translations.[322] Finally, whether *karman* here can be easily translated by the generic 'action' or should be understood in its traditional sense of Vedic ritual action is also questionable.[323]

While Bandyopadhyay painstakingly shows the history of the construction of *Gītā* II.47 as a national motto, through a standardized translation, we should ponder over a few aspects of his criticism. The *mā* in the line, indeed, makes better sense as a prohibitive particle than as a negative one. The translation of the word '*adhikāra*' is also open ended, and 'right' is not necessarily the best option. However, the question that is more fundamental is the exact meaning of *karman* in the *Gītā*, for settling that is necessary not only for translating this particular verse but also for understanding the idea of *karmayoga* in general. The word '*karman*' has several meanings in the Indic tradition. In the Mīmāṃsā philosophy propounded by Jaimini, it indeed signifies Vedic ritual action, and the word is charged with the same sense in the *dharmaśāstra* texts. Many Vedāntic interpreters—especially Śaṅkara—assumed the same sense for *karman* in the *Gītā*. The tradition had such a stronghold on many subsequent thinkers that the Dalit leader B.R. Ambedkar recognized no difference between the *karmayoga* in Jaimini's *Pūrva-Mīmāṃsā* and in the *Bhagavad Gītā*.[324] The difference between the generic idea of 'action' and this limited sense of *karman* is instrumental in Max Weber's paradoxical statement that the originality of the *Bhagavad Gītā* lies in conceptualizing '*karma*-free action'.[325]

However, looking at the word '*karman*' in the *Bhagavad Gītā* in this limited sense actually ignores the context. The strongest advocate of this idea, after all, has been Śaṅkara, a great champion of *jñānayoga* and renunciation. Since the *Gītā*, alongside the Upaniṣads and Bādarāyaṇa's

Brahmasūtra, formed the sacred triad of Vedāntic philosophy, Śaṅkara could not ignore the text. Yet, Kṛṣṇa's emphatic insistence on the mode of activity (*pravṛtti*) was almost an antithesis to Śaṅkara's fascination with renunciation (*nivṛtti*) which was to him a necessary condition for a sojourn into the path of knowledge (*jñānayoga*). Kṛṣṇa, of course, saw no major contradiction between the performance of *karman* and attainment of knowledge. But Śaṅkara and his followers did not show the same catholicity. Overlooking the traditional tripartite division of *karman* in the three categories of *nitya* (obligatory), *naimittika* (occasional), and *kāmya* (desiderative), Śaṅkara ended up with a formulation that any *karman* is a *kāmya karman*. Therefore, *niṣkāma karman* is an oxymoron, because to become *niṣkāma*, one must give up *karman* itself. *Karman* and *jñāna* cannot be fused together, because it is the *sannyāsin* (renunciant) alone, and not the *karmayogin*, who is entitled to *jñāna*.[326] Śaṅkara's follower Sureśvara viewed the relationship between *jñāna* and *karman* like the one between the sun and darkness or between lion and goat. To substantiate this hypothesis with the *Gītā*, Śaṅkara had to resort to an interpretation of the text which may very legitimately be considered distorted. He dismissed the verses not suiting his project, including II.47, as inessential, argued that the verses extolling *karmayoga* are actually a simpler recipe for those who are not fit for *jñānayoga*, and understood *karman* in its limited sense of the performance of Vedic rituals with desire. In this bid, he overstretches the significance of the *eva* in the first line of II.47 to mean 'you have no *adhikāra* for *jñāna*, therefore your *adhikāra* is *karman* alone'.[327] Śaṅkara's irritation has been the highest with the verse IV.18 of the *Gītā* (*Mahābhārata* VI.26.18) that considers a person who can view *karman* and non-*karman* as the same as wise:

> *karmaṇy akarma yaḥ paśyed akarmaṇi ca karma yaḥ/*
> *sa buddhimān manuṣyeṣu sa yuktaḥ kṛtsna karmakṛt.*[328]

While commenting upon this verse, Śaṅkara reprimands the Lord himself for mystifying his own doctrine by unnecessarily confounding all by an 'ambiguous circumlocution' and declares that the word '*buddhimān*' (wise/intelligent) here should be read as a mocking euphemism for fool!

Therefore, Śaṅkara does not seem to be the most reliable interpreter of the *Gītā*, nor is his interpretation the only traditional way of looking at the text. Rāmānuja, the master of Vedāntic Qualified Monism (*viśiṣṭādvaitavāda*) and a great critic of Śaṅkara, considered *karmayoga* a stepping stone—rather than antagonistic—to *jñānayoga*. However, being also a believer in the supremacy of *jñāna*, he also looked at *karman* in its limited sense and equated the negation of *karman* with *jñāna*.[329]

The word '*karman*' has various other implications in traditional literature than the one propounded by Mīmāṃsā, the *Dharmaśāstras*, Śaṅkara, and Rāmānuja. For instance, in the Vaiśeṣika philosophy propounded by Kaṇāda, it denotes physical phenomena of five kinds.[330] The word '*kamma*', in Buddhist philosophy, implies a personal agency.[331] Therefore, to locate the *karman* of the *Bhagavad Gītā* we have to look at the use of the word in Upaniṣadic literature with which the *Gītā* shares its world-view, in the *Mahābhārata* in general, and in other verses of the *Gītā*.

The word '*karman*' has been used in the Upaniṣads both in the limited sense of Vedic rituals (since the Upaniṣads, the *jñānakāṇḍa* of Vedic literature, is contrasted with the *Saṃhitā* and *Brāhmaṇa*—the ritual sections—known as the *karmakāṇḍa*) as well as in the generic sense of 'action'. The latter seems to be the sense when the BU says that one becomes virtuous by virtuous *karman* and bad by bad *karman*.[332] In the *Mahābhārata*, *karman* has the implication of the performance of Vedic rituals mainly in the later didactic sections associated with the *Dharmaśāstra* world-view, such as in the 'Sāntiparvan'.[333] However, in the older narrative sections, it has the sense of action in general. Almost approaching the Buddhist *kamma*, *karman* has been described as human effort.[334] Draupadī declared *karman* simply as what should be done (*kartavyaṃ tv eva karma*).[335]

The *Gītā* seems to have perceived *karman* in a similar way. We have shown earlier how the *Gītā* dismissed the performance of ritual action as an act full of desire. Further, there are verses—of course the ones dismissed by Śaṅkara as inessential—which clearly testify that Kṛṣṇa understood *karman* as action in general:

na hi kaś cit kṣaṇam api jātu tiṣṭhaty akarmakṛt/
kāryate hy avaśaḥ karma sarvaḥ prakṛtijair guṇaiḥ//
karmendriyāṇi saṃyamya ya āste manasā smaran/
indriyārthān vimūḍhātmā mithyācāraḥ sa ucyate.

(Indeed, no one ever remains even for a moment without performing actions, for everyone is compelled to act by modes of nature. Whoever sits curbing his powers of action but dwelling in his mind on sense objects is fooling himself and is said to be of false conduct.)[336]

The statement that one cannot spend a single moment without *karman* definitely uses the word in the sense of 'action' in general. The *mithyācāras* (liars) speaking of the impossible renunciation of *karman* here are possibly the Jainas or proto-Jainas who advocated *nivṛtti*. But it is doubtful if Kṛṣṇa would have spoken more favourably of Śaṅkara had he been familiar with his doctrine. What his reply to Śaṅkara's dismissal of *karman* could have been is also illustrated in the *Gītā* in another verse discarded by Śaṅkara:

niyataṃ kuru karma tvaṃ karma jyāyo hy akarmaṇaḥ/
śarīrayātrāpi ca tena prasiddhyed akarmaṇaḥ.

(Perform the usual actions, for action is better than inaction; without action, your body can't even be kept alive.)[337]

Therefore, Bankim or Tilak, even though they were constructing a national motto, were not divorced from the tradition when they had extended the meaning of *karman* into the generic 'action'. The doctrine of *niṣkāma karman* is basically the performance of action in general without the outcome being the primary concern (the *mā* being understood as prohibitive), as explained in the subsequent verse, *Gītā* II.48, quoted earlier, where the same attitude is solicited for success and failure (*siddhyasiddho samo bhūtvā*). That is how Ramakrishna Paramahansa had understood the essence of these two verses:

Gītā dictates you to dispassionately perform *karma*... It asks you not to crave for the fruits of *karma*."[338]

In this doctrine, Kṛṣṇa sought a unique solution of the basic problem of human existence—the choice between action and non-action. Scholars such as Sukumar Sen and Peter Della Santana conceive the *Gītā*'s doctrine of *karman* as directed against the Śramaṇa doctrine of non-action.[339] However, the doctrine is equally or more directed against the Vedic and Mīmāṃsā doctrine of ritual action for material benefit. The point of emphasis is complete lack of desire for the fruits of the action and complete even-mindedness towards success and failure. The ideal actor in the *Gītā* is the *sthitaprajña* (a man of steady wisdom) who applies *buddhiyoga*. As Malinar points out, the term '*buddhi*' seems to have been used in its Sāṃkhya sense, as the foremost and first of the created cognitive faculties, which helps the individual to distinguish and discriminate.[340] With this faculty, a person can discriminate between the action and desire for its fruits and therefore leave the fruits behind.[341] In this way, he can become a *sthitaprajña* who can go beyond all desires:

prajahāti yadā kāmān sarvān pārtha manogatān/
ātmany ev ātmanā tuṣṭaḥ sthitaprajñas tadocyate//
duḥkheṣv anudvignamanā sukheṣu vigataspṛhaḥ/
vītarāgabhayakrodhaḥ sthitadhīr munir ucyate//
yaḥ sarvatrān abhisnehas tat tat prāpya śubhāśubhaṃ/
nābhinandati na dveṣṭi tasyā prajñā pratiṣṭhitā//
yadā saṃharate cāyaṃ kūrmo'ngān iva sarvaśaḥ/
indriȳan indriyārthebhyas tasyā prajñā pratiṣṭhitā//.

(When a man discards all desires from his mind, Pārtha, and by his own effort becomes content within himself, then he is called a man of steady wisdom. He whose mind is unperturbed in times of sorrow, who has lost the craving for pleasures, and who is rid of passion, fear and anger, is called a sage of steadied thought. His wisdom is secure who is free of any affections and neither rejoices nor recoils on obtaining anything good or bad. When he completely withdraws his senses from the sense objects like a tortoise withdrawing its limbs then his wisdom is secure.)[342]

Control of desire and attachment, control over the senses, is therefore what characterizes a man of steadied wisdom. All the feelings of heat and cold, pleasure and pain, come from the sense objects coming in contact with the material world. Therefore, indifference to them is to be cultivated.[343] Otherwise sense objects create attachment, from attachment is created desire, and from desire anger. From anger comes confusion (*sammohaḥ*). Confusion disturbs the memory (*smṛtivibhramaḥ*). When memory fails, so does understanding (*buddhināśaḥ*). Without understanding, one perishes.[344] On the other hand, a man attains peace by abandoning all desires and acting without craving, selfishness, and ego (*ahaṃkāraḥ*).[345] In serenity (*prasāde*), all sorrows come to an end (*sarvaduḥkhānāṃ hāniḥ*). This is the state of Brahman (*brāhmī sthiti*). Remaining in it even at the time of death, one attains the *nirvāṇa* that is Brahman (*brahmanirvāṇam*).[346]

There is nothing exclusive about this teaching, and the passages could have been transmitted easily as spoken by the Buddha rather than by Kṛṣṇa. When the Buddha would try to find out the cause and solution of human suffering, he would also find the answer in desire. It was in overcoming desire and attachment that the secret of the end of all sorrows would be found by him. And that state would be the state of *nirvāṇa*. In the *Majjhima Nikāya*, the Buddha draws a direct sequence from destruction of craving to dispassion to cessation and to *nibbāna*.[347] In the *Samyutta Nikāya*, he declares:

> Being disenchanted, he becomes dispassionate. Through dispassion he is freed.[348]

Naturally, many scholars tried to understand this concept of *brahmanirvāṇa* in the light of Buddhism. Zaehner views it as an adoption of Buddhist ideal.[349] Van Buitenen views it as a reply to the Buddhists by declaring that even by taking a Brahmanistic stance in life a person can attain the serenity which the Buddhists seek by not being socially active.[350] However, there is hardly any assertion of Brahmanism in the passage. Rather, it shares a common premise with Buddhism that is the criticism of the materialistic ritualism of Vedic Brahmanism. However, outright adoption from Buddhism is also difficult to accept, since the general discussion is within an Upaniṣadic structure. The concept of the soul (*ātman/jivātman*) had already been introduced. Now comes the concept of the *Brahman/paramātman* (the Supreme Soul). With this concept, the idea of the individual and personal self becomes cosmic, for every individual soul is nothing but a fraction of the Supreme Soul. They are separated by the material bodies. However, the ultimate liberation lies in the soul being dissolved in the Absolute. This concept is very much different from the

Buddhist world-view where no singular eternal absolute, and hence no changeless immortal soul, is acknowledged. Thus, to the Buddha, liberation from the cycle of transmigration was attainable through individual discipline and control but not through the process of union with an all-encompassing singular existence. S. Dasgupta rejects any direct connection of the concept with Buddhism.[351] It seems to us that, again, Kṛṣṇa and the Buddha derived much of their thought from a common intellectual pool which was critiquing Vedic ritualism. Therefore, the teachings of the two masters have significant similarities as well as significant discrepancies. Both Kṛṣṇa and the Buddha sought the way of liberation (*nirvāṇa*) from the cycle of transmigration (which both accepted). Yet, to Kṛṣṇa, who believed in the Upaniṣadic *Brahman*, what transmigrated was itself changeless and eternal, a part of the Absolute, which could dissolve in its original source the moment it becomes aware of its true nature. The mental discipline Kṛṣṇa recommends is just a vehicle for preparing one for such realization. Thus, it was a path of union (*yoga*), and liberation was the same with the attainment of the state of *Brahman* (*brahmanirvāṇa*). The ideas seem neither a response to nor a derivative of Buddhism. Rather, it is a presentation of the Upaniṣadic philosophy to bring it in tune with a life of action. Thus, when the Buddha sought to challenge the Upaniṣadic knowledge system and point out that there was nothing permanent and changeless in a transient world, and liberation (*nirvāṇa*) was all about individual effort and discipline, rather than a Union with any all-encompassing Absolute, it was a response to Kṛṣṇa's doctrine as well.

However, Kṛṣṇa's doctrine stands out for its approach to action. The philosophy discussed so far does not differ much from the philosophy of the Upaniṣads. If liberation is the goal and eradication of desire the means, then renouncing seems a better option than an active social life. Ritual action for the sake of heaven has been already dismissed. What is then the need to act socially? The precise question was raised by Arjuna also, in the beginning of the *Gītā*'s third chapter:

jyāyasī cet karmanas te matā buddhir janārdana/
tat kiṃ karmaṇi ghore māṃ niyojayasi keśava//

(Janārdana, if you think that understanding is more important than action, then why are you urging me to this dreadful deed, Keśava?)[352]

Here Kṛṣṇa came up with an exclusive idea. Using the Sāṃkhya concept of *prakṛti*, he dismissed renunciation and non-action as impossibility. No one actually could remain inactive even for a moment, for everyone was compelled to act by the modes (*guṇah*) of the nature (*prakṛti*). Whoever sits curbing his powers of action but dwelling in his mind on sense objects was fooling himself and was said to be of false conduct. Since non-action was impossible, a person excelled by curbing his senses yet remaining active, by acting without attachment. Action had to be performed, for action was mandatory even to keep the body alive.[353]

However, action had to be performed without desire and therefore not for personal gain. Rather, it was to be performed for maintaining the world (*lokasaṃgraha*).[354] In fact, the whole cosmic order was a collection of everybody performing his duty. For the sake of that order, one must perform his duty. Here, we listen to the same person who stated in the 'Udyogaparvan' that action was the highest principle, for it was through action that all the deities became deities. It was for the sake of action that the sun rose and clouds showered and so on. The same principle was elaborated here in a sacrificial metaphor. After discarding ritual sacrifice, Kṛṣṇa interpreted the Cosmic Order as the real sacrifice. Everybody was nourished and sustained on the earth by the Cosmic Order. Whoever enjoyed these Cosmic and natural gifts, but gave nothing in return, was just a thief.[355]

Everyone, thus, must perform the stipulated action and play his part in this Cosmic Sacrifice which had Brahman as its basis.[356] Therefore, performing the action without attachment was the only way to attain the Supreme Self.[357] Kṛṣṇa himself, the *sthitaprajña* teacher, without any desire in the three worlds, performed his duties constantly, because he had to set an example for other ordinary men.[358] Therefore, despite his vigorous criticism of Vedic ritualism, Kṛṣṇa was vigorously opposed to renunciation. He would definitely write off extreme renunciation, such as in Jainism, as false conduct and would hardly consider the moderate renunciation of the Buddhist middle path necessary.

The concept was clear that action was inevitable, so it was better to perform one's duties for the sake of the Cosmic Order. But how did one understand what role he was expected to perform for the Cosmic Order? Kṛṣṇa replied again with a reference to his concept of *svadharma*:

> *śreyān svadharmo viguṇaḥ paradharmāt svanuṣṭhitāt/*
> *svadharme nidhanaṃ śreyaḥ paradharmo bhayāvahaḥ.*
>
> (One's own duty, even if done imperfectly, is better than another's, even if done well. The duty of others is fraught with danger; better to die while fulfilling one's own.)[359]

This verse is often quoted as a staunch espousal of the caste system. However, there is nothing in this verse to suggest that the *svadharma-paradharma* paradigm is based on caste. The basis of *svadharma* is, in fact, not yet totally disclosed. But an indication is there that deeds are performed actually by the modes of nature.[360] Therefore, it is more plausible to think that *svadharma* of a person is defined not by one's birth but by the balance of the three *guṇas* of nature in a person.

We will return to Kṛṣṇa's definition of *svadhrma*. But before that, we have to look at an interesting aspect of his teaching. That one's duty had to be given the maximum importance was something Kṛṣṇa believed in from his adolescent days. It was on the basis of this idea that he had encouraged the cowherds to pay for their cattle and countryside, rather than for a sacrifice to Indra. However, formulating this whole concept in the metaphor of a Cosmic Sacrifice was something novel. And Kṛṣṇa does not seem to be the innovator of this novelty. Rather, if we look at the CU, we will find out that it was one of the concepts that Ghora Āṅgirasa had taught to the young Kṛṣṇa Devakīputra:

> When a man is hungry, thirsty, and without pleasures—that is his sacrificial consecration, and when he eats, drinks, and enjoys pleasures—by that he performs the preparatory rites; when he laughs, feasts, and has sex—by that he sings the chants and performs the recitations; austerity (*tapaḥ*), generosity (*dānam*), integrity (*ārjabam*), non-injury (*ahiṃsā*), and truthfulness (*satyavacanam*)—these are his gifts to the priests.[361]

Kṛṣṇa learnt from his teacher that every action in human life could be for the sake of an eternal sacrifice, and real sacrifice lay in austerity, generosity, integrity, non-injury, and truthfulness and not in rituals. He developed the teaching in a coherent doctrine of desireless action (*niṣkāma karman*) which dealt with both the problems of the misery created by desire and the futility of non-action.

Therefore, overcoming desire and attachment was absolutely essential in this concept. Otherwise desire (*kāma*), which could also be transformed into anger (*krodha*), born of the passionate mode (*rajoguṇasamudbhavaḥ*), could overshadow all knowledge.[362] Kṛṣṇa declares:

> *indriyāṇi parāṇy āhur indriyebhyaḥ paraṃ manaḥ/*
> *manasas tu parā buddhir yo buddheḥ paratas tu saḥ//*
>
> (They say the senses are supreme; but higher than the senses is the mind, higher than the mind is understanding, and higher than understanding is 'he'.)[363]

Here, the word 'he' (*saḥ*) is interesting. The passage has parallels in the KU:

> Higher than the senses (indriyebhyaḥ) are their objects (arthāḥ);
> Higher than the sense objects is the mind (manaḥ);
> Higher than mind is the intellect (buddhiḥ);
> Higher than intellect is the immense self (ātmā mahān);
>
> Higher than the immense self is the unmanifest (*avyakta*);
> Higher than the unmanifest is the person (*puruṣa*);
> Higher than the person there's nothing at all.
> That is the goal, that's the highest state.[364]

If the *Gītā* was expressing the same sentiment, then *saḥ* should mean the Self. However, Malinar notes that the location of the passage is within the description of the harmful effect of desire. So, *saḥ* can also stand for desire (*kāma*). Then the significance of the passage would be that desire is powerful enough to overshadow even the highest cognitive faculty—*buddhi*.[365]

It seems that the author of the *Gītā* deliberately used the vague '*saḥ*', so that both the meanings remain possible. The passage may mean that a desireless self can be secure with complete possession of all its faculties starting from *buddhi* up to the senses. But the scenario can be the opposite for a soul full of desire, in which case desire will take possession of all the faculties. Desire is therefore identified as the main enemy in the battle of human life. The metaphorical battle scene is made clear for once by Kṛṣṇa in his encouragement to Arjuna for fighting, by naming the enemy to be slaughtered—'*jahi śatruṃ mahāvāho kāmarūpaṃ durāsadaṃ*' (slay the formidable foe, mighty-armed one, in the form of desire)[366]—a battle cry to which the non-violent Buddha would have been the first one to respond.

Therefore, the first three chapters of the *Gītā* doctrine have given us a wholesome picture of Kṛṣṇa's philosophy, except a clarification of his concept of *svadharma*. However, what Kṛṣṇa spoke so far was still as a human teacher, like the one speaking in the 'Udyogparvan'. A few passages trying to assert his divinity can be easily identified as interpolations.[367] The fourth chapter, however, opens with a shock, with Kṛṣṇa claiming to be the founder of a lineage of Yoga teachers:

imaṃ vivasvate yogaṃ proktavān aham avyayam/
vivasvān manave prāho manur ikṣvākave' bravīt//
evaṃ paramparāprāptam imaṃ rājarṣayo viduḥ/
sa kāleneha mahatā yogo naṣṭaḥ parantapa.

(I taught this eternal Yoga to Vivasvat, Vivasvat taught it to Manu, and Manu taught it to Ikṣvāku. So the royal sages knew it as passed one to another; but in the long course of time it was lost to the world, enemy-scorcher.)[368]

Arjuna, till then quite unaware of Kṛṣṇa's divinity, wondered how Kṛṣṇa could be the teacher of Vivasvat who was born long back. In his reply, Kṛṣṇa introduced a new set of theories:

bahuni me vyātītāni janmāni tava cārjuna/
tāny ahaṃ veda sarvāṇi na tvaṃ bettha parantapa//
ajo' pi sannavyay ātmā bhūtānām īśvaro' pi san/
prakṛtim svam adhiṣṭhāya saṃbhavāmy ātmamayayā//
yadā yadā hi dharmasya glānir bhavati bhārata/
abhyutthānam adharmasya tad ātmānaṃ sṛjāmy aham//

paritrāṇāya sadhūnam vināśāya ca duṣkṛtām/
dharmasaṃsthāpanārthāya saṃbhavāmi yuge yuge.

(I have had many births, Arjuna, and so have you. I know them all, scorcher of enemies, but you don't. Despite being unborn and essentially imperishable, despite being the lord of all beings, I resort to my phenomenal nature and come into being through my creative power. I send myself forth whenever righteousness declines and unrighteousness is on the rise, Bhārata; age after age I come into being to protect the virtuos, destroy the wicked, and reestablish righteousness.)[369]

The passage is a very important one and also possibly the most popular of the *Gītā* passages. It introduces two important concepts—reincarnation and Kṛṣṇa's divinity—and combines them in a third concept of divine reincarnation. The doctrine of reincarnation had already been implicated by the doctrine of the transmigration of the imperishable soul. Since the soul cannot be destroyed, it will continue to take new forms till it reaches the condition needed for liberation and dissolves in the *Brahman*. However, what about a person like Kṛṣṇa who possessed complete knowledge and should be liberated rather than being born again and again? What kind of divinity did Kṛṣṇa claim here?

Our suggestion would be that Kṛṣṇa did not claim any supernatural divinity yet but one consistent with what he taught so far. He had taught how a person could be equated with *Brahman* (*brāhmī sthiti*) by cultivation of desireless action and control over all the senses. With a perfect knowledge of the things, Kṛṣṇa had to be such a person. So he was inseparable with the *Brahman*, as every soul potentially was. Reaching that potential, Kṛṣṇa now knew the full secret of his previous births, which Arjuna did not. If such a soul, with full knowledge of its true nature, was born again, that was nothing but a *māyā*, since the soul—being inseparable with *Brahman*—was in total control of the *prakṛti*. Why should that soul be born again? For the sake of the Cosmic Order, for preservation of the virtuous, destruction of the wicked, and establishment of righteousness. This was a claim not exclusive to Kṛṣṇa but the source of legitimacy for several prophets. It is the concept behind the 547 previous births of the Buddha, behind God sacrificing his only child for the sake of the mankind, behind the Bodhisattvas delaying their *nirvāṇa* for rescuing other people, and so on. Thus the Buddha declares in the *Saddharmapuṇḍarīka* (XV.7–9):

> Repeatedly am I born in the world of the living ... I see how the creatures are afflicted ... i will reveal to them the true law.[370]

Claiming to be identical with the original Yoga teacher, Kṛṣṇa here gave his teaching a scriptural value, the status of a divine revealation. The reason for what the Vedic poets claimed to be mere seers, the Ten Commandments were revealed to Moses rather than being ordained by him, or the Quran was understood as not a composition of Muhammad but a message sent through him, the *Gītā* now claimed to be an eternal Yoga teaching rather than being what the individual named Vāsudeva Kṛṣṇa taught.

Radhakrishnan explains Kṛṣṇa's use of the first person here by applying the *Vedānta Sūtra* (I.1.30) as an example, which explains the Vedic passage where Indra declares himself to be *Brahman* on the hypothesis that he is only referring to the philosophical truth that *ātman* in man is one with Supreme Brahman. The *Gītā* teaches that an individual freed from passion and fear, and purified by the fire of wisdom, attains the state of God. Kṛṣṇa of the *Gītā* stands for the Infinite in the finite, the God in man, concealed within the folds of flesh and the powers of sense.[371] Therefore, Kṛṣṇa did not claim that status exclusively for himself but for anybody attaining the state:

> *vītarāgabhayakrodhā man mayā mām upāśritāḥ/*
> *bahavo jñanatapasā pūta mad bhāvam āgatāḥ//*
>
> (Many have been rid of passion, fear and anger and, absorbed in me, have taken refuge in me, purified by the austerity of their knowledge; and these have attained my state of being.)[372]

Moreover, this way of attaining divinity had been left totally unsectarian, as Kṛṣṇa declared:

> *ye yathā māṃ prapadyante tāṃs tathaiva bhajāmy aham/*
> *mama vartmānuvartante manuṣyāḥ pārtha sarvaśaḥ//*
>
> (As men approach me, so do I accept them; and there are always men who follow my path, Pārtha.)[373]

Thus, everybody could reach the Supreme Being in his own way, and that own way had to be understood in terms of his *svadharma*. Here, Kṛṣṇa now explained his idea of the *varṇa* system as divinely ordained (*mayā sṛṣṭam*) in accordance with their qualities and actions (*guṇaka rmavibhāgaśaḥ*). The term '*guṇa*' is used in the *Gītā* specifically in the sense of the modes of *prakṛti*. Therefore, Kṛṣṇa understood the *varṇa* system as to be based on the balance of these modes and the natural abilities in a person. Matilal points out how this concept of Kṛṣṇa matched that of Yudhiṣṭhira who gave a fuller exposition of the doctrine in the 'Āraṇyakaparvan'. Yudhiṣṭhira declared that truthfulness, generosity, ability to forgive, goodness, kindness, self-control, and compassion together constituted a *brāhmaṇa*. If a *śūdra* was characterized by all these virtues, he was to be defined as a *brāhmaṇa*, and if a *brāhmaṇa* lacked them, then he was to be regarded as a *śūdra*. Since people copulated through sexual urge and produced children, birth was not a good criterion for these matters. Therefore, the old sages depended upon good conduct as the indicator of a better person. Even one who was a *brāhmaṇa* by birth would be a *śūdra* through poor and despicable conduct.[374] The same concept is espoused in the CU where the sage Haridrumata Gautama accepts Satyakāma Jābāla, the son of a public woman, as a *brāhmaṇa* because of his truthfulness.[375] The Buddha's understanding of *varṇa* did not differ much from it. Kṛṣṇa would again return to this issue while concluding his arguments in the eighteenth chapter, and we will look into the matter further.

Explaining his idea of *varṇa*, Kṛṣṇa returned to an elaboration of his doctrine of desireless action and how all the actions melted away when a person was completely non-attached and free. All his acts being only for the sake of the Cosmic Sacrifice, the act of offering, the oblation, the fire, and the sacrifice all became indistinguishable in the one *Brahman*.[376] This sacrifice was not a ritual, but action, which could be anything—austerity, study, knowledge, and so on.[377] However, Kṛṣṇa did not hide his preference for the sacrifice of knowledge over others.[378]

Since Kṛṣṇa celebrated both knowledge and action in the first four chapters, Arjuna became curious about their relative status in the beginning of the fifth.[379] In his reply, Kṛṣṇa reasserted his support for action against non-action, but clarified that *sāṃkhya* (knowledge) and *yoga* (action) were not essentially different but led to the same state.[380] That ultimate state was when one became *sarvabhūtātmabhūtātmā*.[381] Garbe translates the phrase as a state when one's self has become the self of all beings.[382] Van Buitenen takes it as an identification of one's own self with the selves of all creatures.[383] Schreiner takes it as a state when the person is at once himself and all creatures.[384] Actually, it seems to be the same state when the *yogin* identifies himself with the *Brahman*. The MU, for instance, understands the Cosmic Creator, *Brahman*, as *sarvabhūtāntarā tman*.[385] Being identical with the Supreme Soul, he understood the existence of the same soul everywhere.

Therefore, the *yogin* viewed every being as the same:

> *vidyāvinayasampanne brāhmaṇe gavi hastini/*
> *śuni caiva śvapāke ca paṇḍitaḥ samadarśanaḥ//*
>
> (The wise can see the equivalence between a learned and cultured Brahmin, a cow, an elephant, a dog, and an eater of dogs.)[386]

Such a person did not rejoice in coming across something pleasant nor did he become dismayed when coming across something unpleasant.[387]

He saw himself present in all beings and all beings present in himself (*sarvabhūtastham ātmānaṃ sarvabhūtani cātmani*).[388] He remained steadfast in cold and heat, joy and sorrow, honour and dishonour. His attitude was to be the same towards a clod of earth, stones, or gold. His mental attitude was to be the same towards the friends, allies, foes, and relatives, towards the indifferent, the impartial, and the hateful, and towards good and evil men.[389] This complete equality of vision had also been celebrated in the ĪU:

> When a man sees all beings within his very self, and his self within all beings,
> It will not seek to hide from him.
>
> When in the self of a discerning man, his very self has become all beings,
> What bewilderment, what sorrow can there be, regarding the self of him who sees this oneness.[390]

Similarly says the Gītā:

ātmaupamyena sarvatra samaṃ paśyati yo'rjuna/
sukhaṃ vā yadi vā duhkhaṃ sa yogī paramo mata.

(He who by analogy with his own self sees the same thing everywhere, in joy or in sorrow, is reckoned to be the best yogi.)[391]

This was the state when a person became *Brahman* and attained the state of *brahmanirvāṇa*.[392] This state was comparable with the state of the Upaniṣadic sage who declared:

O Puṣan, sole seer!
Yama! Sun! Son of Prajāpati!
Spread out your rays!
Draw in your light!
I see your fairest form,
That person up there,
I am he![393]

This stage (*brahmasaṃsparśa*) was a state of boundless bliss.[394]

As we have already discussed the general premises shared by Kṛṣṇa and the Buddha, and decided that the latter was possibly countering the ideas of the former, we must appreciate why it was essential for the Buddha to challenge the philosophical foundation of Kṛṣṇa's teaching. Both the masters emphasized on non-attachment and control over senses and desire. The result, for both, was liberation from the suffering caused by the senses and attaining the state of *nirvāṇa*. Kṛṣṇa's *nirvāṇa*, however, was attaining of the *Brahman*, an idea the Buddha denied. While the Buddha advocated a middle path (*majjhima panthā*) as the means, Kṛṣṇa also spoke of moderation in food and sport, sleeping and waking, as the means of the *yoga* that ended suffering (*duḥkhahā*).[395] However, what differentiated the two was Kṛṣṇa's emphasis on desireless action and the Buddha's preference for monastic life. After all, monasticism would be pointless if active life could be desireless and an integral part of a cosmic order which was the manifestation of a singular eternal self.

Therefore, when the Buddha preached, he had to face these doctrines. The 'Alagaddupama Sutta' of the *Majjhima Nikāya* contains one such instance when the Buddha faced the monk Arittha who claimed that there was nothing wrong in engaging in sensual activities, as long as one remained non-attached. The Buddha declared it impossible to simultaneously enjoy an activity and yet have no attachment to it.[396]

Kṛṣṇa did not consider it impossible. He thought:

> *uddhared ātman ātmānaṃ nātmanam avasādayet/*
> *ātmaiva hy ātmano bandhur ātmaiva ripur ātmanaḥ//*
> *bandhur ātmātmanas tasya yenātmaivātmana jitaḥ/*
> *anātmanas tu śatrutve vartet ātmaiva śatruvat.*
>
> (A man should elevate himself by himself and shouldn't degrade himself, for the self is the self's only friend, and the self is the self's only foe. He is his own friend who has conquered himself by himself; but that same self might behave like an enemy hostile to the one bereft of himself.)[397]

Similar words were uttered by the Buddha as well:

> Propel yourself by yourself, control yourself by yourself.[398]

Yet, what Kṛṣṇa emphasized on was that a person in control of himself could, and should, be active. What was necessary was detachment from the desire of results of the action rather than from action itself. Otherwise, renunciation was futile:

> *anāśritaḥ karmaphalaṃ kāryaṃ karma karoti yaḥ/*
> *sa saṃnyāsī ca yogī ca na niragnir na cākriyaḥ//*
>
> (He who disengaged from its fruits, performs the action that ought to be done, is a renouncer and a yogi; but he who has merely given up the sacred fire and ritual acts is not.)[399]

This was the teaching of Kṛṣṇa contained in the first six chapters of the *Gītā*, where Kṛṣṇa, emerging out of the Later Vedic intellectual milieu, was vehemently opposing desire-driven Vedic ritualism but was equally averse to the idea of renunciation as an alternative and had created an ingenious middle ground that asked a person to perform his duties as ordained by his nature and abilities in a self-controlled and desireless manner. The next six chapters suddenly take a turn towards a new direction and dimension. Kṛṣṇa himself appeared as the Supreme Lord, even above *Brahman*. Personal devotion to Kṛṣṇa, rather than to any action, was prescribed as the way of liberation. In the seventh chapter, Kṛṣṇa claimed to be the source of the whole universe as well as its dissolution. Everything was strung on him like sets of pearls in a thread (*sūtre maṇigaṇā iva*).[400] He claimed to be everything—the taste within waters, the light of the moon and the sun, the syllable '*om*' in all the Vedas, the sound in the space, the virility of men, the pure smell of the earth, the radiance of fire, the life in all beings, the austerity of the ascetics, the eternal seed of all beings, the understanding of the wise, the splendour of the splendid, the strength of the strong, and also the desire itself.[401] He gave a fuller exposition of this doctrine in chapter ten, where he explained everything brilliant as his manifestation (*vibhūti*). The climax came in the eleventh chapter where Kṛṣṇa showed Arjuna his Cosmic Form containing all deities in it. There, Kṛṣṇa revealed himself as the destructive Time (*lokakṣayakṛt kāla*) who already destroyed all the warriors and urged Arjuna to be nothing but an instrument (*nimittamātram*) of God's will.[402]

With Kṛṣṇa emerging as the Supreme Deity, the ways of worship were also changed. Now, even the one with desire (*arthārthī*) was considered a valid devotee, though the knowledgeable (*jñānī*) was still considered the best. Vedic practice was thus accepted, but as a way of temporary sojourn to heaven, not as a way to attain Kṛṣṇa.[403] However, all the deities being in Kṛṣṇa, even those faithfully worshipping other deities actually worshipped Kṛṣṇa in an immature way.[404] On the other hand, the right way to worship was devotion to Kṛṣṇa: offering a leaf, a flower, a fruit, water, anything.[405] The result of this devotion was attainment of Kṛṣṇa who was beyond *Brahman*.[406]

The lateness of these six chapters is quite apparent. Not only are they inconsistent with the teaching of the first six, but there are signs of lateness in themselves. In fact, Basham rightly praises the composer of these chapters as a 'literary genius' who could give the text an apparent unity despite his views being diametrically opposed to the teachings of the earlier layer.[407] No doubt, these chapters are the result of a Vaiṣṇavized revision of the text. As we have seen, the philosophy of Kṛṣṇa used certain Sāṃkhya doctrine, but not in its classical form. Kṛṣṇa used the concept of *puruṣa* and *prakṛti*, but superimposed a Vedāntic *Brahman* on them, which would not be accepted when the Sāṃkhya philosophy would be organized as a separate school by Kapila. The first six chapters of the *Gītā*, therefore, seem to be pre-Kapila. But, chapter ten is certainly not, since it describes Kṛṣṇa as Kapila among the *siddhas*.[408] The main actors of this revision can be identified as the Bhārgavas, since three of them appear as Kṛṣṇa's manifestations—Bhṛgu among the great sages,[409] Uśanas among the poets,[410] and possibly Jāmadagnya Rāma among the weapon wielders.[411] Actually, chapter ten of the *Bhagavad Gītā* matches with the praise of Kṛṣṇa by Bhṛgu elsewhere in the *Mahābhārata* as well.[412]

The lateness of these passages is also indicated by the appearance of Brahmā and the Purāṇic conception of Cosmic Time in chapter eight.[413] Deshpande points out the internal contradiction in the text. Chapter twelve takes up directly from chapter ten, tenth verse, without any recognition of Kṛṣṇa's manifestation of the Cosmic Form.[414] Actually, the simple beginning of chapter twelve is an anti-climax after the dramatic events of chapter eleven.

Moreover, Kṛṣṇa's assertion that he had already killed all the warriors was not in conformity with the *Mahābhārata*. We have already discussed how Kṛṣṇa told Arjuna in the 'Udyogaparvan' that he could act only within his human limitations and not control fate. He would argue similarly to Uttaṅka in the 'Āśvamedhikaparvan'. Thus, Kṛṣṇa's sudden appearance as Fate itself is definitely a later Vaiṣṇavized development. Similarly, Arjuna's request to Kṛṣṇa to come back to his familiar four-armed form revealed the nature of these chapters.[415] Kṛṣṇa was nowhere four-armed in the *Mahābhārata* and had no reason to be. However, the Bhāgavatas, identifying him with Viṣṇu, worshipped him in a four-armed form. The eleventh chapter is the only place in the *Gītā* where Kṛṣṇa has been called Viṣṇu. The chapters seven–twelve therefore are no doubt products of later Vaiṣṇavized interpolation in which the Bhṛgus had a notable role to play. However, given that at least some of these verses were possibly known as early as the fifth century BCE, and because the growth of Bhāgavatism as the cult of Vāsudeva Kṛṣṇa can be traced from various sources ranging between the times of Pāṇini and Heliodorus, it seems that the Vaiṣṇvized revision of the *Bhagavad Gītā* took place sometime in the second half of the first millennium BCE.

However, the poet composing these chapters definitely sought to maintain the textual unity of the *Gītā*. Therefore, he subordinated the Vedic ritualism to self-realization, following the Upaniṣadic tradition.[416] The way to liberation, now through devotion, still remained open to all, including women, the *vaiśyas*, and the *śūdras*, the ones supposed to have 'sinful births'.[417] The features of the devotee echoed those of the *yogin*: one who neither perturbed the world nor was perturbed by it; who was free of excitement, indignation, fear, and agitation; who was unconcerned, pure, capable, impartial, and free of distress, and who had given up all undertakings; who neither delighted nor hated, neither grieved nor desired; who had given up both the auspicious and inauspicious; who was the same towards friend and foe, honour and dishonour, cold and heat, pleasure and pain, praise and blame.[418]

In fact, these six chapters are revision and modification of the older teaching. Elements of the older teaching can still be found in them. In the CU, Ghora Āṅgirasa had taught Kṛṣṇa that during the time of death (*antabelāyām*), one should remember *Brahman*—the undecaying (*akṣita*), imperishable (*acyuta*), and fortified by breath (*prāṇasaṃśita*)—which was one's real self.[419] In chapter eight of the *Gītā*, *Brahman* had been replaced by Kṛṣṇa.[420] But the older concept was also present:

kaviṃ purāṇam anuśāsitāram anor anīyaṃ sam anusmared yaḥ/
sarvasya dhātāram acintyarupam ādityavarṇaṃ tamasaḥ paras tāt//
prayāṇakāle manasācalena bhaktyā yukta yogavalena caiva/
bhruvor madhye prāṇam āveśya samyak sa taṃ paraṃ puruṣam upaiti divyam//
yad akṣaraṃ vedavido vadanti viśanti yat yatayo vītarāgaḥ/
yad icchanto brahmacaryaṃ caranti tat te padaṃ saṃgraheṇa pravakṣye//

(Whoever meditates at the time of departure on the primordial poet, the governor who arranged it all, who is subtler than subtle, incomprehensible in form, and the colour of the sun beyond the darkness, his mind unwavering, devoted and disciplined by the power of Yoga, concentrates all his vitality between his eyebrows and reaches that

> supreme person. I will tell you briefly about the state that knowers of the Veda call indestructible; it is that those who have striven to drive off their passions enter, it is this they desired when they took the path of chastity.)[421]

Here, it is the familiar Upaniṣadic Brahman, more minute than an atom,[422] ordainer of all, of form unthinkable,[423] that is sought, in a form celebrated in the ŚU, a late Upaniṣdic text, composed in the second half of the first millennium BCE, where the Upaniṣadic philosophy was given a theistic orientation:

> I know that immense Person, having the colour of the sun and beyond darkness. Only when a man knows him does he pass beyond death; there is no other path for getting there.[424]

Therefore, relinquishment of the fruits of action still remains the supreme virtue:

> *śreyo hi jñānam abhyāsāj jñānād dhyānaṃ viśiṣyate/*
> *dhyānāt karmaphalatyāgas tyāgāc chāntir anantaram//*
>
> (For knowledge is better than regular study, meditation surpasses knowledge, relinquishment of the fruits of action is superior to meditation; and peace follows immediately upon relinquishment.)[425]

So far, we have seen that the first six chapters of the *Gītā* present a consistent doctrine. The next six present another, retaining some connection with the earlier one. The last six explanatory chapters of the *Gītā* are a medley of various ideas. They explain the various ideas initiated in the earlier chapters and contain both earlier and later sections. However, chapters thirteen–sixteen are more closely related with the older teaching than with the newer one, though *bhakti* verses have been inserted in these[426] and much of these have been revised. Chapter fourteen, for instance, discusses in detail the properties of the three modes (*guṇas*) of nature, pivotal for the *Gītā*'s central teachings. The characteristics of one transcending the three *guṇas* are repetitions of the features already mentioned:

samaduḥkhasukhaḥ svasthaḥ samaloṣṭrāśmakañcanaḥ/
tulyapriyāpriyo dhīras tulyo nindātmasaṃstuti//
manāvamanayos tulyas tulyo mitrāripakṣayoḥ/
sarvārambhaparityāgī guṇātītaḥ sa ucyate//

(Who is equable in pain and pleasure; who is self-reliant and resolute; who has the same attitude towards clods of earth, stones, and gold; who is indifferent to pleasant and unpleasant things, to his being praised or blamed, and to honor and dishonor; who behaves the same towards friendly and antagonistic parties; and who has abandoned all undertakings . . . that man is said to have transcended the modes.)[427]

The doctrine is expressed with the metaphor of the eternal *aśvattha* tree:

ūrdhvamūlam adhaḥśākham aśvatthaṃ prāhur avyayam/
chandāṃsi yasya parṇāni yas taṃ veda sa vedavit/
adhas cordhaṃ prasṛtās tasya śākhā guṇapravṛddha viṣayapravālaḥ/
adhas ca mulāny anusaṃtatāni karmānubandhāni manuṣyaloke//
na rūpam asyeha tathopalabhyate nānto na cādir ca saṃpratiṣṭhā/
aśvattham enaṃ suvirūḍhamūlam āsaṅgaśastreṇa dṛḍhena chittvā//

(They speak of the eternal *aśvattha* tree, with its roots above and its branches below, whose leaves are the Vedic hymns: he who knows it, knows the Vedas. Its branches, whose young shoots are the sense objects, spread out below and above, nourished by the modes; and its roots extend downwards, connecting with actions in the human world. Its form cannot be perceived here, nor its end, nor its beginning, nor its foundation. You must cut down this firmly rooted *aśvattha* with the keen axe of non-attachment.)[428]

The metaphor used is a familiar one. Its origin seems to be in a Ṛgvedic verse attributed to Sunaḥśepa, where Varuṇa, the upholder of the order (*ṛta*), is described as holding a collection of radiance with roots above and face downwards. It probably signified that the Cosmic Order was spread throughout the world but deeply rooted in the heaven. The KU, however, uses the metaphor to describe *Brahman* as being present everywhere though originating from heaven:

Its root above, its branches below
This is the eternal banyan tree.
That alone is Bright! That is *Brahman*!
That alone is called the Immortal!
On it all the worlds rest;
Beyond it no one can ever pass.[429]

Similarly, the ŚU describes the eternal *Puruṣa* as a tree planted firmly in heaven.[430]

However, the *Gītā* understands the matter in its original Vedic rather than the Upaniṣadic sense. The imagery cannot be a very suitable one for the all-pervading *Brahman* whose root cannot be in the temporal heaven. Rather, it is the world order, with Vedic hymns as its leaves, which is deep rooted in heaven and spreads its branches in the human world through the modes of nature. Therefore, the tree needs to be chopped down for self-realization. The passage, therefore, reasserts that Vedic ritualism, bound by the three modes, was futile for liberation.

In fact, in chapter sixteen, Vedic ritualism is denounced as a demonic (*āsurī*) act. R.D. Karmakar has tried to identify the 'Asuras' of chapter sixteen as the Buddhists.[431] Schreiner has identified them as the materialist Cārvākas.[432] However, both seem implausible given the sacrificial association of these 'Asuras', as pointed out by Minor and T.G. Mainkar.[433] Kṛṣṇa described the attitude of these 'Asuras' as

idam adya mayā labdham imaṃ prāpsye manoratham/
idam asīdam api me bhaviṣyanti punar dhanam//
asau mayā hataḥ śatrur haniṣye cāparān api/
īśvaro'ham ahaṃ bhogī siddho'ham balavān sukhī//
āḍhyo'bhijanavān asmi ko'nyo'sti sadṛśo mayā/
yakṣye dāsyāmi modiṣya ity ajñānavimohitaḥ//

('Today I have acquired this, and soon I will fulfill that wish too; this much is mine now, and more wealth will be mine alone. I have killed that enemy, and I will kill these others too. I am the lord; I am the enjoyer; I am successful, powerful, and happy. I am rich and of noble birth; who else can match me? I will sacrifice, make donations, and be merry'—that is what they think.)[434]

Clearly, the target was no religious community in particular, but all with a materialistic attitude, including the Vedic sacrificers. As regarding the castes, Kṛṣṇa again asserted that it was not religious affiliation or birth but the attitudes and actions which made a man a deity or a demon.

Therefore, Kṛṣṇa had a certain set of virtues for identifying even the divine beings:

abhayaṃ sattvasaṃśuddhir jñānayogavyavasthitaḥ/
dānaṃ damaś ca yajñaś ca svādhyāyas tapa ārjabam//
ahiṃsā satyaṃ akrodhas tyāgaḥ śāntir apaiśunam/
dayā bhuteṣv aloluptaṃ mārdavaṃ hrīr acāpalam//
tejaḥ kṣamā dhṛtiḥ śaucam adroho nātimānitā/
bhavanti sampadaṃ daivīm abhijātasya bhārata//

(Fearlessness, essential purity, steadfastness in knowledge and yoga, generosity, self-restraint, sacrifice, Vedic recitation, austerity, sincerity, non-violence, truthfulness, freedom from anger, renunciation, serenity, lack of malice, modesty, steadiness, splendor, forgiveness, resolve, purity, harmlessness, and lack of arrogance are the virtues of the man who is born to the divine set of qualities, Bhārata.)[435]

One can easily trace the essential teachings of Ghora Āṅgirasa—*tapaḥ*, *dānam*, *ārjabam*, *satyavacanam*, and *ahiṃsā*—in the list. That Kṛṣṇa's intellectual world was very much shaped by the teachings of his preceptor is quite clear.

What realization do these divine people attain? Kṛṣṇa represented his essentially Upaniṣadic theory in the form of a new doctrine—*puruṣottamayoga*. He took up the Sāṃkhya idea of *puruṣa* but represented the concept in three levels. In the first level, there was the perishable (*kṣaraḥ*) mortal being, then the imperishable (*akṣaraḥ*) soul in him. These two were also presented as the *kṣetra* (field) and *kṣetrajña* (knower of the field), respectively, in the thirteenth chapter. But there was a third one, Supreme Self, above these two—the indestructible lord who possessed and maintained the three worlds.[436] This Supreme Lord would be *Brahman*, according to the first six chapters of the *Gītā*, and Kṛṣṇa, according to chapters seven–twelve. In this way, Kṛṣṇa integrated Vedānta and Sāṃkhya by making the Vedantic *Brahman* the *puruṣottama*, placed over the Sāṃkhya *puruṣa*. Therefore, the imperishable *puruṣa*, the *ksetrajña*, became equivalent to the Upaniṣadic-Vedāntic *ātman* who was nothing but a part of, and in the end identical with, the *Brahman*.

The description of *Brahman*, however, was totally Upaniṣadic in language:

> *sarvataḥ pāṇipādaṃ tat sarvato'kṣiśiromukham/*
> *sarvataḥ śrutimal loke sarvān āvṛtya tiṣṭhati//*
> *sarvendriyaguṇābhāsaṃ sarvendriyavivarjitam/*
> *asaktaṃ sarvabhṛc caiva nirguṇaṃ guṇabhoktṛ ca//...*
> *jyotiṣam api taj jyotis tamasaṃ param ucyate/*
> *jñānaṃ jñeyaṃ jñānāgamyaṃ hṛdi sarvasya visthitam//*
>
> (Enveloping everything, it dwells in the world with hands, feet, eyes, heads, faces and ears everywhere; appearing to have the qualities of all the senses, yet devoid of all senses, detached yet supporting everything, free of the modes yet experiencing those modes ... It is called the light of lights beyond darkness; it is knowledge and the object and purpose of knowledge, settled in everybody's heart.)[437]

This very well-known Upaniṣadic understanding of the *Brahman* is derived from Book X of the *Ṛg Veda*, where the poet Viśvakarman introduced this concept of the Supreme Being:

> That one Lord has eyes everywhere, faces everywhere, hands everywhere, heads everywhere, legs everywhere.[438]

The ŚU describes the *Brahman* as one appearing to possess the powers of all the senses, yet devoid of every sense.[439] The ĪU views it as within this world, yet outside it.[440] The MU acknowledges its presence in everybody's heart,[441] and the BU understands *Brahman* as the 'light of lights'.[442]

Again, the description of the realm of the *Brahman*, the source of all lights, as a place which neither the sun nor the moon nor fire can illuminate (*na tad bhāsayate sūryo na śaśāṅka na pāvakaḥ*)[443] is echoed in the Upaniṣadic verses:

There the sun does not shine, nor the moon and stars;
There lightning does not shine, of this common fire need we speak!
Him alone, as he shines, do all things reflect;
This whole world radiates with his light.[444]

Understanding of this all-pervading, omnipresent *Brahman* leads a person to understand the Oneness of the universe. That person views the same Supreme Lord abiding in all beings. This realization of Unity unites one with *Brahman*.[445]

While chapters thirteen–sixteen thus synthesize the Upaniṣadic ideas of the *Gītā*, chapter seventeen seems to be the latest Brahmanical interpolation which vigorously argues in favour of Vedic Brahmanism and against ascetic practices.

The eighteenth chapter is the *Gītā*'s culmination where Kṛṣṇa summed up his arguments. The interpolators also, therefore, had to deal with it. Here Kṛṣṇa summarized all his arguments, stating that no action was to be denounced but all action should be performed with attachment and fruits relinquished.[446] Here, he took up his final exposition of the *varṇa* system and explained on which basis he understood *svadharma*. He declared that the actions of the *brāhmaṇas*, *kṣatriyas*, *vaiśyas*, and *śūdras* had been assigned according to their *svabhāva* (natural inclination). Therefore, a *brāhmaṇa* was one whose *svabhāva* consisted of calmness (*śamaḥ*), self-restraint (*damaḥ*), austerity (*tapaḥ*), purity (*śaucaḥ*), patience (*kṣānti*), honesty (*ārjabam*), knowledge (*jñānam*), insight (*vijñānam*), and piety (*āstikyam*). A *kṣatriya* was one whose natural inclination was in valour (*śauryam*), vigour (*tejam*), resolve (*dhṛtiḥ*), skill (*dākṣyam*), generosity (*dānam*), mastery (*īśvarabhāvaḥ*), and not fleeing from a battle (*yuddhe apalāyanam*). Agriculture, tending of cattle, and trade were the natural inclinations of a *vaiśya*. A *śūdra* was a man of servile tendencies.[447]

A close reading of these verses may address some important question raised by Arti Dhand about the practical implications of *niṣkāma karman*. Dhand argues that the *karmayoga* taught in the *Gītā* is primarily a soteriology and it works well at that level. The philosophy of performing not what one *wants* but what one *ought*, disengaging the motive for action from its expected rewards and acting in a spirit of non-attachment motivated only by duty, provided a middle path between world renunciation and victimization by worldly pleasures. Outright renunciation serves only individual aspirations, while *karmayoga* serves both the self and the other: the self through mental discipline and the others through one's stipulated work. Thus, *karmayoga* ensures the critical moral function of serving one's function in the social ecosystem, honouring one's responsibilities, and continuing care of one's dependents. It promotes self-abnegating altruism with a concern with *lokasaṃgrahai*, the welfare of the world.[448] Therefore, as a soteriology, it succeeds in establishing itself in between Vedic Brahmanism and the renunciatory traditions.

However, Dhand wonders if it remains similarly laudable at the social realm. After all, it is a philosophy that prioritizes order over ethics. She thinks that *karmayoga* and its correlate *svadharma* both advocate and entail an abdication of moral conscience. The idealization of stability necessitates a deeply suspicious attitude to innovation. The insistent reification of social duty breeds a moral stultification, discouraging social innovation, and all but squelching a quizzical concern with social justice.[449] In *karmayoga*, one must do one's duty, which is one's *svadharma* of class, life stage, gender, and so forth; one's *svadharma*, overwhelmingly predicated upon one's birth, is shaped by one's innate nature (*svabhāva*); this innate nature itself reflects the ratio of one's *guṇas*, which themselves are predetermined by one's supposed *karma* in previous lives.[450] Therefore, this theory of *karma* producing results in subsequent births actually places the blame for one's social disempowerment on one's own shoulders. One has to conform to one's own *svadharma*, practically synonymous with *varṇadharma*, and pin hopes on the next life.[451] This problem might not be visible if the *kṣatriya* hero Kṛṣṇa asked his friend and social equal Arjuna to perform the duty earmarked for him for the sake of duty. But, *karmayoga*, when addressed to the subaltern/underprivileged, becomes a morally loathsome proposition which smothers resistance to one's social circumstance, silences complaint and dissent, and bills these as acts of impiety.[452] Therefore, it signifies appropriation of all positive values from the disenfranchised to the elite and actually cloaks injustice as the transcendental Right and constructs a false consciousness where lack of moral reasoning, lack of resistance, and docility are deemed positive moral values.[453]

Dhand's objection completely holds ground if we associate *karmayoga* with the mystical interpretation of *svadharma*, based on the concept of *karma* producing *saṃskāras* carried on from one birth to another, determining one's social location in the next birth. This would equate *svadharma* with hereditary caste duty, since one's birth would be explained as an outcome of the actions of the previous life, endowing one with the *guṇas* required for the performance of social duties required by the birth. Even though such an interpretation of *karma* is immensely popular in various strands of Brahmanical philosophy, we have seen earlier that there is no internal evidence of the *Gītā* supporting such an explanation. It is not within the scope of this book to analyse the contemporary relevance of *karmayoga* in terms of social justice. However, it is important to note that Kṛṣṇa did not explain either *svabhāva* or *svadharma* as predicated by the results of the actions of prior births in the *Gītā*. Such an interpretation, in fact, would go against the basic premise of Kṛṣṇa's teaching, since that would privilege the sustained results of action over the performance of action itself.

Rather, in the passages quoted earlier, Kṛṣṇa clarified his agreement with Yudhiṣṭhira and the Buddha, Gautama and Satyakāma Jābāla, that his definition of a man's *varṇa* was not based on his birth but on his *svabhāva*, which was determined by the balance of *guṇas* in him. Therefore, a man must perform his duty (*svadharma*) even if it was faulty, for no task was flawless. A man must perform his *svadharma*, being best equipped for that. *Paradharma* was dangerous for him, since he did not have the skill needed for its performance.[454] Buddhadeb Basu, elaborating on how Kṛṣṇa's idea of *svadharma* was not necessarily based on *varṇadharma* but on psychological inclinations (though both of these matched in the case of Arjuna), shows how the *Mahābhārata* demonstrated different kinds of *svadharma* for different people. Thus, following the warrior's code was the *svadharma* of Jarāsaṃdha (and of Arjuna, too). But Yudhiṣṭhira, a man of non-violent inclination, also followed his own *svadharma*. While leading a householder's life and begetting offsprings was part of the expected *varṇa dharma* of the *kṣatriyas*, maintaining his vow of celibacy became the *svadharma* of Bhīṣma who could even disobey and fight his revered *guru* for the sake of it.[455] The principle matches the ideological world-view of the *Mahābhārata* as analysed in Chapter 3. Thus, Kṛṣṇa was preaching an ideology which would resolve the tension between the emerging *varṇa* order and the older notion of free choice of one's vocation according to ability and inclination. Kṛṣṇa would indeed prefer a *varṇa* society, but not one where the accident of birth would fix one's social location. Rather, he would be comfortable with awarding a Vidura or a Karṇa or a Vyāsa a social position much higher than the one determined by birth and allowing a Droṇa and a Kṛpa to choose vocations below what their birth would make them do, since he would privilege *svadharma* determined by *svabhāva* shaped by the balance of *guṇas*. It can easily be compared with Aristotle's view:

> He is best who acts on his own convictions, while he is second best who acts in obedience to the counsel of others.[456]

Explaining the doctrine of *svadharma* and *svabhāva*, Kṛṣṇa reiterated the characteristics of a man who could attain the *Brahman*.[457] Every person had that potential since the Lord sat in the heart of every being—'*īśvaraḥ sarvabhūtānāṃ hṛd deśe'rjuna tiṣṭhati*'.[458] Clarifying his views, Kṛṣṇa asked Arjuna to do whatever he wanted (*yathecchasi tathā kuru*).[459]

With this statement, Kṛṣṇa's lecture practically ended. However, what seems to be a Vaiṣṇavized interpolation follows. There, Kṛṣṇa asserted *bhakti*'s superiority over everything else, culminating in the statement:

> *sarvadharmān parityājya mām ekaṃ śaraṇaṃ vraja/*
> *ahaṃ tvā sarvapāpebhyo mokṣayiṣyāmi ma śucaḥ//*
>
> (Relinquish all your duties and come to me as your sole refuge; I will rescue you from all evils, don't worry.)[460]

The *Gītā*, therefore, is neither a manual endorsing violence and war nor a supporting document for the caste system. It is definitely not an endorser of Vedic Brahmanism. The *Gītā* cannot even be described as directed towards the kings, asking them to be devoted to God, as Malinar thinks. In its present form, it has elements of a devotional scripture but that possibly was not part of Kṛṣṇa's core teaching. Moreover, Arjuna represents more the Human Universal, than the king. Arjuna was not to be the king even in the *Mahābhārata* context. The content of the teaching was the solution to the eternal problem of human misery and not the issues of kingship. Malinar tries to compare some *Gītā* passages with the ideas contained in the *Arthaśāstra*. However, that cannot be very crucial given Kṛṣṇa's clear advice to Arjuna to become *nir yogakṣema*, since *yoga* and *kṣema* (acquisition and maintenance) are the main motives of the Arthaśāstric king. Kṛṣṇa's teaching was a developed form of the Upaniṣadic doctrine taught by Ghora Āṅgirasa.

What Kṛṣṇa taught was basically the performance of one's duty as Cosmic responsibility, without desire and attachment for the fruits of the action. The duty was to be determined by one's *svadharma* based on his *svabhāva* derived from *guṇakarma*. Arjuna, a warrior by that *svadharma*, could not ethically escape fighting. It was his *svabhāva* that made him a warrior, and he could not make an exception for the sake of his kinsmen, which was nothing but mere weakness of heart. The case would have been different for Yudhiṣṭhira, whose *svabhāva* was *ānṛśaṃsya*, for whose sake Kṛṣṇa had become a messenger of peace.

The *Gītā* was the message befitting a man who had urged the cowherds to perform their own duties rather than paying for mindless sacrifices, indulged in amorous relationships with the milkmaids of a free society where *svabhāva* endorsed such behaviour, killed his own maternal uncle for larger good, gave an elaborate discourse on action to Saṃjaya in the 'Udyogaparvn', and went as an ambassador to perform his duty, despite knowing that his mission would fail. Therefore, David Kinsley's contrast between the Kṛṣṇa of the *Gītā* and Kṛṣṇa the lover of Rādhā holds little ground,[461] as in both the cases Kṛṣṇa urged his companion to perform the 'inherent duty' (*svabhāvaja karma*) rather than the dubious *kuladharma*. Rightly comments Jayant Lele:

> They (the women devotees) celebrate the same aspect of duty which Pārtha discovers as true consciousness in dialogue with Kṛṣṇa.[462]

In Kṛṣṇa's philosophy, there was no place for complete non-action. The greatest supporters of non-action (*nivṛtti*), the Jainas, therefore, viewed him as the highest epitome of active life, a *vāsudeva*, for which they condemned him to hell, but could not deny his importance. In the *Ghaṭa Jātaka*, the Bodhisattva was born as Kṛṣṇa's brother Ghaṭa Paṇḍita who had no other role in the story except teaching a grief-stricken Kṛṣṇa, who had lost a son, the doctrine Kṛṣṇa had taught in the *Gītā*:

My son is born, let him not die! Nor man nor deity
Can have that boon; then wherefore pray for what can never be!
Nor Mystic charm, nor magic roots, nor herbs, nor money spent,
Can bring to life again that ghost whom, Kaṇha, you lament.[463]

The intention is clearly to claim a Buddhist origin for Kṛṣṇa's teachings, especially the doctrine of the cycle of birth and death (*jātasya hi dhruvo mṛtyur dhruvo janmaḥ mṛtasya ca*) and the need to go beyond it, given the similarity of the two masters' doctrines. Kṛṣṇa, however, had no qualms about non-action. Conquest of desire was a magic formula through which he eradicated the difference between a *sannyāsī* and a man of action. A true *sannyāsī*, for Kṛṣṇa, would not be the one who renounced the active world but one who became indifferent to its pleasure and pain, who viewed every being as the same, and who worked for the benefit of all (*sarvabhūtahite rata*). As Radhakrishnan puts it:

> It is not an ascetic ideal that the sannyasin adopts. He may be aloof from society, yet he has compassion for all. Mahadeva, the ideal ascetic, seated in the Himalayan snows, readily drinks poison for the saving of humanity.[464]

4.8 '*Yatra yogeśvaraḥ kṛṣṇaḥ yatra pārthaḥ dhanurdharaḥ*': Kṛṣṇa at Kurukṣetra and Beyond

May Lord Kṛṣṇa be the raft that carries you over the flood
Of your enemies—just as Arjuna crossed his flood, the river of war,
Whose sands were arrows and spears, banks were Bhīṣma and Droṇa,
Water Jayadratha, the King of Gāndhāra a whirlpool, Karṇa the waves,
Aśvatthāman a crocodile, Kṛpa the shark, and Duryodhana the torrent.[465]

The verse quoted here comes from Bhāsa's '*Urubhaṅga*', a drama with Duryodhana as its hero. However, even the pro-Duryodhana poet starts with homage to Kṛṣṇa, acknowledging him as the man who had won it for the Pāṇḍavas. Kṛṣṇa did not fight in the Bhārata War. Technically, he was only the charioteer of Arjuna. However, he was the factor that possibly separated the two sides. A close analysis of the battle books actually shows the absurdity of a Kṛṣṇaless *Mahābhārata*. After our analysis of Kṛṣṇa's philosophy as contained in the *Gītā*, in the previous section, we shall now concentrate on Kṛṣṇa's activities in the war.

The *Gītā* ends with Saṃjaya's assertion that the combination of *yogeśvara* Kṛṣṇa and the archer Pārtha would bring victory.[466] His prediction was correct. M.A. Mehendale thinks that the word '*yogeśvara*' in the last verse of the *Gītā* does not mean a 'master of Yoga' but 'the master of expedient means of war stratagems'.[467] Kṛṣṇa was the *yogeśvara*, the master strategist, for the Pāṇḍava-Pañcāla force, whose strategy, combined with Arjuna's archery, brought victory.

However, these strategies of Kṛṣṇa have created a lot of ethical-philosophical debates and controversies. Most of them seem to be not conforming to the code of righteous warfare (*dharmayuddha*) agreed upon before the battle commenced. The man who had lectured on ethics and righteousness throughout his life, and gave Arjuna his best discourse just before the battle, suddenly turned into a shrewd war strategist whose strategies would have made a Kauṭilya or a Machiavelli ashamed. The three greatest Kaurava commanders—Bhīṣma, Droṇa, and Karṇa—fell not in the most acceptable manners. Nor was Duryodhana killed in a fair way. Even the killing of Jayadratha has been seen as controversial. This led various scholars to think over the matter. The extreme case was Holtzmann's Inversion Theory where he conceived the Kauravas as the original heroes of the epic. We have already discussed the drawbacks of such a theory. Bankim Chandra Chattopadhyay dismissed all the inconsistent behaviours of Kṛṣṇa as later interpolations by a devoted poet who wanted to show that God was beyond good and evil and the originator of both.[468] Bimal Krishna Matilal, in his own way, tried to seek a defence for this 'devious divinity', which we will discuss in detail while dealing with the killing of Droṇa. We will briefly deal with Kṛṣṇa's actions during the war and try to understand their significance, both historically and from the point of view of Kṛṣṇa's teachings, rather than trying to formulate a defence for them.

The war started with Bhīṣma as the Kaurava commander. However, the first ten days of the war was more of a mock war than a real one. Bhīṣma had decided not to kill the Pāṇḍavas. On the other hand, Kṛṣṇa's teachings were not enough to persuade Arjuna to kill Bhīṣma. As a result, the real war did not start. Every day, the battle ended in a stalemate with the killing of many ordinary soldiers. The killing of these ordinary soldiers, their number being exaggerated with poetic fancy, would have been a heroic act from the code of heroism prevalent in that time. However, Kṛṣṇa's philosophy, directed towards the benefit of all beings, would not approve of that. A war could be the *svadharma* of some warriors for a justified claim. But if they kept on avoiding each other for personal affection (*kṣudraṃ hṛdayadaurbalyam*) and continued to kill faultless ordinary soldiers, Kṛṣṇa was not a man to be delighted by that. Irritated by both Arjuna and Bhīṣma, Kṛṣṇa decided to break his oath of not fighting and to kill Bhīṣma. Arjuna somehow managed to control him. On the other hand, Bhīṣma, understanding the futility of the life he was living, welcomed Kṛṣṇa to kill him.

This incident has been narrated twice in the *Mahābhārata*, once during the third day of the war and once during the ninth day. It is possible that one of the accounts was added later. The ninth day seems to be the more plausible of the two occurrences by narrative logic. Therefore, after the day's battle was over, Yudhiṣṭhira and Arjuna decided that enough was enough. The matter had to be put to an end. Yudhiṣṭhira suggested that they visit Bhīṣma and ask him for a solution, and Kṛṣṇa readily agreed.

Here we see Bhīṣma, himself weary of his life, asking Yudhiṣṭhira to arrange his killing. He told him that he would not attack the effeminate Śikhaṇḍin because of his own code of war. So, keeping Śikhaṇḍin in front, Arjuna would be able to kill the defenceless Bhīṣma.[469] Arjuna was still reluctant to kill his beloved grandfather,[470] but Kṛṣṇa managed to persuade him to do what was required.[471]

This very first of Kṛṣṇa's 'unethical' acts revealed his attitude towards the war and can help us in understanding his role throughout the war. The ethics Kṛṣṇa seems to have broken repeatedly was the ethics of heroic warfare. We usually expect the epics to be the representatives of a 'heroic age'. Thus, Homer's *Iliad* is a nostalgic recalling of the days when heroes such as Achilles and Hector lived. Even Vālmīki's *Rāmāyaṇa* recalls the deeds of a steadfast hero, Rāma, and his equally heroic antagonist, Rāvaṇa. The Bhārgava redactors of the *Mahābhārata* found their unassailable war hero in Paraśurāma.

However, Vyāsa's *Mahābhārata* seems to be an exception. Vyāsa, as a poet, was not one celebrating the *varṇa* code. Rather than celebrating heroism, he showed the evils of war and violence. The 'Strīparvan' of the *Mahābhārata* stands as an example of how abominable and painful were the consequences of war. Beauty of heroic valour was overshadowed by the lamentations of women mourning their beloved ones. Thus, the champion of *kṣatriya* heroism, Duryodhana, was not Vyāsa's favourite. Rather, he celebrated the pacifist Yudhiṣṭhira who pointed out the cruelty of *kṣatriya* ethics and the futility of glorifying war which was nothing but a power struggle.

Here Kṛṣṇa becomes important. Standing between Yudhiṣṭhira and Duryodhana, he knew that a war had to be fought if the need arose. But war was not a thing to be celebrated; nothing was ethical and heroic about war. For the sake of saving the life of his people, he had decided not to combat Jarāsaṃdha in Mathurā and fled to Dvārakā. Not caring for the respected code of heroism, he went to kill Jarāsaṃdha to save the kings to be sacrificed and accomplished the task with minimum bloodshed. Be it Jarāsaṃdha, Siśupāla, or Kālayavana, Kṛṣṇa got rid of most of his antagonists in a one-to-one duel, avoiding a clash of armies. Even at Kurukṣetra, he continued that tradition. Here it was a massive clash of armies, causing much death and destruction. Still, we would see Kṛṣṇa intervening frequently to stop the useless bloodbath and direct the course of the battle towards the ones who really mattered and away from the clash of the ordinary soldiers.

Bhīṣma, on the other hand, was the epitome of his *varṇa* virtue. Kṛṣṇa respected him for his adherence to his *svadharma* but hardly agreed with his world-view. As a true hero, he remained steadfast to his vow of celibacy and not assuming kingship, although it created a series of confusions and troubles culminating at Kurukṣetra. Affectionate to the Pāṇḍavas, Bhīṣma would not kill them. But he would be steadfast to his virtue of heroism and kill numerous ordinary soldiers. He himself knew that he had failed; the values he stood for were corroding. His vow became the cause of the destruction of the clan for whose sake he took it. His *kṣatriya* valour was to serve the purpose of a person whose behaviour he hardly approved of. He knew his days were gone and acknowledged and worshipped Kṛṣṇa as the hero of the new age. However, he was still dragging his weary body to the battlefield for the sake of the last desire of an ideal *kṣatriya*—a heroic death on the battlefield. Kṛṣṇa and Yudhiṣṭhira obliged him and ended the useless bloodbath in the name of a *dharmayuddha*.

With Bhīṣma's fall, the real war started. In its charge was Droṇa, not a relative but a professional. He had as little regard for the *varṇa* system as had Kṛṣṇa and Yudhiṣṭhira. A *brāhmaṇa* by birth, he chose warfare as his profession. He had no scruples about war being anything glorious. The 'Droṇaparvan' is the most violent, most brutal book of the *Mahābhārata*, with the war in its ugliest form.

The ugliest incident happened on the thirteenth day. A steadfast group of warriors, called the '*saṃsaptakas*', took Arjuna away from the main scene of battle. Then Droṇa arranged his army in a difficult circular formation—*cakravyūha*—that none but Arjuna and Kṛṣṇa, in the Pāṇḍava camp, would have been able to successfully penetrate. Abhimanyu, the son of Arjuna and Subhadrā, was partially taught to penetrate it by his father but did not know the way out. In a mad rush of heroism, he entered the formation and created a terror in the Kaurava camp before being entrapped. Encircled by warriors from all the sides, the young hero died a brutal death.

The grief-stricken Arjuna took a vow to either kill Jayadratha, the man who valiantly guarded the Kaurava formation during Abhimanyu's death, or commit suicide the next day. In this episode, we see Kṛṣṇa in his full composure. Abhimanyu's death was not a minor blow to him. During the thirteen years of Pāṇḍava exile, it was Kṛṣṇa who had raised Abhimanyu. Still, he did not grieve like Arjuna. Not only did he himself use brutal means in the war but he accepted the brutality of the war as a reality when his favourite nephew perished. Rather, he criticized Arjuna for his rash oath.[472] Being unperturbed in sorrow (*duhkheṣu anudvignamanā*) as he taught, he rather went to console the grief-stricken parents in their understandable language, that Abhimanyu had attained his desired heroic death.[473]

The next day's fight showed Kṛṣṇa's skill as a charioteer at its best. The whole battle revolved around protecting Jayadratha from Arjuna. But Kṛṣṇa—driving the chariot with mastery and also providing the horses the necessary rest and care—managed to help Arjuna find Jayadratha before the day's end. There is a strange account that Kṛṣṇa covered the sun with his magic to create an illusion of sunset so that Jayadratha would come out unprotected. The episode has been sometimes rationalized as a solar eclipse. Neither interpretation needs serious consideration. If we read the account carefully, Arjuna had found Jayadratha before and without Kṛṣṇa's magic and started fighting him.[474] After the magic, the same fight continued, and Jayadratha was killed after a very lengthy battle. Kṛṣṇa's magic therefore seems to be nothing but a poorly inserted interpolation by a poet seeking a divine intervention.

The next major event in the battle was the killing of Ghaṭotkaca, the Rākṣasa son of Bhīma and Hiḍimbā. At the nocturnal battle on the fourteenth day, he became dangerous and uncontrollable. None but Karṇa in the Kaurava camp could take him on. Ultimately, Karṇa killed Ghaṭotkaca with a special weapon that he had preserved for killing Arjuna.

The account took a most unexpected turn here. Witnessing Ghaṭotkaca's death, Kṛṣṇa started dancing in joy, embraced Arjuna, and clapped his armpits.[475] When a disturbed Arjuna asked him the reason for this crazy reaction to a beloved one's death, he related the story of Karṇa's divine armour and earrings. These were the gifts to Karṇa from his father, the sun god. Wearing these, he would have been invincible in battle. Indra, Arjuna's father, took them away from Karṇa in the disguise of a beggar, since the great donor Karṇa never refused one begging. However, ashamed by the greatness of Karṇa, Indra compensated him with a divine *śakti* that Karṇa had preserved to kill Arjuna. Now, it being spent, Arjuna was safe.[476] Then Kṛṣṇa went on saying that for the benefit of the Pāṇḍavas, he had killed Jarāsaṃdha, Śiśupāla, and Ekalavya who would have joined the Kaurava side and made them invincible. He had also got the Rākṣasas such as Hiḍimba, Kirmīra, Baka, and Alāyudha killed. Now he had to do the same with Ghaṭotkaca who was an enemy of the *brāhmaṇas* and destroyer of sacrifices.[477]

That the whole section is a gross interpolation is quite apparent. The killings of Jarāsaṃdha, Śiśupāla, and Ekalavya were no doubt accomplished by Kṛṣṇa. But making him the killer of Hiḍimba, Baka, and Kirmīra—three Rākṣasas slain by Bhīma, the first two being slain before the Pāṇḍavas ever met Kṛṣṇa—has no internal support in the *Mahābhārata*. The interpolation therefore seems to be the handiwork of a poet similar to the one who, in the eleventh chapter of the *Gītā*, made Kṛṣṇa the all-destroying Kāla who had already killed all the warriors to be killed. To the Brahmanical sentiment of this poet, a Rākṣasa contributing greatly to the Pāṇḍava victory was possibly disturbing. So, he made Ghaṭotkaca the typical Rākṣasa, disturbing the *brāhmaṇas* and their sacrifices. The deity Kṛṣṇa, whom he would love to see as a protector of the *brāhmaṇas* and sacrifices, could not therefore contain his joy in the death of such a Rākṣasa. Kṛṣṇa, always indifferent to joy and sorrow, who did not shed teardrops even at the death of his beloved nephew, who would not dance even after the deaths of the greater warriors such as Karṇa or Duryodhana or even Jarāsaṃdha, had been credited with this rather obscene dance of joy by this interpolator.

However, that does not mean that we can dismiss every disturbing act of Kṛṣṇa as an interpolation, as Bankim did. Therefore, we have to deal in detail with the killing of Droṇa, since inconsistency in behaviour cannot be the only criteria of labelling some incident as interpolated. After all, it is crisis that brings out the inconsistency in human beings.

Droṇa was no doubt such a crisis. It was his generalship that showed the Kauravas a hope of victory. The Pāṇḍavas lost Abhimanyu and Ghaṭotkaca. The Pāñcālas lost their king Drupada. The Matsya king Virāṭa was also killed. All three dominant forces in the Pāṇḍava-Pāñcāla camp were therefore demoralized, and Droṇa was leading the Kauravas steadily towards victory. In this situation came Kṛṣṇa's most shocking counsel that Droṇa could not be overcome by anyone, even Indra, in a fair battle and, therefore, the Pāṇḍavas should kill him by forsaking righteousness (*dharmam utsṛjya*).[478]

Kṛṣṇa's suggestion was to demoralize Droṇa, as the Pāṇḍava camp was demoralized. He knew Droṇa's weak point to be his son—Aśvatthāman. Therefore, he suggested telling a lie about Aśvatthāman's death, which everybody except Arjuna agreed to. To give the lie a resemblance of truth, Bhīma killed an elephant named Aśvatthāman and told Droṇa that Aśvatthāman was dead.[479] Knowing his students well, Droṇa did not trust Bhīma but asked Yudhiṣṭhira about the matter.[480] However, both Bhīma and Kṛṣṇa persuaded the ever-truthful Yudhiṣṭhira to tell a lie. Yudhiṣṭhira, 'afraid of speaking lies, but anxious to obtain victory' (*jaye sakto*), clearly said that Aśvatthāman was dead, adding indistinctly the word 'elephant' after the name Aśvatthāman.[481] Then Dhṛṣṭadyumna attacked the grief-stricken and exhausted Droṇa. Still, Droṇa continued fighting valiantly until Bhīma admonished him for taking up the warrior's job, despite being a *brāhmaṇa* by birth and for keeping on fighting even after his son was dead.[482] After that Droṇa stopped fighting and sat down to meditate. He might have passed away in meditation when Dhṛṣṭadyumna chopped his head off.

This terrible episode has always troubled readers. The act is unacceptable to those who regard Kṛṣṇa as a deity. Even those who view him as a human character are troubled to see how the person who declared *dharmasaṃsthāpana* as his ideal asked the Pāṇḍavas to leave *dharma* for their benefit. Even more shocking was the act of the ever-truthful '*dharmarāja*' Yudhiṣṭhira whose 'anxiety to obtain victory' made him speak a lie, not a simple white lie, but one carefully spoken to cause the death of his teacher who had full trust in his truthfulness. Matilal tried to explain the act of Kṛṣṇa by viewing him as a deity/human who was not omnipotent. Lacking omnipotence, Kṛṣṇa wanted to assure the relatively righteous side's victory, for which Droṇa had to be killed. The issue was a question of survival and the survival of the righteous. The Kauravas were the more powerful side, and Kṛṣṇa wanted to ensure the victory for the 'right' side. Matilal justifies his argument on the philosophical premise that a world with both good and evil, where sometimes justice is done and sometimes evil forces try to suppress justice, but there is the hope of the good's triumph at the end, is more desirable than either an amoral world or a perfect world with no evil or unhappiness (and therefore no sense of happiness).[483]

However, assuring justice by the means of injustice is a denial of the very sense of justice. It may lead to a vicious circle of unjust behaviours, each justifying itself as a response to an earlier injustice. Kṛṣṇa, of course, did not use such logic. Rather, his logic was different:

> If influenced by rage Droṇa fights only half a day, then I tell you truly, your troops are sure to be destroyed. Save us from Droṇa; under the circumstances as the present falsehood is better than truth. Speaking falsehood for the sake of saving a life one does not become a sinner.[484]

As we have discussed earlier, Kṛṣṇa did not believe in the idea of a 'heroic' or 'glorious' warfare. However, in this case, it was not just the ethics of heroism but also those of truthfulness and trustworthiness, which were at stake. Kṛṣṇa declared that he viewed every value as relative. Values were for the sake of humanity. Human life was the most precious thing. Therefore, no value could be followed if it endangered the fundamental cause of human survival. Therefore, Kṛṣṇa stated that falsehood was better than truth for saving a life.

That is understandable. But the contradiction remains. Here the falsehood was uttered for taking a life rather than for saving one. Kṛṣṇa's idea, here, would be that Droṇa was taking numerous lives. In a war, life and death were the issues at stake. So, if taking a life unlawfully saved several lives, it was virtuous to do so. Taking a life in a war was not wrong, and it was the duty of a warrior to kill an enemy who was taking numerous lives. Since heroism did not matter to Kṛṣṇa, he approached the war as the brute reality it was. Droṇa himself perceived the war as a brute reality and did not desist from brutally butchering Abhimanyu. Similarly, Kṛṣṇa saw no wrong in adopting the same brutality in killing Droṇa who was endangering many precious lives.

The contradiction is not solved by this, and it is not our intention to solve that. What we have tried to do is understand Kṛṣṇa's logic. Since we are not in a bid to prepare a clean chit for Kṛṣṇa, we will leave the contradictions as they are. So did Vyāsa. Despite Kṛṣṇa's logic, he did not fail to note Arjuna's refusal to adhere to the whole scheme. Despite all the persuasions of Kṛṣṇa, Arjuna's refusal to kill Bhīṣma and Droṇa remained. He killed Bhīṣma with much reluctance, but the way of killing Droṇa remained too abominable for him. Moreover, here the preacher of *svadharma* persuaded the anxious Yudhiṣṭhira to leave his *svadharma* of truthfulness. It disturbed the poet intensely. He metaphorically represented his disturbance by saying that Yudhiṣṭhira's chariot, which always remained four feet higher than the earth, now touched the ground.[485] War brings out the evil in man. It brought Yudhiṣṭhira down to the level of an ordinary human. Possibly it brought Kṛṣṇa down as well.

However, the issue leaves a larger ethical question unanswered. Can falsehood be better than truth in a certain situation? Can truth be turned into untruth? Bankim clearly sides with Kṛṣṇa.[486] However, Rabindranath Tagore strongly protests against this understanding:

> In no situation does falsehood become truth. Not even if the honourable Bankimbabu says so. Not even if Śrī Kṛṣṇa himself says so.[487]

This is a discourse of deeper significance in which Kṛṣṇa would get involved even after the killing of Droṇa. The concerned issue occurred on the seventeenth day of the battle. After the killing of Droṇa, the war more or less reached its climax. Everything was now to be decided by the showdown between Karṇa and Arjuna. In this situation, Yudhiṣṭhira once attacked Karṇa and was badly battered. While he was healing his wounds in the tent, Arjuna came to enquire after his health. Yudhiṣṭhira hoped that Arjuna had killed Karṇa. When his hope was dashed, he reviled Arjuna. In the course, he asked Arjuna to give away his famous Gāṇḍīva bow to Kṛṣṇa. Now, Arjuna had a secret vow to kill anybody who would ask him to give his Gāṇḍīva away. The truth-obsessed Arjuna, therefore, decided to fulfill his vow. Kṛṣṇa then stopped him and lectured him on truth and falsehood. In this discourse, Kṛṣṇa made his ethical viewpoint clearer:

> Believing yourself conversant with *dharma*, you are observing it in a way which but indicates your ignorance of it. You believe yourself to be virtuous but you know not, O Pārtha, that it is a sin to slay living beings. Methinks, keeping from doing any injury to any animal is a cardinal virtue. Even an untruth might be told but never an animal be slain.[488]

Thus, Kṛṣṇa defined non-injury and non-violence as the highest virtue, a virtue higher than truthfulness. Then he stated that it was even more sinful to slay someone not engaged in a fight or unwilling to fight or seeking shelter or asking for protection or taking refuge or insane, even if he was a foe. Slaying the righteous elder brother, Yudhiṣṭhira, would therefore be a heinous crime.[489] Kṛṣṇa did not pay much attention to Arjuna's vow which he considered a 'childish act', and it was Arjuna's folly to think of committing an unrighteous act to defend his childish vow.[490]

We have already seen that non-violence (*ahiṃsā*) was a cardinal virtue that Kṛṣṇa had learned from Ghora Āṅgirasa; but so was truthfulness (*satyavacanam*). Then, was Kṛṣṇa denying one of his teachings for the sake of another? Kṛṣṇa did not think so:

> *satyasya vacanaṃ sādhu na satyād vidyate param/*
> *tattvenaitat sudurjñeyaṃ yasya satyam anuṣṭhitam//*
> *bhavet satyam avaktavyaṃ vaktavyam anṛtaṃ bhavet/*

> (One who tells truth is a pious person. Nothing is there higher than truth. It is, therefore, very difficult to understand the details of truth as observed in action.
>
> Truth becomes unutterable and untruth utterable.)[491]

Kṛṣṇa gave three different lists of situations where untruth could be told legitimately. During the killing of Droṇa, he told that untruth could be told to save a life. In the context we are discussing, he approved speaking a lie to save a life, or one's entire fortune, or in a marriage negotiation, declaring that in certain situations the truth becomes untruth and the untruth truth (*yatrānṛtaṃ bhavet satyaṃ satyaṃ cāpy anṛtaṃ bhavet*).[492] The last list accepted speaking untruth when one's life was endangered, at marriage, at the risk of destruction of one's kith and kin, or in the course of business.[493] May be the different lists were added at different times or Kṛṣṇa was quoting some traditional sayings on the issue. But his general idea was very straightforward that one must not be obsessed with truthfulness literally. There were situations where untruth served the purpose of truth and vice versa. If a person exaggerated or did not literally speak the truth when praising a woman while flirting or courting or copulating with her, Kṛṣṇa would not take that as a crime. If a trader lied a bit in advertising his product or a party in a marriage negotiation exaggerated the qualities of the bride/groom, Kṛṣṇa would not view it as a sin. Above all, if a person's life or entire fortune was at stake, and if a lie could save those, that lie would be as virtuous as a truth to Kṛṣṇa. Thus said Kṛṣṇa:

> He who is bent upon always practising the truth alone is a fool and takes truth to be as it is. Indeed it is not a very easy thing to become righteous. He who can distinguish between the niceties of truth and untruth can alone become conversant with *dharma* (*satyānṛte viniścitya tato bhavati dharmavit*).[494]

Kṛṣṇa explained his idea with a story about a truth-obsessed *brāhmaṇa* named Kauśika. The *brāhmaṇa*, steadfast in his vow of truth speaking, once told a group of robbers where some innocent people were hiding themselves. The robbers found those innocent people and killed them. As a result, Kauśika was sent to hell rather than to heaven for telling the 'truth' which was worse than a lie.[495]

Therefore, Kṛṣṇa's understanding of *dharma* was contextual. He did not deny the universality of *dharma* but preferred to apply it contextually. Matilal has shown the opposition between Kṛṣṇa's morality and Kantian morality. Kant thinks that even if a murderer is chasing a man's friend who took refuge in the man's house, the man—if asked by the murderer—must speak the truth. Here Kant's logic is based on the universality of truth. Whatever be the reason, if one can legitimately replace truth with untruth, then the basis of the virtue called truth will be lost. This is the same reason for which Tagore says that falsehood can never become truth, even if Bankim or Kṛṣṇa himself says so.[496] This emphasis on an idea on its face value is seen by Matilal as 'primaficy intuitive reasoning' which is the dominant value of the *Rāmāyaṇa* as well.[497] In fact, the *kṣatriya* ethics, which Rāma represents, was basically based on this kind of primaficy intuitive reasoning. Therefore, Rāma leaves his legitimate claim to the throne and chooses an exile in the forest for the sake of his father's promise. He also abandons his faultless wife for the sake of his own principle. However, even Rāma's steadfastness gets shaken at the end. He starts a discussion with Time Personified by pledging to kill anybody entering the room. Lakṣmaṇa, his beloved brother, has to enter the room to save entire Ayodhyā. Even the steadfast Rāma then seeks a compromise and finds it in abandoning, rather than killing, Lakṣmaṇa.[498] Therefore, primaficy intuitive reasoning always has a limit which can only be solved by 'critical level thinking' represented by the *Mahābhārata*.[499]

That critical-level thinking considers that universality of the truth is important but so is the universality of non-violence. Since there cannot be contradiction within the universal, the two cannot really be antagonistic. The untruth therefore serves the purpose of truth here. In other words, if the purpose of both truth and non-violence is to assure a better living condition for humanity, what contradicts that is untruth. Thus, Kṛṣṇa's *dharma* was not what was there in the scriptures.[500] Rather

prabhavārthāya bhūtānāṃ dharmapravacanaṃ kṛtaṃ//
dhāraṇād dharmam ity āhur dharmo dhārayati prajāḥ/
yaḥ syād dhāraṇasaṃyuktaḥ sa dharma iti niścayaḥ//

(The moral precepts have been made for the well-being of the creatures.

All that is free from any motive of injury to any being is surely *dharma*. For, indeed, the moral precepts have been made to free the creatures from all injuries.

Dharma is so-called because it protects all. Indeed, *dharma* saves all creatures. Surely, then that is *dharma* which is capable of keeping off a creature from all injuries.)[501]

It was not 'Utilitarianism' per say but a concept of universal betterment of all beings, the *sarvabhūtahita* that Kṛṣṇa had emphasized on in the *Gītā*.

This episode, together with the debate around the killing of Droṇa by deceit, indeed illustrates the uniqueness of the ethics propounded by the *Mahābhārata* in general and Kṛṣṇa in particular. Lakshmi Bandlamudi explains the ethical world of the *Mahābhārata* with Bakhtin's idea of answerability, and argues:

> While the *Mahābhārata* does not espouse absolutes, it does not vouch for anything goes relativism either; instead it calls for a context-dependent, history-sensitive nature of ethical action.[502]

Rather than prioritizing phantom, abstract ethics, the *Mahābhārata* deals with context-specific concretes. In moral dilemmas, one must exercise the full force of their agency, accept responsibility for the choices made, and experience the consequences. An ethics of answerability, rather than an abstract ethic, helps one to be imaginative amidst constraints and to compose a persuasive moral argument with the available tools.[503]

This context-dependent sensitivity is important because the *Mahābhārata* upholds many intrinsic values without a strict hierarchy among them. Vrinda Dalmiya and Gangeya Mukherji follows Jonardon Ganeri in arguing that one needs the skill of 'receptivity' to act sensitively in such a scenario, as it is a disposition that makes sense of a value in terms of others and grasps their contextualized significance. Acting righteously is to be creative and adaptive not merely repetitive.[504] Endowed with this skill, Kṛṣṇa deprioritized literal truth in a particular case because of how other values such as compassion and heroism affected what truth speaking meant in that situation. What truth amounts to is conditional on all the intrinsic values relevant in specific contexts. A receptive agent sees this and transforms contextualism in a deep, moral particularism. Kṛṣṇa was receptive in this way and, therefore, open to reconstituting the meaning of 'truth' creatively. On the other hand, Ganeri finds in Yudhiṣṭhira a lack of such receptivity. Being a rule fetishist, he was unable to imagine how deviating from principles could still accord with *dharma*. He failed to see the positive ethical quality (saving numerous lives by taking one) in the 'lie' proposed by Kṛṣṇa to bring Droṇa's downfall and uttered a convoluted truth (by uttering the word 'elephant' discreetly while claiming that Aśvatthaman was dead). Therefore, he missed the *dharma* from both the possible points of view—speaking the truth literally or speaking an untruth that would be equivalent to truth because of its ethically valid purpose.[505]

However, there was no lack of primaficy intuitive reasoning in the *Mahābhārata* either. The strict adherents of the *kṣatriya* virtue were there as well. Thus, Bhīṣma could not be diverted from his vow even when his vow was destroying its very purpose. The same syndrome affected Arjuna. Though Kṛṣṇa described his vow as childish, Arjuna kept on insisting for a compromise formula where his vow could be maintained.[506] Kṛṣṇa provided a childish solution to a childish concern by saying that insulting a senior person would be equivalent to killing him.[507] However, the virtue-obsessed Arjuna felt remorse after insulting Yudhiṣṭhira and wanted to commit suicide. Kṛṣṇa took care of his childish friend using another ready solution, self-praising being made equivalent to suicide.[508] When this melodrama was over, Kṛṣṇa boosted Arjuna's morale with a pep talk like an ideal *sūta*[509] and took him for the decisive encounter with Karṇa.

The battle of Karṇa and Arjuna was no doubt the most intense encounter Kurukṣetra had witnessed. It was possibly fought on muddy terrain. Thus, when Karṇa almost killed Arjuna, Kṛṣṇa protected Arjuna's head by pressing down Arjuna's chariot one cubit deep in the earth.[510] Kṛṣṇa lifted the chariot again. But Karṇa's chariot became stuck in a worse manner moments later. Karṇa, invoking the code of ethical warfare, asked Arjuna to wait for him to lift his chariot. But Kṛṣṇa denied that with a brutal verbal assault on Karṇa:

> You, Duryodhana, Duḥśāsana, and Subala's son Śakuni, brought Draupadī, clad in one piece of cloth, before the court. Then, O Karṇa, this *dharma* of yours, did not display itself.
>
> When Śakuni, a clever hand at dice, defeated Kuntī's son Yudhiṣṭhira who was innocent of the game, where was this *dharma* of yours?
>
> When you laughed at Draupadī while she, spare dressed and in her season, stood before the court at Duḥśāsana's will, where was this *dharma* of yours?
>
> When thirsting for the kingdom and relying on the king of Gāndhāra you invited the Pāṇḍavas to a game of dice, where was this *dharma* of yours?[511]

Ashamed by the true words of Kṛṣṇa, Karṇa started fighting again. With his chariot immobile, he must have been in great difficulty. Arjuna succeeded in killing him.

The words spoken by Kṛṣṇa were all true. Still, what is hurt in this incident is sentiment, the sentiment for the ever-deprived but noble Karṇa who was denied by luck a fair trial even in his final encounter with his arch-enemy. However, what surprises us is Kṛṣṇa's criticism of Karṇa, despite knowing his nobility and generosity (which he had acknowledged in the 'Udyogaparvan'). What went wrong? Was it the moment when Kṛṣṇa pointed out why *paradharma* was dangerous? Karṇa, a great and noble-hearted man, committed so many offences against his own moral sensibilities just to please his friend and benefactor Duryodhana. Adopting Duryodhana's *dharma*, Karṇa lost the course of his own *svadharma*. In 'Udyogaparvan', he at least chose a glorious death over material welfare as the last salvation of his sensibility. Did Kṛṣṇa remind him of that? The last thing that maintained the glory of Karṇa was his indomitable spirit, his generosity. Begging for mercy to Arjuna, Karṇa was on the verge of losing that. Kṛṣṇa's rude words might have reminded him of the purpose of his life. Thus Karṇa fought again, fought for his death, and died a death that would bring tears to the eyes of generations of sensitive readers.

Karṇa's death more or less decided the result of the war. The eighteenth day saw the Pāṇḍavas sweep off the rest of the Kaurava army. However, the man at the centre of everything—Duryodhana—needed to be dealt with. The Pāṇḍavas traced him down, hiding in the Dvaipāyana Lake. However, Yudhiṣṭhira—being the crazy gambler he was—offered him the kingdom if he could defeat any one of the Pāṇḍavas. Kṛṣṇa was utterly irritated with this gambling tendency of Yudhiṣṭhira. He made it clear that none of the Pāṇḍavas could match Duryodhana with a mace, and none but Bhīma could even offer a fight. However, the proud Duryodhana chose Bhīma only and the final battle started.

The final battle was also the scene of Kṛṣṇa's final unethical act—persuading Bhīma to strike Duryodhana under the belt, a strike not allowed in mace fighting. Kṛṣṇa had his logic that Bhīma would not be able to match Duryodhana through fair means, and he had already vowed to avenge Draupadī's humiliation by crushing Duryodhana's lower portions. The act was no exception to Kṛṣṇa's view of warfare, already discussed in detail. In fact, thinking beyond heroic sensibilities makes it clear that a strike above or below the belt was hardly different in a mortal combat.

The event was the occasion of the final split between Kṛṣṇa and Balarāma. The teacher of both Bhīma and Duryodhana, Balarāma, was witnessing the duel. He could not approve of Bhīma's unlawful blow and wanted to punish him. Kṛṣṇa stopped him by reminding him of Bhīma's vow.[512] As always, Balarāma could not go against his brother. However, he expressed his displeasure about the entire episode and Kṛṣṇa's 'fraudulent morality' (*dharmacchalam*). Reviling Bhīma and praising Duryodhana, he left.[513]

Throughout our narrative, we have seen Balarāma as a shadowy presence in Kṛṣṇa's life. The two brothers started their lives together. They always acted together in their adolescence, be it in play or in an amorous dance with milkmaids or in a combat. Together they entered Mathurā, encountered the wrestlers, and killed Kaṃsa. Together they faced the menace of Jarāsaṃdha. However, with Kṛṣṇa's rise as the Vāsudeva, Balarāma gradually receded to the background. Despite his deep love for his brother, he failed to realize the new philosophy Kṛṣṇa was preaching. More comfortable with the traditional *kṣatriya* virtues, he liked his disciple Duryodhana. The Syamantaka episode first revealed the gap between the two brothers. Disturbed and confused, Balarāma stood away from the war. When he returned to witness the final encounter, he could not accept the scenario. Duryodhana remained the virtuous one for him, and Kṛṣṇa's morality seemed fraudulent.

We have mentioned the defiant statements of the dying Duryodhana. He admonished Kṛṣṇa very harshly for all his strategies throughout the war.[514] Kṛṣṇa replied by recounting all the evil deeds of Duryodhana, from the dice game to Draupadī's humiliation to Abhimanyu's killing, and made him responsible for the massacre.[515]

However, Duryodhana remained steady in his faith in his version of virtues. He remembered his Vedic studies and gift-givings, capable administration and heroic fighting, and the poet greeted this with a shower of scented flowers.[516]

The poet celebrates Duryodhana's virtue at the end. Kṛṣṇa and the Pāṇḍavas were ashamed of what they did, and at last Kṛṣṇa accepted that he could have never won the war by 'fair' means.[517] Kṛṣṇa's understanding of war ethics ended up triumphant. However, he did not fail to accept the steadfastness Duryodhana showed in his *svadharma*. After all, Kṛṣṇa had to remind Arjuna, the hearer of the *Gītā*, of his duty repeatedly. Despite believing in an ideology worlds apart, Duryodhana epitomized Kṛṣṇa's teaching '*svadharme nidhanaṃ śreyo*'.

Kṛṣṇa had told Arjuna in the 'Karṇaparvan' that he valued non-violence above everything. It was majorly to stop the useless bloodbath that he maneuvered the downfalls of Bhīṣma and Droṇa. However, Kurukṣetra witnessed an immeasurable bloodbath. With Aśvatthāman, Kṛtavarman, and Kṛpa attacking the Pāṇḍava camp at night and slaughtering all the Pāñcālas, along with the five sons of Draupadī, the great blood sacrifice came to an end. What did Kṛṣṇa accomplish in all these? One wonders. Was it only the performance of one's duty without thinking of the results? One wonders. Surprisingly, everybody from Gāndhārī to Utaṅka regarded Kṛṣṇa as the cause of the bloodbath. Kṛṣṇa told the complaining sage Utaṅka in the 'Āśvamedhikaparvan' that he tried his best to stop the war, within his human limitations, but could not succeed.[518]

The same human limitations possibly tied him down within his own clan. Right from the time of Kaṃsa's killing, Kṛṣṇa's position in Yādava politics was never smooth. We have seen that he was obeyed because of his superiority over others but not universally liked. The Syamantaka episode revealed the dirty and bitter truth and created a misunderstanding between Kṛṣṇa and Balarāma. With Duryodhana's killing, the gap only increased. Kṛṣṇa was now all powerful, but all alone, within the Yādava-Vṛṣṇi politics.

This was the scenario in which Kṛṣṇa spent the last thirty-six years of his mortal life. Just like he could not save the Kurus and Pāñcālas from destruction, despite his best efforts, his earnest efforts could not stop the Yādavas from going towards the path of destruction. Proud of their power and Kṛṣṇa's presence, the Yādavas became an uncontrollable force.

The 'Mauṣalaparvan' of the *Mahābhārata* says that the Yādavas once mocked the three sages Viśvāmitra, Kaṇva, and Nārada by disguising Sāmba, son of Kṛṣṇa and Jāmbavatī, as a pregnant woman. They took him to the sages and asked them to predict the sex of the child to be born. The sages saw through the matter and cursed them that he would produce a pestle that would destroy the Yādavas. When Sāmba produced the pestle, it was destroyed and its dust was thrown into the sea. Kṛṣṇa and Balarāma tried all measures to control the Yādavas. Even manufacturing liquor within Dvārakā was declared punishable by death. However, the practice possibly continued. Therefore, when the Yādavas went for a day out at Prabhāsa, bottles of liquor came out. People like Balarāma, Kṛtavarman, and Gada started drinking. Soon, Sātyaki and Kṛtavarman started a drunken debate about their activities in the Bhārata War. Pradyumna, son of Kṛṣṇa and Rukmiṇī, came in Sātyaki's support. Sātyaki started the massacre by killing Kṛtavarman. Soon some other Yādavas killed Pradyumna and Sātyaki. A huge fight arose in which the Yādavas killed each other. Their weapons were only reeds which turned into pestles. When the massacre was over, Kṛṣṇa sent Akrura to protect the women in Dvārakā and asked Dāruka to inform Arjuna about the incident. Akrura was killed on his way. Kṛṣṇa decided to go to the Himalayas, along with Balarāma, but he found Balarāma already dead. In utter exhaustion, Kṛṣṇa entered a forest and went deep in contemplation. A hunter named Jarā, who was actually an extramarital son of Vasudeva, shot him mistakenly. Kṛṣṇa departed in the humblest possible manner. Thus, as Phyllis Granoff has noted, Kṛṣṇa let the destruction of his clan happen as a consequence of their actions, just like the Buddha let Viḍūḍhava destroy the Śākyas (the Buddha's own clan), though both of them possibly had the ability to save their kinsmen.[519]

But what was the *karman* that merited such a violent end? The story of the pestle is extraordinary. However, there seems to be some significant elements in the account. The Yādavas, indisciplined and given to drinking, probably killed each other off. The account is found everywhere—in the *Mahābhārata*, the *Harivaṃśa*, the Purāṇas, the *Ghaṭa Jātaka*, and the Jaina legends. However, the Buddhist and Jaina accounts add an important dimension to it.

In the *Ghaṭa Jātaka*, the reason of the destruction of the Yādavas was the curse of Kaṇhadīpāyana (Kṛṣṇa Dvaipāyana) whom the sons of Kṛṣṇa killed. The Jaina account also makes the rage of the sage Dīpāyana (Dvaipāyana) responsible for the destruction, after he was stoned to death by some Yādavas. The suggestion is interesting. The *Mahābhārata* practical joke seems too trivial a reason for an incident like an entire clan, that too the clan of Kṛṣṇa himself, perishing. However, an arrogant murder of the greatest mind of the time would be much more deadly a cause. That even the Brahmanical tradition was aware of this account is proven by the *Arthaśāstra* that says that the Vṛṣṇis perished because they maltreated Dvaipāyana.[520] It, therefore, seems that the Yādavas became so arrogant and cruel that they killed Dvaipāyana Vyāsa, the greatest contemporary intellectual and the creator of the *Mahābhārata* tradition. He had been immortalized in his own tradition, but the countertraditions remembered the incident. Even the Brahmanical tradition remembered it at least till the time when the *Arthaśāstra* started to be composed.

If his clansmen really committed such a heinous crime, what would Kṛṣṇa do? Would he still save his kinsmen in his capacity of the Vāsudeva? The episode shows that such was not to be the case. Kṛṣṇa would not allow his affection for his kinsmen to come in the way of his *dharma*. The lecture he had given to Arjuna, '*kṣudraṃ hṛdayadaurbalyaṃ tyaktottiṣṭha parantapa*', was illustrated by him with example at Prabhāsa. He himself killed several Yādavas and ended the tyranny that was based on his own power. Kinship never prevented Kṛṣṇa from meting out justice. He started by killing his own uncle who had turned into a tyrant; he ended by killing his own tyrannical kinsmen.

But was it to be the end of Kṛṣṇa? Was it the end that suited the greatest hero of the *Mahābhārata*? Was the Vāsudeva to perish unnoticed, in a forest, with nobody but a hunter for company? The 'Mahaparinibbāna Suttānta' of the *Dīgha Nikāya* records how the Buddha departed in great grandeur, like a king of kings. Numerous relic *stūpas* still bear the memory of his departure. Jesus's sacrifice of his body for mankind has been a moment canonized, a moment to be relived in every Eucharist and to be inspired by. Mahāvīra's departure is said to have been greeted with Dīpāvalī lamps in the Malla country. Did not Vāsudeva Kṛṣṇa deserve a more ceremonious departure?

Or, maybe, this is what suited Kṛṣṇa most. Karve writes:

> Krishna remains an elusive personality for this very reason. He worked, he thought intensely, he advised others, but we do not find him downcast or mourning because his actions, thought or advice did not bear fruit ... we do not find him mourning even after the terrible end of his clan. He made arrangements that the old, the very young and the women to be taken care of, and then met with his death. This is what he would have called yoga, this calm, this non-involvement.[521]

Kṛṣṇa lived his teachings. He epitomized the desireless action, the non-attached indifference to pleasure and pain he taught. The Buddha perceived death as one of the three great sorrows of human existence. The *stūpas* stand as a testimony to that. Kṛṣṇa taught a philosophy of life, of celebrating action. Death was nothing but one mere step to him, a bodily transformation such as the change from adolescence to youth to old age, like changing a worn-out garment for a new one. Kṛṣṇa passed away with that message, paying little importance to death that did not exist in his philosophy.

Here we find why Kṛṣṇa was Vyāsa's hero. The deserted child born of a premarital union, the sage denounced by the caste orthodoxy, the ugly dark man despised by the beautiful queens, the scholar killed by the crazy Yādavas, Vyāsa still established himself as the greatest mind of his time, as the poet of an immortal *itihāsa*. His composition showed an alternative to the world, the alternative to the hereditary *varṇa* order, the alternative of ability epitomized by his protagonist Yudhiṣṭhira. Countering the Vedic orthodoxy, he composed his 'fifth Veda', the 'Veda of the women and the *śūdras*', that alone outweighed the other four. And he had his hero in Kṛṣṇa—the hero of the changing times: the hero who could question the Vedic ritualism and provide an alternative in the true sacrifice that was action; the man who could question the hereditary *varṇa* on the basis of the doctrine of *svadharma* based on *svabhāva* determined by *guṇakarma*; the man who discarded the mindless adherence to vows as childish and could speak of the *dharma* which emphasized the welfare of all beings. Starting in a free-flowing cowherds' camp, Kṛṣṇa's mortal life ended on a hunter's breast. The time in between saw several ups and downs, from Kaṃsa to Jarāsandha, from Kurukṣetra to Prabhāsa, from Rādhā to Rukmiṇī, from the burning of the Khāṇḍava to the propagation of the *Gītā*. However, as Kṛṣṇa taught, life never ends. The inherent paradox, the surprising iconoclasm, yet the unavoidable charisma in Kṛṣṇa continued his journey. Deification was only a start, since he became the deity to be adopted by whoever sought to challenge the order, to voice a dissent through devotion. Rāma could be the eye-candy hero for those who valorized the orthodoxy and, in recent times, communal fundamentalism. Kṛṣṇa was to be the hero of those who believed like him that it was neither religion nor birth nor sex, but only action and approach, which made someone a god and someone else a demon. His Cosmic Form might have been imagined by a later interpolator, but his character contained all the ingredients of a *viśvarūpa*. Kṛṣṇa's journey as a deity, therefore, has a history no less exciting than the history of his life, and that suits the man who taught that God resides in every human being, that a human being could attain godhood, and that there was indeed no difference between God and the man. However, that journey is a different story to be told in a different context.

Notes

1. Cited in Sukthankar (1957), p. 95.
2. Karve (2007), p. 158.
3. Vyāsa, II.35.15–25; translation slightly modified.
4. Vyāsa, II.38.10–20.
5. Cited in Hiltebeitel (1979), pp. 67–68.
6. Cited in Hiltebeitel (1979), pp. 88–90.
7. Hermann Jacobi, 'Incarnations (Indian)', *Hastings Encyclopaedia of Religion and Ethics* (Vol. VII), Scribner, New York, 1964, p. 195.
8. R.G. Bhandarkar, *Vaiṣṇavism, Saivism and Minor Religious Systems*, Indological Book House, Varanasi, 1965 (reprint), pp. 8–12.
9. Bhandarkar (1965), pp. 37–8.
10. Kosambi (1964), pp. 31–44.
11. Hiltebeitel (1979), p. 67.
12. E. Washburn Hopkins, *Epic Mythology*, Biblo and Tannen, New York, 1969b (reprint), pp. 215–216.
13. Hopkins (1969b), pp. 397–398.
14. Sylvain Levi, 'Tato Jayam Udirayet', *Annals of the Bhandarkar Oriental Research Institute*, Vol. I, 1918–1919, pp. 13–20.
15. Sukthankar (1957).
16. Bankim Chandra Chattopadhyay, 'Kṛṣṇacaitra' in *Bankim Racanavali* (Vol. I, Part II), Pshchimbanga Niraksharata Durikaran Samiti, Calcutta, 1973.
17. H.C. Raychaudhuri, *Materials for the Study of the Early History of the Vaiṣṇava Sect*, Oriental Books Reprint Corporation, New Delhi, 1975 (reprint).
18. Madhav M. Deshpande, 'The Epic Context of the Bhagavadgītā' in Arvind Sharma (ed.), *Essays on the Mahābhārata*, Motilal Banarsidass, Delhi, 2007, pp. 334–348.
19. Cited in Hiltebeitel (1979), pp. 99–107.
20. Karve (2007), pp. 141–161.
21. Van Buitenen (1975a), pp. 14–21.

22. Bhaduri (2004).
23. Cited in Hiltebeitel (1979), p. 95.
24. TĀ, X.1.6.
25. Cited in Bhaduri (2004), p. 26.
26. CU, III.17.6.
27. TS, III.19.9.3; JUB, I.6.1.
28. Pāṇini, IV.3.98.
29. Bhaduri (2004), pp. 29–30.
30. Cited in Raychaudhuri (1975), pp. 45, 60.
31. Kosambi (1964), p. 35.
32. R.C. Majumdar, *Ancient India*, Motilal Banarsidass, Delhi, 1989 (reprint), p. 173.
33. R.C. Majumdar (ed.), *Classical Accounts of India*, Firma K.L. Mukhopadhyaya, Calcutta, 1941, pp. 119–120.
34. Bhaduri (2004), p. 31.
35. Angelika Malinar, *The Bhagavadgītā: Doctrines and Contexts*, Cambridge University Press, Cambridge, 2007, p. 255.
36. Malinar (2007), p. 251.
37. Malinar (2007), p. 252.
38. Malinar (2007), p. 252.
39. Malinar (2007), p. 255.
40. Malinar (2007), pp. 252–253.
41. Bhaduri (2004), p. 61.
42. *The Jātaka* (Vol. IV), pp. 50–57.
43. *The Jātaka* (Vol. VI), pp. 246–247.
44. Karve (2007), p. 149.
45. Sumitra Bai and Zydenbos (2007), pp. 251–273.
46. Majumdar (1989), p. 173.
47. ṚV, VII.19.7.
48. ṚV, VII.18.19.
49. TS, III.19.9.3; TB, III.10.9.15; ŚB, III.1.1.4, XIII.5.4.21; AB, VIII.14.3; JUB, I.6.1.
50. Cited in Raychaudhuri (1975), p. 20.
51. *Viṣṇumahāpurāṇaṃ*, translated by M.N. Dutt, Eastern Book Linkers, Delhi, 2005 (reprint).
52. *The Bhāgavata Purāṇa* (Part IV), translated by G.V. Tagare, Motilal Banarsidass, Delhi, 2002 (reprint), X.1.59–69.
53. *Viṣṇumahāpurāṇaṃ*, V.4.16.
54. Raychaudhuri (1975), p. 45.
55. *Viṣṇumahāpurāṇam*, V.7.
56. ṚV, VIII.96.13–15; ṚV VIII.85.13–15 in Griffith's translation.
57. *Harivaṃśa*, 59.5–18; translation mine.
58. *Viṣṇumahāpurāṇam*, V.10.19–24.
59. *Viṣṇumahāpurāṇam*, V.10.26–30.
60. *Harivaṃśa*, 59.20–61.

61. *Viṣṇumahāpurāṇaṃ*, V.10.37.
62. *Viṣṇumahāpurāṇam*, V.10.38–40.
63. *Viṣṇumahāpurāṇam*, V.12.12; *Harivaṃśa*, 62.43–44.
64. *Viṣṇumahāpurāṇam*, V.13.10–12.
65. Vyāsa, II.38.5–10.
66. Kosambi (1964), p. 40.
67. Bankim Chandra Chattopadhyay (1973), pp. 620–621.
68. *Viṣṇumahāpurāṇam*, V.5.12–13.
69. Hāla (ed.), *The Prakrit Gathasaptasati*, translated by Radhagovinda Basak, Asiatic Society, Calcutta, 1971, II.14.
70. Ilanko Atikal, *The Cilappatikaram: The Tale of an Anklet*, translated by R. Parthasarathy, Penguin, New Delhi, 2004, XVII.5.
71. *Harivaṃśa*, 63.30.
72. *Viṣṇumahāpurāṇaṃ*, V.13.47–50; translation slightly changed.
73. *Viṣṇumahāpurāṇaṃ*, V.13.53–55.
74. *Harivaṃśa*, 63.32–32.
75. *Harivaṃśa*, 63.25.
76. Hāla, II.12.
77. *Viṣṇumahāpurāṇaṃ*, V.13.59.
78. J.L. Mason, 'The Childhood of Kṛṣṇa: Some Psycho-Analytic Observation', *Journal of the American Oriental Society*, Vol. 94, No. 4, Oct–Dec 1974, pp. 454–459.
79. Hāla, I.89.
80. Atikal (2004), XVII.23–25.
81. Vyāsa, II.13.33.
82. *Harivaṃśa*, 65.
83. *Harivaṃśa*, 73.36.
84. *Harivaṃśa*, 73.8.
85. *Harivaṃśa*, 65.96.
86. Vyāsa, II.14.33.
87. Bhaduri (2004), p. 64.
88. *Viṣṇumahāpurāṇaṃ*, V.20.81.
89. Vyāsa, V.7.18.
90. *Harivaṃśa*, 76.19.
91. *Viṣṇumahāpurāṇam*, V.20.84.
92. *Harivaṃśa*, 77.46.
93. Bhāsa, 'The Envoy' in *The Shattered Thigh and Other Plays*, translated by A.N.D. Haskar, Penguin, New Delhi, 2008, p. 69.
94. Bhāsa (2008), p. 69.
95. Vyāsa, V.126.36–37.
96. *Harivaṃśa*, 78.33–35.
97. Vyāsa, XII.341.41.
98. Vyāsa, V.69.3.

99. Vyāsa, II.13.
100. Vyāsa, II.18–22.
101. Cited in J.L. Brockington, 'Jarāsaṃdha of Magadha' in Mary Brockington (ed.), *Proceedings of the Second Dubrovnik International Conference on the Sanskrit Epics and Puranas, August 1999*, Croatian Academy of Science and Arts, Zagreb, 2002, p. 78.
102. Kosambi (1964).
103. Asko Parpola, 'On the Jaiminīya and Vādhūla Traditions of South India and the Pāṇḍu/Pāṇḍava Problem', *Studia Orientalia*, Vol. 55, 1984, pp. 3–42.
104. Cited in Brockington (2002), p. 80.
105. Cited in Brockington (2002), p. 82.
106. Brockington (2002).
107. Van Buitenen (1975a), p. 15. We must mention that many scholars identify Rājagṛha and Girivraja but that was possibly because the latter was gradually absorbed into the greater city of Rājagṛha. The name 'Girivraja' indicates a mountain fastness inhabited by pastoral people.
108. Vyāsa, II.12.8.
109. AV, V.22.14.
110. *Harivaṃśa*, 81.6.
111. Vyāsa, II.13.49.
112. Bhāsa (2008), p. 69.
113. Bhāsa (2008), p. 69.
114. Norvin Hein, 'Kālayavana, a Key to Mathurā's Cultural Self-Perception' in Doris Meth Srinivasan, *Mathurā: The Cultural Heritage*', American Institute of Indian Studies, New Delhi, 1989, pp. 223–235.
115. *Harivaṃśa*, 87.33–41.
116. *Viṣṇumahāpurāṇam*, V.26.1–6.
117. Vyāsa, V.29.68.
118. Vyāsa, II.42.15.
119. Vyāsa, II.42.18–19.
120. Vyāsa, II.13.21–22.
121. Vyāsa, I.211.23.
122. Vyāsa, I.213.3–10.
123. Vyāsa, I.213.15–20.
124. *Viṣṇumahāpurāṇam*, V.29.9–11.
125. Vyāsa, V.29.74.
126. The suspicion over Sītā's 'chastity' after her abduction by Rāvaṇa, in the *Rāmāyaṇa*, can be a point of comparison.
127. Vyāsa, II.14.17–19; translation slightly modified.
128. Vyāsa, II.19–20.
129. Vyāsa, II.22.
130. Vyāsa, II.33.22–23.
131. Vyāsa, II.25–29.

132. Vyāsa, II.34.5–11.
133. Vyāsa, II.34.15.
134. Vyāsa, II.35.6–21.
135. Vyāsa, II.35.22–28.
136. Vyāsa, II.36.1–4.
137. Vyāsa, II.38–39.
138. Vyāsa, II.40.
139. Vyāsa, II.42.7–11.
140. Vyāsa, V.22.24–27.
141. Van Buitenen (1975b), p. 182.
142. Witzel (1997b), p. 304.
143. Vyāsa, V.29.73.
144. Vyāsa, II.13.19.
145. *Viṣṇumahāpurāṇam*, V.34.4–27.
146. Vyāsa, V.29.79–80.
147. Vyāsa, V.28.13.
148. *Viṣṇumahāpurāṇam*, V.36.5–9.
149. Vyāsa, V.128.41.
150. Vyāsa, V.28.11–12.
151. Bhaduri (2004), p. 92; for Yāska's reference and its analysis, see Jogendranath Basu, 'Sources of the Two Kṛṣṇa Legends', *Indian Culture*, Vol. VI, Nos 1–4, July 1939–April 1940, pp. 464–467.
152. *Harivaṃśa*, 29.1.
153. *Viṣṇumahāpurāṇam*, IV.13.42.
154. Jogendranath Basu (1939–1940), p. 467.
155. *The Brahma Purāṇa* (Part I), edited by J.L. Shastri, Motilal Banarsidass, New Delhi, 2001, XIV.25.
156. *Viṣṇumahāpurāṇaṃ*, IV.13.27–28.
157. *Viṣṇumahāpurāṇaṃ*, IV.13.35.
158. *The Brahma Purāṇa*, XV.4–5.
159. *The Brahma Purāṇa*, IV.13.65–68, IV.13.82–86.
160. *Viṣṇumahāpurāṇaṃ*, IV.13.104.
161. *Viṣṇumahāpurāṇaṃ*, IV.13.136.
162. *Viṣṇumahāpurāṇaṃ*, IV.13.150–151.
163. *Viṣṇumahāpurāṇaṃ*, IV.13.74, 79.
164. *The Jātaka* (Vol. VI), pp. 216–217.
165. *Corpus Inscriptionum Indicarum* (Vol. III), pp. 269–270.
166. Vyāsa, V.128.48.
167. *Viṣṇumahāpurāṇaṃ*, V.30.34–37.
168. *Viṣṇumahāpurāṇaṃ*, V.30.46–51.
169. *Harivaṃśa*, 92.
170. Vyāsa, V.1.13–14.
171. Vyāsa, V.1.23–24.

172. Vyāsa, V.2.1–12.
173. Vyāsa, V.5.1–10.
174. Vyāsa, V.7.1–22.
175. Vyāsa, V.7.23–28.
176. Vyāsa, V.19.1.
177. Vyāsa, V.7.30.
178. Vyāsa, V.7.32–33.
179. Vyāsa, V.29.67–79.
180. Vyāsa, V.28.11–14.
181. Vyāsa, V.66.4–14.
182. Vyāsa, V.67.2–3.
183. Vyāsa, V.68.
184. Vyāsa, V.69.
185. Vyāsa, V.67.19–21.
186. Vyāsa, V.128.41–54.
187. Vyāsa, V.25.7.
188. Vyāsa, V.25.9.
189. Vyāsa, V.27.24–25.
190. Vyāsa, V.27.2.
191. Vyāsa, V.28.8.
192. Vyāsa, V.29.1–2.
193. Vyāsa, V.29.6–14.
194. Vyāsa, V.29.21–24; translation slightly modified.
195. Vyāsa, V.29.25.
196. Vyāsa, V.29.27–28.
197. Vyāsa, V.29.31–40.
198. Vyāsa, V.91.5–20.
199. Vyāsa, V.158.31–33; translation slightly modified.
200. Vyāsa, V.158.9; translation slightly modified.
201. Vyāsa, V.130.7; translation slightly modified.
202. Vyāsa, V.130.19–29; translation slightly modified.
203. Vyāsa, V.131.5.
204. Vyāsa, V.131.30–32.
205. Vyāsa, V.132.2.
206. Vyāsa, V.131.13.
207. Vyāsa, V.131.15.
208. Vyāsa, V.132.36–38; translation slightly modified.
209. Vyāsa, V.7046–49; translation modified.
210. Vyāsa, V.70.70–74.
211. Vyāsa, V.70.53–59.
212. Vyāsa, V.70.65–69.
213. Vyāsa, V.70.68.
214. Vyāsa, V.70.42–45.

215. Vyāsa, V.72.1–23.
216. Vyāsa, V.76; V.81.1–4.
217. Vyāsa, V.78.
218. Vyāsa, V.79.1–4.
219. Vyāsa, V.135.16–17.
220. Vyāsa, V.80.31–41.
221. Vyāsa, V.80.16–19; translation slightly modified.
222. Vyāsa, V.71.3–5; translation slightly modified.
223. Vyāsa, V.71.21–24.
224. Vyāsa, V.73.15–23; translation slightly modified.
225. Vyāsa, V.83–84.
226. Vyāsa, V.85.18.
227. Vyāsa, V.89.15–19.
228. Vyāsa, V.89.24–25.
229. Vyāsa, V.122.32–35.
230. Vyāsa, V.127.20–34.
231. Vyāsa, V.128.1–9.
232. Vyāsa, V.77.5.
233. Vyāsa, V.139.20–23.
234. Vyāsa, VI.23.28–37; translation slightly modified.
235. E.W. Hopkins, *The Religions of India*, Ginn, Boston, 1895, p. 389.
236. Cited in Malinar (2007), p. 23.
237. Malinar (2007), p. 23.
238. W.D.P. Hill, *The Bhagavadgītā: Translated from the Sanskrit with an Introduction and Argument and a Commentary*, Oxford University Press, London, 1928, p. 35.
239. F. Edgerton, *The Bhagavad Gītā or the Song of the Blessed or India's Favourite Bible*, Chicago University Press, Chicago, 1925, p. 2; F. Edgerton, 'Review of "The Original Gītā: The Song of the Supreme Exalted One" by Rudolf Otto, translated and edited by J.E. Turner', *Review of Religion*, Vol. 4, p. 448.
240. Cited in Malinar (2007), p. 26.
241. D.D. Kosambi, *Myth and Reality*, Popular Prakashan, Bombay, 1962, pp. 12–41.
242. Cited in Malinar (2007), p. 26.
243. G.M. Bailey, 'On D.D. Kosambi's Interpretation of the Bhagavadgītā', *Indologica Taurinensia*, Vol. 12, pp. 343–353.
244. S.C. Roy, *The Bhagavadgītā and Modern Scholarship*, Luzac, London, 1941.
245. Sukthankar (1957).
246. R.C. Zaehner, *The Bhagavad-Gītā with a Commentary Based on the Original Sources*, Oxford University Press, Oxford, 1969.
247. Cited in Malinar (2007), p. 27.
248. M. Biardeau, 'The Salvation of the king in the Mahābhārata', *Contributions to Indian Sociology*, New Series, Vol. 15, 1981, pp. 75–97; M. Biardeau, 'Some Remarks on the Links between the Epics, the Puranas, and Their Vedic Sources'

in G. Oberhammer (ed.), *Studies in Hinduism: Vedism and Hinduism*, Verlag der Osterreichischen Akademie der Wissenschaften, Vienna, 1997, pp. 69–177.

249. J.A.B. van Buitenen, *The Bhagavadgītā in the Mahābhārata: Text and Translation*, Chicago University Press, Chicago, 1981, p. 5.
250. Nick Sutton, 'What Is *Dharma*? Ethical Tensions within the *Mahābhārata*' in T.S. Rukmani (ed.), *The Mahābhārata: What Is Not Here Is Nowhere Else*, Munshiram Manoharlal, New Delhi, 2005, pp. 91–102.
251. Cited in Malinar (2007), p. 20.
252. R.N. Minor, *Bhagavad-Gītā: An Exegetical Commentary*, Heritage, Delhi, 1982, p. 362.
253. Cited in Malinar (2007), p. 187.
254. Cited in Malinar (2007), p. 21.
255. Malinar (2007), p. 23.
256. J. Charpentier, 'Some Remarks on the Bhagavadgītā', *Indian Antiquary*, Vol. 59, pp. 40–126.
257. Cited in Malinar (2007), p. 25.
258. M. Jezic, 'Textual Layers of the Bhagavadgītā: Traces of Indian Cultural History' in W. Morgenroth (ed.), *Sanskrit and World Culture*, Akademie Verlag, Weimar, 1979, p. 633.
259. Cited in Malinar (2007), p. 22.
260. Malinar (2007), pp. 23–24.
261. G.S. Khair, *Quest for the Original Gītā*, Somaiya, Bombay, 1969.
262. Karve (2007), p. 159.
263. A.L. Basham, *The Origins and Development of Classical Hinduism*, Beacon Press, Boston, 1989, pp. 92–98.
264. Basham (1989), p. 96.
265. Malinar (2007), pp. 5–7.
266. Malinar (2007), pp. 35–53; Madhav M. Deshpande, 'The Epic Context of the Bhagavadgītā' in Arvind Sharma (ed.), *Essays on the Mahābhārata*, Motilal Banarsidass, New Delhi, 2007, pp. 334–348.
267. Kevin McGrath, *Arjuna Pāṇḍava: The Double Hero in Epic Mahābhārata*, Orient BlackSwan, Hyderabad, 2016, pp. 73–106.
268. S. Jaiswal, *The Origin and Development of Vaiṣṇavism*, Munshiram Manoharlal, Delhi, 1967, pp. 223–224.
269. Vyāsa, VI.32.8.
270. Vyāsa, VI.32.23.
271. Vyāsa, VI.32.24.
272. Vyāsa, VI.32.26.
273. Vyāsa, VI.31.26.
274. S. Radhakrishnan, *Indian Philosophy* (Vol. 1), Oxford University Press, New Delhi, 2008 (reprint), pp. 446–447.
275. For a detailed discussion, also see Basham (1989), pp. 87–89.
276. Cited in Malinar (2007), p. 64.

277. A. Hejib and K. Young, 'Klība on the Battlefield: Towards a Reinterpretation of Arjuna's Despondency', *Annals of the Bhandarkar Oriental Research Institute*, Vol. 61, pp. 235–244.
278. Biardeau (1981).
279. Van Buitenen (1981), p. 3.
280. Bimal Krishna Matilal, *Ethics and Epics* (Vol. II), Oxford University Press, New Delhi, 2002, p. 125.
281. Vyāsa, VI.24.6.
282. Vyāsa, VI.23.40–44.
283. Vyāsa, VI.24.3.
284. Vyāsa, VI.24.12.
285. Vyāsa, VI.24.13.
286. Vyāsa, VI.24.22.
287. Vyāsa, VI.24.16–18.
288. Vyāsa, VI.24.24–25.
289. Vyāsa, VI.24.19–21.
290. Vyāsa, V.I.24.27–28.
291. KU, II.18–19.
292. G.V. Devasthali, 'Bhagavad-Gītā and Upaniṣads' in J.N. Agrawal and B.D. Shastri (eds), *Sarupa-bharati or the Homage of Indology*, Vishveshvarananda Indological Institute, Hoshiarpur, 1954, pp. 132–142.
293. Malinar (2007), p. 67.
294. Cited in Malinar (2007), p. 67.
295. BU, IV.4.22.
296. *The Middle Length Discourses of the Buddha*, I.136.
297. *The Connected Discourses of the Buddha*, III.3.
298. Vyāsa, VI.24.31–36.
299. Vyāsa, VI.24.37–38.
300. Vyāsa, VI.24.42–44.
301. Vyāsa, VI.24.45.
302. KU, I.26–28.
303. BU, II.4.2–3.
304. Vyāsa, VI.24.47–48.
305. Sibaji Bandyopadhyay, 'Translating *Gītā* 2.47 or Inventing a National Motto' in *Three Essays on the Mahābhārata*, Orient BlackSwan, Hyderabad, 2016b, pp. 8–190.
306. Bandyopadhyay (2016b), pp. 76–77.
307. Bandyopadhyay (2016b), p. 27.
308. Bandyopadhyay (2016b), p. 37.
309. Bandyopadhyay (2016b), pp. 52–53.
310. Bandyopadhyay (2016b), p. 54.
311. Bandyopadhyay (2016b), pp. 54–55.
312. Bandyopadhyay (2016b), p. 55.

313. Bandyopadhyay (2016b), p. 54.
314. Bandyopadhyay (2016b), p. 90.
315. Bandyopadhyay (2016b), p. 107.
316. Bandyopadhyay (2016b), p. 118.
317. Bandyopadhyay (2016b), p. 122.
318. Bandyopadhyay (2016b), pp. 131–141.
319. Bandyopadhyay (2016b), pp. 24–25.
320. Bandyopadhyay (2016b), p. 55.
321. Bandyopadhyay (2016b), p. 110.
322. Bandyopadhyay (2016b), pp. 72–74.
323. Bandyopadhyay (2016b), pp. 59–71.
324. Bandyopadhyay (2016b), p. 167.
325. Bandyopadhyay (2016b), p. 71.
326. Bandyopadhyay (2016b), p. 85.
327. Bandyopadhyay (2016b), p. 92.
328. Vyāsa, VI.26.18.
329. Bandyopadhyay (2016b), p. 90.
330. Bandyopadhyay (2016b), p. 67.
331. Bandyopadhyay (2016b), p. 70.
332. BU, IV.4.5.
333. Vyāsa, XII.194.11.
334. Vyāsa, III.33.30–32.
335. Vyāsa, III.33.36.
336. Vyāsa, VI.25.5.
337. Vyāsa, VI.25.8.
338. Bandyopadhyay (2016b), p. 110.
339. Cited in Matilal (2002), p. 123.
340. Malinar (2007), pp. 69–75.
341. Vyāsa, VI.24.50–51.
342. Vyāsa, VI.24.55–58.
343. Vyāsa, VI.24.14–15.
344. Vyāsa, VI.24.62–63.
345. Vyāsa, VI.24.71.
346. Vyāsa, VI.24.72.
347. *Middle Length Discourses of the Buddha*, I.136.
348. *Connected Discourses of the Buddha*, IV.47.
349. Zaehner (1969), p. 213.
350. Van Buitenen (1981), p. 163.
351. S. Dasgupta, *A History of Indian Philosophy* (Vol. II), Cambridge University Press, Cambridge, 1952, pp. 437–552.
352. Vyāsa, VI.25.1.
353. Vyāsa, VI.25.3–8.
354. Vyāsa, VI.25.20.

355. Vyāsa, VI.25.12.
356. Vyāsa, VI.25.15.
357. Vyāsa, VI.25.19.
358. Vyāsa, VI.25.22–23.
359. Vyāsa, VI.25.35.
360. Vyāsa, VI.25.27.
361. CU, III.17.1–4.
362. Vyāsa, VI.27.37–39.
363. Vyāsa, VI.25.42.
364. KU, III.10–11.
365. Malinar (2007), p. 92.
366. Vyāsa, VI.25.43.
367. Vyāsa, VI.24.61; VI.25.30–32.
368. Vyāsa, VI.26.1–2.
369. Vyāsa, VI.26.5–8.
370. Cited in Raychaudhuri (1975), p. 74.
371. Radhakrishnan (2008), p. 444.
372. Vyāsa, VI.26.10.
373. Vyāsa, VI.26.11.
374. Matilal (2002), p. 142.
375. CU, IV.4.
376. Vyāsa, VI.26.23–24.
377. Vyāsa, VI.26.28.
378. Vyāsa, VI.26.33.
379. Vyāsa, VI.27.1.
380. Vyāsa, VI.27.2–5.
381. Vyāsa, VI.27.7.
382. Cited in Malinar (2007), p. 111.
383. Van Buitenen (1981), p. 91.
384. Cited in Malinar (2007), p. 111.
385. MU, III.1.4.
386. Vyāsa, VI.27.18.
387. Vyāsa, VI.27.20.
388. Vyāsa, VI.28.29.
389. Vyāsa, VI.28.7–9.
390. ĪU, 6–7.
391. Vyāsa, VI.28.32.
392. Vyāsa, VI.27.21–25.
393. ĪU, 16.
394. Vyāsa, VI.28.28
395. Vyāsa, VI.28.17.
396. *Middle Length Discourses of the Buddha*, I.130–142.
397. Vyāsa, VI.28.5–6.

398. *Dhammapada*, translated by Rhys Davids, Pali Text Society, London, 1979 (reprint), p. 379.
399. Vyāsa, VI.28.1.
400. Vyāsa, VI.29.6–7.
401. Vyāsa, VI.29.8–11.
402. Vyāsa, VI.33.32–4.
403. Vyāsa, VI.30.20–23; VI.31.20–21.
404. Vyāsa, VI.31.23.
405. Vyāsa, VI.31.26–27.
406. Vyāsa, VI.34.5–7.
407. Basham (1989), pp. 87–8.
408. Vyāsa, VI.32.26.
409. Vyāsa, VI.32.25.
410. Vyāsa, VI.32.36.
411. Vyāsa, VI.32.31.
412. Vyāsa, VI.64.2–6.
413. Vyāsa, VI.30.16–19.
414. Madhav M. Deshpande, 'Interpreting the *Mahābhārata*' in T.S. Rukmani (ed.), *The Mahābhārata: What Is Not Here Is Nowhere Else*, Munshiram Manoharlal, New Delhi, 2005, pp. 3–18.
415. Vyāsa, VI.33.46.
416. CU, V.10.1–2; BU, VI.2.15–16; *Praśna Upaniṣad*, I.9–10.
417. Vyāsa, VI.31.32.
418. Vyāsa, VI.34.15–19.
419. CU, VI.17.6.
420. Vyāsa, VI.30.5.
421. Vyāsa, VI.30.9–11.
422. KU, II.20 ; CU, III.14.3 ; ŚU, III.9, III.20.
423. MU, III.1.7.
424. ŚU, III.8.
425. Vyāsa, VI.34.12.
426. Vyāsa, VI.37.13–16.
427. Vyāsa, VI.36.24–25.
428. Vyāsa, VI.37.1–3.
429. KU, VI.1.
430. ŚU, III.7.9.
431. R.D. Karmakar, 'Bhagavadgītā XVI.8 Asatyaṃpratiṣṭhāṃ Te', *Annals of the Bhandarkar Oriental Research Institute*, Vol. 31, pp. 132–137.
432. Cited in Malinar (2007), p. 181.
433. Minor (1982), p. 438; T.G. Mainkar, 'Some Thoughts on the Brahmasūtras and the Bhagavadgītā', *Annals of the Bhandarkar Oriental Research Institute*, Vols 58–59, p. 751.
434. Vyāsa, VI.38.13–15.

435. Vyāsa, VI.38.1–3.
436. Vyāsa, VI.37.16–17.
437. Vyāsa, VI.35.13–17.
438. ṚV, X.81.3.
439. ŚU, III.16–17.
440. ĪU, 5.
441. MU, III.1.7.
442. BU, IV.4.6.
443. Vyāsa, VI.37.6.
444. KU, V.15; ŚU, VI.14; MU, II.2.9.
445. Vyāsa, VI.35.27–30.
446. Vyāsa, VI.40.5–6.
447. Vyāsa, VI.40.41–44.
448. Arti Dhand, '*Karmayoga* and the Vexed Moral Agent' in Sibesh Chandra Bhattacharya, Vrinda Dalmiya, and Gangeya Mukherji (eds), *Exploring Agency in the Mahabharata: Ethical and Political Dimensions of Dharma*, Routledge, London and New York, 2018, pp. 83–85.
449. Dhand (2018), p. 81.
450. Dhand (2018), p. 94.
451. Dhand (2018), p. 91.
452. Dhand (2018), p. 96.
453. Dhand (2018), p. 103.
454. Vyāsa, VI.40.45–48.
455. Buddhadeb Basu (2004), pp. 87–96.
456. Cited in Radhakrishnan (2008), p. 488.
457. Vyāsa, VI.40.51–54.
458. Vyāsa, VI.40.61–62.
459. Vyāsa, VI.40.63.
460. Vyāsa, VI.40.66.
461. David Kinsley, 'Devotion as an Alternative to Marriage in the Lives of Some Hindu Women Devotees' in Jayant Lele (ed.), *Tradition and Modernity in the Bhakti Movement*, E.J. Brill, Leiden, 1981, pp. 90–91.
462. Jayant Lele, 'Introduction' in Jayant Lele (ed.), *Tradition and Modernity in the Bhakti Movement*, E.J. Brill, Leiden, 1981, p. 13.
463. *The Jātaka* (Vol. IV), p. 55.
464. Radhakrishnan (2008), p. 497.
465. Bhāsa, 'Urubhaṅga', translated by Edwin Gerow, in Arvind Sharma (ed.), *Essays on the Mahābhārata*, Motilal Banarsidass, New Delhi, 2011, p. 68.
466. Vyāsa, VI.40.78.
467. Mehendale (1995).
468. Bankim Chandra Chattopadhyay (1973), pp. 747–750.
469. Vyāsa, VI.103.70–82.
470. Vyāsa, VI.103.85–89.

471. Vyāsa, VI.103.90–100.
472. Vyāsa, VII.53.2–3.
473. Vyāsa, VII.50.62–69; 54.12–26.
474. Vyāsa, VII.121.1–15.
475. Vyāsa, VII.155.2–4.
476. Vyāsa, VII.155.11–30.
477. Vyāsa, VII.156.
478. Vyāsa, VII.164.67–68.
479. Vyāsa, VII.164.72–74.
480. Vyāsa, VII.164.94–95.
481. Vyāsa, VII.164.106.
482. Vyāsa, VII.164.27–32.
483. Bimal Krishna Matilal, 'Kṛṣṇa: In Defence of a Devious Divinity' in Arvind Sharma (ed.), *Essays on the Mahābhārata*, Motilal Banarsidass, New Delhi, 2011, pp. 401–418.
484. Vyāsa, VII.164.98–99; translation follows M.N. Dutt.
485. Vyāsa, VII.164.107; translation follows M.N. Dutt.
486. Bankim Chandra Chattopadhyay (1973), pp. 761–771.
487. Cited in Bimal Krishna Matilal, *Niti, Yukti o Dharma*, Ananda, Calcutta, 1988, p. 52.
488. Vyāsa, VIII.49.19–20; translation follows M.N. Dutt.
489. Vyāsa, VIII.49.21–22.
490. Vyāsa, VIII.49.23.
491. Vyāsa, VIII.49.27–28; translation follows M.N. Dutt).
492. Vyāsa, VIII.49.19.
493. Vyāsa, VIII.49.53.
494. Vyāsa, VIII.49.30; translation follows M.N. Dutt.
495. Vyāsa, VIII.49.41–46.
496. Matilal (1988), pp. 59–61.
497. Matilal (1988), p. 48.
498. Matilal (1988), pp. 56–58.
499. Matilal (1988), p. 48.
500. Vyāsa, VIII.49.47.
501. Vyāsa, VIII.49.49–50; translation follows M.N. Dutt.
502. Lakshmi Bandlamudi, 'Answerability between Lived Life and Living Text: Chronotopicity in Finding Agency in the *Mahābhārata*' in Sibesh Chandra Bhattacharya, Vrinda Dalmiya, and Gangeya Mukherji (eds), *Exploring Agency in the Mahabharata: Ethical and Political Dimensions of Dharma*, Routledge, London and New York, 2018, p. 217.
503. Bandlamudi (2018), pp. 222–223.
504. Vrinda Dalmiya and Gangeya Mukherji, 'Introduction: To Do' in Lakshmi Bandlamudi, 'Answerability between Lived Life and Living Text: Chronotopicity in Finding Agency in the *Mahābhārata*' in Sibesh Chandra Bhattacharya,

Vrinda Dalmiya, and Gangeya Mukherji (eds), *Exploring Agency in the Mahabharata: Ethical and Political Dimensions of Dharma*, Routledge, London and New York, 2018, pp. 13–14.

505. Dalmiya and Mukherji (2018), pp. 12–13.
506. Vyāsa, VIII.49.57–63.
507. Vyāsa, VIII.49.67–71.
508. Vyāsa, VIII.49.91.
509. Vyāsa, VIII.51.
510. Vyāsa, VIII.66.10–13.
511. Vyāsa, VIII.67.2–5; translation follows M.N. Dutt.
512. Vyāsa, IX.59.17–21.
513. Vyāsa, IX.59.22.
514. Vyāsa, IX.60.27–38.
515. Vyāsa, IX.60.39–47.
516. Vyāsa, IX.61.48–51.
517. Vyāsa, IX.61.57–66.
518. See Matilal (1988), p. 122.
519. Phyllis Granoff, 'Karma, Curse or Divine Illusion: The Destruction of the Buddha's Clan and the Slaughter of the Yādavas' in Sheldon Pollock (ed.), *Epic and Argument in Sanskrit Literary History: Essays in Honour of Robert P. Goldman*, Manohar, New Delhi, 2010, pp. 75–90.
520. Kauṭilya, I.6.
521. Karve (2007), pp. 160–161.

5

The *Bhārata* beyond the Bhārata War

5.1 Śaunaka and the *Sūta*: Bhārgavizing the *Bhārata*

So far, we have tried to look at the *Mahābhārata* in its original context, as an *itihāsa* text reflecting on and commenting upon the transitions taking place in the Later Vedic period. We have also traced how the author, popularly believed to be Vyāsa, possibly rendered the transition a meaning which would not delight the orthodox followers of the Brahmanical *varṇa* norms and presented a unique and new understanding of *dharma*—with the concept of desireless action driven by *ānṛśaṃsya*—as propagated by new kinds of heroes, such as Yudhiṣṭhira and Kṛṣṇa. Thus, in its original form, the *Mahābhārata* would not have been a comfortable text for the Brahmanical order, and its obsessive insistence on multiple varied meanings of *dharma* would render any normativity futile. Ramanujan thinks that 'it is not *dharma* or right conduct that the *Mahābhārata* seems to teach, but the *sūkṣma* or subtle nature of *dharma*'.[1] Yudhiṣṭhira, the *dharmarāja* himself, opined that *dharma* as a concept was concealed in a cave (*dharmasya tattvaṃ nihitaṃ guhāyām*), in some manuscripts.[2] Goldman has noted how even Yudhiṣṭhira's own conduct did not always conform to the expected level of morality.[3] Therefore, not only the *dharmarāja* acted as an uncontrollable gambler, staked his brothers and wives in a dice game, always remained a silent spectator to his wife's harassment, and told a lie to get his teacher killed but he also cold-bloodedly murdered, with active support from his mother and brothers, six innocent poor *niṣādas*—lured by a prospect of good food—in the lacquer house built for the Pāṇḍavas, only to assure the Kauravas of their own pretended death.[4] As Greg Bailey puts it:

From Dāśarājña to Kurukṣetra. Kanad Sinha, Oxford University Press.
DOI: 10.1093/oso/9780190130695.003.0005

> *Mahābhārata* shows an awareness that despite an unqualified *dharma* having universal validity for the *ārya* ... the foundations of *dharma* are arbitrary and not beyond question.[5]

Arvind Sharma, in fact, thinks that the *Mahābhārata* was either by intention or by actual composition intimately related with the *śūdra* bards, who were closely associated by tradition with the metre *anuṣṭubh* in which most of the text is composed.[6] As we have seen earlier, the *Mahābhārata*, indeed, was initially a bardic composition, though the bards were not necessarily *śūdras*. The most prominent of the bards were the *sūtas*, and there were many other categories whose caste status could be varied.[7] We have already seen that the emergent hereditary *varṇa* system was not well accepted by Vyāsa who himself would not be very favourably located in a *varṇa*-based society. Few texts question the given maxims of its contemporary society as vigorously as the *Mahābhārata* does. G.C. Pande nicely puts it thus:

> Śvetaketu questions the origin of marriage, Yudhiṣṭhira the justification of the state. Arjuna questions the Kṣatriya's duty to fight, Janaka the very need to lead a worldly life.[8]

However, the composition of the text—as already mentioned—had a long journey lasting over a millennium. For a substantial section of its journey, at least after the text was put into writing, the *Mahābhārata* was controlled by the *brāhmaṇas* like other Sanskrit texts. This transformation turned the *itihāsa* into a scripture and increasingly asserted Kṛṣṇa's divinity (supplemented by the divine or demonic births of most of the other principal characters) to integrate the text into Vaiṣṇava theology. The *Mahābhārata* itself is aware of its shift from *kṣatriya-sūta* control to *brāhmaṇa* control. Thus, while Vaiśaṃpāyana had narrated it under *kṣatriya* patronage of the Kuru king Janamejaya, the bard Ugraśravas's narration was for an exclusively *brāhmaṇa* audience headed by Kulapati Śaunaka. That both the narrator and the patron of the first retelling were important Later Vedic figures have been discussed earlier. The second retelling is more symbolic as we have discussed how the names of the bards (Ugraśravas and his father Lomaharṣaṇa) and the location of the telling (Naimiṣa forest) are loaded with metaphorical meanings. However, it also points to a change in the nature of the text which the change of patronage was bound to bring. Deshpande notes that the narrators must have had to reshape their text to suit the needs of their royal and *brāhmaṇa* audience in the two retellings.[9] This is testified by the nature of Ugraśravas's narration in the text. As Sullivan has mentioned, these sections in the text are self-consciously later than the part where Vaiśaṃpāyana is the narrator.[10] More importantly, it is shown that Śaunaka clearly told Ugraśravas that his primary interest lay in the descent of his own clan, the Bhṛgus.[11] Ugraśravas craftily wove the story of the Bhārgava genealogy in a way that it culminated in the theme of Janamejaya's *sarpasatra* from whereon he could take up the story he had intended to tell, the tale of the Pāṇḍavas and the Kauravas.[12] Does this indicate a Bhārgava takeover of the text? Did the *Mahābhārata* undergo a 'Bhārgavization'?

This idea was first propounded by V.S. Sukthankar.[13] Pointing out the huge amount of Bhārgava myths in the text, he opined that the Bhārgavas took from the *sūtas* the *Bhārata* and gave back to the world the *Mahābhārata*, the same book yet different.[14] Goldman also noted the strong recurrence of the Bhārgava myths in both the *Mahābhārata* and the *Rāmāyaṇa* and thoroughly studied those myths.[15] McGrath showed how Bhārgavization created a new theology by associating Kṛṣṇa with an old divinity named Nārāyaṇa, possibly of pre-Aryan origin, and identifying Arjuna with Nara, the companion of Nārāyaṇa, and how often the Bhargavized sections justify their claims by drawing on traditions and stories referring to ancient times, mainly through the authoritative figure of Nārada who is depicted as the repository of divine and all-pervading knowledge and is the representative of oral traditions within the text.[16]

However, the idea of Bhārgavization has also been challenged. Sullivan has noted that the Bhārgava material is only 5 per cent of the text.[17] N.J. Shende, as early as in 1943, had noted that the Bhārgavas are not the only *brāhmaṇa* clan to have been frequently mentioned in the *Mahābhārata*.[18] In fact, there are more references to the Āṅgirasas than to the Bhārgavas in the *Mahābhārata*.[19] Hiltebeitel has rightly pointed out that the separation between a *Bhārata* and a *Mahābhārata* is not supported by the text.[20] Moreover, though it is said that the Naimiṣa sacrifice was headed by Kulapati Śaunaka, there is no suggestion that it was an exclusively Bhārgava affair. The other participants could well have been non-Bhārgava *brāhmaṇas*. In fact, referring to Goldman's study of the Bhārgava legends, Hiltebeitel notices that the Bhārgavas appear in conflict with princes and gods, but never with other *brāhmaṇas*, maybe because they represented them.[21] In other words, the Bhārgavas in the text can be representative of the *brāhmaṇa* myth-makers in general.[22] Hiltebeitel argues:

> There is nothing to suggest that the composing Brahmans were Bhārgavas. Indeed, it is far more likely that they were not, or not just.[23]

The point that these criticisms often miss is that it is not a matter of mere quantitative data. There are several *brāhmaṇa* groups, and their several legends, which appear in the *Mahābhārata*. However, it is only the Bhārgava cycle which is presented as a systematic body of myths—such as the *kṣatriya vaṃśas*—directly commissioned by Śaunaka. Moreover, the Bhārgava myths often appear in clusters, be it in I.5–12 of Ugraśravas's Bhārgava genealogy or in the Bhārgava Mārkaṇḍeya's storytelling sessions with the Pāṇḍavas in the 'Āraṇyakaparvan' or in the 'Śāntiparvan' and the 'Anuśāsanaparvan', indicating the insertion of bodies of separate Bhārgava texts in the *Mahābhārata*. In fact, as McGrath shows, the name of Bhṛgu alone occurs 135 times in the 'Śāntiparvan' and the 'Anuśāsanaparvan' of the *Mahābhārata*.[24] The Āṅgirasas definitely have more references. They must, since three of the major characters of the main narrative—Kṛpa, Droṇa, and Aśvatthāman—were Āṅgirasas. However, the concern is not the older narrative here but the additions and alterations made to the original narrative in subsequent centuries. Hence, the negligible presence of the Bhārgavas in the central narrative and yet the substantial amount of Bhārgava myths in the sections representative of a later context (the ones mentioned earlier) show that at some point of time the Bhārgavas had a prominent role in the history of the *Mahābhārata* text.

However, Hiltebeitel is probably correct in taking the Bhārgava role as representative of all the *brāhmaṇas*. The *brāhmaṇas* of other groups might also have a role in Brāhmanization of the text, but the Bhārgavas were the most prominent of such groups. In fact, the Bhārgavas—particularly the Gṛtsamada-Śaunaka branch—have played a very interesting role in the history of Sanskrit text creation. We have seen that they might have been very prominent in pre-Vedic time, but in the Ṛgvedic history they were subdued by the Āṅgirasas at first and the upstart Vasiṣṭha later. This made them an unorthodox group of *brāhmaṇas* often associated with magic and sorcery (probably remnants of pre-Vedic shamanism). The association of the Bhārgavas with the Asuras (possibly representative of the Indo-Iranians of pre-Vedic days) who are said to have possessed magical power (*māyā*) is probably a result of that.[25] The famous Bhārgava figure Uśanas Śukrācārya is thus also renowned as the teacher of the Asuras. The Bhārgava Śaunakas are the compilers of the most popular recension of the *Atharva Veda*, the *Śaunaka Saṃhitā*, which deals with mainly magic and sorcery. When the Bhārgavas started taking serious interest in the literary field, they also provided their interpretation of the *Ṛg Veda* in the *Bṛhaddevatā*, attributed to a Śaunaka, as discussed in Chapter 2. The Bhārgava myths indicate a close link between the Bhārgavas and the *kṣatriyas* who might have benefitted from the Bhārgava tradition of sorcery and text creation (since both could be sources of royal legitimacy). So, when the Brahmanical authority was questioned by the rise of heterodox religions, many of which received considerable royal patronage, it was the Bhārgavas who might have suffered substantially by losing a good share of their monopolized patronage. This is probably the context of the Bhārgavas emerging as the main mouthpiece for a *varṇa*-ordered society protected by a *dhārmika* king defending the *cāturvarṇya* and patronizing the *brāhmaṇas*. The Bhārgavas seem to be instrumental in articulating this vision of kingship in the post-Maurya period (*c*. BCE 200–300 CE). The most vocal propagation of this theory was presented in the archetypal lawbook *Manu Smṛti* also known as the *Bhṛgu Saṃhitā*. However, this was the period which had witnessed major modification of both the *Rāmāyaṇa* and the *Mahābhārata* as well. The principal additions to the *Rāmāyaṇa* were the 'Uttarakāṇḍa' (the last book) and parts of the 'Bālakāṇḍa', which turned the erstwhile heroic romance in the story of an ideal *dhārmika* king who ruled according to *cāturvarṇya*, and deified the hero Rāma into a Vaiṣṇava incarnation. The Bhārgavas seem to have some role in the process, at least in claiming a Bhārgava identity for the poet Vālmīki if not in anything else.[26] The *Mahābhārata* witnessed a similar process of Brahmanization and Vaiṣṇavization and with a much more pronounced body of Bhārgava myths. In fact, there seems to be a close relationship between the composition of the *Manu Smṛti* and the Bhārgavization of the *Mahābhārata*. Sukthankar has pointed out that about 260 stanzas of the *Manu Smṛti* (about 10 per cent of the total) are found verbatim or with slight variations in the Bhārgava sections of the 'Āraṇyakaparvan' and the later Bhārgava books 'Śāntiparvan' and 'Anuśāsanaparvan'.[27] Hence, Bhārgavization seems to be a very plausible tool to understand the process. However, following Hiltebeitel, we may say that it was not an exclusive process of Bhārgavization but a process of Brāhmanization in which the Bhārgavas had a significant role.

However, it would be wrong to assume that Brahmanization was a one-way process. There seems to be a substantial contest between the *brāhmaṇa* and *kṣatriya* traditions, which is to be discussed in the subsequent sections of this chapter. Therefore, the *brāhmaṇa-kṣatriya* conflict, in the Bhārgava myths attains a very bitter overtone. Death and destruction loom large on the background and the narrative moves towards the violent purge of the demonic *kṣatriyas*. Unlike the apathy towards violence and cruelty in the main narrative—exemplified by the ideal of *ānṛśaṃsya*—the Bhārgava reflection on the war is starkly pro-purge, since Samantapañcaka (Kurukṣetra) is also the location where an earlier complete extermination of the unrighteous *kṣatriyas* had culminated, and that extermination was the single-handed contribution of the most celebrated Bhārgava hero, Paraśurāma. Not surprisingly, Ugraśravas's Bhārgava genealogy merged into the violent *sarpasatra* of Janamejaya, where also the priest leading the violent dark rite was aptly named Caṇḍabhārgava (the angry Bhārgava).[28] No doubt, the story fitted Śaunaka's taste and Ugraśravas could get into his narration.

However, Brahmanizing the *Mahābhārata* was not an easy task. Neither the author Vyāsa, nor the narrator Vaiśaṃpāyana, nor the listener Janamejaya, not even the heroes Yudhiṣṭhira and Kṛṣṇa were characters which would delight the makers of the *Manu Smṛti*. Therefore, the Bhārgavas had to put maximum effort in sanitizing these characters. First and foremost, they had to tackle Kṛṣṇa. He was the affective protagonist of the theology of the Vaiṣṇavized *Mahābhārata*. Yet, Kṛṣṇa's aggressive dismissal of desire-driven Vedic ritualism in favour of his new doctrine of *niṣkāma karman*, as well as his sermon that *cāturvarṇya* was to be based not on birth but on merit (*guṇakarmavibhāgaśaḥ*), would be enough to jeopardize the entire project the Bhārgavas were standing for. One way was of course to revise the *Gītā* with a pro-Brahmanical *bhakti* layer, as shown in Chapter 3. But even that was probably not enough. Therefore, amidst the narrative of the 'Āśvamedhikaparvan', suddenly Arjuna was heard saying that he had completely forgotten what Kṛṣṇa had told him on the battlefield of Kurukṣetra.[29] Kṛṣṇa berated Arjuna for his lack of faith and understanding and refused to provide a repeat performance.[30] Instead, he told Arjuna a set of stories which are known as the *Anugītā*.[31]

Thus, in the *Anugītā*, Kṛṣṇa is made to teach Arjuna afresh, now in more pronouncedly Brahmanical terms. In one of the stories, Kṛṣṇa also narrated the debate between an ascetic (*yati*) who believed in *ahiṃsā* and a *brāhmaṇa* performer of Vedic rituals. The debate ended favourably for the *brāhmaṇa*.[32] The defeated *yati* is no doubt representative of the heterodox religions based on the notion of *ahiṃsā*, such as Jainism and Buddhism (showing a social context much later than that of the Later Vedic Age). Attack on the heterodox religions is not uncommon in the other later sections such as the 'Śāntiparvan', most notably the representation of the materialist philosopher Cārvāka as a demonic associate of Duryodhana, destroyed by the *brāhmaṇas*.[33] However, the ultimate triumph of Vedic ritualism is not just a triumph over heterodox faiths but also over Kṛṣṇa's own dismissal of Vedic rituals in the early sections of the *Bhagavad Gītā*. Interestingly, the *yati* propounds a philosophy of dualism,[34] which might be a dig at the Sāṃkhya school of thought which had substantially influenced the philosophy of both Buddhism and the *Bhagavad Gītā*. However, the greatest inversion of the *Bhagavad Gītā* comes at the end of the *Anugītā* where Kṛṣṇa quotes Brahmā as saying, '[S]ome men who are led by bad understanding speak highly of *karman*. Those, however, who are numbered among the great ancients never speak highly of *karman*'[35] and assures Arjuna that this is what he had taught him on the battlefield.[36] Conveniently, the *brāhmaṇa* redactors thus not only made Arjuna forget the *Gītā* but also transferred the amnesia to Kṛṣṇa himself who not just forgot but discarded his earlier teaching!

But sanitizing Kṛṣṇa would serve only half of the purpose. After all, what the Bhārgavas were looking for was a Brahmanical order where righteous *kṣatriyas* would protect the *varṇa* order and patronize the *brāhmaṇas*. In other words, a righteous king was to be at the centre of the Bhārgava design. The 'Uttarakāṇḍa' of the *Rāmāyaṇa* presents Rāma as that righteous Brahmanical king. Who would be that king in the *Mahābhārata*? It was Yudhiṣṭhira who held the status of the *dharmarāja* in the *Mahābhārata*. Yet, he also happened to be one of the most vigorous critics of the *varṇa* system. Would Yudhiṣṭhira's rule then be a *dharmarājya* where *varṇa* would be inconsequential? This, probably, was the biggest challenge faced by the Bhārgavas. To face this challenge, they needed a hero of their own. Duryodhana, though well suited for the role, could not be the hero because his character had already been associated with a kind of negativity in tradition, and he was defeated and dead as the head of the unrighteous *kṣatriyas*. Therefore, the Bhārgavas needed to find their hero in someone else. And they found one.

Amidst all the turmoil in the *Mahābhārata*, there was one man who stood for the hereditary *kṣatriya* code of valour and clan honour. Like a good *kṣatriya*, he was respectful towards the *brāhmaṇas*, defended his vows with his life, was unassailable in battle, and could be defeated only when he himself embraced his fall for the sake of the *kṣatriya* code of valour that stopped him from fighting someone he suspected to be a female. No wonder, when the Bhārgavas needed to re-educate Yudhiṣṭhira in *rājadharma* (duties of a king), there could not have been a better teacher than Devavrata Bhīṣma, the grand *kṣatriya* patriarch of the Kuru clan, the last pillar of strength for a decaying order in the days of a transition for worse (Dvāpara ended to bring in the abominable Kali Age).

Possibly in the earlier narrative of the *Mahābhārata*, Bhīṣma died on the tenth day of the war, when he refused to fight Śikhaṇḍin (whom he considered a female-in-disguise, a reincarnation of Ambā), and Arjuna took advantage of his being unarmed. In fact, that was what Saṃjaya had reported to Dhṛtarāṣṭra after returning from the battlefield on the tenth day: 'Bhīṣma, the son of Śāṃtanu, the grandfather of the Bharatas, has been slain (*hato bhīṣmaḥ śāṃtanavo bharatānāṃ pitāmahaḥ*)'.[37] However, the Bhārgavas, in their refashioning, did not let their hero die so early. Hence, in the present text of the *Mahābhārata*, Bhīṣma awaited for the opportune moment of his death, lying on a bed of arrows. This opening was utilized by Yudhiṣṭhira in receiving lessons on *dharma*, particularly *rājadharma*, from the great patriarch. These lessons are the themes of the two quintessential Bhārgava books of the *Mahābhārata*, the 'Śāntiparvan' and the 'Anuśāsanaparvan'. We have discussed above how scholars such as Thapar and R.S. Sharma, pointing out the contextual difference between the narrative and didactic sections of the *Mahābhārata*, showed that the 'Śāntiparvan' and the 'Anuśāsanaparvan' reflect a much later social, political, and economic context with a well-formed state and fully developed landed and monetary economy, quite different from the clan society of the narrative sections. Recent studies by McGrath further elaborate on this point. Earlier, we have seen how McGrath characterizes kingship in the *Mahābhārata* narrative as 'corporate kingship' of a clan society in which power is shared by the king with his kinsmen, the opinion of the clansmen are vital in ruling, the king is akin to an oligarchic clan chief than to a full-fledged monarch, there is no claim of the king to be the supreme landholder, and the context is pre-literate, pre-monetary, and pre-urban. However, in the 'Śāntiparvan' and 'Anuśāsanaparvan', kingship is monarchic in its domination and not corporate, autarchic rather than fraternal, 'cultural' rather than 'natural'.[38] McGrath associates this political transition with the coming of money. He argues, following Soren Stark, that, in early social community, membership was based on personal bonds of each member and the 'leader', leading to mutual obligations. Loyal services were compensated by material gifts and social prestige.[39] Thus, pre-monetary exchange is founded upon mutual recognition of loyalties or dependency, whereas a monetary system operates according to supply and demand, which finds equilibrium in terms of impersonal and abstract 'price'. Loyalty possesses a moral agency, whereas price does not. Price concerns contract, not fidelity.[40] As Nigel Dodd has shown, gifts are emotionally charged, morally loaded, and reciprocal. Monetary exchange, by contrast, seems to lack emotional significance, morality, and reciprocity.[41] Therefore, McGrath argues:

> With the development of a money economy and a money-based culture, familial and kinship relations become—by varying degrees—replaced by paid or commercially funded faithfulness: human worth becomes a product that is universally convertible, and not socially entailed, since labour can be rented and not simply exchanged and served.[42]

As a result, paid service replaces dependable kingship in the office of rule.[43] The 'Śāntiparvan' deals with this new kind of kingship and tries to refashion the text according to the Bhārgava engagement with this kind of political power. Therefore, we notice a fully functional state apparatus in this book. Rather than sharing power with kinsmen, the king was advised to fear kinsmen like death (*jñātibhyaś caiva vibhyethā mṛtyor iva yataḥ sadā*).[44] Rather, the king has to rely on the office of the ministers (*mantrins*).[45] Use of open or discreet force and extensive use of spies were considered part and parcel of statecraft.[46] This kingship was definitely not the pre-monetary, pre-literate, clan-based fraternal kingship of the Later Vedic era but representative of a context following the monetization and state formation processes which commenced in North India around the sixth century BCE. These books have no direct connection with the *Mahābhārata* narrative. They make no reference to the event around the Bhārata War. As McGrath says, there is nothing 'epic' in it except the names of the speaker and his interlocutor,[47] and the books would not be affected even if these names were taken away.[48] McGrath furnishes no evidence in support of his assumption that the Bhārgava editors worked under the aegis and commission of the Gupta kingdom, possibly under Samudra Gupta.[49] However, what can be ascertained is that these books represent a much later context than the Later Vedic context of the central narrative and possibly contain materials inserted into the text over a period of time ranging between the post-Maurya period, when the *Manu Smṛti* was composed, and the Gupta period.

However, in this chapter, we shall examine not just the lateness of these sections, but what the Bhārgavas (and others) attempted to do to the text with these late interventions.

When the Bhārata War ended, Yudhiṣṭhira was no novice as a king. Before the fateful dice game, he had ruled quite competently at Indraprastha. Then, why would he suddenly need a lesson in *rājadharma*? The Bhārgavas located the problem in Yudhiṣṭhira's moral inclination. Yudhiṣṭhira, after all, was a believer in *ānṛśaṃsya* and quite opposed to the idea that someone had to follow his violent *varṇadharma* just because one was born a *kṣatriya*. This disregard for *varṇa* and apathy towards violence would be curiously similar to the teachings of the heterodox renunciatory religions. Thus, Yudhiṣṭhira, after knowing that Karṇa was in reality his elder brother, was overcome by grief for the death of Karṇa.[50] Eventually, he decided to abdicate and become a renouncer.[51] He was advised against it by his wife, brothers, and several sages, and ultimately the *aśvamedha* sacrifice was prescribed as an expiatory rite.[52] The narrative could have moved smoothly into the 'Āśvamedhikaparvan' from here. But the Bhārgavas had other ideas.

Yudhiṣṭhira, after settling down as a king, suddenly realized Kṛṣṇa's divinity and enrolled himself as one of his devotees. Kṛṣṇa advised him to receive lessons from Bhīṣma.[53] Thus, they went together to Kurukṣetra where Bhīṣma was awaiting his death. Bhīṣma also celebrated Kṛṣṇa's godhood.[54] Here, Kṛṣṇa narrated to Yudhiṣṭhira the legends of the supreme Bhārgava hero Paraśurāma.[55] After this, Kṛṣṇa urged Bhīṣma to instruct Yudhiṣṭhira.[56] Bhīṣma praised Yudhiṣṭhira for his ascetic and Brahmanic virtues[57] but began his lesson by declaring that the *kṣatriyas* were justified in killing even their fathers, sons, and teachers.[58] Bhīṣma's instructions to Yudhiṣṭhira continued in the rest of the 'Śāntiparvan' and the bulk of the 'Anuśāsanaparvan'.

What do we make out of this? Yudhiṣṭhira's inclinations, as we have noticed, were too close to the heterodox religions. In fact, as James Fitzgerald has noted in his introduction to the translation of the 'Śāntiparvan', it was extremely similar to the remorse of the pro-Buddhist king Aśoka after looking at the carnage resulted by the only military campaign of his life, in Kaliṅga.[59] However, by the post-Maurya period, ideas of renunciation and asceticism had very much entered the Brahmanical religion as well. Hence, such ideas could not be dismissed altogether. The Bhārgavas sought the solution in the *varṇa* order being restored and strictly adhered to. Fitzgerald notes the radical distinction made in the *dharma* practicable for the *brāhmaṇa* and the *kṣatriya*. It was only the *brāhmaṇas* who were to pursue the highest values of the new *dharma* based on asceticism, non-violence, and expunging of all desires. The duty of the *kṣatriya* was to support the *brāhmaṇa*. The *kṣatriya* had to perform violence which was necessary for protection from external enemies and domestic criminals.[60] Thus, the *brāhmaṇa* Utathya told the *kṣatriya* Māndhātṛ that the king existed as the protector of law, and, thus, a king who—neglecting his duty—pursued the highest *dharma* (of renunciation) was evil![61] Yudhiṣṭhira was, therefore, on the verge of becoming an evil king, and he had to be groomed by Bhīṣma who knew the proper code of conduct. In the words of Fitzgerald:

> The narrative argument depicting the ethically ambivalent Yudhiṣṭhira, having him lead a purge of the *kṣatra*, and then making him a proper *brāhmaṇya* king is central to the entire *Mahābhārata* as it stands now.[62]

Thus, what Yudhiṣṭhira learnt from Bhīṣma was basically the necessity of a symbiotic relationship between the *brāhmaṇa* and the *kṣatriya*, with the superiority of the *brāhmaṇa* accepted. After all, this was the knowledge the founder of Yudhiṣṭhira's lineage, Purūravas Aila, had received from the wind god! In fact, the wind god's teachings cited by Bhīṣma were nothing but a retelling of the *puruṣasūkta* from Book X of the *Ṛg Veda*, which first outlined the *varṇa* order. Answering Purūravas's question about the origin of the *varṇas*, the wind god said that the *brāhmaṇas* came from the mouth of Brahmā, the *kṣatriyas* from his arms, the *vaiśya* from his thighs, and the *śūdra* from his feet.[63] With allusion to this Vedic myth (though the Vedic Puruṣa was replaced by the Purāṇic Brahmā), the teaching proclaimed that the *brāhmaṇa* was the lord of all beings and guardian of *dharma*, while the *kṣatriya*, *vaiśya*, and *śūdra* had to protect the earth and its order, provide wealth and food, and serve the other *varṇas*, respectively.[64] Thus, the earth basically belonged to the *brāhmaṇa*. The *kṣatriya* was inferior in status to a *brāhmaṇa* and was expected to rule relying upon the guidance of a learned *brāhmaṇa*.[65] Bhīṣma endorsed the content of the teaching by accepting the *brāhmaṇa* as the first-born of all and the rightful owner of everything,[66] and emphasized on the need of the *brāhmaṇa* and the *kṣatriya* to perform their respective duties properly.[67] The king must guard the wealth of the *brāhmaṇas* and honour and gratify them.[68] He might expropriate the wealth of the non-*brāhmaṇas* when in dire straits but should never use the wealth of the *brāhmaṇas* for public purposes, should never envy the wealth of the *brāhmaṇas*, and should give them wealth if he would be able to.[69] The king's right was over the wealth of all except that of the proper *brāhmaṇas*.[70]

Bhīṣma accepted the king's right to tax, punish, even expel the *brāhmaṇas* who did not perform their duties and engaged in unworthy professions, but only if he failed to bring these *brāhmaṇas* in the right track by providing them adequate support.[71] It was the king's responsibility to make it possible for the *brāhmaṇas* to live by an appropriate livelihood.[72] Moreover, it was alright for a *brāhmaṇa* to live by *kṣatriya* or *vaiśya* professions.[73] If the *kṣatriyas* became offensive towards the order, the *brāhmaṇas* might chastise them through any means, including duplicity and violence.[74] Therefore, the Bhārgava hero Paraśurāma's violent purge of the *kṣatriyas* was not against the *dharma*. This thesis of kingship was legitimized by a new origin myth of rulership, different from the Sūryavaṃśa and Candravaṃśa origin myths, regarding Pṛthu, the first righteous king.

In fact, this was the legend with which Bhīṣma started his instruction. Requested by the deities to provide a ruler for the mortals, Viṣṇu created his mind-born son Virajas to be the first king. However, Virajas, his son, and his grandson, all withdrew from royal responsibility. Rulership was assumed by Virajas's great-grandson Anaṅga who was a good ruler. Anaṅga's son Atibala indulged his senses, and so did Atibala's son Veṇa. Since Veṇa ruled unlawfully, he was destroyed by the sages. To create the next king, the seers churned Veṇa's right thigh which gave birth to the ugly little Niṣāda who was banished to the mountains and forest. Then the seers churned Veṇa's right hand from which the handsome and competent Pṛthu was created. Asked to govern, he agreed to do so only if the *brāhmaṇas* helped him. As the *brāhmaṇas* took their charge, Pṛthu was consecrated and received presents of wealth from the personified Earth, Ocean, Sumeru mountain, and various demigods. The earth was full of grains thanks to him and Viṣṇu himself entered his person.[75]

Thus, the king was entitled to a lot of wealth and divine power, but only when he was subservient to the *brāhmaṇas*. After all, it was the *brāhmaṇas* who could make or unmake a king. They were the custodians of the *dharma* that governed everything. Even if the forest and mountain tribes, such as the Niṣādas, were out of the purview of their *dharma*, it was because of their own design. Otherwise, both the Niṣāda and Pṛthu were their creations.

Yudhiṣṭhira, therefore, received a thorough lesson about the supremacy of the *brāhmaṇas* from Bhīṣma, and the entire teaching was enshrined within a Vaiṣṇava theology. After all, the teaching was commissioned by Kṛṣṇa who was regarded as God by both the teacher and the student. Naturally, in this teaching, *brāhmaṇa* and *bhakti* rituals also received much more importance than the archetypal *kṣatriya* rituals such as *rājasūya* and *aśvamedha*. Both these rituals, performed by Yudhiṣṭhira, were regarded as of lesser merit than generosity to the *brāhmaṇas*,[76] reverence for cows,[77] fasting,[78] visiting pilgrimage centres,[79] and gift-giving,[80] in Bhīṣma's teaching as well as in the other late didactic sections. Even Yudhiṣṭhira's favourite maxim of *ānṛśaṃsya* was reshaped as subservience to one's stipulated *varṇa* duty in the long didactic story of Dharmavyādha in the 'Āraṇyakaparvan'.[81] Yudhiṣṭhira learned from Bhīṣma that the Brahmanical principles were the only guiding principles on the earth for a righteous king, as the virtuous and knowledgable Asura king Prahrāda had taught to his Deva counterpart Indra:

> The wisdom in the mouth of the *brāhmaṇas* is an immortal nectar upon the earth, an unexcelled eye; one goes forward after learning it.[82]

Therefore, the Bhārgavas and their associates were in a conscious project of reshaping the *Mahābhārata* with a fundamentally different meaning from what Vyāsa might have intended or what Janamejaya might have learnt from Vaiśaṃpāyana. Even though the disciples of Vyāsa were given *brāhmaṇa* identity in the 'Śāntiparvan'[83] (whereas, as Sullivan notes, the name of at least Vaiśaṃpāyana suggests a *kṣatriya-sūta* status),[84] the discrepancy was too pronounced to be overlooked. Thus, the *Mahābhārata* text was a battleground among various contending composers. Bhīṣma told Yudhiṣṭhira a very interesting story about how a king named Janamejaya was looked down upon for accidentally killing a *brāhmaṇa*. When he met the sage Indrota Śaunaka, he also reviled him for the act. However, Śaunaka also suggested the expiation of his sin by sacrifices and being respectful to the *brāhmaṇas*. Janamejaya followed the suggestion and attained a lot of merit and success.[85]

The story is interesting because here Bhīṣma was narrating a legend about his yet to be born great-grandnephew, Janamejaya! Moreover, Janamejaya's instructor was a Śaunaka here! And, of course, the eventual listener of the story was Janamejaya himself from Vaiśaṃpāyana, since the entire 'Śāntiparvan' is put inside Vaiśaṃpāyana's narration! Adam Bowles thinks that it is a textual playfulness to vaguely suggest that the principal audiences of the two tellings of the *Mahābhārata* were engaging in a conversation.[86] However, the matter seems more serious than playfulness and the suggestion is anything but vague. The idea that Janamejaya was a fallen and despised individual elevated eventually by the intervention of a Śaunaka probably also comments upon the nature of the *Mahābhārata* itself. Was the text addressed to Janamejaya one of little expiatory merit, only to be elevated by its revision by the Śaunakas? Is this story a Bhārgava dig at the earlier version of the *Mahābhārata*, that Janamejaya could have become more respectful towards the *brāhmaṇas* if he received his instruction not from Vaiśaṃpāyana but from the Śaunakas? This assumption gets consolidated further if we look at how the 'Anuśāsanaparvan' perceived Janamejaya and Vaiśaṃpāyana. Technically still a part of the Janamejaya-Vaiśaṃpāyana dialogue, it quotes Brahmā, the Creator, as saying:

> *śakrasyodasya caraṇaṃ prasthito janamejayaḥ/*
> *dvijastrīṇāṃ vadhaṃ kṛtvā kiṃ daivena na vāritaḥ//*
> *ajñānād brāhmaṇaṃ hatvā spṛṣṭo bālavadhena ca/*
> *vaiśaṃpāyanaviprarṣiḥ kiṃ daivena na vāritaḥ//*
>
> (Forthright Janamejaya privileged Śakra-esque behaviour and killed twiceborn women. Do you think he was not held to account by the gods? Vaiśaṃpāyana the *brāhmaṇa ṛṣi* killed a *brāhmaṇa* accidentally, and was stained by having killed a child. Do you think he was not held to account by the gods?)[87]

Therefore, schooling Yudhiṣṭhira in Brahmanical *rājadharma* propounded by Bhīṣma was the major intervention of the Bhārgavas, but not the only one. Bhārgavization or Brāhmanization of the *Mahābhārata* was part of a very long and complex textual journey in which various traditions fought against each other. The fight could get bitter to the extent that it made the *brāhmaṇa* redactors refashion the *kṣatriya* Janamejaya and his narrator Vaiśaṃpāyana as despicable characters who killed *brāhmaṇas*, women, and children. This reflects a relatively unnoticed side of the *Mahābhārata* tradition, the contest between the *brāhmaṇa* and the *sūta-kṣatriya* narrators and redactors. This book does not have adequate space to do justice to that history. However, just to have a glimpse of it, we shall return at the end to where the textual history of the Bharata-Kurus started, the contest between the two Ṛgvedic priest-poets: Viśvāmitra and Vasiṣṭha.

5.2 Viśvāmitra versus Vasiṣṭha: Reshaping a Vedic Legend

In the previous section we have seen how the *Mahābhārata* had been Brahmanized at the cost of the *sūta-kṣatriya* content of the original narrative. It seems that there were two very clearly contrasted traditions contesting over the text. F.E. Pargiter insists on the distinction between a *kṣatriya* tradition and the Vedic *brāhmaṇa* tradition and tries to establish the former as relatively more valuable, since the *brāhmaṇas* lacked proper historical sense.[88] The view has been strongly contested by A. Berriadale Keith who points out that the so-called *ksatriya* tradition—the *Mahābhārata*, the *Rāmāyaṇa*, and the Purāṇas—have been worked upon by the *brāhmaṇas*.[89]

The existence of *itihāsa-purāṇa* as a tradition parallel to the Vedic tradition is undoubted. The tradition was not a *kṣatriya* tradition as such but a bardic tradition that possibly grew under political patronage. However, this entire tradition was ultimately codified by the *brāhmaṇas*. Not a single text can be found in its original bardic condition. In fact, the existent Purāṇas are nothing but Brahmanical mythological texts endorsing one or the other Brahmanical *bhakti* sect (Vaiṣṇava, Śaiva, Śākta, etc.). The *Mahābhārata* and the *Rāmāyaṇa* possibly were immune from such gross alterations, thanks to their widely known and highly popular storylines. Therefore, attempts to stratify these two texts are still possible. The same cannot be said about the Purāṇas. Therefore, despite Pargiter's insistent efforts to prove the historical accuracy of the Purāṇas, they remain highly doubtful sources for reconstructing the history of Vedic or post-Vedic times. The present Purāṇas, no doubt, contain some remnants of the old *purāṇa* tradition. But identifying those is nearly impossible except in some rare cases where some strongly identifiable supporting evidence is available.[90] Therefore, in our discussion, we will focus mainly on the *Mahābhārata* and the *Rāmāyaṇa*, looking at the Purāṇic stories only occasionally.

However, bracketing the *Mahābhārata* and the *Rāmāyaṇa* together is also problematic and needs qualification. The *Rāmāyaṇa* is not an *itihāsa* text, not even a *purāṇa*, but a piece of poetry (*kāvya*). Still, it can be considered as a source of traditional history, since originally it also seems to be a production of the bards. The central event of the *Rāmāyaṇa* revolves around the Ikṣvākus of Kosala, who have a minor role in the Vedic world. Unlike the Kuru-Pañcāla dominance of the Vedic landscape, which is attested by almost all kinds of sources, the historical role of the Ikṣvākus in the early historical period is highly doubtful. Vedic literature hardly shows any knowledge of the characters, events, or places associated with the *Rāmāyaṇa*. However, by the time of the Buddha, Kosala under the Ikṣvāku kings Mahākosala and Prasenajit was quite prominent. Archaeology also indicates that Kosala's rise possibly started from BCE 700 onwards. The amount of historicity, if any, in the original *kuśīlava* tradition which Vālmīki fashioned into an epic is thus questionable.

Still, in this section, we are taking both the *Mahābhārata* and the *Rāmāyaṇa* together. In the *itihāsa-purāṇa* tradition, the family of the Vasiṣṭhas is invariably associated with the Ikṣvākus. Therefore, the myths concerning the Vasiṣṭhas have a very intimate relationship with the *Rāmāyaṇa*. Moreover, here our main focus is not the original narrative of either text, but the process of Brahmanization which took place more or less simultaneously for both the texts. With these qualifications in mind, we may try to see how the Vedic sages Viśvāmitra and Vasiṣṭha were reinvented by this tradition.

There are several stories and legends in the *Mahābhārata* about the two sages Viśvāmitra and Vasiṣṭha, such as Viśvāmitra testing his disciple Gālava with an extremely difficult demand,[91] Vasiṣṭha ascending to the sun to fetch the sun's daughter—Tapatī—for king Saṃvaraṇa,[92] and Vasiṣṭha slaying some Rākṣasas for the king Mucukunda.[93] Both the sages saved the people from two lengthy droughts.[94] That the conflict generated several legends is indicated by the story that Viśvāmitra, determined to kill Vasiṣṭha, ordered the river Sarasvatī to transport the latter to him. The river, fearing a curse from either, first carried Vasiṣṭha on her current to Viśvāmitra's *āśrama*, and then—while Viśvāmitra was searching for a weapon—carried Vasiṣṭha back to his own hermitage.[95] However, what interests us more is how the Vedic legend of Viśvāmitra, Vasiṣṭha, and Sudās got reshaped in the *Mahābhārata*.

There are two Sudāsas named in the epic-Purāṇic tradition: one a Pāñcāla king and the other an Ikṣvāku. Since Pargiter has a problematic tendency of accepting almost every Purāṇic figure as unqualifiedly historical, he tried to identify the Pāñcāla Sudāsa with Sudās Paijavana. The Purāṇic genealogy places him in a direct line from Mudgala followed by Vadhryaśva, Divodāsa, Mitrāyu, Maitreya Soma, Sṛñjaya, Cyavana Pañcajana, and Sudāsa or Somadatta. Pargiter notes that Mudgala, Vadhryaśva, Divodāsa, and Sṛñjaya are mentioned in the *Ṛg Veda*. Cyavana is probably alluded to in one hymn. Sudāsa possibly drove the Pūru chief Saṃvaraṇa out of Hastināpura, defeating him on the banks of the Yamunā. Saṃvaraṇa built a grand alliance with the Ānava-Śivis,

Druhyus, Matsyas, Turvaśas, and others. Sudāsa defeated them in a great battle near the Pāruṣṇī.[96]

This reconstruction is questionable. Pusalker notes that there is no relationship among Mudgala, Sṛñjaya, and Sudās in the Vedas. The Ṛgvedic Sudās was son of Pijavana, even in the *Nirukta*, the *Mahābhārata*, and the *Manu Smṛti*. The Pūru antagonists of Sudās were clearly Pūrukutsa and Trasadasyu, not Saṃvaraṇa whom Pargiter, following S.N. Pradhan, tries to show as a contemporary of the priest Tura Kāvaṣeya who is connected with the Battle of Ten Kings in later legends only. Moreover, there is no trace of the Vasiṣṭha-Viśvāmitra issue here. The name of Sudāsa is not fixed in the Pāñcāla genealogy, and in many cases it is replaced by Somadatta. Finally, the *Mahābhārata* does not name the Pāñcāla king who drove Saṃvaraṇa out.[97]

However, it is the Ikṣvāku Sudāsa, or his son Mitrasaha Saudāsa Kalmāṣapāda, who has been integrally connected with the Vasiṣṭha-Viśvāmitra conflict. There can be no doubt that Sudās was not an Ikṣvāku. But as the Vasiṣṭhas became Ikṣvāku priests later on, all legends concerning Vasiṣṭha had been possibly reshaped within the Ikṣvāku traditions.

Interestingly, the *Mahābhārata* deals with the Vasiṣṭha legend as an ancient lore that the Gandharva Citraratha narrated to Arjuna. So, its character as an oral tradition is recognized. The story says that king Viśvāmitra, son of Gādhin, once visited the hermitage of Vasiṣṭha who offered him lavish hospitality, with the help of his wish-fulfilling cow Nandinī. Viśvāmitra wanted the cow, but Vasiṣṭha refused. The cow was taken by force. The cow in resistance created an army of the Pahlavas, Śabaras, Śakas, Yavanas, Puṇḍras, Kirātas, Drāviḍas, Siṃhalas, Barbaras, Daradas, and Mlecchas. Viśvāmitra was defeated and realized the futility of military strength in face of spiritual strength:

> *dhig balaṃ kṣatriyabalaṃ brahmatejobalaṃ balam/*
> *balābalaṃ viniścitya tapa eva paraṃ balam//*
>
> (A curse on the power that is *kṣatriya* power! Brahminic power is power. On weighing weakness and strength, asceticism appears the superior power.)[98]

He performed great austerities and ultimately attained Brāhmaṇahood. In the meanwhile, Kalmāṣapāda Mitrasaha Saudāsa, son of Sudās, once hurt Śakti (Vasiṣṭha's son) in a moment of rage, and the priest cursed him to be a Rākṣasa. Viśvāmitra and Vasiṣṭha were having a feud over their patron. Viśvāmitra instigated the Rākṣasa Kiṃkara to take possession of Kalmāṣapāda. Partially unsettled, Kalmāṣapāda offered a *brāhmaṇa* a dish of human flesh, and the latter reiterated Śakti's curse. Now, Kalmāṣapāda became a complete cannibal and devoured Śakti. Viśvāmitra instigated him to kill the other sons of Vasiṣṭha as well. Vasiṣṭha was deeply agonized but did not contemplate revenge. Rather, he attempted suicide time and again, but in vain. He tried to drown himself in a river that cut his ropes. Another river ran off in hundred directions. He named them Vipāśā and Śatadru, respectively. By that time, Śakti's widow met him and informed him that she was pregnant. Vasiṣṭha got some relief and returned. He cured Kalmāṣapāda from the curse and begot a child off his queen.[99]

We can see in this a classic Brahmanical legend where a priestly conflict of the Vedic Age has been reshaped as a story to prove the superiority of Brahmanical virtue over *kṣatriya* power. It is Vasiṣṭha's spiritual power, and Viśvāmitra's pursuit to attain that, which is valorized. The story begins with a valorization of Vasiṣṭha:

> Lust and wrath, invincible even to the Immortals, were defeated by his austerities and massaged his feet. Harboring a great grudge because of Viśvāmitra's offence, he yet nobly did not annihilate the Kuśikas. While mourning the death of his sons, he did not contemplate any dreadful deed to destroy Viśvāmitra, although he was powerful and able to do so. Just as the great ocean does not trespass on its flood line, he did not trespass on Death by bringing his dead sons back from Yama's realm.[100]

Vasiṣṭha himself also outlined the difference between *brāhmaṇa* and *kṣatriya* power in the story:

> *kṣatriyāṇāṃ balaṃ tejo brāhmaṇānāṃ kṣamā balam*
>
> (A *kṣatriya*'s strength is his energy, a brahmin's strength his forbearance)[101]

The story seems to be a very late one, possibly fabricated in post-Maurya times (*c.* BCE 200–CE 300) when several immigrant ruling groups like the Pahlavas, Śakas, and Yavanas (Indo-Greeks) were becoming dominant. Their dominance forced the *brāhmaṇas* to award them *kṣatriya* status, and they were provided a considerable pedigree to rule, being the defenders of Vasiṣṭha's holy cow. Later Purāṇic tradition explains their 'fallen' non-Vedic status as a result of a defeat of the five foreign tribes—Śakas, Yavanas, Pahlavas, Kambojas, and Pāradas—at the hands of King Sagara.[102] Even then, Vasiṣṭha appeared as their protector.[103]

However, the memories of the actual legend are easily traceable. The conflict of Vasiṣṭha and Viśvāmitra over the patron, Viśvāmitra taking away Vasiṣṭha's cow, killing of Śakti and other sons of Vasiṣṭha by the Saudāsas—instigated by Viśvāmitra, Vasiṣṭha's denouncement of their Rākṣasa nature, and Vasiṣṭha ultimately regaining progeny and wealth—all these Later Vedic material have been reshaped in a new pro-*brāhmaṇa* legend. That the two rivers associated with Vasiṣṭha's suicide attempts—Vipāśā and Śatadru—are the two very rivers which Viśvāmitra helped the Bharatas to cross shows that the geographical context of the original legend is also preserved. Even Vasiṣṭha's wish-fulfilling cow does not seem to be an invention. The only Ṛgvedic hymn composed by Vasiṣṭha's chief patron, Sudās, ends with a dramatic prayer for such a cow:

> Do thou bestow upon us her, O Indra, who yields according to the singer's longing,
>
> That the great Cow may, with exhaustless udder, pouring a thousand streams, give milk to feed us.[104]

If we go back to Vasiṣṭha's poetry in the *Ṛg Veda*, discussed in Chapter 2, new observations can be made. To complicate matters, Viśvāmitra alleged Vasiṣṭha to be a *yātudhāna* (black magician) who caused the death of his own sons. Rahurkar cites Sāyaṇa's commentary as an evidence for such an allegation.[105] Findly notes the effect of this allegation on Vasistha's psychology.[106] He suggests that might have made him weary of the materialistic power struggle and conscious of the sin involved in that. This explains why the Ṛgvedic Vasiṣṭha's reply to Viśvāmitra's allegation had been juxtaposed with a Rākṣasa-destruction curse where he emotionally denied the charge, pledged suicide if proven guilty, and identified his opponents (possibly Viśvāmitra and the Saudāsas) as the real culprits who should be punished for falsehood.[107]

Velankar argues that Viśvāmitra and the Bhṛgus were more prone to use charms and spells, while the strictly ritualistic Vasiṣṭha refused to accept these practices.[108] Findly also thinks that Viśvāmitra was more likely to have used magic for achieving his goals, whereas Vasiṣṭha was more grounded in high and solemn ritual.[109] The association of Viśvāmitra with magic is also attested from the Later Vedic literature. As an associate of the Bhārgavas, Viśvāmitra is the author of some Atharvavedic spells. He composed charms for repelling sorceries (V.15–16), curing diseases (VI.44), marking cattle's ears (VI.141), and increasing food grain (VI.142). Therefore, naturally, the false allegations hurt Vasiṣṭha and resulted in his passionate outburst. However, it cannot clearly be said if Viśvāmitra actually practised 'black magic'. Rahurkar notes that none of Viśvāmitra's Atharvavedic compositions is for a harmful purpose.[110] It rather seems that both Viśvāmitra and Vasiṣṭha suspected the other of performing 'black magic', though neither might have actually practised it. But Viśvāmitra definitely used Rākṣasa-like violent measures for revenge on Vasiṣṭha and his sons.

Again, the role of the Bhṛgus seems to be important in this. The Bhṛgus are the family closely associated with magic and sorcery. The *Mahābhārata* contains numerous stories where one Bhṛgu or another is associated with some kind of magic. These being the Bhṛgu version of their own past, there can be no doubt about their pride and confidence in their magical capability. Therefore, Śukrācārya is bestowed with the magical power to resurrect the dead.[111] Cyavana is remembered for burning his mother's abductor to ashes[112] on the very moment of his birth. He is also held responsible for magically paralyzing none lesser than Indra and creating a demon for killing him.[113] One Bhṛgu prepared the infallible potion which made King Yuvanāśva pregnant.[114] Ruru revived his dead lover by sharing his own stipulated lifespan with her.[115] Ṛcīka or some other Bhṛgu prepared the potions which his wife Satyavatī and her mother confused.[116] Jamadagni subdued the sun god who presented him the first shoes and umbrellas.[117] Newborn Aurva blindfolded the Haihayas and later could have destroyed the entire world.[118] Devaśarman hypnotized Ruci by magically entering her body.[119] Probably, Viśvāmitra's own magical practices coupled with his close association with the Bhṛgu sorcerer Jamadagni made Vasiṣṭha suspicious of black magic and sorcery on Viśvāmitra's part.

The *Rāmāyaṇa* version of the story elaborates on the theme of Brahmanical power. The name of the cow involved was Śabalā here, and the holy cow herself gave a long discourse on the superior power of the *brāhmaṇa*:

> They say that a kshatriya has no real power, and that a Brahman is, in fact, more powerful ... The power of a Brahman is divine and much greater than that of the kshatriyas.[120]

Vasiṣṭha refused to hand her over to king Viśvaratha despite the latter's offer of many more cows, elephants, chariots, horses, and gold.[121] Vasiṣṭha's army killed all but one son of Viśvaratha. Defeated by Vasiṣṭha's army, Viśvaratha alias Viśvāmitra performed great austerities and received great weapons from Śiva. But Vasiṣṭha resisted all divine weapons with one *brāhmaṇa*'s stuff, declaring:

> What comparison is there between your kshatriya power and the immense power of a brahman?[122]

This symbolic victory of the *brāhmaṇa*'s stuff over all *kṣatriya* weapons led to Viśvāmitra's quest to become a *brahmarṣi*. Through austerities, Viśvāmitra became a *rājarṣi*. He continued his pursuit and became a *ṛṣi*. He still did not stop performing austerities. However, he was temporarily diverted from his goal when he was seduced by the *apsarā* Menakā. But he returned to his pursuit, and ultimately became a *maharṣi*. Brahmā said that one could not become *brahmarṣi* without conquering one's senses. Viśvāmitra continued his efforts. Now, Rambhā came to seduce him. He was no longer seduced but he cursed Rambhā in wrath, showing his lack of control over anger. Ultimately, through years of severe effort, he became a *brāhmaṇa*. In that state, all enmity was dissolved. He paid homage to Vasiṣṭha.[123]

The *brāhmaṇas*, while reshaping these legends, refused to show the conflict between two great priests as perpetual. The *Rāmāyaṇa* shows a healthy relationship between the two. When Viśvāmitra came to take Rāma and Lakṣmaṇa (significantly for killing the Rākṣasas), he embraced Vasiṣṭha[124] and identified his guidance as the cause of Daśaratha's virtue.[125] On return, Vasiṣṭha described Viśvāmitra as 'righteousness incarnate and the mightiest of men, wisest man on earth and the supreme source of ascetic power'.[126]

In the *Mahābhārata* also, it was Dharma disguised as Vasiṣṭha who granted Viśvāmitra his *brāhmaṇa* status. The story says that Dharma disguised himself as Vasiṣṭha and went to Viśvāmitra's hermitage for food. Viśvāmitra cooked food, and Dharma asked him to wait. Viśvāmitra waited there, holding the food, for hundred years till Dharma returned. Returning, Dharma awarded him brāhmaṇahood.[127]

However, it will be wrong to assume that the epic-Purāṇic tradition is all about a unilineal journey from conflict to cordiality between Vasiṣṭha and Viśvāmitra. After all, the *brāhmaṇa* (possibly Bhārgava) redactors were not working on an empty field but were engaged in a discourse with the existent bardic tradition. It is unlikely that the bards, working under *kṣatriya* patronage, unquestionably accepted the supremacy of the *brāhmaṇas*.

In fact, the hierarchy between the king and the priest in early India has always been a matter of tussle. The Indians were not exactly the neatly hierarchized 'homo hierarchicus', as the sociologist Louis Dumont would make us believe, with the temporal authority of the kings being consistently subordinated to and encompassed by the spiritual authority of the *brahmanas*.[128] Rather, the situation was closer to the understanding of Declan Quigley that

> [t]he relationship between patron and priest is charged with all kinds of difficult tensions and is best characterized as ambiguous and equivocal rather than in terms of higher and lower or superior and inferior.[129]

Therefore, Quigley terms the uncritical acceptance of the notion of superiority of priesthood as a 'fantastic distortion of the evidence'[130] and characterizes the fundamental opposition in caste ideology as not between priests and untouchables, but between priests and kings.[131] Arthur Maurice Hocart views the kings as the 'first caste',[132] he notes the secular power as the final arbiter of caste,[133] and Quigley describes the Indian king as the 'numinous centre of the world' with priests as a part of his regalia.[134]

This debate among the modern sociologists is not without support in the early texts. The Vedic *Saṃhitās*, *Brāhmaṇas*, and *Sūtras* may give a picture of a smooth hierarchy of four *varṇas*. But the *sūta* tradition of the *Mahābhārata* repeatedly questions and denounces the notion of *varṇa* based on birth and any singular interpretation of *dharma*. The choice of the *kṣatriya* Kṛṣṇa as the most venerable guest in Yudhiṣṭhira's *rājasūya*, despite the presence of several *brāhmaṇas*, can be noted. The Upaniṣadic tradition not just problematizes the question whether *varṇa* should be based on birth or ability but also represents several kings—such as Pravahana Jābāli of Pāñcāla, Ajātaśatru of Kāśī, and Janaka of Videha—who challenged the notion of the philosophical superiority of the *brāhmaṇas*. The *Mahābhārata* contains several traditions about actual conflicts between chiefly and priestly power. That a large section of the *kṣatriyas* rated themselves as the highest caste is proven by the fact that the heterodox religions of the sixth century BCE—founded invariably by *kṣatriyas* such as Vardhamāna Mahāvīra and Gautama Buddha—considered the *kṣatriya* as the highest caste. The reshaping of the Viśvāmitra-Vasiṣṭha legend has to be understood in this background.

While the affiliation of the *sūtas* with the *kṣatriyas* is quite well known, the exact nature of the *kusīlava* bards, who preserved the tradition which served as source material for Vālmīki's *Rāmāyaṇa*, can hardly be determined. The text of the *Rāmāyaṇa*, even in its older portions, is more conservative than that of the *Mahābhārata*. Still, the *Rāmāyaṇa* was also a *kṣatriya* tradition, containing legends about the Ikṣvākus and about the *kṣatriya* king Rāma. Therefore, the *Rāmāyaṇa* shared a bardic-*kṣatriya* framework with the *Mahābhārata*. One important effect of that framework was possibly the insertion of a Viśvāmitra in the *Rāmāyaṇa*. The training of the ideal *kṣatriya* Rāma was not to be under only the powerful *brāhmaṇa* family of the Vasiṣṭhas, the family preceptors of the Ikṣvākus, but also under the erstwhile *kṣatriya* Viśvāmitra. The entire Vasiṣṭha-Viśvāmitra cycle was superimposed on the narrative by the *brāhmaṇa* redactors, possibly to nullify this factor. But this long section of the *Rāmāyaṇa* also contains certain pro-Viśvāmitra legends which seem to be the representatives of a counter-tradition.

One classic example is the story of Triśaṅku. This Ikṣvāku king wanted to perform a sacrifice that would enable him to go to the highest realm of the deities in his own body. Vasiṣṭha declared it impossible. Then the king approached Vasiṣṭha's sons. They were enraged by his audacity and cursed him to become a *caṇḍāla* (outcast). Everybody deserted the outcast king. Then, Viśvāmitra, at that time a *rājarṣi*, promised to fulfil his will. Summoned by Viśvāmitra, several Vedic seers assembled for the sacrifice. But Vasiṣṭha and his sons refused to come. Vasiṣṭha's sons declared:

> How can the gods and seers in an assembly partake of the offerings of a man whose sacrificial priest is a kshatriya, especially when he himself is a pariah?
>
> Or is the patronage of this Viśvāmitra sufficient to ensure that the great Brahmans will go to heaven even after eating a pariah's food?[135]

Angrily, Viśvāmitra cursed them that they would become dog-eating outcasts. He also cursed Vasiṣṭha to become an outcaste Niṣāda and to live a long, miserable life. These curses ruined Vasiṣṭha and his sons. But the deities did not come to Viśvāmitra's sacrifice to accept the offerings. Viśvāmitra, through his power, sent Triśaṅku to the heaven in his own body, but Indra dismissed him from there. The angry Viśvāmitra started to create a whole new set of constellations and deities. The fearful deities pacified him by accepting his new constellations and including Triśaṅku in that heaven.[136]

The story is a radical *kṣatriya* one where Viśvāmitra, still a *kṣatriya*, triumphed over Vasiṣṭha. His curses ruined Vasiṣṭha and his family. He defended the desire of another *kṣatriya*, Triśaṅku, against the injunction of Vasiṣṭha. The caste order got rebutted in the ultimate entry of an outcaste in the heaven. That Viśvāmitra stood for an alternative order and idea was shown clearly by his creation of a new heaven and new deities. Wilson rightly points out that the creation of counter-constellations can also be an allusion to some reformation of the Vasiṣṭha school of astronomy.[137] Pargiter also thinks that Viśvāmitra named some planet after Triśaṅku and rightly points out that a planet named 'Triśaṅku' has been referred to in the *Rāmāyaṇa*.[138] Recognition of Viśvāmitra's demands was the only way to stop a religious split. Viśvāmitra thus assumed the role of a *kṣatriya* icon in the *kṣatriya* tradition.

The story was an old tale possibly known to the *Mahābhārata* as well, where there is an allusion to a *mātaṅga*'s (a synonym of *caṇḍāla*) sacrifice where Indra went to drink soma in fear of Viśvāmitra who angrily created a new galaxy of counter-constellations.[139]

Pargiter points out that there is a prelude to this legend in several Purāṇas (*Harivaṃśa, Vāyu Purāṇa, Brahma Purāṇa, Brahmāṇḍa Purāṇa, Śiva Purāṇa, and Liṅga Purāṇa*).[140] In this story, King Trayyaruṇa condemned Prince Satyavrata to live among the dog-eating *caṇḍāla* for an offence of carrying off a bride from a wedding ceremony. The priest, Vasiṣṭha, did nothing to favour the prince. The heart-broken king retired to the forest. Vasiṣṭha took up the charge of governing the kingdom, with other priests as counsellors, with an intention to consecrate Satyavrata's son as the next king. There was a twelve-year famine at that time. During the famine, Satyavrata supported the family of Viśvāmitra who was busy in performing austerities. For supporting Viśvāmitra's family, he even killed Vasiṣṭha's wish-fulfilling cow. This stigmatized him as performer of three sins, 'Triśaṅku'. After returning, Viśvāmitra in gratitude consecrated him as a king and performed sacrifices for him.

Pargiter considers this story historical, and the *Rāmāyaṇa* account an absurd fabrication. He thinks that Vasiṣṭha, by supporting Satyavrata's exile, deliberately ruined the king and his son to capture all power of the kingdom. He ran a theocratic government, without *kṣatriya* counsellors. Lacking in *kṣartiya* support, his regime crumbled when Viśvāmitra brought Satyavrata back, despite his attempts to deny Viśvāmitra *brāhmaṇa* status.

This interpretation is hardly acceptable. The story nowhere says that Vasiṣṭha had any hand in instigating Satyavrata's exile. The *Vāyu Purāṇa* version rather claims that he was against the exile. Vasiṣṭha's intention to hand over the kingdom to Satyavrata's son is also stated. Moreover, accepting this very late Purāṇnic legend as historical at face value is problematic. Rather, the story seems to be a response of the Purāṇic *brāhmaṇas* to the pro-*kṣatriya* pro-Viśvāmitra story of the *Rāmāyaṇa*. The whimsical curse to a righteous king has been rationalized here as a punishment for a crime. Therefore, contrary to Pargiter's assumption, this is the Brahmanical version responding to the earlier *kṣatriya* version of the *Rāmāyaṇa*. In the attempt to show some fault on Triśaṅku's part, the Purāṇic *brāhmaṇas* hastily picked up many elements of the older Vasiṣṭha-Viśvāmitra legends, such as their conflict over patronage and snatching of Vasiṣṭha's holy cow.

The story of Triśaṅku is not the only instance where the pro-Viśvāmitra pro-*kṣatriya* elements were at work. Another interesting instance is the reshaping of the *Aitareya Brāhmaṇa*'s Śunaḥśepa legend, discussed in Chapter 2. In the *Mahābhārata*, the Śunaḥśepa story is repeated, but Śunaḥśepa has been described as the son of Ṛcīka, rather than of Ajīgarta.[141] Ṛcīka was a Bhārgava sage, and the father of Viśvāmitra's preceptor, Jamadagni. The reshaping of the legend is thus a process through which the *kṣatriya* tradition engages in a dialogue with the Bhārgava *brāhmaṇas*. As we have already seen, the Bhṛgu sage Jamadagni was the saviour of Viśvāmitra in his sacrificial debate with Śakti. This element of Bhārgava help to Viśvāmitra, who was an iconic hero in the *kṣatriya* tradition, had to be countered. Therefore, Viśvāmitra is shown as the saviour of a Bhārgava whom his father had sold for money.

The same process is at work in the *Rāmāyaṇa* account where the *kṣatriya* element is even more dominant. Naturally, in the Ikṣvāku text, it would be problematic to show that an Ikṣvāku king did not keep his word and kept on making excuses. Therefore, the story goes that Ambarīṣa (not Hariścandra) was organizing a sacrifice from where the sacrificial victim was stolen. Thus, Ambarīṣa bought Śunaḥśepa, the son of Ṛcīka, as a substitute. Viśvāmitra's kindness is extolled beyond measure when he is said to have asked his sons to be the sacrificial victim, instead of Śunaḥśepa. The sons refused and were condemned by their father to become dog-eating pariahs like Vasiṣṭha's sons.[142] Thus, the legend shares its location with the Triśaṅku legend where Viśvāmitra condemned the sons of Vasiṣṭha to become dog-eaters as well.

Contrary to Pargiter's argument, it is quite apparent that this *kṣatriya* version of the legend is a later creation to counter the Bhārgava help to Viśvāmitra. That the Āṅgirasa sage Ajīgarta, not the Bhārgava Ṛcīka, was the father of Śunaḥśepa is testified not only by the AB but also by the *Ṛg Veda*. That the *brāhmaṇas* carefully preserved their version is testified by the very late and highly Brahmanized *Bhāgavata Purāṇa* which repeats the AB story with all the details.[143] The same version is found, only with the geographical location changed, in a late *māhātmya* section of the *Brahma Purāṇa* (ch.104) as well.[144] Thus, we can see that both the *brāhmaṇa* and the *sūta-kṣatriya* traditions were at work with their distinct outlooks in reshaping the *Mahābhārata* and the *Rāmāyaṇa*. The Bhārgavas, being the most powerful among these groups of redactors, therefore needed a decisive intervention to make their voice hard. This intervention came in the form of a quintessential Bhārgava superhero, Rāma Jāmadagnya.

5.3 The Axe-Wielding Hero of the Bhṛgus

We have seen in the previous section how the *kṣatriya* tradition responded to the Brahmanization of the Vasiṣṭha-Viśvāmitra legend, projecting Viśvāmitra as the hero in their version and implicating him as the saviour of one of the Bhṛgus. However, the Bhṛgu response to this was not limited to a valorization of Vasiṣṭha but led to the introduction of a new character, a Bhṛgu who embodied all the Bhṛgu aspirations. This new Bhṛgu hero was Paraśurāma (the axe-wielding Rāma), son of Jamadagni, who has been extolled to the status of an incarnation of Viṣṇu.[145]

That Jāmadagnya Rāma, or Paraśurāma, was a relatively new entrant in Brahmanical mythology is quite apparent. Vasiṣṭha, Viśvāmitra, and Jamadagni were all Rgvedic figures. But this son of Jamadagni is unknown to the *Ṛg Veda*. Some scholars tried to make Paraśurāma a pre-Vedic hero, referring to the Iranian association of the early Bhṛgus. Amulya Sen thinks that he was a Hittite king of about BCE 1700, interpreting Jamadagni's name as Jamad-Agni, fire-worshipper of Persia.[146] J.M. Chatterjee identifies Jamadagni with Zarathushtra, as both the names mean one who devours fire. He takes the word 'Paraśu-Rāma' as meaning 'Rama of Persia'.[147] However, that Jamadagni was a contemporary of Vasiṣṭha, Viśvāmitra, and Sudās has been discussed earlier. The word 'Paraśurāma' is a very late Purāṇic epithet, and in earlier references the figure is known as Rāma Jāmadagnya, Bhārgava Rāma, or simply Rāma. Therefore, there is no convincing evidence in favour of a historical pre-Vedic Paraśurāma.

It can be argued that the career of Rāma Jāmadagnya makes him unlikely to be a Vedic poet-seer. K.M. Munshi made significant attempts to present Paraśurāma and his antagonist Kārtavīrya as historical figures, but his theory did not gain much acceptance,[148] nor have the attempts of Swami Banagovinda Parampanthi, to establish Paraśurāma as a historical figure, who did not use the tools of historical reconstruction properly, been much successful.[149] It is very unlikely that the entire corpus of the Later Vedic literature would remain almost silent about a figure of so much importance and influence like Jāmadagnya Rāma, had he been known to them.

Some scholars try to suggest a Later Vedic presence of Paraśurāma in the *Aitareya Brāhmaṇa* story of Rāma Mārgaveya championing the cause of the Śyāparṇas, defending their right to officiate in King Viśvāntara's sacrifice.[150] The presence of a figure named Rāma as a defender of a priestly group against a king is interesting. Therefore, attempts have been made to link the epithet Mārgaveya with Bhārgaveya. Przyluski, for instance, suspects an interchange of *ma* and *bha* in this case. However, Pradeep Kant Choudhary rightly points out that such an interchange would mean that the word '*bhṛgu*' is a later development of *mṛgu*, an unlikely suggestion given the presence and prominence of the Bhṛgus even in Ṛgvedic literature.[151] However, in the Bhargavized sections of both the *Rāmāyaṇa* and the *Mahābhārata*, Paraśurāma appears as a highly important figure.

Who was this Rāma Jāmadagnya? His legend has been narrated in the *Mahābhārata* by his follower Akṛtavarṇa to Yudhiṣṭhira. It started with Ṛcīka, the father of Jamadagni, who married Satyavatī, the daughter of King Gādhin. Satyavatī and her mother confused the separate child-bearing potions prepared for them by Ṛcīka. Thus, the queen bore a son of *brāhmaṇa* sensitivities, the future Viśvāmitra. Satyavatī was to bear a son of *kṣatriya* spirit. But, Ṛcīka could defer it for a generation. Thus, Jamadagni was born with *brāhmaṇa* sensibility, but with *kṣatriya* inclinations subdued in his gene. Like his father, Jamadagni married a princess, Reṇukā. They had five sons. One day, Reṇukā was aroused by witnessing the water-sports of king Citraratha and his wives. Angrily, Jamadagni asked his sons to kill her. Though the first four refused to do so, and were cursed by Jamadagni, Rāma obeyed his father's command.

Much attached to his father, Rāma was furious when Jamadagni's hermitage was ransacked by the proud Haihaya king Kārtavīrya Arjuna. With his *kṣatriya* spirit aroused, Rāma went to fight Kārtavīrya whose men (or sons) used Rāma's absence to kill Jamadagni. It caused the world-shattering wrath of Rāma who brutally massacred all *kṣatriyas*. He repeated this feat twenty times more, conquering the entire world. His violent career at last ended when he gifted the earth to the great sage Kaśyapa who banished him at once from his domain.[152] The *Rāmāyaṇa* alludes to the same legend.[153]

The account of Akṛtavarna is the most extensive description of Rāma Jāmadagnya's life in the *Mahābhārata*, but it is not the only one. Sukthankar notes that the birth story of Paraśurāma had been narrated at least four times in the *Mahābhārata*, and his destruction of the *kṣatriyas* referred to at least ten times. In fact, the Bhārgava reading of the *Mahābhārata* has to begin with a connection made between Paraśurāma's destruction of all the *kṣatriyas* and the death of many *kṣatriyas* in the Bhārata War, both culminating at the same venue, Samantapañcaka or Kurukṣetra.[154] Moreover, the new *kṣatriyas* are described as nothing but creation of the *brāhmaṇas* who cohabited with the widows of the *kṣatriyas* killed by Paraśurāma.[155] In the 'Droṇaparvan', the exploits of Paraśurāma are described in vivid details as a part of the Saga of the Sixteen Kings.[156] The 'Karṇaparvan' extends Paraśurāma's exploits to a victory over the Daityas as well.[157] The story of Paraśurāma is narrated in full in the 'Anuśāsanaparvan' too, and there the reversal of the caste-roles of Viśvāmitra and Paraśurāma is further explained as a result of the Bhārgava Cyavana's prophetic blessing to Kuśika who served him like a slave.[158]

However, the Bhārgava accounts in the 'Śāntiparvan' have a milder tone than the ones in the 'Ādiparvan', 'Āraṇyakaparvan', 'Droṇaparvan', 'Karṇaparvan', and 'Anuśāsanaparvan'. Therefore, in the 'Śāntiparvan', the new *kṣartiyas* are genuine *kṣatriyas*, since nature protected some of their ancestors from Paraśurāma's campaign. This 'Śāntiparvan' account of Paraśurāma's career, placed in the mouth of Kṛṣṇa, also differs from Akṛtavarṇa's account in the characterization of Kārtavīrya Arjuna. The cruel, proud, and oppressive king of Akṛtavarṇa's account is a perfectly noble one in Kṛṣṇa's narrative. His sons created the trouble in the latter account.[159] Again, the Saga of the Sixteen Kings, in the 'Śāntiparvan', does not include Rāma Jāmadagnya but an actual king, Sagara, as the sixteenth one.

Goldman thinks that Kṛṣṇa's version of the Paraśurāma legend ended up as an apologia for the warrior race and their right of sovereignty, and perhaps developed later than the Akṛtavarṇa version. He points out that the Akṛtavarṇa version—which contains a long lamentation by Paraśurāma after Jamadagni's death, shows Kārtavīrya as arrogant and brutal, and makes his destruction of the *kṣatriyas* final—is sympathetic to the hero and shows him as a grief-stricken son avenging his father's death. On the other hand, Kṛṣṇa's version shows Kārtavīrya as a pious, dutiful, and generous ruler, contains no lamentation, makes Paraśurāma's successive destruction of the *kṣatriyas* a result of a taunt by Parāvasu who mocked him for a false pledge, makes some *kṣatriyas* survive the slaughter, is pro-*kṣatriya*, and shows Paraśurāma in a negative light as a ruthless murderer who goes on killing people to boost his own ego and whim.[160]

However, a closer scrutiny of the two versions indicates that the distinction may not be so clear. After all, in both the versions, Paraśurāma reacted to the killing of his father by the *kṣatriyas*. The presence or absence of a *vilāpa* does not alter this scenario, and Paraśurāma remains a grief-stricken son in both. The massive slaughter no doubt hurts our sensibilities, but in the epic context it is probably the fulfilment of the pledge that matters most. Therefore, the representation in Kṛṣṇa's version may not be so negative for Paraśurāma as Goldman thinks, and—in any case—the slaughter is equally gruesome in both the accounts. The survival of the *kṣatriyas*, in fact, points to Kṛṣṇa's version's priority in date. If some *kṣatriyas* were not shown as surviving in each round of slaughter, the very myth of twenty-one slaughters could not even be generated. It seems that in later times, when Paraśurāma had attained the status of a superhero, his followers—which Akṛtavarṇa reportedly was—made his slaughters even more complete, turning the later *kṣatriyas* in creations of the *brāhmaṇas*.

Moreover, the way the 'Śāntiparvan' version of the *ṣoḍaṣarājopākhyāna* (Tale of Sixteen Kings) has been Bhargavized in the 'Droṇaparvan' would point towards the priority of the former one. Therefore, it seems that the first collection of the Bhārgava legends, commissioned by the Śaunakas but still composed by the bards, was possibly the eight Bhārgava chapters in the 'Ādiparvan' (I.5–12). The Bhārgava book of 'Śāntiparvan' and, probably, the revision of the *Bhagavad Gītā* followed next. However, with the *brāhmaṇas* hegemonizing the text, more legends infiltrated the other books, with a much more aggressive character, the radical Bhārgava book 'Anuśāsanaparvan' was composed, and a vast amount of radical Bhārgava legends were added to the 'Āraṇyakaparvan'. The Bhārgava hero Jāmadagnya Rāma was attributed more and more achievements, including the honour of being the martial instructor of the three greatest warriors in the Kaurava camp—Bhīṣma, Droṇa, and Karṇa. The older legends, such as the Saga of Sixteen Kings, were also Bhargavized.[161]

Pradeep Kant Choudhary, while studying the Paraśurāma legends, questions this notion of Bhṛguization. Following Shende's line, he argues that there are 3,200 references to the Āṅgirasas in the *Mahābhārata*, 830 references to the Vasiṣṭhas, and 500 references to the Bhṛgus. Therefore, statistically the Bhārgavas are not the most prominent *brāhmaṇa* clan in the text.[162] He assumes that the *ṣoḍaṣarājopākhyāna* was worked on by some southern redactors who really believed Paraśurāma to be a mythical king.[163] Moreover, he thinks that the picture of Paraśurāma in the *Mahābhārata* is not always of the hero par excellence but of one who often loses his battles and trains three heroes ending up in the losing side.[164]

We have already discussed that most of the references to the Āṅgirasas are to Droṇa, Kṛpa, and Aśvatthāman, three major characters of the main narrative. Similarly, the references to the Vasiṣṭhas are inflated because of the numerous references to Vyāsa, who is not just the author of the text but also an active participant in its events. But the Bhārgava materials represent a parallel cycle coexisting with the main narrative but not directly connected to it. Choudhary ignores this qualitative difference in his quantitative argument against the theory of Bhārgavization. The assumption of a southern group assuming Paraśurāma as a mythical king is very unconvincing, since not a single myth about Paraśurāma shows him as a king, and Paraśurāma's hatred towards the kings is unquestionably established in all myths concerning him. Though his three famous disciples—Bhīṣma, Droṇa, and Karṇa—belonged to the losing camp, they remained the most famous warriors in the text, each having a book named after him, and none of them could be overcome in a fair battle. Moreover, being the teacher of Droṇa makes Paraśurāma virtually the *guru* of all the *Mahābhārata* heroes. Above all, in his bid to challenge Bhārgavization, Choudhary avoids the most important evidence in its favour, which is the internal evidence about Ugraśravas's narration under the patronage of the Bhārgava Kulapati Śaunaka who commissioned a Bhārgava mini-epic alongside the narrative about the Bhārata War. However, even if we accept Bhārgavization as a significant intervention in the textual history of the *Mahābhārata*, we still have to ponder over why Paraśurāma was needed.

The highly violent Brahmanical and patriarchal overtone of the Paraśurāma legend is quite apparent. The legend shows a point of rupture when even reconciliation between the *brāhmaṇas* and the *kṣatriyas* seemed improbable, and when the *brāhmaṇa* aspiration was to purge the earth of all the *kṣatriyas*. No more was the symbiotic relationship based on patronage and legitimacy invoked. Paraśurāma did not distinguish the *brāhmaṇa*'s forgiveness and spiritual strength from the *kṣatriya* energy and martial power, as Vasiṣṭha did even in his reshaped role. Rather, the Bhṛgu hero was one who could martially combat the *kṣatriyas*, conquer the world, and gift that to a *brāhmaṇa*. What antagonized the Bhṛgus this much? What necessitated the conception of Jāmadagnya Rāma?

Adheesh Sathaye explains this by referring to the 'psychosocial anxieties' of the *brāhmaṇas* in the changing social milieu of Mauryan and post-Mauryan India. Referring to the concept of mutual dependence of the *brāhmaṇas* and the *kṣatriyas*, in which the *brāhmaṇas* retained their monopoly over the knowledge-based capital of social superiority by giving up all claims to violence on their behalf in favour of the *kṣatriyas*, Sathaye assumes a social anxiety of a section of the *brāhmaṇas* about the questions of power and violence. He thinks that Paraśurāma and Viśvāmitra represent the 'other' kind of *brāhmaṇa*, the exoticized cultural opposite of the *brāhmaṇa* 'self', whose violent behaviour made them antithetical to the self-controlled *brāhmaṇa* identity being established in North India during the epic's composition. In doing so, the legend 'naturalized' *varṇa* as an unchangeable physical property by bringing in the story of how the intermixture of the potions preordained the *brāhmaṇa*-hood of Viśvāmitra and violent inclinations of Paraśurāma.[165] The *brāhmaṇa* fear of maintaining their place as the dominant father-figures in the *varṇa*-based society might have contributed to the 'negative' Oedipal element in these legends in which the son (Bhārgava Rāma) willingly submits to the father (Jamadagni) by self-castration (lifelong celibacy) at the cost of a mother-figure (the chopping off of Reṇukā's head as a punishment for her illicit sexual desire), a model neatly worked out by Goldman.[166]

However, this model does not explain why it was essential to claim, and valorize, the *brāhmaṇa* 'other' if the epic was content with the creation of a non-violent *brāhmaṇa* self as delineated in the 'Śāntiparvan' stories or the reshaped Viśvāmitra-Vasiṣṭha legend, as discussed in the two preceding chapters. Why would the *brāhmaṇas* who reconstructed Vasiṣṭha as the paragon of *brāhmaṇa* superiority over the *kṣatriya* Viśvāmitra try to claim the latter? Why would the *brāhmaṇas*, happy to show spiritual power, non-violence, and forgiveness as the sources of *brāhmaṇa* supremacy, like to not just claim but also champion Bhārgava Rāma? These questions cannot be answered unless we understand them to be the results of two gradual stages in the Brahmanization of the *Mahābhārata*, in response to two different (and not the same, as Fitzgerald or Sathaye would believe) sociopolitical contexts. Therefore, we come back to the question about what sociopolitical context might have necessitated the championing of Bhārgava Rāma over the model *brāhmaṇas* like the reconstructed Vasiṣṭha.

The answer possibly lies in another legend in the *Mahābhārata*. It says that the noble Haihaya king Kṛtavīrya had distributed a huge amount of wealth among the *brāhmaṇas*. However, his descendants—when in distress—wanted the wealth back. Many Bhṛgus returned the wealth, while many others did not. The angry Haihayas killed all the Bhṛgus, down to the children in the womb. Of course, the Bhṛgus did not let the story end in this fashion. They brought in the infant Aurva who blindfolded the Haihaya persecutors and prepared to destroy the evil world. He only stopped when his ancestors appeared to reveal to him the secret that the puny *kṣatriyas* were no match for the Bhārgavas and would never be able to kill them. Actually the Bhārgavas, who were tired of their lives but were virtually immortal (as death feared to approach them), had to create a pretext for dying. Otherwise, they never desired any wealth except the heaven.[167] However, despite this Bhārgavized defence, a large-scale persecution of the Bhārgavas, who hoarded undue wealth, is revealed.

The legend of Aurva indeed had the potential of what the Paraśurāma legend became. But Aurva stopped twice on the verge of becoming a great annihilator. Choudhary assumes several reasons behind this, including the followers of Aurva losing importance, some actual memory of a historical Paraśurāma, and the appeal of a warrior hero than a hero using sacrificial means to accomplish his task.[168] However, it seems that the Aurva legend is a bit older than the Paraśurāma legend, representing an immediate response to the persecution they were facing. An immediate justification of their fate was conceived as a design made by the Bhārgavas themselves. However, when the wave of persecution was over, the Bhārgava vengeance was crystallized in conceiving their ideal hero, one capable of combating the *kṣatriyas* on the battlefield.

This possibly explains the violent anti-*kṣatriya* stance of the Bhṛgus whose relationship with the rulers had a complicated history. Sukthankar rightly explains that the Bhr̥gu legends show their close relationship with the rulers, including several marital ties.[169] It seems that the Bhr̥gus, very prominent in the Indo-Iranian phase, were gradually losing their importance. The Gr̥tsamadas witnessed the early phase of Indo-Aryan intrusion, and the Bhr̥gus might have been the priests of the Yadu-Turvaśas and the Druhyus. However, Sudas's victory in the Battle of Ten Kings pushed them to the background. In the new ethical religion preached by Vasiṣṭha, the Bhārgava tradition of sorcery was not very well accepted. Therefore, a group of the Bhr̥gus and the Āṅgirasas adopted the *Atharva Veda*. Neglected in the days of Kuru-Pañcāla dominance, they possibly sought patronage under some lesser Vedic tribes, may be the Haihayas.

In the Later Vedic Age, Bhr̥gu, like Vasiṣṭha, was attributed a divine birth. The AB says that the seed of Prajāpati had given birth to Āditya, Bhr̥gu, and Aṅgiras.[170] On the other hand, Bhr̥gu is called the son of Varuṇa in several Later Vedic texts.[171] The Bhr̥gus synthesized these two traditions in the Bhārgavized *Mahabharata*, where Bhr̥gu emerged from the seed of Brahmā, fallen in the fire of a sacrifice performed by Mahādeva disguised as Varuṇa.[172] When the process of Bhārgavization intensified further, Bhr̥gu was given an even more glorious birth, directly from Brahmā's heart.[173]

No doubt, the Bhārgavas composed and controlled a good number of texts. But they probably never succeeded in regaining the social prominence they desired. They were engaged in long struggles against the *kṣatriyas*. Their own text, the *Atharva Veda*, speaks of how the Vaitahavyas perished because of the slaughtering of cows of the Bhr̥gus.[174] Choudhary suggests that the Vaitahavyas joined the Haihaya tribe, which is not improbable.[175] The final blow was probably a violent persecution at the hands of the Haihayas. In fact, they could not do much against the existing political power. But in their texts, they could dream of a role reversal led by a Bhr̥gu hero. That could have given birth to Aurva, and ultimately to Jāmadagnya Rāma. Choudhary shows how various components of the legends came together in the formation of this story of the ultimate Bhārgava triumph, including the Jamadagni-Viśvāmitra friendship, the Battle of Ten Kings (in which Sudās once vanquished twenty-one Vaikarṇa communities, which could have been counterbalanced by Paraśurāma's extermination of the *kṣatriyas* twenty-one times), the Bhr̥gu-Vaitahavya conflict for cow (represented in the Haihaya king's forcible capture of the Bhṛgu Jamadagni's sacrificial cow), the Atharvavedic myths of the Bhṛgus fighting the demons Makkha and Vala (turning into Paraśurāma's victory over the demons), King Viśvakarman's land donation to Kaśyapa (transforming into Paraśurāma's donation of the earth to the same sage), and the story of Aurva.[176] Therefore, a conflict between two communities (the Bhṛgus and the Vaitahavyas) transformed into a conflict between a community (Haihayas) and an individual (Aurva), and finally into a conflict between two individuals (Paraśurāma and Kārtavīrya).[177] The Bhārgava individual, in this case, was a superhuman figure who could extend this conflict to all the *kṣatriyas.*

The Paraśurāma legend is also a response to the *kṣatriya* tradition projecting Viśvāmitra as a hero. Viśvāmitra's attainment of brāhmaṇahood has been turned into the mere consequence of the magic performed by a Bhṛgu sage. The assertion is further consolidated by a prophecy by the Bhārgava Cyavana that the grandson of Kuśika would become an ascetic only through the power of the Bhṛgus—*bhṛguṇām eva tejasā.*[178]

Thus, following scholars such as Sukthankar and Kosambi, we can assume that the creation of Paraśurāma was a psychological overcompensation of the Bhārgava *brāhmaṇas* against their subjugated real-life status and to propagate their own social superiority. It is difficult to determine when it occurred.[179] Adalbert Gail thinks that the Paraśurāma myth may be a product of that period when the division between priestly and warrior families had not become rigid. But the nature of the myth suggests otherwise. The violent antagonism portrayed in the myths can exist only between two clearly demarcated rival factions. Moreover, he suggests a priority of the Purāṇic Paraśurāma tradition over the *Mahābhārata*, a suggestion not very tenable.[180] However, one interesting suggestion comes from James L. Fitzgerald. He thinks that the *Mahābhārata* is primarily a religious epic, a response of the 'Brahmanical Renaissance' to the empires of Pāṭalīputra, which patronized the heterodox religions. The principal agenda of the text is to espouse an ideal polity under a king who subjects himself under the *brāhmaṇas* whom he supports materially and preserves from all harm. The ideal society is conceived as one where all the *varṇas* perform their specified duties. The Brahmanical rage against the contemporary ruling class is presented within an overall narrative of demonic, unlawful *kṣatriyas* being purged by the divine *kṣatriyas* allied with the *brāhmaṇas*. The narration unfolds in genocidal hatred of a sacrifice to kill all the Nāgas, with Rāma Jāmadagnya's genocidal rampage against all the *kṣatriyas* at the backdrop, gradually moving towards the violent purge of the *kṣatriyas* in the Bhārata War.[181]

It is difficult to accept Fitzgerald's general proposition about the entire *Mahābhārata* which contains so many different perceptions of *dharma*, so much apathy to the *varṇa* order, and so many allusions to contexts which are certainly pre-Maurya. But about this Bhārgava myth of Rāma Jāmadagnya, the interpretation may hold some ground. The idea of a 'Brahmanical Renaissance' is again quite problematic. But it can be assumed that there was a strong Brahmanical reaction against the patronage of certain rulers to the heterodox religions, and the reaction might have led to prosecution of some *brāhmaṇas*, including the Bhṛgus. The Bhṛgus reacted with much vigour. One result of their frustrated reaction could have been the *Manu Smṛti* which argued staunchly for an orthodox *varṇa*-ordered society, and earmarked the protection of the *varṇa* order as the quintessential duty of a good king. Rāma Jāmadagnya was also a product of that reaction. The assumption that Paraśurāma was a post-Maurya creation is also supported by the earliest reference to this figure, outside the *Mahābhārata*, in a text dated to *c.* first century CE, Aśvaghoṣa's *Buddhacarita*.[182] As the tension increased, Paraśurāma grew into a superhero in the more aggressively Bhārgavized sections, and it did not take long to establish him as the sixth incarnation of Viṣṇu.

However, royal power was not divorced from the *brāhmaṇa* power for long. The Bhāraśiva-Nāgas, the Vākāṭakas, the Guptas, and the Kadambas, all banked on the Brahmanical religion for legitimacy, from the fourth century CE onwards. Many of these ruling families were themselves *brāhmaṇas*. The Purāṇas started to be codified in a Brahmanical manner from roughly the same time. The idea of a noble ruler as the protector of the *varṇāśrama dharma* was becoming popular. The popularity of the boar incarnation of Viṣṇu as a royal symbol, signifying the king's role in protecting and preserving the order, and the idea of kingship in Kalidāsa's *Raghuvaṃśa* testify to this change. Against this background, the violent Rāma Jāmadagnya would not be a very acceptable figure to look up to, either from the point of view of the ruler or from the point of view of the *brāhmaṇa* beneficiaries of the ruler's patronage.

Thus, Rāma Jāmadagnya returned in another set of myths, only to be defeated by the ideal *kṣatriyas*. The *Rāmāyaṇa* has the biggest instance of this, when Paraśurāma challenged Rāma Dāśarathi. Rāma's great feat in winning Sītā's hand by breaking Śiva's bow infuriated Paraśurāma who returned to teach Rāma a lesson. He challenged Rāma to put an arrow to Viṣṇu's bow and face him in a duel. Rāma did that heroically but refused to kill a *brāhmaṇa*. So, he destroyed the fruits of Paraśurāma's austerities. Paraśurāma acknowledged him as Viṣṇu-incarnate and departed.[183]

It is a well-known fact that the divinity of Rāma had been proclaimed in a very late stage of the development of the *Rāmāyaṇa*. This legend seems to be one such very late legend. It shows the victory of the ideal *kṣatriya*, Rāma, over Paraśurāma. However, it is not a story of *kṣatriya* triumph over the *brāhmaṇas* but a story of reconciliation between the two. The victor is not an anti-*brāhmaṇa kṣatriya* like the Haihayas, but Rāma, the future protector of *varṇāśrama dharma*, the one who was reluctant to kill a *brāhmaṇa*. Moreover, Paraśurāma's acknowledgement of Rāma's divinity created a nice continuity between the two. Rāma destroyed Paraśurāma's pride, but not his works. Only, the hero of a new age replaced the hero of older times. With Viṣṇu's bow, the baton passed from the sixth incarnation of Viṣṇu to the seventh.

Even in the *Mahābhārata*, Paraśurāma lost to an ideal *kṣatriya* who, like Rāma, was a man steadfast in his vow. Bhīṣma, tied to his vow of celibacy, preferred to fight Paraśurāma than to accept his order to marry Ambā who sought Paraśurāma's help. Bhīṣma triumphed but remained respectful towards Paraśurāma. The element of continuity is visible even here, Bhīṣma being a student of Paraśurāma. The latter was not vanquished, but happy to be defeated by a virtuous and brave student whom he blessed before departing.

Our journey with Viśvāmitra and Vasiṣṭha comes to a close here. The fierce rivalry between two powerful Vedic poet-seers had long been overshadowed in the tussle between the *brāhmaṇa* and the *kṣatriya* traditions. But, by the Gupta period, the contest was resolved. The mutual relationship of royal patronage in return for legitimacy conferred by the priest was well established. The massive slaughter of all the *kṣatriyas* by Paraśurāma was no more the need of the time. Paraśurāma remained a hero of the past, the persecutor of the evil *kṣatriyas* like Kārtavīrya Arjuna. But, he was now ready to accept defeat at the hands of 'good' *kṣatriyas* such as Rāma and Bhīṣma, who nevertheless continued his legacy.

This legacy was the legacy of Brahmanization. The *Mahābhārata*, an *itihāsa* that emerged around the Later Vedic Kuru-Pañcālas as a commentary on a period of great transition and posed a number of serious questions to the newly emerging Brahmanical hereditary *varṇa* order, had finally been transformed into a Brahmanical scripture under the Bhārgavas. Thus, Ugraśravas provided Śaunaka with a commissioned redressing of what Vyāsa had composed and Vaiśaṃpāyana had narrated to Janamejaya, Kṛṣṇa had to compromise his original radicalism to suit in his new role as the Vaiṣṇava God demanding and rewarding *bhakti*, Yudhiṣṭhira had to swallow his radical anti-*varṇa* world-view to learn *rājadharma* from the patronizing Bhiṣma, and Paraśurāma wielded his axe ruthlessly against the kings who still failed to learn. Even when Paraśurāma would finally be defeated, his footprints would be too well-rooted to eradicate. The 'good' *kṣatriya* might succeed in defeating him, but only to perpetuate the Brahmanical world-view that he stood for, to facilitate the Brahmanization for which the Bhārgavas had created him.

5.4 From the Lost *Itihāsa* of the Bhāratas to the Great Epic of Bhārata: An Epilogue

In this book, we have tried to obtain a glimpse of the history of the creation of a text as a valuable source in understanding the making of an early Indian historical tradition. The tradition named *itihāsa* is as old as the Vedic tradition and existed simultaneously with the Vedic texts. The greatest representative of this tradition is the *Mahābhārata*, though it is clubbed together with the *Rāmāyaṇa* as an epic in popular perception. We have tried to show how the creation of the *Mahābhārata* has a long, complex, multilayered history and attempted to locate the original context of the tradition in the Later Vedic period with the help of corroborative evidence.

The very name *Mahābhārata* invokes the name of a Vedic tribe, the Bharatas. Hence, the pre-history of the text had to start with them. We have charted the course of the migration of some Ṛgvedic tribes to show how the Bharatas, under the chief Sudās, extended their authority from one river valley to another till they established their hegemony by convincingly defeating a grand alliance of ten tribes. This grand alliance was masterminded by the poet-priest Viśvāmitra, who had once served Sudās but was discarded later in favour of the immigrant upstart Vasiṣṭha. The Ṛgvedic compositions of both Viśvāmitra and Vasiṣṭha provide us with valuable information about the early history of the Bharatas. The triumph of Sudās also enhanced the power and prestige of Vasiṣṭha who had left a lasting contribution to Indian religion by bringing together the two cults of Varuṇa and Indra. However, after Sudās's death, his sons became antagonistic to Vasiṣṭha. They killed his sons and took away his cattle which probably were transferred to Viśvāmitra. Vasiṣṭha, however, succeeded in attaining progeny and cattle again.

After Sudās's victory, the Pūrus, one of the ten tribes, returned to join their old allies, the Bharatas. The amalgamation of these two tribes created a new one, the Kurus. Book X of the *Ṛg Veda*, the latest of the Ṛgvedic books, therefore remembers the Kurus as descendants of the Pūru chief Trasadasyu.[184] The last known Kuru figures in the *Ṛg Veda* are king Śaṃtanu and his elder brother Devāpi. The Kurus are the most important figures in the Later Vedic literature and—together with the Pāñcālas—ruled over the heartland of the Later Vedic world, known as the Madhyadeśa. The greater part of the Later Vedic literature was composed under the patronage of these two kingdoms. This period also became a great period of transition. With the coming of sedentary agricultural life, the clan societies were gradually moving towards state formation. Witzel has categorized the Kuru polity under Parikṣit, a ruler praised in the *Atharva Veda* as a contemporary, as a proto-state. Another development that Witzel places in the Later Vedic Kuru region was the growth of Brahmanical orthodoxy and orthopraxy which crystallized with the emergence of the *varṇa* system.

The Later Vedic period was thus a period of great social, political, economic, and intellectual transition. We have tried to locate the *Mahābhārata*, which self-proclaimedly depicts the end of an era, as the *itihāsa* of that transition. The text is based around the history of the Kurus between Śaṃtanu and Parikṣit and is supposed to have had its first complete narration by Vaiśaṃpāyana under the patronage of the Kuru king Janamejaya, both of whom were considerably well-known Later Vedic figures. However, even if we locate the origin of the *Mahābharata* in the time of Janamejaya (*c.* ninth century BCE), the text attained its present shape over a long period of time. Therefore, we tried to see if the text can still be read in its original context. Closely inspecting the key episodes in the main narrative of the text, we have shown how it is not only possible but also extremely necessary to read these episodes with their original Later Vedic context in mind to make sense of them. This way, we have examined the legends around birth and marriage of the central characters, the burning of the Khāṇḍava forest and the creation of Indraprastha, the Later Vedic Kuru ritual of *rājasūya* and the subsequent game of dice, the cattle inspections and cattle raids, and finally the Bhārata War. We have seen how the narrative was woven around a conflict between the two most prominent Later Vedic tribes, the Kurus and the Pāñcālas, in which a junior branch of the Kurus was maritally allied with the Pāñcālas. We have also shown how Kṛṣṇa, a leader of the Vṛṣṇi *gaṇasaṃgha*, had become significant in this essentially Kuru-Pāñcāla affair, and how he—starting from a very humble background—ultimately elevated himself to the demigod status of a '*vāsudeva*'.

Did we mean, then, that the *Mahābhārata* is a historical document and all its characters and episodes are authentically historical? Not really. Therefore, we had started by differentiating between *itihāsa* and history. However, we definitely view the *Mahābhārata* as a historical *tradition*. Moreover, there are reasons to believe that this tradition was well grounded in the historical reality of the Later Vedic Kurus between Śaṃtanu and Parikṣit, their genealogical crisis, their succession struggle, their alliance and antagonism with the Pāñcālas, and the decisive war. Yet, the *Mahābhārata* was not the 'history' of the Bhārata War the way, for instance, Thucydides composed the 'history' of the Peloponnesian War, not because the ancient Indians lacked a sense of history but because the inclination of *itihāsa* as a tradition was quite different from a systematic chronological account of facts.

Therefore, the tale of a significant war involving the Kurus and the Pāñcālas, in all probability grounded in a historical reality, preserved by the *sūta* bards of the Kuru court (such as Saṃjaya), was transformed into an *itihāsa* commenting upon something more. This *itihāsa*, attributed to Vyāsa, became a commentary upon a time rather than an account of events. The succession struggle became a marker of contest between not only two individuals but also two ideals: the hereditary right to primogeniture (the Sūryavaṃśa principle) and the right to succession based on merit (the Candravaṃśa principle). The latter ideal is attributed to

Bharata, the archetypal good ruler, and its subversion by Bhīṣma's vow culminated in a catastrophic war. This clash of two ideals of succession also became a prism through which a greater ideological clash between the newly emerging hereditary *varṇa* order and the principle that ability should score over birth was looked at. Vyāsa, whose own dubious birth would not accord him a respectable social rank in the *varṇa*-based Vedic Brahmanism, had a clear sympathy for the latter, and thus narrated the story of the coming of a new age (the redoubtable Kali) where the *varṇa* order would be the least adhered to. The establishment of this new order was also espoused with the valorization of a new kind of heroes with new codes of righteousness. Thus, Vyāsa's heroes, Yudhiṣṭhira and Kṛṣṇa, had little adherence to the *kṣatriya varṇa* duty of martial heroism and worked for a new ideal of the performance of *svadharma* based on *svabhāba*, without any desire for the outcome, and with extreme regard for non-cruelty (*ānṛśaṃsya*) and empathy (*anukrośa*). Vyāsa's disciple Vaiśaṃpāyana turned it into an ideal narrative for the Kuru court of Janamejaya by showing the war story not as one of Pāñcāla victory but as one of Pāṇḍava survival through Janamejaya's father, Parikṣita.

However, the bardic tradition was Brahmanized later, and the Bhārgavas had an important role in the process of Brahmanization and Vaiṣṇavization of the text. The characters and teachings of Yudhiṣṭhira and Kṛṣṇa were sanitized to suit Brahmanical taste. Kṛṣṇa was elevated to the position of the Supreme Divinity, and his philosophy of desireless action was subdued under his modified role as the champion of *bhakti*. Yudhiṣṭhira had to undergo a coaching in *rājadharma* based on the *kṣatriya*'s respectful submission to the *brāhmaṇa* and maintenance of the *varṇa* order from the ideal *kṣatriya* Bhīṣma in the 'Śāntiparvan'. The Ṛgvedic Bharata priests Viśvāmitra and Vasiṣṭha and their conflict were recreated as a story of *brāhmaṇa-kṣatriya* conflict where Vasiṣṭha's Brahmanism triumphed over Viśvāmitra's *kṣatriya* valour. The *sūta-kṣatriya* tradition responded with counter-myths with Viśvāmitra as their hero.

The text remained a ground of contest between these two traditions till the *brāhmaṇas*, particularly the Bhārgavas, gained complete control over the text. This was possibly in the post-Maurya period when the text was finally being written down. Hence the literate *brāhmaṇas* (mainly the Bhārgavas) controlled it completely, at the cost of the bards who mastered the oral transmission of the text. Now, not only the eventual brāhmaṇahood of Viśvāmitra was shown as the preordained outcome of Bhārgava prophecy and magic, but the Bhārgavas came up with their own superhero, Paraśurāma, who could take on the *kṣatriyas* in their own field of martial valour and slaughter them ruthlessly. The 'Āraṇyakaparvan' and 'Anuśāsanaprvan' accounts of Paraśurāma, in particular, were even more ruthless than the 'Śāntiparvan' account. However, when rulership became much more pro-*brāhmaṇa*, and the *brāhmaṇas* were systematic beneficiaries of *agrahāra* land grants, in the Gupta period, Paraśurāma's ruthlessness had to be tempered. In a new set of myths, he was defeated by the *kṣatriyas*, not all *kṣatriyas*, but the 'good' *kṣatriyas* such as Rāma and Bhīṣma who were respectful to the *brāhmaṇas* and the Brahmanical order and, hence, would perpetuate the ideological legacy (but not the brutality) of the Bhārgava Paraśurāma.

The *Mahābhārata* was now rendered with a scriptural value in both Vaiṣṇava theology (Kṛṣṇa was Viṣṇu himself and Paraśurāma an incarnation of Viṣṇu). The *brāhmaṇa* custodians of the text wanted to give it an encyclopaedic character in the Brahmanization process. All regions and communities of India, while being Brahmanized and Sanskritized, were accorded a place in the text and a role in the Bhārata War. Gradually, at least in apparent reading, the Later Vedic *itihāsa* of the Bharatas would be lost in the great 'epic' of 'Bhārata', the term denoting the Indian subcontinent from the *Viṣṇu Purāṇa* onwards.

***

What happened to the actual Bharatas or, to be precise, the Kurus? We have already referred to the prosperous reign of Parikṣit as described in the *Atharva Veda*.[185] Surveying the Vedic references to him, H.C. Raychaudhuri concludes:

> The only facts that can be accepted as historical are that he was a king of the Kurus, that the people lived prosperously under his rule, that he had many sons, and that the eldest, Janamejaya, succeeded him.[186]

We have already seen how Janamejaya's *sarpasatra* is a reconstruction of an old Vedic rite to provide a narrative context to the *Mahābhārata* story of *ānṛśaṃsya*, in the comparatively late outer frame of Ugraśravas's narration. However, possibly Janamejaya (and Parikṣit) continued the feud with the Nāgas, which they had inherited from Arjuna. In this process, he might have been involved in a clash with the Nāgas of Taxila. The Later Vedic texts remember him as an aspiring conqueror. The AB remembers his conquests and his aspirations to be a *sarvabhūmi* (universal sovereign).[187] The AB and the ŚB refer to his two *aśvamedhas*, with *aindra mahābhiṣeka* and *punarābhiṣeka*, in this bid, with Tura Kāvaṣeya and Indrota Śaunaka as his priests, respectively.[188] He also reportedly had some quarrel with the *brāhmaṇas*.[189] These traditions probably lay at the root of the 'Śāntiparvan' and 'Anuśāsanaparvan' references to Janamejaya and Vaiśaṃpāyana's anti-*brāhmaṇa* activities, and Janamejaya's regaining of his lustre through Indrota Śaunaka. In any case, Janamejaya ruled in a time when the ideal of universal sovereignty was considered worth pursuing, and the Kurus were in a position to pursue it. B.N. Mukherjee has dated this Janamejaya to early eighth or late ninth century BCE, five to six generations prior to the philosopher Yājñavalkya of the BU.[190] This was probably the time when he had patronized the first full narration of the Kuru *itihāsa*.

Thus, it is surprising that within five to six generations, the descendants of Parikṣit became so insignificant that Yājñavalkya had to face the question, "Where in the world are the Pārikṣitas"?[191] Of course, Yājñavalkya still remembered them as the performers of horse sacrifices.[192] However, what had happened to them? If we follow Raychaudhuri's reconstruction of the history of the later Kurus, Janamejaya's nephew Abhipratarin Kākṣasenī and his son Vṛddhadyumna Ābhipratāriṇa are known to Later Vedic literature. Vṛddhadyumna's sacrificial error had earned him a curse from a *brāhmaṇa*, leading to the expulsion of the Kurus from Kurukṣetra.[193] We have mentioned earlier that Witzel assumes the invasion of the Śālvas as the actual cause of the decline of the Kurus. There is also a later Purāṇic account about Hastināpura being flooded by the Gaṅgā during the reign of king Nicakṣu. [194] B.B. Lal's excavations at Hastinapur actually indicate that a heavy flood did wash away the settlement of Period II (*c.* 1100–800 BCE).[195] Therefore, the flood indeed seems to be the reason of the settlement's desertion.

The flood at their principal city was a great setback for the Kurus but was not the factor that led to their immediate end. The Purāṇas say that Nicakṣu had migrated to Kauśāmbī. However, a junior branch of the

Kurus continued to rule at Indraprastha. Thus, the Kuru kingdom was still one of the sixteen *mahājanapadas*, though a less powerful one, in the Buddha's time. The *Dhūmakāri Jātaka*, the *Dasabrāhmaṇa Jātaka*, and the *Mahāsutasoma Jātaka* speak of the Kuru kingdom which was ruled by a dynasty of Yudhiṭṭila (Yudhiṣṭhira) *gotta* from Indapatta or Indapattana. No longer the capital, Hatthinīpura (Hastināpura) was still an important settlement of the kingdom. Vāraṇāvata is also mentioned as a *nigama* in the kingdom.[196]

If we follow the dramas of Bhāsa, the king of Kauśāmbī, Udayana, was regarded as belonging to the Bharata clan. This Udayana (or Udena) is remembered as a contemporary of the Buddha in the Buddhist legends as well. Thus, even after their migration from Hastināpura, legends and stories did not desert the Kurus. A cycle of legends grew around Udayana, involving his romance with Vāsavadattā, his clashes with the Avantī king Pradyot, the wit of his minister Yaugandharāyaṇa, and his eccentric opposition to Buddhism. These legends had been preserved in the *Jātakas*, Bhāsa's *Svapnavāsavadattā* and *Pratijñāyaugandharāyaṇa*, Guṇāḍhya's *Bṛhatkathā*, and Somadeva's *Kathāsaritsāgara*. Kālidāsa had noticed specialized listeners of these legends (*udayana-kathā-kovida*) in the city of Avantī. However, these legends belong to a different kind of tradition, to be dealt with separately, in some other work.

Notes

1. Ramanujan (2007), p. 435.
2. T.R.S. Sharma (2009), p. 28.
3. R.P. Goldman, '*Eṣa Dharmaḥ Sanātanaḥ*: Shifting Moral Values and the Indian Epics' in P. Bilimoria and J.N. Mohanty (eds), *Relativism, Suffering and Beyond*, Oxford University Press, Delhi, 1997, pp. 187–223.
4. Vyāsa, I.135–139.
5. Greg Bailey, 'The *Mahābhārata*'s Simultaneous Affirmation and Critique of the Universal Validity of *Dharma*' in T.S. Rukmani (ed.), *The Mahābhārata: What Is Not Here Is Nowhere Else*, Munshiram Manoharlal, New Delhi, 2005, p. 63.
6. Cited in Deshpande (2005), pp. 5–6.
7. Naina Dayal's PhD thesis indicates that some of them, the *paurāṇikas*, could have been *brāhmaṇas* as well.
8. Pande (2009), p. 56.
9. Deshpande (2005), pp. 3–18.

10. Sullivan (1990), p. 9.
11. Vyāsa, I.5.1–3.
12. Vyāsa, I.5–12.
13. Sukthankar (1936–1937).
14. Sukthankar (1936–1937), p. 75.
15. Goldman (1972); Goldman (1977).
16. McGrath (2016b), pp. 119–167.
17. Sullivan (1990), p. 19.
18. N.J. Shende, 'The Authorship of the *Mahābhārata*', *Annals of the Bhandarkar Oriental Research Institute*, Vol. 24, 1943, pp. 67–82.
19. Shende (1943), pp. 69–70.
20. Hiltebeitel (2001), p. 108.
21. Hiltebeitel (2001), p. 111.
22. Hiltebeitel (2001), p. 110.
23. Hiltebeitel (2001), p. 110.
24. McGrath (2018), p. 150.
25. For detailed discussion on this, see Kanad Sinha, 'The Devas, the Asuras and Gilgamesh: Exploring the Cross-Cultural Journey of Myths', *Vedic Studies*, Vol. VI, 2014, pp. 360–401.
26. For the transformation of the *Rāmāyaṇa*, see Kanad Sinha (2011).
27. Vishnu S. Sukthankar, *Critical Studies in the Mahābhārata*, Karnataka Publishing House, Bombay, 1944, p. 335.
28. Vyāsa, I.48.4–10.
29. Vyāsa, XIV.16.5–6.
30. Vyāsa, XIV.16.10–12.
31. Vyāsa, XIV.16–50.
32. Vyāsa, XIV.28.
33. Vyāsa, XII.39.
34. Vyāsa, XIV.28.22.
35. Vyāsa, XIV.50.30
36. Vyāsa, XIV.50.45–47.
37. Vyāsa, VI.14.2.
38. McGrath (2016a), p. 165.
39. McGrath (2016a), p. 142.
40. McGrath (2016a), p. 142.
41. Nigel Dodd, *The Social Life of Money*, Princeton University Press, Princeton, 2014.
42. McGrath (2016a), p. 149.
43. McGrath (2016a), p. 149.
44. Vyāsa, XII.81.32.
45. Vyāsa, XII.81.86.
46. Vyāsa, XII.57.7, XII.57.39.
47. McGrath (2018), p. 102.
48. McGrath (2016a), p. 153.

49. McGrath (2018), p. 158.
50. Vyāsa, XII.1.19–38.
51. Vyāsa, XII.7.34–40.
52. Vyāsa, XII.7–19, XII.20–38.
53. Vyāsa, XII.45–46.
54. Vyāsa, XII.47–48.
55. Vyāsa, XII.49.
56. Vyāsa, XII.53–54.
57. Vyāsa, XII.55.1–10.
58. Vyāsa, XII.55.11–20.
59. James Fitzgerald, 'Introduction to the Book of Peace' in Vyāsa, *The Mahābhārata* (Vol. VII): Book of Women and Book of Peace Part I, translated by James L. Fitzgerald, The University of Chicago Press, Chicago, 2004b, pp. 117–118.
60. Fitzgerald (2004b), pp. 129–131.
61. Vyāsa, XII.91.3–6.
62. Fitzgerald (2004b), pp. 128–129.
63. Vyāsa, XII.73.1–4.
64. Vyāsa, XII.73.5.
65. Vyāsa, XII.73.6–20.
66. Vyāsa, XII.74.25–30.
67. Vyāsa, XII.74–75.
68. Vyāsa, XII.76.10.
69. Vyāsa, XII.72.20.
70. Vyāsa, XII.78.1–5.
71. Vyāsa, XII.77.
72. Vyāsa, XII.78.1–5.
73. Vyāsa, XII.79.1–5.
74. Vyāsa, XII.79.15–20.
75. Vyāsa, XII.90–130.
76. Vyāsa, XIII.60.15, XIV.93.78.
77. Vyāsa, XIII.72.28.
78. Vyāsa, XIII.110.64.
79. Vyāsa, III.80.107, III.80.117, III.81.6, III.81.16, III.81.75, III.81.172, III.82.69, III.82.88, III.82.113, III.83.76, XIII.26.11, XIII.26.33, XIII.26–53.
80. Vyāsa, XII.12.25–26.
81. Vyāsa, III.198–199.
82. Vyāsa, XII.124.36.
83. Vyāsa, XII.314–315.
84. Sullivan (1990), p. 10.
85. Vyāsa, XII.146–148.
86. Adam Bowles, *Dharma, Disorder and the Political in Ancient India: The Āpaddharmaparvan of the Mahābhārata*, Brill, Leiden, 2007, pp. 317–318.
87. Vyāsa, XIII.6.36–37.

88. F.E. Pargiter, 'Brahmanic and Kshatriya Tradition', *Journal of the Royal Asiatic Society of Great Britain and Ireland*, April 1914, pp. 411–412.
89. A. Berriedale Keith, 'The Brahmanic and Kshatriya Tradition', *Journal of the Royal Asiatic Society of Great Britain and Ireland*, January 1914, pp. 118–126.
90. See R.C. Hazra, *Studies in the Puranic Records on Hindu Rites and Customs*, Facsimile Publications, New Delhi, 2016 (reprint), for a detailed discussion about the Purāṇas.
91. Vyāsa, V.104.1–20, V.117.10–23, XIII.18–38.
92. Vyāsa, VI.160–163.
93. Vyāsa, XII.75.
94. Vyāsa, I.162.10–I.163.21, XII.139.12.
95. Vyāsa, IX.41.
96. Pargiter (1997), pp. 172–173.
97. A.D. Pusalker, 'Traditional History from the Earliest Time to the Accession of Parikṣit' in R.C. Majumdar (ed.), *The History and Culture of the Indian People: The Vedic Age*', Bharatiya Vidya Bhavan, Mumbai, 1996b (reprint).
98. Vyāsa, I.165.42; translation slightly modified.
99. Vyāsa, I.164–168.
100. Vyāsa, I.164.5–8.
101. Vyāsa, I.165.28.
102. This aspect is absent in the *Rāmāyaṇa* version of the Sagara legends. However, this seems to be a very widespread legend among the Purāṇic *brāhmaṇas*. Thus, the legend of Sagara and the foreign tribes appears in the *Harivaṃśa*, *Brahmāṇḍa Purāṇa*, *Vāyu Purāṇa*, *Śiva Purāṇa*, *Brahma Purāṇa*, *Viṣṇu Purāṇa*, *Padma Purāṇa*, and *Nāradīya Purāṇa*.
103. F.E. Pargiter, 'Sagara and the Haihayas, Vasiṣṭha and Aurva', *Journal of the Royal Asiatic Society of Great Britain and Ireland*, July 1919, pp. 353–367.
104. ṚV, X.133.7.
105. Rahurkar (1964), p. 126.
106. Findly (1984), p. 80.
107. ṚV, VII.104.12–16.
108. Velankar (1942), p. 13.
109. Findly (1984), p. 80.
110. Rahurkar (1961), p. 52.
111. Vyāsa, I.71.
112. Vyāsa, I.4.
113. Vyāsa, III.122–124.
114. Vyāsa, III.125.
115. Vyāsa, I.8.
116. Vyāsa, III.115.
117. Vyāsa, XII.95.
118. Vyāsa, I.169–171.
119. Vyāsa, XIII.40–43.

120. Vālmīki (Vol. I), I.53.14.
121. Vālmīki (Vol. I), I.52.
122. Vālmīki (Vol. I), I.55.4.
123. Vālmīki (Vol. I), I.50–64.
124. Vālmīki (Vol. I), I.17–30.
125. Vālmīki (Vol. I), I.18.2.
126. Vālmīki (Vol. I), I.20.10.
127. Vyāsa, V.104.5–20.
128. Louis Dumont, *Homo Hierarchicus: The Caste System and Its Implications*, Oxford University Press, Delhi, 1988.
129. Declan Quigley, *The Interpretation of Caste*, Oxford University Press, New Delhi, 2012 (reprint), p. 85.
130. Quigley (2012), p. 85.
131. Quigley (2012), p. 86.
132. Cited in Quigley (2012), p. 117.
133. Cited in Quigley (2012), p. 149.
134. Quigley (2012), p. 157.
135. Vālmīki, I.58.14–15.
136. Vālmīki, I.56–59.
137. Pargiter (1917), p. 39.
138. Pargiter (1917), p. 39.
139. Vyāsa, I.65.30–40.
140. F.E. Pargiter, 'Viśvāmitra and Vasiṣṭha', *The Journal of the Royal Asiatic Society of Great Britain and Ireland*, October 1913, pp. 885–904.
141. Vyāsa, XII.3.
142. Vālmīki, I.60–61.
143. *The Bhāgavata Purāṇa*, translated by Ganesh Vasudeo Tagare, Motilal Banarsidass, Delhi, 1976, IX.16.29.37.
144. Pargiter (1917), p. 46.
145. It is not implied that these responses followed one another in a neat chronological succession. Rather, the two traditions existed simultaneously and interacted with each other, generating responses and counter-responses.
146. Cited in Choudhary (2010), p. 28.
147. Choudhary (2010), p. 28.
148. K.M. Munshi, 'The Māhīṣmatī of Kārtavīrya', *The Indian Antiquary*, November 1922, pp. 217–221; K.M. Munshi, *The Early Aryans in Gujarat*, University of Bombay, Bombay, 1941; K.M. Munshi, 'The Historical Value of Paraśurāma Tradition', *New Indian Antiquary*, Vol. 6, 1943–1944, pp. 217–224.
149. Swami Banagovinda Parampanthi, 'Paraśurāma Kuṇḍa: A Study in Historical and Geographical Perspective', *Journal of Assam Research Society, Guwahati*, Vol. 19, 1970–1971, pp. 76–89; Swami Banagovinda Parampanthi, *Bhagawan Paraśurāma and Evolution of Culture in Northeast India*, Daya Publishing House, Delhi, 1987.

150. AB, VII.27–34.
151. Choudhary (2010), pp. 27–28.
152. Vyāsa, III.115–117.
153. Vālmīki, I.74–75.
154. Vyāsa, I.2.3–9.
155. Vyāsa, I.98.5.
156. Vyāsa, VII.70.
157. Vyāsa, VIII.34.
158. Vyāsa, XIII.52–56.
159. Vyāsa, XII.48–49.
160. Goldman (1972), pp. 161–173.
161. Sukthankar notes another such instance. A story of the humbling of King Nahuṣa by the sage Agastya in the 'Udyogaparvan' (V.11–17) has been modified in the 'Anuśāsanaparvan' (XIII.99–100) where it is Bhṛgu who humbles the king, Agastya playing only a secondary role. See Sukthankar (1936–1937), pp. 320–321.
162. Choudhary (2010), pp. 116–117.
163. Choudhary (2010), pp. 86–87.
164. Choudhary (2010), p. 120.
165. Adheesh Sathaye, 'The Other Kind of Brahman: Rāma Jāmadagnya and the Psychosocial Construction of Brahman Power in the *Mahābhārata*' in Sheldon Pollock (ed.), *Epic and Argument in Sanskrit Literary History: Essays in Honour of Robert P. Goldman*, Manohar, New Delhi, 2010, pp. 185–207. Also see Adheesh Sathaye, 'How to Become a Brahman: The Construction of *Varṇa* as Social Place in the *Mahābhārata*'s Legends of Viśvāmitra', *Acta Orientalis Vilnensia*, Vol. 8, 2007, pp. 41–67.
166. See Robert P. Goldman, 'Fathers, Sons, and Gurus: Oedipal Conflict in the Sanskrit Epics', *Journal of Indian Philosophy*, Vol. 6, 1978, pp. 325–392; Robert P. Goldman, 'Matricide, Renunciation, and Compensation in the Legends of Two Warrior Heroes of the Sanskrit Epics', *Indologica Taurinensia*, Vol. 10, pp. 117–131.
167. Vyāsa, I.169.10–25.
168. Choudhary (2010), pp. 47–48.
169. Sukthankar (1936–1937), p. 327.
170. AB, III.34.
171. PB, XVIII.9.1; ŚB, XI.6.1.1; JB, I.42; TU, I.3.1.1; TĀ, IX.1.
172. Vyāsa, XIII.85.
173. Vyāsa, I.60.40.
174. AV, V.18.10, V.19.1.
175. Choudhary (2010), pp. 43–44.
176. Choudhary (2010), p. 51.
177. Choudhary (2010), p. 46.
178. Vyāsa, XIII.55.32.

179. Sukthankar (1936–1937); Kosambi (1953), p. 212; D.D. Kosambi, 'The Emergence of National Characteristics among Three Indo-European People', *Annals of the Bhandarkar Oriental Research Institute*, Vol. 20, 1938–1939, pp. 192–206.
180. Cited in Choudhary (2010), pp. 14–15.
181. James L. Fitzgerald, 'Mahābhārata' in Sushil Mittal and Gene Thursby (eds), *The Hindu World*, Routledge, New York, 2004a, pp. 52–74.
182. Aśvaghoṣa, IX.25.
183. Vālmīki (Vol. I), I.74–75.
184. ṚV, X.33.4.
185. We must mention here that in the *Mahābhārata* and the Purāṇas, two Parikṣits are mentioned, one prior to the Bhārata War and one after. If the Vedic references refer to the earlier Parikṣit, then our entire reconstruction shall be defeated. However, the first Parikṣit is a shadowy figure with a very uncertain place even in the epic-Purāṇic genealogy. Raychaudhuri is probably right in assuming that the two Parikṣits represent a bardic duplication of the same original individual. This individual is in all probability Parikṣit, the son of Abhimanyu, while the other Parikṣit is a very vague and uncertain later creation. See Raychaudhuri (2006), pp. 16–17.
186. Raychaudhuri (2006), p. 19.
187. AB, VIII.11, VIII.21.
188. AB, VIII.21; ŚB, XI.5.5.
189. AB, VII.27.
190. Raychaudhuri (2006), p. 569.
191. BU, III.3.1.
192. BU, III.3.2.
193. Raychaudhuri (2006), pp. 40–41.
194. Raychaudhuri (2006), pp. 39–40.
195. Raychaudhuri (2006), p. 571.
196. *The Jātaka* (Vol. III), translated by H.T. Francis and R.A. Neil, Munshiram Manoharlal, New Delhi, 2002 (reprint), pp. 241–242; The *Jātaka* (Vol. IV), pp. 227–231; *The Jātaka* (Vol. V), translated by H.T. Francis, Munshiram Manoharlal, New Delhi, 2002 (reprint), pp. 246–279.

Bibliography

Primary Sources

'Allahabad Pillar Inscription of Samudragupta' in *Corpus Inscriptionum Indicanum*, Vol. 3, edited by J.F. Fleet, The Superintendent of Government Printing, Calcutta, 1888, pp. 203–220.

Āpastamba Śrauta Sūtra, edited by R. Garbe, Bibilotheca Indica, Calcutta, 1881–1903.

Aśvaghoṣa, *Buddhacarita*, translated by E.H. Johnston, Munshiram Manoharlal, New Delhi, 1995 (reprint).

Āśvalāyana Śrauta Sūtra, edited by R. Vidyaratna, Bibliotheca Indica, Calcutta, 1874.

Atikal, Ilanko, *The Cilappatikaram: The Tale of an Anklet*, translated by R. Parthasarathy, Penguin, New Delhi, 2004.

Baudhāyana Śrauta Sūtra, edited by W. Caland, Bibliotheca Indica, Calcutta, 1904–1924.

The Bhāgavata Purāṇa (Parts I–IV), translated by Ganesh Vasudeo Tagare, Motilal Banarsidass, Delhi, 2002 (reprint).

Bhāsa, *Bālacarita*, translated by C.R. Devadhar, Oriental Book Agency, Poona, 1951.

Bhāsa, *Dūtavākya*, translated by C.R. Devadhar, Oriental Book Agency, Poona, 1957.

Bhāsa, *The Shattered Thigh and Other Plays*, translated by A.N.D. Haskar, Penguin, New Delhi, 2008.

Bhāsa, *Urubhaṅga*, translated by C.R. Devadhar, Oriental Book Agency, Poona, 1957.

Bhāsa, 'Urubhaṅga', translated by Edwin Gerow, in Arvind Sharma (ed.), *Essays on the Mahābhārata*, Motilal Banarsidass, New Delhi, 2011.

The Brahma Purāṇa (Part I), edited by J.L. Shastri, Motilal Banarsidass, New Delhi, 2001.

The Connected Discourses of the Buddha, translated by Bhikkhu Bodhi, Wisdom Publications, Boston, 2009.

Dhammapada, translated by Rhys Davids, Pali Text Society, London, 1979 (reprint).

Gopatha Brāhmaṇa, edited by R.L. Mitra, Bibliotheca Indica, Delhi, 1972 (reprint).

Gṛhya Sūtras (Part I), translated by Hermann Oldenberg, Motilal Banarsidass, New Delhi, 1964 (reprint).

Hāla (ed.), *The Prakrit Gāthāsaptaśatī*, translated by Radhagovinda Basak, Asiatic Society, Calcutta, 1971.

Harivaṁśa, edited by P.L. Vaidya, Bhandarkar Oriental Research Institute, Poona, 1969 (reprint).

Hiranyakeśin Śrauta Sūtra, edited by K.B. Agase, Anandasrama, Poona, 1907–1932.

Hymns of the Atharvaveda (Vols I and II), translated by Ralph T.H. Griffith, Munshiram Manoharlal, New Delhi, 2002.

Hymns of the Ṛgveda (Vols I and II), translated by Ralph T.H. Griffith, Munshiram Manoharlal, New Delhi, 1999 (reprint).

Jaiminīya Brāhmaṇa, edited by Raghu Vira, Sarasvati Vihara, Nagpur, 1934.

Jaiminīya Upaniṣad Brāhmaṇa, translated by H. Oertel, *Journal of the American Oriental Society*, Vol. 16, 1896, pp. 79–260.

The Jātaka (Vol. III), translated by H.T. Francis and R.A. Neil, Munshiram Manoharlal, New Delhi, 2002 (reprint).

The Jātaka (Vol. IV), translated by W.H.D. Rouse, Munshiram Manoharlal, New Delhi, 2002 (reprint).

The Jātaka (Vol. V), translated by H.T. Francis, Munshiram Manoharlal, New Delhi, 2002 (reprint).

The Jātaka (Vol. VI), translated by E.B. Cowell and W.H.D. Rouse, Munshiram Manoharlal, New Delhi, 2002 (reprint).

Kane, P.V., *History of Dharmaśāstra*, Vol. 2, Bhandarkar Oriental Research Institute, Pune, 1997.

Kaṭhaka Saṃhitā, edited by L. von Schroeder, Franz Steiner Verlag, Wiesbaden, 1970–1972.

Kauṭilya, *The Arthaśāstra* (Parts I–III), edited and translated by R.P. Kangle, University of Bombay, Bombay, 1960.

Maitrāyaṇī Saṃhitā, F.A. Brockhaus, Leipzig, 1886.

Majumdar, R.C. (ed.), *Classical Accounts of India*, Firma K.L. Mukhopadhyaya, Calcutta, 1941.

Mānava Śrauta Sūtra, translated by J.M. van Gelder, Sata Pitaka Series, Delhi, 1971.

Manu, *The Ordinances of Manu*, translated by Arthur Coke Burnell and Edward W. Hopkins, Oriental Books Reprint Corporation, New Delhi, 1971.

The Middle Length Discourses of the Buddha, translated by Bhikkhu Ñāṇamoli and edited by Bhikkhu Bodhi, Wisdom Publications, Boston, 2009.

Pañcaviṁśa Brāhmaṇa, translated by W. Caland, Asiatic Society of Bengal, Calcutta, 1938.

Pāṇini, *The Ashtadhyayi*, edited by Srisa Chandra Basu, Motilal Banarsidass, New Delhi, 2003 (reprint).

Ṛg Veda Brāhmaṇas, translated by Arthur Berriadale Keith, Harvard University Press, Cambridge, MA, 1920.

Ṛg Veda Saṁhitā (Vols I and II), translated by Romesh Chandra Dutt, Haraf, Kolkata, 2000 (reprint).

Sāma Veda Saṃhitā, edited and translated by Paritosh Thakur, Haraf, Kolkata, 1975.

Sama Vidhana Brahmana with Commentary of Sayana , critically edited by B.R. Sharma, Rashtriya Sanskrit Vidyapeetha, Tirupati, 2004.

Śāṅkhāyana Āraṇyaka, translated by A.B. Keith, Royal Asiatic Society, London, 1908.

Śāṅkhāyana Śrauta Sūtra, translated by W. Caland, Motilal Banarsidass, Delhi, 1980 (reprint).

Śatapatha Brāhmaṇa (Vols I–V), translated by Julius Eggeling, Motilal Banarsidass, New Delhi, 2005 (reprint).

Śaunaka, *The Bṛhaddevatā* (Parts I–II), translated by A.A. MacDonnell, Motilal Banarsidass, Delhi, 1965 (reprint).

Sayings of the Buddha, translated by Rupert Gethin, Oxford University Press, Oxford, 2008.

Taittirīya Āraṇyaka, edited by R.L. Mitra, Bibliotheca Indica, Calcutta, 1872.

Tarkavachaspati, Taranatha, *Vācaspatyam* (Vols I–VI), Chowkhamba Sanskrit Series, Varanasi, 1990.

Upaniṣads, translated by Patrick Olivelle, Oxford University Press, Oxford, 2008.

Vālmīki, *The Rāmāyaṇa* (Vol. I), 'Bālakāṇḍa', translated by Robert P. Goldman, Princeton University Press, Princeton, 1984.

Vālmīki, *The Rāmāyaṇa* (Vol. II), 'Ayodhyākāṇḍa', translated by Sheldon Pollock, New York University Press, New York, 2007.

Vālmīki, *The Rāmāyaṇa* (Vol. VI), 'Yuddhakāṇḍa', translated by Robert P. Goldman, Sally J. Sutherland Goldman, and Barend A. van Nooten, Motilal Banarsidass, Delhi, 2010.

Van Buitenen, J.A.B., *The Bhagavadgītā in the Mahābhārata: Text and Translation*, Chicago University Press, Chicago, 1981.

Vāyu Purāṇa (Part II), translated by G.V. Tagare, Motilal Banarsidass, Delhi, 1988.

The Veda of the Black Yajus School Entitled Taittirīya Saṁhitā, translated by Arthur Berriedale Keith, Motilal Banarsidass, Delhi, 1967 (reprint).

The Vinaya Texts, translated by T.W. Rhys Davids and Hermann Oldenberg, The Clarendon Press, Oxford, 1881.

Viṣṇumahāpurāṇaṃ, translated by M.N. Dutt, Eastern Book Linkers, Delhi, 2005 (reprint).

Vyāsa, *Mahābhārata* (Book Nine, Shalya, Vols 1 and 2), translated by Justin Meiland, New York University Press, New York, 2007.

Vyāsa, *Mahābhārata* (Book Six): Bhishma (Vols 1 and 2), translated by Alex Cherniak, New York University Press, New York, 2008.

Vyāsa, *The Mahābhārata* (Vol. I), translated by J.A.B. van Buitenen, University of Chicago Press, Chicago, 1973.

Vyāsa, *The Mahābhārata* (Vol. I, Parts I–II), 'Ādiparvan', edited by V.S. Sukthankar, Bhandarkar Oriental Research Institute, Poona, 1997.

Vyāsa, *The Mahābhārata* (Vol. II), translated by J.A.B. van Buitenen, University of Chicago Press, Chicago, 1975.

Vyāsa, *The Mahābhārata* (Vol. II), 'Sabhāparvan', edited by Franklin Edgerton, Bhandarkar Oriental Research Institute, Poona, 1995.

Vyāsa, *The Mahābhārata* (Vol. III), 'Āraṇyakaparvan', edited by V.S. Sukthankar, Bhandarkar Oriental Research Institute, Poona, 2002.

Vyāsa, *The Mahābhārata* (Vol. III), translated by J.A.B. van Buitenen, University of Chicago Press, Chicago, 1978.

Vyāsa, *The Mahābhārata* (Vol. V), 'Virāṭaparvan', edited by Raghu Vira, Bhandarkar Oriental Research Institute, Poona, 1936.

Vyāsa, *The Mahābhārata* (Vol. VI), 'Udyogaparvan', edited by Sushil Kumar Dey, Bhandarkar Oriental Research Institute, Poona, 1940.

Vyāsa, *The Mahābhārata* (Vol. VII), 'Bhīṣmaparvan', edited by Shripad Krishna Belvalkar, Bhandarkar Oriental Research Institute, Poona, 1947.

Vÿasa, *The Mahābhārata* (Vol. VII), translated by James Fitzgerald, Chicago University Press, Chicago, 2004.

Vyāsa, *The Mahābhārata* (Vols VIII–IX), 'Droṇaparvan', edited by Sushil Kumar Dey, Bhandarkar Oriental Research Institute, Poona, 1958.

Vyāsa, *The Mahābhārata* (Vol. X), 'Karṇaparvan', edited by P.L. Vaidya, Bhandarkar Oriental Research Institute, Poona, 2003.

Vyāsa, *The Mahābhārata* (Vol. XI), 'Śalyaparvan', edited by R.N. Dandekar, Bhandarkar Oriental Research Institute, Poona, 1961.

Vyāsa, *The Mahābhārata* (Vol. XII), 'Sauptikaparvan', edited by Hari Damodar Velankar; and 'Strīparvan', edited by Vasudev Gopal Paranjpe, Bhandarkar Oriental Research Institute, Poona, 1948.

Vyāsa, *The Mahābhārata* (Vols XIII–XVI), Śāntiparvan', edited by Shripad Krishna Belvalkar, Bhandarkar Oriental Research Institute, Poona, 2005.

Vyāsa, *The Mahābhārata* (Vol. XVII), 'Anuśāsanaparvan', edited by R.N. Dandekar, Bhandarkar Oriental Research Institute, Poona, 1966.

Vyāsa, *The Mahābhārata* (Vol. XIX), 'Āśramavāsikaparvan', 'Mausalparvan', 'Mahāprasthānikaparvan', and 'Svargārohaṇaparvan', edited by Shripad Krishna Belvalkar, Bhandarkar Oriental Research Institute, Poona, 1959.

Yāska, *The Nighaṇṭu and the Nirukta*, edited by Lakshman Sarup, Motilal Banarsidass, New Delhi, 1962.

The Yuga Purāṇa, critically edited with an English translation and detailed introduction by John E. Mitchiner, The Asiatic Society, Calcutta, 1986.

Secondary Sources

Achar, B.N. Narahari, 'Planetarium Software and the Date of the Mahābhārata War' in T.S. Rukmani (ed.), *The Mahābhārata: What Is Not Here Is Nowhere Else*, Munshiram Manoharlal, New Delhi, 2005, pp. 247–246.

Adarkar, Aditya, 'Karṇa's Choice: Courage and Character in the Face of an Ethical Dilemma' in T.S. Rukmani (ed.), *The Mahābhārata: What Is Not Here Is Nowhere Else*, Munshiram Manoharlal, New Delhi, 2005, pp. 117–130.

Adluri, Vishwa, 'Hermeneutics and Narrative Architecture in the Mahabharata' in Vishwa Adluri (ed.), *Ways and Reasons for Thinking about the Mahābhārata as a Whole*, Bhandarkar Oriental Research Institute, Pune, 2015, pp. 1–28.

Adluri, Vishwa, 'Introduction' in Vishwa Adluri (ed.), *Ways and Reasons for Thinking about the Mahābhārata as a Whole*, Bhandarkar Oriental Research Institute, Pune, 2015, pp. vii–xxxii.

Agrawal, D.P., 'Protohistoric Chronology and Technology and Ecological Factors: A Synthesis' in B.P. Sahu (ed.), *Iron and Social Change in Early India*, Oxford University Press, New Delhi, 2006, pp. 49–59.

Allen, N.J., 'Arjuna and Odysseus: A Comparative Approach', *South Asia Library Group Newsletter*, Vol. 40, 1993, pp. 39–42.

Allen, Nick, 'Bhīṣma as Matchmaker' in Simon Brodbeck and Brian Black (eds), *Gender and Narrative in the Mahābhārata*, Routledge, London, 2007, pp. 176–188.

Altekar, A.S., *The Position of Woman in Hindu Civilization: From Prehistoric Times to the Present Day*, Motilal Banarsidass, New Delhi, 2005.

Auboyer, Jeannine, 'Some Games in Ancient India', *East and West*, Vol. 6, No. 2, July 1955, pp. 123–137.

Bagchee, Joydeep, 'Ruru, Etymology from Hell' in Vishwa Adluri (ed.), *Ways and Reasons for Thinking about the Mahābhārata as a Whole*, Bhandarkar Oriental Research Institute, Pune, 2015, pp. 119–134.

Bailey, G.M., 'On D.D. Kosambi's Interpretation of the Bhagavadgītā', *Indologica Taurinensia*, Vol. 12, pp. 343–353.

Bailey, Greg, 'The *Mahābhārata's* Simultaneous Affirmation and Critique of the Universal Validity of *Dharma*' in T.S. Rukmani (ed.), *The Mahābhārata: What Is Not Here Is Nowhere Else*, Munshiram Manoharlal, New Delhi, 2005, pp. 63–78.

Baldick, Julian, *Homer and the Indo-Europeans: Comparing Mythologies*, I.B. Tauris, London, 1994.

Bandlamudi, Lakshmi, 'Answerability between Lived Life and Living Text: Chronotopicity in Finding Agency in the *Mahābhārata*' in Sibesh Chandra Bhattacharya, Vrinda Dalmiya, and Gangeya Mukherji (eds), *Exploring Agency in the Mahabharata*, Routledge, London and New York, 2018, pp. 214–231.

Bandyopadhyay, Sibaji, 'A Critique of Non-violence' in *Three Essays on the Mahābhārata: Exercises in Literary Hermeneutics*, Orient BlackSwan, Hyderabad, 2016, pp. 267–307.

Bandyopadhyay, Sibaji, 'Of Gambling: A Few Lessons from the Mahābhārata' in Arindam Chakrabarti and Sibaji Bandyopadhyay (eds), *Mahābhārata Now*, Routledge, New Delhi, 2014, pp. 1–28.

Bandyopadhyay, Sibaji, 'Translating *Gītā* 2.47 or Inventing a National Motto' in *Three Essays on the Mahābhārata*, Orient BlackSwan, Hyderabad, 2016, pp. 8–190.

Basham, A. L., *The Origins and Development of Classical Hinduism*, Beacon Press, Boston, 1989 (reprint).

Basu, Buddhadeb, *Mahābhārater Kathā*, M.C. Sarkar and Sons, Kolkata, 2004 (reprint).

Basu, Jogendranath, 'Sources of the Two Krsna Legends', *Indian Culture*, Vol. VI, Nos 1–4, July 1939–April 1940, pp. 464–467.

Bhaduri, Nrisinha Prasad, 'Artha—Puruṣārtha' in Kalyan Kumar (ed.), *Text and Variations of the Mahābhārata: Contextual, Regional and Performative Traditions*, Munshiram Manoharlal, New Delhi, 2009, pp. 301–320.

Bhaduri, Nrisinha Prasad, 'Karṇa in and out of the *Mahābhārata*' in Arindam Chakrabarti and Sibaji Bandyopadhyay (eds), *Mahābhārata Now*, Routledge, New Delhi, 2014, pp. 95–111.

Bhaduri, Nrisinha Prasad, *Mahābhārater Bhāratyuddha o Kṛṣṇa*, Ananda Publishers, Kolkata, 2004.

Bhandarkar, R.G., 'Inaugural Address at Bhandarkar Oriental Research Institute, delivered on December 15, 1918' in Narayan Bapuji Utkigar and Vasudev Gopal Paranjpe (eds), *Collected Works of Sir R.G. Bhandarkar* (Vol. 1), Bhandarkar Oriental Research Institute, Poona, 1933, pp. 516–521.

Bhandarkar, R.G., *Vaiṣṇavism, Saivism and Minor Religious Systems*, Indological Book House, Varanasi, 1965 (reprint).

Bhargav, P.L., *India in the Vedic Age*, Lucknow, 1956.

Bhate, Saroja, 'Methodology of the Critical Edition of the Mahābhārata' in Arindam Chakrabarti and Sibaji Bandyopadhyay (eds), *Mahābhārata Now*, Routledge, New Delhi, 2014, pp. 29–36.

Bhate, Saroja, 'The Mahābhārata: The Global Epic' in Kalyan Kumar (ed.), *Text and Variations of the Mahābhārata: Contextual, Regional and Performative Traditions*, Munshiram Manoharlal, New Delhi, 2009, pp. 37–50.

Bhattacharya, Pradip, 'Was Draupadī Ever Sought to Be Disrobed?' in Kalyan Kumar Chakravarty (ed.), *Text and Variations of the Mahābhārata: Contextual, Regional and Performative Traditions*, Munshiram Manoharlal, New Delhi, 2009, pp. 89–100.

Bhattacharya, Sibesh, 'Significance of the Early Parvans: Modes of Narration, Birth Stories and Seeds of Conflict' in Arindam Chakrabarti and Sibaji Bandyopadhyay (eds), *Mahābhārata Now*, Routledge, New Delhi, 2014, pp. 37–56.

Bhattacharya, Sibesh Chandra, '*Mahābhārata. Itihāsa.* Agency' in Sibesh Chandra Bhattacharya, Vrinda Dalmiya, and Gangeya Mukherji (eds), *Exploring Agency in the Mahabharata*, Routledge, London and New York, 2018, pp. 31–44.

Bhattacharya, Swasti, 'Voices from Hinduism's Past: Kuntī and Gāndhārī's Victory Over Infertility' in T.S. Rukmani (ed.), *The Mahābhārata: What Is Not Here Is Nowhere Else*, Munshiram Manoharlal, New Delhi, 2005, pp. 265–280.

Biardeau, M., 'The Salvation of the King in the Mahābhārata', *Contributions to Indian Sociology*, New Series, Vol. 15, 1981, pp. 75–97.

Biardeau, M., 'Some More Considerations about Textual Criticism', *Purāṇa*, Vol. 10, No. 2, 1968, pp. 115–123.

Biardeau, M., 'Some Remarks on the Links between the Epics, the Puranas, and Their Vedic Sources' in G. Oberhammer (ed.), *Studies in Hinduism: Vedism and Hinduism*, Verlag der Osterreichischen Akademie der Wissenschaften, Vienna, 1997, pp. 69–177.

Black, Brian, 'Eavesdropping on the Epic: Female Listeners in the *Mahābhārata*' in Simon Brodbeck and Brian Black (eds), *Gender and Narrative in the Mahābhārata*, Routledge, London, 2007, pp. 53–78.

Bloch, Marc, *The Historian's Craft*, Knopf, New York, 1953.

Bowles, Adam, *Dharma, Disorder and the Political in Ancient India: The Āpaddharmaparvan of the Mahābhārata*, Brill, Leiden, 2007.

Brekke, Torkel, 'Between Prudence and Heroism: Ethics of War in the Hindu Tradition' in Torkel Brekke (ed.), *Ethics of War in Asian Civilizations*, Taylor and Francis, London, 2005.

Brekke, Torkel, 'Breaking the Thigh and the Warrior Code' in Raziuddin Aquil and Kaushik Roy (eds), *Warfare, Religion and Society in Indian History*, Manohar, Delhi, 2012, pp. 43–61.

Brekke, Torkel, 'The Ethics of War and the Concept of War in Asia and Europe', *Numen*, Vol. 52, 2005b, pp. 59–86.

Brereton, Joel P. 'The Race of Mudgal and Madgalānī', *Journal of the American Oriental Society*, Vol. 122, No. 2, April–June 2002, pp. 224–234.

Brockington, John, 'Jarāsaṃdha of Magadha' in Mary Brockington (ed.), *Proceedings of the Second Dubrovnik International Conference on the Sanskrit Epics and Puranas, August 1999*, Croatian Academy of Science and Arts, Zagreb, 2002, pp. 73–88.

Brockington, John, *The Sanskrit Epics*, Brill, Leiden, 1998.

Brodbeck, Simon, 'Gendered Soteriology: Marriage and the *Karmayoga*' in Simon Brodbeck and Brian Black (eds), *Gender and Narrative in the Mahābhārata*, Routledge, London, 2007, pp. 144–175.

Brodbeck, Simon, *The Mahābhārata Patriline*, Ashgate, Surrey, 2009.

Brodbeck, Simon, 'Solar and Lunar Lines in the Mahābhārata', *Religions of South Asia*, Vol. 5, Nos 1–2, 2011, pp. 127–152.

Brodbeck, Simon, 'Some Textological Observations on the Analytic and Synthetic Modes' in Vishwa Adluri (ed.), *Ways and Reasons for Thinking about the Mahābhārata as a Whole*, Bhandarkar Oriental Research Institute, Pune, 2015, pp. 135–154.

Brodbeck, Simon and Brian Black, 'Introduction' in Simon Brodbeck and Brian Black (eds), *Gender and Narrative in the Mahābhārata*, Routledge, London, 2007, pp. 1–34.

Carr, E.H., *What Is History*, Penguin, Basingstoke, 1986.

Chakrabarti, Arindam, 'Can the Subhuman Speak or Act? Agency of Sagacious Serpents, Benevolent Birds, Rational Rodents, and a Mocking Mongoose in the *Mahābhārata*', in Sibesh Chandra Bhattacharya, Vrinda Dalmiya, and Gangeya Mukherji (eds), *Exploring Agency in the Mahabharata*, Routledge, London and New York, 2018, pp. 143–161.

Chakrabarti, Arindam, 'Just Words: An Ethics of Conversation in the *Mahābhārata*' in Arindam Chakrabarti and Sibaji Bandyopadhyay (eds), *Mahābhārata Now*, Routledge, New Delhi, 2014, pp. 244–283.

Chakrabarti, Shirshendu, 'Irresolution and Agency: The Case of Yudhiṣṭhira' in Sibesh Chandra Bhattacharya, Vrinda Dalmiya, and Gangeya Mukherji (eds), *Exploring Agency in the Mahabharata*, Routledge, London and New York, 2018, pp. 129–142.

Chakravarti, Ranabir, *Warfare for Wealth*, Firma KLM Private Limited, Calcutta, 1986.

Chakravarti, Uma, *Of Meta-narratives and 'Master' Paradigms: Sexuality and the Reification of Women in Early India*, Centre for Women's Development Studies, Delhi, 2009.

Chakravarti, Uma, 'A Sutaputra in a Royal Household: The *Kshatriya* World of Power and its Margins' in Kumkum Roy (ed.), 'Looking within and Looking without: Exploring Households in the Subcontinent through Time', Primus, New Delhi, 2015, pp. 173–201.

Chakravarti, Uma, 'Textual-Sexual Transitions: The Reification of Women in the *Mahābhārata*' in Sibesh Chandra Bhattacharya, Vrinda Dalmiya, and Gangeya Mukherji (eds), *Exploring Agency in the Mahabharata*, Routledge, London and New York, 2018, pp. 162–178.

Chakravarti, Uma, 'Who Speaks for Whom: The Queen, the *Dāsī* and Sexual Politics in the *Sabhāparvan*' in Arindam Chakrabarti and Sibaji Bandyopadhyay (eds), *Mahābhārata Now*, Routledge, New Delhi, 2014, pp. 132–152.

Chakravarty, Kalyan Kumar, 'Introduction' in Kalyan Kumar Chakravarty (ed.), *Text and Variations of the Mahābhārata: Contextual, Regional and Performative Traditions*, Munshiram Manoharlal, New Delhi, 2009, pp. xi–xxiii.

Chandra, Lokesh, 'The Mahābhārata in Asian Literature and Arts' in Kalyan Kumar Chakravarty (ed.), *Text and Variations of the Mahābhārata: Contextual, Regional and Performative Traditions*, Munshiram Manoharlal, New Delhi, 2009, pp. 25–36.

Chapple, Christopher Key, 'Karṇa and the *Mahābhārata*: An Ethical Reflection' in T.S. Rukmani (ed.), *The Mahābhārata: What Is Not Here Is Nowhere Else*, Munshiram Manoharlal, New Delhi, 2005, pp. 131–144.

Charpentier, J., 'Some Remarks on the Bhagavadgītā', *Indian Antiquary*, Vol. 59, 1930, pp. 40–126.

Chatterjee, Amita, 'In Search of Genuine Agency: A Review of Action, Freedom and *Karma* in the *Mahābhārata*' in Sibesh Chandra Bhattacharya, Vrinda Dalmiya, and Gangeya Mukherji (eds), *Exploring Agency in the Mahabharata*, Routledge, London and New York, 2018, pp. 45–61.

Chatterjee, Gautam, 'The Ethical Foundations of Bhīṣma's Promises and Dilemmas' in T.S. Rukmani (ed.), *The Mahābhārata: What Is Not Here Is Nowhere Else*, Munshiram Manoharlal, New Delhi, 2005, pp. 145–162.

Chattopadhyay, Bankim Chandra, *Bankim Racanāvalī* (Vol I, Part II), Pashchimbanga Niraksharata Durikaran Samiti, Calcutta, 1973.

Chattopadhyaya, B.D., 'Indian Archaeology and the Epic Traditions' in *Studying Early India*, Permanent Black, New Delhi, 2003, pp. 29–38.

Chattopadhyaya, B.D., 'State's Perception of the Forest and the "Forest" as State in Early India' in B.B. Chaudhuri and Arun Bandyopadhyaya (eds), *Tribes, Forest and Social Formation in Indian History*, Manohar, New Delhi, 2004, pp. 23–37.

Choudhary, Pradeep Kant, *Rāma with an Axe*, Aakar, New Delhi, 2010.

Chousalkar, Ashok, 'The Concept of *Apaddharma* and the Moral Dilemma of Politics in the *Mahabharata*' in T.R.S. Sharma (ed.), *Reflections and Variations on the Mahabharata*, Sahitya Akademi, New Delhi, 2009, pp. 115–132.

Clarke, Ronald W., *Einstein: The Life and Times*, World Publishing Co., New York, 1971.

Collingwood, R.G., *The Idea of History*, Oxford University Press, Oxford, 1994.

Crothers, Lisa W., 'Duryodhana's Pride and Perception: The Dynamics of Distrust in the Moment of Counsel at the Kaurava Court' in T.S. Rukmani (ed.), *The Mahābhārata: What Is Not Here Is Nowhere Else*, Munshiram Manoharlal, New Delhi, 2005, pp. 197–210.

Custodi, Andrea, 'Show You Are a Man! Transsexuality and Gender Bending in the Characters of Arjuna/Bṛhannaḍā and Ambā/Śikhaṇḍin(ī)' in Simon Brodbeck and Brian Black Brian, *Gender and Narrative in the Mahābhārata*, Routledge, London, 2007, pp. 208–229.

Dalmiya, Vrinda, 'Care Ethics and Epistemic Justice: Some Insights from the *Mahābhąrata*' in Arindam Chakrabarti and Sibaji Bandyopadhyay (eds), *Mahābhārata Now*, Routledge, New Delhi, 2014, pp. 115–131.

Dalmiya, Vrinda and Gangeya Mukherji, 'Introduction: To Do' in Sibesh Chandra Bhattacharya, Vrinda Dalmiya, and Gangeya Mukherji (eds), *Exploring Agency in the Mahabharata*, Routledge, London and New York, 2018, pp. 1–27.

Dandekar, R.N., 'The Human Universal in the *Mahabharata*' in T.R.S. Sharma (ed.), *Reflections and Variations on the Mahabharata*, Sahitya Akademi, New Delhi, 2009, pp. 38–45.

Dandekar, R.N., 'The *Mahābhārata*: Origin and Growth', *University of Ceylon Review*, Vol. 12, No. 4, April 1954, pp. 65–85.

Dange, Sadashiva A., 'The Birth of Vasiṣṭha', *Quarterly Journal of the Mythic Society*, Vol. LV, Nos 3–4, October 1964–January 1965, pp. 83–91.

Dasgupta, S., *A History of Indian Philosophy* (Vol. II), Cambridge University Press, Cambridge, 1952.

Dayal, Naina, 'Tellers of Tales, Paurāṇikas, Sūtas, Kuśīlava, Vyāsa and Vālmīki', PhD thesis submitted to the Jawaharlal Nehru University, New Delhi, 2009.

Den Boer, W., 'Greco-Roman Historiography in Its Relation to Relation to Biblical and Modern Thinking', *History and Theory*, Vol. 7, 1968, pp. 60–75.

Deshpande, Madhav M., 'The Epic Context of the Bhagavadgītā' in Arvind Sharma (ed.), *Essays on the Mahābhārata*, Motilal Banarsidass, Delhi, 2007, pp. 334–348.

Deshpande, Madhav M., 'Interpreting the Mahābhārata' in T.S. Rukmani (ed.), *The Mahābhārata: What Is Not Here Is Nowhere Else*, Munshiram Manoharlal, New Delhi, 2005, pp. 3–18.

Deshpande, Madhav M., 'The Kshatriya Core of the Bhagavad-Gita' in S.P. Narang (ed.), *Modern Evaluations of the Mahābhārata: Professor R.K. Sharma Felicitation Volume*, Nag Publishers, New Delhi, 1995, pp. 182–193.

Devasthali, G.V., 'Bhagavad-Gītā and Upaniṣads' in J.N. Agrawal and B.D. Shastri (eds), *Sarupa-Bharati or the Homage of Indology*, Vishveshvarananda Indological Institute, Hoshiarpur, 1954, pp. 132–142.

Dhand, Arti, '*Karmayoga* and the Vexed Moral Agent' in Sibesh Chandra Bhattacharya, Vrinda Dalmiya, and Gangeya Mukherji (eds), *Exploring Agency in the Mahabharata*, Routledge, London and New York, 2018, pp. 81–106.

Dhand, Arti, 'Paradigms of the Good in the *Mahābhārata*: Śuka and Sulabhā in Quagmires of Ethics' in Simon Brodbeck and Brian Black (eds), *Gender and Narrative in the Mahabharata*, Routledge, London, 2007, pp. 258–277.

Dhand, Arti, 'The Subversive Nature of Virtue in the *Mahābhārata*: A Tale about Women, Smelly Ascetics and God', *Journal of the American Academy of Religion*, Vol. 72, No. 1, March 2004, pp. 33–58.

Dumont, Louis, *Homo Hierarchicus: The Caste System and its Implications*, Oxford University Press, Delhi, 1988.

Dunham, John, 'Manuscripts Used in the Critical Edition of the *Mahābhārata*: A Survey and Discussion' in Arvind Sharma (ed.), *Essays on the Mahābhārata*, Motilal Banarsidass, New Delhi, 2007, pp. 1–18.

Edgerton, F., *The Bhagavad Gītā or the Song of the Blessed or India's Favourite Bible*, Chicago University Press, Chicago, 1925.

Edgerton, F. 'Review of "The Original Gītā: The Song of the Supreme Exalted One" by Rudolf Otto, translated and edited by J.E. Turner', *Review of Religion*, Vol. 4, p. 448.

Emmeneau, M.B. and B.A. van Nooten, 'The Young Wife and Her Husband's Brother: Ṛgveda 10.40.2 and 10.85.44', *Journal of the American Oriental Society*, Vol. 111, No. 3, 1991, pp. 481–494.

Findly, Ellison Banks, 'Vasiṣṭha: Religious Personality and Vedic Culture', *Numen*, Vol. 31, Fasc 1, July 1984, pp. 74–105.

Fitzgerald, James L., 'Bhīṣma beyond Freud: Bhīṣma in the *Mahābhārata*' in Simon Brodbeck and Brian Black (eds), *Gender and Narrative in the Mahābhārata*, Routledge, London, 2007, pp. 189–207.

Fitzgerald, James L., 'Mahābhārata' in Sushil Mittal and Gene Thursby (eds), *The Hindu World*, Routledge, New York, 2004, pp. 52–74.

Fitzgerald, James, 'India's Fifth Veda: The *Mahabharata*'s Presentation of Itself' in Arvind Sharma (ed.), *Essays on the Mahābhārata*, Motilal Banarsidass, Delhi, 2007, pp. 150–170.

Fitzgerald, James, 'Introduction to the Book of Peace' in Vyāsa, *The Mahābhārata* (Vol. VII): Book of Women and Book of Peace Part I', translated by James L. Fitzgerald, The University of Chicago Press, Chicago, 2004.

Foucault, Michel, 'What Is an Author?' in Josue V. Harari (ed.), *Textual Strategies: Perspectives in Post-Structuralist Criticism*, Cornell University Press, Ithaca, 1979, pp. 141–160.

Framarin, Christopher G., 'The Theory of *Karma* in the *Mahābhārata*', in Sibesh Chandra Bhattacharya, Vrinda Dalmiya, and Gangeya Mukherji (eds), *Exploring Agency in the Mahabharata*, Routledge, London and New York, 2018, pp. 62–80.

Gailey, Christine Ward, *Kinship to Kingship: Gender Hierarchy and State Formation in the Tongan Islands*, University of Texas Press, Austin, 1987.

Ghosh, A., 'City in Early Historical India' in B.P. Sahu (ed.), *Iron and Social Change in Early India*, Oxford University Press, New Delhi, 2006, pp. 100–113.

Gitomer, David, 'King Duryodhana: The *Mahābhārata* Discourse of Sinning and Virtue in Epic and Drama', *Journal of the American Oriental Society*, Vol. 112, 1992, pp. 222–232.

Gitomer, David L., 'Rākṣasa Bhīma: Wolfbelly among Ogres and Brahmans in the Sanskrit *Mahābhārata* and the *Veṇīsaṁhāra*' in Arvind Sharma (ed.), *Essays on the Mahābhārata*, Motilal Banarsidass, New Delhi, 2007, pp. 296–323.

Goldman, R.P., 'Akṛtavarṇa vs Srikṛṣṇa as Narrator of the Legend of the Bhārgava Rāma: Apropos Some Observations of Dr. V.S. Sukthankar', *Annals of the Bhandarkar Oriental Research Institute*, Vol. 53, 1972, pp. 161–173.

Goldman, R.P., '*Eṣa Dharmaḥ Sanātanaḥ*: Shifting Moral Values and the Indian Epics' in P. Bilimoria and J.N. Mohanty (eds), *Relativism, Suffering and Beyond*, Oxford University Press, Delhi, 1997, pp. 187–223.

Goldman, R.P., 'Fathers, Sons, and Gurus: Oedipal Conflict in the Sanskrit Epics', *Journal of Indian Philosophy*, Vol. 6, 1978, pp. 325–392.

Goldman, R.P., *Gods, Priests and Warriors*, Columbia University Press, New York, 1977.

Goldman, R.P., 'Matricide, Renunciation, and Compensation in the Legends of Two Warrior Heroes of the Sanskrit Epics', *Indologica Taurinensia*, Vol. 10, pp. 117–131.

Goldstein, Leon, *Historical Knowing*, University of Texas Press, Austin, 1976.

Gombach, Barbara, 'Born Old: Story, Smṛti and the Composition of the Sanskrit *Mahābhārata*' in T.S. Rukmani (ed.), *The Mahābhārata: What Is Not Here Is Nowhere Else*, Munshiram Manoharlal, New Delhi, 2005, pp. 19–34.

Gonda, Jan, 'Dumezil's Tripartite Ideology: Some Critical Observations', *Journal of Asian Studies*, Vol. 34, 1974, pp. 139–149.

Gonda, Jan, 'Some Observations on Dumezil's Views on Indo-European Mythology', *Mnemosyne*, Vol. 4, 1960, pp. 1–15.

Gonda, Jan, *Vedic Literature*, Otto Harragsemitz, Wiesbaden, 1975.

Gonzalo-Reimann, Luis, 'Time in the *Mahābhārata* and the Time of the *Mahābhārata*' in Sheldon Pollock (ed.), *Epic and Argument in Sanskrit Literary History: Essays in Honor of Robert P. Goldman*, Manohar, New Delhi, 2010, pp. 61–73.

Granoff, Phyllis, 'Karma, Curse or Divine Illusion: The Destruction of the Buddha's Clan and the Slaughter of the Yādavas' in Sheldon Pollock (ed.), *Epic and Argument in Sanskrit Literary History: Essays in Honour of Robert P. Goldman*, Manohar, New Delhi, 2010, pp. 75–90.

Greer, Patricia, 'Ethical Discourse in Udyogaparvan' in T.S. Rukmani (ed.), *The Mahābhārata: What Is Not Here Is Nowhere Else*, Munshiram Manoharlal, New Delhi, 2005, pp. 211–224.

Grierson, George A., 'A Note on Mr. Keith's Note on the Battle between the Pāṇḍavas and Kauravas', *Journal of the Royal Asiatic Society of Great Britain and Ireland*, Vol. 40, No. 3, July 1908, pp. 837–844.

Guha, R., *History at the Limit of World History: An Indian Historiography of India*, Columbia University Press, New York, 2002.

Guha, Ranajit, 'Introduction' in Ranajit Guha (ed.), *Subaltern Studies* (Vol. 1), Oxford University Press, New Delhi, 1982, pp. 1–8.

Habib, Irfan, 'Unreason and Archaeology: Painted Grey Ware and Beyond' in K.M. Shrimali (ed.), *Reason and Archaeology*, Association for the Study of History and Archaeology, Delhi, 2007, pp. 17–27.

Hara, Minoru, 'A Note on the Rākṣasa Form of Marriage', *Journal of the American Oriental Society*, Vol. 94, No. 3, 1974, pp. 296–306.

Harzer, Edeltraud, 'Bhīṣma and the *Vrātya* Question' in *The Mahābhārata: What Is Not Here Is Nowhere Else*, Munshiram Manoharlal, New Delhi, 2005, pp. 163–178.

Hazra, R.C., *Studies in the Puranic Records on Hindu Rites and Customs*, Facsimile Publications, New Delhi, 2016 (reprint).

Heathcote, T.A., *The Military in British India: The Development of British Land Forces in South Asia 1600–1947*, Manchester University Press, Manchester, 1995.

Heesterman, J.C., *The Ancient Indian Royal Consecration*, Mouton and Co., The Hague, 1957.

Heesterman, J.C., *The Inner Conflict of Tradition: Essays in Indian Ritual, Kingship and Society*, Oxford University Press, New Delhi, 1985.

Hein, Norvin, 'Kālayavana, a Key to Mathurā's Cultural Self-Perception' in Doris Meth Srinivasan, *Mathurā: The Cultural Heritage*', American Institute of Indian Studies, New Delhi, 1989, pp. 223–235.

Hejib, A. and K. Young, 'Kliba on the Battlefield: Towards a Reinterpretation of Arjuna's Despondency', *Annals of the Bhandarkar Oriental Research Institute*, Vol. 61, pp. 235–244.

Held, G.J., *Mahabharata: An Ethnological Study*, Kegan, Paul, Trench, Trubner and Co., London, 1935.

Hill, W.D.P., *The Bhagavadgītā: Translated from the Sanskrit with an Introduction and Argument and a Commentary*, Oxford University Press, London, 1928.

Hiltebeitel, Alf, 'Among Friends: Marriage, Women, and Some Little Birds' in Simon Brodbeck and Brian Black (eds), *Gender and Narrative in the Mahābhārata*, Routledge, London, 2007, pp. 110–143.

Hiltebeitel, Alf, 'Buddhism and the *Mahābhārata*' in F. Squarcini (ed.), *Boundaries Dynamics and the Construction of Tradition in South Asia*, Firenze, 2005.

Hiltebeitel, Alf, 'The Burning of the Forest Myth' in Bardwell L. Smith (ed.), *Hinduism: New Essays in the History of Religion*, E.J. Brill, Leiden, 1982.

Hiltebeitel, Alf, 'Draupadī's Question' in Kathleen Erndl and Alf Hilebeitel (eds), *Is the Goddess a Feminist? The Politics of South Indian Goddesses*, New York University Press, New York, 2000, pp. 113–122.

Hiltebeitel, Alf, 'Kṛṣṇa and the Mahābhārata', *Annals of the Bhandarakar Oriental Research Institute*, Vol. LX, 1979, pp. 65–107.

Hiltebeitel, Alf, 'New Possibilities in Considering the Mahabharata's Intention as "History"' in Vishwa Adluri (ed.), *Ways and Reasons for Thinking about the*

Mahābhārata as a Whole, Bhandarkar Oriental Research Institute, Pune, 2015, pp. 29–62.

Hiltebeitel, Alf, *Rethinking the Mahābhārata: A Reader's Guide to the Education of the Dharma King*, University of Chicago Press, Chicago, 2001.

Hiltebeitel, Alf, *The Ritual of Battle: Krishna in the Mahābhārata*, State University of New York Press, Albany, 1990.

Hiltebeitel, Alf, 'Two Kṛṣṇas, Three Kṛṣṇas, Four Kṛṣṇas, More Kṛṣṇas: Dark interactions in the *Mahābhārata*' in Arvind Sharma (ed.), *Essays on the Mahābhārata*, Motilal Banarsidass, Delhi, 2007, pp. 101–109.

Hopkins, E. Washburn, *Epic Mythology*, Biblo and Tannen, New York, 1969 (reprint).

Hopkins, E. Washburn, *The Great Epic of India*, Punthi Pustak, Calcutta, 1969 (reprint).

Hopkins, E. Washburn, *The Religions of India*, Ginn, Boston, 1895.

Hudson, Emily T., 'Heaven's Riddles or the Hell-Trick: Theodicy and Narrative Strategies in the *Mahābhārata*' in T.S. Rukmani (ed.), *The Mahābhārata: What Is Not Here Is Nowhere Else*, Munshiram Manoharlal, New Delhi, 2005, pp. 225–234.

Hudson, Emily T., 'Listen But Do Not Grieve: Grief, Paternity, and Time in the aments of Dhṛtarāṣṭra' in Simon Brodbeck and Brian Black (eds), *Gender and Narrative in the Mahābhārata*, Routledge, London, 2007, pp. 35–52.

Huizinga, J., 'A Definition of the Concept of History', in Ernst Cassirer, R. Klibansky and H.J. Paton (eds), *Philosophy and History*, Harper and Row, New York, 1963, pp. 1–10.

Hunt, Lynn, *Writing History in the Global Era*, Norton, New York, 2014.

Ingalls, Daniel H.H., and Ingalls, Daniel H.H. Jr., 'The *Mahābhārata*: Stylistic Study, Computer Analysis and Concordance' in Arvind Sharma (ed.), *Essays on the Mahābhārata*, Motilal Banarsidass, New Delhi, 2007, pp. 19–56.

Jacobi, Hermann, 'Incarnations(Indian)', *Hastings Encyclopaedia of Religion and Ethics* (Vol. VII), Scribner, New York, 1964, p. 195.

Jacobsen, Knut A., 'Kapila in the *Mahābhārata*' in T.S. Rukmani (ed.), *The Mahābhārata: What Is Not Here Is Nowhere Else*, Munshiram Manoharlal, New Delhi, 2005, pp. 35–48.

Jaini, P., 'Jaina Purāṇas: A Puranic Counter Tradition', in W. Doniger (ed.), *Purana Perennis*, New York, 1993, pp. 207–247.

Jaiswal, S., *The Origin and Development of Vaiṣṇavism*, Munshiram Manoharlal, Delhi, 1967.

Jezic, M., 'Textual Layers of the Bhagavadgītā: Traces of Indian Cultural History' in W. Morgenroth (ed.), *Sanskrit and World Culture*, Akademie Verlag, Weimar, 1979.

Johnson, Gesta, 'Varuṇa and Dhṛtarāṣṭra', *Indo-Iranian Journal*, Vol. 9, 1965–1966, pp. 245–265.

Junck, Robert, *Brighter Than Thousand Suns: A Personal History of the Atomic Scientists*, translated by James Cleuch, Penguin, Harmonsworth, 1985.

Kantawala, S.G., 'Genetic Episode of the Pandavas' in T.R.S. Sharma (ed.), *Reflections and Variations on the Mahabharata*, Sahitya Akademi, New Delhi, 2009, pp. 89–98.

Karmakar, R.D., 'Bhagavadgītā XVI.8 Asatyaṃpratiṣṭhāṃ Te', *Annals of the Bhandarkar Oriental Research Institute*, Vol. 31, pp. 132–137.

Karve, Irawati, *Yuganta*, Orient Longman, Hyderabad, 2007.

Katz, Ruth, 'The *Sauptika* Episode in the Structure of the *Mahābhārata*' in Sharma, Arvind (ed.), *Essays on the Mahābhārata*, Motilal Banarsidass, Delhi, 2007, pp. 130–149.

Katz, Ruth Cecily, *Arjuna in the Mahābhārata*, Motilal Banarsidass, Delhi, 1989.

Keith, A. Berriedale, 'The Brahmanic and Kshatriya Tradition', *Journal of the Royal Asiatic Society of Great Britain and Ireland*, Vol. 46, No. 2, January 1914, pp. 118–126.

Keith, A. Berriedale, 'The Battle between the Pāṇḍavas and the Kauravas', *Journal of the Royal Asiatic Society of Great Britain and Ireland*, Vol. 40, No. 3, July 1908, pp. 831–836.

Kennedy, J., 'The Child Krishna and His Critics', *Journal of Royal Asiatic Society*, 1908, pp. 505–521.

Kennedy, J., 'The Child Krishna, Christianity and the Gujars', *Journal of Royal Asiatic Society*, 1907, pp. 951–991.

Khair, G.S., *Quest for the Original Gītā*, Somaiya, Bombay, 1969.

Kinsley, David, 'Devotion as an Alternative to Marriage in the Lives of Some Hindu Women Devotees' in Jayant Lele (ed.), *Tradition and Modernity in the Bhakti Movement*, E.J. Brill, Leiden, 1981.

Kosambi, D.D., 'The Autochthonous Element in *Mahābhārata*', *Journal of the American Oriental Society*, Vol. 84, No. 1, January–March 1964, pp. 31–44.

Kosambi, D.D., 'Early Stages of the Caste System in Northern India', *Journal of the Bombay Branch of the Royal Asiatic Society*, New Series, Vol. 22, 1946–1947, pp. 33–48.

Kosambi, D.D., 'The Emergence of National Characteristics among Three Indo-European People', *Annals of the Bhandarkar Oriental Research Institute*, Vol. 20, 1938–1939, pp. 192–206.

Kosambi, D.D., *An Introduction to the Study of Indian History*, Popular Prakashan, Bombay, 1998 (reprint).

Kosambi, D.D., 'On the Origin of Brahmin Gotras', *Journal of the Bombay Branch of the Royal Asiatic Society*, New Series, Vol. 26, 1950–1951, pp. 21–80.

Kosambi, D.D., 'The Study of Ancient Indian Tradition' in *Indica, The Indian Historical Research Institute Silver Jubilee Commemoration Volume*, St. Xavier's College, Bombay, 1953, pp. 196–214.

Kosambi, D.D., *Myth and Reality*, Popular Prakashan, Bombay, 1962.

Kuiper, F.B.J., 'Some Observations on Dumezil's Theory', *Numen*, 1961, pp. 34–45.

Kulke, H., 'Historiography in Early Medieval India' in G. Berkemer (et al.), *Exploration in the History of South Asia: In Honour of Dietmar Rothermund*, Manohar, Delhi, 2001, pp. 71–83.

Kunhan Raja, C., 'Dāśarājña', *Indian Historical Quarterly*, Vol. XXXVII, No. 4, December 1961, pp. 261–278.

Kunjunni Raja, K., 'Architectonics of the *Mahabharata* and the Place of Legends in its Structure' in T.R.S. Sharma (ed.), *Reflections and Variations on the Mahabharata*, Sahitya Akademi, New Delhi, 2009, pp. 63–69.

Lal, B.B., 'The Two Indian Epics vis-à-vis Archaeology', *Antiquity*, Vol. LV, 1981, pp. 27–34.

Lal, Vinay, *The History of History: Politics and Scholarship in Modern India*, Oxford University Press, New Delhi, 2003.

Larson, Gerald James, 'A Magadha Tale and Some Reflections on the Many-Sidedness of the *Mahābhārata*' in T.S. Rukmani (ed.) *The Mahābhārata: What Is Not Here Is Nowhere Else*, Munshiram Manoharlal, New Delhi, 2005, pp. 79–90.

Lath, Mukund, 'The Concept of *Anrshamsya* in the *Mahabharata*' in T.R.S. Sharma (ed.), *Reflections and Variations on the Mahabharata*, Sahitya Akademi, New Delhi, 2009, pp. 82–88.

Leavitt, John, 'Himalayan Variations on the Epic Theme' in Arvind Sharma (ed.), *Essays on the Mahābhārata*, Motilal Banarsidass, New Delhi, 2007, pp. 444–474.

Lele, Jayant, 'Introduction' in Jayant Lele (ed.), *Tradition and Modernity in the Bhakti Movement*, E.J. Brill, Leiden, 1981.

Lerner, Gerda, *The Creation of Patriarchy*, Oxford University Press, New York, 1986.

Levi, Sylvain, 'Tato Jayam Udīrayet', *Annals of the Bhandarkar Oriental Research Institute*, Vol. I, 1918–1919, pp. 13–20.

Levi-Strauss, Claude, *Structural Anthropology*, Penguin, New York, 1972.

Lommel, Herman, 'Vasiṣṭha und Viśvāmitra', *Oriens*, Vols 18/19, 1965/1966, pp. 200–227.

Lord, A.B., *The Singer of Tales*, Harvard University Press, Cambridge, MA, 1960.

Macdonnell, A.A., *History of Sanskrit Literature*, Motilal Banarsidass, Delhi, 1900 (reprint).

Macdonnell, A.A., and A.B. Keith, *Vedic Index of Names and Subjects* (Vol. II), Motilal Banarsidass, Delhi, 1922.

Mahey, Arjun, 'Epic Mediations: Text, Book and Authority in the Organization of the *Mahabharata*' in T.R.S. Sharma (ed.), *Reflections and Variations on the Mahabharata*, Sahitya Akademi, New Delhi, 2009, pp. 365–386.

Mainkar, T.G., 'Some Thoughts on the Brahmasūtras and the Bhagavadgītā', *Annals of the Bhandarkar Oriental Research Institute*, Vols 58–59, 1977–78, pp. 745–751.

Majumdar, R.C., *Ancient India*, Motilal Banarsidass, Delhi, 1989.

Majumdar, R.C., 'Ideas of History in Sanskrit Literature' in C.H. Philips (ed.), *Historians of India, Pakistan and Ceylone*, Oxford University Press, London, 1961, pp. 13–28.

Malamoud, Charles, *Cooking the World*, Oxford University Press, New Delhi, 1996.

Malinar, Angelika, 'Arguments of a Queen: Draupadī's View on Kingship' in Simon Brodbeck and Brian Black (eds), *Gender and Narrative in the Mahabharata*, Routledge, London, 2007, pp. 79–96.

Malinar, Angelika, *The Bhagavadgītā: Doctrines and Contexts*, Cambridge University Press, Cambridge, 2007.

Malinar, Angelika, 'Duryodhana's Truths: Kingship and Divinity in the *Mahābhārata* 5.60' in J.L. Brockington (ed.), *Battle, Bards and Brahmins*, Motilal Banarsidass, Delhi, 2012, pp. 63–68.

Mason, J.L., 'The Childhood of Kṛṣṇa: Some Psycho-analytic Observation', *Journal of the American Oriental Society*, Vol. 94, No. 4, Oct–Dec 1974, pp. 454–459.

Matilal, Bimal Krishna, *Ethics and Epics* (Vol. II), Oxford University Press, New Delhi, 2002.

Matilal, Bimal Krishna, 'Kṛṣṇa: In Defence of a Devious Divinity' in Arvind Sharma (ed.), *Essays on the Mahabharata*, Motilal Banarsidass, Delhi, 2011, pp. 401–418.

Matilal, Bimal Krishna, *Nīti, Yukti o Dharma*, Ananda Publishers, Calcutta, 1988.

Mauss, Marcel, *Forms and Functions of Exchange in Archaic Societies*, Norton, New York, 1967.

McGrath, Kevin, *Arjuna Pāṇḍava: The Double Hero in Epic Mahābhārata*, Orient BlackSwan, Hyderabad, 2016.

McGrath, Kevin, *Bhīṣma Devavrata: Authority in Epic Mahābhārata*, Orient BlackSwan, Hyderabad, 2018.

McGrath, Kevin, *Heroic Kṛṣṇa: Friendship in Epic Mahābhārata*, Harvard University Press, Cambridge, MA, 2013.

McGrath, Kevin, *Jaya: Performance in Epic Mahābhārata*, Harvard University Press, Cambridge, MA, 2011.

McGrath, Kevin, *Rājā Yudhiṣṭhira: Kingship in Epic Mahābhārata*, Cornell University Press, Ithaca, 2016.

McGrath, Kevin, *The Sanskrit Hero: Karṇa in Epic Mahābhārata*, Brill, Leiden, 2004.

McGrath, Kevin, *Strī: Feminine Power in the Mahābhārata*, Orient BlackSwan, Hyderabad, 2011.

Mehendale, M.A., 'The Critical Edition of the Mahābhārata—Its Constitution, Achievements, and Limitations' in Kalyan Kumar Chakravarty (ed.), *Text and Variations of the Mahābhārata: Contextual, Regional and Performative Traditions*, Munshiram Manoharlal, New Delhi, 2009, pp. 3–24.

Mehendale, M.A., 'Draupadi's Question', *Journal of the Oriental Institute, Baroda*, Vol. 35, Nos 3–4, 1985, pp. 179–194.

Mehendale, M.A., *Reflections on the Mahābhārata War*, Indian Institute of Advanced Study, Shimla, 1995.

Mehta, J.L., 'Dvaipayana, Poet of Being and Becoming' in T.R.S. Sharma (ed.), *Reflections and Variations on the Mahabharata*, Sahitya Akademi, New Delhi, 2009, pp. 70–81.

Minkowski, C.Z., 'Janamejaya's *Sattra* and Ritual Structure', *Journal of the American Oriental Society*, Vol. 109, No. 3, 1989, pp. 401–420.

Minkowski, Christopher, 'Snakes, *Sattras* and the *Mahabharata*' in Arvind Sharma (ed.), *Essays on the Mahābhārata*, Motilal Banarsidass, New Delhi, 2007, pp. 384–400.

Minor, R.N., *Bhagavad-Gītā: An Exegetical Commentary*, Heritage, Delhi, 1982.

Mital, S.K., *Kauṭilīya Arthaśāstra Revisited*, Centre for Studies in Civilization, Delhi, 2000.

Mitchiner, John E., *Traditions of the Seven Ṛṣis*, Motilal Banarsidass, Delhi, 1982.

Mitra, Enakshi, 'Understanding Yudhiṣṭhira's Actions: Re-casting Karma-Yoga in a Wittgensteinian Mould' in Arindam Chakrabarti and Sibaji Bandyopadhyay (eds), *Mahābhārata Now*, Routledge, New Delhi, 2014, pp. 57–81.

Mohanty, Prafulla Kumar, 'The *Mahābhārata*: A Reading in Political Structuring' in T.R.S. Sharma (ed.), *Reflections and Variations on the Mahabharata*, Sahitya Akademi, New Delhi, 2009, pp. 133–140.

Momigliano, A., 'The Place of Herodotus in the History of Historiography', *History*, 43, 1958, pp. 1–13.

Morton-Smith, R., *Deaths and Dynasties in Early India*, Motilal Banarsidass, Delhi, 1973.

Mukherji, Gangeya, 'Complexities in the Agency for Violence: A Look at the *Mahābhārata*' in Sibesh Chandra Bhattacharya, Vrinda Dalmiya, and Gangeya

Mukherji (eds), *Exploring Agency in the Mahabharata*, Routledge, London and New York, 2018, pp. 109–128.

Mukherji, Gangeya, '*Hiṃsā-Ahiṃsā* in the *Mahābhārata*: The Lonely Position of Yudhiṣṭhira' in Arindam Chakrabarti and Sibaji Bandyopadhyay (eds), *Mahābhārata Now*, Routledge, New Delhi, 2014, pp. 219–243.

Munshi, K.M., *The Early Aryans of Gujarat*, University of Bombay, Bombay, 1941.

Munshi, K.M., 'The Historical Value of the Paraśurāma Tradition', *New Indian Antiquary*, Vol. 6, 1943–1944, pp. 217–224.

Munshi, K.M., 'The Māhīṣmatī of Kārtavīrya', *The Indian Antiquary*, November 1922, pp. 217–221.

Nabar, Vrinda, 'Whose *Mahabharata*? A Point of View' in T.R.S. Sharma (ed.), *Reflections and Variations on the Mahabharata*, Sahitya Akademi, New Delhi, 2009, pp. 201–214.

Nagy, Gregory, *The Ancient Greek Hero in Twenty-Four Hours*, Harvard University Press, Cambridge, MA, 2013.

Nagy, Gregory, *Homer the Preclassic*, University of California Press, Berkeley, 2010.

Nagy, Gregory, *Homeric Questions*, University of Texas Press, Austin, 1996.

Nagy, Gregory, *Homeric Responses*, University of Texas Press, Austin, 2003.

Nair, Sreedevi K., 'One Story, Many Texts: Conceptualising a Seed Text in Epics Retold' in T.R.S. Sharma (ed.), *Reflections and Variations on the Mahabharata*, Sahitya Akademi, New Delhi, 2009, pp. 301–315.

Nandy, A., 'History's Forgotten Doubles', *History and Theory*, Vol. 34, No. 2, 1995, pp. 44–66.

Nath, Vijay, 'Women as Property and Their Right to Inherit Property up to the Gupta Period', *Indian Historical Review*, Vol. 20, Nos 1–2, 1993–1994, pp. 1–15.

O'Flaherty, Wendy Doniger, 'Horses and Snakes in the Ādi Parvan of the Mahābhārata' in Margaret Case and N. Gerald Barrier (eds), *Aspects of India: Essays in Honour of Edward Cameron Dimmock Jr.*, Manohar, New Delhi, 1986, pp. 16–43.

Pande, G.C., 'The Socio-cultural Milieu of the Mahabharata: An Age of Change' in T.R.S. Sharma (ed.), *Reflections and Variations on the Mahabharata*, Sahitya Akademi, New Delhi, 2009, pp. 46–62.

Parampanthi, Swami Bangovinda, *Bhagawan Parasurama and Evolution of Culture in Northeast India*, Daya Publishing House, Delhi, 1987.

Parampanthi, Swami Bangovinda, 'Paraśurāma Kuṇḍa: A Study in Historical and Geographical Perspective', *Journal of Assam Research Society, Guwahati*, Vol. 19, 1970–1971, pp. 76–89.

Parasher-Sen, Aloka, '"Foreigner" and "Tribe" as Barbarian (Mleccha)' in Aloka Parasher-Sen (ed.), *Subordinate and Marginal Groups in Early India*, Oxford University Press, New Delhi, 2004.

Parasher-Sen, Aloka, 'Introduction' in Aloka Parasher-Sen (ed.), *Subordinate and Marginal Groups in Early India*, Oxford University Press, New Delhi, 2004.

Parasher-Sen, Aloka, 'On Tribes, Hunters and Barbarians: Forest Dwellers in the Mauryan Period', *Studies in History*, Vol. 14, No. 2, 1998, pp. 173–191.

Pargiter, F.E., *Ancient Indian Historical Tradition*, Motilal Banarsidass, Delhi, 1997(reprint).

Pargiter, F.E., 'Brahmanic and Kshatriya Tradition', *Journal of the Royal Asiatic Society of Great Britain and Ireland*, Vol. 46, No. 2, April 1914, pp. 411–412.

Pargiter, F.E., *Dynasties of the Kali Age*, Motilal Banarsidass, Delhi, 1975 (reprint).

Pargiter, F.E., 'The Nations of India at the Battle between the Pāṇḍavas and Kauravas', *Journal of the Royal Asiatic Society of Great Britain and Ireland*, Vol. 40, No. 2, April 1908, pp. 309–336.

Pargiter, F.E., 'Sagara and the Haihayas, Vasiṣṭha and Aurva', *Journal of the Royal Asiatic Society of Great Britain and Ireland*, Vol. 51, No. 3, July 1919, pp. 353–367.

Pargiter, F.E., 'Viśvāmitra and Vasiṣṭha', *Journal of the Royal Asiatic Society of Great Britain and Ireland*, Vol. 45, No. 4, October 1913, pp. 885–904.

Pargiter, F.E., 'Viśvāmitra, Vasiṣṭha, Hariścandra and Śunaḥśepa', *Journal of the Royal Asiatic Society of Great Britain and Ireland*, Vol. 49, No. 1, January 1917, pp. 37–67.

Parpola, Asko, 'On the Jaiminīya and Vādhūla Traditions of South India and the Pāṇḍu/Pāṇḍava Problem', *Studia Orientalia*, Vol. 55, 1984, pp. 3–42.

Parry, M., 'Studies in the Epic Technique of Oral Versemaking: II, The Homeric Language as the Language of Oral Poetry', *Harvard Studies in Classical Philology*, Vol. 43, 1932, pp. 1–50.

Patel, Manilal, 'A Historical Hymn of the Ṛgveda (RV.VII.33)', *Journal of the Gujarat Research Society*, I, October 1939, pp. 143–148.

Patton, Laurie L., 'How Do You Conduct Yourself? Gender and the Construction of a Dialogic Self in the *Mahābhārata*' in Simon Brodbeck and Brian Black (eds), *Gender and Narrative in the Mahābhārata*, Routledge, London, 2007, pp. 97–109.

Pollock, S., 'Mīmāṁsā and the Problem of History in Traditional India', *Journal of the American Oriental Society*, Vol. 109, No. 4, 1999, pp. 603–610.

Potdar, K.R., 'Contribution of the Vasiṣṭha Family', *Oriental Thought*, Vol. V, No. 4, December, 1961, pp. 1–8.

Pradhan, S.N., *Chronology of Ancient India*, Cosmo Publications, Calcutta, 1927.

Prahladachar, D., 'Puruṣārthas: Values of Life' in Kalyan Kumar Chakravarty (ed.), *Text and Variations of the Mahābhārata: Contextual, Regional and Performative Traditions*, Munshiram Manoharlal, New Delhi, 2009, pp. 281–294.

Preciado-Solis, Benjamin, 'The Episode of the Mausalaparvan' in T.S. Rukmani (ed.), *The Mahābhārata: What Is Not Here Is Nowhere Else*, Munshiram Manoharlal, New Delhi, 2005, pp. 239–244.

Pusalker, A.D, 'Aryan Settlements in India' in R.C. Majumdar (ed.), *The History and Culture of the Indian People: The Vedic Age*, Bharatiya Vidya Bhavan, Mumbai, 1996 (reprint), pp. 245–267.

Pusalker, A.D., *Studies in the Epics and Purāṇas*, Bharatiya Vidya Bhavan, Bombay, 1958.

Pusalker, A.D., 'Traditional History from the Earliest Time to the Accession of Parikṣit' in R.C. Majumdar (ed.), *The History and Culture of the Indian People: The Vedic Age*', Bharatiya Vidya Bhavan, Mumbai, 1996 (reprint), pp. 271–322.

Quigley, Declan, *The Interpretation of Caste*, Oxford University Press, New Delhi, 2012 (reprint).

Radhakrishnan, S., *Indian Philosophy* (Vol. 1), Oxford University Press, New Delhi, 2008 (reprint).

Rahurkar, V.G., *Seers of the Ṛgveda*, University of Poona, Poona, 1964.

Rahurkar, V.G., *The Vedic Priests of the Fire Cult*, Vivek Publication, Aligarh, 1982.

Rahurkar, V.G., 'Viśvāmitra and the Viśvāmitras in the Ṛgveda', *Oriental Thought*, Vol. V, No. 1, January 1961, pp. 25–56.

Ramanujan, A.K., 'Repetition in the Mahābhārata' in Arvind Sharma (ed.), *Essays on the Mahābhārata*, Motilal Banarsidass, Delhi, 2007, pp. 419–443.

Ramanujan, P., 'Computational Database of the Mahābhārata for Assisting Research/ Analysis' in Kalyan Kumar Chakravarty (ed.), *Text and Variations of the Mahābhārata: Contextual, Regional and Performative Traditions*, Munshiram Manoharlal, New Delhi, 2009, pp. 101–112.

Rao, D. Venkat, 'Learning in the Labyrinth: Irony, Contingency and the Question of Responsibility in the Texts of the Mahabharata' in T.R.S. Sharma (ed.), *Reflections and Variations on the Mahabharata*, Sahitya Akademi, New Delhi, 2009, pp. 141–171.

Rapson, E.J. (ed.), *The Cambridge History of India* (Vol. 1), Cambridge University Press, Cambridge, 1922.

Ratnagar, Shereen, 'Archaeology and the State' in B.P. Sahu (ed.), *Iron and Social Change in Early India*, Oxford University Press, New Delhi, 2006, pp. 179–190.

Raychaudhuri, H.C., *Materials for the Study of the Early History of the Vaiṣṇava Sect*, Oriental Books Reprint Corporation, New Delhi, 1975 (reprint).

Raychaudhuri, H.C., *Political History of Ancient India*, new edition with a commentary by B.N. Mukherjee, Oxford University Press, New Delhi, 2006.

Reich, Tamar C., 'The Critic of Ritual Reviler in the Āśvamedhikaparvan' in T.S. Rukmani (ed.), *The Mahābhārata: What Is Not Here Is Nowhere Else*, Munshiram Manoharlal, New Delhi, 2005, pp. 281–292.

Richman, Paula, 'Why Did Bhima Wed Hidimba? A Comparative Perspective on Marriage to the Other' in T.R.S. Sharma (ed.), *Reflections and Variations on the Mahabharata*, Sahitya Akademi, New Delhi, 2009, pp. 172–200.

Roy, Kaushik, *Hinduism and the Ethics of Warfare in South Asia*, Cambridge University Press, New Delhi, 2012.

Roy, Kumkum, *The Emergence of Monarchy in North India*, Oxford University Press, New Delhi, 1994.

Roy, S.C., *The Bhagavadgītā and Modern Scholarship*, Luzac, London, 1941.

Rubin, Gayle, 'The Traffic in Women: Notes on the Political Economy of Sex' in Joan Wallach Scott (ed.), *Feminism in History*, Oxford University Press, Oxford, 1996, pp. 105–151.

Rukmani, T.S., 'Dharmaputra in the Context of the Rājadharma and Āpaddharma of the Śāntiparvan' in T.S. Rukmani (ed.), *The Mahābhārata: What Is Not Here Is Nowhere Else*, Munshiram Manoharlal, New Delhi, 2005, pp. 179–194.

Sahgal, Smita, 'Locating Female Sexuality: A Study of Polyandrous Representation', *Social Science Probings*, Vol. 18, No. 2, December 2006, pp. 33–52.

Sahgal, Smita, *Niyoga*, Primus, Delhi, 2017.

Sahi, M.D.N., 'Agricultural Production during the Early Iron Age in Northern India' in B.P. Sahu (ed.), *Iron and Social Change in Early India*, Oxford University Press, New Delhi, 2006, pp. 191–197.

Sahu, B.P., 'Introduction' in B.P. Sahu (ed.), *Iron and Social Change in Early India*, Oxford University Press, New Delhi, 2006, pp. 1–34.

Saklani, Atul and Rajpal Singh Negi, 'The Living Legend of Rājā Duryodhana: Socio-historical Constructions on the *Mahābhārata* in Himalayan Society' in T.S. Rukmani (ed.), *The Mahābhārata: What Is Not Here Is Nowhere Else*, Munshiram Manoharlal, New Delhi, 2005, pp. 293–308.

Sarkar, S.C., *Some Aspects of Earliest Social History of India*, Oxford University Press, London, 1928.

Sathaye, Adheesh, 'How to Become a Brahman: The Construction of *Varṇa* as Social Place in the *Mahābhārata*'s Legends of Viśvāmitra', *Acta Orientalis Vilnensia*, Vol. 8, 2007, pp. 41–67.

Sathaye, Adheesh, 'The Other Kind of Brahman: Rāma Jāmadagnya and the Psychosocial Construction of Brahman Power in the *Mahābhārata*' in Sheldon Pollock (ed.), *Epic and Argument in Sanskrit Literary History: Essays in Honour of Robert P. Goldman*, Manohar, New Delhi, 2010, pp. 185–207.

Scharf, Peter M., '*Rāmopākhyāna:* The Story of Rāma in the *Mahābhārata*, a Web-Based and Printed Reader for Sanskrit Students' in T.S. Rukmani (ed.), *The Mahābhārata: What Is Not Here Is Nowhere Else*, Munshiram Manoharlal, New Delhi, 2005, pp. 49–60.

Selvanayagam, I., 'Aśoka and Arjuna as Counter-Figures Standing on the Field of Dharma: A Historical-Hermeneutical Perspective', *History of Religions*, Vol. 32, No. 1, 1992, pp. 59–75.

Sen, Prabal Kumar, 'Moral Doubts, Moral Dilemmas and Situational Ethics in the *Mahābhārata*' in Arindam Chakrabarti and Sibaji Bandyopadhyay (eds), *Mahābhārata Now*, Routledge, New Delhi, 2014, pp. 153–202.

Shah, Shalini, *The Making of Womanhood (Gender Relations in the Mahābhārata)*, Manohar, Delhi, 1995.

Shah, Shalini, 'The Principle of Kāma Puruṣārtha in the Mahābhārata' in Kalyan Kumar Chakravarty (ed.), *Text and Variations of the Mahābhārata: Contextual, Regional and Performative Traditions*, Munshiram Manoharlal, New Delhi, 2009, pp. 321–330.

Sharma, R.S., *Aspects of Political Ideas and Institutions in Ancient India*, Motilal Banarsidass, New Delhi, 1996 (reprint).

Sharma, R.S. 'Material Background of the Genesis of the State and Complex Society in the Middle Gangetic Plains' in B.P. Sahu (ed.), *Iron and Social Change in Early India*, Oxford University Press, New Delhi, 2006, pp. 150–168.

Sharma, R.S., 'Material Background of the Origin of Buddhism' in B.P. Sahu (ed.), *Iron and Social Change in Early India*, Oxford University Press, New Delhi, 2006, pp. 42–48.

Sharma, R.S., *Material Culture and Social Formations in Ancient India*, McMillan, Delhi, 1983.

Sharma, R.S., *Perspectives in Social and Economic History of Early India*, Munshiram Manoharlal, New Delhi, 1983.

Sharma, T.R.S., 'Introduction: Many Makers, Many Texts/Contexts' in T.R.S. Sharma (ed.), *Reflections and Variations on the Mahabharata*, Sahitya Akademi, New Delhi, 2009, pp. 1–37.

Shende, N.J., 'The Authorship of the *Mahābhārata*', *Annals of the Bhandarkar Oriental Research Institute*, Vol. 24, 1943, pp. 67–82.

Shulman, David, 'Towards a Historical Poetics of the Sanskrit Epics', *International Folklore Review*, Vol. 11, 1991, pp. 9–17.

Singh, Sarva Daman, *Ancient Indian Warfare with Special Reference to the Vedic Period*, E.J.Brill, Leiden, 1965.

Singh, Sarva Daman, *Polyandry in Ancient India*, Motilal Banarsidass, Delhi, 1978.

Singh, Upinder, *Ancient Delhi*, Oxford University Press, New Delhi, 1999.

Sinha, Braj M., '*Arthaśāstra* Categories in the Mahābhārata: From *Daṇḍanīti* to *Rājadharma*' in Arvind Sharma (ed.), *Essays on the Mahābhārata*, Motilal Banarsidass, New Delhi, 2007, pp. 369–383.

Sinha, Kanad, 'The Devas, the Asuras and Gilgamesh: Exploring the Cross-Cultural Journey of Myths', *Vedic Studies*, Vol. VI, 2014, pp. 360–401.

Sinha, Kanad, 'Redefining *Dharma* in a Time of Transition: *Ānṛśaṃsya* in the *Mahābhārata* as an Alternative End of Human Life', *Studies in History*, Vol. 35, No. 2, 2019, pp. 147–161.

Sinha, Kanad, 'Sporting with *Kāma*: Amusements, Games, Sports and Festivities in Early Indian Urban Culture', *Journal of the Asiatic Society*, Vol. LV, Nos 1–2, 2013, pp. 73–120.

Sinha, Kanad, 'A Tale of Three Couples and their Poet: *Rāmakathā*, Love and Vālmīki in South Asian Tradition', *Studies in Humanities in Social Sciences*, Vol. XVIII, Nos 1–2, 2011, pp. 43–80.

Sinha, Kanad, 'When the *Bhūpati* Sought the *Gopati*'s Wealth: Locating the *Mahābhārata* Economy', *Proceedings of the Indian History Congress*, Vol. 76, 2015, pp. 66–73.

Sinha, Manoj Kumar, 'Hinduism and International Humanitarian Law', *International Review of the Red Cross*, Vol. 87, Part 858, 2005, pp. 285–286.

Sircar, D.C., 'Myth of the great Bhārata War' in D.C. Sircar (ed.), *The Bhārata War and Puranic Genealogies*, University of Calcutta, Calcutta, 1969.

Smith, Mary Carroll, 'Epic Parthenogenesis' in Arvind Sharma (ed.), *Essays on the Mahābhārata*, Motilal Banarsidass, New Delhi, 2007, pp. 84–100.

Sreedharan, Janaki, 'Imaging Venegeance: Amba and Draupadi in the *Mahabharata*' in T.R.S. Sharma (ed.), *Reflections and Variations on the Mahabharata*, Sahitya Akademi, New Delhi, 2009, pp. 99–114.

Staal, Frits, *Discovering the Vedas*, Penguin, New Delhi, 2008.

Stein B., 'Early Indian Historiography: A Conspiracy Hypothesis', *Indian Economic and Social History Review*, Vol. 6, No. 1, pp. 41–60.

Sternbach, L., *Judicial Studies in Ancient Indian Law*, Part I, Motilal Banarsidass, Delhi, 1965.

Subedi, Surya P., 'The Concept in Hinduism of Just War', *Journal of Conflict and Security Law*, Vol. 8, No. 2, 2003.

Sukthankar, V.S., 'The Bhṛgus and the Bhārata: A Text Historical Study', *Annals of the Bhandarkar Oriental Research Institute*, Vol. 18, 1936–1937, pp. 1–76.

Sukthankar, V.S., *On the Meaning of the Mahābhārata*, The Asiatic Society of Bombay, Bombay, 1957.

Sullivan, B.M., *Kṛṣṇa Dvaipāyana Vyāsa and the Mahābhārata: A New Interpretation*, E.J.Brill, Leiden, 1990.

Sullivan, B.M., *Seer of the Fifth Veda*, Brill, Leiden, 1999.

Sullivan, Bruce M., 'The Epic's Two Grandfathers, Bhīṣma and Vyāsa' in Arvind Sharma (ed.), *Essays on the Mahabharata*, Motilal Banarsidass, Delhi, 2007, pp. 204–211.

Sumitra Bai, J.N. and Robert J. Zydenbos, 'The Jaina Mahābhārata' in Arvind Sharma (ed.), *Essays on the Mahābhārata*, Motilal Banarsidass, Delhi, 2007, pp. 251–273.

Sutherland, Sally J., 'Sītā and Draupadī: Aggressive Behaviour and Female Role-Models in the Sanskrit Epics', *Journal of the American Oriental Society*, Vol. 109, No. 1, January–March 1989, pp. 63–79.

Sutton, N., 'Aśoka and Yudhiṣṭhira: A Historical setting for the Tensions in the *Mahābhārata*', *Religion*, Vol. 27, No. 4, 1997, pp. 331–341.

Sutton, Nick, 'What Is *Dharma*? Ethical Tensions within the *Mahābhārata*' in T.S. Rukmani (ed.), *The Mahābhārata: What Is Not Here Is Nowhere Else*, Munshiram Manoharlal, New Delhi, 2005, pp. 91–102.

Thapar, Romila, *Early India*, Penguin, New Delhi, 2002.

Thapar, Romila, *Exile and the Kingdom*, The Mythic Society, Bangalore, 1978.

Thapar, Romila, *From Lineage to State*, Oxford University Press, New Delhi, 2008.

Thapar, Romila, 'Genealogical Pattern as Perceptions of the Past' in Romila Thapar, *Cultural Pasts*, Oxford University Press, New Delhi, 2008 (reprint), pp. 709–753.

Thapar, Romila, 'The Historian and the Epic' in Romila Thapar, *Cultural Pasts*, Oxford University Press, New Delhi, 2008 (reprint), pp. 613–629.

Thapar, Romila, *The Past before Us*, Permanent Black, Ranikhet, 2013.

Thapar, Romila, 'Perceiving the Forest: Early India', *Studies in History*, Vol. 17, No. 1, 2001, pp. 173–191.

Thapar, Romila, 'Society and Historical Consciousness: The *itihāsa-purāṇa* Tradition' in *Cultural Pasts*, Oxford University Press, New Delhi, 2008 (reprint), pp. 123–154.

Thapar, Romila, 'Some Aspects of the Economic Data in the *Mahābhārata*' in Romila Thapar, *Cultural Pasts*, Oxford University Press, New Delhi, 2008 (reprint), pp. 630–646.

Tokunaga, Muneo, 'Bhīṣma's Discourse on *Śokāpanodana*' in Robert P. Goldman and Muneo Tokunaga (eds), *Epic Undertakings*, Motilal Banarsidass, Delhi, 2009, pp. 371–382.

Trautmann, Thomas R., *Elephants and Kings*, Permanent Black, Ranikhet, 2015.

Trautmann, Thomas R., *Kauṭilya and the Arthaśāstra: A Statistical Investigation of the Authorship and Evolution of the Text*, Brill, Leiden, 1971.

Tripathi, Radhavallabh, 'Aesthetics of the Mahābhārata: Traditional Interpretations' in Arindam Chakrabarti and Sibaji Bandyopadhyay (eds), *Mahābhārata Now*, Routledge, New Delhi, 2014, pp. 85–94.

Tubb, Gary A., '*Śāntarasa* in the *Mahābhārata*' in Arvind Sharma (ed.), *Essays on the Mahābhārata*, Motilal Banarsidass, New Delhi, 2007, pp. 171–203.

Urubshurow, Victoria, and T.R. Singh, 'The Battle of Kurukṣetra in Topological Transposition' in Arvind Sharma (ed.), *Essays on the Mahābhārata*, Motilal Banarsidass, New Delhi, 2007, pp. 349–368.

Van Buitenen, J.A.B., 'Introduction to the Book of Beginning' in Vyāsa, *The Mahābhārata* (Vol. I), translated by J.A.B. van Buitenen, University of Chicago Press, Chicago, 1973, pp. 1–16.

Van Buitenen, J.A.B., 'Introduction to the Book of the Assembly Hall' in Vyāsa, *The Mahābhārata* (Vol. II), translated by J.A.B. van Buitenen, University of Chicago Press, Chicago, 1975, pp. 3–30.

Van Buitenen, J.A.B., 'Introduction to the Book of the Forest' in Vyāsa, *The Mahābhārata* (Vol. II), translated by J.A.B. van Buitenen, University of Chicago Press, Chicago, 1975.

Van Buitenen, J.A.B., 'Introduction to the Book of Virāṭa' in Vyāsa, *The Mahābhārata* (Vol. III), translated by J.A.B. van Buitenen, University of Chicago Press, Chicago, 1978.

Van Buitenen, J.A.B., 'The Mahābhārata: Introduction' in Vyāsa, *The Mahābhārata* (Vol. I), translated by J.A.B. van Buitenen, University of Chicago Press, Chicago, 1973a, pp. xiii–xlviii.

Van Buitenen, J.A.B., 'On the Structure of the Sabhāparvan of the *Mahābhārata*' in Ludo Rocher (ed.), *Studies in Indian Literature and Philosophy: Collected Articles of J.A.B. van Buitenen*, Motilal Banarsidass, New Delhi, 1988, pp. 305–321.

Velankar, H.D., 'The Family Hymns in the Family Mandalas', *Journal of the Bombay Branch of the Royal Asiatic Society*, Vol. XVIII, 1942, pp. 1–22.

Veyme, P., *Writing History*, Middletown, 1984.

Von Simson, Georg, 'Kṛṣṇa's Son Sāmba: Faked Gender and Other Ambiguities on the Background of Lunar and Solar Myths' in Simon Brodbeck and Brian Black (eds), *Gender and Narrative in the Mahabharata*, Routledge, London, 2007, pp. 230–257.

Watkins, Calvert, *How to Kill a Dragon: Aspects of Indo-European Poetics*, Oxford University Press, Oxford, 1995.

Weller, Hermann, 'Who Were the Bhriguids?', *Annals of the Bhandarkar Oriental Research Institute*, Vol. 18, Part 3, pp. 296–302.

West, M.L., *Indo-European Poetry and Myth*, Oxford University Press, Oxford, 2007.

Winternitz, Maurice, *History of Sanskrit Literature* (Vol. I), translated by V. Srinivas Sarma, Motilal Banarsidass, New Delhi, 1987.

Witzel, Michael, 'The Development of Vedic Canon and Its Schools: The Social and Political Milieu' in Michael Witzel (ed.), *Inside the Text, Beyond the Text: New Approaches to the Study of the Vedas*, Harvard Oriental Series, Opera Minor 2, Cambridge, MA, 1997, pp. 257–348.

Witzel, Michael, 'Early Sanskritization. Origin and Development of the Kuru State' in B. Kolver (ed.), *The State, the Law, and Administration in Classical India*, R. Oldenbourg, Munich, 1997, pp. 27–52.

Witzel, Michael, 'On the Localisation of Vedic Texts and Schools' in G. Pollet (ed.), *India and the Ancient World: History, Trade and Culture before A.D.650*, Department Orientalistiek, Leuven, 1987, pp. 173–215.

Witzel, Michael, 'Ṛgvedic History: Poets, Chieftains and Polities' in George Erdosy (ed.), *The Indo-Aryans of Ancient South Asia*, Munshiram Manoharlal, New Delhi, 1995, pp. 307–354.

Witzel, Michael, 'The Vedas and the Epics: Some Comparative Notes on Persons, Lineages, Geography and Grammar' in Petteri Koshikallio (ed.), *Epics, Khilas and Purāṇas: Continuities and Ruptures*, Croatian Academy of Sciences and Arts, 2005, pp. 21–80.

Woods, Julian F., 'Destiny and Human Initiative in the *Mahābhārata*' in T.S. Rukmani (ed.), *The Mahābhārata: What Is Not Here Is Nowhere Else*, Munshiram Manoharlal, New Delhi, 2005, pp. 103–114.

Wulff, Daniel, *A Global History of History*, Cambridge University Press, Cambridge, 2011.

Wulff, Fernando Alonso, 'Greek Sources in the Mahābhārata' in Vishwa Adluri (ed.), *Ways and Reasons for Thinking about the Mahābhārata as a Whole*, Bhandarkar Oriental Research Institute, Pune, 2015, pp. 155–184.

Zaehner, R.C., *The Bhagavad-Gītā with a Commentary Based on the Original Sources*, Oxford University Press, Oxford, 1969.

Zimmermann, Francis, *Jungle and the Aroma of Meat*, Motilal Banarsidass, New Delhi, 1999.

Index

For the benefit of digital users, indexed terms that span two pages (e.g., 52–53) may, on occasion, appear on only one of those pages.

abduction, 104–5, 203–4, 241, 287, 288, 289, 298, 301–2, 307–8
Abhimanyu, 19, 112, 114–15, 127, 163, 175–78, 203, 240–41, 245–46, 291, 312, 327–28, 392–96, 403
Abhinavagupta, 13
Abhipratarin. 466
Abhiras, 242, 244
absence
  of bardic tradition, 183
  of biological offspring, 101–2
  of extramarital affairs, 90–91
  of historical texts, 4–6
  of Kṛṣṇa, 298, 304
  of monetization, writing, and urbanization, 26–27
  of Pāṇḍavas, 32
  of Rāma, 451
  of *vilāpa*, 453
account
  about Kṛṣṇa's life, 249–58, 264, 265–66, 271, 272–73, 275–77, 284, 285–86, 298–99, 308, 310–11, 390, 405–6
  about Paraśurāma, 452–53, 464–65
  epic, 22–23, 30
  genealogical, 84, 108
  historical, 7–9, 12, 28, 71, 242
  Mahābhārata, 127–28, 180, 392–93
  of Pāṇḍu, 91
  Purāṇic, 2–3, 241, 246–47, 466
  Rāmāyaṇa, 448–49
  Vedic, 86–87, 178
Achilles, 18–20, 23, 124, 125, 196, 390
action
  path of, 206–7, 214, 252–53, 263, 277, 319, 321, 322–23, 331–32, 338–39, 344–45, 355, 360–62, 365–67, 369–70, 371–72, 373–74, 378, 383–87, 407–8, 423, 464
  ritual, 345–46, 358, 364
  women's, 203–4
  of Yudhiṣṭhira, 208–9, 215
acquisition
  of cattle, 154
  of pleasure and power, 353–54, 386–87
additions
  to the *Mahābhārata*, ix–x, 1–2, 12–13, 66, 67–68, 104, 278, 281, 343–44, 426
  to the *Rāmāyaṇa*, 426–28
  to the *Ṛg Veda Saṃhitā*, 44, 54
Adhiratha, 160, 197–98, 332
Ādiparvan, 26–27, 115, 452, 453
Ādityas, 52, 136–37, 261, 319
administration, 403
adoidos, 185–86
adoption, 43–45, 46–48, 53–54, 67, 70–71, 87, 93–94, 97–98, 109, 194–95, 198–99, 250–51, 260, 299, 332–33, 363–64, 388, 402, 407–8, 456–57
adultery, 237–38, 266, 269, 270–71
advances
  military, 292
  sexual, 126–27, 151
advantage
  geopolitical, 129
  material, 283
  military, 430–31
  political, 289–90
  strategic, 284

advice
of Kṛṣṇa, 242–43, 293, 314–15, 329, 386–87, 406
of Nārada, 70
of Śiva, 114
of Vidura, 130
of Vyāsa, 201, 251–52
affiliation
political, 446
priestly group, 46–48
sectarian, 279–80, 281, 292–93, 381
Agamemnon, 19
Agathokles, 249
Aghamarṣaṇa, 45
Agni, xiv, 49–50, 51, 52–54, 67, 112, 113, 114, 115–16, 117, 121–22, 123–24, 125, 127–28, 134–35, 143–44, 374
Agni Purāṇa, 147–48
agnosticism, 51, 346–47
agriculture, 1, 25, 88–90, 96–98, 105–7, 115–16, 148–49, 153–54, 155, 157–58, 159, 258, 263, 301, 335–36, 383, 462
ahiṃsā, x–xi, 200–3, 366, 381, 397, 429
Ahura, 47
aindra mahābhiṣeka, 23, 465–66
Ajāmīlha, 45
Ajas, 53, 62–63
Ajātaśatru, 166, 281–82, 283, 297, 445–46
Ajīgarta, 70–71, 449–50
Akṛtavarṇa, 451–53
Al-Biruni, 4, 6
Alexander, 169, 211, 286
Alinas, 52–53, 61–62
allegations
against Kauravas, 138
against Vasiṣṭha, 55, 69, 442–43
against Yudhiṣṭhira, 207
alliance
Bharata-Pūru, 9–10, 59, 62–63, 462
with forest people, 121
Jarāsaṃdha and his supporters, 241, 250–51, 257, 279, 283, 286, 298–300, 301–2
of Kṛṣṇa against Kaṃsa, 274, 303
Kuru-Pañcāla, 30, 463
with Nāgas, 126
Pāṇḍava-Matsya, 312
Pāṇḍava-Pāñcāla, 128, 159–60, 289–90
Pāṇḍava-Vṛṣṇi, 112, 177–78, 240–41, 289–91, 311, 313, 314
of ten kings, 49, 52–53, 59–60, 61–63, 439–40, 461–62
allusion
to educational reform, 447
to gods, 98–99
to historical past, 5
to Kṛṣṇa's divinity, 278
to *niyoga*, 99–100
to pre-Vedic context, 459
to ritual contests, 136–37
to Triśaṅku legend, 447
to Vedic myth, 433–34
alternative
ideologies, 194, 197–98, 200–1, 208–9, 331–32, 374–75, 407–8, 447
kinds of sons, 93–94
options of procreation, 100–1
traditions, 247, 261–62
versions, 188
voices, 105–7
Amarakośa, 117
Amarasiṃha, 117, 118–19
Ambā, 104, 105–7, 203–4, 298–99, 460
Ambālikā, 100–1, 102–4, 149–50, 201, 212–14
ambassador, 167, 172–73, 195, 198, 322, 387
Ambikā, 100–1, 102–4, 149–50, 201, 212–14
amnesia, 5, 429
Anāhitā, 16
analysis
historical, x–xi, 14–16
psychohistorical, 56–57
Analytical Theory, 12–16, 20–21, 24, 336–37, 339–40, 343–44
Ānandavardhana, 13
Anaṅga, 435

ancestors, 30, 45, 58–59, 70–71, 83, 84, 88–90, 204, 349, 452, 456
Andhakas, 188–89, 249–52, 253–54, 258–59, 272–73, 286–87, 302, 318
Āṅgirasas, 44–48, 58–60, 62–63, 67, 70, 136–37, 191, 242, 244, 247, 259–60, 344–46, 366, 377, 381, 386–87, 397, 425–28, 449–50, 454, 456–57
animals, xiv, 91, 98–99, 113–17, 121–22, 126–27, 131, 147–48, 153, 193–94, 254, 294, 296–97, 397
Aniruddha, 250–51
Añjanā, 251–52
ānṛśaṃsya, x–xi, 200–4, 206–9, 212–15, 322, 345–46, 387, 423, 428, 432, 435–36, 463–64, 465–66
anṛtadeva, 55
antagonism
  between *brāhmaṇas* and *kṣatriyas*, 458–59
  between Devas and Asuras, 47
  between forest dwellers and settled people, 118, 119–20, 121–23, 301
  between Karṇa and Arjuna, 332, 333
  between Kṛṣṇa and Indra, 261
  between Kṛṣṇa and Jarāsaṃdha, 241, 245–46, 252–54, 281, 334–35, 391
  between Kurus and Paāñcālas, 178–79, 463
  between Mauryas and Brahmanical religion, 183–84
  between Nāgas and Garuḍas, 127–28, 129
  between Nāgas and Kurus, 127
  between Paraśurāma and Kārtavīrya, 450–51, 458–59
  between pastoralism and agriculture, 335–36
  between Rāma and Rāvaṇa, 390
  between ritual and knowledge, 345–46, 359–60
  between Sudās and the ten kings, 52–53, 61, 440
  between Viśvāmitra and Vasiṣṭha, 57–62, 66, 68–69, 461–62
  between water and fire, 125
anthropology, 25, 138, 244
Antialchidas, 248–49
antiquity of a text, 304–5, 329, 334–35
antithesis, 116–17, 336, 358–59
Anugītā, 428–29
anukrośa, x–xi, 201, 463–64
Anus, 48, 61–63
Anuśāsanaparvan, 12, 25, 28–29, 180, 183, 426–28, 430–31, 432–33, 436–37, 452–53, 464–66
anuṣṭubh, 424
Āpastamba, 64–65, 98–99, 149
Aphrodite, 19–20
araṇya, 111–12, 116–17, 121–23
Āraṇyakaparvan, 28–29, 115, 139–40, 143, 155, 160–61, 202–3, 205, 371, 426–28, 435–36, 452, 453, 464–65
archaeology, 22–23, 25, 27–28, 438–39
archery, 151, 167–68, 172, 195, 237, 289–91, 332, 389
archetype, 15–16, 20–21
architect, 114, 124–25, 174
Ariṣṭa, 265–66, 267
Ariṣṭanemi, 252–54
Aristotle, 385–86
Arjuna, xii–xiii, 16, 17, 19–20, 24, 27–28, 30, 31, 32–33, 94, 95, 102, 104, 105, 112, 113, 114–15, 123–29, 135–36, 146, 150–51, 156, 157–58, 160–61, 163, 170, 171, 174–75, 182–83, 185, 196–98, 200, 202–3, 205, 208–9, 239, 240–41, 243, 245–46, 247, 248, 251–52, 260, 277, 279, 288, 289–92, 294–95, 300, 312–13, 314–15, 326–28, 331, 332, 333, 334, 336–41, 342–49, 352, 353, 354, 355, 364, 367–70, 371–72, 374–75, 376–77, 384–87, 388–97, 401–6, 424, 425, 428–29, 430–31, 440, 465–66
Arjuna Kārtavīrya, 451–52, 460
army, 26, 120, 127–28, 133, 141, 156, 157, 163–67, 168–74, 193, 248, 250–51, 261, 264, 274, 279, 284, 286, 312, 314–15, 333, 334, 340–41, 391, 392, 402, 440, 444

Arrian, 169
arrows, x, 18, 88, 102, 113, 164–65, 172, 251–52, 254, 388, 430–31, 459–60
artisan, 115–16, 133–34
Aryan, xiv, 1, 2–3, 11, 43–44, 47, 118, 119–20, 126, 127–28, 164–65, 261, 280, 306, 335–36, 424, 456–57
Aryanization, 115–16, 119–20
Āryāvarta, 1
ascetics, 30, 108–9, 121–22, 195, 203, 213–14, 254, 336, 339–40, 348, 374–75, 383, 388, 429, 432–33, 440, 444–45, 458
Aśoka, xx, 118–23, 156, 183–84, 200, 338–39, 433
aspirations
  Bhṛgu, 450, 454–55
  economic, 158
  individual, 383–84
  of Janamejaya, 465–66
Assam, 171, 241, 250–51, 292–93
assault, 129, 156, 205, 206, 401
assembly, 146, 150, 206, 257, 272–73, 274, 275, 284–85, 296, 312, 447
Aṣṭaka, 45, 95–96
Asti, 279
Āstīka, 188, 212
Asuras, 12, 21, 44–45, 47, 51, 67, 82–83, 114, 124, 126, 137–38, 165, 193, 212, 380, 426–28, 435–36
asurayuddha, 174
Aśvaghoṣa, 188–89, 459
Āśvalāyana Gṛhya Sūtra, 8, 11, 24
Aśvamedha, 43–44, 50–51, 58–60, 70–71, 72–73, 107, 133–34, 283–84, 432, 435–36, 465–66
Āśvamedhikaparvan, 188, 376–77, 404, 428–29, 432
Aśvatthāman, 19–20, 163, 175–79, 192–93, 196, 208, 213–14, 245–46, 388, 394, 400–1, 404, 426, 454
Aśvins, 16, 45, 48, 52, 96–97, 98–99, 127–28
Atharva Veda, 8, 9–10, 23, 28–29, 30, 31, 47, 64, 65, 67, 81, 90–91, 96–97, 148, 154, 155, 158, 159, 165, 179, 188–89, 211, 282–83, 426–28, 443, 456–58, 462, 465
Atibala, 435
Atithigva, 58–59
Atri, 45, 47–48, 49, 58–59, 60–61, 63, 84, 86, 96
attack
  military, 119–20, 163, 171, 175–76, 250–51, 253–54, 279, 284, 286, 294–95, 298, 299, 301, 305–6, 390, 394, 396–97
  nocturnal, 19–20, 176, 208, 404
  verbal, 55, 203–4, 296–97, 314, 353, 429
attainment
  of brāhmaṇahood, 458
  of ends, 57
  of knowledge, 345–46, 358–59
  of liberation, 363–64, 375
  of status, 277, 302
audience, xii, 25–26, 28, 84, 179, 180, 182, 246–47, 256, 424–25, 436–37
Aurva, 443, 456, 457–58
authority
  economic, 149
  over women, 105, 148, 149–50
  political, 1–2, 26–27, 71, 121–23, 160–61, 207, 305, 309–10, 311–12, 445, 461–62
  religious, xiii
  Vedic, 28–29, 31–32, 426–28
authorship, 179–80, 184–85, 186–88, 338–39, 343
avatāras, 20–21, 336
axes, 115–16, 164, 165, 168, 379, 450, 461
ayajyus, 62
Ayodhyā, 71, 143–44, 398–99
Āyus, 8–9, 15–16, 30, 82–83, 84–85, 86

Babhru, 297, 300
Babhruvāhana, 95, 127
background
  economic, 155
  intellectual, 7, 49, 251–52, 445–46

political, 31–32, 123–24, 170, 184–85, 245–46, 459, 462–63
social, 7, 199, 307–8
stories, 212, 428
Bailey, G.M., 335–36, 423
Baka, 121, 126–27, 393–94
Baka Dālbhya, 30, 64–65
Bakhtin, 400
Bālacarita, 249–50, 258–59, 260, 266
Baladeva, 30–31, 249, 251–53, 277, 287–88
Bālakāṇḍa, 426–28
Balarāma, 126, 249–55, 258–59, 265–66, 267, 271, 274, 277, 284, 285–86, 290, 301, 304, 306, 313–15, 403–5
Balin, 99–100, 102–3
Bandyopadhyaya, Bibhutibhushan, 122–23
Bandyopadhyay, Sibaji, 145, 200–1, 355–56
bards, ix–x, xxii–xxiii, 1–3, 7, 8, 11, 15–16, 24–28, 32, 67–68, 155–56, 159, 166, 167, 180–86, 189–90, 282–83, 292–93, 316–17, 334–35, 340–41, 343, 424–25, 438–39, 445, 446, 453, 463–65
barley, 159
baron, 157–58, 271, 297
Basham, A.L., 338–39, 375–76
Basu, Buddhadeb, 20–21, 115, 125, 139–40, 385–86
Basu, Jogendranath, 304–5
battle, x, 10, 11, 18, 51, 69, 124, 125–26, 137–38, 153–54, 159–60, 163–70, 172–79, 192, 194, 198–99, 202–3, 208, 239, 243, 245–46, 253–54, 261, 272, 275, 284, 285–86, 294–95, 296, 309–10, 323, 327, 328, 333–34, 342–48, 353, 367–68, 383, 388–94, 396–97, 401, 402–3, 428–31, 436, 454, 456
Battle of Ten Kings, 5, 7–8, 32–34, 47–48, 53, 57–63, 72–73, 153–54, 256, 439–40, 456–58
Baudhāyana Dharma Sūtra, 248, 259
Baudhāyana Gṛhya Sūtra, 341–42
Baudhāyanas, 64–65
Baudhāyana Śrauta Sūtra, 64–65, 211
begging, 175, 194, 318, 324, 325, 393, 402
behavioural fitness, 71–72, 191–92, 196, 203–4, 212, 276
benefit of all beings, 388, 389–90
Bengal, 299, 357
Bengali literature, 122–23, 243–44, 255–56, 358
Bhadrā Kakṣīvatī, 93
Bhaduri, Nrisinha Prasad, 159–60, 244, 271, 273, 304–5
Bhaga, 17, 52, 127–28
Bhagadatta, 168, 171, 237–422
bhāgadugha, 132–33, 135–36
Bhāgavata Purāṇa, 241, 246–47, 257, 265, 269, 287, 449–50
Bhāgavatism, 248–49, 335, 337–39, 341–42, 376–77
bhakti, 20–21, 24, 57, 125, 175, 195, 335–37, 341, 377, 378, 386, 428–29, 435–36, 438, 461, 464
Bhalanas, 61–62, 244
Bhandarkar, R.G., 242, 247
Bharadvājas, 46, 48, 58–59, 60–61, 63, 103, 108, 191–92
Bhārata, 11, 26–27, 182, 188, 211, 253–54, 425–26
Bharata Dāśarathi, 169
Bharata Dauṣyanti, 30, 83, 105–8, 109–10, 191–92, 463–64
Bharatas, 7–8, 9–10, 31–34, 43–44, 48–53, 56–59, 62–66, 68–69, 72–73, 81, 82, 85, 95, 108, 113–14, 131–32, 134–35, 137–38, 165, 178–79, 193, 213, 239, 256, 290–91, 294, 295–96, 329, 330, 350, 368–69, 381, 430–32, 437, 442, 461–62, 464, 465, 467
Bhārata War, 3–4, 10, 11, 21, 26–27, 28–29, 32–34, 81–82, 95, 109–10, 159–61, 163–64, 167–68, 172, 174, 175–78, 186, 189–90, 213, 276–77, 284, 316–17, 388–89, 404–5, 452, 454, 458–59, 462–63, 464–65

Bhargava, P.L., 2–3
Bhārgava Rāma, 450, 455–56
Bhārgavas, xiii, 24, 43–45, 46–48, 60–61, 62–63, 65, 67–68, 143, 144, 180, 375–76, 390, 424–37, 443, 445, 448–50, 452, 453–54, 456–61, 464–65
Bhārgavization, 46–47, 424–37, 451, 453–54, 456–59
Bhāsa, 194–95, 197–98, 249, 254–55, 256, 258–59, 266, 275, 276–77, 285, 388–89, 467
Bheda, 53
Bhīma, xii–xiii, 16, 84, 99–100, 121, 124–25, 126–27, 130, 139–40, 146, 149–50, 151, 156, 160–61, 163, 167–68, 175–76, 192, 193–94, 196, 200, 202–3, 205, 206–7, 208, 240–41, 250–51, 254, 279, 281, 294–95, 297, 298, 299, 323, 326–28, 329, 331–32, 393–94, 402–3
Bhīṣma, x, 11, 15–16, 17, 18–20, 26–27, 28–29, 99–101, 102–4, 105–7, 109–10, 130, 146, 157, 159–60, 161–62, 163, 178–79, 180, 182, 185, 191–92, 194–95, 198–99, 203–4, 238, 243, 245–46, 295–97, 298–99, 301–2, 312–13, 317, 328–29, 340–41, 385–86, 388, 389–92, 396, 401, 404, 430–31, 432–36, 437, 453, 454, 460–61, 463–65
Bhīṣmaka, 279, 286, 288, 289
Bhīṣmaparvan, 173–74, 333
Bhojas, 240–41, 244, 249–50, 254, 271–72, 275, 288, 297, 302
Bhṛgu, 46–47, 60, 375–76, 426, 457
Bhṛgus, 12, 13, 46–47, 49–50, 52–53, 59–60, 61–63, 67, 68, 82–83, 164, 376–77, 424–25, 426–28, 443, 448–49, 450–51, 454–55, 456–59
Bhūmanyu, 108, 191–92
bhūpati, 1, 153, 158
Bhūriśravas, 163, 175–76, 245–46
Biardeau, Madeleine, 20–21, 114, 123–24, 179–80, 244, 280, 336, 348
bile, 116–17
birds, 113–14, 126
birth legends, 18–19, 21, 55–56, 68, 100–1, 102, 103, 111–12, 159–60, 174, 201–2, 213–14, 245–46, 249–50, 251–52, 253–54, 257, 274, 286–87, 292–93, 319, 332, 341, 371, 424–25, 435, 443, 452, 457
birthright/birth status, 142, 191–92, 196–99, 203, 209, 212, 214, 239, 263, 307, 319, 322–23, 324, 325, 329, 366, 377, 380–81, 384–86, 392, 394, 407–8, 428–29, 445–46, 462–64
Black and Red Ware, 280
Black, Brian, 191–92
black complexion, 261
black magic, 55, 442–43
Black Yajur Veda, 64–65
blindness, 191–92, 212–13
bloodbath, 391, 404
blood drinking, 203–4
bloodline, 107–8, 177–78
blood relationship, 163, 177–78, 289–90
blood sacrifice, 281, 283–84, 404
bloodthirst, 212, 314
blow below the belt, 175–76, 203–4, 403
Bowles, Adam, 436–37
bows, 114–15, 164, 165, 166–68, 205, 263, 327, 396–97
Brahmā, 86–87, 96, 187–88, 376, 429, 433–34, 436–37, 444, 457
Brahman, 319, 338–40, 345–46, 362–64, 365, 369–70, 371, 373, 374–76, 377, 378, 379, 380, 381–82, 383, 386
brāhmaṇas, x, 1–2, 4, 5, 12, 16, 21, 24, 25–26, 33, 43, 66, 70, 84, 90, 91, 95–96, 99–101, 102–3, 118–19, 132–34, 154, 160–61, 172–73, 178, 180–85, 186, 187, 188, 189–90, 191, 195–96, 197–98, 199, 200–1, 208–10, 212, 264, 272, 281, 283–84, 294–95, 296, 344–45, 371, 372, 383, 392, 393–94, 398, 424–30, 433–38, 440–42, 444–47, 448–50, 451, 452, 453–56, 458–60, 464–66
Brahmāṇḍa Purāṇa, 448
Brahmanical religion, x, 2–4, 7, 8, 25–27, 28–29, 32–33, 57, 70–71, 87–89, 108–9, 117–18, 119–20, 127, 149,

175, 178, 180–85, 187, 188–90, 191, 193–94, 195, 210, 249, 254, 259, 277, 282, 337–39, 345–46, 363–64, 383–85, 386–87, 393–94, 405–6, 423, 426–30, 432–33, 435–36, 437, 438, 441, 444, 448, 450, 454–55, 458–60, 461, 462, 463–65
brahmanirvāṇa, 345–46, 362–64, 373
Brahmanization, 7, 12, 21, 24–26, 32–33, 67–68, 81, 159–60, 187, 188–89, 260, 345–46, 426–29, 437–38, 439, 449–50, 455–56, 461, 464, 465
Brahmaṇspati, 52
Brahma Purāṇa, 241, 246–47, 305–6, 448, 449–50
brahmarṣi, 68, 444
Brahmasūtra, 187–88, 191, 357, 358–59
Brahmavaivarta Purāṇa, 241, 269, 270–71
Brahmāvarta, 1
branches
  of Kurus, 66, 82, 86, 107, 110–11, 112, 163, 178–79, 191–92, 289–90, 462–63, 466–67
  of Vedic priestly families, 64–65, 67, 238, 426–28
  of Yadus, 256
branding of cattle, 155–56
brawl, 240–41, 251–52
Brekke, Torkel, 173–74, 175
Bṛhadaśva, 143–44, 145–46
Bṛhaddevatā, 66–68, 69, 96, 108–9, 426–28
Brockington, John, 180–82, 281, 282, 298
Brodbeck, Simon, 15, 86, 88–89, 91, 95, 97–98, 101, 107, 108, 191–92
Buddha, 1, 5, 114–15, 129, 166, 172, 188–89, 255, 282, 297, 344–48, 352, 363–64, 367–68, 369–70, 371, 373–74, 385–86, 404–5, 406, 407, 438–39, 445–46, 466–67
Buddhacarita, 459
Buddhaghoṣa, 118
buddhi, 265, 344–45, 353, 359, 361–63, 364, 367–68
Buddhism and Buddhist tradition, x–xi, 2–3, 4, 5, 7, 22–23, 30–31, 32–33, 87–88, 118, 119–20, 163–64, 166, 172, 173–74, 177–79, 183, 184, 188–89, 200–1, 249, 252, 254–55, 256, 257, 258–59, 271, 274, 277, 278, 279–80, 281, 282, 297, 304, 337, 338–39, 344–48, 349, 352, 355, 360, 363–64, 365, 380, 388, 405, 429, 433, 467
Budha, 86, 87–88, 94
bulls, 154, 265–66, 267
burning
  of evil spirits, 53–54
  of forest, xiv, 33–34, 82, 110–17, 119–20, 123–24, 126, 129, 159–60, 240–41, 291–92, 301–2, 407–8, 463
  of Vārāṇasī, 300
butter, 87, 158, 237–38, 241, 266

cakra, 239, 251–52, 297
Cakravartī, Mukundarāma, 122–23
cakravartin, 252–53, 276–77
camp
  of cowherds, 155–56, 255, 257, 258, 259, 267, 407–8
  of Duryodhana, 155–56, 240–41, 245–46, 331, 392, 393, 453, 454
  of Jarāsaṃdha, 286, 287, 299–300, 301–2
  of Kṛṣṇa, 303–4
  of Pāṇḍavas, 175–76, 208, 240–41, 311–12, 314–15, 317, 392, 394, 404
campaign
  against Naraka, 307–8
  of Paraśurāma, 452
  against Śambara, 49
Cāṇakya, 120, 183–84
Caṇḍabhārgava, 428
caṇḍālas, 117, 118–19, 307, 446–48
Caṇḍīmaṅgala, 122–23
Candragupta Maurya, 120, 170, 183–84, 255, 283
Candra Gupta II, 126
Candravaṃśa, 83, 84–85, 86, 87–88, 94, 107, 108, 109–10, 137–38, 191–92, 434, 463–64
canonization, 31–32, 254–55
Cāṇūra, 249–50, 251–52, 253–54, 271

capital
  of Kurus, 22–23, 30–31, 129, 240–41, 466–67
  of Magadha, 22, 281–82, 283–84
capture of booty, 52–53
capture of cow, 458
capture of Duryodhana, 160–61
capture of Elephants, 169
captured kings and barons, 160–61, 279, 293–94, 297
captured women, 89, 104, 292, 293
cardinal
  sins, 143, 144
  virtues, 200, 202–3, 338–39, 397
career
  of Kṛṣṇa, 239, 276–77, 284, 287, 291–92, 299–300, 301–2, 311, 346–47
  of Paraśurāma, 450–51, 452
  of Sudās, 62
carnage, 113, 120, 433
Cārvākas, 344–45, 380, 429
caste, xi, 5, 133, 166, 192, 199, 209–10, 302, 307, 322–23, 325, 347–48, 349, 381, 384–85, 386–87, 407–8, 424, 445–46, 452
categories of heirs, 92–93
cattle, 1, 25, 33–34, 44, 50, 52, 68–69, 81–82, 111, 120, 131, 133, 134–35, 142, 149, 153–54, 155–56, 157–58, 159–61, 163, 165–66, 251–52, 258, 263, 264, 274, 276, 290–91, 312, 366, 383, 443, 462–63
cāturvarṇya, 426–29
cavalry, 155–56, 164, 165–66, 168, 169, 170, 172, 173–74
Chakravarti, Ranabir, 153–54
Chakrabarti, Shirshendu, 208–9
Chakravarti, Uma, 90, 92, 105–7, 151, 198
challenge
  to a duel, 279, 294–95
  to a game of dice, 130, 136, 137, 145–46, 147, 152
  to the idea of Bhārgavization, 425–26
  to Kṛṣṇa, 301–2, 312–13, 373
  to the law of primogeniture, 107, 110–11
  to Rāma, 459–60
  to the Vedic orthodoxy, 28–29, 199, 209, 264, 282–83, 291–92, 301–2, 309–10, 322–23, 363–64, 407–8, 429–30, 445–46, 454
changes reflected by the *Mahābhārata*, xi–xii, 115–16, 169, 194–95, 214, 424–25
charioteer, 27–28, 132–34, 135, 164–67, 173, 175–76, 215, 240–41, 242, 333, 334, 340–41, 343, 346–47, 388–89, 392–93
chariots, 26–27, 52–53, 113, 131, 132–34, 135–37, 148, 153, 155–56, 164–68, 169–70, 171–72, 173–74, 193, 198–99, 287–88, 290–91, 298, 329, 332, 346–47, 353, 392–93, 396, 401, 402, 444
Chatterjee, Gautam, 109–10
Chatterjee, J.M., 450
Chattopadhyay, Bankim Chandra, 243–44, 259, 265, 304, 357, 361, 389, 394, 396, 398–99
Chattopadhyaya, B.D., 22–23, 122–23
Cherniak, Alex, 355–56
chief ministers, 166–67
chief queen/wife/consort, 132–33, 135–36, 253–54, 270–71, 307
chiefs/chieftains, xiv, 1, 5, 7–8, 9–10, 25, 26, 32–33, 43–44, 49, 50, 52–53, 58–59, 61, 62–63, 64, 70–71, 72–73, 82–83, 86, 108–9, 112, 118, 121, 122–23, 127, 129, 131, 132, 137, 153–54, 155, 160–63, 165, 169, 171, 180, 191–92, 209–10, 237, 240–41, 243, 244, 249–51, 256–57, 260, 276–77, 278, 279, 281, 282–84, 286, 292–95, 298, 299, 300, 301, 303–4, 306, 307, 319, 333, 430–31, 439–40, 445–46, 461–62
Childe, V. Gordon, 1–2, 22–23
childhood of Kṛṣṇa, 237–38, 241, 242, 244, 249–50, 251–52, 255–56, 257–59, 265, 269, 271, 274, 275, 296, 314–15
childless man, 100–1, 195
childless widow, 95, 98–99
Chinese, 6, 20, 131, 341

choice
of Karṇa, 332–33
of ruler, 191–92
of sexual partner, 92–93, 96, 100–1, 102–3, 104, 105–7, 110–11, 289–91, 293, 299
Choudhary, Pradeep Kant, 60, 451, 454, 456, 457–58
Christ, 11, 242
Christianity, 356–57
chronology, 2–3, 7, 9, 12–13, 28, 338–39, 463
churning of the Ocean, 113, 124, 309
Cilappaṭikāram, 22–23, 255, 267, 270
Citramahas, 46
Citrāṅgada, 110
Citrāṅgadā, 94, 95, 127
Citraratha, 440, 451
Citravāhana, 94
clan system, xi, 11, 25, 26–27, 32–33, 44–45, 46–47, 51, 65, 67–69, 83, 84, 89, 90–91, 95, 96, 97–98, 102, 104, 105, 110–11, 126, 131, 135, 137–38, 146, 149–50, 151, 152–53, 155–56, 159, 160–63, 168, 172, 177–79, 183, 184–85, 186, 191–92, 203–4, 208, 209–10, 213, 238, 239–41, 247–48, 249–52, 256, 257, 258–59, 272–73, 289–90, 305, 306, 307–8, 312, 337, 338–39, 344–45, 391, 404–6, 424–25, 454, 462, 467
clash
of clans, xiii, 191–92, 215, 314
of ideas, 105–7, 348
with Nāgas, 159, 260, 465–66
with non-Vedic people, 172
of succession norms, 212, 463–64
classical epics, 17, 26–27, 28, 340–41
classical religion, 44, 71–72, 124, 136–37, 263, 284, 322–23, 344–45, 375–76
Classical historians, 6, 342–43
clearance of forest, 111–12, 115–17, 119–20, 127–28, 129, 291, 293–94
code of valour, 19, 27–28, 104, 110, 124, 126, 138, 163, 175–76, 196–97, 208–10, 212, 243, 324, 385–86, 389–91, 401, 424–25, 433, 463–64
codification of a text, 11, 67–68, 254–55
coins, 154, 169, 184, 249
collaterals, 1–2, 83, 84, 88–89, 107, 110
collection
of hymns, 44, 52, 54, 60–61, 63
of legends, 188, 246–47, 249, 453
of poems, 255
of tax and tributes, 132, 133, 258, 293, 299
colonial learning, 4, 5
combatants, 163, 172–73, 175, 240–41, 242
combats, 11, 173–74, 177, 193, 264, 391, 402–3, 454–55, 456
commentaries of texts, 249, 356–57, 442
commentators, 13, 356–57
committee, 180–82, 186
compassion, x–xi, 98–99, 193, 324, 371, 388, 400–1
competition, 131, 154, 289–90
complex society, 1, 122–23, 149–50, 191
components
of army, 163–64, 168, 169, 171
of an ideal, 212–13
of a legend, 457–58
of wealth, 153–54
composers, 7–8, 46, 51, 82–83, 188–89, 190, 198–99, 375–76, 436
composition of texts, ix–x, 1–3, 7–8, 12–13, 24, 25–27, 43–45, 46–47, 49–50, 51, 52, 56, 70–71, 72–73, 163–64, 180–82, 184–85, 186, 286–87, 300, 338–39, 343, 370, 407–8, 424–25, 426–28, 443, 455, 461–62
conditions of marriage, 94, 293
conduct, 200, 207, 324, 361, 365, 371, 423, 433
confederacy
of Vedic tribes, 7–8, 53, 61–62
of the Yādavas, 249–50, 256, 283
conflict
between Aryans and non-Aryans, 118, 127–28, 155–56, 260
between *brāhmaṇas* and *kṣatriyas*, 12, 43, 178, 425–26, 428, 445–46, 457–58, 464
between Devas and Asuras, 21

conflict (*cont.*)
between/within clans, x–xii, 107, 111–12, 178, 191, 203, 213, 240–41, 242, 250–51, 254, 272, 278, 280, 282, 293–94, 298, 299–300, 305, 306, 312, 462–63
between sects, xiii, 260, 281, 284, 291–92, 300
between succession norms, 108–9, 177–78, 191–92
between Viśvāmitra and Vasiṣṭha, 43–44, 54, 66, 68, 69, 72–73, 439, 440, 441, 442, 444–45, 448, 464
consecration, 133–34, 135, 170, 286, 331
consequences
of action, 356–57, 404–5
of choice, 400
of curse, 68, 212–13, 214
of dicing, 142, 145–46
of magic, 458
of ritual, 152
of war, 28–29, 159, 390–91
conspiracy, 203, 271–72, 274, 276, 302, 303
contest
between *brāhmaṇas* and *kṣatriyas*, 428, 437–38, 460, 464–65
between settled society and forest, 126
between Sudās and the ten kings, 52–53
between *vāsudeva* and *prativāsudeva*, 241, 242, 284, 302
for marriage, 105–7, 267
in a sacrifice, 55–56, 69, 70
in a war, 175–76, 194–95
over succession, 133–38, 151, 162–63, 196, 463–64
over a woman's womb, 94, 95–96
context
historical, xiii, 12–13, 15–16, 26–28, 32, 33–34, 43–44, 48, 50–51, 72–73, 81–82, 88–89, 90–91, 92, 96, 98–99, 100, 102, 105–7, 110–12, 117, 129, 131–32, 148, 152–53, 155, 156, 157, 158, 159–60, 163–64, 167, 168, 170, 171–72, 173–74, 179–80, 182–83, 186, 187–88, 194, 196–97, 200–1, 203–4, 214, 244–45, 282–83, 338–39, 340–41, 344–45, 357, 423, 426–28, 429, 430–32, 442, 455–56, 459, 461, 462–63
narrative, xii–xiii, 19–20, 83, 86, 108, 133, 135, 139–40, 143, 151, 188–90, 201–3, 244, 298, 304–5, 334, 335, 336, 340, 343, 346–47, 358–59, 386–87, 398, 453, 465–66
ritual, 8, 121–22, 133–34, 137–38, 145–46, 152
contextuality of *dharma*, 398–99, 400–1
continuity of family line, 55–57, 90, 245–46
continuity of polyandry, 96–97
contrasting ideas, 17, 54–55, 105–7, 119–20, 121–22, 173–74, 200–1, 205, 340–41, 347, 360, 387, 430–31, 437–38
contribution
of Paraśurāma, 428
of Vasiṣṭha, 43–44, 56–57, 461–62
of Vyāsa, 188, 189–90
control
over a territory/clan, xii, 50–51, 52–53, 71, 120, 153–54, 155–56, 159, 184, 240–41, 258, 283, 314–15, 404–5
over a text, 8, 25, 180–82, 187, 424–25, 457–58, 464–65
over a woman, 19, 90–91, 92–93, 95, 102–3, 147, 148–49
over senses, 316, 319, 331, 362–64, 369–70, 371, 373, 374–75, 444, 455
core of a text, xiii–xiv, 11, 14, 152–53, 337, 386–87
corpus
Bhārgava, 67
Brahmanical, 113
Buddhist, 32–33
Occidental, 6
Vedic, 28–29, 31–33, 52, 64–65, 67, 69–70, 72–73, 86–87, 179–80, 182–83, 191, 450–51
corroboration, 2–3, 12, 15–16, 24, 25, 30, 82, 461

costume, 115
counsel, 240–41, 243, 245–46, 302, 333, 386, 394
counsellors, 130, 160–61, 240–41, 260
court, 24, 130, 142, 145–46, 180, 185–86, 195, 203–4, 205, 206, 247–48, 271, 275, 286, 311, 317, 321, 322, 331, 334–35, 343, 348, 401–238, 463–64
courtesans, 148–49, 329
cousins, 26–27, 105, 135–36, 152, 163, 208, 240–41, 253–54, 287, 290, 297, 312, 317, 323
cowardice, 204, 243, 324, 328, 329, 349
cowherds, 155–56, 157–58, 239–41, 249–50, 251–52, 255, 257, 258–59, 260, 261, 264–65, 266–67, 268–70, 271, 274, 276–77, 278, 286–87, 291, 297, 298, 302, 303, 311–13, 314–15, 320, 334–35, 344–45, 366, 387, 407–8
cows, 52–53, 54–55, 70, 111, 135, 154, 155–56, 158, 159, 173–74, 238, 261–62, 263, 265, 267, 272, 372, 435–36, 440, 441–44, 448, 457–58
Creation, 51, 85, 101, 145–46, 345–46
Creator, 187–88, 331, 341, 371–72, 436–37
creatures, 85, 87, 113–14, 116–17, 119–20, 152, 193–94, 207, 278, 300, 301, 315–16, 318–19, 323, 370, 371–72, 399
crime, 206, 297, 306, 312, 320, 321–22, 397, 398, 406, 433, 448
crisis, 28–29, 100–1, 161–62, 191–92, 313–14, 338, 346–48, 349, 394, 463
Critical Edition, xiii, 14–16, 20–21, 26–27, 28–29, 154, 243, 285–86
critique, 200–1, 208, 259–60
crops, 158, 261–62
crossing of rivers, 47–48, 50–51, 59, 62, 65
crown gem, 208
cruelty, 120, 203, 207–8, 213, 214, 321–22, 390–91, 428
cult
 of *bhakti*, 57
 of fertility, 344–46
 of fire, 53–54, 67
 of heroes, 27–28
 of Indra, 43–44, 56–57, 71–72, 260, 263, 264, 274, 285–86, 291–92, 301–2, 318, 461–62
 of Kāmākhyā, 292–93
 of Kṛṣṇa, xiii, 177–78, 182–83, 243, 310–11, 338–39, 376–77
 of Nāgas, 259–60, 291–92, 301–2
 of Varuṇa, 43–44, 56–57, 71–72, 461–62
 of Yakṣas, 260
cultivation, xiv, 114, 115–17, 121–22, 141, 154, 263, 264, 319, 362–63, 369–70
Curtius, 169, 248
custodians, 8, 98–99, 177–78, 435, 465
customs, 84, 92–93, 95–100, 102, 103–4, 105–7, 349
Cyavana, 439–40, 443, 452, 458
cycle
 of legends, 43–44, 126, 242, 426, 446, 454, 467
 of transmigration, 345–46, 363–64, 388
 of *yuga*, 27–29, 144, 277, 280
Cypria, 18

Dabhīti, 48
Dadhikrā, 52
Dahlmann, Joseph, 13, 21
Dakṣa, 84–85, 88
Dākṣāyanī, 85, 88
dalliance, 241, 249–50, 271
Damana, 99–100
Damayantī, 105–7, 143–46
dānastuti, 5, 7–8
Dānavas, 113–14, 127–28, 193–94, 265
dance, 155–56, 255, 260, 266–68, 269–70, 274, 354, 393–94, 403
Dange, Sadashiva A., 55–56
darkness, 21, 111–12, 195, 261–62, 316, 327, 358–59, 377–78, 382, 407–8, 428
Dasabrāhmaṇa Jātaka, 30–31, 129, 466–67
Daśajyoti, 85
daśapeya, 135

dāśarājña, 7–8, 10, 32–33
Daśaratha, 131, 444–45
Dāśārha, 295–96, 327, 328, 329–30
Daśārṇas, 171
Dāsas, xi–xii, 43–44, 48, 49, 50, 52–53, 58–59, 117, 166–67, 172, 261
dāsīs, xi–xii, 100–1, 102–3, 142, 177–78, 195, 214
dasyus, 50, 52, 56, 70–71, 172, 206, 261
date of Kṛṣṇa legends, 243, 246–47, 254–55, 281, 286
date of the *Mahābhārata*, x, 4, 11, 12–13, 22, 23, 24, 81, 131, 163–64, 182, 194, 209–10, 334–35, 336, 338–39, 341–42, 344–45, 453, 465–66
daughters, 30, 59–60, 82, 85, 86, 87–89, 94, 95–96, 99–100, 109, 149, 151, 178, 213–14, 249–54, 257, 258, 267, 273, 279, 283, 286, 288, 289–91, 292, 303–4, 312, 439, 451
Dawn, 51, 54–55
Dayal, Naina, 25–26
death of
  Abhimanyu, 392
  Bhīṣma, 18–19
  Droṇa, 395
  Duryodhana, 173–74, 192, 193–94, 195
  Ghaṭotkaca, 202–3, 393–94
  Haṃsa, 284
  Jarāsaṃdha, 295
  Kaṃsa, 247, 274, 275, 279, 284–85
  Karṇa, 196, 198–99, 332–33, 402, 432
  Kīcaka, 157–58
  Kṛṣṇa, 254, 407
  the Pāñcālas, 178–79
  Parikṣit, 126
  Śalya, 11
  Satrājit, 306, 307
  Śiśupāla, 297, 298
  Vasiṣṭha, 56–57
  Vasiṣṭha's sons, 68, 69, 441, 442
  Vyāsa, 188–89, 254, 405–6
Death, 54, 134–35, 136–37, 199–200, 239, 247, 272, 279–80, 315–16, 325, 328, 343, 345–46, 348, 351, 352, 354, 362–63, 377, 378, 388, 391, 428, 452, 456
debates, x–xi, 1, 5, 9, 43–44, 50–51, 59–60, 91, 138, 146, 147, 148, 149–50, 173, 206–7, 214, 239, 295, 297, 311–13, 322, 327, 333, 335, 336, 340, 389, 400, 404–5, 429, 445–46, 448–49
decay, 27–28, 133–34, 430
deceit, 172, 197–98, 203, 243, 281, 400
dedication to deities, 49–50, 51, 52, 55–56, 60–61, 115–16, 340–41
deer hunt, 201–2
defeat, 43–44, 48–49, 52–53, 59, 62–63, 66, 69, 104, 105–7, 113, 114–15, 125, 136–37, 138, 143–44, 152, 160–61, 168, 214, 249–51, 253–54, 256, 279, 281, 282, 283–84, 285, 289, 298–99, 300, 301, 303–4, 308, 309–10, 315–16, 317, 325, 326, 327, 334–35, 353, 401, 402, 429–30, 439–40, 441–42, 444, 459–62, 464–65
defection, 62–63
definition
  of history, 6
  of *itihāsa*, 8–9, 10
  of just war, 175
  of *svadharma*, 366
  of *varṇa*, 385–86
  of *vāsudeva*, 278
deforestation, 155
deformities, 195, 201, 212–13
deification, 28–29, 55–56, 125, 129, 239, 264–65, 302, 331–32, 334–35, 407–8
deities, 12, 16, 18, 21, 47, 49–51, 52, 53–54, 57, 70–71, 85, 86, 88, 95, 98–100, 125, 127–28, 143–44, 198–99, 237–38, 242, 246–48, 250–52, 253–54, 255, 259, 261–62, 263, 264–65, 274, 280, 283–84, 291–92, 296, 299, 309–10, 331, 334–35, 337, 338–39, 365, 374–75, 381, 388, 393–94, 395, 407–8, 435, 446–47
demand
  of devotion, 336–37, 357, 461
  of gifts, 50–51

of heir, 95, 102
of narrative, 67–68
of sacrifice, 71, 121
of succession, 109
demigod, 242, 243, 264–65, 280, 302, 311–12, 435, 462–63
demons, 18, 21, 111–12, 137–38, 174, 194, 241, 249–50, 265–66, 282–83, 292–93, 380, 381, 407–8, 424–25, 428, 429, 443, 457–59
descent, 83, 133–34, 424–25
Deshpande, M.M., 244, 340, 376, 424–25
designs, 71, 90–91, 105, 139, 177–78, 212–13, 249–50, 258–59, 281, 284, 289, 290, 291, 293–94, 429–30, 435, 456
desire, 50–51, 90, 91, 126–27, 154, 188–89, 194, 210, 214, 247, 268, 272, 276–77, 304, 305–6, 308–9, 317, 319, 320, 321, 322–23, 326–27, 333, 353–54, 358–59, 360, 361–63, 364, 365, 366–68, 374–75, 388, 397, 447
desireless action, 345–46, 355–56, 361–63, 365, 366–67, 374, 387, 463–64
despot, 182, 200, 275
destruction, 30, 50–51, 55, 114, 124, 131, 137–38, 145–46, 172, 192, 193, 260, 315, 317, 350, 363, 369–70, 391, 398, 404, 428, 442, 452–53
destruction of the Yādavas, 18, 188–89, 252, 304, 307, 404–6
determinism, 115–16, 145
Devagabbhā, 251–52, 258–59
Devaka, 249–50
Devakī, 247–48, 249–50, 253–54, 257–58
Devāpi, 7–8, 9–10, 30, 64, 108–9, 110, 191–92, 462
Devas, 12, 21, 47, 51, 52, 114–15, 124, 137–38, 169, 212, 261, 292, 435–36
Devaśarman, 443
Devasena, 253–54
Devaśravas, 51, 58, 62–63
devastation, xiv, 28–29, 172, 288, 317
Devasthali, G.V., 352
Devavat, 52–53, 58–59
Devavrata, 109, 191–92, 430
Devayānī, 82–83, 105–7, 203–4
devotees, 57, 124, 125, 174, 237–38, 241, 248–49, 269, 287, 297, 320, 357, 375, 377, 387, 432–33
devotion, 8, 26–27, 54, 57, 93, 125, 196, 252–53, 254–55, 336–37, 341, 374–75, 377, 386–87, 407–8
dexterity, 238, 296
Dharma, 16, 115, 191–92, 202–3, 313, 442
dharma, 9, 13, 28–29, 90–91, 92–93, 105, 114, 121–22, 125, 146, 173–75, 190, 192, 198–99, 200–1, 202–4, 207, 209–10, 212–13, 215, 243, 263, 310–11, 312, 313, 317, 318, 322–23, 325, 327, 328, 330, 331–32, 336, 348–49, 353, 368–69, 385–86, 394, 395, 397, 398–99, 400–1, 402, 406, 407–8, 423–24, 430–31, 433–35, 445–46, 459–60
Dharmarāja, 144, 150, 200, 201, 313, 327, 395, 423, 429–30
dharmarājya, 429–30
Dharmaśāstras, 98–99, 104, 180–82, 186, 358, 360
Dharmasūtras, 98–99, 148–49, 248, 259
Dharmavyādha, 200–1, 435–36
dharmayuddha, 173–76, 177–78, 389, 391
Dhaumya, 135–36, 160–61
Dhṛṣṭadyumna, 101, 102, 108, 127, 175–76, 178–79, 302, 394
Dhṛtarāṣṭra, 17, 24, 30, 64–65, 81, 84, 100–1, 108–9, 110, 112, 126, 130, 139–40, 144, 145–46, 151, 152, 155–56, 160–62, 167–68, 175, 177–78, 180, 183, 185–86, 191–92, 195, 202–4, 211, 212–13, 290, 297, 312–13, 314, 316, 317, 318, 320, 321, 322, 325, 329, 333–34, 343, 430–31
dialogues, 8–9, 166, 342–43, 387, 436–37, 448–49
dice game, 33–34, 81–82, 129, 130–31, 132–37, 139–40, 141–44, 145–46, 148, 149, 151, 152–53, 159–61, 174, 176, 202–3, 205, 240–41, 253–54, 311, 313–14, 327, 401, 403, 424, 432, 462–63

didactic sections, xiii, 9, 12, 13, 25–26, 28–29, 33–34, 66, 81–82, 124, 152–53, 201, 241–42, 335, 337, 360, 430–31, 435–36
diet, 117
dignitaries, 133–34, 240–41
dilemmas, 124, 174, 208–9, 312, 336, 337, 340–41, 346–47, 400
Diodorus, 131
Dionysus, 286
diplomacy, 121, 159–60, 163, 173–74, 290–91, 299–300, 303, 307–8, 311, 312
diplomats, 128, 239, 276, 291–92, 294–95, 302, 303, 306, 311–12, 343
Dīrghatamas, 99–100, 102–3
discourse, 15–16, 28–29, 151, 180, 200–1, 207, 213–14, 237–38, 333, 335, 342–43, 346–47, 387, 389, 396–97, 444, 445
discrepancies, 84, 363–64, 436
disguise, 98–99, 151, 152–53, 156, 157–58, 201–3, 206, 279, 289–90, 294–95, 311, 314, 348, 393, 430–31, 445, 457
disjuncture, 191–92
dismissal of an idea, 356–57, 361, 428–29
display
  of Cosmic Form, 331, 336–37
  of power, 120
  of sexual desire, 126–27, 151
  of supernatural ability, 193
  of wealth, 155–56
disregard, 109–10, 176, 293, 325, 328, 432
dissent, xi–xii, 191, 384, 407–8
distinction
  between *adoidos* and *rhapsoidos*, 185–86
  between *brāhmaṇa* and *kṣatriya*, 433, 437–38
  between different versions of the same legend, 453
  between forest dwellers and settled people, 121
  between history and historical tradition, ix
  between just and unjust war, 173–74, 175
  between mind and body, 356–57
  between subordinate and marginalized groups, 117
distribution of wealth, 132, 154, 155, 456
divinity, 12, 20–21, 100, 134–35, 187, 237–38, 240–41, 243, 266, 270–71, 297, 299, 302, 312–13, 315, 316–17, 331, 334–35, 338–39, 340, 343, 346–47, 368, 369–70, 389, 424–25, 432–33, 460, 464
division of kingdom, 33–34
division of property, 97, 146
divisions
  of the army, 166–67, 170
  of *karman*, 358–59
  of knowledge, 263
Divodāsa, 31, 43–44, 49, 58–59, 62, 439–40
Doab, xii, 64, 115–17, 157–58, 173–74, 257, 258, 283, 287
doctrines, 209, 247, 299–300, 322, 335–39, 340–41, 343–44, 348, 351, 354, 355–57, 359, 361–62, 363–64, 366–67, 368, 369, 371, 374–76, 378, 379, 381–82, 386–87, 388, 407–8, 428–29
dog-eaters, 447, 448, 449
dogs, 202–3, 214, 325, 372
doubts about norms, 200, 317, 338–39, 344–45, 353
Draupadī, x, 13, 16–17, 18, 19–21, 26, 30–31, 32–33, 96, 97, 101, 102, 105–7, 108, 112, 130, 135–36, 138, 142, 144, 145–47, 148, 149–50, 151–52, 153, 156, 178–79, 197–99, 202–3, 205, 206–8, 240–41, 242, 253–54, 262, 289–90, 291, 299, 302, 311, 312–13, 314, 321, 323, 327, 328, 360, 402–3, 404
drinking, 254, 318, 404–5
drinking of blood, 203–4
Droṇa, 11, 101, 103, 157–58, 160, 163, 175–76, 178–79, 194–95, 196, 197–98, 203, 242–43, 245–46, 284, 295–96, 302, 314, 317, 340–41, 385–86, 388, 389, 392, 394–97, 398, 400–1, 404, 426, 453, 454
Droṇaparvan, 392, 452, 453

Dṛṣadvatī, 59, 64–65
Druhyus, 48, 52–53, 59–60, 61–63, 82–83, 439–40, 456–57
drunkenness, 240–41, 242–43, 251–52, 254, 404–5
Drupada, 30, 101, 160, 163, 178, 289–90, 295–96, 312–13, 314–15, 317, 394
dualism, 340–41, 429
duels, 124, 163, 167–68, 175–76, 240–41, 253–54, 279, 294–95, 297, 303–4, 391, 403, 459–60
Duḥśalā, 213–14
Duḥśāsana, 130, 135–36, 160, 163, 203–4, 327–28, 401
Dumezil, Georges, 16–17, 19, 21, 244
Duryodhana, 11, 19, 104, 110, 129, 130, 135–36, 137, 138, 145–46, 150, 151, 152, 155–56, 157, 159, 160–62, 163, 167–68, 172–74, 175–76, 182, 191–95, 196–98, 200, 203–4, 207, 208, 213–14, 240–41, 242–43, 245–46, 274, 275, 278, 285, 301–2, 304, 306, 312–15, 317, 320, 321, 322–24, 325, 326–27, 328, 329–30, 331–33, 353, 388–89, 390–91, 393–94, 401, 402–4, 429–30
Dūtavākyam, 194, 249, 275, 285
duty, 8–9, 16, 21, 98, 139–40, 147, 151, 160–61, 166–67, 190, 206–7, 210, 214, 310–11, 312, 318, 320, 321, 322–23, 328, 332, 338–40, 343, 346–48, 349, 352, 353, 356–57, 365, 366, 374–75, 383–86, 387, 396, 403–4, 424, 430, 433–34, 435–36, 458–59, 463–64
Dvaipāyana, 21, 30–31, 32, 179–80, 188–89, 190–91, 251–52, 254, 295–96, 405–6
Dvaipāyana Lake, 402
Dvaita forest, 81–82, 120, 155–56, 157–58, 193–94, 258
Dvāpara, 10, 28–29, 123–24, 143–44, 145–46, 430
Dvārakā/Dvārāvatī, 30–31, 129, 240–41, 242, 244–45, 250–54, 278–79, 285, 287, 297, 298, 304, 305–6, 307, 391, 404–5
Dyaus, 52
dynasty, 107, 466–67
Dyumnīka, 46

Early Medieval period, 13, 209–10
Early Vedic period, 9–10, 43, 98–99, 127–28
Earth (goddess), 18, 104, 287–88, 292–93, 319, 435
ecology, 116–17
economy, 1, 8–9, 25, 26–27, 28, 88–89, 90–91, 129, 148–49, 152–54, 155, 157, 158, 163, 283–84, 285, 329, 335–36, 430–31, 462–63
ecosystem, 383–84
edicts, x, 119–20, 121, 183–84
education, 4, 8, 148–50, 201
Ekalavya, 195, 393–94
elementary hero, 196
elephants, 29, 113–14, 119–20, 131, 153, 154, 155–56, 164, 165–66, 168–72, 173–74, 206–7, 276, 329, 372, 394, 400–1, 444
embodiment of all deities, 49–50
emergence
  of *janapadas*, 22–23
  of kingship, 168
  of new kind of heroes, 214, 243, 259
  of philosophical schools, 189–90
  of rituals, 5
  of towns, 166–67
  of *varṇa* system, 189–90, 462
empathy, x–xi, 201–3, 210, 212, 463–64
emperors of Magadha, xiii, 122–23, 156, 281, 282
empires, 21, 171, 184, 209, 283, 458–59
ends, 57, 104, 174, 175–76, 237
enemy, 18, 30, 48, 50–51, 52, 53–54, 55, 58–59, 102, 104, 111, 113–14, 124, 146, 172, 175, 192, 207, 214, 240–41, 253–54, 282, 285–86, 289, 294–95, 298, 300, 314, 326, 327–29, 333, 340–41, 367–68, 369, 374, 380, 388, 393, 396, 402, 433
enigma, 237, 239, 312–13
Enkidu, 124, 125–26
enmity, 50–51, 155–56, 294–95, 314, 444

environment, 18, 117, 328
envoy, 165, 166, 170, 248–49, 317, 321, 322–23, 328, 330, 331, 333
envy, 129, 157–58, 433–34
Epic of Gilgamesh, 124
epics, ix–x, xi–xiv, 11–12, 13, 16–17, 18–19, 20–23, 25–26, 27–28, 30, 83, 94, 119, 120–21, 124, 126, 147, 160–61, 168, 173–74, 175, 179–82, 187–88, 190, 196–97, 198, 203–4, 205, 211, 212–13, 237, 239, 242, 243, 244, 255, 267, 270, 335–37, 340–41, 343, 389, 390, 431–32, 438–40, 445, 453, 454, 455–56, 458–59, 461, 465
epitaph, 55–56
Erikson, Erik, 56
escape, 113, 167–68, 185–86, 193, 249–50, 387
essayist, 243–44
essays, 119–20, 179, 244, 356–57
establishment
  of hegemony, 9–10
  of hereditary monarchy, 105, 169
  of Indraprastha, 33–34, 81–82, 112, 129, 159–60, 240–41, 291, 293–94
  of new kind of heroes, 201, 203, 208
  of righteousness, 369–70, 464
  of sedentary agricultural culture, 88–89, 117, 128, 159–60, 369–70, 463–64
eternal
  Brahman, 363–64, 373, 374–75
  dharma, 91, 92–93, 105–7, 208, 210, 312, 313, 322, 325, 330, 331–32, 349
  dilemma, 346–47, 386–87
  glory, 198–99
  knowledge, 354, 368, 370
  opposition, 125
  poet, 185–86, 187–88
  sacrifice, 366–67
  sages, 19–20, 370, 373, 374–75, 379, 380, 386–87
  soul, 350, 351, 352
  tree, 379, 380
  union, 345–46
ethics, 13, 124–25, 163–64, 172, 173–74, 175–76, 208–9, 243, 293, 294–95, 296, 303, 311, 312–13, 317, 323, 331–33, 337–38, 340–41, 384, 387, 389, 390–91, 395, 396–97, 398–99, 400–1, 403–4, 433, 456–57
ethos, x, 172–73
European historiography, 2, 6
evidence, 12–13, 15–16, 19, 22, 25, 32–33, 57, 62, 67–68, 69, 82, 154, 165, 183–84, 186, 188, 338–39, 341–42, 384–85, 431–32, 438, 442, 445, 450, 454, 461
evil, 17, 25–26, 53–54, 92, 118, 122–23, 134–35, 139–40, 144, 172–73, 175, 205, 271, 317, 321, 325, 326, 328–29, 333, 353, 372, 386, 389, 390–91, 395, 396, 403, 433, 456, 460
evolution of military ethics, 173–74
excellence, 55–56, 67, 121–22, 164, 167–68, 237–38, 454
exceptions, 4–5, 51, 100, 163, 387, 390–91, 402–3
exchange
  of children, 251–52, 253–54
  of curses, 58
  of gifts, 25, 131, 137, 154
  of signals, 269
  of value, 154, 430–31
  of women, 89–90
  of youth, 82
exclusion, 60–61, 117–18
exile, xii–xiii, 99–100, 120–21, 130, 142, 144, 152–53, 155–56, 160, 161–62, 169, 203, 240–41, 245–46, 253–54, 285–86, 307–8, 311, 312, 323, 392, 398–99, 448
expansion of power, 43–44, 280
expeditions, 120–21, 155–56, 241, 250–51
expiation, 436
exploits, 48, 50, 249, 252, 259, 452
exposition, 311–12, 318, 328, 331–32, 334–36, 342–43, 371, 374–75, 383
expression, 90–91, 205, 259, 334
expulsion, 44–45, 282–83, 434
extermination, 211, 212, 256, 428, 457–58

fabrication, 242, 258–59, 274, 306, 448
facts, 2–3, 5–6, 7, 9, 12–13, 15–16, 19–20, 22–23, 28, 89–90, 103, 115–16, 463, 465
faith, 175, 279–80, 326–27, 338, 403, 428–29
faithfulness, 141, 206, 375, 431
faithlessness, 92, 272
fall of a hero, 11, 95–96, 176, 194, 245–46, 343, 349, 392, 400–1, 404, 430
falsehood, 55, 395–97, 398–99, 442
family books, 31, 43, 44–47, 49–50, 51, 60–61, 67
family, 7–8, 13, 18, 52–53, 56–57, 62–63, 67–68, 70, 71–72, 81, 82, 94, 96–99, 105–7, 110–11, 121, 139, 148–49, 155–56, 161–62, 164, 212–13, 239, 276, 298, 305, 311, 326–27, 329, 333–34, 349, 431, 439, 443, 446, 447, 448
fantasy, xii, 14, 111–12, 120–22, 126–27, 259, 445
fasting, 435–36
fate, 44, 139, 167, 245–46, 331, 333, 376–77, 456
fathers, 18, 49, 51, 55–56, 58–59, 68–69, 82, 86, 87, 88, 91, 93–94, 95–96, 101, 108, 113, 114–15, 118–19, 126, 127–28, 137–38, 141, 148–49, 154, 160–61, 191–92, 194–95, 197–99, 200, 201–4, 205, 208, 210, 238, 249–50, 253–54, 257, 263, 269, 272, 275, 277, 295–96, 297, 307–8, 314, 325, 327–29, 333–34, 392, 393, 398–99, 424–25, 432–33, 448–50, 451, 452–53, 455, 463–64
feud, 62, 110–11, 155–56, 212–13, 239, 311, 326, 440–41, 465–66
fight, 11, 18, 51, 65, 105–7, 124, 125, 129, 137–38, 163, 164, 165, 167–68, 170, 171, 172–73, 175–76, 178–79, 204, 208, 214, 240–41, 245–46, 248, 252–53, 261, 264–65, 274, 279, 284–86, 296, 297, 301–2, 309–11, 312–13, 322–23, 325, 327–28, 333, 334, 338–39, 340, 346–48, 350, 352, 353, 359–60, 367–68, 385–86, 387, 388–89, 392–93, 394, 395, 397, 402–3, 404–5, 424, 429–31, 437, 451, 457–58, 460
fighters, 65, 171, 173–74, 298
Findly, Ellison Banks, 56, 442, 443
fire, xiv, 49–50, 53–55, 67, 68, 69, 101–2, 112, 113–14, 115–16, 120, 121–22, 124, 125–26, 129, 141, 185–86, 206–7, 251–52, 287–88, 301, 318, 327–28, 350, 370, 371, 374–75, 382, 383, 450, 457
Firishta, 4
fishermen/fisherwomen, 109, 119–20, 187, 191–92
fishes, 61, 86–87, 113, 325
Fitzgerald, James, 21, 190, 433, 455–56, 458–59
flight, 242
flirting, 239, 398
flood, 22–23, 31–32, 66, 86–87, 388, 441, 466–67
flute, 239, 266, 267
foe, 57, 146, 194–95, 203, 237, 261, 284, 285–86, 302, 317, 328, 346–47, 348, 367–68, 372, 374, 377, 397
foetus, 90–91, 101–2, 272
folk
  beliefs, 337
  hero, 241
  legends, 143–44, 246–47, 254–55
  poems, 255
followers
  of Aurva, 456
  of Duryodhana, 192–93
  of Kṛṣṇa, 177–78, 237–38, 261, 277, 293–94, 334–35
  of Paraśurāma, 451, 453
  of Śaṅkara, 358–59
  of Varcin, 49
  of *varṇa* order, 200, 423
folly, 139–40, 272, 299, 314, 397
fondness, 241, 287
food, 12, 111, 238, 264, 272, 296–97, 329, 330, 373, 423, 433–34, 443, 445, 447

force, 28–29, 48, 49, 66, 82–83, 102–3, 104, 105–7, 111–12, 113, 119–20, 124, 125–26, 128, 141, 160–61, 163, 164, 165–66, 169, 171, 173–74, 185, 193–94, 239, 240–41, 245–46, 265, 274, 284, 286, 287, 290–91, 300, 314, 320, 329, 346–47, 389, 394, 395, 400, 404, 431–32, 440, 441–42
foreign elements, 5, 62, 117, 152, 441–42
forest, xii, 33–34, 65, 81–82, 85, 89, 99–100, 103, 110–14, 115–29, 139–40, 143–44, 152–53, 155–56, 159–60, 161–62, 170, 180–82, 185–86, 193–94, 206–7, 211–12, 239–41, 245–46, 250–51, 254, 258, 263, 264, 276, 290, 291–92, 293–94, 301–2, 303–4, 311, 323, 327, 348, 398–99, 404–5, 406, 424–25, 435, 448, 462–63
forgiving, 207, 212, 309, 317, 324, 371, 381, 454–56
formation
  of alliances, 159–60, 163
  of army, 167–68, 392
  of empire, 282–83
  of a legend, 457–58
  of state, 105, 110–11, 115–16, 344–45, 431–32, 462
  of Vedic orthodoxy, 31,
formula, 59–60, 64–66, 243, 248, 388, 401
forts, 48, 49, 163–64, 166–67, 298–99
foster daughter, 30
foster parents, 197–98, 241, 243–44, 260, 332–33
Foucault, Michel, 180–82
foundation of ideas, 208–9, 351, 357, 373
frames, 86, 180–83, 184–86, 211, 465–66
framework, 4, 7, 15, 27–28, 83, 173–74, 191–92, 200–1, 252–53, 335, 339–41, 446
freedom, 1–2, 54, 91, 92–93, 102, 105–7, 110–11, 147, 148–50, 151, 157–58, 208–9, 284–85, 381
friends, 26–27, 43–44, 49, 59–60, 62–63, 104, 112–13, 140, 141, 142, 160, 163, 172, 192, 205, 240–41, 249–50, 251–52, 265, 272, 273, 274, 287, 288, 290, 291–92, 295, 300, 302, 305–6, 314, 315, 316, 317, 321–22, 326, 332–33, 334–35, 338, 346–47, 348, 372, 374, 377, 384, 398–99, 401, 402
friendship, 19, 193, 258–59, 272, 290, 313, 314, 457–58
frigidity, 82
fringe, 155–56, 258
frivolity, 155–56
frogs, 52, 54–55
fruits, 111, 118, 149, 158, 318, 341, 353–54, 355–57, 361–62, 374, 375, 378, 383, 387, 406, 459–60
frustration, 191–92, 459
functionaries, 132, 133
functions, 6, 16, 17, 33–34, 52–53, 57, 91, 134–35, 180–82, 186, 213, 346–47, 383–84
futility, 191, 301–2, 366–67, 389–91, 440
future, 6, 10, 180–82, 185–86, 187–88, 332–33, 451, 460

Gaḍa, 404–5
Gādhin/Gāthin, 45, 51, 59–60, 440, 451
Gājāyanī Pārāśarīputra, 249
Gālava, 95–96, 439
gallantry, 168, 238, 290–91, 296
gambling, 31, 130, 131, 139–40, 141–46, 147, 152, 323, 402, 423
games of dice, 33–34, 82, 129, 130–31, 133–40, 142, 143–46, 148, 151, 152–53, 159–61, 176, 202–3, 240–41, 253–54, 311, 401, 403, 423, 432, 462–63
gamester, 138, 140–41, 142, 206
gaṇasaṃgha, 191, 240–41, 249–50, 256–57, 271, 275, 276, 286, 311–12, 344–45, 462–63
Gāndhāra, 48, 168, 300, 388, 401
Gāndhārī, 19, 97, 203–4, 213–14, 312–13, 322, 331, 404
gāndharva marriage, 105–7
Gandharvas, 104, 120, 155–56, 194, 265, 319, 440
Gandhi, 56, 357

Gāṇḍīva, 115, 333, 396–97
Gaṅgā, xiv, 19–20, 22–23, 30, 46, 64, 86–87, 105–7, 109, 115–16, 157–58, 168, 203–4, 257, 258, 283, 287, 292, 466
Garga, 46
Gārgya Jyotiṣa, 29
Gārgya Śiśirāyaṇa, 286–87
gāthās, 5, 7–8, 305
Gāthāsaptaśtī, 255, 259, 266, 269–71
Gaurīviti, 46
Gautamas, 45, 60, 67, 101–2, 103, 178, 371, 385–86
gāyatrī, 51
Gehrts, Heino, 20–21, 244
gems, 131, 153, 208, 329
gender, 90, 384
genealogy, 2–3, 5, 23, 32–33, 58–59, 68, 82, 83, 84–86, 87, 88–90, 91, 95, 100–1, 102, 105, 107, 110–11, 180–82, 196, 214, 305, 424–25, 426–28, 439–40, 463
General of forces, 18–19, 165, 176, 178–79, 180–82, 186, 343, 394
generosity, 7–8, 52–53, 324, 366–67, 371, 381, 383, 402, 435–36, 452–53
genitor, 87, 97–98
genres, xiii, 182
geography, xii, 65, 126–27, 128
geopolitics, 128, 129, 240–41, 291
Ghaṭotkaca, 126–27, 163, 202–3, 393–94
Ghora Āṅgirasa, 191, 242, 244, 247, 259–60, 344–46, 366, 377, 381, 386–87, 397
ghoṣayātrā, 155
Ghoshal, U.N., 5, 132
Ghosh, Amalananda, 22–23, 115–16
Ghosh, Aurobindo, 357
Ghoṣūṇḍī Inscription, 249
gifts, 7–8, 25, 48, 50–51, 62–63, 68–69, 93, 104, 131, 135–36, 137, 141, 145–46, 149, 153, 154, 155, 169–70, 185, 192, 196, 290, 293–94, 295, 308, 310, 319–20, 329, 365, 366, 393, 401, 430–31, 435–36, 451, 454–55
Gilgamesh, 124, 125–26
Girivraja, 22, 282–83
Gītā, 17, 46–47, 54–55, 163, 173–74, 176, 188–89, 191, 215, 239, 241–43, 244, 252–53, 259–60, 311–12, 331, 334–48, 352, 353, 355–62, 364, 367–68, 369, 370, 371, 373, 374–77, 378, 380, 381–82, 383–85, 386–87, 388–89, 393–94, 400, 403–4, 407–8, 428–29, 453
Gītagovinda, 270–71
glorification, 172, 278, 281, 296–97, 300, 390–91
glory, 54, 63, 146, 196–97, 198–99, 205, 276, 278, 282–83, 288, 295, 297, 315, 338–39, 343, 392–93, 402, 457
goals, 28, 69, 293–94, 355, 364, 367, 443, 444
Gobala Vārṣṇa, 247–48
godhood, 50, 407–8, 432–33
gods/goddesses, 16, 18, 47, 51, 53–56, 57, 83, 85–86, 88, 98–99, 101–2, 111, 112–13, 121–22, 124, 125, 141, 142, 149, 155, 158, 160–61, 174–75, 192, 193, 198–99, 213, 237, 239, 243, 248–49, 251–52, 262, 263, 264, 265, 277, 278, 287–88, 291–93, 300, 313, 316, 318–19, 331, 335, 336–37, 338–40, 345–47, 369–70, 374–75, 386–87, 389, 393, 407–8, 425–26, 433–34, 435–36, 437, 443, 447, 461
gojit, 153, 157–58
Gokula, 249–50, 257, 258, 259
Goldman, Robert P., 67–68, 188, 205, 423, 425–26, 452–53, 455
Gomanta, 285–86
Gopā, 114–15
Gopālī, 286–87
gopas, 114–15, 157, 265, 268, 269, 274, 310–11
gopati, 1, 153–54, 158
Gotama, 60–61
Gotama Rāhugaṇa, 45, 115–16
gotra, 60, 305
Govardhana, 249–50, 264, 285–86, 296–97
government, 133–34, 157–58, 160–61, 448

Govinda, 160–61, 238, 248, 259, 264, 308, 315–16, 333
grace, 50–51, 52–53, 54–55, 142, 287–88, 308
grains, 50, 52, 64–65, 131, 153, 262, 341, 435, 443
grandchildren, 312
grandeur, 155–56, 194, 246–47, 406
grandfather, 187–88, 201–2, 312, 324, 390, 430–31
grandsons, 52–53, 58–59, 107, 126, 179, 212, 333–34, 435, 458
Greek mythology, 17–18, 19–20, 196–97
Greeks, 4, 118, 248–49, 250–51, 255, 286–87, 342–43
Greer, Patricia M., 13–14
grief, 195, 352, 387, 392, 394, 432, 452–53
Grierson, George, 12, 178–79
Gṛtsamadas, 44–45, 46–47, 48, 60–61, 63, 67, 426–28, 456–57
guardian, 124, 433–34
guards, 118, 160–61, 164, 167, 249–50, 297, 392, 433–34
guidance, 27–28, 62, 164, 239–41, 253–54, 300, 303, 338, 346–47, 433–34, 444–45
guidebook, 66–67
guidelines, 8–9, 17–18
guṇakarma, 371, 387, 407–8, 428–29
guṇas, 345–46, 360, 365, 366, 367, 371, 378, 379, 384–86
Gupta period, 98–99, 121, 122–24, 126, 148, 211, 246–47, 335–36, 341–42, 345–46, 431–32, 459, 460, 464–65
guru, 160–61, 195, 208–9, 238, 319, 326, 385–86, 454

hagiography, 237–38, 246–47, 265–66
harassment of Draupadī, 423
Hari, 267, 268, 288, 315–16
Haridrumata Gautama, 371
Hariścandra, 44, 70–72, 135, 147–48, 449
Harivaṃśa, 1–2, 86, 87, 105–7, 147–48, 187–88, 241, 245, 246–47, 249–50, 253–55, 256, 257, 260, 261, 266, 267, 268–69, 271–73, 275, 276–77, 278–79, 284, 285–86, 287, 288, 292–93, 300, 301–2, 304–6, 307–8, 310, 405, 448
harmony, 111–12, 121–22
Haryana, 64
Hastināpura, 22–23, 31–32, 66, 112, 128, 129, 131, 195, 242, 329, 332, 439–40, 466–67
Hastings, Warren, 356–57
Hāthibāḍā Inscription, 249
hatred, 21, 70–71, 140, 239, 330, 372, 377, 454, 458–59
heaven, 54, 88–89, 92–93, 95–96, 98–99, 133–34, 136–38, 173–74, 192–93, 194, 202–3, 214, 237, 308, 313, 315–16, 322–23, 353–54, 364, 375, 379, 380, 398, 447, 456
Hector, 17, 19, 23, 390
hegemony, 7–8, 9–10, 43–44, 66, 72–73, 122–24, 283–84, 453, 461–62
Heimdall, 19
Helen, 18, 19–20
Heliodorus, 248–49, 277, 376–77
Hellenization, 286–87
Heracles, 19–20, 31, 248
herdsmen, 156, 157–58, 258, 264, 265
heredity, 88–89, 105, 108, 110–11, 162–63, 166–67, 191–92, 196–97, 199, 239, 322–23, 344–45, 347–49, 384–85, 407–8, 424, 430, 461, 463–64
hermeneutics, 14, 15–16, 20–21
hermitages, 111–12, 120–22, 180–82, 194, 439, 440, 445, 451
hermits, 161–62, 319
Herodotus, 4, 6
heroes, 11, 12, 18, 20–21, 22–23, 27, 28–29, 30–31, 32, 51, 52, 113, 115–16, 124, 125–26, 129, 144, 157, 167–68, 173, 175–76, 177, 187–88, 191, 192–93, 194, 195, 196–97, 198–99, 201, 203–4, 214, 215, 237, 239–44, 248, 256, 259, 260–61, 282–83, 289, 292–93, 302, 312–13, 315, 329, 337, 338–39, 340–41, 342–43, 384, 388–89, 390–92, 406, 407–8,

423, 426–31, 432–33, 434, 448–49, 450, 452–55, 456, 457–58, 459, 460, 463–65
heroic epics, 17, 27, 426–28
heroines, 18, 22–23, 179, 203–4, 205
heroism, x, 20, 25, 26–28, 110, 124, 172–74, 175, 196–97, 198–99, 208–9, 322–23, 324, 326, 338–39, 340–41, 389–92, 395–96, 400–1, 402–3, 459–60, 463–64
heron, 202–3
Hesiod, 19
heterodoxy, 21, 28–29, 182, 183–85, 200, 208, 209–10, 344–45, 426–28, 429, 432, 433, 445–46, 458–59
Hiḍimba, xii–xiii, 121, 126–27, 393–94
Hiḍimbā, xii–xiii, 105–7, 127
Hillebrandt, A., 52–53, 352
Hiltebeitel, Alf, 15–16, 20–21, 33, 114–15, 151, 180–83, 184–85, 186, 187–88, 190–91, 200–3, 244, 279–80, 425–28
Hinduism, 26–27, 124, 196, 356–57
historicity, ix, 7–8, 9, 242, 244–45, 438–39
historiography, 5, 9, 33–34, 123–24, 179
Holtzmann, Adolf, 12, 15–16, 126, 242–43, 279–80, 337, 348, 353, 389
homage, 141, 188–89, 239, 277, 299, 325, 330, 388–89, 444
Homeric epics, xii, 19–20, 22–23, 27–28, 32, 111–12, 341, 390
honour, 14, 25, 51, 62–63, 151, 155–56, 163, 198–99, 240–41, 249–50, 261, 279, 295–96, 320, 332, 372, 377, 383–84, 396, 430, 433–34, 453
Hopkins, E. Washburn, 12–13, 186, 243, 335
horses, 19–20, 29, 48, 50, 52–53, 62–63, 131, 140, 153, 154, 159, 164, 165–66, 167, 168, 169–70, 173–74, 256, 265–66, 290–91, 354, 392–93, 444
horse sacrifice, 23, 121–22, 256, 297, 466
Huizinga, Jan, 6
humankind, 87, 199–200
Humbaba, 124, 125–26
humiliation, 101, 107, 142, 151, 155–56, 193–94, 208, 311, 312, 321, 327, 402–3
humours, 116–17
hunters, 118, 119–20, 122–23, 155–56, 201–2, 239–41, 251–52, 404–5, 406, 407–8
hunting, 117–18, 120–21, 155–56
husbands, 19–20, 30–31, 87, 88, 90–91, 92–94, 95–96, 97–100, 102–3, 105–7, 130, 143–44, 147, 148–50, 151, 159, 203–4, 205, 206–7, 251–52, 269, 279, 309, 310–11
hymns, 5, 19–20, 44–46, 49–51, 52–56, 57, 59–61, 62–64, 69, 70–71, 82–83, 87–88, 92, 108–9, 111–12, 122–23, 142, 260, 264, 337, 379, 380, 439–40, 442
hypothesis, 19–20, 114, 125, 134–35, 343–44, 358–59, 370

Iḍā, 86, 87–88, 94
ideal
  action, 353
  ascetic, 388
  balance, 116–17
  hero, 456
  king, 193–94, 426–28
  kṣatriya, 196–97, 392, 446, 459–60, 464
  landscape, 117
  past, 28, 179, 211
  person, 70–71, 259, 361–62
  polity, 21, 182, 458–59
  sacrifice, 54–55, 121–22
  society, 21, 25–26, 458–59
  sūta, 401
  wife, 105–7
idealization, 182, 384
ideals, 175, 200, 201–3, 207, 208–9, 212, 215, 338–39, 345–46, 356–57, 363–64, 388, 395, 428, 463–64, 465–66
ideas, x–xi, 1, 4–5, 7, 13, 20–21, 32–33, 54–55, 62, 83, 85–86, 87–90, 105–7, 108–9, 116–17, 119–20, 127–28, 133–34, 135, 147–48,

ideas (*cont.*)
149–50, 153, 172, 173, 176, 177–78, 180–82, 184–85, 188, 191–92, 194, 200, 206–7, 208–9, 239, 245–46, 257, 260, 263, 271, 277, 284, 286, 299–300, 313–14, 321, 322–23, 325, 331–32, 339–40, 344–47, 352, 363–64, 365, 366, 371, 373, 374–75, 378, 381–82, 383, 385–87, 395–96, 398–99, 400, 425–26, 432–33, 436–37, 447, 459
identities, 33–34, 43, 50, 60, 61–62, 83, 84, 85, 100, 137–38, 160–61, 177–78, 196–99, 264–65, 294–95, 299, 306, 307, 312, 342, 348, 426–28, 436, 455
Ideology, 20–21, 87–88, 303, 321, 322–23, 385–86, 403–4, 445
Ikṣvākus, 44, 69, 70, 71–72, 83–84, 85, 86, 368, 438–40, 446–47, 449
Iliad, 17–18, 19, 23, 27, 32, 124, 125–26, 390
illusion, 114, 174, 298, 392–93
imagination, xii–xiii, 23, 52, 54, 105–7, 111–12, 167–68, 180–82, 183, 242
impotence, 90–91, 201–2, 208
incarnation, 18, 21, 114, 125, 187–89, 198–99, 239, 243, 251–52, 292–93, 426–28, 430–31, 444–45, 450, 459–60, 465
incest, 87–89, 94, 100
Indo-Aryans, 43–44, 456–57
Indo-Europeans, 16–17, 21, 27–28, 96–97, 124, 125–26, 132, 196–97
Indo-Germanic, 67
Indo-Greeks, 33, 286, 441–42
Indo-Iranians, 47, 67, 82–83, 426–28, 456–57
Indra, 16, 21, 30, 43–44, 48, 49–51, 52–54, 56–57, 59–60, 62–63, 69–70, 71–72, 98–99, 103, 112–13, 114–15, 124–25, 127–28, 129, 134–35, 143–44, 159, 164, 169, 172, 196–98, 241, 247–48, 249–50, 260–63, 264, 274, 285–86, 290–92, 301–2, 303, 308–11, 318, 329–30, 366, 370, 393, 394, 435–36, 442, 443, 447, 461–62
Indraprastha, xiv, 22–23, 30–31, 33–34, 81–82, 112, 114, 128, 129, 159–60, 177–79, 240–41, 245–46, 291, 293–94, 432, 462–63, 466–67
Indrota Śaunaka, 436, 465–66
Indus, 11, 46, 47–48, 65
infallibility, 139–40, 191, 443
infantry, 155–56, 164, 165, 166, 167–68, 169, 170, 172, 173–74, 248
inscriptions, x, 118, 122–23, 249, 292–93, 307
insertion, 32–33, 310, 331, 335, 378, 392–93, 426, 431–32, 446
insight, 3–4, 119, 132, 155, 355, 383
inspection of cattle, 81–82, 120, 155–56, 157–58, 258, 462–63
institutionalization, 98, 191, 345–46
instructions, 86–87, 92–93, 99–100, 116–17, 178, 203–4, 238, 245–46, 335, 432–33, 435, 436–37
instructor, 436–37, 453
intelligentsia, 5, 46–47
intercourse, 101, 199–200
interpolations, ix–x, xiii, 1–2, 12–13, 14, 20–21, 28, 33–34, 81–82, 84, 87–88, 152–53, 241–42, 243–44, 298, 304, 310, 331, 334–36, 338–39, 341, 343–44, 368, 376–77, 383, 386, 389, 392–94, 407–8
interpretations, ix–x, 7, 9, 11, 20–21, 62, 67, 71, 98, 114, 115–16, 134–35, 139–40, 145–46, 177–78, 180–82, 193–94, 265, 279, 280, 334, 339–40, 347–48, 355–57, 358–60, 365, 384–85, 392–93, 426–28, 445–46, 448, 450, 459
interventions, 11, 28–29, 43, 71, 151, 175–76, 184–85, 212–13, 245–46, 258–59, 338–39, 392–93, 432, 436–37, 449–50, 454
intrigues, 203, 272, 284–85
introduction
of elephants and horses in army, 173–74

of iron tools, 115–16
of new characters, 450
to a sacrificial session, 133–34, 346–47
of saddle and stirrup, 170
introspection, 56–57
invasions, 31–32, 33, 62, 66, 156, 157–58, 279, 284, 286–87, 298–99, 303, 466
Inversion Theory, 12–13, 15–16, 242–43, 389, 429
Iran, 43–44, 47, 53–54, 59, 82–83
Iranians, 16, 47–48, 53–54, 82–83, 450
iron, 27–28, 32, 115–16, 280
irony, 196–97, 208
irrigation, 153–54
itihāsa, 1–2, 4, 5, 6, 7–10, 11, 25–26, 28, 43, 81, 83, 105–7, 110–11, 179, 183, 189–90, 212, 214, 239, 246–47, 255, 256, 311–12, 407–8, 423, 424–25, 438–39, 461, 462–66

Jacobi, Hermann, 242, 335, 337
Jahṇu, 45
Jaimini, 188–89, 358
Jaina tradition, 2–3, 7, 9, 30–31, 117, 183–84, 188–89, 252–55, 256, 257, 258, 259, 272–73, 274, 276–77, 278, 284, 291–92, 295, 301–2, 345–46, 347, 405–6
Jainism, 173–74, 184, 200–1, 252–53, 338–39, 344–46, 348, 361, 365, 387, 429
Jamadagni, 43–44, 46–47, 50–51, 59–61, 67, 68, 69–71, 443, 448–49, 450, 451, 452–53, 455, 457–58
Jāmbavān, 303–4, 306
Jāmbavatī, 250–52, 303–5, 306–8, 404–5
jana, 62–63, 118
Janakas, 3–4, 154, 424, 445–46
Janamejaya, 3–4, 23, 24, 30, 31–32, 64–65, 67–68, 81, 126, 161–62, 179, 180–83, 185, 211–12, 245–46, 260, 424–25, 428–29, 436–37, 461, 462–64, 465–66
janapadaniveśa, 119–20
janapadas, 22–23, 209
Janārdana, 113–14, 205, 238, 315–16, 325, 326, 329–30, 333–34, 349, 364
jaṅgala, 116–17
Jarāsaṃdha, 11, 22, 98, 167–68, 182, 191, 240–41, 242, 243, 244, 245–46, 250–54, 257, 264, 273, 278–87, 288, 289, 292–95, 296–97, 298, 299–300, 301–2, 303, 311, 312–13, 330, 334–35, 385–86, 391, 393–94, 403
Jarūtha, 53–54
jāti, 118–19, 130, 263, 349
Jaṭilā, 96
Jaya, 11, 177–78, 182, 195
Jayadeva, 270–71
Jayadratha, 163, 203, 205, 245–46, 388, 389, 392–93
Jayaswal, K.P., 132
Jetṛ, 45
Jinasena, 9
journeys, 17, 64, 155–56, 185–86, 202–3, 297, 299, 307
judgement, 56, 144, 149–50, 309
Judge, William Quan, 356–57, 358
jungle, 115–16
just war, 11, 173–75, 336, 343, 354, 363–64, 365, 388, 389, 395, 402, 404–5, 426, 429–30, 432, 437, 441, 445–46, 454, 455–56
justice, 384–85, 395, 406
justifications, 5, 96, 124, 144, 146, 172, 175, 312, 336, 395, 424, 425, 432–33, 437, 456

Kaikeyī, 203
Kālaketu, 122–23
kālavāda, 28–29
Kālayavana, 250–51, 264, 286–87, 303–4, 391
Kali, 10, 18, 25–26, 28–30, 123–24, 143–46, 174, 430, 463–64
Kālidāsa, 111, 121–22, 467
Kaliṅga, 94, 104, 171, 184, 300, 433
Kālīya, 126, 241, 249–50, 260, 274
kāma, 9, 200, 209–10, 367
Kāmākhyā, 158
Kāmarūpa, 158

Kaṃsa, 238, 240–41, 242, 248–54, 255, 257, 258–59, 265–66, 271–74, 275–77, 278–79, 283, 284–85, 286–87, 294–95, 296–97, 298, 301–2, 303, 305–6, 309–10, 312–13, 314–16, 403, 404, 407–8
Kaṇāda, 360
Kant, 398–99
Kaṇva. 30, 105–7, 404–5
Kāṇvas, 44, 46, 48, 60–61, 62–63, 65–66, 182, 184
kapha, 116–17
Karandikar, A.J., 47, 53–54
karman, 209, 355–62, 366–67, 383–84, 405, 428–29
Karṇa, 11, 17, 19, 93, 97, 130, 147, 151, 155–56, 160, 163, 167, 171, 176, 196–99, 203–4, 212, 245–46, 302, 312–13, 317, 332–33, 340–41, 385–86, 388, 389, 393–94, 396–97, 401–2, 432, 453, 454
Karṇaparvan, 404, 452
Karṇapravaras, 118
Karve, Irawati, 126, 138, 151, 244, 338, 406
Kāśīputra Bhagabhadra, 248–49
Kāśisundarī, 188–89
Kāśī, 104, 105–7, 300, 445–46
Kata, 45, 51
kathā, 190, 196–97
Kaṭhaka Saṃhitā, xv, 30, 81
Kathāsaritsāgara, 118
Kauravas, 11, 12, 17, 22–23, 30–31, 33–34, 131, 139–40, 155–56, 163, 176, 177–79, 212, 213–14, 240–41, 242–43, 245–46, 252, 254, 279, 299–300, 301–2, 317, 326, 343, 389–90, 392, 393, 394–95, 402, 423, 424–25, 453
Kauravya, 158
Kauśika, 398
Kauṭilya, 119–20, 121, 143, 156, 163, 173–74, 389
Kavaṣa, xi–xii, 52–53, 61–62, 139–40, 142, 144
Kavi, 46–47
Keith, Arthur Berriedale, 1–2, 12, 178–79, 247, 437–38
kernel, 243, 336, 356–57
Keśava, 29, 238, 248, 259, 265–66, 287–88, 315–16, 329–30, 333, 364
Keśin, 265–66
Keśin Dārbhya, 64–65, 66, 136–37
Khāṇḍava forest, xiv, 33–34, 65, 81–82, 110–14, 115–17, 120, 123–24, 125–26, 128, 129, 159–60, 211–12, 240–41, 245–46, 291–92, 293–94, 315, 407–8, 462–63
Khāṇḍavaprastha, 112, 114, 128, 211, 290
Khāravela, x, 184
khila hymns, 64, 81
Kīcaka, 151, 156, 157–58, 203, 206–7
Kīkaṭas, 59, 282–83
killing
  of Abhimanyu, 203, 403
  of Bhīṣma, 203–4, 390
  of brāhmaṇas, 436
  of children, 257, 274, 275
  of creatures, 113–14, 119–20, 296–97
  of demons, 241, 265–66, 272
  of Droṇa, 203, 284, 389, 394, 396–97, 398, 400
  of Duryodhana, 404
  of Ghaṭotkaca, 393
  of Jarāsaṃdha, 242, 245–46, 278, 295, 296–97, 298, 301–2, 393–94
  of Jayadratha, 389
  of Kaṃsa, 242, 248–50, 255, 259, 271, 274, 275, 276–77, 284, 294–95, 296–97, 314–15, 404, 406
  of Karṇa, 176, 402
  of kinsmen, 333, 348–49, 406, 432–33
  of Kṛtavarman, 404–5
  of Nāgas, 212
  of Namuci, 172
  of Naraka, 293, 308
  of people, 18, 104, 175–76, 177, 301, 312, 326, 328, 389–90, 452–53
  of Prasena, 305
  of Rākṣasas, 167–68, 444–45
  for revenge, 205, 212, 286, 443, 453
  of sages, 188–89, 201–2
  of Śiśupāla, 250–51, 280, 299, 301–2
  of Vālin, 126

of Vasiṣṭha's sons, 69, 442
of Vāsudeva of Puṇḍra, 299, 301–2
kingdoms, xi, 31, 33–34, 71–73, 81–82, 94, 97, 108–10, 128, 130, 133, 137–38, 143–44, 145–46, 155–56, 157–58, 159, 160–61, 176, 177–78, 182, 194–95, 202–3, 209–10, 211, 212, 215, 240–41, 244, 251–52, 254, 256–57, 258, 274, 276, 282–83, 286, 289–90, 312, 313–14, 317, 323, 326, 327, 332, 333–34, 344–45, 401, 402, 431–32, 448, 462, 466–67
kingmakers, 165, 166, 239, 276–77
kings, x, 2–3, 4, 5, 7–8, 11, 18, 21, 22, 24, 26, 30–31, 32–34, 47–48, 49, 50, 52, 53, 54, 55–56, 57–58, 64–66, 67–68, 69, 70–73, 82, 83, 84, 95–96, 99–101, 107, 108–9, 114, 115–16, 118, 122–23, 130, 131–37, 141, 142, 143–44, 146, 147–48, 150, 151, 153–54, 155–58, 159, 160–63, 166–67, 168, 169, 170, 171, 179, 182, 184, 188–89, 190, 191–95, 196–98, 200, 201–2, 203–4, 206, 212, 214, 239, 248–49, 250–52, 255, 256, 258, 261–62, 264, 275, 276–77, 279, 281–82, 283–84, 285, 286–87, 288, 289, 290, 292, 293–98, 299, 300, 302, 306–7, 312, 313, 314, 315–16, 319, 320, 321, 323, 324, 325, 327, 328–30, 332, 333, 336, 339–41, 386–87, 388, 391, 394, 401, 406, 424–25, 426–28, 429–36, 439–40, 441–42, 443, 444, 445–47, 448, 449, 450, 451–54, 456–59, 461, 462–63, 465, 466, 467
kingship, x, 26–27, 84, 88–89, 90, 108–10, 132, 133, 134–38, 139–40, 147, 153–54, 160–63, 168–69, 177–78, 191–92, 194, 209–10, 249–50, 257, 275, 293–94, 295, 296, 332, 344–45, 353, 386–87, 391, 426–28, 430–32, 434, 459
kinship, 25, 89–90, 160–61, 163, 406, 431
Kinsley, David, 387
kinsmen, 26, 102, 105–7, 131, 137, 146, 151, 160–61, 163, 172, 194–95, 240–41, 275, 284, 285, 286–87, 298, 303–4, 312, 317, 326, 328, 333–34, 348–49, 387, 404–5, 406, 430–32
Kirmīra, 121, 126–27, 393–94
knowledge, 5, 26–27, 46, 50, 51, 56, 64–65, 98–99, 126–27, 138, 139–40, 173–74, 178, 180–83, 238, 263, 272, 296, 302, 316, 318, 344–46, 354, 355, 358–59, 363–64, 367, 369–70, 371–72, 378, 381, 382, 383, 425, 433–34, 438–39, 455
Kosala/Kośala, 23, 65, 66, 169, 171, 438–39
Kosambi, D.D., 12–13, 47, 61–62, 126, 242, 248, 265, 280, 335–36, 341–42, 458–59
Kṛpa, 103, 160–61, 163, 175–76, 192–93, 196, 197–98, 245–46, 314, 317, 385–86, 388, 404, 426, 454
Kṛpī, 103
Kṛṣṇa, xiii, 11–12, 20–21, 23, 26–29, 30–31, 46–47, 104, 105–7, 112, 113–14, 124–25, 126, 127–29, 151, 160–61, 162–63, 167, 174–75, 176, 177–78, 179, 183, 185, 188, 191, 192–93, 194–95, 196–99, 203–4, 205, 212, 215, 237, 238–39, 272, 273–82, 284–317, 318, 320, 321–23, 324, 325, 326–28, 329–48, 349, 350, 351, 352, 353–54, 355, 358–59, 360, 361–62, 363–72, 373–77, 380–82, 383–408, 423, 424–25, 428–30, 432–33, 435–36, 445–46, 452–53, 461, 462–64, 465
Kṛṣṇacaritra, 243–44
Kṛṣṇā, 21, 30–31, 147, 151
Kṛṣṇa Dvaipāyana, 21, 30–31, 32, 179–80, 188–89, 190–91, 251–52, 405–6
kṣatṛ, 132–33
kṣātradharma, 146, 192, 194, 195, 200, 203–4, 212, 324, 325, 328, 329, 330, 331–32, 338–39, 348, 353
Kṣatraśrī, 58–59
kṣatrasya dhṛti, 133–34
kṣatriyas, x, 1–3, 12, 16, 18, 21, 24, 26–28, 33, 43, 50, 57, 66, 67–68, 69, 70, 84, 88–89, 90, 99–100, 102, 103–4,

kṣatriyas (*cont.*)
105–7, 109, 110, 118–19, 126, 137–38, 172–73, 178, 182, 184–85, 192, 194, 195, 196–97, 198–99, 201–2, 203–4, 206–7, 208–10, 238, 243, 282–83, 287, 294, 296, 312, 320, 322–25, 328, 329, 330, 337, 338–39, 344–45, 347–48, 352, 353, 383, 384, 385–86, 390–91, 398–99, 401, 403, 424–25, 426–28, 429–30, 432–34, 435–36, 437–38, 440, 441–42, 444, 445–46, 447, 448–50, 451–53, 454–61, 463–65
kṣetraja putra, 97–98, 99–100, 110, 149–50
kṣetrajña, 356–57, 381–82
kula, 137–38, 160–61, 203–4, 349
kuladharma, 84, 338–39, 349, 353, 387
Kulapati Śaunaka, 24, 180–82, 424–26, 454
Kumbhakarṇa, 17, 126–27
Kunhan Raja, C., 58–59, 62
Kuntī, 19, 91, 92–93, 98, 99–100, 102–3, 149–50, 177–78, 191–92, 196–99, 203–4, 208, 253–54, 312–13, 322, 323, 324–23, 327, 332, 333, 353, 401
Kurukṣetra, x, 10, 11, 22, 25, 48, 64–66, 128, 132, 178–79, 247, 253–54, 331, 348, 391, 401, 404, 407–8, 428–29, 432–33, 452, 466
Kurus, xii, 3–4, 9–10, 11, 12, 24, 30–34, 43, 64–66, 67–68, 72–73, 81, 82, 84, 85–86, 91, 94, 97, 100–1, 103, 107, 108–9, 110–11, 112, 115, 117, 120, 126, 128, 129, 131–32, 134–36, 137–38, 139–40, 150, 152–53, 155–56, 157–58, 159–60, 162–63, 166, 171, 175, 177–79, 180, 182, 185–86, 188–90, 191–92, 195, 205, 211–13, 215, 239–42, 245–46, 247, 253–54, 256–57, 258, 275, 281, 282–83, 289–90, 293–94, 295–96, 298–99, 311–12, 313, 314, 317, 318, 321, 322, 326–28, 329–30, 331, 332, 334–35, 343, 344–45, 404, 424–25, 430, 437, 438–39, 456–57, 461, 462–64, 465–67
Kuruśravaṇa, 64
Kuṣāṇas, 170, 184
Kuśikas, 45, 47–48, 49–51, 62–63, 68–69, 71–72, 441, 452, 458
Kutsa, 49, 52–53, 58

lacquer house, 203, 289–90, 423
Lakṣmaṇa, 252–53, 398–99, 444–45
lakṣmaṇas of a *Purāṇa*, 246–47
Lal, B.B., 22–23, 81, 115–16, 466
land, xii, 88–89, 97, 115–17, 120, 121, 122–23, 126, 131–32, 141, 146, 148–49, 153, 158, 159, 171, 240–41, 261–62, 282–83, 320, 345–46, 430–31, 457–58, 464–65
landmark, 7–8, 271, 282–83
landscape, 1, 9–10, 23, 64–65, 67–68, 116–17, 119–20, 121–22, 191, 282–83, 438–39
language, xiv, 111–12, 121–22, 178, 199–200, 330, 382, 392
Lassen, Christian, 11, 241–42
later additions into texts, x, 12, 25–27, 28–29, 32–34, 44, 46–47, 54, 59–60, 64, 81–82, 84, 85, 96–97, 98–99, 131, 152–53, 170, 175, 185–86, 196, 241–42, 243–44, 258–59, 281, 293–94, 296, 298, 304–5, 306, 310, 331, 334–36, 337–40, 341, 343–44, 360, 375–77, 378, 389, 390, 407–8, 424–25, 426–28, 429, 430–32, 449–50, 452–53
Later Vedic literature, xi, 3–4, 5, 9–10, 24, 30, 31, 43, 64, 65, 66–67, 68, 69–72, 81, 87–88, 90–91, 92, 101, 128, 148, 158, 162–63, 169, 171, 172, 178, 183, 190, 211, 247–48, 256, 282–83, 304–5, 424–25, 443, 450–51, 457, 462–63, 465–66
Later Vedic period, 1, 9–10, 23, 24, 27–29, 30, 43, 64, 66, 67–68, 72–73, 81–82, 88–90, 91, 92, 96–97, 98–99, 102, 104, 105, 108–9, 110–12, 116–17, 128, 129, 131–32, 135–36, 142, 143, 151, 152–53, 154, 155, 158, 159–60, 162–64, 168–69, 172, 173–74, 179–80, 182–83, 184–85, 186,

188–90, 191, 200–1, 239, 247, 256, 282–83, 293–94, 322–23, 334–35, 338–39, 374–75, 423, 429, 431–32, 442, 457, 461, 462–63, 465
Lath, Mukund, 200–1
lawbooks, 426–28
lawgivers, 149
laws, 10, 13, 57, 91, 92, 105–7, 108–10, 160–61, 175, 194, 206, 208, 238, 290–91, 313, 315–16, 319, 320, 321, 322, 323, 324, 325, 327–28, 330, 333, 370, 433
layers, 2–3, 11, 14, 24, 91, 110–11, 131, 180, 187, 188, 241–42, 334–35, 336–37, 338–39, 344–45, 375–76, 428–29
leaders, 50–51, 61–62, 133, 141, 165–66, 177, 240–41, 247, 249–50, 260, 261, 264–65, 272–73, 303, 305–6, 307–8, 311, 312–13, 314–15, 334–35, 342–43, 344–45, 356–57, 358, 430–31, 462–63
learning, 144, 238, 253–54, 296, 314, 436
legacy, 56–57, 108, 109–10, 301, 460–61, 464–65
legends
  Bhārgava, 67, 425–26, 451–58, 460
  Buddhist, 30–31, 249, 250–51, 252, 257, 258–59, 467
  Christian, 11, 242
  historical, 12, 120, 309, 467
  Jaina, 252–53, 254–55, 276–77, 278
  Kṛṣṇa-relaterd, 126, 188–89, 241, 242, 243–47, 248–49, 250–51, 254–56, 257, 258–59, 270, 276–77, 286–87, 292, 293, 303–5, 307–8, 310–11, 405
  Mahābhārata, 12, 24, 81–82, 83, 88, 94, 107, 114, 117, 118, 129, 143, 152–53, 159–60, 280, 281–82, 432–33, 435, 436–37, 439, 440, 441, 444–46, 450, 451, 452–53, 454–58, 462–63
  Purāṇic, 448, 449–50
  Vedic, 43–44, 49–51, 53–54, 57, 59–60, 66, 67–68, 70–72, 133–35, 440, 442, 448–49
legitimacy, x, 93, 100, 101, 102, 132, 134–35, 137, 139–40, 152, 160–61, 175–76, 191–92, 194, 197–98, 283–84, 293–95, 348, 359, 369–70, 398–99, 426–28, 454–55, 459, 460
Lellement, Joseph, 17
Levi, Sylvain, 243
levirate, 97–98, 177–78
Levi-Strauss, Claude, 89–90
liberality, 238, 281, 282–83, 296
liberation, 54, 338, 339–40, 345–46, 348, 363–64, 369, 373, 374–75, 377, 380
lineage, xi, 1, 3–4, 25, 30–31, 55–56, 64, 68–69, 82, 83, 84, 85, 88, 89–90, 94, 95–96, 100–1, 105–7, 114–15, 126, 129, 177–79, 196, 289, 290–91, 368, 433–34
list
  of allies and rivals, xii, 159–60, 163–64, 166, 169, 171, 299
  of conquests, 300, 317
  of crimes, 297, 298
  of cruel acts, 203
  of deities, 127–28
  of forest tribes, 118
  of forms of marriage, 104
  of genealogical information, 82, 83, 88, 95
  of gifts, 131, 153
  of military ethics, 173–74, 175–76
  of plunder, 292
  of protected animals, 119–20
  of *ratnins*, 132–33
  of sacrificed animals, 121–22
  of *śalākāpuruṣas*, 252–53
  of seven sages, 60–61, 97–98, 121–22, 127–28, 131, 132–33, 153, 159–60, 163–64, 166, 171, 173–74, 203, 292, 298, 300, 381, 398
  of suitable heirs, 92–93, 97–98
  of virtues, 381, 398
listeners, 428–29, 436–37, 467
literacy, 25, 26–27, 180–82, 464–65
literature, xii, 1, 2–3, 4–6, 10, 15, 17, 19–20, 23, 30, 31, 32–33, 43, 60, 64, 66–67, 68, 69–70, 71–72, 82, 88, 100–1, 102–4, 111–12, 118, 121–22, 128,

literature (*cont.*)
143, 147, 149, 169, 173–74, 178–79, 183, 211, 213–14, 247–48, 249, 255, 256, 259, 282–83, 335, 356–57, 360, 438–39, 443, 450–51, 462, 466
livelihood, 149, 196, 200–1, 258, 328, 434
Livy, 4
location, xii, 44–45, 65, 81, 116–17, 159, 168, 171, 289–90, 335, 340, 343, 367, 384–86, 424–25, 428, 449–50
Lomaharṣaṇa, 180–82, 424–25
Lommel, Herman, 69
Lord, A.B., 27–28
lord
of cowherds, 255, 264–65
of death, 354
of devotees, 187–88, 237–38, 270, 315–16, 327–28, 341–42, 357, 359, 374–75, 382, 383, 386, 388
of Dvārakā, 241
of heaven, 261–62
of the people, 328, 350, 380, 433–34
of *pralaya*, 114
of the world, 114–15, 238, 261–62, 369, 381–82
of women, 238
love, 90–91, 104, 105–7, 130, 143–44, 197–99, 201–2, 214, 239, 259, 265, 266, 269, 270–71, 287, 288, 306–8, 317, 323, 326, 330, 332–33, 387, 393–94, 403, 443
lure, 140, 214, 423
lying, 55, 237, 238, 361, 394–95, 398, 400–1, 423

MacDonnell, A.A., 4, 5–6
Mādhavī, 95–96
Madhuchandas, 45
Madhyadeśa, 64–65, 116–17, 171, 178, 462
Madras, 105–7, 171
Mādrī, 97, 100, 149–50, 177–78, 202–3, 253–54
Magadha, 11, 22, 129, 170, 171, 173–74, 182, 184, 191, 200, 209–10, 240–41, 250–51, 253–54, 257, 276, 279–84, 285, 289, 292–93, 294–95, 300
māgadhas, 1–2, 8, 282–83, 292–93
magic, 50–51, 55, 67, 141, 165, 166, 194, 239, 249–50, 282–83, 310, 345–46, 388, 392–93, 426–28, 442–43, 458, 464–65
mahābhāratācārya, 24, 183
Mahākosala, 438–39
Mahāpadma Nanda, 209–10, 282, 285
mahāprasthāna, 202–3
Mahāvṛṣas, 65, 69
mainstay of an army, 156, 245–46
mainstream, 118, 119, 281, 283–84
maintenance of order, 349, 386–87, 464
Majumdar, R.C., 4
Malinar, Angelika, 193–94, 339–40, 352, 361–62, 367, 386–87
Mamatā, 96, 102
maṇḍala theory, 163
Māndhātṛ, 2–3, 433
mantras, 47, 64–65
Manu, 47–48, 84–85, 86–87, 88, 94, 98–99, 104, 116–17, 118–19, 143, 149, 188, 368, 423
manuscripts, 13, 14, 15–16, 20–21, 114, 243, 285–86
Manu Smṛti, 25, 426–29, 431–32, 440, 459
marches, 64–65, 164, 166–67, 193
Mārkaṇḍeya, 28–29, 426
Mārkaṇḍeya Purāṇa, 147–48
marriages, x, 30–31, 32–33, 59–60, 82, 85, 87, 89, 90, 93–94, 95, 98, 104–7, 109, 111–12, 114–15, 126, 128, 133–34, 148–49, 159–60, 161–62, 178, 203–4, 212, 240–41, 245–46, 249–52, 253–54, 257, 258–59, 273, 279, 283, 287, 288, 289–90, 291, 293, 297, 303–4, 306, 307–8, 311, 312, 398, 424, 451, 460, 462–63
martial
contests, 105–7, 136–37
ecstasy, 124–25, 340–41
qualities, 16, 196–98, 208, 210, 338–39, 454–55, 463–65
teacher, 101, 453

Maruts, 52, 96–97, 164–66
masquerade, 142, 312
master
of animals, 159
of dicing, 142
of diplomacy, 306
of a house, 180–82
of muster, 170
of people, 150
of philosophy, 356–57, 359–60, 363–64, 373, 388
of stratagems, 176, 389
of three worlds, 309
of a territory, 253–54
of treasury, 132–33
mastery, 50, 151, 154, 383, 392–93
Mātariśvan, 49–50, 59–60
Mathurā, 12, 18, 19, 22, 31, 128–29, 177–78, 240–41, 242, 244–45, 246–47, 248, 249–52, 257, 258, 259, 264–65, 270–72, 273–74, 276, 278–79, 280, 283, 284–86, 287, 291–92, 293–95, 391, 403
Matilal, Bimal Krishna, 348, 371, 389, 395, 398–99
Matsya, 33–34, 61–62, 81–82, 142, 145–46, 156, 157–58, 163, 206, 240–41, 245–46, 258, 312, 348, 394, 439–40
Mauryan period, x, 119–20, 121, 166–67, 188–89, 282, 455
Mausalaparvan, 18, 404–5
Mauryas, 120, 170, 171, 182, 183–85, 255, 281, 283
maxims, 13, 188–89, 356–57, 424, 435–36
Maya, 114, 124–25
māyā, 114, 194, 369–70, 426–28
Māyon/Mayavan, 255, 267, 270
McGrath, Kevin, 26–28, 33–34, 160–63, 177–78, 185–86, 193–94, 196–97, 203–4, 340–41, 425, 426, 430–32
meat eating, 105–7, 116–17, 325
meat seller, 200–1
medieval period, 4, 6, 255–56, 270–71
meetings, 141, 313, 315
Megasthenes, 31, 170, 177–78, 248, 338–39
Mehendale, M.A., 151, 175–77, 389
memory, xiii–xiv, 5, 6, 49, 70–71, 82–83, 98, 184–86, 286, 343, 362–63, 406, 442, 456
merchants, xiii, 263
mercy, 54, 142, 175, 237, 238, 402
merit, 109–10, 142, 173–74, 200, 321, 322, 332–33, 428–29, 435–37, 463–64
Mesopotamia, 6, 86–87, 90
message, 71, 212, 215, 317, 318, 321, 323, 324, 326, 330, 331, 356–57, 370, 387, 407
messenger, 132–33, 240–41, 245–46, 328, 330, 331–32, 387
metaphors, 55, 71–72, 128, 133–35, 145–46, 174, 184–85, 346–47, 365, 366, 367–68, 379, 396, 424–25
methodology, 6, 12–13, 22–23, 81, 123–24, 186
methods of analysis, 15–16, 336–37
methods of history writing, 6
metre, 424
migration, xiv, 43–44, 72–73, 83, 252, 255, 461–62, 467
milieu
historical, 28, 58, 87–88, 148–49, 153–54
philosophical, 345–46, 355, 374–75, 455
military, 7–8, 52, 57, 70–71, 163–64, 165, 166, 167–68, 171, 172, 173–74, 197–98, 248, 257, 264–65, 283, 284, 292, 299–300, 315, 322–23, 433, 440
milk, 54–55, 87, 155, 158–59, 198, 261–62, 265, 442
milkmaids, 238, 239, 241, 266, 387, 403
Mīmāṃsā, 5, 358, 360, 361–62
mind-born sons, 96
Mithilā, 200–1, 304
Mitra, 16, 49–50, 52, 55–57, 86, 87, 103, 127–28, 133–35
mlecchas, 117–18, 171, 440
modification, 60, 87–88, 94, 377, 426–28, 464
mokṣa, 9, 200, 209–10, 336

molestation, 151, 203, 205, 271, 323
monarchs, 1, 57, 122–23, 159, 162–63, 430–31
monarchy, xi, 25–26, 105, 162–63, 168–69, 215, 430–31
monetization, 431–32
monopoly, 92, 191, 209–10, 426–28, 455
Moon god, 68, 83, 86, 212, 251–52, 277, 309, 318, 374–75, 382–83
morale, 183, 343, 401
morality, 56–57, 122–24, 149–50, 172–73, 175, 208–9, 237, 270–71, 336, 340–41, 383–84, 398–99, 400–1, 402, 403, 423, 430–31, 432
mother, 18–20, 30, 55–56, 88, 91, 94, 95, 100–1, 102, 103, 111, 113, 118–19, 127–28, 137–38, 140, 141, 160, 177–78, 201, 202–4, 208, 210, 212–14, 241, 260, 265, 269, 275, 292, 306–8, 322, 325, 332–33, 423, 443, 451, 455
mountains, 48, 49, 54–55, 113–14, 171, 193, 261–62, 264, 281–82, 283, 292, 301, 341, 435
Mucukunda, 286, 439
Mukherjee, B.N., 465–66
multiplicity
  of authorship, 187, 338–39
  of dharma, 173–74, 345–46, 423
murderers, 200, 398–99, 452–53
murders, 275, 285, 289–90, 303–4, 305–6, 405–6, 423
Mūṣṭika, 249–50, 251–52, 253–54, 271
mysticism, 241, 259, 384–85, 388
mythology, 16, 19–20, 46–47, 57, 67, 70–71, 83, 86–87, 124, 125–26, 128, 137–38, 184–85, 191–92, 252–53, 260, 277, 295, 438, 450
myths, 11, 12–13, 16–17, 19–20, 53–54, 55–56, 59–60, 67, 71, 86–88, 103, 114, 123–24, 125–26, 127–28, 137–38, 187–88, 237–38, 244, 260, 265, 280, 425–28, 433–34, 439, 453, 454, 457–60, 464–65

Naciketas, 154, 354
Nāgas, 12, 95, 119, 126–28, 211–12, 241, 249–50, 259–60, 291–92, 301–2, 382, 458–59, 465–66
nāgavana, 119–20
Nahuṣa, 82–83, 84–85, 86, 126
Naimiṣa forest, 65, 85, 89, 180–82, 424–26
nairuktakas, 9
Nakula, 16, 156, 160–61, 163, 167–68, 171, 200, 202–3, 326–27
Nala, 31, 143–46
Namuci, 48, 172
Nanda, 249–50, 253–54, 258–59, 262, 265, 271
Nandagopā, 251–52, 258–59
Nandas, 166–67, 170, 171, 209–10, 282, 283
Nara, 46, 125, 199, 243, 291–92, 425
Nārada, 19–20, 70–71, 98–99, 257, 310, 404–5, 425
Naraka, 241, 243, 250–51, 292–93, 307–8, 309–10, 315–16
Nārāyaṇa, 125, 187–88, 243, 247, 249, 253–54, 278, 291–92, 425
Nārāyaṇīya army, 240–41, 274, 314–15
narrations, 7–8, 21, 24, 84, 85, 211, 212, 245–46, 297, 343, 424–25, 428, 436–37, 454, 458–59, 462–63, 465–66
narratives, ix–xi, xii, 2–4, 5, 7–8, 9–10, 11, 13–14, 21–23, 24–27, 28–29, 30, 32–34, 64, 66, 72–73, 81–82, 84, 93, 97–98, 100–1, 104, 105–12, 114–15, 125, 129, 149, 152–53, 155–56, 158, 159–63, 168, 170, 171, 175, 180, 183, 184–85, 186, 188, 196–97, 200–1, 208, 209–10, 211, 212–13, 215, 239, 241, 244, 256, 288, 289–90, 291, 311–12, 335, 337, 338–39, 343–44, 360, 390, 403, 426–29, 430–32, 433, 446, 452, 454, 462–64, 465–66
narrative sections, xiii, 13, 25, 28–29, 30–31, 33–34, 66, 72–73, 81–82, 97, 149, 152–53, 158, 159, 160–61, 168, 335, 360, 430–31
narrators, 24, 84, 180–82, 213–14, 343, 346–47, 428–29, 437
nationalism, 243–44, 357
nationalist historians, 4, 5
Nearchus, 169

nephews, 121, 392, 393–94, 436–37, 466
Nirukta, 9, 30, 69, 118, 248, 304–5, 440
Niṣādas, 118–19, 121, 171, 423, 435, 447
niṣkāma karman, 215, 355–57, 358–59, 361, 366–67, 383–84, 428–29
nivṛtti, 152, 200, 209, 214, 345–46, 358–59, 361, 387
non-violence, x, 124, 172, 173–74, 200–1, 208, 312, 338–39, 347, 357, 381, 397, 399, 433, 455–56
normativity, 71–72, 110–11, 119, 121–22, 168, 423
norms, 25, 86, 88–89, 90–91, 92, 94, 97, 105–7, 108–11, 120–22, 149–50, 155, 423
novelist, 243–44
nṛśaṃsa, 203, 208

objectives, 68, 307–8
objectivity, 5–6, 14–16
observance of rules, 121–22, 126, 175–76, 200, 317, 328, 397
observances of rituals, 301, 310
observations, 26–27, 28–29, 57, 90, 93, 298–99, 442
obsession, 47–48, 55, 61, 131, 139–40, 196–97, 199, 317, 322, 396–98, 401, 423
obsessive compulsive disoreder, 145–46
Occidental scholarship, 6, 17, 356–57
occupation of new areas, 115–16
odour, 102–3
Odysseus/Ulysses, xii–xiii, 17, 19–20
Odyssey, xii, 19–20, 111–12
Oedipal elements, 455
offerings, 87, 101–2, 133–34, 198, 279, 287–88, 329, 341, 349, 371, 375, 447
offspring, 50, 52, 68, 85, 87, 88, 94, 95–96, 97–98, 101, 102, 108, 109, 203–4, 214, 290–91, 324, 385–86
Oldenberg, H., 12, 52–53, 57, 335
Onesikritas, 211
orality, 1–2, 8, 15–16, 24, 25, 180–83, 194, 246–47, 254–55, 425, 440, 464–65
order
  of army, 164
  of cosmos, 56, 145, 174, 193–94, 321, 365, 369–70, 373, 379, 380
  of human society, 87–88, 133, 148, 149–50, 179, 182, 191, 209–10, 384
  of morality, 122–23
  of primogeniture, 90–91
  of a religion, 56–57, 72–73
  of the state, 123–24
  of varṇa, 25–26, 28–29, 31, 44, 117, 191, 193, 195, 208–9, 320, 321, 322–23, 344–46, 347–48, 349, 353, 385–86, 407–8, 423, 426–28, 429–30, 433–34, 447, 459, 461, 463–65
orderliness, 89, 193–94
organization
  of a ceremony. 286
  literary, 5, 44
  military, 163–64, 165, 166–67
  philosophical, 338–39, 345–46, 375–76
  of a sacrifice, 23, 67–68, 137, 139–40, 152, 154, 180, 240–41, 261, 293, 449
  socio-political, 1, 88–89, 110–11, 117, 183, 209, 261, 286, 292–93, 344–45
orientation, 1–3, 5, 148–49, 161–62, 196, 349, 354, 378
origin, 3–4, 5, 14–15, 24, 32–33, 43, 47, 50, 54, 65, 67–68, 69, 82–83, 84–86, 87–88, 126–27, 133–34, 137–38, 154, 180–82, 184, 187, 189–90, 209–10, 239, 341, 342, 352, 379, 388, 389, 424, 425, 433–34, 462–63
original homeland, 82–83, 211
original context, ix–x, xiii, 8, 11, 12, 14, 22–23, 25, 43–44, 86–87, 94, 110–11, 114, 133–34, 136–37, 159–60, 196, 241, 242–46, 249, 275, 280, 282–83, 304–5, 331, 335, 337, 338–39, 341, 343–44, 357, 358, 363–64, 389, 423, 426, 437–39, 442, 461, 462–63
orthodoxy, 31, 72–73, 132, 183–84, 189–90, 282–83, 407–8, 423, 459, 462
orthopraxy, 31, 72–73, 132, 189–90, 462
Ouranos, 19
outcastes/outcasts, 70, 122–23, 141, 187, 189–90, 195, 307, 446–47

pacification, 93, 304, 447
pacifism, 200, 204, 214, 311–12, 322, 323, 328, 329, 331–32, 338–39, 390–91
Padapāṭha, 54
Padmanabhayya, A., 47
Pakthas, 52–53, 61–62
Pañcāla, 9–10, 11, 12, 30, 31, 33–34, 48, 64–66, 72–73, 81, 97, 101, 117, 128, 131–32, 134–35, 136–37, 159–60, 163, 171, 178–79, 182, 186, 191–92, 215, 239–42, 245–46, 247, 256–57, 282–83, 289–90, 293–94, 311–12, 314, 327, 334–35, 389, 394, 404, 439–40, 445–46, 456–57, 461, 462–64
Pāṇḍavas, xii, 11–12, 17, 21, 32–34, 94–96, 99–101, 111–12, 114–15, 121, 128, 129, 130, 135–36, 138, 144, 145–46, 147, 149–50, 151, 152–53, 155–56, 157–58, 159–62, 163, 174–76, 177–79, 185, 192–93, 194–95, 198–99, 200, 201–2, 203, 205, 208, 212, 213–14, 240–41, 242–43, 245–46, 252–55, 278–79, 289–90, 291–92, 293–94, 298, 299–300, 301–2, 304, 307–8, 311–12, 313, 314–15, 317–18, 320, 321, 322–23, 327, 328, 329–30, 331, 332, 333, 334–35, 336, 340, 348, 388–90, 391–92, 393–95, 401, 402, 403–4, 423, 424–25, 426, 463–64
Pande, G.C., 209, 424
Pāṇḍu, 12, 17, 30–31, 91, 92–93, 98–101, 102, 105–7, 110, 147, 161–62, 177–78, 191–92, 197–98, 201–2, 280, 314, 322, 324
panic, 329
Pāṇini, 24, 31, 32–33, 125, 182, 183, 248, 277, 338–39, 342, 376–77
Panjab, 45–47, 64
paradox, 139–40, 237–38, 239, 358
Parāśara, 46, 100–1
Parasher-Sen, Aloka, 117, 119–20
Paraśurāma, 390, 428, 432–33, 434, 450–51, 452–61, 464–65
Parāvasu, 452–53
Pargiter, F.E., 1–4, 12–13, 23, 71–72, 81, 159–60, 437–38, 439–40, 447–50
Parikṣit, 3–4, 9–10, 23, 30, 31–33, 64, 65, 66, 72–73, 81, 115, 126, 158–59, 160–61, 177–78, 179, 183, 188–89, 212, 245–46, 260, 282–83, 462–64, 465–66
parivṛkti, 132–33
Parjanya, 52, 158, 194, 251–52, 262
partition, 81–82, 112, 137, 145–46, 159–60
party, 131, 155–56, 178, 272, 300, 314–15, 398
Pāruṣṇī, 48, 52–53, 62, 439–40
Pāśadyumna, 55–56, 61–62
passages, 33–34, 48, 131, 158, 165, 193, 247, 248, 296, 329, 335–36, 337, 341–42, 352, 363–64, 367–68, 369, 370, 376, 380, 385–87
passion, 142, 144, 145–46, 172, 191–92, 254, 287–88, 289, 290, 354, 362, 367, 370, 377–78
past, ix–x, xiv, 5–9, 10, 25, 28, 33, 69, 104, 180–83, 185–86, 248–49, 291, 292–93, 443, 460
pastoralism, 1, 25, 98, 120, 154, 157–58, 239, 241–42, 258, 264, 280, 283–84, 335–36
pasture, xiv, 156, 283–84
Pāṭaliputra, 21–22, 281–82, 458–59
path
  of action, 200
  of balance, 345–46, 365, 373, 383–84
  of *dharma*, 203–4, 206–7, 331
  of hell, 272
  of knowledge, 358–59, 378
  of liberation, 338, 363–64, 370
  of peace, 173–74, 318
  of renunciation, 200
  of self-control, 316, 377–78
  of violence, 208
patriarch, 151, 430–31
patriarchy, 89, 94, 149–50, 454–55
patrimony, 204
patronage, xiii, 1–2, 21, 24, 25–26, 31–32, 43, 47, 50–51, 62–65, 67–68, 160, 182, 183–84, 190, 200, 209–10,

281, 424–25, 426–28, 429–30, 438, 445, 447, 448, 454–55, 456–57, 458–59, 460–61, 462–63, 465–66
patrons, 7–8, 24, 51–53, 62, 67–68, 70–71, 185–86, 191, 194–95, 242, 280, 282, 292–93, 316, 424–25, 440–41, 442, 445
paurāṇika sūtas, 25–26
Pāyu, 46, 58–59
peace, 31–32, 54–55, 56–57, 89, 158, 165, 172, 173–74, 179, 207–8, 311–12, 314, 317, 318, 321–22, 323, 326–28, 329–30, 331–33, 338–40, 362–63, 378, 387
pedigree, 44–45, 65, 68, 69, 332–33, 441–42
penance, 68
performance
of bards, 26–27, 185–86, 343, 428–29
of black magic, 55
of duties, 310–11, 321, 331–32, 339–40, 347, 356–57, 358–59, 361, 384–86, 387, 404, 463–64
of leaders, 177
of rituals, 90–91, 133, 135–36, 345–46, 358–59, 360
performers
of poetry, 180–82, 185–86
of rituals, 55, 137–38, 160–61, 211, 429, 466
of sin, 448
Persia, 47, 450
Persians, 4
PGW, 22–23, 27–28, 115–16, 131
philosopher, 154, 180–82, 186, 187–88, 241, 244, 343, 429, 465–66
philosophy
of Brahmanism, 384–85
of Buddhism, 352, 360
of Gandhi, 357
of *Gītā*, 191, 334–35, 345–47, 356–57, 368, 375–76, 384, 387, 388–89
of Jainism, 277
of *Mahābhārata*, 203, 214, 237–38, 239, 259, 311–12, 321, 342–43, 356–57, 389–90, 403, 407, 429, 464
of Mīmāṃsā, 5, 358
of Sāṃkhya, 344–45, 354, 375–76, 429
of Vaiśeṣika, 360
of Vedānta, 189–90, 337, 344–45, 351, 357, 358–59, 363–64, 378
Phrygians, 47
Pijavan, 52–53, 58–59, 440
pilgrimage, 64–65, 310, 435–36
Pinnāi, 255, 267, 269–71
pitta, 116–17
playfulness, 174, 265–66, 270, 297, 315–16, 436–37
playing dice, 130, 138, 139–40, 141, 142, 144–46, 150, 152
plays, 194, 256, 267
play of love, 269
playing the flute, 239, 266
playing tricks, 143–44, 174
pleasure, 8–9, 10, 112, 192, 202–3, 209–10, 214, 254, 303, 317, 319, 330, 333–34, 352, 353–54, 355, 362–63, 366, 377, 379, 383–84, 388, 407
Pliny, 170
plots, 17, 26–27, 194, 271, 272–73, 305–6
ploughshare, 115–16
Plutarch, 170
poems, ix–x, 13, 19, 27, 45, 48, 118, 242, 255, 335, 356–57
poetry, 23, 51, 52, 54, 57, 63, 67, 162, 209, 259, 269, 270–71, 308, 309, 310, 389–90, 438–39, 442
poets, ix–x, xii–xiii, 7–8, 10, 12, 23, 27–28, 33–34, 43–48, 51, 52, 54, 58–60, 67, 70–71, 72–73, 111–12, 121–22, 123–24, 126–27, 140, 152, 167–68, 174, 179–80, 183, 185–86, 188, 191, 192–93, 195, 198–99, 202–3, 207, 209, 211, 213–14, 241, 242, 246–47, 255–56, 259, 261, 268, 269, 270–71, 274, 281, 284, 286, 293–94, 295, 298, 304–5, 311, 331, 335, 340–41, 342–43, 346–47, 370, 375–76, 377–78, 382, 388–89, 390–91, 392–94, 396, 403–4, 407–8, 426–28, 437, 450–51, 460, 461–62
policies of kings, 119–20, 183–84, 204, 338–39

politics, xi, 1–2, 7–8, 17–18, 28, 58, 66, 69, 83, 89, 90, 104, 111–12, 122–23, 131–32, 135, 139–40, 153–54, 160–61, 162–63, 191–92, 195, 237–38, 240–41, 244, 250–51, 255–56, 257, 258–59, 263, 274, 276–77, 284–85, 287, 289–90, 291, 292–94, 298, 299–300, 301–2, 303, 305–6, 307–8, 311, 312, 357, 404, 430–32, 438, 457–58, 462–63
polity, 21, 132, 133, 135–36, 146, 152–53, 157–58, 160–63, 168, 209, 249–50, 257, 458–59, 462
polyandry, x, 13, 26, 32–33, 96–98, 100, 178, 197–98, 205
Porus, 169, 248
Positivism, 5–6, 9, 15
post-Gupta period, 345–46
post-Maurya period, x, 98–99, 170, 184, 282, 286, 426–28, 431–32, 433, 441–42, 455, 459, 464–65
post-Vedic period, xi, 143, 144, 163–64, 166, 438
Potdar, K.R., 54–55, 56–57, 71–72
Pradyumna, 251–52, 253–54, 307–8, 404–5
Prahrāda, 435–36
praises, 5, 19–20, 31, 52, 62, 65, 111, 157–58, 159, 167–68, 180–82, 188–89, 194–95, 196, 198, 202–3, 206–7, 238, 261, 265, 268, 272, 275, 322, 343, 375–76, 377, 379, 432–33, 462
Prajāpati, 45, 47, 51, 84, 85, 88, 101, 134–35, 373, 457
prank, 241
Prāpti, 279
Prasenajit/Pasenadi, 166, 438–39
Prasvāpinī, 307–8
Pratardana, 58–59, 95–96
prativāsudeva, 252–53, 278, 284, 295, 301–2
pravṛtti, 200, 214, 345–46, 358–59
prayers, 50–51, 52, 54–55, 70–71, 96–97, 153, 172, 247, 264, 442
preaching, 1, 194–95, 202–3, 237, 239, 243, 310–11, 335, 336–37, 354, 374, 385–86, 396, 403, 456–57
preclassical, 71–72, 136–37
predominance, 1, 153–54, 208–9, 279–80, 345–46
preliterate society, 26–28, 180–82, 183, 343
premarital children, 100–1, 187, 203–4, 332, 407–8
premonetary economy, 26–27, 161–62, 329
presents, 155, 251–52, 435
priests, 2–3, 5, 7–8, 12, 23, 30, 32–33, 43–44, 46, 47–48, 49–51, 52–53, 54, 55–57, 58–59, 61–63, 66–73, 115–16, 132–36, 153, 160–61, 164, 165, 166–67, 169, 286–87, 295–96, 366, 428–29, 437, 440–41, 444–46, 447, 448, 451, 456–57, 458–59, 460, 461–62, 464, 465–66
primogeniture, xi, 83, 86, 88–89, 94, 105, 107, 108–10, 191–92, 463–64
princes, 8, 29, 71, 92, 94, 102–4, 105–7, 108–9, 126, 127, 143–44, 155, 160–61, 163, 167, 172, 178, 179, 191–92, 194, 195, 197–98, 214, 238, 240–41, 245–46, 250–52, 253–54, 258, 262, 281, 289–90, 327, 328–29, 332–33, 425–26, 448, 451
princesses, 92, 94, 102, 104, 105–7, 126, 127, 143–44, 179, 214, 240–41, 245–46, 250–51, 253–54, 289–90, 327, 451
principles, 28–29, 44, 60–61, 109–10, 208–9, 239, 344–46, 365, 385–86, 398–99, 400–1, 435–36, 463–64
privileges, 23, 198, 309–11, 356–57, 384–86, 437
process
  of Brāhmanization, 426–28, 439, 457, 464, 465
  of deification, 334–35
  of migration and settlement, xiv, 62, 128
  of sacrificial rituals, 49–50, 133–35
  of Sanskritization, 115–16
  of social organization, 90
  of spiritual liberation, 363–64
  of state formation, 105, 431–32

of text creation, ix–x, 15–16, 25–27, 72–73, 128, 180–82, 201, 214, 239, 258–59, 448–49
of translation. 355–57
production of wealth and goods, 115–16, 131, 148–49, 154
professional bards, 185, 315
professional soldiers, 26, 166–67, 392
professions, 200–1, 251–52, 263, 434
profit, 10, 140, 313, 322, 330, 353
progeny, 44, 69, 92–93, 96–97, 102, 442, 461–62
projects, xi–xii, 3–4, 20–21, 195, 358–59, 428–29, 436
proliferation
of artisanal production, 115–16
of meanings, 180–82
of sources, 256
of Vāsudeva worship, 338–39
promises, 10, 70, 94, 173, 203, 243, 261, 264, 305–6, 310, 321, 340–41, 398–99, 401, 446–47, 461
propagation of doctrines, 13, 55, 243, 245–46, 252–53, 259, 264–65, 303, 321, 322, 353, 356–57, 407–8, 423, 426–28, 458–59
property, 88–89, 90–91, 97–94, 105–7, 130, 131, 147–50, 160, 177–78, 309–10, 312, 320, 455
prophecy, 249–52, 254, 258–59, 458, 464–65
prophets, 53–54, 338, 369–70, 452
proposals, 139, 157, 198–99, 287, 318, 321
prose *vaṃśa*, 84–85, 86, 107, 108
prosecution, 459
prosperity, 54–55, 157–58, 197–98, 238, 296, 332–33, 465
prostitutes, 155–56, 188–89
Pṛṣatī, 101, 102–3
Pṛthivī, 52
Pṛthu, 118, 193–94, 434–35
prudence, 96, 143–44, 160–61
psychoanalysis, 269
psycho-history, 56
psychology, 57, 145–46, 149–50, 338, 385–86, 442, 458–59
pukkasas, 117
Pulindas, 70, 117, 118
punishments, 70–71, 88, 105–7, 108–9, 126–27, 204, 275, 290, 320, 321, 323, 403, 404–5, 434, 442, 448, 455
Purāṇas, 1–3, 5–8, 9–10, 12, 22–23, 29, 45, 57, 60, 83, 92, 107, 147–48, 149–50, 179–82, 183, 187–88, 189–90, 196–97, 241, 244, 246–47, 249–50, 256, 257, 259, 260, 261, 262, 265–66, 267, 269, 270–71, 273–74, 276–77, 278, 279, 282–83, 284, 286, 287, 288, 292–93, 299, 300, 301, 304–6, 308, 310–11, 376, 377, 405, 433–34, 437–40, 441–42, 445, 448–50, 458–59, 465, 466–67
purge, 21, 428, 433, 434, 454–55, 458–59
Purocana, 203
purpose, ix, 6, 11, 15–16, 17–18, 25–26, 28–29, 55, 96–97, 115–16, 126, 155–56, 180–82, 192, 210, 246–47, 249–50, 271, 295, 296, 309–10, 313–14, 323, 337, 357, 382, 391, 398, 399, 400–1, 402, 429–30, 433–34, 443
Purukutsa, 49, 58–59, 62–63, 98–99, 440
Purumīlha, 45
Purūravas, 7–8, 9–10, 30, 84–85, 86–87, 94, 433–34
Pūrus, 9–10, 30, 32–33, 43–44, 48, 49, 52–53, 58–59, 61–64, 66, 72–73, 81, 82–83, 85, 95–96, 107, 161–62, 239, 256, 439–40, 462
Puruṣa, 344–46, 351, 354, 367, 375–76, 380, 381–82, 433–34
puruṣasūkta, 433–34
Pusalker, A.D., 62–63, 440

qualitative differences, 454
qualities, 17–18, 126–27, 143–44, 166, 202–3, 296–97, 371, 381, 382, 398, 400–1
quantitative data, 426, 454
queens, 97, 101, 111, 132–33, 135–36, 151, 177–78, 191–92, 195, 249, 306–7, 332–33, 407–8, 440–41, 451

questioning, x, 1, 12–13, 17, 20–21, 22–23, 24, 27–28, 110–11, 121–22, 138, 149–50, 161–62, 191, 196–97, 200, 203–4, 208–10, 237–38, 242, 244–45, 259–60, 292, 301–2, 338–39, 344–46, 358, 407–8, 426–28, 438–39, 440, 454
questions, ix, 19, 20, 25, 83, 86, 110–11, 128, 130, 135–36, 138, 146, 149–50, 151, 152, 179–80, 184–85, 186, 196–97, 199, 205, 211, 215, 241, 303, 312–13, 341, 358, 364, 383–84, 395, 396, 424, 433–34, 445–46, 455–56, 461, 466
quests, 355, 444

races, 133, 135, 136–37, 148
Rādhā, 198, 241, 266, 269, 270–71, 387, 407–8
rage, 21, 99–100, 188–89, 206, 243, 253–54, 285, 286, 327–28, 395, 405–6, 440–41, 446–47, 458–59
Rahurkar, V.G, 52, 53–54, 57, 61–62, 68–69, 70–71, 442–43
Rai, Lala Lajpat, 357
raids, 1, 25, 33–34, 81–82, 120, 133, 134–35, 153–54, 155, 156–58, 159–60, 163, 165–66, 258, 283–84, 292–93, 298–99, 312, 462–63
rain, 52, 54–55, 64, 108–9, 158, 194, 261–62, 268, 319
rājadharma, 430–31, 432, 437, 461, 464
rājasūya, 20–21, 33–34, 64–65, 81–82, 107, 129, 131–32, 133–38, 139–40, 145–46, 148, 149–50, 151, 152–53, 159–61, 170, 191, 203, 240–41, 245–46, 250–51, 281, 283–84, 293–94, 295, 297–98, 299–300, 435–36, 445–46, 462–63
rākṣasa marriage, 104, 105–7
Rākṣasas, 50, 52, 55, 68, 69, 113–14, 118, 119, 120–21, 122–23, 126–28, 167–68, 190, 203, 393–94, 439, 440–41, 442–43, 444–45
Rāma, 2–3, 23, 83, 169, 203, 252–54, 390, 398–99, 407–8, 426–28, 429–30, 444–45, 446, 459–60
Rāma Jāmadagnya, 21, 99–100, 375–76, 449–56, 457–60, 464–65
Rāmānuja, 358, 359–60
Ramanujan, A.K., 13–14, 423
Rāmāyaṇa, 1–2, 17, 23, 25–26, 32–33, 72–73, 83, 88–89, 118, 126–27, 147, 169, 188, 195, 205, 306, 307, 323, 390, 398–99, 425, 426–28, 429–30, 437–39, 444–45, 446, 447, 448, 449–50, 451, 459–60, 461
Rapson, E.J., 4, 5–6
Ratnagar, Shereen, 115–16
ratnins, 132–36, 137–38, 145–46, 160–61, 165
Rāvaṇa, 169, 252–53, 390
Ravi river, 48
Raychaudhuri, H.C., 1–2, 3–4, 23, 81, 178–79, 244, 259, 304, 344–45, 465, 466
Ṛbhus, 50, 52
Ṛcīka, 59–60, 85, 443, 448–50, 451
reaction, 183–84, 193–94, 303, 306, 393, 453, 459
reality, 28–29, 50, 71, 121–22, 173, 175, 177, 345–46, 392, 396, 432, 463–64
recensions, 27, 64–65, 114, 426–28
reception
  of a jewel, 305–6
  of kingdom, 112
  of knowledge, 24, 26–27, 430–31, 432–34, 435–37
  of legitimacy, 132
  of news, 195
  of patronage, 1–2, 50–51, 52–53, 58–59, 165, 426–28
  of power, 243, 356–57
  of recognition, 197–98, 296
  of revelation, 69–70
  of sons, 108
  of a text, 356–57
  of tributes, 135–36, 145–46, 170, 435
  of weapons, 115, 444
recitations, 23, 24, 67–68, 133–34, 212, 366, 381
reconciliation, 56–57, 336, 339–40, 454–55, 460
reconstructions, ix, 2, 3–4, 7–8, 15–16, 28, 49, 244, 256, 334–35, 355–56,

438, 440, 442, 450–51, 455–56, 465–66
records, xi–xii, 1–3, 4, 5, 6, 7–8, 10, 48, 49, 64–65, 66, 67–68, 107, 118, 140, 154, 185–86, 189–90, 195, 215, 342–43, 406
recurrence, 243, 425
redactions, 11, 81, 139–40, 144, 152–53, 175, 187, 194, 211, 390, 429, 437, 445, 446, 449–50, 454
reincarnation, 251–52, 369, 430–31
relationships, 32–33, 43, 45, 49–50, 52–53, 58, 59–60, 68–69, 71–72, 81, 82–83, 111–12, 117, 120–22, 131, 133–34, 187–88, 212, 260, 265, 278, 286–87, 289–90, 340, 345–46, 358–59, 426–28, 433–34, 439, 440, 444–45, 454–55, 456–57, 460
religions, xiii, 1–3, 7, 11, 15–16, 17–18, 20–21, 28–29, 43–44, 46–47, 52, 56–57, 62, 72–73, 86–87, 90–91, 129, 148, 149–50, 182, 183–84, 191, 200–1, 203, 208, 209–10, 244, 259–60, 264–65, 281, 292–95, 301, 306, 322–23, 335–36, 337, 338, 342, 344–46, 348, 353, 354, 357, 381, 407–8, 426–28, 429, 432, 433, 445–46, 447, 456–57, 458–59, 461–62
reluctance
  to copulate, 102–3, 195
  to fight, 215, 245–46, 289–90, 314, 324, 347, 390, 396, 460
remorse, 206–7, 326, 401, 433
Renaissance, 6, 21, 208–9, 458–59
renouncers, 111–12, 120–22, 160–62, 200, 254, 336, 344–45, 358–59, 374, 388, 432
Reṇu, 45
Reṇukā, 451, 455
renunciants, 200, 358–59
renunciation, 200, 214, 239, 345–46, 348, 358–59, 361, 365, 374–75, 381, 383–84, 432, 433
repetitions, 7–8, 378
replies, 238, 263, 275, 285, 288, 316, 317, 318, 325, 354, 361, 363–64, 365, 368, 371–72, 403, 442
representations, 12, 13, 16, 18, 24–28, 30, 32–33, 55–56, 60–61, 71–73, 83, 84, 87–89, 93, 104, 105–7, 110–11, 114, 115–16, 119, 123–24, 126–28, 129, 131, 133–34, 135, 136–37, 142, 145–46, 148–49, 153, 157–58, 159–60, 162–63, 164, 172, 173–74, 179–83, 184–86, 188, 190, 191, 193–94, 196, 198–99, 200, 208–9, 238, 242, 244, 254–55, 260, 264, 280, 282, 286, 291–92, 298–99, 313, 314, 329, 335–36, 340–41, 343, 345–47, 348, 356–57, 381–82, 386–87, 390, 396, 398–99, 429, 431–32, 445–46, 453, 454, 455, 456, 457–58, 461
reproduction, 87, 89, 90–91, 92–93, 98, 101, 102–3, 105–7, 345–46
repulsion, 62, 102–3, 201, 212–13
requests, 18, 91, 100–1, 102, 113, 130, 161–62, 251–52, 273, 286, 292, 326–27, 376–77, 435
rescue, 155–56, 160–61, 205, 241, 321–22, 386
resistance, 49, 59, 69, 87–88, 95–96, 102, 120, 121, 122–23, 126–28, 130, 151, 205, 247–48, 269, 272, 275, 279, 280, 285, 384, 440, 444
resolution, 108–9, 126, 141, 142, 212, 238, 250–51, 296, 317, 338–39, 353, 381, 383, 385–86, 460
resources, 7, 90, 97, 119–20, 121, 122–23, 155–56, 209–10, 283, 284, 291
responses, 21, 55, 110–11, 182, 184–85, 200–1, 263, 296, 328, 344–45, 363–64, 367–68, 395, 448, 450, 455–56, 458–59, 464
responsibilities, 62, 67–68, 95, 139–40, 145, 188–89, 201, 314, 338–39, 383–84, 387, 400, 403, 405–6, 434–35, 443
restoration, 28–29, 114, 249–50, 275, 276–77, 279, 433
result
  of action, 207, 214, 321, 332, 337, 374, 384–85, 404
  of devotion, 375
  of game of dice, 138, 144

result (*cont.*)
of *niyoga*, 100–1, 149, 177–78
of non-attachment, 345–46, 373
of sacrifice, 101
of war, 178–79, 208, 402, 433, 441–42
retelling, 4, 11, 343, 424–25, 433–34
revenue, 156
reverence, 62, 141, 239, 334–35, 385–86, 435–36
revision, 1–2, 72–73, 187, 238, 296, 297, 337, 343–44, 375–77, 378, 436–37, 453
revulsion, 201
reward, 50–51, 58–59, 153, 154, 159, 203, 204, 207, 324, 383–84, 461
Ṛg Veda, xi, 1, 5, 7–8, 9–10, 30, 31, 43–45, 46–50, 52, 57–61, 63–64, 66–67, 68, 81, 82–83, 86–88, 96–97, 98–99, 103, 104, 108–9, 111–12, 122–23, 140, 145–46, 169, 173–74, 183, 211, 247, 256, 260, 261, 264, 344–45, 382, 426–28, 433–34, 437, 439–40, 442, 449–50, 451, 462, 464
Ṛgvedic age, 43, 44, 48, 49, 58–59, 66–67, 68, 70–71, 87–89, 94, 96–97, 99–100, 140, 148, 149–50, 153–54, 163–64, 165, 169, 172, 173–74, 182, 256, 258, 379, 426–28, 461–62
rhapsoidos, 185–86
rice, 115–16, 121–22, 158, 349
riches, 51, 140, 141, 159, 290–91, 308
righteousness, 47–48, 56–57, 174, 175–76, 194–95, 200–1, 206–7, 208, 237, 301, 329, 332–33, 338–39, 352, 369–70, 389, 394, 395, 397, 398, 400–1, 429–30, 435–36, 444–45, 448, 463–64
rights, xii, 7, 8, 86, 89–90, 95, 102, 110, 124, 136, 138, 146, 148, 149–50, 151, 174, 194, 196–97, 203–4, 206–7, 208, 271, 309–10, 313–14, 355–56, 358, 433–35, 451, 452–53, 463–64
Rigspula, 19
rise
of agriculture, 258
of the Bharatas, 239
of heterodox religions, 338–39, 426–28
of Kosala, 438–39
of Kṛṣṇa, 129, 239–41, 255–56, 259, 265, 298, 302, 303, 306, 311–12, 403
of Magadha, 170, 280, 281–83
of the *mahājanapadas*, 115–16, 132
of the Pāṇḍavas, 111–12, 129, 291, 298
in status, 198
of unrighteousness, 369
ritualism, 5, 50–51, 52, 191, 209, 337, 340–41, 344–46, 363–64, 365, 374–75, 377, 380, 407–8, 428–29, 443
rituals, 5, 6, 7–8, 44, 56–57, 62, 64–65, 66, 88–89, 90–91, 102, 107, 121–22, 131, 132, 133–37, 146, 149–50, 152, 161–63, 178, 190–91, 209–10, 293–94, 295, 301, 302, 322–23, 336, 340–41, 345–46, 358–59, 360, 361–62, 364, 366–67, 371, 374, 429, 435–36, 443, 462–63
rivalries, 30, 178, 303–4, 460
rivals, 50–51, 52–53, 55, 70–71, 89, 136–38, 152, 160–61, 299, 458–59
rivers, 30, 48, 50–51, 52–53, 59, 62, 64–65, 86–87, 115–17, 124, 128, 142, 153–54, 193–94, 247, 248, 260, 319, 341, 388, 439, 440–41, 442, 461–62
Ṛjiśvan, 46, 48
robbers, 159, 398
romance, 143, 249–50, 266, 270–71, 426–28, 467
Romans, 4, 19, 248
Romulus, 19
root, 19, 43–44, 83, 118, 304–5, 379–80, 388, 465–66
Roy, Kaushik, 173–74, 175
Roy, Kumkum, 137
Ṛṣabha, 45, 51
ṛṣis, 60, 120–21, 180–82, 188, 191, 209–10, 437, 444
ṛta, 56–57, 379
Ṛtuparṇa, 143–44
Ruben, Walter, 11, 242, 245–46, 279, 335–36
Ruci, 443

Rudra, 52, 54, 88, 155, 290–91, 319
Rukmin, 286, 287, 288, 289
Rukmiṇī, 105–7, 241, 244–45, 250–51, 253–54, 279, 286, 287–88, 290, 291, 298, 307–8, 310, 404–5, 407–8
rulers, 1–2, 5, 23, 30–31, 105–7, 108–9, 118, 126, 131, 152, 157–58, 159–60, 162, 170, 177–79, 182, 195, 243, 252–53, 260, 276–77, 292–93, 435, 452–53, 456–57, 459, 462, 463–64
rulership, 22, 56–57, 66, 108–10, 122–23, 131–32, 144, 157–58, 159, 161–62, 169, 182, 184, 192, 198–99, 202–3, 251–52, 260, 307, 313, 315–16, 319, 426–28, 429–30, 431–32, 433–35, 441–42, 462, 464–67
rules, 91, 109–10, 121–22, 137–38, 160–61, 173, 175–76, 400–1
Ruru, 443

sabhā, 146, 148, 149–50
Sabhāparvan, 28, 152–53, 288, 297
Śacī, 308–9
sacrifices, 1, 7–8, 20–21, 23, 25–26, 33–34, 43–44, 49–51, 54–56, 61, 62–63, 67–68, 69–72, 81, 87, 101, 102, 108, 114, 115–16, 118, 121–24, 125, 129, 131, 132, 133–37, 153–54, 160–62, 174, 179, 191, 211, 249–50, 256, 259–60, 261, 262, 271, 279–80, 281, 283–84, 293–95, 297, 301–2, 319, 320, 324, 336, 339–40, 345–46, 365, 366–67, 369–70, 371, 380–81, 391, 393–94, 404, 406, 407–8, 425–26, 432, 436, 446–49, 451, 457–59, 466
saga, 12, 242, 452, 453
Sagara, 2–3, 441–42
sages, 19–20, 30–31, 43, 46–47, 50–51, 53–54, 57, 59–61, 70, 85, 91, 95–96, 99–101, 102–3, 105–7, 108–9, 114, 125, 139–40, 142, 143, 144, 152–53, 180, 188–89, 190, 195, 201–2, 208–9, 212–13, 239, 251–52, 253–54, 286, 292, 322, 341, 344–46, 362, 368, 371, 373, 375–76, 380, 404–6, 407–8, 432, 435, 436, 439, 448–50, 451, 457–58
Sahadeva, 16, 156, 157–58, 160–61, 163, 200, 279, 296–97, 349
Sahasrajyoti, 85
Sahi, M.D.N., 115–16
Śaivism, 279–80, 281, 284, 300, 438
Śākalya, 54
Śakti, 46, 68–69, 324, 393, 440–41, 442, 448–49
Śakuni, 129, 130, 138, 144, 152, 160, 176, 401
Śakuntalā, 30, 105–7, 161–62, 203–4
śalākāpuruṣas, 252–53
salvation, 8–9, 10, 151, 209–10, 336, 337, 348, 402
Śālva, 31–33, 66, 105–7, 286–87, 292, 298–99, 301, 466
Śalya, 11, 97, 163, 167, 176, 245–46, 317
Sāmā, 149
Samaṅga, 155–56
Samantapañcaka, 428, 452
Sāma Veda, 65, 165–66
Samavidhāna Brāhmaṇa, 165–66, 188–89
Sāmba, 304, 307, 404–5
Śambara, 43–44, 49, 58–59, 62, 315–16
Saṃjaya, 24, 26–27, 84, 86, 135–36, 160–61, 175, 184–86, 201–2, 204, 214, 312–13, 315, 316–17, 324, 331–32, 334–35, 343, 346–47, 387, 389, 430–31, 463–64
Sāṃkhya, 338, 344–46, 351, 352, 354, 355, 361–62, 365, 371–72, 375–76, 381–82, 429
Saṃkṣobha, 122–23
Śaṃtanu, 7–8, 9–10, 30, 31, 64, 66, 72–73, 81, 108–10, 183, 191–92, 290–91, 430–31, 462–63
Samudra Gupta, 121, 122–23, 126, 260, 431–32
Samudravijaya, 253–54
Saṃvaraṇa, 30, 45, 439–40
sanction, 88–89, 137–38, 145–46, 240–41, 258
sanitizing, 96–97, 345–46, 428–30, 464
Śaṅkara, 356–57, 358–60, 361
Śāṅkhāyana Srauta Sūtra, 8, 66
Sanskrit, 4–5, 25, 31, 143, 424–25, 426–28

Sanskritization, 122–23, 126–27, 292–93, 465
Śāntiparvan, x, 12, 25, 26–27, 28–29, 148, 170, 180, 183, 277, 278, 360, 426–28, 429, 430–31, 432–33, 436–37, 452, 453, 455–56, 464–66
Śāradaṇḍāyinī, 99–100
Sarasvān, 52
Sarasvatī, 30, 45, 46, 52, 59, 64–66, 142, 439
Śarmiṣṭhā, 82–83, 105–7
sarpasatra, 211–12, 424–25, 428, 465–66
Sarpedon, 19
Śatapatha Brāhmaṇa, xiv, 23, 30, 48, 62–63, 65–66, 86–87, 88, 115–16, 120, 131–32, 133, 154, 178–79, 465–66
Sātvatas, 242, 247, 248, 256, 290–91
Satyabhāma, 250–51, 303–6, 307–11
Sātyaki, 163, 175–76, 314–15, 331, 404–5
Satyavatī, 59–60, 100–1, 102–3, 109–10, 191–92, 201, 203–4, 214, 443, 451
Saudāsas, 68–69, 70–71, 99–100, 440–41, 442
Śaunaka, 24, 46–47, 65, 66–68, 180–82, 184–85, 424–28, 436–37, 453, 454, 461, 465–66
Sāvitṛ, 51, 52, 127–28, 134–35
Sāvitrī, 105–7
schools, 5, 9, 64–65, 345–46, 375–76, 429, 447
science fiction, 298–99
sciences, 14–15, 263
scripture, 166, 316, 335, 357, 370, 386–87, 399, 424–25, 461, 465
sects, x, 172, 438
seeds, 86–87, 90–91, 93, 96–97, 98, 103, 149, 323, 374–75, 457
segments, ix, 83, 84
separation
  of army units, 166–67
  of body and mind/soul, 337, 352, 363–64
  of a couple, 143–44
  of different Kṛṣṇas, 247, 291
  of different layers of a text, 2–3, 12, 242, 243–44, 336–37, 338–41, 425–26
  of home and workplace, 148–49
  of settled society and forest. 122–23, 352, 425–26
sequels, 130, 241, 300
sermons, 239, 428–29
serpents, 199–200, 260
services, 105–7, 122–23, 430–32
settled society, xiv, 1, 46, 48, 49, 111–12, 115–17, 119–23, 126–28, 129, 153, 155, 157–58, 240–41, 250–52, 258, 278–79, 283–84, 286, 287, 292, 301, 304, 466–67
shamanism, 52, 193–94, 426–28
Shamash, 124
Sharma, Arvind, 424
Sharma, R.S., 26, 28, 33–34, 81–82, 115–16, 131–33, 135, 147, 148, 153, 160, 163, 335, 430–31
Sharma, T.R.S., 199
shelter, 155, 178, 206, 397
Shende, N.J., 425–26, 454
shepherd, 56, 62
shift, 1, 10, 16, 22–23, 25, 48, 64, 83, 166, 211, 258, 279, 289, 355–56, 424–25
ship, xii–xiii, 86–87, 151, 298
Śibi, 95–96
Śigrus, 53
Śikhaṇḍin, 163, 178–79, 185, 390, 430–31
Singh, Sarva Daman, 96–97, 163–65, 167
singing, 155–56, 159, 194, 268
Sinha, Manoj Kumar, 175
sins, 50, 54, 56–57, 92, 143, 144, 193, 238, 272, 320, 321, 328, 349, 352, 353, 377, 395, 397, 398, 436, 442, 448
sisters, 86, 87–88, 103, 104, 105–7, 112, 127–28, 137–38, 240–41, 245–46, 251–52, 253–54, 274, 290, 301–2, 307–8
Śiśupāla, 105–7, 203, 238, 240–41, 243, 245–46, 250–51, 265–66, 279, 280, 281, 282, 283, 286–87, 288, 295–99, 301–2, 303–4, 311, 312–13, 334–35, 391, 393–94
Sītā, 205, 206–7, 459–60

Śiva, 20–21, 57, 114, 127–28, 145–46, 243, 279–80, 281, 283–84, 286, 444, 459–60
Śivā, 105–7
Śivadevī, 253–54
Śiva Purāṇa, 448
Śivas, 52–53, 61–62
sixteen kings, 452, 453
sixteen *mahājanapadas*, 466–67
skirmish, 155–56, 165–66, 264, 312
slaughter, 120, 167–68, 173, 264, 346–47, 367–68, 404, 452–53, 457–58, 460, 464–65
slaves, 130, 131, 148–49, 151, 152, 153, 166–67, 172, 329, 452
slaying
  of Baka, 121, 393–94
  of Bhīṣma, 430–31
  of Droṇa, 200
  of Duryodhana, 193
  of foemen, 57, 113–14, 367–68
  of Hiḍimba, 393–94
  of Jarūtha, 53–54
  of Kaṃsa, 251–52, 319
  of Kirmīra, 393–94
  of living beings, 397
  of relatives of a girl, 71–72
  of Śiśupāla, 280
  of soldiers, 177
  of Vasiṣṭha's sons, 68, 69, 319, 333–34, 367–68, 397
  of Vṛtra, 51
Smith, Mary Caroll, 103
snake sacrifice, 21, 211
snakes, 21, 52, 112–14, 194, 211, 260, 328–29
solar deities, 11, 17, 85, 261
solar dynasty, 83, 86
solar eclipse, 392–93
Soma, 50, 52, 60–61, 84, 86, 101, 134–35, 137–38, 140, 439–40, 447
Somadatta, 317, 439–40
Somadeva, 467
Somāhūti, 44–45
Somavaṃśa, 83, 84, 86
sons, xi–xii, 18, 23, 30–32, 44–47, 48, 49, 50, 51, 52–53, 55–57, 58–60, 63, 68–69, 70–71, 81, 82–83, 84, 85–88, 90–91, 92, 93–94, 95–96, 97–101, 102–3, 107–10, 112, 113, 114–15, 127, 141, 142, 148–49, 150, 154, 163, 167, 177–79, 180–82, 188, 191–92, 195, 196–98, 201–4, 205, 206, 208, 210, 212, 213–14, 240–41, 245–46, 247–48, 249–52, 253–54, 258, 260, 265–66, 272, 275, 277, 279, 281, 286–87, 290–91, 292–93, 294–96, 300, 303–4, 307–8, 313, 314, 317, 320, 322, 324, 326, 327–28, 331, 332–34, 371, 373, 387–88, 392, 393, 394, 401, 404–6, 430–31, 432–33, 435, 440–41, 442–43, 444, 446–47, 448–50, 451–53, 455, 457, 461–62, 465, 466
sorcery, 67, 426–28, 443, 456–57
sources of history, ix, 1–4, 9–10, 15–16, 19–20, 22–23, 24, 25, 30, 49–50, 81–82, 90, 111–12, 185–86, 194, 237, 244–45, 247, 255–56, 259, 265–66, 269–70, 287, 292, 304, 311–12, 334–35, 352, 363–64, 376–77, 438–39, 446, 461
sources of revenue, 121, 122–23, 156, 180–82
specialists, 6, 115–16, 148–49, 467
spectators, 172–73, 240–41, 242, 312–13, 423
speeches, 50–51, 158, 203–4, 295, 303, 314, 321, 331, 342–43, 357
spirit
  of evil nature, 53–54, 260
  of truth and righteousness, 47–48, 62, 333
spirituality, 28, 56–57, 191, 209, 237–38, 243, 263, 296, 303, 340–41, 440, 441, 445, 454–56
spoils, 51, 60
Śramaṇas, x, 183–84, 361–62
Śramaṇic religions, xiii, 7, 9, 200–1, 203, 345–46
stages
  of development of a text, 24, 25–26, 94, 182, 241, 242, 455–56, 460
  of human life, 121–22, 328, 384

stages (*cont.*)
of Kṛṣṇa's career, 274, 311
of rituals, 133
of social evolution, 117
of spiritual liberation, 345–46, 373
stakes, 89, 129, 130, 131, 142, 143–44, 145–46, 147, 149–50, 151, 152, 153, 155–56, 395–96, 398, 423
state, xi, 1, 3–4, 25–26, 31, 88–89, 94, 105, 110–11, 115–16, 119–20, 121, 122–24, 131, 132, 133, 149, 159, 163–64, 168, 169, 182, 183, 209, 344–45, 367, 424, 430–32, 462
status, xi, 25–26, 69, 89–90, 100, 118–19, 135, 137, 139–40, 148–50, 157–58, 166, 167, 170, 192, 196–99, 209–10, 243, 264, 269, 277, 278, 298, 302, 311–12, 334–35, 356–57, 370, 371–72, 424, 429–30, 433–34, 436, 441–42, 445, 448, 450, 453, 458–59, 462–63
stealing, 238, 241, 266, 269, 270, 310, 320
stepmother, 202–3
stepson, 203
stereotypes, 5–6, 50, 121, 322–23, 328
stories, xi, 18, 20–21, 28–29, 43, 68–69, 70–73, 81–83, 84–85, 86–88, 89, 91, 92, 93–94, 96, 99–100, 102–3, 105–7, 108–9, 111–12, 114–15, 118, 120, 125–26, 131, 135, 143–44, 179–82, 184–86, 188–92, 195, 201, 204, 211, 212–13, 241, 242, 244, 245–47, 249–50, 252–53, 254–56, 258–59, 260, 270, 271, 279, 284, 285–86, 297, 300, 307, 310, 324, 387, 393, 398, 405, 407–8, 424–25, 426–29, 435–37, 438, 439, 440, 441–42, 443–44, 445, 446–50, 451, 452, 455–56, 457–58, 460, 463–64, 465–66, 467
story-tellers, 25–26, 28–29, 180
strata of a text, 28–29, 158
stratagems, 176, 204, 301–2, 389
stratification, 1, 12–13, 14, 25, 115–16, 149, 438
strength, 50, 52, 124, 169–70, 205, 211, 238, 250–51, 261–62, 286, 291, 295, 296, 306, 319, 323–24, 326, 327, 374–75, 430, 440, 441, 454–55
Strīparvan, 27, 390–91
structure
philosophical, 363–64
political, 131–32
social, xi, 335–36, 344–45
textual, 13–14, 17, 24, 27–28, 179, 246–47, 341–42
struggle
between ability and heredity, 191, 197–98
between *brāhmaṇas* and *kṣatriyas*, 457–58
between *dharma* and *adharma*, 13
between Divodāsa and Śambara, 49
between Greeks and Persians, 4
between Kṛṣṇa and Jarāsaṃdha. 299–300, 301–2, 306
between Kṛṣṇa and Kaṃsa, 303, 306
between Viśvāmitra and Vasiṣṭha, 67, 68
for power, 44, 325, 390–91, 442
for succession, 33–34, 82, 112, 289–90, 463–64
students, 5, 15, 191, 312, 394, 435–36, 460
subduing, xii, 62–63, 126, 157–58, 159–60, 249–50, 260, 299, 302, 305, 426–28, 443, 451, 464
Subhadrā, 19, 32–33, 104, 105, 112, 114–15, 177–78, 179, 180, 245–46, 290–91, 392
subjugation, 5, 102, 104, 105–7, 241, 317, 326, 458–59
subordination, xi–xii, 117, 118–19, 122–23, 145–46, 160–61, 164, 177–78, 200, 293–94, 335–36, 338–40, 377, 445
subservience, 435–36
subsistence, 115–16, 263
subversion, 204, 463–64
succession, 28–29, 33–34, 82, 91, 102, 105, 107, 109–10, 112, 127, 131, 137–38, 152, 161–63, 174, 177–78, 179, 191–92, 213–14, 215, 289–90, 293–94, 463–64

successors, 1–2, 23, 32, 45, 58–59, 66, 91, 110, 127, 158, 159, 160, 177–78, 179, 191–92, 214
Sudās, 7–8, 31, 32–33, 43–44, 47–48, 49, 50–51, 52–53, 58–60, 61–63, 68–69, 70–71, 72–73, 256, 439–41, 442, 450, 456–58, 461–62
Sudeṣṇā. 99–100, 102–3, 206
śūdras, 117, 118–19, 195, 209–10, 288, 320, 324, 371, 377, 383, 407–8, 424, 433–34
Sudyumna, 86
suffering, 91, 109, 164, 175, 202–3, 206, 208, 210, 214, 270–71, 275, 323, 363, 373, 426–28
Sugrīva, 126–27
Śukrācārya, 47, 82–83, 426–28, 443
Sukthankar, V.S., xiii, 12, 13–14, 24, 67–68, 243, 336, 425, 426–28, 452, 456–57, 458–59
Sullivan, Bruce M., 186, 187–88, 190, 424–26, 436
Sumeru, 341, 435
Sun, 54–56, 83, 84–86, 124, 125–26, 133–34, 198–99, 212, 251–52, 261–62, 277, 318, 358–59, 365, 373, 375, 377–78, 382–83, 392–93, 439, 443
Śunahotra, 44–45, 46
Śunaḥśepa, 44, 70–72, 133–34, 135, 379, 448–50
Śunaka, 44–45
Sunandā, 108
Śuṅgas, 32, 182, 183–84
superiority, 50–51, 56–57, 138, 144, 166, 167–68, 172, 207, 238, 248, 296, 309–10, 315–16, 342, 378, 386, 404, 433–34, 440, 441, 444, 445–46, 455–56, 458–59
supervisors, 132–33, 157–58
supplements, 136, 245, 246–47, 256, 337, 424–25
supremacy, 104, 303, 345–46, 359–60, 435–36, 445
supreme
  apparatus, 167
  hero, 27, 432–33
  landholder, 430–31
  position, 56–57, 277, 298, 299
  power, 51, 170, 193
  principle, 28–29, 367
  varṇa, 102
  virtue, 378
Supreme Being, 8, 12, 47, 243, 296, 302, 315–16, 331, 335, 336–37, 338–39, 341, 345–46, 363–64, 365, 370, 371–72, 374–75, 377–78, 381–82, 383, 464
Śūrpaṇakhā, 126–27
surplus, 115–16
surrogates, 120, 201–2, 214
survival, xi, 19–20, 47, 61–62, 86–87, 89, 109–10, 114, 129, 179, 192–93, 213–14, 251–52, 265, 285–86, 301–2, 307, 395, 452–53, 463–64
Sūrya, 49–50, 52, 93, 96–97, 134–35, 197–98, 262, 277
Sūryavaṃśa, 83, 84–86, 88–89, 105, 107, 108, 109–10, 191–92, 434, 463–64
Suśarman, 156–58
Sutanu, 273
sūtas, 1–3, 8, 11, 24–26, 67–68, 86, 132–34, 135–36, 160–61, 166, 180, 184–85, 197–99, 206, 282–83, 315, 332–33, 340–41, 343, 346–47, 353, 401, 424–25, 436, 437–38, 445–46, 449–50, 463–64
Sutherland, Sally J., 205
Sutlej, 50–51, 59
suzerainty, 137, 293–94
svabhāva, 383–86, 387, 407–8
svadharma, 263, 321, 331–32, 336, 347–48, 352, 365, 366, 368, 371, 383–86, 387, 389–90, 391, 396, 402, 403–4, 407–8, 463–64
svayaṃvara, 104–7, 114–15, 240–41, 242, 253–54, 286, 290, 312–13
Śvetaketu, 91, 92–93, 424
Śvetakī, 114
Syamantaka jewel, 241, 250–51, 303–4, 305, 403, 404
sympathy, xii, 163, 313, 452–53, 463–64
symposium, 180–82, 184–85
Synthetic Method, 13–14, 15–16, 24, 336

taboo, 87–89, 269
Tagore, Rabindranath, 396, 398–99
Taittirīyas, 64–65
Takṣaka, 112–13, 126, 127, 211–12
tales, 8, 12, 32, 188–89, 190–91, 241–42, 246–47, 304–5, 424–25, 447, 453, 463–64
Tapatī, 439
Taranatha Tarkavachaspati, 8–9
taste, 242–43, 374–75, 428, 464
taxation, 1, 26, 132–33, 153, 434
Taxila, 169, 211, 465–66
teachers, 5, 24, 47–48, 59–60, 83, 101, 103, 160, 163, 188–90, 212, 238, 244, 247–48, 295–96, 312, 314, 333–35, 340–41, 345–46, 365, 366–67, 368, 370, 395, 403, 423, 426–28, 430, 432–33, 435–36, 454
teachings
  of Bhīṣma, 435–36
  of Gautama Buddha, 345–46, 363–64
  of Ghaṭapaḍita, 251–52, 387
  of Ghora Āṅgirasa, 344–45, 366–67, 370, 381
  of the Gītā, 244, 337–38, 343–46, 347–48, 349, 353, 357, 363–64, 366, 370, 373, 374–76, 377, 378
  of heterodox religions, 172, 348, 432
  of Kṛṣṇa, 255–56, 310–11, 318, 331–32, 333, 334–35, 338, 342–46, 347–48, 349, 353, 357, 363–64, 366, 370, 373, 374–76, 384–85, 386–87, 388, 389–90, 397, 403–4, 407, 429, 432, 464
  of Ramakrishna, 358
  of the *Rāmāyaṇa*, 25
  of Vyāsa, 188–89
  of wind god, 433–34
  of Yuḍhiṣṭhira, 326–27, 464
technology, 115–16, 209
telling, 10, 25–26, 72–73, 87, 93, 159–60, 180, 184–85, 246–47, 297, 394, 398, 424–25, 436–37
terminology, 56, 98
territory, 22–23, 25, 33, 65, 114, 120, 153, 157–58, 184, 258, 260, 283–84, 290, 291, 294–95, 299, 344–45
terror, 113–14, 357, 392
tests, 82, 109–10, 114–15, 180–82, 199, 202–3, 214, 254, 284, 439
textiles, 131, 153
Thapar, Romila, 1, 3–4, 6, 7–8, 25, 28, 33–34, 81–82, 83, 88–89, 115–16, 120, 131, 146, 335, 430–31
Thebes, 18
themes, 17, 20–21, 43, 52, 114, 115, 118, 123–24, 133–34, 143–44, 175, 179, 211, 248–49, 331, 336–37, 347–48, 424–25, 430–31, 444
Theogony, 19
theology, 2, 5, 51, 270–71, 424–25, 428–29, 435–36, 465
theories, 12–13, 14, 15–16, 28–29, 114, 133, 135, 163, 174, 209, 242–43, 317, 334–35, 354, 368, 381–82, 384, 389, 426–28, 450–51, 454
thesis, 2–3, 25–26, 115–16, 133–34, 196–97, 245–46, 280, 336, 434
Thetis, 19–20
thighs, 151, 329, 433–34, 435
thinker, 17, 121–22, 191, 298, 358
Thucydides, 342–43, 463
Tilak, Bal Gangadhar, 357, 361
Time, 28–29, 113–14, 144, 145–46, 280, 315–16, 374–75, 376, 398–99
tools, 14, 15–16, 20–21, 27–28, 115–16, 122–24, 125, 209, 324, 400, 426–28, 450–51
tormenting, 58, 59–60, 141, 202–3, 261–62, 350
tract, 112, 118, 243
trade, 131, 209, 320, 383
trader, 131, 155–56, 263, 398
traditions
  familial, 56–57
  historical, ix–x, xi, 1–4, 5–10, 11, 12, 15–16, 20–21, 22–23, 24–25, 27–28, 30–31, 32–34, 43, 47–48, 60, 62–63, 66, 67–68, 83, 87–89, 96–97, 98–99, 114, 117, 119, 125–26, 127–28, 142, 159–60, 179–83, 184–86, 188–90, 191, 194, 209–10, 239, 241–42, 246–47, 249, 252, 254–55, 256, 258, 269–70, 271, 274, 277, 278, 282–83, 291–92, 302, 340–41, 342, 343, 405–6, 424, 425, 426–28,

429–30, 437–40, 441–42, 445–46, 447, 448–50, 457, 458–59, 460, 461, 463, 464–66, 467
military, 170, 391
religious, 125, 132, 140, 145–46, 200, 209, 336, 338–39, 348–49, 358–60, 361, 377, 383–84, 403, 445–46, 456–57
social, 149
transcendentalism, 56, 122–23, 213, 384
transfer
of amnesia, 429
of authorial role, 180, 184–86
of crown gems, 208
of diseases, 282–83
of gifts, 461–62
transition, xi, 1, 9–10, 12, 24, 28–29, 72–73, 88–89, 90, 105–7, 110–11, 166, 168, 172, 173, 179–80, 196–97, 209, 214, 215, 239, 311–12, 338, 423, 430–31, 461, 462–63
translation, 97–98, 201, 334, 355–58, 371–72, 433
transmigration of soul, 338–39, 345–46, 363–64, 369
transmission
of property, 88–89, 90–91, 105
of textual traditions, 8, 89, 90–91, 183, 254–55, 363, 464–65
of ways of life, 56
Trasadasyu, 52–53, 58–59, 62–64, 98–99, 440, 462
Trautmann, Thomas R., 168–70
travellers, xii–xiii, 4, 180–82, 249
treasures, 49, 285
treatises, 277, 331–32, 336, 337
treatment
of the brāhmaṇas, 158
of the 'other', xii, 122–23
of pacifism, 329
of the Pāṇḍavas, 161–62
of women, 147, 148, 213–14
tribes, xiii–xiv, 1, 7–8, 9–10, 22–23, 26, 43–44, 47, 48, 52–53, 59–60, 61–62, 69, 70–71, 82–83, 98–99, 117–21, 126–27, 129, 131, 133, 135, 148, 149–50, 153–54, 155–56, 160, 171–72, 178, 191–92, 242–43, 258–59, 261, 264–65, 266, 280, 281–82, 283–84, 292, 298–99, 301, 306, 435, 456–58, 461–63
tricks, 12, 138, 139, 143–44, 145–46, 174, 193, 237–38, 240–41, 270, 279, 284, 286–87, 336
Trigartas, 156–57, 163
Trikartas, 65
Triśaṅku, 446–49
triumph, 48, 56, 88–89, 105–7, 108–9, 111, 177–79, 212, 261, 284, 296–97, 299–300, 301–2, 395, 403–4, 429, 447, 457–58, 460, 461–62, 464
Trojan horse, 19–20
Trojan War, 18
Troy, xii–xiii, 18, 22–23
Tṛtsu, 52–53, 62–63
truth, 19–20, 30, 47–48, 55–57, 141, 196, 198, 203–4, 303, 304, 315–16, 319, 350, 357, 366–67, 370, 371, 381, 394, 395–99, 400–1, 404
truth-claim, 48, 50
turmoil, 195, 250–51, 430
Turvaśa, 48, 49, 52–53, 59–60, 61–63, 82–83, 439–40, 456–57

Udayana, 467
Udyogaparvan, 167, 173–74, 204, 278, 297, 300, 311–12, 333, 340, 347, 365, 376–77, 402
Ugraśravas, 24, 84, 85–86, 89, 180–82, 184–86, 190, 424–25, 426, 428, 454, 461, 465–66
Ulūpī, 95, 102, 105–7, 126, 127, 212
Umā, 243
unity
of a clan, 306
with cosmic entities, 13, 54, 336, 340–41, 345–46, 383
of a text, 13–14, 20–21, 24, 336, 338, 375–76, 377
universal
author, 188
creator, 187–88
dharma, 398–238, 400, 424
epic themes, 17
human, 125, 291–92, 386–87
sovereignty, 57, 465–66

untouchables, 117, 118–19, 122–23, 445
Upakaṃsa, 251–52
Upaniṣad, 13, 23, 58–59, 111–12, 154, 155, 165–66, 172, 189–90, 191, 200, 242, 244, 247–48, 256, 259–60, 335–37, 341–42, 344–46, 349, 350, 351, 352, 354, 355, 358–59, 360, 363–64, 373, 377, 378, 380, 381–82, 383, 386–87, 445–46
Upasāgara, 251–52
Upayāja, 101
upholder of order, 56, 125, 379
upstarts, 426–28, 461–62
urbanization, 26–28, 115–16, 127–28, 340–41
Urvaśī, 7–8, 9–10, 55–56, 103
Ūṣā, 52, 54–56
Uśanas, 46–47, 67, 82–83, 375–76, 426–28
Utathya, 96, 433
Utilitarianism, 400
Utkala, 86
Utkīla, 45, 51
utopia, 105–7, 111–12, 121–22
Uttara, 167
Uttarakāṇḍa, 195, 426–28, 429–30
Uttarakuru, 105–7
Uttarpara, 357
Uttar Pradesh, 48
Uttarā, 240–41, 245–46, 312

Vāc, 45, 51
vacabhūmika mahāmātras, 156
Vācaspatyam, 8–9
Vahista, 47–48
Vaidya, C.V., 115–16
Vaikarṇa tribes, 52–53, 61–62, 457–58
Vaiśaṃpāyana, 24, 26–27, 64–65, 81, 84, 85–86, 179, 180–82, 183, 184–86, 188, 211, 212, 424–25, 428–29, 436–37, 461, 462–64, 465–66
Vaiśeṣika, 360
Vaiṣṇavism, xiii, 12, 95, 125, 160–61, 196, 255–56, 270–71, 279–80, 281, 284, 287, 300, 335, 424–25, 426–28, 435–36, 438, 461, 465
Vaiṣṇavization, 25–26, 28–29, 196, 278, 302, 343–44, 375–77, 386, 426–29, 464
vaiśyas, 16, 70, 320, 324, 377, 383–84, 433–34
Vālmīki, 126–27, 188, 390, 426–28, 438–39, 446
valour, 27–28, 29, 104, 196–98, 202–3, 209–10, 252–53, 309, 332, 383, 390–91, 430, 464–65
value, 9, 26–27, 70, 95, 114, 148, 170, 173–74, 197–98, 200, 202–4, 215, 294–95, 336, 340–41, 346–47, 356–57, 370, 384, 391, 395, 398–99, 400–1, 404, 433, 448, 465
Vāmadeva, 45, 46–47, 48
vaṃśānucarita, 305
vaṃśas, 84–85, 86, 88, 94, 95–96, 107, 108–9, 426
vana, 111–12, 119–20, 263, 323
van Buitenen, J.A.B., 23, 81, 97–98, 128, 131, 136, 143, 157–58, 188, 244, 281–82, 298, 336, 348, 363–64, 371–72
Varcin, 49, 58–59, 62
varṇa system, xi–xii, 21, 25–26, 28–29, 31, 43, 72–73, 88–89, 102, 110–11, 117–19, 189–90, 191, 196–97, 199, 200, 203–4, 206–7, 209, 210, 263, 319, 320, 321, 322–23, 325, 331–32, 344–46, 347–49, 353, 371, 383, 384, 385–86, 390–92, 407–8, 423, 424, 426–28, 429–30, 432, 433–34, 435–36, 445–46, 455, 458–60, 461, 462, 463–64
Varuṇa, 17, 43–44, 49–50, 51–52, 54, 55–57, 70–72, 86, 87, 98–99, 103, 113, 125, 127–28, 134–35, 137–38, 143–44, 251–52, 292, 379, 457, 461–62
Vasiṣṭha, 7–8, 32–34, 43–44, 46–48, 49–51, 52–63, 66–73, 82–83, 96, 98–100, 103, 426–28, 437, 439–42, 443–50, 454–57, 460, 461–62, 464
Vāstospati, 52

Vasudeva, 253–54, 257, 258–59, 265–66, 271–74, 277, 284–85, 295–96, 404–5
Vāsudeva, xiii, 21, 29, 30–31, 182–83, 215, 237–422, 462–63
Vasumanas, 95–96
vāvātā, 132–33
Vāyu, 16, 52, 158
Vāyu Purāṇa, 187–88, 246–47, 448
Vedānta, 189–90, 337, 344–46, 351, 355, 356–60, 370, 375–76, 381–82
Velankar, H.D., 49, 50, 249, 443
Veṇa, 118, 435
Vibhīṣaṇa, 126–27
Vicitravīrya, 100–1, 102, 104, 105–7, 110, 195, 201, 203–4
victims, 44, 70–71, 126, 195, 279, 383–84, 449
victory, xiii, 7–8, 12, 19–20, 43–44, 47–48, 49, 50, 52–54, 55–57, 58–59, 61, 62–64, 69, 125, 130, 133, 160–61, 168, 172, 174–75, 176, 179, 191, 237–38, 243, 272, 274, 278, 298–99, 300, 315–16, 317, 320, 326, 332, 333, 336, 340, 343, 353, 389, 393–95, 444, 452, 456–58, 460, 462, 463–64
vidatha, 165, 166
Vidathin, 48
Videgha Maṭhava, xiv, 115–16, 120
Videha, xiv, 3–4, 23, 65, 66, 115–16, 154, 445–46
Vidura, 17, 100–1, 130, 138, 139, 160–61, 195, 198, 200, 204, 214, 298, 301, 308, 312–13, 317, 321, 324, 329, 330, 331, 383, 385–86
Vidurā, 204, 324, 325
Vikarṇa, 130, 146, 147, 317
villages, 111, 121–23, 154, 239, 241, 249–50, 251–52, 253–54, 257, 258–59, 265, 266, 267, 268–69, 271, 301, 307, 313
violence, x–xi, 21, 69, 105–7, 111–12, 113, 120, 123–24, 126, 128, 130, 136–37, 139–40, 172, 173–74, 175, 200–1, 203–4, 206–7, 208, 210, 212, 215, 239, 291–92, 312, 325, 326–27, 338–40, 346–48, 353, 357, 381, 386–87, 390–91, 392, 397, 399, 404, 405, 428, 432, 433, 434, 443, 451, 454–59
Virajas, 435
Virāṭa, 142, 156, 157–58, 163, 206, 312, 323, 394
Virāṭaparvan, 151, 156, 157, 158
virility, 204, 206, 374–75
Viṣāṇins, 52–53, 61–62
vision, 185–86, 239, 311, 335, 372, 426–28
Viṣṇu, 20–21, 52, 54, 57, 125, 187–88, 241, 246–49, 256, 257, 259, 261, 262, 264, 265, 267, 269, 273, 274, 277, 278, 288, 291–93, 294–95, 299, 300, 301, 304–6, 308, 310–11, 317, 335, 337, 376–77, 435, 450, 459–60, 465
Viśvadevas, 51–52, 96–97
Viśvāmitra, 7–8, 32–34, 43–45, 46–48, 49–52, 54–61, 62–63, 66–73, 95–96, 147–48, 404–5, 437–38, 439–41, 442–43, 444–50, 451, 452, 455–56, 457–58, 460, 461–62, 464–65
viśvarūpa, 239, 407–8
Vivasvat, 84–87, 88, 368
voice
  of the author, 180–82
  of bards, 25
  of Bhārgavas, 449–50
  of dissent, 191, 407–8
  of Kaṃsa, 273
  of Kṛṣṇa, 259–60, 311–12
  of Naimiṣeya *ṛṣis*, 180–82
  of people, 26–27, 162
  of Sahadeva, 327
  of Satyabhāmā, 309–10
  of Vikarṇa, 146
  of Vyāsa, 212
  of women, 105–7, 110–11
vows, 19, 55, 71–72, 92, 100–1, 109–10, 130, 135, 154, 191–92, 203–4, 212, 293, 310, 333, 385–86, 391, 392, 396–97, 398, 401, 402–3, 407–8, 430, 460, 463–64

Vraja, 156, 238, 269
Vratinī, 307–8
Vṛcivats, 69
Vṛddhadyumna, 466
Vṛddhakṣatra, 182
Vṛndāvana, 241, 246–47, 249–50, 255, 258, 259–60, 264, 265–66, 271, 318
Vṛṣaparvan, 82
Vṛṣṇis, xiii, 112, 128–29, 162–63, 188–89, 191, 240–41, 242, 244, 247–48, 249–50, 253–54, 256, 258–59, 283, 284, 286–87, 294–95, 302, 303, 305, 311–12, 314, 318, 334–35, 404, 405–6, 462–63
Vṛtra, 51, 57
Vyāsa, 21, 23, 24, 26–27, 28–29, 31–32, 67–68, 100–1, 102–3, 110, 179–82, 184–92, 194–95, 196, 199, 201, 203–4, 209–10, 212–15, 245, 289–90, 343, 385–86, 390–91, 396, 405–6, 407–8, 423, 424, 428–29, 436, 454, 461, 463–64
Vyuśitāśva, 93

wars, 2–3, 10, 11, 18–20, 21, 23, 24, 26–27, 28–29, 31–34, 52, 81–82, 89, 95, 104, 107, 109–10, 128, 153, 159–61, 163–64, 165–70, 171–80, 184–86, 198, 202–3, 205, 208, 213, 214, 240–43, 248, 256, 276–77, 279–80, 284, 294–95, 309, 311–12, 313–15, 316–17, 318, 320, 321, 322, 323, 324, 325, 326, 327, 329, 331–32, 333, 334–35, 336, 337, 338–39, 340–41, 343, 347, 348–49, 352, 353, 386–87, 388–92, 396–97, 402, 403–5, 428, 430–32, 452, 454, 458–59, 462–64, 465
war books, 26–27, 185–86
war elephants, 169–70, 171
war ethics, 403–4
warfare, 19, 26–27, 124, 126, 148, 153–54, 163–65, 166–70, 171–74, 176, 200, 283–84, 338–39, 389, 390, 392, 395, 401, 402–3
war heroes, 52, 390
warmongers, 314–15, 331–32
war narratives, 24, 184–85, 337, 343
war reporters, 175–76, 309
warriors, 11, 18–19, 26–28, 68–69, 113, 124–25, 126, 132–33, 148, 163, 164, 165, 166–68, 173–74, 175–76, 192–93, 198, 206, 215, 241–42, 247–48, 259, 279, 291–92, 322, 327–28, 331–32, 340–41, 343, 347, 348–49, 353, 374–75, 376–77, 385–86, 387, 389–90, 392, 393–94, 396, 452–53, 454, 456, 458–59
water, 49, 54, 64–66, 87, 113, 116–17, 124, 125–26, 135–36, 154, 193–94, 261–62, 270, 301, 318, 319, 329–30, 341, 349, 350, 374–75, 388
watershed, 10
water-gods/goddesses, 18, 113, 125
water-sports, 451
weakness, 206–7, 242, 243, 279, 349, 387, 440
wealth, xiii, 14–15, 33–34, 50, 52–53, 54, 61–62, 70, 90, 118, 131, 137–38, 139–40, 141, 147–48, 153–54, 155–56, 157–58, 192, 292, 303, 318, 320, 321, 324, 329, 333–34, 348–49, 354–55, 380, 433–34, 435, 441, 456
weapons, 113–14, 125, 164, 165, 172, 175, 209, 238, 248, 260, 297, 299, 350, 375–76, 393, 404–5, 439, 444
Weller, F., 352
Weller, Hermann, 47
widows, 93, 95, 98–99, 100–1, 102, 110, 148–49, 195, 202–3, 213–14, 440–41, 452
Wikander, Stig, 16–17, 244
wind, xii–xiii, 54–55, 65, 116–17, 124, 125–26, 158, 193–94, 261–62, 318, 350
wind god, 433–34
wisdom, 138, 199–200, 210, 238, 285–86, 316, 321–22, 324, 325, 330, 350, 351, 358–59, 361–63, 370, 372, 374–75, 436, 444–45
witnesses, 1, 9–10, 102, 132, 142, 146, 151, 154, 165, 206, 213–14,

Yudhiṣṭhira (*cont.*)
435–36, 437, 445–46, 451, 461, 463–64, 466–67
Yuvanāśva, 443
Zarathushtra, 53–54, 450
Zeus, 18–19
Zimmermann, Francis, 116–17
Zoroastrians, 53–54